本书的出版得到江苏省十三五重点教材、扬州大学出版基金及研究生双向跨文化交际能力的国际化培养路径研究项目（JGLX2020_002；132030985）的资助

新时代高等院校大学英语系列教材

大学通识教育课程系列

总主编 俞洪亮

跨文化交际学
——理论·方法·应用

Intercultural Communication Studies
——Theories · Methods · Applications

田德新 俞洪亮 编著

图书在版编目(CIP)数据

跨文化交际学:理论·方法·应用:汉文、英文 / 田德新,俞洪亮编著. —西安:西安交通大学出版社,2022.9(2024.1重印)
新时代高等院校大学英语系列教材 / 俞洪亮主编
ISBN 978-7-5693-2695-6

Ⅰ.①跨… Ⅱ.①田…②俞… Ⅲ.①文化交流—高等学校—教材—汉、英 Ⅳ.①G115

中国版本图书馆 CIP 数据核字(2022)第 118092 号

书　　名	跨文化交际学——理论·方法·应用
编　著	田德新　俞洪亮
责任编辑	牛瑞鑫
责任校对	庞钧颖
出版发行	西安交通大学出版社 (西安市兴庆南路1号　邮政编码710048)
网　　址	http://www.xjtupress.com
电　　话	(029)82668357　82667874(市场营销中心) (029)82668315(总编办)
传　　真	(029)82668280
印　　刷	陕西奇彩印务有限责任公司
开　　本	880 mm×1230mm　1/16　印张　28　字数　920千字
版次印次	2022年9月第1版　2024年1月第2次印刷
书　　号	ISBN 978-7-5693-2695-6
定　　价	68.00元

如发现印装质量问题,请与本社市场营销中心联系。
订购热线:(029)82665248　(029)82667874

版权所有　侵权必究

　　当今世界正处在百年未有之大变局,以新能源、新材料、大数据、人工智能等为代表的新一轮科技革命加速演进。中国制造2025、教育现代化2035等国家重大战略布局,对高等教育发展尤其是人才培养和人才供给产生了深刻的影响,也提出了全新的命题。我们要把准新一轮科技革命和产业革命的脉搏,坚持以社会需求为导向,深入推进本科专业布局调整和教育教学改革,让一流本科教育真正满足新时代对一流本科人才的需求。

　　世界现代大学发展史表明,本科教育是高等教育的立命之本、发展之本。回归本科教育已经成为世界一流大学共同的行动纲领。党和国家加快推动本科教育振兴,持续推进本科人才培养模式改革,从"四新建设"到"双万计划",从构建高校思政工作体系到全面实施课程思政……推进一流本科教育的步伐行稳致远、张弛有度。2019年9月,教育部印发《关于深化本科教育教学改革 全面提高人才培养质量的意见》,同年12月,教育部印发《普通高等学校教材管理办法》,对立德树人的人才培养根本任务、课程建设质量的全面提高和高水平教材的编写及使用等方面提出了意见。

　　发展外语教育是全球的共识,外语教育伴随国家发展阶段的变化而变化。进入新时代,外语教育的使命与责任更加重大,高等外语教育的发展关系到高等教育人才的培养质量。在中国新一轮的高等教育改革中,大学英语教育教学要立足新的发展阶段,主动服务国家战略需求,主动融入新文科建设,适应高等教育普及化阶段的需求和特点,拥抱新未来和新技术,在建设更高质量的课程中获取改革与发展的新动能,在融合发展中开辟大学英语课程建设的新路径。

　　教材关乎国家事权,是铸魂工程,是构建高质量高等教育体系的重要内容,也是课堂教学的重要载体和实现人才培养的有力保障。因此,推进新时代教材建设,必须体现马克思主义中国化要求,体现中国和中华民族风格,体现党和国家对教育的基本要求,体现国家和民族基本价值观,体现人类文化知识积累和创新成果。2021年是中国共产党成立100周年和"十四五"规划开局之年,也是开启全面建设社会主义现代化国家新征程的第一年,我们在这个重要历史节点上,以全面贯彻党的教育方针,落实立德树人根本任务为宗旨,紧扣国家对推进新文科建设的需求,并以《大学英语教学指南(2020版)》为指导,组织编写了这套"新时代高等院校大学英语系列"教材,力求培养心系祖国发展、积极参与全球竞争、思维方式创新、融贯中西文化的新时代人才。

　　本系列教材分为两个子系列,分别为"大学通识教育课程系列"和"专门用途英语系列",以知识、能力、素养和价值为本位,体现通识教育与专业教育的有机结合。具体来讲,本系列教材的特色如下。

1. 思政统领,落实立德树人的根本任务,坚持价值和能力双重导向

　　"新时代高等院校大学英语系列"教材全面贯彻党的教育方针,落实立德树人根本任务，扎根中国大地，站稳中国立场，充分体现社会主义核心价值观，强化爱国主义、集体主义、社会主义教育，展现中华优秀传统文化，将构建人类命运共同体、"一带一路"倡议、中国制造2025等热点话题有机融入教材编写，使学生在真实场景中习得知识，提升能力，引导学生坚定道路自信、理论自信、制度自信、文化自信，增强学生"讲好中国故事"的底气和能力。

2. 聚焦一流建设，融入"双万计划"，发挥示范引领作用

本系列教材遵循高起点、高标准、高要求的原则，融入一流专业和一流课程建设，对标金课"两性一度"，反映学科发展的最新进展，引入高等外语教育改革最新成果。我们力求从体系搭建、内容架构、问题设置等方面打造全方位、多维度的示范性教材。

3. 融入"四新"建设，体现学科交叉融合，服务创新人才体系

大学英语教育在新工科、新医科、新农科和新文科建设中被赋予了新的责任和使命。面对新一轮的科技浪潮和全球变局，大学英语教育成为创新型、复合型、应用型、国际化人才培养体系的重要一环，也是服务跨学科创新人才培养的不可或缺的基础。本系列教材中不仅有对人工智能、大数据和区块链发展等新兴交叉学科的探讨，也有对医学、艺术、教育、科技、农业等传统领域的拓展。这些教材能够帮助不同学科背景的学生拓宽视野，培养创新思维，增强思辨能力。

4. 坚持"学生中心"育人理念，尊重个体差异，实现教学资源多样化

智能教育时代学生的思维特点、学习习惯和现代信息技术的持续发展都对教材的内容和形态提出了新的要求。学生学习的方式和获取资源的渠道日趋多样化，教材也要走好线上线下融合的道路。同时，教师的教育观、教学观、教材观、学生观、质量观等均发生了变化。多形态的教材建设和数字化学习资源供给成为新一轮大学英语建设的重要内容。本系列教材配套慕课、示范微课、在线练习、音频和视频等各类知识服务资源，产生"教"与"学"的互动，提升学生的参与感、获得感和成就感。

5. 面向中西部高校，推动优质教育均衡发展，满足学生更高水平的需求

高等教育的整体质量是我国构建高质量教育体系的重要影响因素。本系列教材加强东部与西部高校间协同合作，观照中西部地区高等院校目标读者，增加展现中西部地区人文特色以及社会和科技发展成果的最新内容，依据中西部高校的教学实际编写，适应国家和区域经济社会发展需求。

"新时代高等院校大学英语系列"教材编写团队成员均是具有丰富教学经验、专业知识背景和先进教学理念的骨干教师，来自西安交通大学、兰州大学、西北工业大学、西安电子科技大学、扬州大学、西北师范大学、宁夏大学、河南科技大学、西安外国语大学、西北政法大学等多所院校。

一流人才培养须"知行合一"。我们组织编写的这套具有中西部特色，体现东部与西部合作的高水平、高质量、高起点的"新时代高等院校大学英语系列"教材正是对国家人才培养战略部署的积极响应，希望它如同一艘航船，带领老师和同学们驶向更广阔的海洋。

跨文化交际指具有不同文化背景的人士之间的交际活动,其英文有使用"Intercultural Communication"表示的,也有使用"Cross-Cultural Communication"表示的,而且有人认为两者可以互换。严格地说,两个概念都表示具有不同文化背景的人士之间的交际活动。但是,前者着重探讨来自两个或两个以上文化背景的人士之间的跨文化交际行为本身,而后者注重对来自两个或两个以上文化背景的人士之间的跨文化交际行为进行比较研究。跨文化交际学(Intercultural Communication Studies)的诞生以美国人类学家爱德华•霍尔 1959 年出版《沉默的语言》(*The Silent Language*)为标志,跨文化交际学主要涉及文化观念、语言交际、非语言交际和交际语境四个层面。文化观念是人们基于其价值体系对现实世界的感知而形成的信念、态度、价值观与世界观。语言交际关注语言与文化的关系,特别是文化对语言使用的影响。非语言交际探究肢体,行为和时空对人们分享思想和感受的影响。交际语境研究文化、社会、感知、时空等内在和外在环境对语言和非语言交际的影响。随着全球化的发展,世界范围内的文化交流活动和人员交流频次呈指数级剧增,当今的跨文化交际学事实上涵盖了政治、经济、文化、教育、军事、科技、旅游等各个方面的学术研讨。

跨文化交际学自 20 世纪 80 年代引入国内,主要用于外语教学方面的应用与研究,起初注重母语与目的语在语言文化方面的差异,随后逐渐拓展到跨文化意识、文化习俗、文化价值、文化冲突、心理认知及跨文化交际能力等层面。近几年来,相关研究持续发展壮大,涵盖了语言学、心理学、传播学、社会学及哲学等多个学科。目前跨文化交际学在实践方面出现了囿于外语教学之一隅,或无限度地与其他学科嫁接,催生交叉学科不断问世的现象。在学术研究方面,跨文化交际学的相关研究也大有从作为传播学的一个分支学科向任何与两种以上文化有关的学科大踏步迈进的趋势。

出于正本溯源并从根本上推动跨文化交际学的系统性、科学性与有效性发展的目的,笔者编写《跨文化交际学——理论•方法•应用》一书。本书基于文化观念、语言交际、非语言交际和交际语境的四大传统板块,共囊括 12 个章节,各个章节由 2 篇经典阅读课文、3 篇与课文内容相关的论文摘要范例及包含课程思政与学术论文写作内容的 6 项口头与书面习题组成,旨在从理论、方法和应用 3 个层面,实现学生对全书各章主题内容的融会贯通与实际应用。其中,各章主题内容包括跨文化交际与跨文化交际学;跨文化交际史与跨文化交际研究史;语言、文化与研究方法;环境、权利与跨文化交际;身份与跨文化交际;语言跨文化交际;非语言跨文化交际;东西方跨文化交际学理论;跨文化交际研究方法;新媒体与跨文化交际;跨文化交际关系与冲突;文化化、文化休克与跨文化交际能力。另外,与本书配套的 PPT 课件与跨文化交际学术语词汇表,可供教师备课和学生查阅相关术语与难词时参考。本书适合用作本科高年级和研究生跨文化交际课教材,也是致力于跨文化交际学研究的有关专家、学者及各类涉外人士的重要参考资料。

本书特色有如下三个方面。

第一,总体设计集中跨文化交际学的最新、最权威和最有代表性的理论、研究方法和实际应用于一体,以体现跨文化交际学研究与教学的系统性、科学性和有效性。

第二,书中各章由2篇经典阅读课文、3篇与课文内容相关的论文摘要及包含课程思政和学术论文写作内容的6项口头与书面习题组成,便于使用本书的师生和其他读者将书中内容融会贯通。

第三,本书基于作者数十年来在国内外教学的丰富经验编著而成,同时得到首批国家级一流本科课程"跨文化交际通识通论"、江苏省"十三五"重点教材、扬州大学出版基金及研究生双向跨文化交际能力的国际化培养路径研究项目(JGLX2020_002;132030985)基金的资助。

本书的撰写得到了扬州大学人文社科处及扬州大学外国语学院领导的倾心关怀与帮助,西安交通大学出版社的领导与编辑也为本书的出版付出了很多的心血与努力,在此一并表达真诚感谢与由衷敬意!

由于编著者水平有限,书中疏漏之处在所难免,恳请有关专家和读者朋友批评指正。

扬州大学　田德新　俞洪亮
2021年8月26日

UNIT ONE Intercultural Communication and Intercultural Communication Studies (1)
  Readings (3)
    Text A An Introduction to Intercultural Communication (3)
    Text B Introducing Critical Intercultural Communication (19)
  Applications (29)
  Interactive Activities (30)

UNIT TWO History of Intercultural Communication and History of Intercultural Communication Research (33)
  Readings (35)
    Text A Notes in the History of Intercultural Communication: The Foreign Service Institute and the Mandate for Intercultural Training (35)
    Text B Murky Waters: History of Intercultural Communication Research (48)
  Applications (63)
  Interactive Activities (64)

UNIT THREE Language, Culture, and Research Methods (67)
  Readings (69)
    Text A Language and Culture from a Linguistic Perspective (69)
    Text B Language and Culture: Research Methods (83)
  Applications (95)
  Interactive Activities (96)

UNIT FOUR Contexts, Power, and Intercultural Communication (99)
  Readings (101)
    Text A Culture, Communication, Context, and Power (101)
    Text B Culture Power and Intercultural Communication (113)
  Applications (123)
  Interactive Activities (124)

UNIT FIVE Identity and Intercultural Communication (125)
  Readings (127)
    Text A Identity and Intercultural Communication (127)
    Text B Ideology, Identity, and Intercultural Communication: An Analysis of Differing Academic Conceptions of Cultural Identity (151)
  Applications (162)

  Interactive Activities ……………………………………………………… (163)

UNIT SIX Verbal Intercultural Communication ……………………… (165)
  Readings …………………………………………………………………… (167)
   Text A Verbal Communication: How Can I Reduce Cultural
       Misunderstandings in My Verbal Communication? ………… (167)
   Text B Verbal Communication across Cultures ……………………… (181)
  Applications ……………………………………………………………… (192)
  Interactive Activities ……………………………………………………… (194)

UNIT SEVEN Non-verbal Intercultural Communication ……………… (197)
  Readings …………………………………………………………………… (199)
   Text A The Non-verbal Code ……………………………………… (199)
   Text B A Cultural Look at Non-verbal Cues ……………………… (223)
  Applications ……………………………………………………………… (231)
  Interactive Activities ……………………………………………………… (232)

UNIT EIGHT Eastern and Western Theorizing about Intercultural
       Communication ……………………………………………… (235)
  Readings …………………………………………………………………… (237)
   Text A Theorizing about Intercultural Communication:
       An Introduction ……………………………………………… (237)
   Text B Theorizing Culture and Communication in the Asian Context:
       An Assumptive Foundation ………………………………… (262)
  Applications ……………………………………………………………… (274)
  Interactive Activities ……………………………………………………… (276)

UNIT NINE Research Methods of Intercultural Communication ………… (277)
  Readings …………………………………………………………………… (279)
   Text A Methods for Intercultural Communication Research ……… (279)
   Text B Thinking Dialectically about Culture and Communication … (294)
  Applications ……………………………………………………………… (308)
  Interactive Activities ……………………………………………………… (309)

UNIT TEN New Media and Intercultural Communication ……………… (311)
  Readings …………………………………………………………………… (313)
   Text A The Impact of New Media on Intercultural Communication
       in Global Context …………………………………………… (313)
   Text B New Media and Intercultural Communication ……………… (322)
  Applications ……………………………………………………………… (329)
  Interactive Activities ……………………………………………………… (330)

UNIT ELEVEN Intercultural Relationships and Conflicts ……………… (333)
  Readings …………………………………………………………………… (335)
   Text A Culture, Communication, and Conflict …………………… (335)

  Text B Understanding Intercultural Conflict Competence: Multiple
      Theoretical Insights ·· (353)
 Applications ·· (365)
 Interactive Activities ·· (367)

UNIT TWELVE Acculturation, Culture Shock, and Intercultural
       Communication Competence ······································ (369)
 Readings ·· (371)
  Text A Acculturation, Culture Shock, and Intercultural
      Communication Competence ·· (371)
  Text B Understanding and Assessing Intercultural Competence:
      A Summary of Theory, Research, and Practice ··············· (390)
 Applications ·· (410)
 Interactive Activities ·· (412)

Glossary of Intercultural Communication Studies ···························· (414)

UNIT ONE

Intercultural Communication and Intercultural Communication Studies

Readings

Text A An Introduction to Intercultural Communication

After James W. Neuliep

▸ Introduction

As we enter the 21st century, there is a growing sense of urgency that we need to increase our understanding of people from **diverse** cultural and ethnic backgrounds. From interpersonal misunderstandings to intercultural conflicts, frictions exist within and between cultures. With rapid changes in global economy, technology, transportation, and immigration policies, the world is becoming a small, **intersecting** community. We find ourselves in increased contact with people who are culturally different, working side by side with us. From workplace to classroom, different cultural beliefs, values, and communication styles are here to stay. In order to achieve effective and appropriate intercultural communication, we have to learn to manage differences flexibly and mindfully.

Actually, humans have always been diverse in their cultural beliefs and practices. However, as new technologies have led to the perception that our world has shrunk, and political changes have brought attention to cultural differences, we communicate with people across cultures much more frequently than ever before. The oceans and continents that separate us can now be **traversed** instantly with an e-mail, phone call, tweet, or status update. Additionally, our workplaces, schools, and neighborhoods have become more **integrated** in terms of race and gender, increasing our interaction with diversity. The fact that we are **exposed** to more cultural differences doesn't mean we genuinely appreciate the differences and fully understand the subsequent impacts.

▸ Communication

Communication is everywhere. Every day, everywhere, people are communicating. Even when alone, people are **bombarded** with communication. Communication professor Charles Larson estimated that in 2010 most U.S. citizens were exposed to more than 5,000 persuasive messages every day. Most people would be miserable if they were not allowed to communicate with others. Indeed, solitary **confinement** is perhaps the worst form of punishment for humans. Human communication—that is, the ability to symbolize and use language—separates humans from animals. Communication with others is the essence of what it means to be human. Through communication, people conduct their lives. People define themselves via their communication with others. Communication is the vehicle by which people initiate, maintain, and terminate their relationships with others. Communication is the means by which people influence and persuade others. Through communication, local, regional, national, and international conflicts are managed and resolved. Ironically, however, communication—and particularly one's style of communication—can be the source of many interpersonal problems. Marriage counselors and divorce lawyers indicate that a breakdown in communication is one of the most frequently cited reasons for relational issues in the United States. A specific kind of communication—that is, public speaking—is one of the most frequently cited fears, even more feared than death. **Intercultural communication** occurs whenever two or more people from different cultures come together and exchange verbal and non-verbal messages. Throughout the course of this book, you will be introduced to a whole host of concepts and theories that explain the process of people from differing cultural backgrounds coming together and exchanging verbal and non-verbal messages.

Human Communication

Because of its **ubiquitous** nature, communication is difficult to define. If you were to go to your university library and select 10 different introductory communication texts, each would probably offer a different definition of communication. Although there are no universally agreed-on definitions of communication, most communication scholars agree on certain dimensions of communication that describe its nature. Communication is a process. A process is anything that is ongoing, ever changing, and continuous. A process is not static or at rest; it is always moving. Communication is always developing; it is never still or motionless. That communication is a process means that communication is **dynamic**. The terms process and dynamic are closely related. Part of what makes communication a process is its dynamic nature. Something that is dynamic is considered active or forceful. Because communication is a dynamic process, it is impossible to capture its essence in a written definition or graphic model. Communication is interactive and **transactional** because it occurs between people. Communication requires the active participation of two people sending and receiving messages at the same time—that is, as we are sending messages we are simultaneously receiving messages (transactional). That communication is symbolic is another fundamental assumption guiding most communication scholars. A symbol is an **arbitrarily** selected and learned stimulus that represents something else. Symbols can be verbal or non-verbal. They are the vehicle by which the thoughts and ideas of one person can be communicated to another person. Messages are constructed with verbal and non-verbal symbols. Through symbols, meanings are **transferred** between people. Symbols (i.e., words) have no natural relationship with what they represent (they are arbitrarily selected and learned).

Non-verbal symbols are arbitrary as well. Showing someone your upright middle finger may not communicate much in some cultures. Verbal and non-verbal symbols are meaningful only to people who have learned to associate them with what they represent. People can allow just about any symbols they want to represent. For example, you and your friends probably communicate with one another using private symbols that no one else understands. You have your own secret code. You have words, phrases, gestures, and handshakes that only you and your friends know, understand, and use. This allows you to communicate with one another in your own "foreign" language. Most communication is intentional, meaning that it is performed consciously. Intentional communication exists whenever two or more people consciously engage in interaction with some purpose. Unintentional communication may exist, however. For example, you pass a friend in the hallway of your dorm, say hello, and your friend does not respond. Perhaps your friend simply didn't see you and was thinking about the exam he or she just failed and was not intentionally ignoring you. In this book, the type of communication that will be discussed is intentional communication. This book takes the position that intentional communication, either verbal or non-verbal, is more informative than unintentional communication. Communication is dependent on the context in which it occurs. **Context** refers to the cultural, physical, relational, and perceptual environment in which communication occurs. In many ways, the context defines the meaning of any message. With whom and where you interact significantly alters the messages sent. That communication is ubiquitous simply means it is everywhere, done by everyone, all the time. Wherever one goes, some communication is happening.

Finally, culture shapes communication, and communication is culture **bound**. People from different cultures communicate differently. The verbal and non-verbal symbols we use to communicate with our friends and families are strongly influenced by our culture. Perhaps the most obvious verbal communication difference between two cultures is language. Even cultures speaking the same language, however, have different meanings for different symbols. For example, although English is the dominant language spoken in the United States and Britain, many words and phrases have different meanings between these two cultures. In Britain, to "bomb" an examination is to have performed very well. However, it means to "flunk," "blow" or "fail" an examination in the United States.

Communication, then, is the ubiquitous, dynamic, interactive process of encoding and decoding verbal and non-verbal messages within a defined cultural, physiological, relational, and perceptual context. Although many of our messages are sent intentionally, some others—perhaps our non-verbal messages—can unintentionally influence other people.

Human Communication Apprehension

Although communication is difficult to define, we know that people begin to communicate at birth and continue communicating throughout their lives. We also know that many people experience fear and anxiety when communicating with others, particularly in situations such as public speaking, class presentations, a first date, or a job interview. The fear or anxiety people experience when communicating with others is called communication **apprehension.** In the past 50 years, a **substantial** body of research has accumulated regarding the nature and prevalence of communication apprehension. The late Jim McCroskey, considered the father of this concept, believed that nearly everyone experiences some kind of communication apprehension sometimes, but roughly one in five adults in the United States may suffer from communication apprehension every time they communicate with others. McCroskey said that experiencing communication apprehension is normal; that is, all of us experience it occasionally. McCroskey argued that there are four types of communication apprehension: trait-like, context based, audience based, and situation-based. Trait-like communication apprehension is an enduring general personality tendency where an individual experiences communication apprehension most of the time across most communication situations. Of all adults in the United States, 20% experience trait-like communication apprehension.

Context-based communication apprehension is restricted to a certain generalized context, such as public speaking, group meetings, or job interviews. Persons with context-based communication apprehension experience anxiety only in certain contexts. Audience-based communication apprehension is **triggered** not by the specific context but by the particular person or audience with whom one is communicating. Hence, persons with audience-based communication apprehension may experience anxiety when communicating with strangers or their superiors. For example, college students with audience-based communication apprehension may experience anxiety when communicating with professors but not when communicating with other students. Finally, situation-based communication apprehension, experienced by virtually everyone, occurs with the combination of a specific context and a specific audience. For example, students may feel anxious interacting with professors only when they are alone with the professor in the professor's office. At other times, perhaps in the hallways or in the classroom, interacting with the professor may not be a problem. To repeat, virtually everyone experiences communication apprehension at some time; if you experience such anxiety, it does not mean you are abnormal or sick.

▶ Culture

Like communication, culture is ubiquitous and has a profound effect on humans. Culture is simultaneously invisible yet **pervasive**. As we go about our daily lives, we are not **overtly** conscious of our culture's influence on us. How often have you sat in your dorm room or classroom, for example, and consciously thought about what it means to be a Chinese or U.S. citizen? As you stand in the lunch line, do you say to yourself, "I am acting like a Chinese or U.S. citizen"? As you sit in your classroom, do you say to yourself, "The professor is really acting like a Chinese or U.S. citizen"? Yet most of your thoughts, emotions, and behaviors are culturally driven. One need only step into a culture different from one's own to feel the immense impact of culture.

Culture has a direct influence on the physical, relational, and **perceptual** contexts. For example, the next time you enter your communication classroom, consider how the room is arranged physically, including where you sit and where the professor teaches, the location of the chalkboard, windows, and so on. Does the professor lecture from behind a lectern? Do the students sit facing the professor? Is the chalkboard used? Next, think about your relationship with the professor and the other students in your class. Is the relationship formal or informal? Do you interact with the professor and students about topics other than class material? Would you consider the relationship personal or impersonal? Finally, think about your perceptual disposition—that is, your attitudes, motivations, and emotions about the class. Are you happy to be in the class? Do you enjoy attending? Are you nervous when the instructor asks you a question? To a great extent, the answers to these questions are dependent on your culture. The physical arrangement of classrooms, the social relationship between students and teachers, and the perceptual **profiles** of the students and teachers vary significantly from culture to culture.

Definitions of Culture

Like communication, culture is difficult to define. To be sure, more than 50 years ago, two well-known **anthropologists**, Alfred Kroeber and Clyde Kluckhohn, found and examined 300 definitions of culture, no two of which were the same. Perhaps too often, people think of culture only in terms of the fine arts, geography, or history. Small towns or rural communities are often accused of having no culture. Yet culture exists everywhere. There is as much culture in New Mexico as there is in New York. The two cultures are just different. Simply put, culture is people.

The origin of the Latin word *cultura* is clear. It originates from the verb *colo* (infinitive colere), meaning "to tend," "to cultivate," and "to till," among other things. It can take objects such as *ager*, hence *agricultura*, whose literal meaning is "field tilling." Another possible object of the verb *colo* is animus ("character"). In that case, the expression would refer to the cultivation of the human character. Consequently, the Latin noun *cultura* can be associated with education and refinement.

The **etymological** analysis of "culture" is quite uncontroversial. But in the field of anthropology, the situation is much more complex. Definitions of culture abound and range from very complex to very simple. For example, a complex definition was proposed by Kroeber and Parsons: "transmitted and created content and patterns of values, ideas, and other symbolic-meaningful systems as factors in the shaping of human behavior." An even less easily comprehensible definition was provided by White: "By culture we mean an external, temporal **continuum** of things and events dependent upon symbolizing." Often cited is also a definition by Kluckhohn:

> Culture consists in patterned ways of thinking, feeling and reacting, acquired and transmitted mainly by symbols, constituting the distinctive achievements of human groups, including their **embodiments** in artifacts; the essential core of culture consists of traditional (i.e. historically derived and selected) ideas and especially their attached values.

At the other extreme is a well-known simple and narrow definition. Culture is shared mental software, "the collective programming of the mind that distinguishes the members of one group or category of people from another" as provided by Hofstede in 2001. The group or category can be a national society but Hofstede believes that his definition applies also to other collectives, such as regions, ethnicities, occupations, organizations, or even age groups and genders.

According to Jahoda, "culture" is the most **elusive** term in the vocabulary of the social sciences and the number of books devoted to the topic would fill many library shelves. A practical solution was proposed by Segall, who believed that it was not worth the effort to enhance the concept's clarity or attempt to **articulate** a universally acceptable definition. In his view, cultural analysts should abandon the struggle to conceptualize culture. Instead, they should "turn to the real business at hand," which is to "intensify the search for whatever ecological, sociological and cultural variables might link with established variations in human behavior."

Segall's call for pragmatism in cross-cultural analysis is laudable. Theoretical debates about the meaning that "should" be attributed to the concept of culture are pointless. There is no absolute reason why one abstract theoretical concept of it should be better than another. However, disagreements have been voiced not only with respect to abstract definitions of culture but also concerning specific matters, such as whether artifacts should or should not be considered part of culture. The answer to a question of this kind can have practical consequences: It may determine what should or should not be studied for the purpose of a **dissertation** on culture or be published in a journal devoted to culture.

Although there may not be a universally accepted definition of culture, there are a number of features of culture that most people would agree describe its essence. In this book, culture is defined as an **accumulated** pattern of values, beliefs, and behaviors shared by an identifiable group of people with a common history and verbal and non-verbal symbol systems.

Features of Culture

In their book, *Understanding Intercultural Communication* published in 2012, Ting-Toomey and Chung discussed four defining features of culture.

Culture as a learned meaning system

Culture is basically a learned system of meanings—a value-laden meaning system that helps you to "make sense" of and explain what is going on in your everyday intercultural surroundings. It fosters a particular sense of shared identity and solidarity among its group members. It also reinforces the boundary of "we" as an ingroup and the "dissimilar others" as belonging to distant outgroups. Ingroup identity basically refers to the emotional attachments and shared fate (i.e., perceived common treatment as a function of category membership) that we attach to our selective cultural, ethnic, or social categories. Outgroups are groups from which we remain psychologically or emotionally detached, and we are skeptical about their words or intentions.

In sum, culture is defined in this book as a learned meaning system that consists of patterns of traditions, beliefs, values, norms, meanings, and symbols that are passed on from one generation to the next and are shared to varying degrees by interacting members of a community. Members within the same cultural community share a sense of traditions, worldviews, values, rhythms, and patterns of life. We explore some of the key definitional ideas of culture—popular culture, meanings, symbols, norms, values, beliefs, and traditions—in the following subsections.

Culture is like an iceberg: the deeper layers (e.g., traditions, beliefs, and values) are hidden from our view. We tend to see and hear only the uppermost layers of cultural artifacts (e.g., fashion, pop music, and mass-appeal commercial films). We can also witness the exchange of overt verbal and non-verbal symbols (see Figure 1.1). However, to understand a culture—or a person in a cultural community—with any depth, we must match their underlying values coherently with their respective norms, meanings, and symbols.

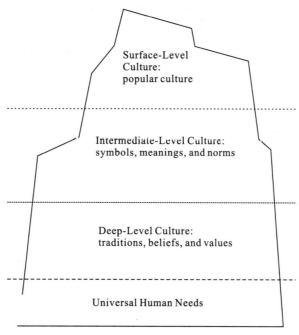

Figure 1.1 Culture: An Iceberg Metaphor

It is the underlying set of cultural beliefs and values that drives people's thinking, reactions, and behaviors. Furthermore, to understand commonalities between individuals and groups, we must dig deeper into the level of universal human needs. Some universal human needs, for example, can include the needs for security, inclusion, love/connection, respect, control, and creating meaning. Although people in diverse cultures are dissimilar in many ways, they are also alike in many aspects—especially in the deep levels of the needs for human respect, connection, and security. Unfortunately, using the analogy of the iceberg, individuals usually do not take the time or effort to discover the deeper layers of universal human needs and connections.

Popular culture at the surface level

On the most surface level, we often learn about another culture via the representation of its popular culture. Popular culture is often referred to as "those cultural artifacts, processes, effects, and meanings that are popular by definition, derivation, or general understanding." Popular culture covers a wide range of mediums—from pop music to pop gadgets, from pop karaoke to pop icons, and from global TV shows to global hip-hop fashion.

Popular culture (or pop culture) basically refers to cultural artifacts or systems that have mass appeal and that penetrate into our daily life. Popular images as portrayed in television, film, advertising, pop music, and even comic strips often reinforce cultural and gender **ideologies** in a society. The daily bombardment of television is one of our main sources of pop culture. Despite a limited number of women and ethnic minorities on television, for example, the media actually do offer some strong female gender roles and positive images of ethnic roles. It is also important to remember that all popular media are businesses that aim for mass consumption and profit-generating outcomes.

In this context, U.S. popular culture tends to dominate the global market. In 2010, *Crime*

Scene Investigation (*CSI*) won the **prestigious** International Television Audience Award for a Drama TV Series at the Fiftieth Monte Carlo TV Festival. *CSI* has won the award three times in the five-year history of the audience awards and is the highest rated global television show across five continents. The reasons for the global appeal of *CSI* could be because it is a fast-paced suspense drama, featuring attractive-looking actors, and depicting crimes committed and solved smartly within a one-hour span. Furthermore, many U.S. television shows are exported globally, such as *Glee*, *House*, *Lost*, and *The Big Bang Theory*. Contemporary television programming of reality shows (e.g., *American Idol*, *Jersey Shore*, and *Pawn Stars*) appeals widely across multiple national boundaries, especially with global online video streaming.

Furthermore, U.S. popular culture in the category of films also dominates on a worldwide level. Films like *Avatar* and *Inception* reflect the surface layer of U.S. commercial pop culture. Other films, such as *Iron Man*, *Pirates of the Caribbean*, and *The Bourne Identity*, promote sweeping adventure, romance, open frontiers, and a spirit of exploration—images that reinforce the notion of the United States as a carefree, action-packed, adventure-seeking culture. Although the United States is one of the highest movie-producing countries, do you know which country is the top-ranked highest movie-making country? Take a guess and check out Table 1.1, which lists the top five movie producing countries in 2011. Beyond films, people also receive images of another country via news magazines and television shows.

Table 1.1   Top Five Movie Producing Countries in 2011

Country	Features Produced
India	1,288
United States	677
China	456
Japan	448
France	158

Besides, icons, such as Disneyland, McDonald's, Coca-Cola, and Starbucks brand names, together with pop music, television shows, and films, are some prime examples of global popular culture. Some forms of popular culture have a direct **correlation** with the culture's underlying values and norms, but other forms of popular culture have been created for sheer entertainment purposes and profit-making objectives. Popular culture is often driven by an economic industry with a money-making target audience in mind. Boosting global appeal is another aspect of popular culture driven by strong economic interests.

As the music industry continues to suffer a severe decline in revenue and **rampant** piracy issues, music labels are finding alternative ways to **evolve** and achieve success. Digital downloads are one way. Another alternative is the unique manifestation of hip-hop and rap. Chile's Ana Tijoux was nominated in 2011 for her rap in Spanish in the Grammy category of Best Latin Rock, Alternative, or Urban Album. Korean pop's (K-pop) domination in Asia is slowly **infiltrating** the United States, with artists like Rain selling out in New York and the Wonder Girls opening up for the Jonas Brothers. Finally, the combinations of ethnic minorities singing hip-hop/rap and social networks (YouTube and Facebook) have appealed to the masses. For example, the group Far East Movement. These Koreatown, Los Angeles rappers hit **platinum** with their song "Like a G6." It was the first time an Asian American group had a No. 1 digital single, eliciting about 10 million views on YouTube.

Some individuals consume a particular form of popular culture as a way to be informed and included in their cultural community. By commenting on the headline news as reported on CNN, for example, individuals have a common symbol to **rally** around and to trade reactions with one another. Although having some information is better than no information before we visit another culture, all of us must remain alert in questioning the sources of where we receive our ideas or images about another culture. We should ask ourselves questions such as the following: Who are the decision makers behind the production of these popular images, icons, or sounds? Have we ever had a meaningful conversation with someone directly from that particular culture concerning his or her specific cultural or personal standpoints? Do we actually know enough people from that particular culture who are able to offer us multiple perspectives to understand the diverse reality of that culture? Do we actually have any acquaintances or close friends from that group who could help us to comprehend their culture on both a broad and a deep level?

In other words, we must be more watchful about how we process or form mental images about a large group of people under the broad category of "culture" or "race." Although we can travel in time to many far-flung places through the consumption of various media, we should remain mindful that a culture exists on multiple levels of complexity. Popular culture represents only one surface slice of the **embedded** richness of a culture.

Symbols, meanings, and norms of culture at the intermediate level

A symbol is a sign, artifact, word, gesture, or non-verbal behavior that stands for or reflects something meaningful. We use language as a symbolic system (with words, idioms, and phrases), which contains rich culture-based categories to organize and dissect the fluctuating world around us. Naming particular events (e.g., "formal gathering" versus "hanging out") via distinctive language categories is part of what we do in everyday communication activities. Expressions such as "Where there's a will there's a way" (a U.S. expression) or "The nail that sticks out gets hammered down" (a Chinese expression) reveal something about that culture's attitude toward self-determination or group-value orientation. Intercultural frictions often arise because of the ways we label and attach meanings to the different expressions or behaviors around us.

The meanings or interpretations that we attach to a symbol (e.g., a national flag or a non-verbal gesture), for example, can **cue** both objective and subjective reactions. People globally can recognize a particular country by its national flag because of its design and color. However, people of different cultural or ethnic backgrounds can also hold subjective meanings of what the flag means to them, such as a sense of pride or oppression. Other symbolic meaning examples can include the use of different non-verbal gestures across cultures. An animated "OK" non-verbal gesture sign from the United States, for example, with the thumb and forefinger signaling a circle, can mean money to the Japanese, a sexual insult in Brazil and Greece, a vulgar gesture in

Russia, or zero in France.

Cultural norms refer to the collective expectations of what constitutes proper or improper behavior in a given interaction scene. For example, whether we should shake hands or bow to a new Japanese supervisor when being introduced reflects our sense of politeness or respect for the other individual in the scene. However, to enact a proper "getting acquainted" interaction script, we must take the setting, interaction goal, relationship expectation, and cultural competence skills into account.

The setting can include the consideration of cultural context (e.g., the interaction scene takes place in Japan or the United States) or physical context (e.g., in an office or a restaurant). The interaction goal refers to the objective of the meeting—a job interview meeting is quite different from a chance meeting in a restaurant. A meeting to "show off" that you are an expert about the Japanese culture (therefore, you bow appropriately) is quite different from a chance meeting with a Japanese supervisor in an American restaurant (therefore, maybe a slight head nod will do).

The relationship expectation feature refers to how much role formality/informality or task/social tone you want to **forge** in the interaction. Last, cultural competence skills refer to the cultural knowledge you have internalized and the operational skills you are able to apply in the interaction scene. For example, if you do not have a good knowledge of the different degrees of bowing that are needed in approaching a Japanese supervisor, you may make a fool of yourself and cause awkward interaction. You may end up with an improper performance in the "getting-acquainted bowing" scene. By not differentiating the different levels of bowing (e.g., lower bowing for supervisors and shallow bowing for low-ranking staff), you may have committed a cultural **bump** without conscious realization.

To understand a culture, we must master the operational norms of a culture. However, beyond mastering the prescriptive rules of what we "should" or "should not do" in a culture, we must dig deeper to understand the cultural logics that frame such distinctive behaviors. Although norms can be readily inferred and observed through behaviors, cultural beliefs and values are deep seated and invisible. Cultural traditions, beliefs, and values intersect to influence the development of collective norms in a culture.

Traditions, beliefs, and values at the deep level

On a communal level, culture refers to a patterned way of living by a group of interacting individuals who share a common set of history, traditions, beliefs, values, and interdependent fate. This is known as the normative culture of a group of individuals. On an individual level, members of a culture can attach different degrees of importance to these complex ranges and layers of cultural beliefs and values. This is known as the subjective culture of an individual. Thus, we can talk about the broad patterns of a culture as a group membership concept. We can also think about the culturally shared beliefs and values as subjectively subscribed to by members of a group, demonstrating varying degrees of **endorsement** and importance as Ting-Toomey suggested in 2011.

Culturally shared traditions can include myths, legends, ceremonies, and rituals (e.g., celebrating the New Year, or Thanksgiving) that are passed on from one generation to the next via an oral or written medium. They serve to reinforce ingroup solidarity, communal memory, cultural stability, and continuity functions. Culturally shared traditions can include, for example, the celebrations of birth, coming-of-age rituals, courtship rituals, wedding ceremonies, and seasonal change celebration rituals. They can also include spiritual traditions, such as in times of sickness, healing, rejuvenation, mourning, and funeral rituals for the dead.

Culturally shared beliefs refer to a set of fundamental assumptions or worldviews that people hold dearly to their hearts without question. These beliefs can revolve around questions as to the origins of human beings, the concept of time, space, and reality, the existence of a supernatural being, and the meaning of life, death, and the afterlife. Proposed answers to many of these questions can be found in the major religions of the world, such as Christianity, Islam, Hinduism, and Buddhism.

Beyond fundamental cultural or religious beliefs, people also differ in what they value as important in their cultures. Cultural values refer to a set of priorities that guide "good" or "bad" behaviors, "desirable" or "undesirable" practices, and "fair" or "unfair" actions. Cultural values (e.g., individual competitiveness versus group harmony) can serve as the motivational basis for actions. For example, an Israeli psychologist, Shalom Schwartz believes that we should understand the underlying motivational values that drive human actions. Those motivational values or basic value needs include the following: satisfying biological needs, social coordination needs, and the survival and welfare needs of the group.

From his various research studies in more than fifty countries, Schwartz has further identified ten value clusters that motivate people to behave the way they do in different cultures. These motivational value clusters or value types include the following: self-direction, stimulation, and hedonism; security, tradition, and conformity; power and **benevolence**; achievement; and universalism. Although self-direction, stimulation, and hedonism appear to reflect individualistic value tendencies, security, tradition, and conformity appear to reflect group-based, collectivistic value patterns. Power and benevolence seem to reflect whether individuals crave social recognition or deeper meaning in life. Achievement and universalism reflect whether individuals are ambitious and crave material success or whether they are universalistic oriented in wishing for a world at peace and inner harmony. More important, Schwartz's research indicates that a clear structure of values does emerge in reflecting people's underlying needs. The value structure and the relationship between value types appear to be consistent across cultures. However, cultures vary in terms of how strongly or how weakly they endorse a particular cluster of values. To understand various communication patterns in a culture, we must understand the deep-rooted cultural values that give meanings to such patterns.

▲ Intercultural Communication

Ideally, we now have an understanding of the word communication and the idea of culture. So what happens when people from different cultures come together and communicate with one another? We call that process "intercultural communication." Compared with many other academic disciplines, the study of intercultural communication is young. The histories of other academic fields such as math, biology, philosophy, and psychology date back hundreds and, in some cases, thousands of years. But the academic discipline of intercultural communication can be traced back only a few decades—specifically, to the year 1959 and the publication of Edward T. Hall's book *The Silent Language*.

Historical Development of Intercultural Communication

Hall is generally recognized as the founder of the academic discipline we call intercultural communication. Although the term intercultural had been used prior to Hall's work, it is thought that Hall was the first to use the term intercultural communication. Hall held three university degrees (i.e., BA, MA, and Ph.D.) in anthropology. Anthropology is the study of the origin, behavior, and physical, social, and cultural development of humans. Hall earned his doctorate in anthropology in 1942 when the United States was involved in World War II. During this period, traditional approaches in anthropology focused on studying a single culture at a time. So a particular anthropologist might focus his or her studies on, say, the Navajo or Hopi Indians of the American Southwest, as did Hall. Hall often referred to this as a macro-level approach to culture. Among the many significant influences on Hall's approach to his studies was anthropologist Franz Boas. The term cultural relativism is often **attributed** to him.

Boas believed, as did Hall, that humans are inherently ethnocentric (i.e., believing that one's native culture is the standard by which other cultures are observed and judged) and that our observations of other cultures are necessarily biased in favor of our native cultural background. Consequently, an individual from a particular culture cannot draw conclusions about some other culture's traditions, values, and customs without some inherent bias. Moreover, Boas believed that any particular culture is an adaptation to and a distinctive product of a unique set of historical, social, and environmental conditions. As these conditions vary, cultures vary accordingly—and, in this sense, there is no correct culture.

Following World War II, the U.S. Congress established the Foreign Service Institute (FSI). FSI is the federal government's primary training institution for officers and support personnel of the U.S. foreign affairs community, preparing American diplomats and other professionals to advance U.S. foreign affairs interests overseas and in Washington. In the early 1950s, Hall taught at FSI and soon discovered that the traditional ways of teaching about macro-level culture, from an anthropological perspective, were not effective in training FSI personnel how to interact with persons from different cultures. So Hall and others began to rethink how to teach about culture and soon developed a new curriculum that eventually became known as intercultural communication.

In this new curriculum, scholars focused on intercultural communication—that is, how people from different cultures interact with one another—rather than on how members of a particular culture interact within their culture. This new curriculum also emphasized the non-verbal elements of intercultural communication. Hall was especially interested in the study of how cultures manage the non-verbal channels of time (chronemics), space (**proxemics**), and body language (**kinesics**). One of Hall's most fascinating insights was how invisible culture is to its own members—that is, how most people are so unaware of their own cultural ways of living.

This new approach also embraced Boas's idea of cultural relativism in that cultures should be judged only from within their specific cultural context, and cultural traditions, beliefs, and behaviors are to be evaluated on that culture's unique set of historical, social, and environmental conditions.

In 1959, Hall published *The Silent Language*, which sold more than 500,000 copies in its first 10 years and is considered the seminal work in the field. In the book, Hall asserted that culture is communication. By the late 1960s, we saw the first intercultural communication courses being offered at universities. In 1970, the International Communication Association established a Division of Intercultural Communication. L.S. Harms's 1970 book, *Intercultural Communication*, is thought to be the first textbook on the subject. By 1975, the Speech Communication Association established the Division of Intercultural Communication, and in 1977, the *International Journal of Intercultural Relations* began publication.

Differences between Intercultural Communication and Cross-Cultural Communication

Intercultural communication, as the name indicates, is concerned with communication across cultures. In 2000, Gudykunst a communication studies scholar, **distinguished** intercultural researches from cross-cultural studies of communication as follows:

> "Cross-cultural" and "intercultural" are often regarded as interchangeable. They are, nevertheless, different. Cross-cultural research involves comparing behavior in two or more cultures (e.g. comparing self-disclosure in Japan, U.S. and Iran when individuals interact with members of their own culture). Intercultural research involves examining behavior when members of two or more cultures interact (e.g. examining self-disclosure when Japanese and Iranians communicate with each other).... Understanding cross-cultural differences in behavior is a prerequisite for understanding intercultural behavior.

This is a useful distinction, but it immediately raises a more fundamental issue: how can cultures be defined and how can intercultural communication thus be distinguished from intracultural communication? This is a very complex question, which requires an in-depth theoretical discussion.

In our usage, "cross-cultural" applies to something which covers more than one culture. For example "a cross-cultural study of education in Western Europe" would be a comparison of chosen aspects of education in various countries or regions, but would consider each country or region separately and would not suggest any interaction between the various educational systems. On the other hand, the term "intercultural" implies interaction. From an intercultural perspective, it would be possible to study the experiences of students or teachers who move from one educational system to another, or to examine the interactions of students from different countries enrolled in a specific class or program. "Culture shock" and "cultural adaptation" are thus intercultural notions.

Fundamental Assumptions about Intercultural Communication

A central **premise** of this book is that intercultural communication is a complex combination of the cultural, micro-cultural, environmental, perceptual, and socio-relational contexts between two people who are encoding and decoding verbal and non-verbal messages. Because of the complexity of this process, a fundamental assumption about intercultural communication is that during intercultural communication the message sent is usually not the message received.

ASSUMPTION #1: During intercultural communication, the message sent is usually not the message received. Whenever people from different cultures come together and exchange messages, they bring with them a whole host of thoughts, values, emotions, and behaviors that were planted and cultivated by culture. As we have said, intercultural communication is a symbolic activity in which the thoughts and ideas of one person are encoded into a verbal or non-verbal message format and then transmitted through some channel to another person who must decode it, interpret it, and respond to it. This process of encoding, decoding, and interpreting is filled with cultural noise. Noted intercultural communication scholar Gudykunst has **asserted** that during intercultural communication, culture acts as a filter through which all messages, both verbal and non-verbal, must pass. To this extent, all intercultural exchanges are necessarily, to a greater or lesser extent, charged with ethnocentrism. Hence, during intercultural communication, the message sent is not the message received.

Ethnocentrism refers to the idea that one's own culture is the center of everything and all other groups (or cultures) are scaled and rated with reference to it. Sociologist W.G.Sumner argued that **ethnocentrism** nourishes a group's pride and vanity while looking on outsiders, or out-groups, with contempt. Although culture may mediate the extent to which we experience ethnocentrism, it is thought to be universal. One of the effects of ethnocentrism is that it clouds our perception of others. We have a tendency to judge others, and their communication, based on the standards set by our own culture. Neuliep and McCroskey have argued that the concept of ethnocentrism is essentially descriptive and not necessarily pejorative. Ethnocentrism may serve a valuable function when one's ingroup is under attack or threatened. Moreover, ethnocentrism forms the basis for patriotism, group loyalty, and the willingness to sacrifice for one's own group. To be sure, however, ethnocentrism can be problematic. In not looking past their own culture, people see little importance in understanding other cultures. At high levels, ethnocentrism is an obstacle to effective intercultural communication.

ASSUMPTION #2: Intercultural communication is primarily a non-verbal act between people. Some foreign language teachers might have us believe that competency in a foreign language is tantamount to effective and successful intercultural communication in the culture that speaks that language. To be sure, proficiency in a foreign language expedites the intercultural communication experience, but intercultural communication is primarily and fundamentally a non-verbal process. The expression of intimacy, power, and status among communicators is typically accomplished non-verbally through paralinguistic cues, proxemics, **haptics**, **oculesics**, and **olfactics**. In Korea, for example, one's hierarchical position is displayed via vocal tone and pitch. When a subordinate is offered an important piece of paper, such as a graded exam from a respected professor, he or she grasps it with both hands (not just one) and accompanies this action with a slight nod of the head and indirect eye contact—all non-verbal signs of respect.

The well-known anthropologist Hall has argued that people from different cultures live in different sensory worlds. Hall claims that people from different cultures engage in a selective screening of sensory information that ultimately leads to different perceptions of experience. Regarding olfactics (smell), most cultures establish norms for acceptable and unacceptable scents associated with the human body. When people fail to fit into the realm of olfactic cultural acceptability, their odor alerts others that something is wrong with their physical, emotional, or mental health. In the United States, we are obsessed with masking certain smells, especially those of the human body. In Western and Westernized cultures, body odor is regarded as unpleasant and distasteful, and great effort is expended in its removal.

ASSUMPTION # 3: Intercultural communication necessarily involves a clash of communicator style. In the United States, talk is a highly valued commodity. People are routinely evaluated by their speech. Yet silence—that is, knowing when not to speak—is a fundamental **prerequisite** for linguistic and cultural competence. The use and interpretation of silence varies dramatically across cultures. In many collectivistic cultures, such as Japan and Korea, silence can carry more meaning than words, especially in the maintenance of intimate relationships. In fact, the Japanese and some Native American Indian tribes in the United States believe that the expression of relational intimacy is best accomplished non-verbally. They believe that having to put one's thoughts and emotions into words somehow cheapens and discounts them.

In the United States, people value, and employ, a direct and personal style of verbal communication. Personal pronouns are an essential element in the composition of just about any **utterance**. The American mottos include "Get to the point," "Don't beat around the bush," "Tell it like it is," and "Speak your mind." Many cultures, however, prefer an indirect and impersonal communication style. In these cultures, there is no need to articulate every message. True understanding is implicit, coming not from words but from actions in the environment, where speakers provide only hints or insinuations. The Chinese say, "One should use the eyes and ears, not the mouth," and "Disaster **emanates** from careless talk." The Chinese consider the wisest and most trustworthy person to be the one who listens, watches, and restricts his or her verbal communication.

ASSUMPTION #4: Initial intercultural communication is a group phenomenon experienced by individuals. Whenever we interact with a person from a different culture, especially early in our relationship with him or her, we carry with U.S. assumptions and impressions of that other person. The specific verbal and non-verbal messages we exchange are usually tailored for the person based on those assumptions and impressions. Often, these are based on characteristics of the other person by virtue of his or her membership in groups related to culture, race, sex, age, or occupation, for example, we have a tendency to see others not as individuals with unique thoughts, ideas, and goals, but rather as "an Asian American" or "a woman" or "an old person" or "a cab driver." In other words, we do not see the person—we see the groups to which the person belongs. The problem with this is that group data may not be a reliable source on which to construct our messages. Because someone belongs to a specific racial, ethnic, sex, or age group does not necessarily mean that he or she takes on the thoughts, behaviors, and attitudes associated with that group. Thus, the potential for miscommunication is great. So during initial intercultural communication, we have to be mindful that while the person with whom we are interacting is from a different cultural group, he or she is also an individual. Once we further develop a relationship with that person, we will start to see the relationship as interpersonal rather than intercultural.

ASSUMPTION #5: Intercultural communication is a cycle of stress, adaptation, and growth. As mentioned earlier in this chapter, when we come together with a person from a different culture we may feel uncertain, apprehensive, and anxious. Such feelings are stressful. Hence, sometimes intercultural communication is stressful. The good news is that we can learn and adapt to such stress and eventually grow. During intercultural communication, we have to be mindful that the communication strategies we use with persons with whom we are familiar may not be effective with persons from other cultures. Thus, we have to learn to adapt and adjust our communication style. We have to recognize that we will make mistakes, learn from them, adapt, and move on. From these experiences, we grow as humans. A good beginning point is to recognize that people from different cultures are different—not better or worse, but simply different. Once we are able to do this, we can adjust and adapt our verbal and non-verbal messages accordingly and become competent interactants.

▶ Benefits of Intercultural Communication

Although the challenges of an increasingly diverse world are great, the benefits are even greater. Communicating and establishing relationships with people from different cultures can lead to a whole host of benefits, including healthier communities; increased international, national, and local commerce; reduced conflict; and personal growth through increased tolerance.

Healthy Communities: Joan England argues that genuine community is a condition of togetherness in which people have lowered their defenses and learned to accept and celebrate their differences. England contends that we can no longer define equality as "sameness" but, instead, must value our differences—whether they be in race, gender, ethnicity, lifestyle, or even occupation or professional discipline. Healthy communities are made up of individuals working collectively for the benefit of everyone, not just their own group. Through open and honest intercultural communication, people can work together to achieve goals that benefit everyone, regardless of group or culture, including the global community in the home, business, or neighborhood. Healthy communities support all community members and strive to understand, appreciate, and acknowledge each member.

Increased Commerce: Our ability to interact with persons from different cultures, both inside and outside our borders, has immense economic benefits. In 2015, the top 10 countries with which the United States traded—in terms of both imports and exports—were, in order, China, Canada, Mexico, Japan, Germany, the Republic of Korea, the United Kingdom, France, and India. In 2015, U.S. trade with these countries accounted for nearly \$3 trillion (i.e., \$3,000,000,000,000). Only through successful intercultural communication can such economic potentials be realized.

Reduced Conflict: Conflict is inevitable; we will never be able to erase it. We can, however, through cooperative intercultural communication, reduce and manage conflict. Often, conflict stems from our inability to see another person's point of view, particularly if that person is from a different culture. We develop blatant negative generalizations about the person, which are often incorrect and lead to mistrust. If we can learn to think and act cooperatively by engaging in assertive (not aggressive) and responsive intercultural communication, we can effectively manage and reduce conflict with others.

Personal Growth: Through tolerance as you communicate with people from different cultures, you learn more about them and their way of life—including their values, history, and habits—and the substance of their personality. As your relationship develops, you start to understand them better, perhaps even empathizing with them. One of the things you will learn (eventually) is that although your cultures are different, you have much in common. As humans, we all have the same basic desires and needs; we just have different ways of achieving them. As we learn that our way is not the only way, we develop a tolerance for difference. This can be accomplished only when we initiate relationships with people who are different from ourselves. We could learn far more about English culture by initiating and maintaining a relationship with an English student at our college or university than we could by traveling to Britain for a 2-week or 3-week vacation. Moreover, although this may sound contradictory, the more we learn about others and other cultures, the more we begin to learn about ourselves. When we observe how others conduct their lives, we begin to understand how we conduct our own lives.

Text B Introducing Critical Intercultural Communication

After Rona Tamiko Halualani

▲ Introduction

Text B introduces a unique approach to understanding intercultural communication; that is, a critical approach. This approach explores and views intercultural communication **encounters** through a specific focus on power and how cultural groups are positioned in different ways through larger, unseen sociopolitical structures, histories, and conditions. These unseen or invisible structures of power that play out in intercultural communication are the taken-for-granted shapers of intercultural relations such as the media, government, economy, history, global markets, and popular culture. A critical approach to intercultural communication will heighten your awareness and analytical skills, as well as raise new and interesting questions to explore. Moreover, a critical approach to intercultural communication enables you to make important observations about the world around you and equips you with insights so that you can take meaningful action and change in improving our world toward more positive and **equitable** intercultural relations. We all can make a difference in this world, and this text will guide you on this path.

▲ Critical Intercultural Communication

A critical approach to intercultural communication provides a perspectival view of the world in terms of the structures and contexts of power that surround us and impact our lives and experiences. This approach examines the invisible **dimensions** of intercultural communication, or the taken-for-granted shapers of intercultural relations such as the media, governmental institutions, economic structures, historical memories, global markets and brands, and popular culture (television, film social media, fashion, cultural trends). The key highlighted element through a critical approach to intercultural communication is power, or the **constraining** force by which larger dominant structures, and sometimes, groups and individuals, are able to gain in position and achieve their aims and interests over or against the will of others. It is important to note that whether we notice or not, invisible dimensions of power frame our intercultural communication encounters, relationships, and everyday experiences.

As stated earlier, intercultural communication is much more than in-person, face-to-face contact between two or more persons or micro interactional episodes. Instead, a critical approach to intercultural communication expands this focus to contain all multi-layered dimensions of power in specific contexts and operate beneath the surface of intercultural communication in hidden and subtle ways.

Definitions of Power

In the words of Martin Luther King, the U.S. Civil Rights leader, "power properly understood is nothing but the ability to achieve purpose. It is the strength required to bring about social, political, and economic change." Power in today's reality refers to the capacity of individuals or groups to determine: who gets what, who does what, who decides what, and who sets the agenda.

Thus, power in the context of the United States can be defined as the degree of control over material, human, intellectual and financial resources exercised by different sections of society. The control of these resources becomes a source of individual and social power. The extent of power of an individual or group is correlated to how many different kinds of resources they can access and control. Different degrees of power are sustained through social divisions such as gender, age, caste, class, ethnicity, race, north-south; and through institutions such as the family, religion, education, media, law, etc. There is a continuous process of resistance and challenge by less powerful and marginalized sections of society, resulting in various degrees of change in the structures of power. When these challenges become strong and extensive enough, they can result in the total transformation of a power structure.

In a sense, power is a relationship between persons, social classes, genders, ethnic groups, generations, territories, states, and institutions, often one in which some are dominate and others are subordinate. It is also a relationship in which resistance, confrontation, and negotiation arise. These relationships can give rise to **upheavals** and breakdowns as people seek to change the relationships of power toward relationships of equality and a world without discrimination or subordination. In addition, power is dynamic and multidimensional, changing according to context, circumstance and interest. Its expressions and forms can range from domination and resistance to collaboration and transformation.

Characteristics of Power

All types of power share three noteworthy characteristics:

(a) A context of power is based on an obvious and/or subtle (visible and or hidden) hierarchy of dominant and subordinate parties.

(b) A context of power revolves around an ongoing struggle for power between dominant and subordinate parties/interests.

(c) Each context is both independent and interdependent of each other.

Hierarchy of Power. This first characteristic highlights how a context of power is based on an obvious and/or subtle (visible and or hidden) **hierarchy** of dominant and subordinate parties. A dominant party can be defined as one that possesses the legal, economic, and governmental authority to enforce rules, laws, policies, taxes and fees onto others—a trait that most individuals do not themselves possess. In addition, this dominant party (or parties) exerts great influence in widely projecting and circulating specific ideas and views about what the "truth" is— how the nation and its government should be viewed and how others are to be seen. A dominant party benefits the most economically and socially, given that its position and power capacities allow it to maintain, reproduce, and strengthen its own supremacy and authority over others. A subordinate party is defined in opposition to that of a dominant one, meaning that a subordinate party does not possess the larger authority to make and enforce laws (and imprison individuals), impose fees, or control media content, nor does it have the great financial and political resources of a dominant party at its feet to exert influence over society. A subordinate party (an individual, a group or community), instead, is often the one who is at the other end of (and who experiences the blow of) the dominant party's full reach of power and authority and who must creatively use its own resources to fight domination and marginalization in society.

As an example, in many cities throughout the United States (and possibly in other countries as well), housing developers and city **"revitalization"** programs (which are funded by state and local grant monies), have targeted rundown, crime-infested, worn-out, and economically struggling city spaces for the building of "new" residential communities that can take advantage of more affordable land and housing prices. Such a process is also known as gentrification, in which housing developers and urban planners make over and re-occupy a city composed of poor and struggling minority groups, such as East Palo Alto in California or Harlem in New York. In such a context, the housing developers (who are mostly White/European American-run corporations that make billions of dollars in revenue), as well as the city/urban planners and redevelopment agencies, represent the dominant parties, while those at the other end, the longtime racialized minority residents (most often Black/African American, Latino, and Southeast Asian communities), who are pushed out of the housing market and eventually out of the new, gentrified cities, represent the subordinate party. The hierarchy of power between these two interests, in this context, positions them in starkly unequal positions, with city developers and planners making all the decisions about redevelopment and with longtime minority residents excluded from the planning process and the economic benefits of gentrification (for they cannot afford to buy the new homes in their own area).

Moreover, there are tense and often hostile interactions and economic competition among the historically established minority residents and those new residents (who are mostly professional class White/European American and Asian Americans) who buy into homes for more reasonable prices and can experience the benefit of remaking a new city (that is, by taking over seats on city councils and enlisting the help of local police officers to watch over and protect their new neighborhoods over the under-resourced areas). Changes in neighborhoods, therefore, indicate a specific hierarchy of socioeconomic class and racial/ethnic interests as intercultural interactions among these parties are, at the outset, already unequal.

Contexts of power with their embedded hierarchy of power interests make seemingly equalized and balanced intercultural interactions more complicated and questionable in terms of mutual understanding and agreement. Instead, the contexts of power that touch intercultural communication encounters and relationships require us to unpack the hierarchies involved that can frame and push an intercultural interaction in a specific direction (and toward affirming one party over the other).

A Struggle for Power: A context of power revolves around an ongoing struggle for power between dominant and subordinate parties/interests. In this hierarchy, dominant and subordinate parties compete with one another to gain societal power. Dominant parties (large structures, such as governmental administrations, court system, corporations, and educational institutions, among others) work hard to establish and maintain the power they have over smaller communities and cultural groups in terms of race, ethnicity, gender, sexual **orientation**, nationality, region, and socioeconomic class, among others. The moves by dominant parties are not always guaranteed in exacting power over others with less power resources; instead, subordinate parties/interests also participate in this feud for power by creatively and strategically using their resources at bay in order to resist such dominant parties and liberate themselves. Thus, this struggle of power is characterized by an unpredictable fight for, on one hand, in terms of dominant parties, domination and control, and, on the other, in terms of socially marginalized groups, freedom, and resistance. No one side is guaranteed of always winning the fight, which is ongoing with new challenges and obstacles. Of course, dominant interests have more wide-reaching resources and capacities of power to make and enforce laws, policies, and taxes, but this does not mean that individuals and groups naturally yield to such forces. Through alternative forms, such as music, art, writing, independent media, the power of protest and mobilization, as well as crafty usages of dominant law and policy, individuals and groups can indeed resist and defy dominant forces, but with great risk and costs to them, including societal rejection, imprisonment, and even death.

Using the aforementioned context of power—redeveloping neighborhoods—the struggle occurs among the housing development corporations, city planners, and the longtime minority residents who are economically pushed out of their homes to make way for more affluent homeowners. As city planners and developers remake certain aspects of a neglected community for upper middle-class homeowners, focus on revenue, push for redistricting changes, and solicit retail franchises to establish businesses in the area, minority residents circulate petitions and create propositions that resist the gentrification process. In addition, minority residents also invite local media coverage to "hear the true story" of how the city (and the housing developers) are "chasing us" out of our homes. Here, housing developers work for profit and territorial control over a neighborhood with the interests of new, affluent residents in mind while current residents fight for the preservation of their communities.

Contexts of power, therefore, stand as **arenas** where struggles of power play out and dominant parties/interests and subordinate parties/interests vie for power—more specifically, for the former, the power to rule over and control all others, and for the latter, the power of freedom and independence from dominant forces.

An Independent and Interdependent Context: The third characteristic of contexts of power in our lives is that each context is both independent and interdependent of each other, meaning that contexts of power typically have their own unique attributes and envelop specific forms of struggles between dominant and subordinate parties/interests. At the same time, these contexts also work in cooperation with one another, providing support for similar and/or shared struggles of power. In the neighborhood context, for example, the city government creates and operates a city redevelopment agency to increase revenue for its fledgling city and attract new and more affluent homeowners (and taxpayers). As an independent unit, the city government context, therefore, possesses its own tailored interests in making profits and **stabilizing** its community base. Within the city context, there also lies an ongoing struggle between city leaders and planners who have made commitments with housing corporations, incoming retail businesses, and city officials and workers who fear that all of these "redevelopment" changes will displace the majority of the residents in the community. Thus, this context is driven by its own interests of power and is characterized by specific struggles over power, such as those between city leaders and other leaders and city workers, as well as a struggle between minority residents and new residents.

But, contexts of power also become **intertwined** with one another and become interdependent in terms of a shared interest in making money, establishing generic communities that "sell," increasing tax revenue, and securing state monies to help support a stable and growing city. Thus, the contexts of local government and economic corporations work together to "redevelop" a racialized neighborhood into an attractive, marketable, and non-minority-focused living community. Such an alliance makes the contexts of local government and economic corporations even more powerful than when each works alone. Contexts of power often operate in cooperation with one another so as to achieve shared interests and goals, especially in terms of gaining and maintaining power and control in a particular setting.

Contexts of Power

There are several overlapping contexts of power in our lives that shape intercultural communication encounters and relations in unique ways. These are as follows:

(a) The economic context.
(b) The governmental context.
(c) The legal context.
(d) The educational context.

(e) The family context.

(f) The media context.

(g) The tourism context.

These settings are constituted by larger, unseen power forces that help to demarcate how we understand and approach culturally different persons and communities. The following section features several main contexts of power that operate in our lives in terms of culture and intercultural communication.

The Economic Context: The context of the economy affects how we live day to day, influencing everything from how much money we make in our jobs to what products or items are deemed important to consume, to which region we will live in based on our socioeconomic class. The economic context is based on material capital (money) and a shifting global/national/regional marketplace of consumer services and goods in which the public (always marked as consumers), in some way, participates, some more than others. The main unit of material capital and how much of it one has, outlines intercultural communication relations by "classing" specific racial/ethnic groups into a hierarchy of socioeconomic classifications—lower class, working class, middle class, upper middle class, upper class.

These classed distinctions determine the type of neighborhoods that individuals will live in, as cities represent complex "racial maps" of ethnic enclaves separated from one another. This impacts our intercultural communication encounters because the economic context influences some cultural groups living in one part of town and away from others. Ethnic enclaves are located in differentially classed areas such as the "slums," "the **ghetto**," "the suburbs," and the "metropolitan downtown," which also further label its residents in racially spatialized ways. The economic context, therefore, places cultural groups in specific areas and in contact with only one to two different groups.

In the greater Bay Area in Northern California, for instance, inner city "ghettoes" and **"dilapidated"** areas house mostly Latino/as Southeast Asians and Pacific Islanders, while the suburbs and ritzier "residential communities" enclose mostly Whites, African Americans, and, in some cases, Asian Americans. Residents, therefore, tend to interact mostly with those other cultural groups that live within their racialized space, and beyond these, many do not have any interactions with other cultures. The economic context also plays a role in placing us in certain professions and jobs, schools and universities, and in friendships and romantic relationships with individuals within our own class **designation**. The economic context therefore frames who and which cultural groups will interact with each other and how often.

The Governmental Context: There are several overlapping levels of governmental power that impact us. The U.S. national government engages in foreign relations and diplomatic missions with other nations. These specific foreign relationships that are forged, and the way in which the U.S. government perceives these relations (as "friendly," "cordial," "tense," "hostile," "at a standstill") inevitably frames the U.S. perspective of the world's nations and their culture(s). The mood that is set through foreign relations not only touches on nation—nation dealings on a formal level, but also how we view their national and ethnic counterparts who have immigrated to the United States.

In the case of World War Ⅱ, when the United States faced off against Japan, the government launched a massive **detainment** of all Japanese who lived in the country, even though the majority of them had been born as American citizens. In the midst of the proclaimed war on Iraq, individuals of Middle Eastern descent, many of whom came to the United States more than 10 years ago, become easy targets of anger and resentment that stem from the U.S. government's view and approach to the Middle East. How the U.S. country treats and interacts with other nations historically also affects how these nations perceive America and by extension, Americans.

We, as private individuals who do not operate at the governmental level, are therefore always considered aligned with the U.S. government and thus, their "relational baggage" becomes our own as citizens from other nations may grow to emulate and or scorn the U.S. government and culture. The enormous power of governmental structures to solidify nation-to-nation relations, organize alliances with specific nations, and declare war on others, greatly frames and configures our views and attitudes about other national cultures and our private one-on-one relationships with individuals who come from (by citizenship) or descend from (by ethnicity/ancestry) other countries.

As another example, state and local governmental bodies also work together with the legal system to define the cultural meaning of marriage. From 2008 through 2012, many state governments and supreme courts reasserted their definition that marriage is a legalized union between a biological male and female. There is no question then that the governmental context (along with the legal context) shapes our cultural definitions of marriage and family, which greatly structure the cultural views of these notions and those individuals who do not fit neatly into the state's definitions. Thus, although same-sex marriages have been **federally** recognized in recent years, this context has pre-determined our contact with and shaped our understanding of same-sex couples before any interaction has taken place in the past and still can today.

The Educational Context: The educational sphere is a major setting that sets into place our knowledge about other cultures and culturally different persons, as well as how we approach diversity and intercultural interactions. Elementary, middle, and high school social studies curricular materials are not neutral, comprehensive resources that describe other nations, their specific histories, and the historical and contemporary role of the United States in relation to the rest of the world. Individuals employed by public/state school districts and who come from specific cultural vantage points (in terms of gender, age/generation, race/ ethnicity, nationality, regional origin, languages spoken, and socioeconomic class, among others) determine such curricula which in turn, shape our views and perceptions of different nations, cultures, and even languages.

What we learn during our childhood education about, for example, the Native Americans and their contentious history with early European settlers in North America, or World War Ⅱ and the designated "allies" and "enemies" of the United States, therefore is not the sole definitive account of "what actually happened" and "how cultures truly are." Instead, the public educational system, with its bureaucratic structures, political interests, and dependency on governmental funding, selectively constructs a specific version of knowledge about other nations and cultures. Under the guise of state-approved curricular standards (which mandates the dissemination of uniform teaching materials to students), unvarying versions of knowledge are continually reproduced throughout schools and with successive generations.

It is questionable as to why many parents and students do not question the supposed "facts" about history and culture that are repeated year after year. Other questions with regard to this context include "Why are only the languages of French and Spanish taught at most public schools, as opposed to other European, African, Asian, and Pacific Islander languages? Why do we only read literary accounts from the 'classic' White American writers such as John Steinbeck and Ernest Hemingway? Who makes these curricular decisions? Why did we not learn more about the original inhabitants of the Americas and how their lives changed when Columbus arrived?"

The Family Context: The sacred space of family is also a context of power in ways that are not completely obvious. Our parents, grandparents, and other family members greatly influence how we see the world and other cultures by **adapting** ourselves into their shared world views and attitudes about others. Rejecting our family's views is not an option, as our families possess great resources of power: their approval, love, financial support, and recognition of us as true family members. Certainly, none of us want to alienate ourselves from the caring and security and emotional/financial support that our family can provide us. But, this becomes difficult when it relates to how to choose to live our lives, the professions we strive for, and the relationships that we build with others. For example, parents and family members have already selected professions for their children before they even enter high school—doctors, engineers, lawyers, business entrepreneurs, teachers, and so on. Their decisions about their children's future determine the kind of schools she or he is to enroll in and the type of social networks she or he must engage in.

Racial/ethnic groups seem to have preferred professions and careers for their children, which derive from cultural and community expectations and priorities. Many Asian Americans, for example, have shared that their parents wanted them to be doctors, engineers, or lawyers as opposed to teachers, social workers, and artists. This creates tension and conflict within families as the children break away from their parents' expectations and pursue different venues. Difficult relations between parents and their grown children are linked to societal beliefs that benefit certain power interests. Racial, ethnic, and cultural communities invoke the societal belief that if children enter the fields of medicine, science, or business, lucrative and socially elevated positions will follow, resulting in financial prosperity and social mobility. These beliefs are not just isolated views of a group that serve only those directly involved; in the larger picture, these beliefs also "feed" the science and business arenas, with a tailored workforce, and help these sectors gain immense esteem (and social respect), privilege, and, of course, profits. Thus, societal structures, such as the economy and government, indirectly and directly touch on our family units and relations.

Throughout our childhood, there may also be ongoing conversations with our parents and elders about who is "appropriate" to be friend, date, and even marry. Seemingly innocent comments such as "You should hang out more with your own kind and not those _____" or, "Those _____ are not good for you" may slip by without notice. Comments such as these may reflect on how a family and or a cultural group view and perceive specific racial, ethnic, religious, socioeconomic, or sexual-identity groups. Learning about their parents' intercultural do's and don'ts of friendship and marriage creates enormous pressure for individuals, and oftentimes forces them to have to choose between their families or their friends, romantic partners, and/or spouses from different backgrounds. There is much at stake in these relational decisions wrought by familial and cultural pressures. Even to this day, parents worry that intercultural and interracial marriages (with specific racial/ethnic group members) will threaten their cultural and religious beliefs and that such unions will not be accepted by society. Cultural communities fear the dilution of cherished cultural traditions and practices and the loss of language over time due to growing rates of intercultural relationships and marriages. Intercultural dating and marriage taboos then indirectly serve to maintain ideals of cultural, racial, or ethnic purity and discourage relationships across difference.

The Media Context: The media context is undoubtedly a powerful shaper of intercultural communication and relations, given the overly media-saturated world in which we live. With access to radio, television, film, and the Internet, individuals all over the world are exposed to representations of the world and its many different cultural groups. We may not see such mediated images, content, and portrayals as representations embedded with specific world views, cultural/national slants, and power interests of capitalism. Instead, more often than not, these images are accepted and invoked with little critical analysis, which could be largely due to the seductive nature of hyper-real, almost life-like, and visually stunning moving images captured on the screen. But when peering closer at mediated images and content, we must remember that these are created in a context driven by economic motives, governmental control (the FCC in the United States, or the BBC in England), and nationalistic interest in negatively depicting certain nations over others.

Thus, given this backdrop of power, the local and national news coverage that we receive often provides imbalanced and distorted views of world events and national occurrences. How, for example, the U.S. media depicts and discusses the war in the Middle East, or the relations between the United States and the Democratic People's Repulblic of Korea, China, Mexico, France, and other national powers with a vested interest in positively valorizing U.S. world views (of democracy, equality, and freedom) and justifying past and present governmental actions—how we understand the depictions of foreign nations and their cultures depends largely on the kind of knowledge constructions and representations that are circulated in various forms of media. For many individuals, with limited economic capital to traverse the world and little leisure time to gather alternative perspectives, the news, therefore, becomes the primary source of supposedly neutral and truthful "information" about other cultures.

The power of the media also lies in our own willing suspension of critical judgment regarding news coverage because of the immediate trust that we place in the journalistic principles of objective fact and the responsibility to tell the truth. How do we as Americans really know what is going in the world's wars and hostile confrontations and what constitutes those conflicts? What ultimately lies beyond the image of nations who supposedly clamor for United States' intervention, aid, and liberation from tyranny? How does news coverage depict and portray immigrants as always "illegal" and swarming and desperate to realize the American dream? How are specific minorities portrayed in terms of being "criminals," "poor," and/or "model citizens"? What do media enterprises and national governments gain by producing certain kinds of representations? Taken together, these questions encourage us to see our media in a different light and in terms of how mediated images reveal different, vested views of cultures, nations, and world events.

▶ Calling for Critical Reflections and Actions

Because we exist in a globalized, media-saturated, and profit-centered world, we stand at the crossroads of great uncertainties, complex questions, and difficult times. The uncertainty lies in the kind of life we can have for ourselves and loved ones in this complex power-laden world in which we, and cultural groups and nations, may have limited resources of power (money, influence, authority) at our disposal. In addition, there is great angst over issues of war and hostility as we consider the many historically-based and "new" conflicts between, among, and within nations and cultural groups. Will only the military-strong and rich nations prevail, while all others are doomed to cultural decimation? Are there actually some cultural differences that cannot be worked out and mediated no matter how much we try? And, what of the cultural groups and nations whose voices are silenced and not considered—what happens to them? How do oppressed cultural groups and nations resist, remake, and tip the contexts of power in their favor? What interpersonal acts and larger efforts can be made to bridge cultures and bring about conditions of equality and empowerment for all cultural groups? How might we incorporate a more just and **transformative** way of approaching cultures and intercultural communication in our lives?

All of these questions further emphasize the importance of critical intercultural communication as an area of study. Simply put, we need to examine, study, and care about intercultural communication in terms of issues of power because there is a great deal at stake if we do not. With a great sense of urgency, then, there is a need for us to enact a critical intercultural communication approach in our lives. This perspective enables us to look beyond and beneath the obvious aspects of power as well as dig down into the hidden dimensions.

This text is written from a critical intercultural communication perspective and it is expected to guide you through this lens of seeing and knowing. This perspective requires that we seriously consider and engage the following questions as we go about our daily routines and encounters:

(a) What dimensions, structures, and forces of power are embedded in my own intercultural encounters and relationships? To what extent are these dimensions, structures, and forces of power invisible and/or obvious?

(b) What kind of power dynamic deeply exists in these encounters and relationships, meaning, what is the hierarchy of power interests and how are different individuals and cultural groups positioned in relation to one another? To what extent does one individual or group have more power than the other?

(c) How am I positioned in the intercultural relationships and encounters in my life? In different contexts (family, work, school, and to the government, corporations, courts of law, and the media)? To what extent do I gain a power advantage over others in some contexts than in others? To what degree am I marginalized and put at a disadvantage in certain contexts over others?

(d) What can I do to change and mediate the power differences between individuals and cultural groups? How might I help others who are marginalized and oppressed in society? What are some small and large acts that I can engage in to bring about equality, reconciliation, positive/cordial relations, and build strong communities?

(e) How can I take advantage of my own position in specific contexts that may be used to help marginalized communities?

(f) How can I raise important questions about culture and power with those around me (my family, friends, classmates, co-workers, and community/cultural members)?

These questions encourage us to seriously consider the different power dimensions that occur in intercultural interactions and relations. Think of how much we all could help one another if we made it a practice to step out of our normal routines and conveniences to question and analyze issues of intercultural interaction in terms of power. We may gain great insight on others from different backgrounds and the experiences they are having in relation to structures of power. We may also learn about our own selves and the taken-for-granted aspects of our cultural identities and experiences. Herein, we can become more attuned thinkers, analysts, cultural members, and societal participants as humans attached to larger communities. These gains represent only some of the amazing gifts that can be proffered through the active practicing of the critical intercultural communication perspective in our lives and, more specifically, in terms of our intercultural communication encounters and relationships.

Applications

1. Intercultural Communication from an Interdisciplinary Perspective

Sadri, A. H. (2011). Intercultural communication from an **interdisciplinary** perspective. *U.S.-China Education Review*, 8(1), 103–109.

Abstract: The need for effective communication among the people of the world has never been more pressing than it is at the start of the 21st century in this post-9/11 world. Recent breakthroughs in such fields as transportation, computing and telecommunications have combined to increase the ease and frequency of communication among members of different cultures. At the same time, developments in world politics have made the need for meaningful communication among different people a necessity for the survival of everyone on the planet. This paper describes a course that prepares students for global citizenship. The course helps students develop an informed understanding of global challenges and the skills to address those challenges. The paper offers specific teaching strategies and assignments that can be adapted to many disciplines.

Keywords: intercultural communication, global citizenship, mindfulness, international relations

2. Intercultural Research: The Current State of Knowledge

Dahl, S. (2004). Intercultural research: The current state of knowledge. Middlesex University Discussion Paper No. 26. Available at http://dx.doi.org/10.2139/ssrn.658202.

Abstract: This paper has focused on two main aspects: The definition of culture and a review of different approaches to research into cultural value dimensions. By presenting a short overview of the main concepts and theories in intercultural and cross-cultural communication, this paper has provided a brief introduction into the field of **empirical** research into culture-based value variations and providing a short outline of the major works in this area. Hall's classic patterns, Hofstede's cultural dimensions, and the value dimensions of Trompenaars and Hampden-Turner have been discussed and compared.

Keywords: intercultural research, current state of knowledge, review, approaches, value dimensions

3. Issues in Intercultural Communication: A Semantic Network Analysis

Barnett, G. & Jiang, K. (2017). Issues in intercultural communication: A semantic network analysis. In L. Chen (Ed.), *Handbook of Intercultural Communication*, 99–118. Mouton de Gruyter: Berlin.

Abstract: This chapter describes a number of critical issues facing the field of intercultural communication including, the discipline's definition, power relations among various ethnic or national groups and nation-states, voice—who speaks for an ethnic group or nation-state, and globalization. But the major portion of the paper takes a different approach to discussing the issues facing intercultural communication. Rather than focusing on what topics, areas of study, or issues the idealized field of international/intercultural communication should concentrate on, it describes the topics that it has examined in the published articles in those journals devoted to the subject over the last fifteen years. It employs a semantic network analysis of the abstracts of articles to answer the questions, "What nations/cultures have intercultural scholars examined?" and "What topics or issues have intercultural communication scholars investigated?" By doing so, we define the field and the issues it faces in the future.

Keywords: power, voice, globalization, semantic network analysis

Interactive Activities

1. Individually, please finish reading Text A, Text B, and the application abstracts and work out the meanings of the terms in bold type by consulting the dictionary or glossary whenever necessary.

2. In pairs, please summarize the content in 2 to 3 sentences of each sub-heading in the unit outlines of Text A and Text B based on your reading and understanding of the texts.

3. In groups, share your gains, comments and suggestions regarding the three application abstracts. Based on your interests, locate and finish reading the full-length papers of your interested abstracts.

4. Q&A: Questions are encouraged about any uncertain or confused part or parts in the unit and seek answers either from other fellow students or the instructor.

5. Complete the Personal Report of Communication Apprehension, a scale designed to measure your degree of communication apprehension. Take a few moments and complete the scale of the self-assessment for Unit 1.

6. A **paper title** constitutes one of the most important components of the entire paper. A successful paper title should: (a) present the reader a clear idea of what the paper will be about; and (b) catch the readers' attention. The techniques for working out paper titles include: (a) use a colon or dash; (b) ask a question; (c) begin with "on"; (d) begin with an "-ing" verb; (e) use an image or word play. Please examine the two titles in Text A and Text B and the other three titles in the abstract applications by underlining the key words in the titles for idea clarification and rephrasing one or two titles for catching readers' attention.

Work out a potential title for an academic or research paper, which is concerning a meaningful intercultural topic or phenomenon and is likely to facilitate "Chinese culture going global."

UNIT TWO

History of Intercultural Communication and History of Intercultural Communication Research

Readings

Text A Notes in the History of Intercultural Communication: The Foreign Service Institute and the Mandate for Intercultural Training

After Wendy Leeds-Hurwitz

Introduction

Many articles discussing some aspect of intercultural communication begin with a paragraph in which the author reviews the history of the field and the major early publications. Typically, Edward T. Hall's book, *The Silent Language*, published in 1959, is listed as the first work in the field, and often specifically mentioned as the crucial starting point. The lack of attention to his motives and sources for the work is not surprising, since the young field still has little history written about it. But no book develops without a context, and no author invents a field without a reason. This study looks at the context in which Hall's work was produced and describes some of the events that led to the creation of the field of intercultural communication. Using this historical record, I argue that the **parameters** of the field were established in response to a particular set of problems. If we are to understand why we include some topics as appropriate and do not consider other types of work, we must understand the urgencies that generated the first study of intercultural communication.

Briefly, I argue that intercultural communication emerged from occurrences at the Foreign Service Institute (FSI) of the U.S. Department of State (DOS) between 1946 and 1956. Because intercultural communication grew out of the need to apply abstract **anthropological** concepts to the practical world of foreign services, this early focus on training American diplomats led to the later, now standard use of intercultural communication training. Only recently (beginning with Gudykunst in 1983) has intercultural communication begun to discuss theoretical approaches; initially the concepts were accompanied only by examples, not by an elaboration of theory. In their first writings on the subject, Hall and Whyte made no explicit attempt to create a new academic field with a novel research tradition. Establishing a new academic field was, rather, a secondary phase, based on Hall's early attempt to translate anthropological insights into cultural differences to an audience that wanted immediate and practical applications, not research studies.

My discussion offers four major arguments: first, that Hall's work was important to the development of the field of intercultural communication; second, that Hall's work originated in and was shaped by the specific context of the FSI; third, that this context resulted in a number of crucial decisions, which were continued by later researchers; and fourth, that these decisions **illuminate** some features of the contemporary literature. Assuming that the readers of this article will be most familiar with the contemporary literature, my effort focuses upon illuminating the historical context which set the stage for the current practices in the field.

The following specific connections between the work of Hall (and others) at the FSI and current intercultural communication research will be demonstrated:

(a) Instead of the traditional anthropological focus on a single culture at a time, or at best, a comparison of two, Hall responded to the critique of his foreign service students by stressing interaction between members of different cultures. Hall is most explicit about this in a publication written jointly with William Foote Whyte:

> In the past, anthropologists have been primarily concerned with the internal pattern of a given culture. In giving attention to intercultural problems, they have examined the impact of one culture upon another. Very little attention has been given to the actual communication process between representatives of different cultures.

This shift from viewing cultures one at a time to studying interactions between members of different cultures has been enormously influential on the study of intercultural communication and is what most completely defines the field today.

(b) Hall narrowed the focus of study from culture as a general concept (macro-analysis) to smaller units within culture (micro-analysis). This occurred in response to a particular problem: the students in the FSI classes had no interest in generalizations or specific examples that applied to countries other than the ones to which they were assigned; they wanted concrete, immediately useful, details provided to them before they left the U.S., and they thought it appropriate that the anthropologists involved in their training should focus their energy on this level of culture. Hall, eventually agreeing that the complaints of his students were justified, began the move from a focus on the entire culture to specific small moments of interaction.

(c) Hall enlarged the concept of culture to include the study of communication; he viewed much of his work as an extension of anthropological insight to a new topic, interaction between members of two or more different cultures. Those who study intercultural communication continue to use the concepts taken from anthropology in the 1940s and 1950s (culture, **ethnocentrism**, etc.), but this cross-fertilization moved primarily in one direction: now only a few anthropologists study proxemics, time, **kinesics** or paralanguage, or focus on interactions between members of different cultures. Although anthropology and intercultural communication were once closely allied, the two fields have grown apart as reflected in the shift from the qualitative methods of anthropology to the quantitative methods of communication generally used in intercultural communication today and in the recent **surge** of interest in applying traditional American communication theories to intercultural contexts. While intercultural communication sprang from anthropological insights, it has been on its own for some thirty years, and some shift in focus was predictable.

(d) Implicit in Hall's work is the view that communication is patterned, learned, and analyzable, just as culture had been previously described. Researchers today make the same assumptions about communication. Without these assumptions, we could not have the abstract theorizing about intercultural communication that now marks the field.

(e) Hall decided that the majority of information potentially available about a culture was not really essential in situations of face-to-face interaction with members of that culture; only a small percentage of the total need be known. Thus he categorized several types of microcultural behavior as the focus of study: tone of voice, gestures, time, and spatial relationships. That intercultural research still pays extensive attention to these types of interaction over many other possibilities is a **tribute** to the influence of his work.

(f) Several aspects of the training established by Hall are accepted as part of the **repertoire** of training procedures used today: First, Hall created teaching materials out of experiences abroad which students in the training sessions were willing to provide; Second, Hall encouraged his students to meet with foreign nationals as part of the preparation for a trip abroad, as one way to increase their knowledge of other cultures. Third, Hall presented his insights as a beginning for his students, but assumed they would continue the learning process once they arrived at their destination.

(g) Hall and his colleagues at FSI are responsible for the use of descriptive linguistics as the basic model for intercultural communication, a model which still implicitly serves as the basis for much current research. Explicit discussion of linguistic terminology is currently enjoying a rebirth through attention to what are now termed the "**etic**" and "**emic**" approaches to intercultural communication.

(h) Hall expanded his audience beyond foreign diplomats to include all those involved in international business, today one of the largest markets for intercultural training. Intercultural communication continues to serve the function of training Americans to go abroad, although it has grown substantially beyond this initial mission to include such areas as the training of foreign students, recent immigrants, and teachers who work with students of different cultural backgrounds; it has established a university base now, and many practitioners engage in research, as well as teaching large numbers of undergraduate students the basics of an intercultural communication approach.

The innovations listed here were picked up by the new field of communication, and they were crucial in the establishment of the area known as intercultural communication. They are today hallmarks of intercultural communication.

▶ Background: The Foreign Service Institute

The story of intercultural communication begins at the Foreign Service Institute. In the 1940s many persons recognized that American diplomats were not fully effective abroad, since they often did not speak the language and usually knew little of the host culture. After World War II Americans began to reevaluate their knowledge and understanding of other countries, both in terms of their languages and in terms of their cultural **assumptions**. Along with general concern about the ability of Americans to interact with foreign nationals, the training and knowledge of American diplomats were issues, since deficiencies in those areas have substantial consequences. In 1946 the U.S. Congress passed the Foreign Service Act, which reorganized the

Foreign Service, and established a Foreign Service Institute to provide both initial training and in-service training on a regular basis throughout the careers of Foreign Service Officers and other staff members.

As one part of the preparation of the bill, in 1945 the *American Foreign Service Journal* sponsored a contest for ideas to improve the training program of the Foreign Service; Foreign Service personnel from around the world contributed essays. Those judged to be the best were published as a series of articles in the journal, and the comments are fascinating. Many themes recur, among them the recommendation for better language training. Because American representatives abroad were often not well trained in foreign languages, many contributors argued that they would be more successful if they had fluency in at least one language other than English. Many authors also urged fuller education about the history, political structure, economics, and international relations with the United States, not only of the country to which the diplomat would be sent, but of the entire geographic region.

About the same time, a series of articles not submitted for the contest, but generally addressing the issue of change in the Foreign Service, was published. One of these specifically criticized the generally limited language fluency in the foreign services and highlighted the need for individuals who knew more than basic grammar and who could converse in a language other than English. In an unpublished history of the beginnings of FSI, Boswell points out that "Prior to 1946 the American Foreign Service placed less emphasis on language qualifications for entry than any other nation's foreign service." He attributed the deficiency to the poor language training available in American schools.

One factor which changed attitudes towards language training in the Foreign Service was the extensive language training program begun by the Army during World War II, which demonstrated the feasibility of language training on a large scale. Little excuse remained for Foreign Service diplomats to have inadequate language skills.

In 1939 Mortimer Graves, then the Executive Secretary of the American Council of Learned Societies (ACLS), reasoned that linguists who were capable of analyzing Native American Indian languages (often funded through ACLS grants) should be able to analyze other, perhaps more politically useful, languages. Convinced that world-wide conflict was inevitable, he obtained funding from the Rockefeller Foundation to put a small group of linguists to work. Mary Haas, the first hired, was asked to analyze Thai from native speakers, to prepare basic teaching materials, and then to teach a group of students the language, combining the spoken words of native speakers with the written materials she had prepared.

When the United States formally entered World War II, Graves brought J. Milton Cowan to Washington; together they organized the linguists to serve the war effort through what became known as the Intensive Language Program (ILP). Those who had been inducted served on the military side of the project, and those who had not participated as civilians through the ACLS. Henry Lee Smith, Jr., who was trained as a linguist, was in the Army Reserves at the time; he was recalled to active duty and put in charge of the military side.

The method, developed as the "linguistic method" of language training, became the "the Army method." Instead of the traditional focus on learning to read and write a language and on grammar as the key to a language, the method emphasized appropriate use of the spoken language, an innovative approach. Because the classroom teacher was a native speaker, students heard the idiomatic usage and pronunciation. These native speakers were under the close **supervision** of professional linguists, who worked with them on consistent organization of the materials. Ideally the material was organized as a series of natural speech situations: asking directions, going shopping, finding housing, etc. Through this division of labor, a small number of linguists supervised a large number of native speakers, and dozens of languages could be taught simultaneously with a minimum of full-time staff members.

Initially the Army program, formally one part of the larger Army Specialized Training Program (ASTP), was to serve 1,500 of the brightest and most qualified army recruits. However, believing that having a larger number of soldiers qualified to speak a variety of languages was desirable, officials increased the number of participants to 15,000. Not all of the techniques that had been established for 1,500 transferred easily to the larger group but, on the whole, the program was remarkably effective. The primary problem with ASTP was not in the training, but in the follow-through. For various reasons, soldiers trained to speak particular languages were assigned **randomly** and only rarely were able to use their linguistic training.

All of these efforts came together when the Foreign Service Institute was officially established. Because of the experience within an Army setting and due in part to the widespread agreement of a need for language training within the Foreign Service, FSI was immediately able to establish a language training program that had already been developed, tested, and proven effective. Frank Hopkins, the first Director of FSI, had studied linguistics and anthropology while at Harvard and had been impressed there with the work of Clyde Kluckhohn. "Hopkins was the **linchpin** in recruiting Haxie [Henry Lee] Smith and in the bringing of Social Science into FSI." Smith moved from the Army, where he had been serving as Director of the Language School, to a position as Director of Language Studies in the Division of Training Services for the Foreign Service in 1946; when the new Foreign Service Institute was formally established in 1947, he was made director of the School of Languages, one of the four schools established within FSI. Smith was later responsible for recruiting well-known linguist George L. Träger into the School of Languages, as well as Edward Kennard, an anthropologist who ran the School of Area Studies. Bringing to FSI the knowledge of how to run a linguistically-based language training program, Smith adapted his experience to a new audience.

Smith maintained the model of native speakers in the classroom, combined with trained linguists available to prepare additional written materials where these were needed, although much of this work had already been prepared under ILP and ASTP **auspices**. The linguists could also work occasionally with the students. For the classes in descriptive linguistics, linguists such as Träger prepared the materials.

Träger summarized the basic approach quite well in this statement, described as the efforts of the entire group working together:

Language has been indicated as being only one of the systematic arrangements of cultural items that societies possess. A culture consists of many such systems—language, social organization, religion, technology, law, etc. Each of these cultural systems other than language is dependent on language for its organization and existence, but otherwise **constitutes** an independent system whose patterning may be described. In theory, when one has arrived at the separate statements of each such cultural system, one can then proceed to a comparison with the linguistic system. The full statement of the point-by-point and pattern-by-pattern relations between the language and any of the other cultural systems will contain all the "meanings" of the linguistic forms, and will constitute the meta-linguistics of that culture.

Two important assumptions are apparent here: first, that the analysis of culture was dependent upon a prior linguistic model; and second, that linguistic meaning comes not from words alone but from a combination of the linguistic and what was then termed the "metalinguistic" levels. Both ideas are basic to Hall's 1959 book; both have influenced the contemporary field of intercultural communication.

The other members of the group to which Träger refers were: John M. Echols, Charles A. Ferguson, Carleton T. Hodge, Charles F. Hockett, Edward A. Kennard, Henry Hoenigswald, and John Kepke. Träger, Ferguson, and Hodge all had the advantage of having worked previously with Smith within the Army program. Edward Hall came into the group later than the others, in 1951, and frequently served a different administrative structure, although he was part of the FSI staff, and did participate in most of the **orientation** programs for Foreign Service personnel. In addition to learning how to speak a particular language, the students attended a seminar on general linguistics and another on discussing general principles for analyzing human societies. There Hall found his role, working to ensure that the students obtained general anthropological training to complement their specific language training. Shortly before Hall's arrival, Edward Kennard published an article describing the role of anthropology at the FSI, in which he mentions developing the course, "Understanding Foreign Peoples," to combine anthropological insights with actual Foreign Service experiences.

Although a full member of the FSI staff with the rank of professor, Hall was under a different administrative branch of the Department of State, the Technical Cooperation Authority (TCA) also widely referred to as Point IV. He worked closely with the linguists and anthropologists at FSI from 1951 to 1955 to provide the training TCA required, since no separate staff was available. A contemporary described TCA as "a stepchild in the organization (FSI)" for various reasons, a fact that did not facilitate its work. Hall points out that FSI acquired a reputation for having a large number of anthropologists. Later problems were attributed to the inappropriate numbers of anthropologists on staff, and two new directors were sent into the organization with orders to "get rid of the anthropologists." Hall writes in detail about the administrative problems that academics in government faced: many of them could not use the proper procedures effectively, seeing them as unnecessary interference. Thus, they spent an inordinate amount of time trying to get their work done, and struggling to offer the training they were hired to provide. The basic four-week training course that Hall and the others offered to Point IV technicians was a modified version of the training given to foreign service personnel, including beginning instruction in the language of the country of assignment, orientation to the mission and its philosophy, limited study of the country and area, and a small amount of time devoted to anthropological and linguistic generalizations, including culture as a concept, change as a process, and common American assumptions.

Micro-Cultural Analysis

The idea of culture, one of the central concepts taught in the anthropology seminars, was, and still is, one of the cornerstones of intercultural communication. Today, of course, the notion that each group of people has what can be described as a unique culture, consisting of traditional ways of doing things, traditional objects, oral traditions and belief systems, is taken for granted. In the 1940s and 1950s this was a newer concept, requiring extensive discussion. Much to the astonishment of the anthropologists, many participants in the seminars viewed the concept itself as vague and viewed discussing it as a waste of time; instead, they wanted concrete information about how to interact with persons in the specific culture to which they were being sent. As Hall later wrote, "There seemed to be no 'practical' value attached to either what the anthropologist did or what he made of his discoveries." Faced with this reaction, Hall resolved to focus on what he termed micro-cultural analysis: on tone of voice, gestures, time, and spatial relationships as aspects of communication. These smaller units of a culture, having obvious and immediate impact on interaction between members of different cultures, were very attractive to the foreign service personnel. Hall writes: "Micro-cultural analysis, when used, seems to be much more acceptable and more readily handled by the layman." Thus, the focus of his training efforts gradually became all those parts of culture which are learned and used without conscious notice. By the time he published *The Silent Language*, this emphasis on aspects of interaction generally ignored by others was even more obvious: "If this book has a message it is that we must learn to understand the 'out-of-awareness' aspects of communication. We must never assume that we are fully aware of what we communicate to someone else."

Sometimes Hall termed these discussions "informal culture," which he contrasts with "formal culture," defined as traditional parts of knowledge, and "technical culture," the most explicit elements of knowledge, and those generally associated with particular sciences or technologies. In presenting this **scheme**, Hall emphasized that although lay persons assumed that informal culture has no rules or patterns governing it, the job of the anthropologist was to prove otherwise. At one time he explained informal culture through an extended description of the difference between what we assume schools are supposed to teach students, the formal and technical, and what they really teach, the informal. In the latter category he included: All things are subservient to time; Bureaucracies are real; What happens in the classroom is a game, and the teachers set the rule, and the teacher's primary mission is to keep order.

While discussing the complexity of the cultural systems governing interaction, Hall provides a clear statement of culture as a system of patterns which must be learned:

> The anthropologist knows that in spite of their apparent complexity, cultural systems are so organized that their content can be learned and controlled by all normal members of the group. Anything that can be learned has structure and can ultimately be analyzed and described. The anthropologist also knows that what he is looking for are patterned distinctions that transcend individual differences and are closely integrated into the social matrix in which they occur.

The extension from this view of culture to assuming that communication, as culture's **counterpart**, is equally patterned, learned, and analyzable is implicit in Hall's work, although others, writing later, made the point explicitly. These assumptions about culture and communication and the ways in which they are similar lie at the heart of much current research in intercultural communication; Hall's influence here is crucial. Hall views culture as communication, and others after him have had to come to terms with the ways in which the two overlap.

For Hall, the practical implication of this theoretical extension of culture into communication was the **feasibility** of training those going overseas to attend deliberately to the more **subtle** aspects of interaction and to understand more fully the implications of their own behavior for others. Hall notes that the beginnings of his awareness of cultural impact on behavior occurred through observing his own interactions with others. While preparing the orientation materials for Americans going overseas, he was surrounded by people who represented many of the major languages and cultures of the world, some of whom would stop by his office to visit. "I would find myself impelled (as though pulled by hidden strings) to hold myself, sit, respond, and listen in quite different ways. I noted that when I was with Germans I would (without thinking) hold myself stiffly, while with Latin Americans I would be caught up and involved." It was exactly this sort of awareness of behavior that he then tried to foster in others. His instruction stressed understanding that others do not necessarily interpret our behavior as we do nor as we expect them to. Unlike typical anthropology students, the students in these classes were unwilling to arrive in a culture and simply observe interaction for several months before trying to draw conclusions as to what was occurring. In response, Hall gradually concluded that the majority of information potentially available about a culture was not really essential in situations of face-to-face interaction with members of that culture: only a small percentage of the total need be known, although that portion was critical.

One problem in implementing this insight was the lack of information at the level of micro-cultural analysis. Hall had to create his own materials, primarily using details about experiences abroad which students in the training sessions were willing to provide. In addition, Hall was able to travel abroad to check the effectiveness of his program; he specifically listened to the problems Americans were having once they arrived at their destinations. These stories served as an additional resource for improving training.

In his earliest articles Hall already demonstrated what was to become a mark of his approach: providing a few generalizations, along with a large number of specific examples documenting interaction differences between members of different cultures. His students at FSI encouraged this approach, because they would tolerate only a few theoretical statements, although they paid attention to concrete details of real occurrences and were able to learn from them by drawing their own generalizations. This style also served him well with a broader audience, although scholars within intercultural communication, who hope for more extensive, less anecdotal, perhaps more traditionally academic studies, sometimes criticize it. As late as 1979, Nwanko suggested that most intercultural communication instructors "focus on the identification of communication barriers and on description and application rather than theory-building." This can be attributed largely to the origins of the field as a practical tool for training diplomats rather than as discipline based within a university setting, where the focus would have been on abstract theorizing. By 1983 this had changed with the publication of a volume specifically devoted to theories within intercultural communication.

Hall notes that the four weeks total training time for the general sessions as well as specific language training only provided a direction for students; he saw four months as ideal. A series of shortcuts designed to maximize the amount of learning possible despite a lack of available teaching time were used to make the endeavor feasible. For example, he mentions the need to put Americans in touch with someone from the local culture with the task of discovering how many times they had to meet with someone in the country before they could begin official business. Through such assignments, Americans destined for the Middle East learned not to pursue business too quickly. Intercultural communication training still takes this approach of providing basic orientation to some problems that occur in intercultural interaction, leaving the balance of the learning to the student.

▲ Proxemics, Time, Para-language, and Kinesics

Major early statements on proxemics and non-verbal communication developed out of the training program at the Foreign Service Institute. In trying to adapt anthropological concepts for presentation to a new audience, Hall and the others established a whole new series of concepts: Hall's proxemics and related discussions of the use of time, occasionally called **chronemics**, Träger's **paralanguage**, and Birdwhistell's **kinesics**, were all initially begun by the group of linguists and anthropologists who were involved in the training courses presented through FSI. These areas are today standard parts of courses on intercultural communication and of other shorter training sessions, as well as standard parts of much research in other areas of communication.

Not until 1963 did Hall separate his work on cultural differences in use of space from the other aspects of micro-cultural analysis, and give it the name now popular, "**proxemics**." He reported having considered a series of other possible labels, including: "topology," "chaology," the study of empty space, "oriology," the study of boundaries, "choriology," the study of organized space. But he decided that proxemics was most descriptive. Since the widespread adoption of a new field of study is often delayed until a name has been chosen, this choice of a name was critical. Later, in 1972, he reunited the various aspects of non-verbal communication, saying "proxemics represents one of several such out-of-awareness systems which fall within the general rubric para-communication." "Para-communication," not a term generally used in the field then or now, served as one of a series of ways of referring to the entire complex of what are today more generally termed non-verbal "channels" of communication. Other early terms included Träger's "meta-linguistics," again not the term of choice today.

The materials Träger wrote while at FSI between 1948 and 1953 allude to meta-linguistics and the importance of extending the study of linguistics to more than words. Originally, all non-verbal communication was categorized under the rubric "meta-linguistics," and all was viewed as being potentially of equal interest to linguists. Träger saw no reason for linguists to limit themselves to the study of language, arguing that non-verbal behaviors had an influence both on language choice and on how such choices were interpreted by participants in an interaction. Since virtually no one else was studying non-verbal communication at the time, there was little competition, and no one to complain if Träger and the others crossed the boundary between language and other aspects of culture and/or communication to "**trespass**" on territory covered in other disciplines. Although Träger's **seminal** article on paralanguage was not published until 1958, after research experience with *The Natural History of an Interview* team, among other influences, his position on the significance of that research was established while he was at FSI, as a direct result of the effort to put linguistic generalizations into a form which diplomats would be able to appreciate and put to immediate use.

Träger not only published general statements on the importance of meta-linguistics as an extension of language study and the specific programmatic statement for research in paralanguage, but he was also the group member most directly involved in Hall's writings. In all of his early publications, Hall credits Träger as a collaborator. The draft for *The Silent Language* was actually published jointly, as *The Analysis of Culture*. This jointly authored text was issued only as a prepublication draft, by FSI in 1953, although at various times Hall commented that it was to be published shortly. Träger later decided it was not the best possible analysis, commenting in 1971: "No other edition ever published; no published criticism or discussion. GLT has completely replaced this scheme by another." His assessment reflects his effort to refine his work rather than **substantive** disagreements with the content of the work. In a parallel fashion, Hall also revised his understandings of intercultural communication as the years went by. He noted "My own description does not **deviate** in any significant degree from the joint version. However, I have come to feel that it was somewhat oversimplified and this I shall attempt to correct." In *The Silent Language* Hall sometimes uses the plural first person form and refers often to an idea or a problem as being a joint effort between himself and Träger. In later publications Träger's role has become significantly reduced, though still noticeable.

Since one of Hall's major statements about his work was published in *Current Anthropology* and accorded the CA treatment (being subjected to critique by peers, their comments published with the article), Träger had the opportunity to comment in print on the development of the work. After objecting to a rather minor linguistic point (Hockett's comment that language has the characteristic of **duality**, which he feels Hall has misunderstood and consequently misused), he adds that he is able to "commend this article unreservedly." As this statement shows, and as Hall confirms, any disagreements were minor.

Although Ray L. Birdwhistell was at FSI only during the summer of 1952, his publication of *Introduction to Kinesics* through FSI established his reputation as the expert in that area of communication. In spite of his brief tenure, discussion at FSI during the time, particularly the need to focus attention on a micro-analytic level, influenced his work. Like Träger he was later a part of *The Natural History of an Interview* team and developed his early insights in that context, adapting them to a new audience of **psychiatrists**. As with the study of proxemics, time, and paralanguage, kinesics obviously can be and now is fruitfully applied to almost any context of interaction. But all four originated with a particular context in mind, a context which shaped the way they developed.

My concern here is not to distinguish between the specific contributions of each member of the group at FSI, but rather to stress the importance of understanding that the influential work produced at FSI was partly due to the particular combination of talents drawn together at one time and place for a single purpose. As the person most immediately involved with Hall's work, Träger merited the title of co-author on the original major publication, but the presence of other scholars was equally significant since their ideas contributed to the whole. Although it is customary to attribute specific ideas to individual writers, sometimes an unusually **fortuitous** combination of individuals, brought together for the purposes of a specific research agenda, can encourage the development of new insights by all. Because he is the author of most of the early work on intercultural communication, giving Hall sole credit for the ideas is easy. However, the **catalyst** of the particular context, and informal discussions with particular individuals available, may well have been crucial to his thinking.

The Linguistic Model

Modelling para-language, kinesics, and proxemics after the analysis of language provided by descriptive linguistics was a deliberate attempt to make at least some aspects of culture as readily available to **verbalization**, and as readily taught, as language. Linguistics in the 1940s had acquired the reputation of being the most "scientific" of the social and behavioral sciences, and the FSI group wanted anthropology to be equally scientific. That two of the most influential descriptive linguists of the 1950s, Smith and Träger, were part of the group of peers Hall found at FSI was obviously a contributing factor. Not only did linguistics as a whole have the reputation of being scientific, but representatives were available daily and influenced Hall's ideas as they developed. Hall emphasized that the material he included in micro-cultural analysis was intended to be learned "in much the same way that language is learned," eventually making explicit the connection between linguistic analysis and cultural analysis: "Language is the most technical of the message systems. It is used as a model for the analysis of the others." In later writings he related this parallel more specifically to micro-cultural analysis:

> A micro-cultural investigation and analysis properly conducted can provide material which can be compared in the same way that phonetic and phonemic material from different languages can be compared. The results of such studies are quite specific and can therefore be taught in much the same way that language can be taught.

Occasionally Hall has been explicit about why he saw the linguistic model as a particularly useful one, as when he specifically listed the strengths of linguistics: "It has distinguished between etic and emic events..., and has been able to handle greater and greater complexity." He wished to utilize these strengths in intercultural communication. If anything, the linguistic model is even more important today to intercultural communication research, as the concepts of "etic" and "emic," in a slightly adapted form, are undergoing a strong **revival** as key terms in the field.

For many of the same reasons that prompted Hall to utilize the model of descriptive linguistics in developing proxemics, Träger and Birdwhistell used descriptive linguistics as their model in developing para-language and kinesics. Träger's interest in para-language was an extension of his interest in language; he considered it obvious that para-language as a field of study would closely parallel formal linguistic analysis of language. Although the majority of his early work focused on a rather abstract level of analysis, developing the categories to be used in studying paralinguistic behavior, he subsequently published a description of paralinguistic behavior for a Native American language, Taos. Later authors described in detail the problems that divergent paralinguistic norms can cause when, members of different cultures attempt to interact, the application of the topic most directly relevant to the study of intercultural communication. Birdwhistell has been equally explicit about the deliberate use of descriptive linguistics as the model for kinesic analysis in his outlines of the historical development of kinesics, and about the influence of linguists such as Träger and Smith on his ideas. Hall was responsible for recommending to Kennard that Birdwhistell be brought into the FSI group; his intention was to permit him to work with the linguists there in refining his early model of kinesics.

In addition to the ready and appropriate model linguistics provided for analysis of human symbolic behavior, Hall points out that the linguists at FSI were more successful in their efforts to teach language than the anthropologists were in their efforts to teach culture and adds that this **disparity** led to direct comparisons of the methodologies of the two fields. "Träger and Smith thought that if language is a part of culture, and can be taught so that people speak with little or no accent, why would it not be possible to analyze the rest of culture in such a way so that people could learn by doing and thereby remove the accent from their behavior?" This provided yet another reason to use a linguistic model.

▶ Culture and Communication

One goal of Hall's work was to extend the anthropological view of culture to include communication. At the time anthropologists paid attention to large cultural systems (e.g., economics or kinship) only and did not document directly interaction patterns in any detail. Statements relating culture and communication abound in his work; both *The Silent Language* and *The Hidden Dimension* have entire chapters devoted to the subject. In the early work, culture is seen as primary, communication as secondary, since it is only one aspect of culture. In the later work, Hall suggests "culture is basically a communicative process," thus reversing the order: communication is now viewed as primary. In light of this, it is important to note that *The Silent Language* was proposed as the first presentation of "the complete theory of culture as communication," not as the establishment of a new field to be called intercultural communication, not even as an outline of proxemics and/or the study of time as new **foci** for research.

Much of Hall's work is explicit about citing anthropological precedents, from the grandfather of American anthropology, Franz Boas to the most significant of the early American linguists: Edward Sapir, Leonard Bloomfield, and Benjamin Lee Whorf. Indeed, Whorf's essays were first gathered together and published by FSI during Hall's tenure there. Whorf's influence on Hall's work is obvious in *The Silent Language*, where he is called "one of the first to speak technically about the implications of differences which influence the way in which man experiences the universe. " In *The Hidden Dimension*, Hall specifically says: "The thesis of this book and of *The Silent Language*, which preceded it, is that the principles laid down by Whorf and his fellow linguists in relation to language apply to the rest of human behavior as well—in fact to all culture. "

The changing connections between intercultural communication and anthropology **merit** explicit comment. Culture as a concept had been and still is traditionally the domain of anthropology. Yet, for a variety of reasons, many of them political and bureaucratic in nature, anthropologists were no longer a part of FSI after the late 1950s. For other reasons relevant to disciplinary boundaries in American universities, anthropologists are not generally involved in intercultural communication as currently taught, whether as a full course or as a workshop.

Hall's first publication on intercultural communication, in 1955, was titled "The Anthropology of Manners," not "proxemics" or "the silent language," and not "intercultural communication. " He suggests that:

> The role of the anthropologist in preparing people for service overseas is to open their eyes and sensitize them to the subtle qualities of behavior—tone of voice, gestures, space and time relationships—that so often build up feelings of frustration and hostility in other people with a different culture. Whether we are going to live in a particular foreign country or travel in many, we need a frame of reference that will enable us to observe and learn the significance of differences in manners. Progress is being made in this anthropological study, but it is also showing us how little is known about human behavior.

Hall's focus on establishing a "frame of reference" that would enable one to observe better and that would help us to discover the significant differences in manners (or, as more commonly described today, interaction styles), has remained important in the field. His emphasis on how much is still to be discovered, rather than what had already been learned, was an appropriate emphasis for a new field. His statement also illustrates how Hall clearly positioned his new field in relation to the discipline of anthropology, not communication. Only in looking back on the past thirty years of work, do we know communication would provide an intellectual home to the new field rather than anthropology; in the 1950s there was no way to predict its future course. My suggestion is not that anthropology in some way abandoned intercultural communication, but that the expanding field of communication turned out to be an appropriate "foster home" for the new research into intercultural interaction, readily accepting the "infant" as a member of its extended "family. "

Anthropology originally addressed an academic audience, along with a smaller group in various government agencies. The original audience of intercultural communication was the reverse: primarily a sector of government (foreign service officers) with a small audience among academics. But this division changed over time. Intercultural communication today addresses a varied audience: Americans who travel for pleasure or business or school as well as foreign nationals coming to this country for any of the same reasons. Hall himself made this shift away from the original audience of diplomats. In at least one article, Hall drew explicit connections between his work with diplomats and what has become one of the largest groups interested in the results of intercultural communication research and training: international business. The rationale for this new, broader audience assumed that the same wide variety of factors that played a role in diplomatic interactions must play an equal role in business. Even in this early application, Hall saw the value of the case study approach; a major section of his article describes how a business deal **"soured"** due to cultural differences in timing, use of space, etc. Comparable case studies still abound in intercultural communication training today as one of the best ways to provide participants concrete examples of problems caused by cultural differences in communication patterns.

▶ Conclusion

FSI hired some of the best linguists and anthropologists of the day to train members of the Foreign Service. These academics had to adapt their knowledge for the new audience in a variety of ways; this adaptation led to new ideas about their work and to a **burst** of creativity in the late 1940s and early 1950s. The need to teach immediately practical aspects of their subject led to the study of small elements of culture, rather than the traditional topics anthropologists taught their college students. This shift, in turn, led to the creation of new fields of research, all centered on the role of non-verbal communication in social interaction: proxemics, time, kinesics, paralanguage. Since the academics who had been assembled were not adept at nor interested in the political **maneuvering** necessary to survive in the federal bureaucracy, the group was disbanded in the mid-1950s. But by that time their role in establishing what is now known as the field of intercultural communication had been completed and their influence assured.

Hall's writings have been **instrumental** in the development of intercultural communication as it is currently practiced; further, since Hall's approach was created in response to the context provided by the FSI, the field today owes much to the explicit requests of a small group of diplomats in the 1940s and 1950s for a way to apply general anthropological insights to specific problems of international discourse. Intercultural communication as a field obviously has changed in many ways over the past forty years, and no doubt will continue to change; understanding the roots of our own discipline and the reasons for some of the decisions that have come to be accepted as **doctrine** can only increase our ability to deliberately shape it to meet future needs.

Text B Murky Waters: History of Intercultural Communication Research

After John Baldwin

▶ Introduction

Determining the beginnings of the field of intercultural communication research is problematic. Many consider Edward T. Hall to be the founder of the modern study of intercultural communication; there were no departments with specialization in intercultural communication before his day. But this claim requires three **caveats**: (a) The history of research in communication and culture precedes Hall. (b) There are **domains** of research outside of the mainstream of "intercultural communication" that at times have forcefully entered the discipline. And (c) most histories of the study of intercultural communication consider primarily what has occurred within or in relation to the United States or English-speaking countries. In this essay, we consider the background and main **trajectory** of the study of intercultural communication, some newer "histories" of research that have challenged that main trajectory, and issues that these approaches present to the field. Through a glimpse here at different histories we will see that the fields of inquiry, authors, and histories upon which one draws have major implications for what one considers to be culture, how one approaches the study of culture and communication, and the interaction of that research with issues of ethics and **civic** engagement.

▶ Competing Histories of Intercultural Communication Research and Theory

Wendy Leeds-Hurwitz relates the emergence of the field of intercultural communication with the work of Edward. T. Hall and others within the Foreign Service Institute of the United States during the 1940s and 1950s. This marks an important point in one history of intercultural communication research, as it framed an approach to research that continues to the present day; however, before we consider this specific influence, we must consider the roots prior to this time, and then look ahead to the intellectual results of a movement that Hall and his colleagues began.

The Prehistory of the Modern Study of Intercultural Communication

Everett Rogers and William Hart, outlining the histories of international, development, and intercultural communication, note the common focus in communication between peoples who have characteristic group differences, based on different group-held values and beliefs. They **contend** that, although development and international communication have been informed by macro-level concerns (e.g., sociology, national or group-based agendas), interpersonal communication theory and research have been the primary drivers of intercultural communication. Framing their discussion in terms of Thomas Kuhn's work on the evolution of scientific **paradigms**, they argue that, while the work of the Foreign Service Institute solidly establishes a "paradigm" for intercultural research, there is—as Kuhn suggests there always will be—"pre-paradigmatic" work in which scholars debate issues and ways of seeing things until one perspective becomes dominant.

Specifically, they summarize authors, beginning in the European anthropology (Boas, Sapir) and psychology (Freud). Sociologist Charles Darwin had both a direct influence, through his study of ethology (the study of animal behavior) and non-verbal behavior, and indirectly through the social evolutionary theories of Karl Marx and Herbert Spencer, who impacted other authors. Darwin's ethology related to Edward T. Hall's work, for example, as he compared human use of space to that of birds, and Marx's view impacted future authors who looked at the evolution of cultures.

An early anthropologist, Franz Boas, critiqued the **ethnocentrism** in the work of Tylor and others, promoting, instead, a view of *cultural relativism*—the idea that the cultural standards of one culture cannot be used to judge other cultures. Some of Boas' students (Edward Sapir, Ruth

Benedict, Margaret Mead) were influenced by Freud's notions of the subconscious, which ultimately influenced the idea later used by Edward T. Hall in 1959 that people follow unconsciously learned patterns of culture. Figure 2.1 visualizes these cross-cutting influences. Rogers and Hart continue to describe how these and other authors began early research on standard topics of intercultural research, such as cross-cultural differences, non-verbal communication, ethnocentrism, cultural adjustment, competence, prejudice, and the notion of the stranger. Content analysis of top intercultural journals demonstrates that these topics continue to hold importance among scholars today.

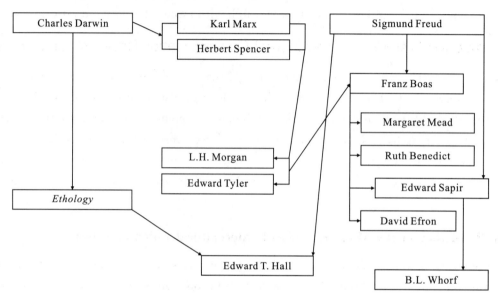

Figure 2.1 Roots of Intercultural Communication

While focusing on things such as the mind, social evolution, sociology, or anthropology, these authors touched upon topics that are communicative in nature. Many of the early anthropological ethnographies include at least some component of communication. Steven Kulich, who later takes a biographical approach to the roots of the study to intercultural communication, wonders whether an early article by Francis J. Brown in 1939 may be one of the first journal articles focusing specifically on culture and communication. In this article, Brown contrasts ethnocentrism to cultural **pluralism**, which he defines as "the continuation of the folk culture of the many racial and national group," with implications for intercultural education.

The Foreign Service Institute and Edward T. Hall

Many contemporary intercultural authors consider Edward T. Hall and the work of the Foreign Service Institute to be central to the history (at least this history) of intercultural research—a hinge to which previous work looks forward and later work looks back. Hall and other scholars, under the **impetus** of U.S. President Truman, began a training program for U.S. diplomats that "conceptualized the new field of ICC (intercultural communication)." Rogers and Hart see this work as the foundation of a paradigm for seeing intercultural communication. In 1990, Wendy Leeds-Hurwitz outlines the origins of intercultural communication in the Foreign

Service Institute, detailing the specific work of Edward T. Hall, the collaboration of scholars that worked together to create the training programs used in the Foreign Service Institute, and, most importantly for our discussion, the impact of these origins on the study of intercultural communication.

Hall began outlining his view of intercultural communication in a 1955 article in *Scientific American* on the "anthropology of manners" and expanded this through a series of books based on his own experiences and interaction with **expatriates**, including *The Silent Language* (1959/1973), *The Hidden Dimension* (1966/1982), *Beyond Culture* (1976/1981), and *The Dance of Life* (1983). In these books, Hall presented **constructs** that scholars and trainers still use today—such as high and low context communication, **monochromic** and **poly-chronic** time orientations, the zones of personal space and the idea of high and low contact cultures and others. He saw culture as patterned, much like language, and patterns being invisible to most people, who follow them without thinking. Culture is an "irrational force," with the result that "people in culture-contact situations frequently fail to really understand each other."

Leeds-Hurwitz describes Hall's contributions to the discipline in detail, including his shift from a wide-based anthropological and theoretical focus to a "micro-cultural" focus—that is, what were the specifics of cultural behavior that diplomats could learn and become adept in—aspects of space, time, verbal and non-verbal communication, and other behaviors. This shift turned attention fully to the focus of communication in cultural contexts, with a special focus on communication between people of different national backgrounds. Hall saw culture as "patterned, learned, and analyzable," using descriptive linguistics as a model for studying culture. He promoted training techniques still used today and expanded the relevant audience for intercultural knowledge beyond diplomats. Interestingly, Hall did not intend to start a new **discipline**, leading Kulich to conclude that he should "not be labeled as 'founder,' but more indirectly as an inspiration, **impetus**, or 'grandfather,' just as Margaret Mead, Clyde and Florence Kluckhohn, and Ruth Benedict were surely intercultural 'grandparents'."

Regardless of how we see Edward T. Hall's role, Leeds-Hurwitz notes that the historical **juncture** of the Foreign Service Institute, and the paradigm of research that it inspired, was not due to Hall alone, but to a critical group of scholars gathered by the U.S. government within the Foreign Service Institute. These include many scholars who also form the history of the modern U.S. social scientific study of non-verbal communication (rather than a semiotic or critical view)—scholars who looked at aspects of non-verbal communication, but always with an eye on cultural differences. Central to the work of these scholars were the disciplines of anthropology and linguistics. Hall himself was an anthropologist, and Frank Hopkins, the director of the institute, had also studied both anthropology and linguistics. These authors used the "model of descriptive linguistics" as their approach to culture, to suggest that cultural behavior was patterned and learnable, even without an "accent." Important to our review here, linguistics at this time (1940s–1950s) "had acquired the reputation of being the most 'scientific' of the social and behavioral sciences," with the Institute seeking to make anthropology "equally scientific."

Rogers and Hart note that the Institute established a firm paradigmatic base for the study of intercultural communication. We can see four important points based on these origins: (a) In modern terms, even though based largely in anecdotal research (Hall's narratives from diplomats and his own experience), the discipline saw the valid approach to culture and communication to be one that was "social scientific." (b) In terms of the analysis of definitions of culture by Faulkner, Baldwin, Lindsley and Hecht, the view of culture was a "structural" definition of culture—with culture treated much as a patterned set of components passed down, like a suitcase, from one generation to another. (c) The focus of training and education became highly pragmatic, a "skills" approach, giving the travelers the "micro" information that the trainers felt they most needed to be effective in the host culture. (d) Both the stories on which much of the work is based and the training the Institute provided were focused on individuals traveling to and from nations; thus, "culture" was treated largely in national terms, "used by relatively large numbers of people," with cultural boundaries "usually, but not always" fitting with political or national boundaries.

A Trajectory of Research

As we have noted, Rogers and Hart suggest that the Foreign Service Institute began a paradigm of research that informed a generation of researchers. Several authors have done an excellent job outlining this history provide a useful outline, roughly by decade, which can guide us through the work of this period with titles for each period borrowed from Baldwin, Coleman, González and Shenoy Packer.

The 1950s: The Decade of Beginnings. We have already seen the impetus or beginning of the modern academic study of intercultural communication in the Foreign Service Institute.

The 1960s: The Decade of Silence. Rogers and Hart argue that during this decade (and into the next), the paradigm of intercultural communication begun by the Foreign Service Institute became accepted and developed into what Thomas Kuhn, in his approach to the revolution of science (applied frequently to communication discipline) called "normal science"—an accepted way of doing things. In 1998, Chen and Starosta noted two major books in this era—Robert Tarbell Oliver's *Culture and Communication*—a book of lectures by the author in 1962, and Alfred Smith's *Communication and Culture*, an edited book of essays contributed by scholars from a variety of disciplines in 1966, which focus specifically on culture and communication. Michigan State University and the University of Pittsburg began teaching courses on the subject.

The 1970s: The Decade of Research. During the next few years, intercultural communication courses began to **prosper**. The first doctorate in intercultural communication may have been given to William Starosta. Doctoral programs began at several schools that offered coursework in intercultural communication. Both Chen and Starosta and Rogers and Hart **enumerate** the large number of first editions of intercultural texts that emerged during this period. In addition, edited books of readings appeared, as well as the first issue of the long-running *International and Intercultural Communication Annual*. The latter was similar to a semi-annual journal, with up-to-date research by a variety of scholars; similarly, William Starosta established *The Howard Journal of Communications*, which continues to publish articles related to intergroup communication, sex and gender, national cultures, and so on; and Dan Landis edited the first issue of the *International Journal of Intercultural Relations*, a multi-disciplinary journal focused on all aspects of international and intercultural training and communication. Finally, divisions in intercultural communication began in the International Communication Association (ICA) in 1970 and in what is now the National Communication Association (NCA) in 1975—both U.S.-based; each is now one of the largest divisions in the respective association.

What characterizes this era of this history of intercultural communication is the focus on research. Chen and Starosta suggest that intercultural research in the 1970s was characterized by "disorder," with scholars pursuing their own directions, with little theoretical focus. It was an area of great growth in the discipline—with an array of new course texts and with edited books, journals, and scholarly associations dedicated to the study of intercultural communication.

The 1980s: The Decade of Theory. This era runs from 1981 to the present. Chen and Starosta suggest that many scholars trained in the 1960s and 1970s (often in rhetoric), such as Molefi Kete Asante (formerly Arthur Smith), John Condon, Michael Prosser and William Howell, were now teaching intercultural communication courses. They list five edited volumes that promoted theory specifically in the 1980s: *Intercultural Communication Theory* by Gudykunst in 1983, *Theories in Intercultural Communication* by Kim in 1988, *Handbook of Intercultural Communication* by Asante, Gudykunst and Newmark in 1989, *Methods for Intercultural Communication Research* by Gudykunst and Kim in 1984, and *Communication Theory: Eastern and Western Perspectives* by Kinkaid in 1987. The focus on theory continued to the present time with two other major volumes, *Intercultural Communication Theory* by Wiseman in 1995 and *Theorizing about Intercultural Communication* by Gudykunst in 2005. In addition, two new journals began in the 1980s: *Intercultural Communication Studies* and *World Communication*.

We can make several observations about the development of the field in the 1980s. First, we see the outstanding influence of William Gudykunst in the theorization in this history of intercultural communication. Steve Kulich notes both Gukykunst and Young Yun Kim among the most cited intercultural scholars in an author analysis of the *International Journal of Intercultural Relations*. Further, if we trace the history of the *International and Intercultural Communication Annual*, we will see that all editors of the books from the 7th to the 19th editions (1983—1995) included Gudykunst, Kim, or their close colleagues. Along with this, we see the influence of the *International and Intercultural Communication Annual* in shaping the mainstream direction of the discipline, along with the intercultural divisions of the International Communication Association (ICA) and the National Communication Association (NCA). These are not the only authors, of course. A special issue of the *International Journal of Intercultural Relations* in 2012 turned from the focus on articles, books, or even events to focus on biographies of authors, with scholars contributing essays on 12 different authors, including Nobleza Asunción-Lande, Dean Barnlund, and others. Finally, we see ongoing debate about the direction and purposes of intercultural communication research. Scholars debated whether focus should be empirical or practical and what should be the topics of interest. Robert Shuter initiated and continues to lead a charge to keep the notion of "culture" central in our studies and has **critiqued** the narrow focus of intercultural research on a few selected nations or regions of the world.

If we trace the theories from the first volume in 1983, we note a trajectory. The first volume includes chapters on rules, theories, rhetoric, grounded theory, and **phenomenology**, with Larry

Sarbaugh and Nobleza Asunción-Lande in 1983 outlining each of these perspectives. The authors also regret the largely western bias in theorization in the field. The second volume by Kim and Gudykunst in 1988 included several social scientific theories, but also coordinated management of meaning—a rules perspective, and Collier and Thomas's essay on cultural identity theory, seemingly forced into the social scientific mold by including one out-of-place **"theorem"** among a series of assumptions that are much more interpretive in nature. In 2005, Gudykunst, however, included theories that could be used interpretively or even that were explicitly based on power and social imbalance.

The (causal) theories in intercultural communication often drew upon a set of core constructs, including the ideas of high and low context by Edward T. Hall in 1976 and Geert Hofstede's **dimensions** of cultural difference in 1980. Principal among these has been the construct of individualism-collectivism, which several scholars hold to be the primary driver of cultural difference. After the 1987 publication of an article critiquing Hofstede's dimensions and suggesting a new dimension—Confucian work dynamism, Hofstede added that to his four original dimensions (individualism/collectivism, power distance, masculinity/femininity, and uncertainty avoidance), and recently added a sixth dimension, restraint versus **indulgence.**

In 1995, Min-Sum Kim added to individualism-collectivism the personal-level variable of **self-construal**, one's perception of one's self in connection to those around one's self, adapted from Markus and Kitayama. She argued at that time that one could not predict behavior well from only cultural-level variables (that is, "individualism" describes a whole culture orientation, not specific individuals), but also needed individual-level variable (does an individual consider himself or herself independent from or dependent on others in making personal life and communicative choices?). Current versions of several theories now include self-construal; it has become conventional wisdom that theories of intercultural communication must account for both "cultural-level and individual-level effects."

Content decisions in what to study in intercultural communication in the early 1980s ranged from highly practical reasons of increased cultural **adjustment**, job skills, and development of personal relationships to personal **cosmopolitanism** and social change. By 1984, Young Yun Kim outlined the main areas of focus of intercultural research: **therapy**/counseling, business/organizations, politics, immigrant acculturation and **sojourner** adjustment, education, and technology transfer. The field still treated "culture" largely as national cultures, with intercultural communication occurring between people of different nations (despite inclusion of media, interethnic communication, and rhetoric, occasionally, in books from the early 1980s on). Theoretical and topic **foci** in this area included much work on the diffusion of innovations, intercultural competence, mass media effects, cross-cultural relationships, intergroup communication and prejudice.

The 1990s: The Decade of Bebate. Rogers and Hart report that "the ICC paradigm in the 1990s shows few signs of the unusual and exhausting stages, displayed few major shifts in research perspectives, and little important questioning of core tenets occurred;" rather, they suggest, scholars extended the existing paradigm to Japan and other nations. However, there seems to be more to the story, as evidenced what some might consider a split, and others, simply growing diversity in the discipline from the mid-1990s to today. We can anticipate this split/growth in diversity by considering several characteristics of the "history" of intercultural communication so far presented.

First, much, though not all, of this work characterizes a specific view of theory popular in the intercultural communication discipline at this time—a social scientific perspective based on a view of the world (**ontology**) that is grounded in cause and effect (often beyond the awareness of the communicator); a view of knowledge (**epistemology**) based on the accumulation of "fact" or evidence-based research and the use of some version of the scientific method, including survey or experimental research or controlled, quantitative field studies; and an approach to values (**axiology**) that sought to minimize their role in the communication research process. The purpose of the theory is not to provide specific understanding of behavior within the context of a specific culture, but to use "cultural differences as **operationalizations** of dimensions of cultural variability (e.g., individualism versus collectivism)." Such a view could be related to the fact that intercultural communication entered the communication discipline in the 1970s, at a time when one of the major influences in the field was social psychology as it relates to relational growth, with a view that intercultural communication is merely a context of interpersonal communication.

This is not to say that the writers were unaware of other perspectives. As noted above, compilations of essays throughout the period included essays on rules and systems perspectives, reflecting application of the famous 1977 debate in the *Quarterly Journal of Speech* on "covering laws," rules, and systems approaches to understanding communication. At the same time, authors sometimes made limiting choices. For example, Young Yun Kim, in her survey of "Current Research in Intercultural Communication," notes that "other research endeavors such as historical, critical, rhetorical, or linguistic studies will not be included in this review." Gudykunst and Nishida note that the early rhetorical work of Prosser and others, but suggest, in 1989, that "there has been little recent work in this area." If we consider ethnic and co-cultural groups as "cultures," as well as regions of a country, and so on, a search of rhetorical research in the 1970s and 1980s would likely reveal much work that is cultural in focus, such as work on protest and countercultural rhetoric. At some point, several of these authors have used qualitative research in their own studies.

Authors and editors of the driving theoretical works were also aware of the major "**ferment** in the field" reflected in a 1983 issue in *Journal of Communication*, an issue in which communication scholars debated scientific (**post-positivistic**), humanistic (**interpretive**), and critical "paradigms" of research. Karl Erik Rosengren, in that issue, introduced the sociological paradigm-organizing work of Gibson Burrell and Gareth Morgan. Burrell and Morgan's original point is that research ranged from more objective (cause-driven behavior, predictability, reality external to observer) to more subjective (choice-making behavior, rule-following, reality as individual perspective). Our authors applied this **continuum** to understand theory of the time. Gudykunst and Nishida divide theories into objective and subjective theories, the latter including linguistic theory, ethnography of communication and Collier and Thomas' theory of cultural identity. Others reproduce this bi-fold distinction of theories. Young Yun Kim characterizes objective theories as "analytic-**reductionistic**-mechanistic-behavioral-quantitative" and subjective theories as "synthetic-holistic-ideographic-contextual." While the authors describe some theories covered as humanistic/interpretive, "the influence of atomistic, reductionistic assumptions as to how understanding is produced played a significant role" in the theorizing of this time period.

An alternative voice in these volumes includes perspectives of intercultural communication that are phenomenological, rhetorical, observational, or based in grounded theory. Further, the volumes evidence the presence of a focus on media and culture from as early as 1983; however, the "theory" books focus little on qualitative and media research. Chen and Starosta note the strongly quantitative (or social scientific focus) of intercultural theory books through the 1980s and mid-1990s. Other work may have evaded the range of theory-book editors because their work did not coincide with the narrow view of theory noted above, an approach that is, admittedly, a Western, Eurocentric social construction.

A second issue is that this tradition represents only one of the two continua in Burrell and Morgan's—the continuum that pertains to the ontology and epistemology of the theories. A second dimension of theory includes axiology—specifically whether theory or research merely observes (and reproduces) the status quo ideas of a discipline or society, or whether it deliberately seeks to change it. Although Gudykunst and Nishida admit the need to recognize the "ideology" that is "inherent in any communication theory"—and the need to address ideology in future coverage of communication theory, as it is so present in the theorizing of other countries and regions, it receives little attention in the theory books.

▲ Ferment in the Field: Revisionist "Histories" of the Study of Intercultural Communication

Over the next several years, major changes came about within the discipline, as authors seemingly sought to "correct" for Edward T. Hall's additions to the field of intercultural communication. Rather than seeking to understand communication only within its physical and geographical contexts, scholars proposed that communication should be understood also in social, economic, historical, and other power contexts. Michael Hecht and his colleagues, for example, suggested that we could not understand Black-White communication within the United States apart from 400 years of shared and often conflictual history. Scholars were against the highly pragmatic focus of much intercultural research that sought to make businesses better, instead wondering whom such research really benefits. From within the social science discipline, people began to challenge traditional intercultural inquiry, such as the use of Hofstede's dimensions. Judith Martin and Thomas Nakayama (1999) suggested that we think more **dialectically** both about different aspects of communication (e.g., similarity and difference), but even the way we understand ideas such as "objective" and "subjective."

Newer researchers challenged our traditional notion of how to do research, of what constitutes "theory" and of what the focus of our studies should be. Increasingly, studies looked at co-cultures within larger cultures, at **marginalized** cultures on the "borderlands," and textbooks developed to present the voices of members of marginalized groups and to teach interracial communication. Whereas Kroeber and Kluckhohn assembled some 150 definitions of culture in 1952, Baldwin, Faulkner, Hecht and Lindsley collected 313 in 2006, noting new patterns in the way of defining culture since the 1950s, especially in the directions of interpretive and critical research. The interpretive and critical strands represent different "histories" in the study of intercultural communication, for, even though they became prominent in the discipline after 1995, they were present long before, either within or beyond the disciplinary walls of intercultural communication.

The Rise of Interpretive Approaches

The first major approaches that, while long present in some form within the field of intercultural communication research, received major impetus in the field from the 1990s forward is the field of qualitative and interpretive inquiry of different sorts. We introduce two strands of that approach.

The Ethnography of Communication: **Ethnography** is not new and was a principal tool of the anthropologists noted above in the backgrounds of the discipline. Many authors credit linguist and anthropologist Dell Hymes with laying the groundwork for a focus of observational research specifically on communication behavior. Ethnographic writers, talking about theory, provide an explanation of connections between phenomena within a specific speech community regarding a specific action. This theory (e.g., grounded theory) is developed through systematic observation, note-taking, and **verifying** findings with local participants, with criteria to ensure systematic and quality results that reflect the realities of research participants. Through time, researchers' stance toward the research has changed, with earlier researchers describing what they saw as if it was real and they were neutral observers, but more recent researchers admitting their own role in co-constructing their findings with the participants.

Communication studies of people in specific cultures are not new in the field of intercultural communication. Gerry Philipsen's now-classic study, "Speaking 'like a Man' in Teamsterville," which describes the communication of White, working class men in a Chicago neighborhood, would be considered "cultural" communication by today's standards and clearly under the broad umbrella of the studies of culture and communication. As early as 1986, Philipsen and one of his students, Donal Carbaugh, published a list of 250 studies of communication from local cultures around the world. From these studies, Philipsen presents a theory with **propositions** about the nature of culture and communication. Today, observational studies, either using a speech codes approach or not, are frequent fare in intercultural journals. In sum, ethnography of communication has a long history, though is more recent to mainstream of intercultural research.

Phenomenological, Semiotic, and Other Traditions: Rather than use a pre-set approach like speech codes theory, some scholars follow the work of social science researchers such as Alfred Schutz, Edmund Husserl, and Maurice Merleau-Ponty, investigating the perspectives of participants in a cultural situation from within their own life situations, an approach known as phenomenology. As one example of this, in 1998 Mark Orbe has developed a theory based on in-depth analyses of the life/communicative perspectives of African Americans in dominant White U.S. American culture as well as many other co-cultural groups (people with disabilities, and so on) to develop co-cultural theory. Phenomenological perspectives, which usually seek to impose no previous theory, are common in intercultural research today.

Another perspective that has gained force is **semiotics**. Following the work of the wide field of semiotics, including but not limited to writers such as Ferdinand de Saussure, Umberto Eco, Charles Sanders Peirce, Roland Barthes, and others, many students of culture, language and communication are relying on semiotics. Leeds-Hurwitz applied this approach to culture in a 1993 book that considers aspects of culture as representative of underlying values and belief systems. She later applied this and other approaches to understand how weddings represent cultural identities. This approach does not have as much traction in studies of face-to-face communication (with more research on semiotics and communication occurring, for example, in the journal, *Semiotica*, than in communication journals), though it is very prominent in studies of media culture and identity.

Cultural Criticism

Dreama Moon defines culture as "a contested zone" in which "different groups struggle to define issues in their own interests" with unequal access to "public forums to voice their concerns, perspectives, and the everyday realities of their lives." This approach breaks from earlier "histories" that sought either to predict communicative outcomes with cultural variables or to simply provide in-depth, contextual understanding of the communicative lives of research participants from their own perspectives. But rather than seeing this approach as a new development, like observational research, we should realize that it has a long history outside of the intercultural field. Some aspects include traditional critical theory, cultural studies, critical semiotics and language studies, **queer** theory, feminist theory, postmodernism, and new approaches related to anti-racism and **post-colonialism**—each with its own history.

Critical Theory and Cultural Studies. Recent authors have outlined a new critical agenda for intercultural communication, with impacts on how we see culture, intercultural communication, and research. Critical theory has roots in the ideas of Karl Marx, Vladimir Lenin, and others. Marx's original theory focused on how the elite gained control over the means and relations of production, seeking a cheap labor pool for the production of goods. One way the elite maintain control is through deliberate **manipulation** of the idea structures (**ideology**) of the masses, known as false consciousness. The Frankfurt School, a group of Marxist scholars fleeing Nationalist Germany in the 1930s, introduced critical theory through such works as the classic edited book on **anti-Semitism** and other forms of prejudice, *The Authoritarian Personality*, with an objective, variable-analytic (but politically motivated) view of the word. Later authors (e.g., Althusser, Gramsci) modified Marxist ideas, with more complex notions of ideology and **hegemony**. The work of these authors had immediate relevance in how one viewed social struggle between ethnic groups and the ideological control of those groups.

As one of the key tools for shaping the sets of ideas and assumptions (*ideology*) held by a group of people within a culture, the media became a ready focus for the application of these conceptual tools. Thus, a group of scholars in Britain began a cross-disciplinary approach to understanding how popular culture produces and reproduces ideology that serves the interests of some groups over others, calling this new field cultural studies. Raymond Williams and Richard

Hoggart wrote as early as the 1950s and 1960s. In 1979, Dick Hebdige wrote *Subculture: The Meaning of Style*—an analysis of how British youth use fashion to mark their identities; and in 1981, Paul Willis describes how communication within the social environment of the British working class reproduces job expectations. Throughout this time, Stuart Hall wrote several essays analyzing popular culture, with specific application to British **racism**. By 1992, Larry Grossberg, Cary Nelson and Paula Treichler produced a compendium of cultural studies essays on an array of aspects of cultural ideas, identities, of hegemony and resistance and empowerment, of radio broadcasts and interpersonal messages—though with little attention from scholars traditionally seen as from the intercultural communication "discipline."

Feminist Studies and Queer Theory. Increasingly, as intercultural scholars turned their attention away from strictly national "cultures," any topic of group-based difference became useful material for research, including supposed gender differences in communication (a review of which is beyond the scope of this unit). Feminist authors summarize various views of **feminism** that have importance in studies of culture, difference, and **patriarchy**, such as liberal, radical and ecofeminism.

Sharon Marcus notes that feminism and queer theory share similar aims; while feminism challenges patriarchy and restrictive ideological constructions and structures that limit women's options and potential.

Postmodernism. Also influenced by the ideas of Michel Foucault, along with Jacques Derrida and others, postmodernism rejects traditional notions of single narratives to explain all reality, of order and centrality, and so on. Postmodern assumptions have become largely **embedded** in modern thought and intercultural research, though Rueyling Chang makes them explicit, arguing for an end to studies that "essentialize" other cultures, especially by treating a culture as some score on a Hofstedian value like individualism. Chang opposes such dualisms as individualism/collectivism, but also **disdains** logical positivistic research in favor of studies that promote "**multivocality** and inclusivity." Further, postmodern research considers how groups negotiate power through discourse (language, images, etc.).

Whiteness, Critical Race Theory, and Post-Colonialism. Where the traditional paradigm of intercultural research treated intercultural communication largely as an extension of interpersonal communication (between individual of diverse cultural backgrounds), these new approaches consider larger social structures, arguing that sex and gender, sexual orientation, "race," and other identities exist within larger social structures that include media representation, legal policy, job discrimination, educational opportunities, and so on. This final set of aspects of the critical tradition extends this structural-communicative approach into new directions.

Whiteness research, often traced to the early roots of works by Richard Dyer and Ruth Frankenberg focuses on how "Whiteness" is and is maintained as an invisible center of power. That is, being White (in European and North American and some other cultures) gives one privileges of which one is not aware. Whiteness is "a tremendous social force in mobilizing how people act and interact ... in the ways they think of themselves and others." It is maintained through discourses such as only describing White in terms of it being "not" something else, promoting "color blindness," or confusing Whiteness with nationality, such as assuming in one's mind that an American will be White. The purpose of Whiteness research is to **expose** how cultures think in White terms and promote White welfare, usually unintentionally, with an aim at resisting White dominance.

Critical race theory, a perspective that arises in the field of legal studies, begins with a critique of injustices in the legal system, arguing that countercultural groups within a larger culture have a different view of social reality than the "reigning order." Critical race theory includes such notions as how knowledge is structured in a way to privilege Whites over those of other races. Similar to radical feminism, which challenges the very structures of patriarchy rather than simply promoting women's equality within the existing system (liberal feminism), critical race theory is **overtly** political, advocating "engaged, even **adversarial** scholarship." Scholars across disciplines have adopted this perspective, with communication scholars noting its usefulness, for example, in discussion of hate speech and naming.

Finally, post-colonialism relates to ideas articulated by Edward Said in his 1978 book, *Orientalism*. In this work, Said discusses the way that the European West rhetorically constructs the Middle East and its peoples through literature and art. Key ideas from this perspective include the idea of **othering**—thinking and speaking of those who are of different groups in a way that treats them as exotic and different (and thus justifies domination, marginalization, or oppression). Like other critical notions outlined above, **Orientalism** has received acclaim, critique, and debate across disciplines. A search in my own Illinois university library system reveals over 12,000 book entries referencing Orientalism. Post-colonialism extends orientalism to look at the politics of colonizing nations and peoples and the results of that colonization on various aspects of life. Raka Shome and Radha Hegde, in the opening essay of an entire issue of *Communication Theory* devoted to postcolonialism, note that the approach is, above all, "interventionist and highly political." Informed by Marxism and other approaches, it breaks markedly from postmodernism. Where the latter proposes that there are no overarching discourses that can explain all social life, post-colonialism proposes a distinct approach not only to colonized cultures but those that colonized, as Western knowledge and life situation is based in some way upon the conquest of colonized countries by the Western world. This perspective is often interested in ideas such as migration, resistance to colonial ideas, the **hybridity** of cultural influences (usually with a power disparity in who determines and manages the mixture), **diasporic** peoples, and so on. Notably, rather than promote intercultural communication competence as a way to ease tensions and promote good business contexts in a globalized world, post-colonialism tends to complicate globalization by noting its adverse effects on economically weaker nations.

The various perspectives used here (aside from postmodernism, which rejects metanarratives) are sometimes used together. In fact, the cultural and critical perspectives detailed in this section, each with their own histories, and using a wide variety of ethnographic, rhetorical, historical, and other methods, are prominent in the field today. Thomas Nakayama and Rona Hualalani edited a specific handbook of essays and studies based on this array of critical perspectives. These approaches are prominent in communication fields in many countries outside of the United States, as well as in the intercultural division of the NCA, with traditional research being more common in the ICA (based on my own perception of conference offerings). Of course, such summarizations merit caution. What we can say is that cultural and critical perspectives have long histories outside of the field of intercultural communication and that they were both admitted and even used by many scholars within the field even in the early 1980s. What I am arguing here is that these perspectives received little attention and were perhaps even marginalized (with no intent of said marginalization implied here) until the latter part of the 1990s.

Challenges to a Eurocentric Tradition

In contrast to even the critical perspectives noted above, there is one last set of "histories" of intercultural communication research that we must consider: Those histories that object to any attempt of Western theorists to impose a framework to understand people of specific groups, including even feminism, Marxism, or other critical approaches. Ironically, these approaches might imply a postcolonial approach that resists initiatives by Western writers to impose a narrative upon them; but they do provide a single narrative to describe people of a particular descent.

Early communication researchers had already promoted the study of rhetoric and forms of communication from China, India, and other countries. At this same time, communication scholar Arthur Smith adopted a new name, Molefi Kete Asante. As long time director and chair of African American studies at Temple University, Asante describes **Afrocentrism** as "placing African ideals at the center of any analysis that involves African culture and behavior" and, by extension, the communication behavior of any African-descended peoples. He argues that Eurocentric ideas,—be they universalism and objectivity, are "limiting, restricting, and **parochial**", often promoting unrealistic dualisms (e.g., mind-body). Instead, African behavior must be understood in terms of the interrelationship between "feeling, knowing, and acting," in terms of the "generative and productive power of the spoken word," and circular, rather than linear view of the world. Asante's work serves as a foundation to much intercultural research, to the point that he received focus as one of the most influential intercultural communication scholars in the 2012 IJIR issue noted above.

In like fashion, Yoshitaka Miike promotes an **"Asiacentric"** perspective based on harmony between individuals and between elements of human existence (material, behavioral, and mental aspects). He suggests that we should learn *from* other cultures, rather than *about* them, as the former approach makes us more humble in our investigation of other cultures, while the latter treats other cultures like texts and "their members like objects of analysis." Traditional Eurocenrtric research "otherizes" other people and their cultures, often comparing the communication of other cultures with that of the United States (creating the U.S. as another invisible "center" in communication research). The Asia-centric perspective rests on the notion of non-separateness: "Communication is a process in which we remind ourselves of the interdependence and interrelatedness of the universe." Shinsuke Eguchi blends the dialectical approach described above with Asia-centric notions to suggest dialectical tensions in identities of U.S. Asian Americans.

Conclusion: Future Histories of Intercultural Communication

As we have seen, rather than a single history of intercultural communication research, there are **concurrent, confluent** traditions: Much like the murky **backwaters** of the Amazon river, we sense currents of all approaches in each of the others, but each has separate origins, separate histories, as it flows in and out of the domain of what we have socially constructed (and politically argued through competing discourses) as the appropriate "history" of intercultural communication research. Starosta and Chen discuss the field of intercultural communication as a dialogue about whether there is truth to the claim of a "critical turn" in the field, using the same metaphor of "ferment" that we saw in the communication field at large in 1983. They introduce the critique of Edward T. Hall's approach, which "reifies," crystalizes, or essentializes our views of national cultures and urge a dialogic approach among those of different perspectives as we enter the next age of inter-cultural research: "Should 'qualitative and quantitative approaches have to run like two parallel rivers without the hope of possibility of reconciliation'? Certainly not." They later argue for a more complex view of identity in inter-cultural research—one that is fluid and reflects "tensions, shifting definitions and boundaries, temporary alliances across differences, or cultural morphing." In a similar way, S. Lily Mendoza argues that we should avoid monolithic claims about cultures and see them, rather, as complex and in "motion," as she takes a radically political, historical, and dialogic view to theorizing about cultures. At the same time, she admits the usefulness of a generalized understanding of a group as a starting point in understanding that group. In brief, one valuable direction for the history of our field would be increased dialogue between those of different views to see how these can work together to inform our understanding of culture, identity, intercultural communication, and related themes.

At the same time, we will continue to see growth in traditional domains of intercultural research, though they need more focus on specific geographic regions and cultures, such as Africa. As old lines of adjustment, competence, business and health communication and others grow, so will the new field of social media and computer mediated communication, as exemplified by the work of Robert Shuter, and the Center for Intercultural New Media Research. Other researchers will continue to collect research to demonstrate the growing history of intercultural communication research in different regions of the world, such as the work of Steve Kulich, Michael Prosser, and colleagues at the Shanghai International Studies University (SISU) to document not only the history of intercultural communication scholarship in general, but that in China specifically, a project also **embraced** by other scholars, or similar efforts to document the history of intercultural communication in France, Germany, or other countries. And, while new communication research will continue to investigate traditional areas like "face," competence, and adaptation, it is also turning its attention to health communication and to less studied cultures. Communication research appears in a wide number of mainstream communication journals, as well as journals dedicated to the discipline, such as *Journal of International and Intercultural Communication* and *Journal of Intercultural Communication Research*.

The various streams of history—social scientific, interpretive/humanistic (including ethnography, phenomenology, and rhetorical theories), critical theories (including post-colonialism, Whiteness research, feminist approaches, and others) each continue to flow forcefully in the field of intercultural communication, sometimes with dialogue and cross-over between the streams, much as the backwaters of the Amazon meet, flow together for a while, and then separate. Each approach has its own **implications** for how we understand culture, our ethical role as researchers and communicators, and the way we treat others in our everyday lives. Our best understanding of issues of identity, of intolerance, of culture and cultural communication will likely come from dialogue among these seemingly competing perspectives.

Applications

1. Intercultural Communication: Where We've Been, Where We're Going, Issues We Face

Croucher, M. S., Sommier, M., & Rahmani, D. (2015) Intercultural communication: Where we've been, where we're going, issues we face. *Communication Research and Practice*, 1, 71–87.

Abstract: The purpose of this review is to critically analyze the state of intercultural communication literature. This review has three purposes. First, this review summarizes where the discipline has been, paying close attention to the discipline's history and some key areas of research. Second, this review discusses where the discipline is going, with an emphasis on how the discipline is expanding into new contextual areas of research. Finally, the review presents challenges, issues, and areas for future discussion for intercultural communication.

Keywords: intercultural communication; identity; competence; adaptation; health care; social media

2. Writing the Intellectual History of Intercultural Communication

Leeds-Hurwitz, W. (2010). Writing the intellectual history of intercultural communication. In T. K. Nakayama and R. T. Halualani (Eds.), *The Handbook of Critical Intercultural Communication*, 21–33. Malden, MA: Wiley-Blackwell.

Abstract: To document some of the other strands that should be considered when writing the history of intercultural communication, this paper outlines people and organizations that have been important in the history of intercultural communication, but which are generally ignored by current scholars. One obvious question is why these people and organizations have been so thoroughly forgotten by communication scholars, when they helped to establish the direction of our work today.

Keywords: history of intercultural communication; other strands of people and organizations; contributions; ignore; reasons

3. Edward T. Hall and the History of Intercultural Communication: The United States and Japan

Rogers, M. E., Hart, B. W., & Miike, Y. (2002). Edward T. Hall and the history of intercultural communication: The United States and Japan. *Keio Communication Review*, 24, 3 - 26.

Abstract: Here we trace the role of anthropologist Edward T. Hall in founding the scholarly field of intercultural communication during the 1951 - 1955 period when he was at the Foreign Service Institute of the U.S. Department of States. The scholarly field of intercultural communication was then mainly advanced by university-based scholars of communication in the United States and Japan, and in other countries. The development of intercultural communication in the U.S. and Japan is analyzed here.

Keywords: Edward T. Hall; founder of intercultural communication; scholars of communication; the Foreign Service Institute; other countries

Interactive Activities

1. Individually, please finish reading Text A, Text B, and the application abstracts and work out the meanings of the terms in bold type by consulting the dictionary whenever necessary.

2. In pairs, please summarize the content in 2 to 3 sentences of each sub-heading in the unit outlines of Text A and Text B based on your reading and understanding of the texts.

3. In groups, share your gains, comments and suggestions regarding the three application abstracts. Based on your interests, locate and finish reading the full-length papers of your interested abstracts.

4. Q&A: Questions are encouraged about any uncertain or confused part or parts in the unit and seek answers either from other fellow students or the instructor.

5. Complete the Personal Report of Intercultural Communication (ICC) Apprehension, a scale designed to measure your degree of ICC apprehension. Take a few moments and complete the self-assessment for Unit 2.

To facilitate the implementation of the One Belt, One Road initiative in terms of intercultural communication, please carry out a trial survey by using the Personal Report of Intercultural Communication (ICC) Apprehension.

6. Please choose one of the texts in this unit and work out **an annotated bibliography** entry. It is an excellent way to write annotated bibliography entries so as to get prepared for a research project. Besides the title, author, publisher, and date of each of the sources, an annotated bibliography usually makes a summary, an evaluation, or a reflection of each source. The format of it can vary, but it is usually written in paragraph form from a couple of sentences to a couple of pages. Below is a sample in APA (American Psychological Association) style:

Ehrenreich, B. (2001). *Nickel and dimed: On (not) getting by in America*. New York, NY: Henry Holt and Company.

In this book of nonfiction based on the journalist's experiential research, Ehrenreich attempts to ascertain whether it is currently possible for an individual to live on a minimum wage in America. Taking jobs as a waitress, a maid in a cleaning service, and a Walmart sales employee, the author summarizes and reflects on her work, her relationships with fellow workers, and her financial struggles in each situation.

As an experienced journalist, Ehrenreich is aware of the limitations of her experiment and the ethical implications of her experiential research tactics and reflects on these issues in the text. The author, Ehrenreich, is forthcoming about her methods and supplements her experiences with scholarly research on her places of employment, the economy, and the rising cost of living in America.

UNIT THREE

Language, Culture, and Research Methods

PART THREE

Readings

Text A Language and Culture from a Linguistic Perspective

After Ee Lin Lee

▲ The Fundamentals of Language

A major task of language researchers is to understand the complexities in the structures of talk in order to unfold and understand sociality, including human nature, cultural values, power structure, social inequality, and so on. Researchers in language, culture, and communication study language situated in cultural **nuances** in order to understand language use in enhancing intergroup and intercultural dialogue. Although language enables learning and interactions, it also confuses **interlocutors** with contradictory yet deep and rich multi-layered meanings, such as (mis)interpretation of intentions, violation of normative conduct, and repair of conversations that have gone awry.

In a way, language not only makes sense of our perception, but also constructs our social reality by manifesting actual social consequences. For example, the word *race* represents something that does not exist in physical reality, but it has real implications and consequences (e.g., discrimination, social disparity, unequal access to healthcare, etc.). Here, language allows the creation of actual and persistent **perceptions** (e.g., bad, inferior, non-deserving, and so on) that determine aspects of people's lives. In fact, the role of language in influencing interlocutors' perception and communication remains one of the most popular opening lines in empirical studies focusing on language and culture.

How Language Shapes Perception

Known as linguistic relativity, the notion that language influences our thinking about social issues derives from Edward Sapir's works in anthropology and linguistics in the 1920s. Sapir studied the lexical categorization and grammatical features from the **corpora** obtained during his fieldwork over several decades. While studying the languages of different North American Indian tribes, including those living in Washington and Oregon in the U.S. and Vancouver in Canada, Sapir found, for example, that the Hopi language did not have lexical equivalents for the English words *time*, *past*, or *the future*. Therefore, he suggested that the Hopi worldview about **temporal** communication was different from the English worldview. In his lectures Sapir promoted the understanding of language as a system embedded in culture. Thereafter, based on

Sapir's findings, researchers studying language inferred that if there was no word for, say, *you* in a certain language, then speakers of that language treat *you* as nonexistent.

Benjamin Lee Whorf, a student of Sapir's, later suggested that language could, to some extent, determine the nature of our thinking. Known as the Sapir-Whorf **hypothesis**, or linguistic determinism, the notion that language is a shaper of ideas or thought inspired further **empirical** testing. This led some researchers to conclude that speakers of different languages (e.g., Polish, Chinese, Japanese, English, etc.) see their realities differently. The investigation of the effects of languages on human behaviors, as influenced by Sapir's and Whorf's works, continues to be a popular topic in various academic disciplines.

During its postwar rebuilding efforts overseas in the 1930s, the U.S. government recruited linguists and anthropologists to train its personnel at the Foreign Service Institute (FSI). While linguists researching the micro-level elements of languages successfully taught FSI officers how to speak different languages, anthropologists studying the macro-level components of culture (e.g., economy, government, religious, family practices, etc.) taught the officers how to communicate effectively with people from different cultures. The research and training collaboration between linguists, anthropologists, psychologists, and sociologists at FSI showed that the learning of a foreign culture was not merely about acquiring language skills or translating from one language to another, but a **holistic** understanding of language in a wider context.

While the teaching of foreign languages to FSI officers was efficient, teaching anthropological understanding of foreign cultures was more challenging. Moreover, during the 1940s the Sapir-Whorf hypothesis and the notion that language frames people's worldview were contested in empirical findings. In 1966, Edward T. Hall, who is credited with founding the field of intercultural communication, strongly promoted his belief that effective communication between two people from different cultural backgrounds (i.e., intercultural communication) should combine verbal (i.e., speech) and non-verbal (i.e., non-linguistic) communication embedded in a cultural context.

Citing efficiency, researchers at the time developed language translation programs that enabled the quick learning of intercultural communication. In this approach of linguistic universalism, researchers assumed structural equivalence across languages—that word-by-word translation can foster cultural understanding according to Chomsky's research in 1972. This shift of direction in academic research challenged Sapir's proposition of the understanding of culture and communication based on common conceptual systems—the notion that meanings and values of concepts cannot be truly understood without understanding the cultural system.

Regardless of the competing viewpoints, research on how speakers of different languages operate under different language and communication systems continues to date. Researchers have also widened the scope of the language and culture program to include the study of language use and functions (i.e., communicative purposes) in and across different cultural systems. Although the translation of the linguistic **corpora** into the English language is commonly featured in proprietary research publications, analyzing discourse data in the native languages is preferred. Language is therefore treated as intact with the cultural system. This line of study, despite differences in methodological and theoretical frameworks, forms the basis for a specific discipline within the communication field called language and social interaction (LSI).

Language and Social Interaction

The LSI discipline focuses on the study of human discourse and human interaction in various situations. Scholars pursuing this line of research seek to understand the development of speech and language processes in various settings, from small group to interpersonal, including face-to-face and those **mediated** by technology. The scholarship employs qualitative and quantitative methods and includes verbal (i.e., speech) and non-verbal communication (i.e., nonlinguistic cues). The various methodological and theoretical frameworks used include social psychology, ethnography of speaking, discourse analysis, conversation analysis, and narrative analysis. Although well-established and housed in the communication field, works in LSI are **interdisciplinary**.

While LSI studies also include non-verbal communication as a language system, scholarship on speech—whether naturally occurring, **elicited**, mediated, or written—outnumber those focusing on non-verbal communication. The insufficiency of non-verbal scholarship in the LSI discipline underscores the challenges of recording non-verbal communication for data analysis. Although studies pertaining to how social life is lived in situated conversation and language is used in various interactional settings dominate LSI research discourse, the study of non-verbal communication as language deserves its own coverage as a (sub)discipline. Consequently, this essay focuses on the scholarship on speech in LSI. The following sections review a selection of the LSI sub-disciplines organized by research methods, or more commonly conceptualized as analytical frameworks and procedures: language pragmatics, conversation analysis, discourse analysis, and the ethnography of communication. This review highlights a few major theories or theoretical frameworks in each sub-discipline, namely the speech act theory, Grice's maxims of **implicatures**, politeness theory, discursive psychology, critical discourse analysis, the ethnography of speaking, speech codes theory, and cultural discourse analysis.

Language Pragmatics

Pragmatics is the study of language usage or talk in interaction. Researchers who study language pragmatics investigate the meanings of utterances in relation to speech situations in the specific contexts of use. Two theoretical frameworks that are commonly cited in language pragmatics are the speech act theory and Grice's maxims of conversational implicatures, from which the influential politeness theory derives. These theoretical frameworks emerged from the examination of language independently from context, including situational factors that influence the cultural assumptions of the speaker and hearer.

Speech Act Theory. In an attempt to understand **utterances** in interaction, Austin explained speech acts as communicative acts in which speakers perform actions via utterances in specific contexts. Called *performatives*, these are **illocutionary** acts in which the speaker asserts a demand through utterances. Illocutionary acts contain *force*—that is, they allow the speaker to perform an act without necessary naming the act (e.g., apology, question, offer, refuse, thank, etc.). Austin illustrated three types of force: (a) *locution*, the words in the utterances;

(b) *illocution*, the intention of the speaker; and (c) **perlocution**, the consequential effects of the utterance upon the thoughts, feelings, or actions on the hearer.

The speaker's illocutionary act is said to be *happy* when the hearer understands the locution and illocutionary forces. In order for the speaker's illocutionary act to be happy, the utterance has to fulfill luck conditions. Lucky illocutionary acts are those that meet social and cultural criteria and bring about effects on the hearer that the speaker intended. Thus, illocutionary acts are conventionalized messages, because their performance is an engagement in rule-governed behavior.

Searle extended Austin's concept of speech acts and elaborated on the speech act theory by identifying the conditions necessary for the realization of speech acts. For example, to promise, the speaker needs sincerity and intentionality; to declare the marital union of two partners, a priest or a judge has to be present. Hence the successful performance of a speech act depends on whether the constituent conditions of a particular speech act are fulfilled, or a particular speech act is realized in a contextually appropriate manner (i.e., in relation to sociocultural factors).

Searle developed a **typology** to categorize speech acts: (a) *representatives*, where the speaker says how something is, like asserting; (b) *directives*, the speaker tries to get the hearer to perform some future action, such as requesting and warning; (c) *commissives*, the speaker commits to some future course of action, such as promising; (d) *expressives*, the speaker expresses his or her psychological state of mind about some prior action, such as apologizing and thanking; and (e) *declaratives*, performatives that require non-linguist institutions, such as baptizing or sentencing. These conditions must be fulfilled for the speaker to effect the specific act.

The speech act theory can be used to describe utterance sequences—for example, to predict antecedents and consequents in a conversation. Thus, when a violation of the typology occurred, speech act theory successfully predicted repairs and other signs of troubles in the conversational moves. However, Searle's **taxonomy** was criticized for several reasons. First, while Searle treated illocutionary acts as consisting of complete sentences in grammatical form, such acts can be very short utterances that do not follow the complete object-verb-subject structure (e.g., forge on). On the other hand, the speaker may need to utter several sentences to bring about effects on the hearer (e.g., advising). Second, Searle assumed that the luck conditions for successful performances are universal, but later studies found that the conditions are indeed specific to the culture.

Furthermore, Searle subscribed to a linear, speaker-to-hearer view of transaction that dismissed the interactional aspect of language. The hearer's role was minimized; specifically, the hearer's influence on the speaker's construction of utterances was ignored. Searle also neglected perlocutionary acts, which focus on the intention of the speaker. Instead, he focused solely on the linguistic goal of deliberate expression of an intentional state while overlooking extra-linguistic cues. In short, the speech act theory could not account for intentionality and variability in discourse.

Grice's Maxims of Implicatures. By moving beyond the linear (i.e., speaker-to-hearer) view of transaction, Grice proposed the cooperative principle. He observed that interlocutors engage in collaborative efforts in social interaction in order to attain a common goal. In Grice's view, collaborative efforts do not mean agreement; they mean that the speaker and the hearer work together in the conversation. According to the principle, participants follow four conversational maxims: *quantity* (be informative), *quality* (be truthful), *relation* (be relevant), and *manner* (be clear, be brief). Since these four maxims vary by culture, the interlocutors need to have culturally nuanced knowledge to *fulfill* these maxims.

According to Grice, meaning is produced in a direct way when participants adhere to the maxims. When the speaker's intentions are conveyed clearly, the hearer should not have to interpret the speaker's intentions. This occurs with conventional implicatures where standard word meanings are used in the interaction. However, in actual social interaction, most meanings are implied through conversational implicatures in which one or more of the conversational maxims are violated. Due to normative constraints, a speaker who says p implicates q, and the hearer would then need to infer the implied meanings; for example, what is being said and what is beyond words in a recommendation letter.

In short, Grice's maxims of conversational implicatures are used to explain why people engage in different interpretations rather than rely on the literal meanings of utterances. The maxims attend to implied meanings that constitute a huge part of conversation and also the role of the hearer. Nonetheless, the cooperative principle was criticized for **privileging** the conversational conventions of middle-class English speakers. Additionally, Grice did not examine strategic non-cooperation, which remains a primary source of inference in conversation.

Politeness Theory. Influenced by Grice's maxims, Brown and Levinson proposed the politeness theory in 1987 to explain the interlocutor's observation of conversational implicatures in order to maintain the expressive order of interaction. Brown and Levinson observed politeness strategies that consistently occurred in their field data across several languages: Tzetzal and Tamil languages in Asia, and the British and American forms of English. Despite the distinctive cultures and languages, they observed outstanding parallelism in interlocutors' use of polite language to accomplish conversational goals. Politeness is the activity performed to enhance, maintain, or protect face or the self-image of the interlocutors.

To illustrate language universality in politeness, Brown and Levinson proposed a socialized interlocutor—nicknamed a model person (MP)—as a face-bearing human with rationality and intentionality when communicating. To avoid breaking social balance, the MP, whom Brown and Levinson identified as the speaker, conforms to social norms to be polite. In performing a speech act, the MP **cultivates** a desirable image (i.e., positive social worth), pays attention to the hearer's responses, and ensures that nobody loses face in social interactions (e.g., feels embarrassed, humiliated, awkward, etc.).

Since face is emotionally **invested** (e.g., actors get upset) and sanctioned by social norms, actors are said to engage in rule-governed behavior to pay respect to their face. Due to the emotional investment, face threats are likely to occur when actors perform facework. Brown and Levinson described two basic face wants: *positive face*, the desire for one's actions to be accepted by others, such as approval from others; and *negative face*, the desire for one's actions to move smoothly to others. A threat to positive face decreases approval from the hearer (e.g., acknowledging one's **vulnerability**), whereas a threat to negative face restricts one's freedom to act (e.g., requesting a favor).

According to the politeness theory, the speaker can choose whether or not to perform face-threatening acts (FTAs). When performing FTAs, the speaker will go *on* or *off* record. In going off record, the speaker uses hints or utterances that have more than one intentions, so that he or she does not appear to have performed a speech act. For example, the speaker who utters "Oops, I don't have any cash on me" to the hearer after they have dined together in a restaurant is using an off-record strategy to suggest that the hearer **foot** the bill. In contrast, going on record means that the speaker performs the FTA (i.e., baldly without saving face) with or without redress. With redress, the speaker indicates that he or she does not intend to violate social balance by performing the FTA. Without redress, the speaker directly expresses his or her desire; for instance, the speaker commands the hearer to pay for lunch by saying, "You should pay this time."

The speaker can use either positive or negative politeness strategies when performing FTAs with redress. Positive politeness strategies are used to attend to the hearer's positive face. For example, in the restaurant scenario, the speaker can choose to **compliment** the hearer in order to establish solidarity by saying, "You have always been so generous..." On the other hand, negative politeness strategies are used to avoid imposing on the hearer's negative face. For example, by seeking permission, "Would you consider paying for lunch? I will return the favor in the future," the speaker acknowledges that the hearer does not have to foot the bill.

According to the politeness theory, the speaker wants to use the least amount of effort to maximize ends by considering the weight of performing the FTA. Brown and Levinson put forward a formula: $Wx = P(S, H) + D(S, H) + R$, where W stands for the weight of the FTA; P the relative power of hearer (H) over speaker (S), which is asymmetrical (e.g., if H is an authority); D the social distance between H and S, which is symmetrical (if H speaks another dialect); and R the ranking of imposition of the FTA in a particular culture. They suggested that P and D were universal with some emic correlates. Thus, in calculating Wx, S will consider the results of each strategy. For example, in using positive politeness strategies, S may appear to be friendly, whereas in using an off-record strategy, S may appear **manipulative** by imposing on H, who gets S's hints and then performs a future act. In using an on-record strategy, S may choose to be efficient, such as in an emergency (e.g., Ambush!).

After three decades, politeness theory remains one of the most tested theories. However, amongst its criticisms, the theory is said to account for intentional politeness, but not intentional impoliteness. The significant attention paid to the speaker's utterances, albeit with a consideration for the hearer's face, reveals the assumption of conversations as mono-logic. In some respects the theory followed the trajectory of Searle's and Grice's works in that the performance of utterances is conceptualized as a rational activity of the speakers. In particular, speakers are assumed to generate meanings and actions, whereas hearers are treated as receivers who interpret the speech performances. Therefore, the politeness theory is unable to fully explain interactional organization in talk exchanges.

UNIT THREE
Language, Culture, and Research Methods

▶ Conversation Analysis

During the 1960s, empirical science centered on the prediction of the effects of abstract ideas on communication and social life. Common predictors tested include personality types, cognition, biological sex, income level, and political stance. Social scientists who studied language commonly adhered to the quantitative paradigm; they conducted experiments, used **elicited** conversations, and analyzed responses containing rehearsals of recollected conversations. The study of everyday rituals, however, was not of academic concern.

Erving Goffman, a sociologist, later made a radical theoretical move that differed significantly from the mainstream empirical studies. Goffman stated that orderliness was empirically observable from everyday conversation. He argued that since socialization shapes the social actor's competencies, conversation maintains moral codes and institutional order. In other words, sequential ordering of actions in social interaction reflects the macro social institution (e.g., politics, business, legal systems, etc.).

Goffman's works were viewed as a paradigm shift in the social sciences. He called attention to the orderliness that is observable in ordinary conversation—an area of investigation that other scientists neglected. Furthermore, unlike the early works in language study, Goffman's theoretical framework no longer focused solely on the performance of speakers in conversations. Instead, meaning making—that is, the examination of the participants' understanding of one another's conduct—took precedence. Goffman did not test his ideas, nor did he develop any set of empirical methods that allowed the testing of his ideas.

In search of an empirical analysis of conversation, Harold Garfinkel, another sociologist, expanded on Goffman's ideas. In 1967, Garfinkel proposed that ethno-methods (i.e., the study of people's practices or methods) inform the production of culturally meaningful symbols and actions. He noted that social actors use multiple tacit methods (e.g., presuppositions, assumptions, and methods of inference) to make shared sense of their interaction. Thus, conversation is a place where participants engage in everyday reason analysis, and conversational sequential structure—the organization of social interaction—reveals membership categorization.

The sub-discipline of conversation analysis (CA) was further expanded when Harvey Sacks and Emanuel Schegloff, who were later joined by Gail Jefferson, studied suicide calls made to the Center for the Scientific Study of Suicide, Los Angeles. They investigated how sequential structure is managed in institutional talk. Conversation analysts study conversation sequence organization, turn design, turn taking, lexical choices, the repair of difficulties in speech, and the overall conversational structure. They analyze linguistic mechanisms (e.g., grammar and syntax, lexis, intonation, prosody, etc.) in naturally occurring conversations.

Institutional talk, as examined in later CA studies, focused on those that have fewer formal constraints as institutional practices (e.g., phone calls, doctor-patient interaction, and classroom instructions), but not those that have rigid structures within formalized rituals (e.g., a religious wedding ceremony, a sermon, etc.). Institutional CA studies picked up speed in the past few decades, allowing the identification of macro-level societal shifts through the management of social interaction in talk.

In general, CA theory postulates that talk is conducted in context. Participants' talk and actions call forth context, and context is constructed by participants. Sequencing position in conversations reflects the participants' understanding of the immediate preceding talk. As such, sequential structure reveals socially shared and structured procedures. Thus, CA is the study of action, meaning, context management, and **inter-subjectivity**.

CA is qualitative in methodology, even though later scholarship involved statistical analysis. The method is criticized for several weaknesses, among them: (a) the analysis and presentation of select segments of conversation lack rationale; (b) most CA studies are restricted to studying conversations in North America and Europe; (c) since multiple identities are at play in conversations, those that are consequential for social interaction remain ambiguous and debatable in analyses; and (d) the boundaries between pleasantries (e.g., small talk) and institutional talk are at times fuzzy in institutional CA. Nevertheless, with a range of sub-areas quite well developed, CA is said to form its own discipline.

▶ Discourse Analysis

Discourse Analysis (DA) is a broad term for different analytical approaches used to examine text and talk. Discourse is considered language use in general, and language is viewed as a form of action. The distinctions between the different approaches used in DA are based on the influences of the early works or traditions in conversation analysis and ethnomethodology, **discursive** psychology, critical discourse analysis and critical linguistics, Bakhtinian research, Foucauldian research, and even interactional sociolinguistics. However, the very different approaches and practices in DA have sparked disagreements among researchers about their applications and distinctions.

Data used in DA range from written to spoken, such as recorded spontaneous conversation, news articles, historical documents, transcripts from counseling sessions, clinical talk, interviews, blogs, and the like. Socio-historical contexts are often included in DA. As a tool for analyzing text and talk, DA has significantly influenced the study of language and culture. Two of the most popular DA approaches used in communication studies are Discursive Psychology (DP) and Critical Discourse Analysis (CDA).

◻ Discursive Psychology

DP evolved in the early 1990s from Derek Edwards and Jonathan Potter's works, in which they expressed dissatisfaction with the ways psychologists treated discourse. In psychology, utterances are treated as a reflection of the speaker's mental state. Hence, talk is considered *reflective*. However, in DP talk is considered *constructive*; language use is thus viewed as a social action or function. This means that people use language to make sense of what they do in a socially meaningful world. Therefore, language is treated as a tool to get things done.

In DP, researchers study the details of what people say (e.g., descriptions, terms, lexicons, or grammar). Researchers are concerned with how these features have particular effects or bear functions, such as shifting blame, denying responsibility, and providing counterarguments. DP researchers seek to understand the interests, attitudes, and motives of the speakers, particularly, why people use language the way they do and how they manage and construct identities.

Language use in news media coverage provides a good example for DP analysis. For example, the August 2015 news coverage about corruption in Malaysian government offices supplies rich vocabularies for analyzing the speakers' motives. Under the leadership of *Bersih* (an organization whose name literally translates to *clean* in the Malay language), an estimated half a million people went to the streets and urged the Prime Minister, Najib Razak, to resign following a critical expose published in *The Wall Street Journal*. The Prime Minister was reported to have transferred the equivalent of U.S. $11 billion from a government development firm into his personal bank account. Prior to the Prime Minister's counterattack, the press labeled the demonstrators *rally goers*. However, the Prime Minister and his supporters in government in turn used descriptors such as *criminals*, *crazy*, *unpatriotic*, and *shallow-minded criminals* to label the demonstrators *traitors* to their country.

The description above shows the way the speakers used language to construct their reality and their relationship to that reality. In this case, DP researchers would analyze and illustrate how the Prime Minister and his government officials co-construct shared meanings in interaction, such as particular realities, beliefs, identities, or subjectivities. For instance, the government can be seen as attempting to exercise control over the public demonstrators (through discourse) in order to defend governmental power. Thus, by labeling the demonstrators *criminals*, the government asserted its identity as the *authority*—the *elite power* that runs the country and decides what goes.

DP researchers assume that each speaker has multiple identities, and the identities can only be performed successfully with the consent of the listeners. The researchers also assert that the productive examination of discourse must be considered within the context of language use, such as the institutional setting and local sequential organization of talk. For example, a proper analysis of the Malaysian public demonstration above must include an understanding of the context of the public demonstrators' dissatisfaction with governmental corruption and citizen's demand for transparency in governance—a longstanding issue since the country's independence from Britain. Thus, **indexicality**—the understanding that the meaning of a word is dependent on the context of use—is essential in DP analysis.

Perhaps one of the strongest criticisms of DP is the researchers' reluctance to interpret macro-social concerns. DP researchers insist that the analysis of text and talk should depend on the context exactly as construed by the language used. This means that extra-textual information should not be inserted in the analysis. Therefore, DP cannot be utilized to **interrogate** broader social concerns, such as politics, ideology, and power. As such, context is limited to and constituted by the interactional setting and functions of utterances.

DP is also criticized for casting speakers as conscious and **agentic**—that is, as autonomous subjects who manipulate language to do things. Speakers' intentionality in attribution is thus considered fixed in their minds. Such an assumption in fact closely resembles that of traditional psychology—the very idea that DP researchers attempted to shift away from. Moreover, the analyst's interpretation is crucial in unfolding an understanding of the discourse. The analyst's knowledge and statuses thus influence his or her interpretation of the language used by speaker and can be a weakness if the analyst may conform to some sort of ideology that impacts data interpretation.

Critical Discourse Analysis

Of all the approaches used to study DA, CDA is one that takes a macro-societal and political standpoint as opined by van Dijk in 1993. Critical discourse analysts examine how societal power relations are enforced, **legitimated**, maintained, and dominated through the use of language. The socio-historical context of the text is emphasized. The examination of social problems requires the analyst to be well versed in multiple disciplines. Commonly, the analysts are motivated by particular political agendas or ideologies, and they seek to challenge certain ideologies as remarked by Fairclough in 2005. Therefore, based on, say, the motivation to fight social inequality and oppression, an analyst may seek out selected texts or talks for study. It is in CDA studies that the abuse, dominance, and unequal distribution of social goods are called into question.

Social theorists whose works are commonly cited in CDA include Pierre Bourdieu, Antonio Gramsci, Louis Althusser, Karl Marx, Jürgen Habermas, and Michel Foucault. Typical vocabulary in CDA studies includes *power*, *dominance*, *hegemony*, *class*, *gender*, *race*, *discrimination*, *institution*, *reproduction*, and *ideology*. Topics examined include gender inequality, media discourse, political discourse, racism, ethnocentrism, nationalism, and anti-Semitism. Critical discourse analysts seek to answer questions such as: How do elite groups control public discourse? How does such discourse control the less powerful group (in terms of mind and action)? What are the social consequences of such discourse control? The dominant social groups in politics, media, academics, and corporations are **scrutinized** in terms of the way they produce and maintain the dominant ideology.

According to van Dijk in 1993, critical discourse analysts explore three contextual levels of discourse: the macro, meso, and micro. At the macro level, analysts focus on the understanding of relationship between the text and broader social concerns and ideologies. At the meso level, analysts examine the contexts of production and reception of the text, and the ideologies portrayed. The analysts ask questions such as: Where did the text originate? Who is (are) the author(s) and the intended audience of the text? What perspectives are being promoted? At the micro level, analysts scrutinize the forms and contents of the text through linguistic features and devices in order to reveal the speaker's perspective or ideology. Linguistic features and components studied include direct and indirect quotations, terms used to refer to individuals or groups, sentence structure and grammar (e.g., active and passive voice), and pre-modifiers (e.g., non-violence).

While analysts frequently favor institutional texts (e.g., a journalistic report) in their analyses, everyday conversation is also included. In fact, everyday conversation is considered social group discourse that can be used to reveal societal norms and shared beliefs. According to van Dijk's studies of racism in everyday conversation, he found that the speakers' utterances of "I am not racist, but…" and "We are not a racist society, but…" are in fact a reproduction of institutional talk. He called this specific type of talk a double strategy of positive self-representation and negative other-denigration.

While the multidisciplinary nature of CDA seems beneficial, it is also one of its biggest criticisms. In particular, critical discourse analysts are often accused of not productively using a combination of multiple approaches. Indeed, more linguistically-oriented studies of text and talk overlooked theories in sociology and political sciences that focus on social and power inequality issues. In addition, those that focus on sociology and political sciences did not **rigorously** engage in DA. Moreover, the relationship between discourse and action coupled with cognition remains inconclusive.

▶ The Ethnography of Communication

The ethnography of communication originated from ethnology in the 1800s and found a home in anthropology. Bronislaw Malinowski, a Polish anthropologist, pioneered the ethnographic methods. He intensively recorded the methods he used in his fieldwork when studying the Trobrian Islanders of Papua New Guinea in 1914, including intrinsic details about the people, their language, and their daily life. Franz Boas, a German anthropologist who lived among the Inuit in the late 1800s, further stressed the necessity for language training among ethnographers who wished to decode the emic (i.e., native) perspective.

Ethnographers study social norms, meanings, and patterns of life by examining symbolic activities ranging from speech to social artifacts. By writing on culture, recording people, and natural history, ethnographers describe, analyze, and compare people from different communities. The painstaking work involved in ethnography provides rich data that are highly nuanced. Ethnographic works are said to be the portraits of social life. Oftentimes, interviews are used **concurrently**, along with other methods (e.g., textual analysis) to obtain community members' interpretation and explanation of the communicative activities. Data analyses are conducted along with (i.e., not after) data recording in the field.

While an ethnographer may generate questions for investigation before entering the field, he or she must remain flexible and receptive to other important questions that may emerge on site. The focus of investigation might shift because theoretical sensitivity—the review of literature prior to fieldwork—may not sufficiently orient the ethnographer to actual interactions. This is because the behaviors and activities that the ethnographer intends to study may have changed due to culturalshift. The use of such an inductive method allows the study of language and culture without theoretical limitations.

Ethnographers may compare the behaviors cross-culturally when a sufficient number of studies of the cultures of interest become available. Since the voices of community members are given precedence, ethnographic reports rely heavily on and present people's utterances, as well as fine details of observations. In fact, early ethnographic works in anthropology tend to **exhaustively** cover many life aspects about a community, though the search for nuances and painstaking details, coupled with the ethnographer's prolonged engagement in the community, pose **constraints** of time and resources. However, in the 1960s, ethnography took a new turn with the greater emphasis on the study of language use.

The Ethnography of Speaking

The prominence of ethnographic studies focusing on speech in language and culture began in the 1960s with Dell Hymes's study of language use. Hymes, who was trained in anthropology and linguistics, sought to understand speech patterns, functions, and speaking in situatedness. He departed from micro-linguistics (which focuses on semantics, turn-taking, prosody, and conversational structure) to pursue a more holistic account of interaction in context. Hymes emphasized the examination of non-verbal cues, tone of conversation, evaluation of the interlocutors' conduct, the setting of the interaction, and so forth.

Speaking is considered fundamental in understanding social reality. Hymes's ethnography of speaking (later called ethnography of communication) is a method for analyzing communication in different cultural settings. In 1972, Hymes developed as an etic framework for the etic understanding of social interaction, provides an inductive tool for examining social and cultural elements through the means and ways of speaking. Each letter in the SPEAKING **mnemonic** represents a different element of a speech act: S represents the setting or scene; P, the participants and participant identities; E, the ends; A, the act sequence and act topic; K, the key or tone; I, the instrumentalities; N, the norms of interaction and interpretation; and G, the genre.

The SPEAKING mnemonic is one of the most widely used theoretical and analytic frameworks in ethnographic studies. Although Hymes developed it to study spontaneous conversation, recent communication studies has broadened the scope of the data to include textual analysis and computer-mediated communication. Such pluralities are, in fact, inherent in people's ways of speaking and despite some criticisms, the ethnography of speaking's theoretical framework has withstood the test of time. It was the inspiration for Gerry Philipsen's speech codes theory—another important **heuristic** theory in the ethnographic study of language and culture.

Speech Codes Theory

In addition to Hymes' ethnography of speaking, Philipsen drew from Bernstein's coding principle to **postulate** his speech codes theory. Bernstein argued that different social groups manifest different communicative practices and linguistic features. These differences are influenced by and, in turn, reinforce the groups' coding principles—the rules that govern what to say and how to say it in the right context.

According to Philipsen, people's ways of speaking are woven with speech codes—the system of symbols, meanings, premises, and rules about communication conduct that are historically situated and socially constructed. Therefore, examining a community's discourse can tease out people's understanding of the self, society, and strategic action. Philipsen posited five propositions for studying the relationship between communication and culture:

(a) People in different speech communities exhibit different ways of speaking, with different rules for communicative conduct informed by their socially constructed symbols and meanings.

(b) Each code gives practical knowledge about the ways of being in a speech community.

(c) People attach different cultural meanings to speech practices.

(d) Metacommunication (i.e., talk about talk) reveals important worldviews, norms, and values of the people.

(e) The common speech code reveals the morality of communication conduct.

Using the five propositions, Philipsen argued that the speech codes theory can reveal the ways of speaking and reinforce a group's speech codes. Indeed, the theory has informed the vibrant scholarship on ways of speaking and meaning-making across different global cultural communities. For example, Lee and Hall's study of Chinese Malaysian discourse of dissatisfaction and complaint-making, with and without a formal goal of resolution—called, respectively, *thou soo* and *aih auan*—unearthed previously unexplored cultural values of the speech community. Lee developed the study further to understand the assumptions of personhood among Chinese Malaysians.

Cultural Discourse Analysis

The speech codes theory also served as the foundation for the development of Donal Carbaugh's cultural discourse analysis theory in 1996. Carbaugh, a former student of Philipsen's, proposed the cultural discourse theory (CuDT) as a way to understand culturally shaped communication practices. According to CuDT, cultural discourses are constituted by cultural communication and codes. Culture is an integral part but also a product of communication practices that are highly nuanced and deeply meaningful and intelligible to cultural participants. Cultural participants draw on diverse communication practices and thus create diversity within and across cultural communities.

Cultural discourse analysts study key cultural terms that are deeply meaningful to the participants; for example, *oplakvane*, which is a distinctive way of speaking to assert Bulgarian personhood. Such cultural terms are an ongoing meta-cultural commentary that reveals implicit cultural knowledge, the taken-for-granted knowledge, such as beliefs, values, and assumptions about the self.

Three types of questions typically guide cultural discourse analysis (CuDA) are: (a) *functional accomplishment* (What is getting done when people communicate in this specific way?); (b) *structure* (How is this communicative practice conducted? What key cultural terms are used to give meaning to the participants? What deep meanings do the terms create?); and (c) *sequencing* or *form* (What is the act sequence of this communicative practice, in terms of interactional accomplishments, structural features, and sequential organization?).

The analyst approaches a CuDA project with a particular stance or mode of inquiry. Carbaugh identified five modes of inquiry that enable analysts to tease out important cultural ingredients in a topic of investigation: the theoretical, descriptive, interpretive, comparative, and critical. For example, the theoretical mode enables analysts to understand the basic communication phenomena in the speech codes of a community and therefore to refine what and how to listen for culture in their discourse before venturing into the field. The five modes chart a rough linear design; the analyst must accomplish the preceding mode before starting on the subsequent mode. The first three modes (i.e., theoretical, descriptive, and interpretive) are mandatory in any CuDA project; however, the last two (i.e., comparative and critical) may or may not be accomplished in a single study (e.g., in an exploratory study).

Cultural discourse analysts typically use Hymes's SPEAKING framework and Philipsen's speech codes theory as guidelines for their subsequent analyses in the descriptive and interpretive stages. The analysis of implicit cultural meanings in CuDA can be structured using five semantic **radiants** or hubs: *being*, *acting*, *relating*, *feeling*, and *dwelling*. Using CuDA, analysts can tease out people's understanding of who they are (being); what they are doing together (acting); how they are linked to one another (relating); their feelings about people, actions, and things (feeling); and their relationship to the world around them (dwelling). The cultural discourse analyst's task, then, is to advance cultural propositions (i.e., statements containing the taken-for-granted knowledge) and premises (i.e., values or beliefs). These are statements that shed light on the importance of a particular communicative practice among members of a speech community (e.g., beliefs about what exists, what is proper, or what is valued).

While the theories in the ethnography of communication have gained a lot of prominence in the LSI discipline, they have also enriched it. For example, Hymes's SPEAKING framework, Philipsen's speech codes theory, and Carbaugh's CDT have all added depth and rigor to LSI data analysis. Evidently, to navigate through the language and social interactions of a community to which the researcher is not an insider, he or she needs to gain communicative competence. Specifically, the researcher needs to know how to communicate like the insiders in order to articulate and explain the behaviors and communicative phenomena to other outsiders. The researcher also needs to gain competence particularly in the multidisciplinary methods of LSI.

However, neither reliance on English as *lingua franca* for LSI research nor the practice of hiring translators are sufficient for undertaking this line of inquiry successfully. Therefore, many LSI studies recruit international scholars to participate in their research projects. While this is a common practice, especially in CuDA, the researchers' cultural interpretations and the subsequent translation of the data into the English for publications need to be done with utmost care in order to maintain the integrity of cultural nuances. Moreover, while the scholarship has strived to give voice to muted, non-dominant groups internationally, the dearth of cross-comparative studies—a goal and a tradition of ethnography—is a great concern. In that sense the study of intercultural interaction using the ethnography of communication has not yet come of age in this increasingly globalized and complex world.

Conclusion

This essay outlines the history and evolution of the study of language and culture by the main areas of study in the LSI discipline. The four main areas summarized are language pragmatics, conversation analysis, discourse analysis, and the ethnography of communication. Influential methodological and theoretical frameworks reviewed cover the Sapir-Whorf hypothesis, speech act theory, Grice's maxims of implicatures, politeness theory, discursive psychology, critical discourse analysis, the ethnography of speaking, speech codes theory, and cultural discourse analysis. Finally, the essay examines major criticisms of the theories and applications, as well as possible future directions of scholarship, when and where appropriate in the discussion.

UNIT THREE
Language, Culture, and Research Methods

Text B Language and Culture: Research Methods

After Claire Kramsch

Given the overwhelming diversity of areas covered by the field of research called "Applied Linguistics" as reviewed by Knapp in 2014, I focus here on the area acknowledged by Knapp as "by far the biggest and best known,", namely language studies or language education. The publication in 1998 of the little book *Language and Culture* by Kramsch in 1998 was a first attempt to **stake out** an area of Applied Linguistics focused specifically on the relation between language and culture. There had been before that several efforts to include "culture" in language education, but culture was not a concept that was echoed by scholars in second language acquisition/applied linguistics, who were more psycho- and socio-linguistically oriented and preferred to study language in its social or situational context. With the growing influence of anthropology and linguistic anthropology in particular, the concept of culture in Applied Linguistics began to shift from a stable national or social group entity to portable representations, and from products, beliefs and behaviors to processes of identification, symbolic power struggles and identity politics. Duranti and Goodwin book titled *Rethinking Context* published in 1992 served as inspiration to Kramsch.

By the end of the nineties, the modernist concept of culture was coming to be replaced by late modernist concepts like **historicity** and subjectivity that put the focus on the historical and subjective nature of culture, conceived as co-constructed "membership in a discourse community that shares a common social space and history, and common imaginings. Even when they have left that community, its members may retain, wherever they are, a common system of standards for perceiving, believing, evaluating, and acting" according to Kramsch in 1998. Such a definition suggests that the relation of language and culture has been studied from a variety of disciplinary and methodological perspectives ... This survey is organized around the aspects of language and culture mentioned above. It **takes stock** of the research questions and the research methods used then and now. Given the ill-defined boundaries between Applied Linguistics and Psycho- and Sociolinguistics and especially Linguistic Anthropology with regard to language and culture, it will not always be possible to distinguish research in applied linguistics from research done in these related fields. In the end I consider some important analytical and methodological trends for the future.

▲ How Is Cultural Meaning Encoded in the Linguistic Sign?

Taking language as cultural semiotic, this section considers the advances made in recent decades in three major areas that illuminate the way culture is encoded in the linguistic sign and its use: language and thought; language, **cognition** and emotion; and language and embodied knowledge. These areas of research fall roughly under the concept of language relativity.

Research on language relativity that studies the way language shapes the way people think, has picked up since the 1990s in Linguistic Anthropology. While Whorf claimed that speakers were prisoners of the grammatical and lexical structures of their language this strong version of the linguistic relativity hypothesis has now been rejected and researchers tend to agree more with Sapir's more moderate statement: "Language is a guide to social reality … it powerfully conditions all our thinking about social problems and processes…. The 'real world' is to a large extent unconsciously built up on the language habits of the group. No two languages are ever sufficiently similar to be considered as representing the same social reality. The world in which different societies live are distinct worlds, not merely the same world with different labels attached." This weaker version of the Sapir-Whorf hypothesis is now non-controversial and is researched in Applied Linguistics under three different aspects: semiotic relativity, linguistic relativity and discursive relativity according to Kramsch in 2004.

Semiotic Relativity, or How the Use of a Symbolic System Affects Thought

This aspect of language relativity draws on the insights of Soviet psychologists like Lev Vygotsky. According to Vygotsky, a semiotic system is both a linguistic sign and cognitive tool. By learning to speak and to communicate with others, children learn to think, by first internalizing the words and thoughts of others on the social **plane**, then making them their own on the psychological plane. According to Vygotsky and sociocultural theory (SCT), a community's culture and an individual's mind are in an inherently dialectical relationship as semiotically organized functional systems. In 1999, Lantolf described the process of cultural acquisition in children as follows: "during ontogenesis the bio-logically specified mental endowment of children is shaped in specific ways once it interfaces with cultural forces as children are apprenticed into their native culture." Cultural development here is taken to mean socialization into a given social group, be it the family, the school or the sports-team.

In second language acquisition (SLA) research, the enthusiastic embrace of SCT by one of SLA's most prominent scholars, Merrill Swain, in the nineties composed a sea change in the way SLA was conceived. Notions such as "comprehensible input," "interaction and negotiation," and "comprehensible output," which had nothing to do with culture, gave way to concepts such as "internal speech," "zone of **proximal** development," and the "help of more capable peers." This raised the possibility that children's speech and cognition were shaped by those of cultural others. The question arose then as to whether second language learners can appropriate for themselves the culture of the native speakers of that language. As long as culture acquisition only means the ability to momentarily see the world through the eyes of a native speaker or to occasionally behave in ways that conform to native speaker expectations, culture acquisition should be a desirable goal of language learning. As Lantolf shows, language learners are able to adopt the conceptual metaphors of native speakers, for example, they can be taught to say in English "Thanks for your time," and "I want to respect your privacy." But they might have quite a different view of time and privacy from native English speakers. Indeed, if culture is, as Lantolf writes, drawing on Clifford Geertz, *"an historically transmitted semiotic network* constructed by humans and which allows them to develop, communicate, and perpetuate their knowledge, beliefs and attitudes about the world," then non-native speakers by definition cannot have this semiotic network transmitted to them historically since it is, as Geertz calls it, a "system of inherited conceptions. " However, they can gain secondary access to it and make it their own in a manner that will be different from that of native speakers.

Researchers in the SCT tradition have drawn on Vygotsky's work as well as on activity theory to develop more dialogic or dynamic ways of assessing learners' competences based on the difference between what a learner can do alone and what he/she can do with the assistance of others, and to design a task-based pedagogy in which learners cooperate on solving problems that mirror those encountered in real-world cross-cultural exchanges.

That SCT theory is now being put into question by the arrival of complexity theory, a theory that is more in tune with our decentered, global world shows how the theory of semiotic relativity itself is affected by larger sociocultural and sociopolitical forces like the collapse of the Soviet Union and globalization. If Vygotsky lived today in our world of videogames, social networks, tweets, and 24/7 media outlets, he might have developed a different view of cognitive development. Not one based on the notion that "the mechanism of individual developmental change is rooted in society and culture," but on the notion that individual development emerges in a non-linear way from much less stable and less predictable connections in a complex "network society."

With the growing importance of visual forms of communication and research on multimodal semiotic systems, the **interpenetration** of the verbal and the non-verbal has created additional links between text and context, linguistic and visual forms of meaning making. Particularly online communication that looks both at and through language, blurs the distinction between text and context in a complex virtual culture that creates additional layers of reality.

Linguistic Relativity, or How Speakers of Different Languages Think Differently

Linguistic relativity in language education has been researched from a psycholinguistic perspective by Slobin in 1996 in his path-breaking study of children's narratives, based on one story in pictures *Frog, Where Are you*? narrated by different children in their different native languages. Slobin argues that in order to speak at all, speakers must attend to the syntactic and lexical choices offered by their grammars, and that the cumulative occurrence of these choices can have cognitive and affective effects on the listener. For example, the obligation to attend to honorifics in Japanese or to T/V distinctions in German, French or Spanish, forces learners of these languages to pay attention to social hierarchies that they might not need to attend to in their mother tongue. Based on the typology of each of these languages, Slobin proposed to replace the Whorfian static nominal phrase "thought-and-language" with the more dynamic phrase "thinking-for-speaking," which moves culture from Whorf's focus on the linguistic *sign* to the activity of *signing* by living speakers and writers. Culture becomes indeed, as Brian Street suggested, a verb rather than a noun.

Recent psychological experimental research on linguistic relativity has further confirmed the influence of linguistic form on cognitive processes. For example, psychologists have explored whether and how the grammatical gender of **inanimate** objects influences speakers' associations. Speakers of Russian who have two words for "blue," *siniy* (light blue) and *goluboy* (deep blue) have a quicker reaction time when asked to identify kinds of blue than English speakers who only have one word for both. The recent discovery of a tribe of Australian Aborigines, the Guugu Yimithirr, that position themselves in space not according to the orientation of their bodies (right/left/in the front of/in the back of), but according to the four cardinal points of the compass (north/south/east/west) has triggered a flurry of studies on the cultural differences in people's conceptions of time and space.

Because linguistic relativity has recently attracted renewed attention from the popular media, there have been virulent debates about it. Responding to what Gopnik calls "pop Whorfianism," McWhorter argues that while the idea of linguistic relativity is clearly fascinating, it is, he says, plainly wrong. It is language that reflects culture and worldview, he argues, not the other way around. The fact that a language has only one word for eat, drink, and smoke, doesn't mean its speakers don't process the difference between food and beverage.

Since the eighties cognitive linguists like Lakoff and Johnson have made cognitive science into a major approach to understanding the metaphoric structure of the mind and the close relationship of language, cognition and emotion. Cultural signs can become idealized cognitive models or ICMs that channel our thinking and make it more difficult to grasp other people's words because of the different underlying ICMs associated with them. For example, the prototypical ICM for "woman" will be different in Saudi Arabia and in the United States or between gays and heterosexuals. The linguists who separate cognition from morality and emotions have a noble belief in the rationality of human action. Surely we know what *torture* means, Gopnik exclaims. If Cheney calls it *enhanced interrogation*, he argues, this still doesn't change the meaning of the word *torture*, which Cheney and the public know perfectly well. But cognitive linguists like Lakoff remind us that the public can be manipulated into believing that torture is "merely" an enhanced interrogation technique and thus does not protest. Indeed this is exactly what a marketing strategist like Frank Luntz manages to get corporations and political parties to do when he persuades them, for example, that calling the estate tax a "death tax" will lead citizens to vote against it, because, after all, it is not fair to tax people for dying. As citizens of our languages, we must be aware that words don't change meaning on their own; they can be made to change meaning in order to arouse different emotions and thus serve different political interests through discourse.

Discursive Relativity, or How Different Speakers Have Different Cultural Worldviews

As Scherzer remarked: "It is discourse that creates, recreates, focuses, modifies, and transmits both culture and language and their intersection." Speakers use the resources of discourse—contextualization cues, like affective and **epistemic** stance markers, speech acts and identity markers, and other communicative practices to link what they say to the larger context of culture. This link has been researched through discourse analysis of audio and, increasingly, video recordings of spontaneous interactions and their transcriptions. Advances in computer technology have enabled researchers to study the construction of culture in and through communicative exchanges in the minute details of gaze, posture, gestures and facial expressions.

Research in socialization studies, drawing on Bourdieu's notion of the *habitus* or embodied knowledge, has shown **indexicality** to be one of the major ways in which linguistic signs point to other signs to create a universe of meaning that can be shared by members of a speech community. But communicability brings with it several risks. First the sign, that following de Saussure might have been called "arbitrary" in its nature, becomes "motivated" in its use, as communication entails intentionality, choice and expectation. Second, motivated signs can sediment or solidify through time to form condensation symbols also called stereotypes. These condensation symbols appeal less to our rational apprehension of social reality than to our emotions and imagination. Sociolinguists have worked on the commodification of language and culture used for marketing and political purposes; they have studied the keywords of neoliberal thought and the use of multimodal signs.

For example, Heller shows how the French language used in Quebec is now used as an **exotic** commodity that serves to sell French Canadian products on the global market. Holborow uses Raymond Williams' keywords, i.e. "ideologically sensitive words" such as *ideology*, *liberalism*, *folk*, *genius*, *citizenship*, *gender*, to show how their associations and connotations change with the changing political, social and economic situation. She applies Williams' analysis to the current sloganization of political and academic life. In 2010, Kress identified three principles of sign-making: that (a) *signs are motivated conjunctions of form and meaning*; that conjunction is based on (b) *the interest of the sign-maker*; using (c) *culturally available resources*. He defines culture as follows: "*Culture*, in my use, is the domain of socially made values; tools; meanings; knowledge; resources of all kinds; *society* is the field of human (inter)*action* in groups; of 'work' or practices; of the use and effects of power." Heller, Holborow and Kress use a critical approach to discourse phenomena that links the motivated sign to cultural and political interest and power.

In sum, various fields of research related to Applied Linguistics have made it easier in recent decades to conceptualize how culture is encoded in the linguistic sign and its use. Culture is linked to language in three major ways: semiotically, linguistically, discursively. Language does not determine our cognition nor our emotions; torture means torture in any language. But by calling it something else, like "enhanced interrogation technique," one can change the degree of the cognition and the intensity of the emotion triggered by the words. Not in a deterministic way, and not in the dictionary meanings of words, but in the **enunciative** choices of speakers and writers and in the affective, social, and political meanings they assign to these words. It is to these enunciative choices that I now turn.

▶ How Is Cultural Meaning Expressed Pragmatically through Verbal Action?

In this section I focus on three emblematic studies: The cross-cultural speech act realization project, Moerman's ethnographic conversation analysis, and Tannen's frame analysis to discuss how applied linguistic research studied language and culture in the 1980s and 1990s. I will discuss in the next section the move toward a more constructivist approach and a greater role given to performativity.

Cross-Cultural Speech Act Realization Research

The multinational cross-cultural speech act realization project (CCSARP) conducted by

Blum-Kulka, House and Kasper in the eighties was a path-breaking project that compared how requests and apologies were realized across different national languages and their national cultures. Discourse completion tests (DCT) and situational role-plays were used to elicit plausible rejoinders uttered by native speakers in distinct pragmatic situations, such as requesting that a roommate clean up the kitchen, or apologizing for not returning a book to your professor on time. This methodology was the object of frequent adjustments, first requesting an open-ended utterance, then providing a contextual constraint in the form of a third rejoinder. But still the DCT left too much to the imagination of the respondents and their idiosyncratic understandings of the situation to be able to provide a reliable measure of pragmatic competence pegged to "the native speaker."

Culturally Inflected Conversation Analysis

As conversation analysis (CA) gained in importance in Applied Linguistics as a method to measure gains in grammatical and discourse competence, the need was felt to incorporate a cultural dimension in a method that remained strictly focused on what the participants were orienting to in the conversation itself. Culture was brought into the picture by Moerman in 1988, based on his work in Thailand and his memorable transcriptions of conversations between rice farmers and the local authorities. Moerman, who like Schegloff was based at UCLA, was the first applied linguist to include cultural and historical knowledge in the field of conversation analysis that had been conceived by Schegloff as the pure study of the here-and-now turns at talk in conversation. In his book titled *Culture* in 1988, Moerman was largely rejected by pure CA analysts who refused to take into account anything that did not emerge from the analysis of the interaction/transcript itself, and they wouldn't consider culture as one such emergent category. However, Moerman's work enabled applied conversation analysts to include perceptions, memories, and cultural beliefs into their data as long as it could be shown that the participants were orienting to them at the time of utterance.

Cultural Frames

The work of Deborah Tannen was the third sociolinguistic influence on the way Applied Linguistics approached culture. In *Framing in Discourse* in 1993, Ervin-Tripp and others, Tannen showed the importance of cultural frames to understand events. These "frames of expectation" were studied as social roles (e.g., what men and women expect of each other in conversation) or characteristics of a conversational style (e.g., California vs. New York Jewish style). Researchers gained access to these invisible frames by eliciting narratives from pictures or videos without words, such as Wallace Chafe's *The Pear Story*, that make visible a storyteller's assumptions about stories and their culturally-specific expectations about human motives and actions. Tannen found that, when they retold the pear story, her American informants paid much more attention to the cinematic aspects of the video than her Greek informants, who focused more on evaluating the motives and intentions of the characters and on passing moral judgments.

However, there were researchers who showed that such mappings of language on to culture were too simplistic and had to be studied with much greater differentiation. In her work on bilingualism, Ervin-Tripp, who had studied the different completions of the same story told by bilinguals in English and in Japanese to find out whether the differences were attributable to their different cultural backgrounds, had found that there was much more deviation between and within national groups than expected.

Even the monolingual norms needed differentiating. Like many psychologists interested in bilingual children, Ervin-Tripp used a range of tests to measure the relation of language and culture in bilinguals, e.g., Thematic Apperception Tests, storytelling, word associations, sentence completions, semantic differentials and story completions. She studied the difference between foreign born Japanese of the first generation of immigrants to the U.S. (the Issei) and second generation Japanese-Americans (the Nisei) and their distance from American norms, distance from Japanese norms, and relative dominance of the two distance scores. She found that, when asked to give associations of words in Japanese, both Issei and Nisei gave associations typical of women in Japan; but when speaking English, the Issei gave typically American associations. For instance, Japanese women more often say "what I want most in life … is peace." Americans say "… happiness." But the Japanese responses were very much dependent on how long they had lived in the U.S., how many Anglo-American friends they had, whether they read American magazines, to what extent they kept the two cultures separate or not, and, ultimately, whether they could picture for themselves what a "typical" Japanese or American response would be. The over-all effect was that content shifted with language for both groups.

In sum, culture as enacted pragmatically by speakers and writers has been studied by psycho- and sociolinguists who have been quick to map the pragmatics of one language on to psychological and social characteristics of groups that speak that language. The dissatisfaction with such structuralist approaches to pragmatic cultural variation has prompted some researchers in recent years to turn to post-structuralist approaches that explore how language and culture co-construct each other in intercultural encounters.

How Is Culture Co-constructed by Participants in Spoken Interaction?

If the main insight gained by research on language and culture in the 1980s and 1990s was that culture was expressed by participants in and through the very structure of spoken interaction, the post-structuralist turn in the last fifteen years has focused the attention on its co-constructed nature and on the non-structural aspects of this co-construction, such as identities, ideologies, timescales, and orders of indexicality.

From Structuralism to Post-Structuralism

In the 1980s and 1990s, applied linguists were interested in finding out how interlocutors in conversation express social and cultural identities through their use of language in social contexts and how they reproduce well-bounded ethnic, familial, and social cultures. They drew, for example, on Gumperz's notion of contextualization cue and its role in cross-ethnic communication, on Ochs' study of family narratives and their role in reproducing a family culture of "father-knows-best." In the last 15 years, with globalization, applied linguists have had to deal with the multilingual uses of language in multicultural contexts and the co-construction of multiple, changing and sometimes conflictual cultural flows. They have explored the code-switching and code-meshing practices of bilingual youngsters in classrooms, in large urban centers and online exchanges, the **trans-idiomatic** practices of transnational immigrants and the rise of **hyper-reflexivity** in an era of super-diversity. In so doing, they have broadened and diversified their research methodology.

For example, while Gumperz was intent in cataloguing the different types of code-switching and in identifying their discrete pragmatic functions in countries which traditionally keep different linguistic codes strictly separated, Canagarajah, studying the code-switching in ESL classrooms in Sri Lanka, went beyond a structuralist typology. He recognized that, by allowing in the classroom code-switching and even code-meshing, i.e., the seamless blending of several languages as if they were one, the school was preparing the students for the hybrid culture of the real world outside, where such trans-languaging is common currency. Going beyond Gumperz's typological interest, Canagarajah not only observed secondary school teachers in the classrooms but also discussed the teacher's views on code-switching after each lesson. He found that code-switching fulfilled both micro-functions, such as classroom management and content transmission, and macro-functions that dealt with socio-educational implications, such as the status of English as reserved for the formal content of the lesson and Tamil for personal and unofficial interactions. Thus he was able to draw inferences as to the emotional identification of the students with each of the languages: English perceived as impersonal, **detached** and alien; Tamil perceived as informal, personal and homely. By allowing code-meshing, the school was in effect allowing the students to appropriate and personalize English and integrate it into a post-structuralist hybrid culture of the future. However, in this post-structuralist culture people's identities are no longer unitary, stable and unproblematic, but multiple, changing, and more often than not the site of conflictual allegiances and memories.

Scholars like Canagarajah and those engaged in the study of English as a **Lingua Franca** would want to replace the outdated and even pernicious, because too deterministic, concept of culture with the much more agentive, fluid and hybrid notion of "cosmopolitan practice," in which interlocutors seek alignment, not intercultural understanding, multilayered affiliations, not uni-dimensional identities, and communicate with one another in the absence of any shared values. As Canagarajah argues: "Nothing may be shared in such communities other than the objectives that bring people together (e.g., professional, business, faith, etc.).... People come from their respective communities to negotiate their differences and find alignment by adopting constructive strategies." This cosmopolitan view of global citizenship does seem more suited to our mobile, decentered world, but it is a fallacy to think that it does away with culture. It has only replaced local culture as the negotiation of worldviews, attitudes and beliefs among families and friends with global culture as the negotiation of purposes and interests in joint professional, business, or faith projects. Indeed, one could say that in this new dispensation individuals share the value of negotiation and collaborative project management on a global scale and that is their "culture." In his latest book *Communication Power* in 2009, the sociologist Manuel Castells, having defined culture as "the set of values and beliefs that inform, guide, and motivate people's behavior," distinguishes between global culture and local cultures as follows:

What characterizes the global network society is the contraposition between the logic of the global net and the affirmation of a multiplicity of local selves".... The common culture of the global network society is a culture of protocols of communication enabling communication between different cultures on the basis *not of shared values but of the sharing of the value of communication*.

Not surprisingly, speakers of English as a Lingua Franca favor this cosmopolitan view of culture, that befits English as the global language of business and technology and that gets constructed anew at every new global encounter. Such a view **correlates** well with a constructivist perspective on culture in interaction.

Toward a Constructivist View of Language and Culture in Spoken Interaction

The turn from a structuralist to a post-structuralist approach to language and culture has been spearheaded by critical sociolinguists. For these researchers, culture is not a fixed, stable institutional reality that individuals belong to by virtue of having been socialized in it and that pre-exists the individual. Culture is, rather, a process of language use that is integrated with other semiotic systems such as "ritual, dance, music, graffiti, beat-boxing, clothing, gestures, posture, ways of walking and talking." Speakers and writers do not just perform culture, they construct it in interaction with others. In so doing, they often make use of the stereotypical views of traditional cultures, but in order to draw a profit of distinction and further their interests.

This constructivist view is inspired by the work of Michel Foucault. In his famous preface to the *Order of Things* in 1970, Foucault recounted his laughter at reading Borges' story about a fictional Chinese encyclopedia that classifies animals according to a totally absurd system of classification such as: a) belonging to the emperor, b) embalmed, c) tame, d) sucking pigs, etc. What we lack, Foucault says, to grasp the logic of this classification are the "fundamental codes of [the] culture" that guided the system of thought of the people living at the time. What we lack is an understanding of the conventions, presuppositions and norms of discourse that such a classification performs. Moreover, we fail to see the relation between this way of classifying animals and the classification of other phenomena, such as diseases, school children, citizens and historical events. A given culture is not only performed by its members in the form of such encyclopedias, but encyclopedias, like dictionaries, instruction manuals, examinations, child rearing practices and, today, social networking, are constantly creating and constructing the culture that people live by.

From Performance to Performativity

Deborah Cameron has characterized this constructivist perspective as "post-modern," which doesn't mean that it has superseded the modern, but that the emphasis has shifted from an essentialist view of culture as the performance of pre-existing values and beliefs to a view of culture as a performative process in which old words can be given new meanings and can give birth to new thoughts. In her reanalysis of one of her students' work, Cameron gives a brilliant example of this performative turn in the study of language and culture. In the example, the gendered culture of white males perform heterosexual **masculinity** by making fun of a colleague's homosexuality in his absence. The point of this exchange is not so much, Cameron argues, to **bash** gays, but, rather, to reconstruct their own heterosexual identity that might have been put into question by their association with a gay man.

It is in this sense that we must read Judith Butler's argument in *Excitable Speech. A Politics of the Performative* in 1997 about the linguistic vulnerability brought about by harmful speech. In her analysis of legal documents like "Don't Ask, Don't Tell," Butler shows how a culture of silence or of hate speech can wound by reactivating past contexts of discrimination into the present. But, she adds, because the performative can break with the past and be indeed transformative, it can "open up the domain of the sayable" and actually transform the meaning of, say, the word "queer" or "gay" from a term of insult to a marker of pride. Butler expands Austin's study of performatives into the more general notion of performativity that applies directly to the relation of language and culture. Quoting Toni Morrison, she wrote in 1997: "We die. That may be the meaning of life. But we *do* language. That may be the measure of our lives." Like Austin's performatives that do things with words, meaning making acts, both verbal and non-verbal, have a performative illocutionary force that not only performs but brings about social reality. In his analysis of popular **hiphop** culture, Pennycook has called such a performativity "a semiotic reconstruction." He wrote in 2007: "This move from the performative to the transformative is crucial for our understanding of performativity as neither merely the playing out of public roles, nor the acting out of conventional behavior, but the refashioning of futures."

From Culture to Historicity and Subjectivity

With performativity, time has re-entered the picture of a field that tended to consider culture only spatially or geographically. In anthropological research, the vague notion of "culture" has given way to culture as historicity and subjectivity. Researchers, inspired by insights from complexity theory, cultural memory studies, look at the data with increased reflexivity and attention given to the subjective perspectives of both researcher and researched. In 2008 Kramsch and Whiteside, using a complexity theory framework, examined the exchanges between Yucatec Maya immigrants and Asian shop owners in the Hispanic district of San Francisco and showed that, rather than performing expected linguistic and cultural identities, these immigrants operated on multiple timescales and positioned themselves subjectively in multiple ways so as to get along with others and avoid the police. In 2014 Samata, drawing from cultural memory theory, conducted interviews with immigrants to the UK who had no or limited knowledge of the language of their parents, but a strong **affiliation** with the culture of their parents' language. She too takes into account history and memory in her analyses and reflects on her own subject position as a multilingual and multicultural researcher. In his study of classroom discourse, Wortham in 2006 drew on Silverstein's meta-semiotic theory to illuminate the "meta-pragmatic models" or characteristic types of students and their actions and relationships to other students, that persist over the school year and influence how students perceive themselves and are perceived by others. Performative models of culture enable us to imagine another relation to time and space, one based not on linearity and simplistic views of causality, but on the emergence of phenomena and on the "layered simultaneity" of timescales.

In sum, the performative turn in the study of language and culture within a post-structuralist perspective does not, as many have feared, transform culture into a merely discursive process, open to all the relativity and subjectivity of individuals' verbal utterances and with no clear agreed upon social boundaries. It does underscore the man-made nature of culture, its historicity, its disciplining power and its power to impose on a social group definitions of what is taken-for-normal, the shared understanding of people and events. But at the same time, the performative shows that the very political forces that have constructed culture can also be used to deconstruct and reconstruct culture in different ways. Performativity can indeed be seen as **transformativity**.

How Are Language and Culture Affected by Language Technologies?

In this section I consider the uses of literacies (written, print, online, multimodal) in shaping what we call culture. Literacy education and writing technology, inheritors of a print culture that started in the 16th century and that ever since has raised the interest of scholars in literacy issues such as genre, style, register, and norms of interpretation, has provided the foundation for applied linguists' understanding of language and culture. Indeed, the structuralist approaches to language and language use discussed in previous sections of this paper come from an intellectual tradition steeped in print culture. For example, the very scholarly culture that enables applied linguists to transcribe spoken data and analyze and interpret them from a structuralist perspective belongs to an eminently literate culture that has academic legitimacy only to the extent that it is literate, not oral. Similarly, the application of Hallidayan systemic functional linguistics to teach register and genre and to reshape foreign language and literature curricula along genre-based principlesis in line with an academic culture anxious to maintain the boundaries between oral and literate speech genres and their use. Such policing of literacy practices has been the hallmark of national cultures eager to use print technology to distinguish educated from less educated citizens, and to inculcate in the young the political and moral values that go along with such technology.

Enter online technology and the Internet. Applied linguistics has been slow to research in any critical depth the effects of the new technology and its uses in language education. The pressure to prepare language learners for the "real" world of online communication has led most researchers to consider the computer as just another tool for the realization of print literacy goals, including the communicative competence that is taught in instructional environments. The virtual culture of computer-mediated communication has been viewed by many as the ideal instructional environment to implement the post-structuralist turn in the teaching of language and culture. This environment matches the communicative goals of language education: communication with native speakers, interaction with other non-native speakers, collaborative learning with more capable peers, learner autonomy, and the learning through tasks that mirror those of the real world. All this at the click of a mouse. But the new environment also ushers in: a decentered view of the individual at the mercy of public opinion, distributed cognition and the danger of plagiarism, multiplicity of identities and a distinctly addictive reliance on the judgment of others, a blurring of oral and literate genres (e.g., email, Skype, blogs), and in general, a reshuffling of the usual axes of time, space, and reality. The very technology that promised to give all learners access to any foreign culture and its members is exacting its own price: shallow surfing of diversity instead of deep exploration of difference, leveling of aspirations and expectations, bullet-like ability to process information but loss of the ability to follow a complex argument, amazing ability to multitask but limited ability to problematize the task and question the question.

The political and ideological issues raised by each new technology, from print culture to multimodal forms of expression to the virtual culture of the Internet, have been addressed by Critical Discourse Analysis (CDA). I mentioned in the previous section the poststructuralist turn in Applied Linguistics, inspired by Foucault asking about the historic conditions of possibility of cultural phenomena, and the subject positions of the producers, reproducers and transformers of the discourses that constitute culture. In the same way as cultural theorists are rethinking concepts such as historical tradition and authenticity in an era of simulacrum and second life, so are critical applied linguists starting to question the authenticity of cultures in the age of the hyper-real and the virtual. For this they need another kind of CDA than the one pioneered by Norman Fairclough. They need to draw on complexity theory and ecological approaches to language and culture.

In his book *Discourse: A Critical Introduction* in 2005, Blommaert recounted how, in preparation for a workshop on "Frame and Perspective in Discourse" held in the Netherlands on the 60th anniversary of the 1944 Warsaw Uprising, the participants had been handed the texts of various speeches made on the occasion and were asked to subject them to various forms of discourse analysis. Blommaert was able to show how the events themselves had been **entextualized** in different ways and how each of these texts was operating on various timescales: the time of the uprising itself, the time of the Allied invasion, the time of the Soviet restraint, as well as the present time in which most Western narratives follow the U.S. American interpretation, heavily tainted by a Cold War rhetoric that, as present events suggest, has not died down since the official end of the Cold War. All these timescales operate in what Blommaert calls "layered **simultaneity**." He wrote:

> We have to conceive of discourse as subject to layered simultaneity. It occurs in a real time, synchronic event, but it is simultaneously condensed in several layers of historicity, some of which are within the grasp of the participants, while others remain invisible, but are nevertheless present …. People can speak from various positions on these scales. The **synchronicity** of discourse is an illusion that masks the densely layered historicity of discourse.

Thus, while the actual workshop took place in 2004, the participants positioned themselves on different timescales, some more global, some more local, associated with different memories and anticipations of the future, within the various discourses surrounding the historical event called "the Warsaw uprising." This way of reading texts as entextualizations positioned on different timescales and in different orders of indexicality offer a more complex reading than traditional CDA and can serve as a model to analyze online texts with their equally complex relations to time, space and reality.

In sum, the relation of language and culture in Applied Linguistics is inseparable from the issues surrounding the use of language technologies. The print culture of the book, the virtual culture of the Internet, the online culture of electronic exchanges all have their own ways of redrawing the boundaries of what may be said, written and done within a given discourse community. They are **inextricably** linked to issues of power and control.

Applications

1. The Paradox of Culture
Hall, T. E. (1970). The paradox of culture. In B. Landis and E. S. Tauber (Eds.), *In the Name of Life. Essays in Honor of Erich Fromm*, 218–235. Holt, New York: Rinehart and Winston.

Abstract: The best minds of each age inevitably come to grips with alienation in its various forms. Today one can observe at least three areas in which serious alienation occurs: in the self; between men; and between man and nature. Basically, the American culture, once vigorous and viable, has become much less so today. If we are to survive and adapt successfully, we must change, and this change will not be easy. It involves, among other things, a recognition of the fact that life is rooted both in context and in content, and that without both, life makes little sense. So far, Western man has been dealing with the content part of the equation. The context part of their behavior had escaped the bureaucrats entirely. The paradox is that, in his strivings for order, Western man has created chaos, denying that part of himself that integrates, while enshrining the part that fragments experience.

Keywords: alienation; American culture; context and content; order vs. chaos; paradox

2. The Relationship between Language and Culture
Elmes, D. (2013). The relationship between language and culture. National Institute of Fitness and Sports in Kanoya International Exchange and Language Education Center. Available at: www.libnifsk.ac.jp/HPBU/annals/an46/46-11.

Abstract: With first language learners immersed in their own culture, connections between language and culture often never come to question. For foreign language learners, where true cultural intricacies and understandings are situated well beyond the textbook, an understanding of language assumes a very different form. While it is possible to separate language and culture, one has to question the validity and implications such separation brings. This paper introduces the concepts of language and culture, and explores the viability of their relationship based on the three possible relationships proposed by Wardhaugh, i.e. the structure of the language determines the way we use language, cultural values determine language usage, and the neutral claim that a relationship does not exist. The importance of cultural competency is then considered for its importance to language education and the implications it holds for language learning and policy.

Keywords: language; culture; Sapir-Whorf Hypothesis; language education

3. Language and Words: Communication in the *Analects of Confucius*

Chang, H. C. (1997). Language and words: Communication in the *Analects of Confucius*. *Journal of Language and Social Psychology*, 2, 107-131.

Abstract: Despite attention to effects of Confucianism on Asian communication, views of Confucian philosophy are hampered by predilection to look at its social implications rather than Confucius's many observations about words and speaking. Comprehensive examination of *Confucian Analects* yields four principles: (a) words define and reflect moral development, (b) beautiful words lacking substance are blameworthy, (c) actions are more important than words, and (d) appropriate speaking relies on rules of propriety. Five weaknesses are found in current views linking Confucianism and Asian communication: (a) collectivist metaphors are inappropriately foregrounded, (b) social position is assumed incompatible with individual will, (c) moral character is excluded from discussion of language in Confucian societies, (d) personal freedom is thought the essence of ability to reason and formulate messages, and (e) Confucianism is used retroactively to explain observed communication behaviors in Confucian societies. Research suggestions from several disciplines and methodologies are offered.

Keywords: effects of Confucianism; *Analects of Confucius*; comprehensive examination; principles; language and words

Interactive Activities

1. Individually, please finish reading Text A, Text B, and the application abstracts and work out the meanings of the terms in bold type by consulting the dictionary whenever necessary.

2. In pairs, please summarize the content in 2 to 3 sentences of each sub-heading in the unit outlines of Text A and Text B based on your reading and understanding of the texts.

3. In groups, share your gains, comments and suggestions regarding the three application abstracts. Based on your interests, locate and finish reading the full-length papers of your interested abstracts.

4. Q&A: Questions are encouraged about any uncertain or confused part or parts in the unit and seek answers either from other fellow students or the instructor.

5. Complete the Personal Report of Cross-Cultural Awareness, a scale designed to measure your degree of awareness of intercultural or cross-cultural communication. Take a few moments and complete the self-assessment for Unit 3.

6. **Abstracts** allow readers interested in a longer work to quickly decide whether it is worth their time to read it. Also, many online databases use abstracts to index larger works. Therefore, it is essential to appreciate abstracts and learn to write abstracts yourself. Abstracts differ by field, but in general, they need to summarize a longer work or full-length paper in about 200 words, including the following elements: (a) a statement of the problem and objectives; (b) a statement of the significance of the work; (c) a summary of the employed research methods; (d) a summary of the findings or conclusions of the study; and (e) a description of the theoretical and practical implications of the findings.

Based on your reading of the two texts and the applications of the three abstracts, please check the library or the website, search for an academic paper concerning the relationship between the Chinese language and Chinese culture in either English or Chinese, and then translate the abstract of the paper from Chinese to English or the other way round.

UNIT FOUR

Contexts, Power, and Intercultural Communication

Readings

Text A Culture, Communication, Context, and Power

After Adrian Holliday

Introduction

Text A reviews a struggle between two sociological paradigms which govern the way we think about and research the intercultural. Table 4.1 summarizes these. On the one hand, **post-positivism** leads to neo-essentialism and a post-positivist research methodology. On the other hand, postmodernism leads to a critical **cosmopolitan** approach and a constructivist ethnography. I argue that the post-positivist paradigm fails because of its neo-essentialist inability to escape from Center methodological nationalism and structural-functionalism, whereas the success of the postmodern paradigm is its engagement with a de-Centered small culture formation on the go. Throughout, I use large cultures to refer to the bounded, essentially separate, homogenous, national, continental, ethnic, religious or other entities that are falsely constructed by the post-positivist paradigm as defining the cultural behavior of people who reside "within" them.

I use Kuhn's concept of paradigm in 1970 as scientific revolution. This means that post-positivism and post-modernism do not stand side-by-side as choices but that the latter is an advancement of the first. It needs however to be acknowledged that Kuhn himself is postmodern in that he sees the career politics and ideological positioning in science, which contributes to the difficulties that old paradigms have with adopting the new. It also therefore needs to be acknowledged that Table 4.1 is written from the postmodern perspective in the right hand-column, therefore framing post-positivism in the left-hand column as "weakened" by different aspects of a pull back to positivism. It may also be argued that, in Kuhn's terms, post-positivism is not a paradigm but an unsuccessful break from positivism, or positivism pretending to be something else. The implications of this **anomaly** are discussed below.

Table 4.1 Two Paradigms

Postpositivist paradigm	Postmodern paradigm
A belief in diverse social realities But weakened by maintaining a positivist belief in an objectivist structural-functional sociology	Realising that so-called objective social realities are ideological grand narratives
Neo-essentialist approach to the intercultural Claiming attention to cultural diversity But weakened by a methodological nationalism that always begins and finishes with behaviour-defining large cultures as the default entities Maintaining Centre structures that define and reduce the Other Interculturality tolerates the cultural Other	**Critical cosmopolitan approach to the intercultural** Believing in de-centered realities that — are hidden, unrecognised and therefore marginalised by Centre structures — possess creative agency that transcends and dissolves Centre structures The centrality of small culture formation on the go underlying universal cultural processes and personal cultural trajectories Interculturality is a messy exploration of Self in Other and Other in Self
Postpositivist methodology Qualitative But weakened by a perceived need to minimise subjectivity with researcher distance and a priori 'mixing' with quantitative methods	**Constructivist ethnography** Treating the realities of all parties including the researcher as socially and subjectively constructed Juxtaposition of subjective instances through thick description Applying disciplines to manage the subjectivity of the researcher Allowing multiple methods to emerge in response to the research setting

▶ Historical Perspectives

To place these paradigms within a historical context, it is necessary to go back to some of the basics of sociological theory.

Positivism and Structural-Functionalism

The post-positivist paradigm can be traced back to the positivist sociological tradition of structural-functionalism of Emile Durkheim which presented society as an organic system which achieves **equilibrium** through the functioning of its parts. Derived from biological science, this gave the impression of a society as a solid object, and enabled the development of social theory based on detailed descriptions of how the parts of society, such as the institutions of education, the military, the family and politics contributed to the whole. In 1951, Talcott Parsons' social system developed this notion and provided a detailed description of all the interconnected parts of society, and contributed greatly to our understanding of the way in which society works.

However, problems arise when these descriptions are used to explain and indeed predict cultural behavior and values as though they are contained within the system, giving the impression that individual behavior is determined rather than autonomous. Therefore, if a large culture is deemed collectivist, any behavior within it can be explained as contributing to (or as an exception to) its collectivism. Each large culture is also considered to be a differentiated unit between which precise comparisons can be made. This approach underpins the influential work of Hofstede, who draws on Talcott Parsons to gain support for the notion of a culture as a "complete" social system which is "characterized by the highest level of self-sufficiency in relation to its environments," according to Hofstede in 2001. There is also a strong normative sense to this thinking, which enables the evaluation of behavior and values depending on whether they are functional or dysfunctional to the equilibrium of the whole.

Postmodernism and Social Action Theory

Postmodernism within the social sciences might be traced to the postmodern condition by Lyotard and Berger in 1979 and social construction of reality by Luckmann in 1979. Both made it clear that the idea of a confining and defining social system can be no more than a construction for the political purpose of instilling social cohesion. There is also an important contribution to this thinking from Max Weber's social action theory in 1964. This maintains that the precise nature of human behavior can never be determined. Part of his strategy against pinning things down was remembering that coherent ideas about societies should be regarded as "ideal types"—imagined models or **heuristic** devices—which might be used to imagine what society might be like but which should never be taken as descriptions of how things actually are. While Weber did much to describe the social structures of **Protestantism** and Confucianism, it was made very clear that the social action of individuals could be expressed in dialogue with them. While political and other circumstances may severely reduce the degree to which individual social action can be acted out, this does not mean that the potential is not there. The example of critical thinking, which has become a common focus in intercultural communication studies, can be used to clarify the difference of the two sociological approaches:

The Structural-Functionalist View. If a society is structured in such a way that students are not allowed to express critical views in the classroom, they will lack critical thinking everywhere.

The Social Action View. Not being allowed to express critical views in classrooms in one particular social system does not mean that students do not think critically in private or that they cannot express critical views when moving to other social systems.

Unlike the neat layering depicted by structural-functionalism, social action theory indicates a messy, shifting, and uncertain complexity of cultural reality which is ideologically dependent on the perspectives of the people concerned. One must however avoid projecting too neat a case for Weber's social action theory. It has been argued that he was still **preoccupied** with nation to the degree that he failed completely "to treat it as problematic social and historical construction."

The Centrality of Ideology

The key to the postmodern critique of positivism and post-positivism is the positioning of ideology. Whereas structural-functionalism positions ideology as a feature of the structure of the culture being investigated, postmodernism places ideology within the **domain** of the investigator and therefore maintains that the descriptions of culture are themselves ideological, and that the structural-functionalists' claim to scientific neutrality and objectivity comprise a naive denial of ideology.

However, of more concern here, related to the false, objectivist notion of large cultures, ideology can be defined as a system of ideas which are "systematically distorted" or "bent out of shape," to promote the interests of a particular group of people. Mannheim explains that "these **distortions** range all the way from conscious lies to half-conscious and unwitting disguises." In this sense we need to be wary even of what he describes as the other, "more inclusive" notion of "the ideology of an age or of a concrete historic-social group."

Of particular relevance to how we think about the intercultural is the role of ideology in perceptions of the Center and the de-Centered. Here, Stuart Hall is helpful in explaining the importance of the de-Centered where he refers to "the de-centered cultural" as the basis of a "most profound cultural revolution" in which the "margins" can "**reclaim** some form of representation for themselves" and threaten "the discourses of the dominant régimes." He states that "by, as it were, recovering their own hidden mysteries, they have to try to retell the story from the bottom up, instead of from the top down." I use a capital "C" to emphasize the reality and importance of the Center. The Center can take different forms. Within the current historical climate, it is placed very much within a global politics where the power of "the West defines the **Periphery** non-West" within a Center image of **globalization** which is driven by global markets. The Center could however also be other dominant structural forces such as **patriarchy**, the neoliberalism that encourages the quantification of the intercultural within the post-positivist paradigm or the ideology of native-speakerism that encourages the positivist equating of English and a false notion of large Western cultures according to Holliday in 2018.

The problem with neo-essentialism, on the left of Table 4.1, is that it takes Center-constructed images of cultural diversity as a sufficient truth and works with them rather than appreciating that they are ideological and hiding other de-Centered representations. A recent example of neo-essentialism is Lindholm and Mednick Miles's book on the intercultural classroom. On the one hand, it appears to support immense cultural diversity, even to the extent of referring to the highly critical notion of inter-sectionality. However, on the other hand, much of their text is based on Center essentialist large culture definitions and stereotypes following Hofstede and others that divide the world into separate cultural blocks. Diversity therefore remains locked within essentialist large culture boundaries.

▸ Critical Issues and Topics

The second row in Table 4.1 indicates the approach to thinking about and researching the intercultural that gives rise to critical issues and topics.

Critical Cosmopolitanism

Critical cosmopolitanism is the sociological approach that develops from postmodernism and can be employed as the basis for a powerful critique of the positivist and post-positivist views of the intercultural. The critical cosmopolitan argument, supported by critical and postcolonial sociology, claims that it is a Center Western grand narrative that has falsely defined and **marginalized** non-Western cultural realities. It therefore recognizes that in the hidden, marginal world, there is unrecognized complexity and fluidity in social processes and multiple ways through which the social world is constructed in different contexts with different modernities, and acknowledges that cultural realities are built at an individual level around personal circumstances that dissolve structural and spacial boundaries.

Methodological Nationalism and Neoliberal Accounting

On the left of Table 4.1, methodological nationalism is referred to as the basis for the neo-essentialist adherence to large cultures as the primary category. This is attributed to the politics of 19th Century European nationalism and is considered by the critical cosmopolitan position and others to be the major ideological force that presents large cultures as the default starting place in social science. Its support for structural-functionalism feeds the requirement within the academy for accountability, especially marked during the Reagan and Thatcher era of the 1980s. This requirement has developed with the increased neoliberal desire to show quantifiable success in "adding value" in intercultural learning. Shuter argues that the need for quantification encourages tightly specialist concepts such as "uncertainty reduction," "initial interaction," "intercultural communication competence," "communication apprehension," intercultural adaptation" and "relationship development." Kumaravadivelu makes a similar point about the proliferation of technical terms such as "accommodation, acculturation, adaptation, adoption, assimilation, enculturation, integration."

An Individualist versus Collectivist Imagery

A particularly influential example of such post-positivist concepts that falsely attempts to categorize and define large cultures is the so-called collectivism-individualism distinction. This is most commonly associated with Triandis, who maintains that "people from individualist cultures"—"North Americans of European backgrounds, North and West Europeans, Australians, New Zealanders"—are associated with autonomy, personal goals, improvement, achievement, assertiveness, self-reliance, consistency, openness to change, fun, equality, and choice. In contrast, "people from collectivist cultures"—"Latin Americans, Southern Europeans, East and South Asians, Africans"—are associated with group and family membership and loyalty, interdependence, circular thinking, stability, conservatism, circular thinking, silence, and few choices. These large culture "prototypes" have taken on a **disproportionately** powerful reality that extends in different ways into current literature and practice.

The critical **cosmopolitanism** critique is that the collectivist-individualist distinction is an ideological construction that represents a veiled **demonization** of a non-Western Other by an idealized Western Self, and that the collectivist attributes thus represent cultural deficiency. The outcome is therefore essentialist Othering—the defining of a particular group of people or a person by means of negative characteristics—so that the behavior of someone from a so-called "collectivist culture" is explained entirely according to these imagined and negative collectivist characteristics. That the collectivism description relates more to a generalized notion of low-achievement, rather than what might be attributed to large cultures, is evidenced by the use of the same descriptions for low-achieving mainstream American school children. Triandis himself gives away how he associates collectivism with characteristics that seem to be framed as deficient.

Neo-racism

This characterization of a particular cultural group as culturally deficient amounts to what has been termed by some writers as neo-racist. This is where race is hidden and denied under the "nice" heading of culture. At a macro level, the self-perception of a democratic West as "de facto anti-racist" leads to the idea of "race." At a micro level there are everyday "disclaimer" statements of denial—"I have nothing against ..., but," "my best friends are ..., but," "we are tolerant, but," "we would like to help, but ...".

There is also an implicit ethos of a deeply patronizing "tolerant" "helping" of the non-Western Other which can be connected with a modernistic desire to tie down identities and to hide aggression beneath education, progress and civilization. I have framed this process of Othering as an apparently well-wishing, and therefore easily sustained, though in reality deeply **patronizing** West as steward discourse. It is this **psychotic** disorder that in many ways underpins the neo-essentialist mixing of care for diversity and desire for large culture definition while denying the neo-racist implications.

The Struggle for De-Centered Cultural Recognition

It is therefore part of this West as steward discourse to argue that the collectivism-individualism distinction preserves the integrity of non-Western large cultures in their resistance of Western values. The critical cosmopolitan response is that the distinction itself is constructed by Western academia—that definitions of the Other which are produced by the West are so powerful that they remove any recognition of non-Western realities—and that a "West versus the rest" discourse that bases its resistance on essentialist categories such as collectivism is also essentialist. This gives rise to a complex debate around the **detrimental** nature of self-Othering, while appreciating that "strategic essentialism," in the form of an apparent buying into imposed stereotypes, is a means of resistance against powerful symbolic violence.

Here it is also important to note the difference between critical cosmopolitanism and a Center picture of a cosmopolitan world which has been variously termed "global cosmopolitanism," "globalism," and "global mass culture," which falsely suggests an attractive, liberalization and **integration** of markets. All this serves progress, democracy and prosperity, global villages and silicon valleys of the Western economies.

The critical cosmopolitan viewpoint counters this picture of harmony with a purposefully uncomfortable picture of global inequality. It presents a hidden, alternative, and local cosmopolitanism which struggles for recognition, but which "has always been there in non-Western communities" with villagers dealing easily across small linguistic boundaries, but which has largely been destroyed by colonial powers by dividing these communities arbitrarily into nation-states for their convenience. Various theorists are relatively optimistic about a revolutionary reclaiming of cultural space from the margins—a de-Centered globalization from below.

📖 Competing Views of Multiculturalism, Third Space and Hybridity

The reclaiming of de-Centered cultural space from Center definitions **pivots** around what these spaces are like. Three concepts play an important role here: multiculturalism (how we can acknowledge cultural diversity); the third space (where we can step out of Center definitions); and **hybridity** (how we can be ourselves especially in the search for postcolonial spaces). However, they have taken on both essentialist Center as well as de-Centered definitions in different places in the literature. In 2019, MacDonald provided an excellent analysis of how the third space has shifted in meaning as it has become **routinized** in the literature. The de-Centered definitions, which I argue are the original intention behind the terms, should therefore be recovered.

A Center interpretation of multiculturalism has been accused of reducing "other cultures" to an essentialized and packaged spectacle of festivals, food and costumes, and has been responsible for essentialist representations in school textbooks and the "shopping for difference." However, a de-Centered multiculturalism appreciates the diversity of cultural realities without avoiding "assimilationist" and "separationist" tendencies through "collaboration and identification with others."

Similarly, the Center interpretation of the third space has been accused of being a limited intermediate space between bounded large cultures. In contrast, a de-Centered third space is a creative space within which all people at all times can work out intercultural identity "without an assumed or imposed hierarchy," eluding "the politics of **polarity**," so that we can "emerge as others out of selves" and avoid the colonial discourse. However, as part of the struggle for de-Centered recognition, it needs to be an uncomfortable space.

A Center notion of hybridity suggests that cultural values and identities remain mixed-up between un-crossable large culture boundaries. However, a de-Centered hybridity is present in all our identities and cultural realities as the normal nature of culture and the intercultural—where "new identities of hybridity" are replacing "national identities" for all of us. It is the nature of culture per se and how we all are, it is the nature of the cosmopolitan, and it represents an "**upsurge** of new forms of life."

The essentialist forms of multiculturalism, third space and hybridity however remain powerful in the academy and in everyday discourse. That they lead to an appearance of support for diversity but in effect do the opposite fits well the paradoxical nature of neo-essentialism. Hence, what appears to be an inclusive, celebratory recognition remains in effect an Othering of non-Western groups by a Center Western definition of who they are. The example that whatever any "Asian" says or does is interpreted with stunning regularity as a consequence of their "Asianness," their "ethnic identity," or the "culture" of their "community" is thus still **resonant**.

▶ Current Contributions and Research

The persistence of Center imagery which continues to marginalize de-Centered realities requires research which can at least try to put aside Center structural lines.

Focusing on the Small and Messy

This can be achieved by taking the focus away from large cultures to discourses or small culture formation on the go. Small cultures could be a wide range of social groupings from neighborhoods or communities to work, friendship or leisure groups. They are built from the micro basics of how individuals manage image within the group to how groups are formed and routinized. They represent the "intermediate level of social structuring" in which there are identifiable discourses according to Fairclough in 1995; and it is at the level of discoursal strategies that we see the individual's ability to acquire the social competence to move through a multiplicity of cultural experiences within the complexity of society. It is at this level that we can see the detail of the building of "normal" thinking through social construction, normalization and **reification**—in the formation of "imaginary representations of how the world will be or should be within strategies for change which, if they achieve hegemony, can be **operationalized** to transform these imaginaries into realities." These are the bases for the social action which is in dialogue with and not confined by social structure within the Weberian social action view of society described above.

Small culture formation *on the go* moves a step further in the sense that it concerns the changeable process though which we all engage with the intercultural on a daily basis from an early age. This is different to the more common view of communities of practice in that it is not a normative process of building cultural unity, but instead represents possibly transient relationships which can be culturally discordant and therefore far from the Center expectation of "success."

Finding More Complex, Hidden Realities

This messier picture of the intercultural can be seen in Baumann's **ethnographic** study of how people in the multicultural London **borough** of Southall construct different narratives of culture in different ways at different times depending on who and what they are relating to, and also in school children from diverse backgrounds showing unexpected agency in working creatively with cultural identities in urban classrooms, and similarly with study abroad university students.

Political positioning, as discussed by the critical cosmopolitanists above, can make the difference here. Where cultural struggle is **underpinned** by the intense desire to throw off the stereotypes imposed by a Center Western order, the emphasis on the ability to dissolve cultural lines and take ownership of the foreign becomes all important. Implicit in this struggle is the dissatisfaction with the Western monopoly of key concepts of cultural proficiency such as modernity and self-determination. An interesting text on this subject is Honarbin-Halliday's ethnography of Iranian women claiming all of the modern world as their own cultural heritage and tracing it back to the deep indigenous modernity implicit in their grandmothers' generation.

Implicit in this **assertion** that people are not what they appear to be is a stand against the Orientalist trope that the non-West is characterized as culturally deficient in the opinion of Edward Said in 1978, which is associated with the false image of collectivist cultures described above. One example is the ongoing stand against negative and indeed neo-racist constructions of so-called "non-native speakers" and against the collectivist stereotyping of East Asian students and their imagined cultural inability to take part in educational activities.

Blocks, Threads and Uncomfortable Third Spaces

My own attempt to resolve this relationship between de-Centered reality and the Center illusion is in my grammar of culture, of which there is a simplified representation in Figure 4.1. "Grammar" here is as used to mean the basic work of the social scientist to make sense of society. Small culture formation on the go is positioned as the core domain of the intercultural in which we share the underlying universal cultural processes that begin in childhood and enable us to engage with the intercultural wherever we find it. There is therefore immediately a blurring of the distinction between the cultural and the intercultural. The particularities of national and other structures and cultural **artefacts** and products on the right and left, rather than defining us, as with the Center perception, provide the resources and influences that populate the substance of the intercultural with which we engage and the discourses and narratives that we produce. There are also, at the core of the grammar, very personal cultural **trajectories** which themselves defy national structures in their connections with family, ancestry, peers and profession according to Halliday in 2010.

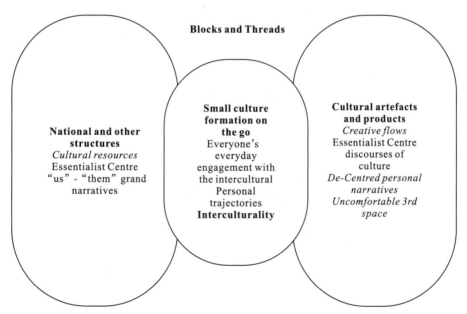

Figure 4.1 Grammar of Culture

However, as this personal **engagement** with the intercultural in small culture formation on the go struggles to make sense of the politics of Self and Other, it can result in both essentialist and non-essentialist outcomes which I refer to as blocks which separate us through essentialist references and threads (marked in italics in the figure) which connect us through shared experience respectively. Both of these forces can be found in all parts of the grammar.

The national and other structures on the left of the grammar govern the way in which we are brought up differently with different education systems, economies, political systems and media influences. They can provide valuable resources than we can carry with us into other social settings and help us to forge threads. They can also produce the Centre grand narratives about large culture difference that create blocks by placing us in opposition to each other. The cultural artefact and products domain, on the right of the grammar concern the physical, visible aspects of society. As well as art, music, architecture, cuisine and so on, they might include everyday aspects of the appearance of a society and what people do in it, from how buses and streets look to how animals are killed and where screws are sold. All of these elements are present in the global cultural flows that provide the substance of threads that bring us together.

On the other hand, they can be the superficial focus of the essentialist multiculturalism discussed above, and can become the basis ideologically driven statements about culture that may confirm Center structures. These blocks are common in statements about culture. These are what people say or otherwise project consciously about their "culture." These are not descriptions of what their cultural group is actually like. They are cultural acts—artefacts produced by the culture. Thus when people state that their culture is individualist and is marked by self-determination, it does not necessarily mean that self-determination is a defining characteristic of their group, but that this is the ideal with which they wish to be associated. This ideal then feeds the Center "us" vs. "them" grand narratives on the left of the figure.

In contrast to a constructed certainty about blocking, essentialist statements about culture, creating threads about personal cultural identity might not be a straight-forward process in that it requires us to search for who we are in perhaps unexpected places. Hence, as indicated on the right of the figure, it takes us into perhaps a necessarily uncomfortable third space, which fits with the messy, deep-digging nature of **interculturality** as defined by Dervin above.

The Defined or Undefined Non-Western Other

What has become a classic preoccupation within English language education and the internationalization agenda in universities—of students from outside the West being quiet in Western educational settings—can be used to illustrate the contrast between the neo-essentialist and critical cosmopolitan views:

The Dominant Neo-essentialist View. Silence derives from collectivist national cultures in which loyalty to the group inhibits individual expression, which in turn reflects a lack of self-determination. This therefore reflects different values which have to be appreciated and understood. Western teachers (from individualist cultures) need to be sensitive and to adjust their expectations.

The Critical Cosmopolitan View. Silence may well be influenced by national traditions and educational practices; but the students do not have to be confined by them. The behavior reflects the employment of universal **discoursal** strategies within small culture formation on the go to deal with unfamiliar cultural practice (different structures of power and authority). Silence may be a form of resistance which involves strategic withdrawal. The particular de-Centered cultural experience and criticality that students bring with them may enable them to bring new, innovative behavior and successfully change the dynamics of the classroom.

The critical cosmopolitan view is partly informed by doctoral and masters dissertations in which Japanese language students who are noisy in Japan go quiet in front of British teachers who demand controlled talk, and Chinese language students who are quiet because they do not understand task instructions and then get what they need outside the classroom. More recently, current "non-Western" Ph.D. students are researching their own **positionality** and that of their peers with regard to **resilience**, Othering, constructions of "Britishness," how they are constructed as "foreign," and radical personal cultural change. To do this, they employ auto-ethnographic methods and include themselves as participants to investigate their own personal cultural trajectories. In all cases, they take great care not to use any cultural stereotypes of themselves or others, in an attempt to de-Center who they are.

There is also the important factor that when people are newcomers in a particular cultural domain, they must not be seen negatively as deficient in the foreign practices they find, but as people with enhanced cultural skills because they have travelled, building positively on their cultural experience as they go—hence the very real possibility that "international" students who have the opportunity to rationalize more than one educational institutional experience are in a better position to contribute creatively than "home" students who have not travelled according to Halliday in 2011. In contrast, the neo-essentialist reading, while pretending sensitivity and understanding, in effect represents the **patronizing** Othering implicit in the essentialist multiculturalism described above by positioning the foreign in another place from which it is not able to contribute.

Main Research Methods

The critical cosmopolitan approach suggests a research methodology which seeks to allow meanings to emerge from the non-aligned, de-Centered piecing together of what is found, rather than imposing the a priori narratives implicit in a neo-essentialist approach. If de-Centered cultural realities are to be revealed, the aim must therefore be (a) to put aside established descriptions, (b) to seek a broader picture, and (c) to look for the hidden and the unexpressed. This is a difficult aim to achieve within the ideological and politicized domain which critical cosmopolitanism attributes to culture. It is also difficult because it must not take at face value statements about culture as described in the right of Figure 1, and must dig deeper to fathom the messiness and politics of interculturality.

Constructivist Ethnography

I therefore recommend a broadly constructivist ethnographic approach which acknowledges the subjective implicatedness of researchers as interactants in the research event. Research sites are thus places where all parties co-construct meaning and make sense of the world. This relates especially to the interview, which is "a potentially creative space between people." Researchers themselves "cannot, in a sense, write stories of others without reflecting" on their "own histories, social and cultural locations as well as subjectivities and values." As with the Ph.D. researchers mentioned in the previous section, they have no choice but to employ themselves as participants in the research, which becomes a prime example of small culture formation on the go in which all parties are struggling to make sense of each other's social constructions within a third space interculturality.

Cultural Studies

It is also important to think of all participants in the intercultural as researchers. Moving away from the post-positivist paradigm necessitates no longer thinking of intercultural newcomers as people who have to achieve a new "intercultural competence" through an initiation into being tolerant of a large culture which is separate to where they come from. Small culture formation on the go implies that they are instead developing an interculturality brought from childhood. Again, ethnography is relevant here, as already seen in young people using narrative and autobiography to develop their intercultural awareness. However, it must move away from the dominant neo-essentialist discourse, where it can easily remain framed around large culture differences and can lack the constructivist element.

One good example of not focusing on large culture difference is in the materials produced by IEREST (Intercultural education resources for Erasmus students and their teachers). Their aim is to help the students to co-construct who they are in interaction with others beyond national identities. This resonates strongly with a cultural studies pedagogy in which there is a radical project to re-interrogate "self among others" through a reflexive critique of Center structures and "a critical understanding of lived cultures and a consideration of people's experience and struggles and the forms of consciousness which established them as people."

The section in the IEREST materials on racism and anti-discrimination addresses directly the dark side of the cultural resources that we all have from the national structures within which are brought up on the left of Figure 4.1—the grand narratives of nation and history that create blocks that position us against each other. The cultural studies approach, driven by the work of Stuart Hall and Raymond Williams, seeks to "rescue" education from Centre forces that oppress or alienate cultural creativity. The focus of the "radical project" on class, ethnicity and gender and the importance of diverse membership as a crucial point of focus in the classroom "to alter forms of consciousness" implies a two-way process. In the case of intercultural education, this approach would encourage all parties to become conscious of the hitherto unrecognized cultural contribution of the newcomer, and an understanding of how Centre structures have acted to conceal this. This would not be to enable the non-West to behave well in the West. It would instead be to follow a de-Centering agenda of opening the West to understand the non-West—by removing the "non" of the West's imagined "collectivist" Other, and understanding the politics of how the collectivist label has been imagined in the first place.

Future Directions

A **predominant** theme running through the discussion in this chapter has been that of a global inequality which underpins the manner in which a Center image of culture and cultural difference has been **projected** both in the academy and in everyday life. The result has been a sustained and profound cultural disbelief with regard to an imagined non-Western Other. Adding to this issue has been the denial of this inequality in the dominant approach to the intercultural, where it has been falsely believed that cultural descriptions such as those of falsely labelled collectivist and individualist societies, though possibly overgeneralized, are technically neutral.

Future directions therefore need to be in two areas. Research into cultural difference and education towards cultural awareness both need to focus on cultural belief rather than disbelief. This very subtle change in gear suggests that we focus on what the cultural Other can do and contribute—that the Center-constructed line between large cultures can be **dissolved** by means of a de-Centered, third-space understanding. An important aspect of this focus is the concept of small culture formation on the go, which provides the potential for a de-Centered interculturality that is not located within any particular **culturality**. These underlying, common processes need to be observed and understood as the basis for threads that bring us together and enable us to read critically both what is going on between us and what fuels the ideologies of the blocks that keeps us apart.

Text B Culture Power and Intercultural Communication

After Rona Tamiko Halualani

▶ A Power-Based Perspective: Re-thinking Culture and Intercultural Communication

The concepts of culture and intercultural communication are difficult to define and reveal a multi-layered nature that is often forgotten or ignored. We learned earlier that power is the constraining force by which larger dominant structures, groups, and individuals are able to gain in position and achieve their aims over/against the will of others. This chapter will focus on the power-based perspective of culture that will be used throughout this book and help ground our understanding of intercultural communication. Several examples of how a power-based perspective frames culture differently from our everyday outlook will be shared. After reading this chapter, you will be anchored in the notion of culture as a field of forces that encompass multiple layers, contexts, and elements of power.

A perspective that focuses on power reveals great insights about aspects of culture and intercultural communication relations. But, what exactly is power? Is it something we all have, or just something some of us engage in? Is power an entity that we can see and touch? Is it a positive or negative force? The next section delineates a power-based perspective as it relates to understanding culture, communication, and intercultural communication in a different light.

Typically, individuals view power as "physical coercion" in which one individual dominates over another. In addition, for many, power seems to connote a type of social influence over others to act and think in a specific way. The underlying assumption of these popular conceptions is that power is defined from the standpoint of someone who is exerting or enacting power, or someone who is deemed *powerful*. But, lest we forget that power is multidimensional, it can push and be pushed. Power can destroy and create. These dimensions are grounded, though, in the specific context of power at hand and the position one occupies in relation to dominant power.

For example, Asian Pacific American communities occupy a unique position in relation to dominant power. Within the last 15 years, a multitude of East Asians—Chinese, Koreans,

Japanese—and Asian Indians, who have recently emigrated into the U.S. and conduct transnational business around the globe, have emerged as the upper professional class among all racial/ethnic groups. Many members of these groups have purchased expensive homes in largely White/European American affluent neighborhoods and gained high-ranking leadership positions in city and state government. These Asian Americans also enroll their children into prestigious schools and universities, many of whom go on to earn scholastic honors. With such increased affluence, society has labeled Asian Americans as the new "Whites": an ethnic group that has achieved economic and political success and, in turn, pushed out all other racial/ethnic groups from gains in power. This example belies a more complex relationship between Asian Americans and their relationship to dominant power. While they may have financially established themselves, Asian Americans, especially those that have emerged in the upper, professional, and middle classes, still experience systemic and social discrimination.

As a contrast, Southeast Asian communities have established a presence in the U.S. with population numbers running at two million and residing in states such as California, Illinois, Minnesota, and New York, among others. However, according to a 2000 report jointly released by the Asian Pacific American Legal Center, Asian Law Caucus, and National Asian Pacific American Legal Consortium, Southeast Asians stand as one of the poorest Asian groups in California, with Hmong, Cambodian, and Laotian communities being the poorest. Thus, Southeast Asians do not have the economic and political resources that other Asian Americans do, which means that they are relegated to **dilapidated** neighborhood areas, lower-tier jobs, economically deficient schools, and diminished means to voice their needs to governmental and social agencies. All of this translates into a heavily imbalanced relationship between this cultural group and the larger structures of power and dominant interests. However, it is important to note that while Southeast Asians face more significant challenges to financial and political empowerment, they *do have the power* to express their frustrations, voice their concerns, resist institutional and economic racism, and push for transformation, albeit in more confined channels.

Thus, the particular relationship between a cultural group and dominant power, therefore, determines the kind of push-pull dynamic a cultural group will face in a power-laden world. Meaning, the degree to which a cultural community (or even a member) will face resistance from structures of power and dominant parties will determine how much leeway it can have for resistance and how creative it must be in overcoming structural and power obstacles. Given their limited hold on formal power resources such as economic and political influence, Southeast Asians have relied on the one resource in their favor: community **mobilization**. They have been able to bring together and mobilize Southeast Asians across regions to protest societal dominance over them. One example of this can be seen in the collective organization, SAKHI for South Asian Women, a community-based organization in the New York metropolitan area committed to ending the exploitation and violence against women of South Asian origin. Another stands in the form of the Southeast Asian Resource Action Center (SEARAC), which is a national organization that advances the interests of Cambodian, Laotian, and Vietnamese Americans through advocacy and leadership development.

Somewhere in between the struggling Southeast Asian groups and the upper-class East Asian

Americans and Asian Indians, there lie several other Asian American groups who have lived in this country for over 20 years, and bought homes, settled into stable jobs, and managed to send their now-grown children to college. Chinese Americans, Japanese Americans, and Korean Americans have, for example, established a presence in the United States since their initial period of immigration.

Given their settled status in the U.S., middle class Asian Americans stand in a tricky position in relation to dominant power. They feel vested in the American system of power given their hard work and sacrifice all these years and thus, work hard to strike a balance between gaining societal acceptance (and improving their social status) and resisting persistent discrimination issued against them for being "forever foreign" immigrants. Thus, these middle class Asian Americans are not likely to express outright hostility against and make trouble for structures of power; instead, they feel compelled to protect what they (and their families) have and blend into society as Americans as best as possible. Though middle class Asian Americans face similar discrimination like all other Asian American groups (but in different ways), they still feel more attached to and dependent on dominant power and thus will behave in ways that do not threaten that relationship although, when needed, these communities will protest and demand recognition as hard-working ethnic Americans. Again, the position a cultural group occupies in relation to dominant power and structures of power helps to shape that group's relationship to dominant power and larger society, as well as the kind of push-pull dynamic (whether in the extreme, medium, or subdued sense) that will ensue.

These examples, therefore, demonstrate that the power dynamic between cultural groups (and members) and structures of power and dominant parties can vary from context to context and from group to group. In addition, the aforementioned examples illustrate the double-sided nature of power, or the constraining and enabling aspects of power. Power can be both a controlling force that seeks to restrict the movements and experiences of individuals and groups as well as an enabling force that individuals and groups can deploy in dramatic or subtle form against larger structures.

With this in mind, power can be defined as the following:

(a) A constraining force by which individuals, groups, and structures are able to achieve their aims and interests over/against the will of others, and

(b) An enabling and creative force that individuals and groups can use against larger structures.

Characteristics of Power

Power is characterized by several **attributes** or qualities that solidify its force. There are several key characteristics of power that complicate the relationship between cultural groups, dominant parties, and structures of power:

Power Is Invisible and Hidden. As discussed earlier, we cannot see all of the power structures in our lives. Think about the set of friendships that you have in your life. These friendships are special, precious, and very private. It even seems that we voluntarily choose, out of all the possible options, who our friends will be based on common interests, personality, group associations, and similar backgrounds. However, friendships remain a hidden context shaped by historical, economic, and power forces. The settings through which we forge friendships are not neutral, blank slates. Rather, without our conscious attention, these settings are already layered over with power influences such as history, economics, and cultural or social inequalities. For instance, the neighborhoods that we reside in, the workplaces that we are part of, and the social outlets to which we attend have a predetermined set of relations laid out for us due to history and economics. Through historical patterns of migration and conflict, certain cultural groups have been placed in closer contact and shared settings with one another. In specific cities, one or two cultural groups stand as the primary residents of particular areas—Whites/European Americans dominating one area and in another, Whites/European Americans, Asian Americans, and Latinos/Latinas.

Economics further shape these settings because economic cycles and **hierarchies** of people place us in neighborhoods, schools, workplaces, and social outlets with other individuals of *similar socioeconomic status* (and detach us from individuals outside of our class status). Thus, if historical and economic cycles and hierarchies position us with one or two other racial/ethnic groups, it is likely that most of our everyday contact and friendships will occur with members of these groups. Friendships, then, are social contracts that are based on some degree of limited choice and are invisibly framed by historical and economic conditions and the resulting cultural/social inequalities. This example suggests that power dimensions are unseen, invisible, and untraceable. **Ponder** other everyday experiences, choices, relationships, and interactions that fill your life and how these may be framed, to some degree and in invisible form, by macro-power influences. Just because we do not "see" such power domination or daily wars in our streets does not mean that they do not exist. Social control and power gains even more potency through its invisible nature. Power can move swiftly and easily when unsuspected and forgotten, especially when it touches our intercultural and interpersonal relationships and interactions.

Power Is Material. Power also manifests itself differently within and among groups, creating inequalities and a society of haves and have-nots. Power is material in that it results in concrete, tangible consequences for all those involved, especially in terms of economic implications, or the amount of money we have, the type of jobs that we are able to enter in, the kind of lifestyle we are able to lead, and how we, as different groups, are economically exploited. Simply put, the degree of material power that you possess (or do not) determines, in part, how you are able to live, how others (and even yourself) view you, and society's valuation of you in terms of the economic context. Material power, while operating mostly through the economic mode of production, also impacts the social spheres of our lives: how we think and relate to one another through issues of money, status, and economic gain or loss at home, school, work, places of worship, and in times of leisure. In its materiality, power then carries real effects on individuals and groups; it can hit a person hard in his or her pocketbook and affect how society treats him or her. Material power can even determine that person's very survival in, for example, war-torn countries and top-heavy national economies that exploit the working and immigrant classes.

Cultural group members are undoubtedly affected by material power in that there are distinct economic differences among, between, and within specific racial, ethnic, religious, and regional groups. Ponder how, in the U.S., certain racial/ethnic group members, such as Mexicans/

Mexican Americans, Southeast Asian Americans, and under-classed Whites/European Americans that make up the working class, take on "blue collar" tier manual labor (housekeeping, janitorial services, gardeners, construction) and factory jobs and are often treated with disdain, avoidance, and pity. Because of material power, these groups often experience social marginalization and economic exploitation as they are paid small wages for taxing labor in horrific working conditions. The experiences of these groups are markedly different from those of their racial/ethnic group counterparts of all different backgrounds but most notably Whites/European Americans, Asian Americans, and Asian Indians in the upper professional classes who are in a position to practice more economic freedom and enter and participate in American society and institutions although minority upper professional classes still experience discrimination and resentment from society because they are posed as "economic threats." Thus, in comparison to the upper professional classes, the working class is looked down upon and they are deemed "lowly," as well as the professions associated with them, which become racially/ethnically marked jobs, and receive limited (if any) medical and family benefits and protection on the job. Likewise, this class is considered to be a disposable and easy-to-replace labor force and is granted a disproportionate amount of power to influence the political, economic, and social arenas of society with little money, and possess limited political representation as well as a restricted voice to express discontent with jobs. These material differences set the stage for often tense, **contentious**, and even a lack of intercultural encounters and relationships between different economic classes. Power and domination are not light matters; these forces, especially in the material sense, affect every fiber of our being and carry real implications for various cultural groups in different ways.

Power Is Constraining. When we are placed in a subordinate social, economic, or political position to a larger power—like when a manager reprimands an employee for critiquing the company's weak organizational culture or when a parent disciplines a daughter for being too "bold" and aggressive for a "girl"—we are made to feel repressed, punished, and inferior. The taxing and painful experience of being dominated reveals the constraining and dominating tendency of power. For example, Filipinos all over the world have been made to feel dominated for several decades, first with colonization by Spain and then colonization by the U.S. Such domination has reflected throughout the hearts, minds, and souls of Filipinos for centuries. Filipinos punish themselves for being naturally "weak" and "inferior" to colonial powers, questioning the value of their culture, language, and traditions which become a form of internal colonialism in which the oppressed marginalize and rebuke their own selves.

Consider also the African and Asian slave trades throughout Europe, Asia, and across the Atlantic, which today still have far-reaching effects throughout the world and how individuals were stripped of their rights and individual freedoms as humans, and their citizenship and power to control aspects of their lives. The toll exacted on enslaved individuals by colonialist governments is unimaginable as they experienced, according to Mendoza and Strobel in 2015, a form of **epistemic** violence that undermines and devalues their own cultural identities. Through such epistemic violence and extreme subjugation, individuals and cultural groups are constrained by governmental, legal, economic, institutional, and social forces, as their movement, desires, and perceptions are contained. The **conceptualization** of power as constraining, therefore speaks to the type of power—one through coercion, force, and violence—that has been historically established in the age of exploration, conquest, and domination and is synonymous with martial states and colonialist administrations. However, constraining types of power still linger and seep into the experiences and lives of many different cultural groups and countries. Thus, given its long-established and still-active presence, the constraining and dominant mode of power must be named and exposed as it relates to intercultural communication encounters and relations.

Power Is Enabling and Creative. In the same turn, though, while power can restrain, limit, and contain us, power can also be productive and creative. It is not just a force that subjects us to top-down **configurations**. Instead, individuals' capacity to change, or at least challenge, their dominated structures and conditions can be enabled through power. We, as individuals and cultural groups, possess a different type of power than larger power structures and forces. We have the ability to resist and act through social means, meaning, oppressed cultural groups can mobilize members and protest structures like the government, law enforcement, military, and corporate powers via rallies, picketing, strikes, marches, riots, and activist organizing. In regard to the earlier example of the Filipinos, Filipino communities in the Philippines and the U.S. have used their power to develop a grass roots indigenous Filipino movement that renews the "original" languages, traditions, and practices that were cast aside by colonial powers. Filipino movement groups challenge the Westernized constructions of Filipino culture and re-narrate their indigenous historical origins. It is their hope to recreate the Philippines as an indigenous sovereign nation, much like the Native Hawaiians seek to do with Hawaii. The Filipino case illustrates that even in the most repressive conditions of domination, power can be remade by marginalized individuals and groups in creative and complicated ways.

Dominant forms of power can even be **re-deployed** by individuals and groups to work in their interests. Indigenous Native American and Latin American groups, for example, use the prevailing courts system, and international law and legal loopholes to stop corporate development, modernization, and encroachment of their sacred cultural lands. In the United States, during the 1960s, Chicanos/Chicanas used group mobilization and activist organizing to resist dominant society's unfair and harsh treatment of Mexican migrant workers. These activists also used the power of the law in a resistive way to charge police with excessive force and brutality during peaceful protests. Hawaiian nationalists have used the state and federal supreme court venues to "sue" the United States for illegally seizing Hawaiian land in 1893 and demand that Hawaii be returned completely to the Hawaiian people as a separate nation from the U.S. Thus, there is wiggle room within dominant contexts, structures, and conditions to maximize the enabling aspect of power; power—even dominant forms—can be used to recreate and remake conditions for marginalized cultural groups.

These last two attributes—power as constraining and power as enabling—seem, at first glance, to be contradictory. How can power be both extremes? Such a contradiction represents the dialectical tensions of power. We feel overwhelmed and determined by power at times (and constrained), but we also can use power productively, strategically, and creatively in any setting and circumstance and within the terms of our individual lives and experiences to fight against power domination. These two linked dimensions capture the complexity of social power in today's world as critical scholars have attributed to and highlighted as deriving from theorist Karl Marx: Individuals "make history in conditions not of their own making" in the words of Hall in 1980. That is, we work within the **parameters** of the power dynamic that are embedded in our lives. Thus, hope is not lost in that cultural groups who live amid power forces and structures can **maneuver** around and maximize the power-laden conditions of their lives. Individuals and cultural groups have agency or the ability to act and possibly change their lives for the better. It is important to remember that our experiences as cultural group members are structured and embedded by dimensions of power that frame but do not dominate or lock in our actions.

A power-based perspective therefore enables a uniquely rich view of intercultural communication and the concrete power pressures, demands, and realities of individuals and cultural groups in their intercultural communication relationships and encounters.

Culture as a Field of Forces: Four Premises

Different power interests shape uneven, contradictory, and even contentious framings of cultures, which carries serious political and social implications for those cultural groups. Culture, in this way, should be viewed as a larger field of forces. This reconceptualization rests on four **premises** that merit discussion.

First Premise. The core meanings that make up culture derive not just from the cultural group itself, but from a myriad of competing structures and parties that seek to define culture in such a way that privilege their own interests. Meanings that constitute the "face" of a culture come from a variety of power sources and do not merely serve the needs of a cultural community. Instead, meanings and representations of culture that are created and circulated by specific structures and parties of power enable these entities to, above all else, meet their needs and advance their own agendas. Dominant structures of power prioritize the goals of maintaining and increasing their dominance in society and thus, participate in the act of defining, constituting, and representing cultures with these goals in mind according to Said in 2012. For instance, governments can justify tighter control and restrictions over cultures that they deem (and in turn come to define) as a people "in need" or that pose as militaristic or economic threats to the nation. African Americans, Native Americans, Puerto Ricans, and Hawaiians have historically been labeled and defined by the federal government as "inferior people" who are in need of "development" and "guidance" by U.S. governmental bodies. Such definitions have served as vehicles to justify slavery, segregation, illegal occupation, and the containment and dispersion of peoples in specific cultural ethnic enclaves, villages, homesteads, or reservations.

Second Premise. The meanings of culture that are created by structures of power mostly benefit these dominant structures rather than the actual cultural groups that are being represented. Indeed, meanings carry political weight and are considered to be the driving "capital" for some structures of power to gain much more than the actual cultures being depicted. Thus, cultures that are being represented and depicted by specific structures of power gain little, if any. The definitions created do not contribute to the substance and structure of a cultural group in such a way that the group benefits economically and politically. For instance, consider the corporations and retailers who create and promote specific economic profiles of culture groups and how much money they make from ethnic marketing strategies. Such revenue is not apportioned out to, or even enjoyed by, the cultural groups of focus. Oftentimes, the representations are created at the expense of the cultural group and end up stereotyping or simplifying the nature of that group's cultural system. For example, fast-food chains such as McDonald's have advertisements that feature only Latino or African American patrons, while Whole Foods ads display only younger White customers. Basketball shoe and apparel companies have advertising campaigns that showcase African American hip-hop and rap artists and influencers and African American customers. Corporate brands have long created Spanish language advertising campaigns to "court" Latino consumers and thus, presume that all Latinos/Latinas speak Spanish and/or want to be reached through that language. These marketing representations work to benefit the corporate brands and do not fully consider the needs of the cultural groups themselves.

Third Premise. The meanings created by influential structures of power tend to "stick," gain more credibility, and therefore, are considered to be the "real" face of a culture. Ironically, although structures of power are external sources of representation for cultural groups, there is no way to differentiate between externally created meanings (those created by forces other than the group itself) and internally created meanings (those created by the actual groups themselves) of culture. Instead, all the meanings seem to be "natural," "truthful," and "real," and as if they originated from the groups themselves. What occurs here is that the meanings created by structures of power may incorporate the culture's native language or imagery and therefore become blurred and naturalized as authentic reflections of that culture. With access to money and resources that enable the circulating of specific images of culture, dominant structures and parties of power gain a foothold. In addition, dominant structures of power, such as the government and the media, often rely on the authoritative discourses of "scientific fact" and "cultural expertise."

A culture is continually perceived and valued based on the more sensationalized and widely reproduced meanings and the incorporation of seemingly authentic elements, such as symbols, imagery, and voices that come from within that cultural group. With culture as a field of forces, there is a dual process at work: structures of power create definitions of culture to meet their own needs and goals, and, in turn, these definitions take on a life of their own and are widely reproduced by these structures and society as the actual reflections of that culture.

Complicating matters, what also happens is that cultural groups being represented often internalize these meanings and project these as their own "authentic" reflections of who they are. Meanings and images created by structures of power enter in and become fused with a larger collection of representations, portrayals, world views, and beliefs of a cultural group. There are no distinctions between these meanings in terms of their source of origin; instead, they all appear equally convincing, credible, and "real." Cultural group members, therefore, internalize meanings and representations that may not have derived from their own cultural systems and may, in fact, benefit others rather than themselves.

Native Hawaiian culture stands as a primary example of the naturalization and **incorporation** of externally created meanings. To this day, Hawaiians believe that one of their most important cultural values is the "Aloha spirit," which is based on the notion that the Hawaiian culture (meanings, world view, cultural practices, and even resources such as land and artifacts) is to be equally shared, not only among all Hawaiians, but also among non-Hawaiians. Think about the reproduced notions that you hear about when you travel to Hawaii: "Hawaiians are inherently generous" and "the Hawaiian culture is about giving and sharing." This widely held interpretation of the Aloha spirit represents a meaning shaped by external structures and parties of power, such as the colonialist government in Hawaii (the British and the U.S.) that mimics a "native" value within the Hawaiian culture and distorts such a value for economic and social gain.

The colonialist government from the 18th and 19th centuries, and foreign business representatives in the Hawaiian islands, extracted and re-interpreted the notion of "Aloha" from the Hawaiian philosophical concepts of *aloha 'aina* (love and respect for the land) and *Aloha* (sharing, exchange in reciprocity), so as to guarantee and naturalize a one-way line of compassion and charity between foreigners and Hawaiians. Consider also that the Aloha spirit was created during a time when Hawaiian warfare was at its height (during King Kamehameha's rise to power and ongoing battles between Hawaiian chiefs), which suggests that the Aloha spirit was distorted and then used to depict and naturalize the inherently "friendly" and "peaceful" nature of Hawaiians at a time when it was in the best interest of the colonialist government to tame native unrest. This dominant representation of the Aloha spirit is slippery because Hawaiian culture does indeed invoke values based on caring, unity, collectivity, and giving.

Hawaiian Studies scholar and historian Lilikala Kame'eleihiwa describes *Aloha* as it was meant in the Hawaiian culture: as a relation of reciprocity between status-similar Hawaiians who would exchange goods and resources with one another. This was to *Aloha* your neighbor. Thus, the cultural value of *Aloha* was appropriated by Western outsiders as a means of power to naturalize Hawaiian giving for the benefit of colonial explorers, American business representatives and government interests, and even tourists. Thus, *Aloha*, as the distorted Aloha spirit, stems from a structure of power rather than a cultural essence of "Hawaiianness." As a result, the representation of Hawaiians as naturally **benevolent** and willing to share everything further opens and extends native belonging and residency to all non-Hawaiians.

Fourth Premise. The power imbalance between structures of power and the cultural group being represented has a major impact on the cultural group itself and its ability to define itself on its own terms and for its own needs. Representations created and projected by structures of power carry serious consequences for the cultural groups being represented. Cultural groups have a challenging time trying to shake off these external representations of their cultures, especially those that incorporate historically based **stereotypes** and myths and do not provide a full portrait of their cultures.

For instance, Asian Americans have been depicted by mainstream film, television, and music culture as one-dimensional caricatures such as Kung Fu masters and martial arts fighters, foreign immigrants, and in the case of Asian American women, docile and subservient. These images of Asian Americans, through persistent reproduction over time, have come to represent Asian American cultures (and their members) and stand in the place of other meanings and representations.

Such depictions have plagued the Asian American community over the years as they constantly face these stereotypes in all aspects of life. For example, Asian Americans in classified government positions often fall under suspicion by the U.S. government because of the long-held representation of Asian Americans as foreign immigrants whose national loyalty rests with their homeland. The stereotype of the Asian American model minority labels all Asian Americans as "aggressively driven overachievers who assimilate well" and as "super-intelligent students," meaning that this group represented the model immigrant minority via its successful educational, economic, and social integration into U.S. society. These dominant representations of Asian Americans cast a negative light on those Asian Americans who do not fit the profile of being assimilated, economically successful, and demonstrating academic excellence. Many Asian American immigrant families explain that they are often mocked or ridiculed for not having a command of the English language or adopting the American lifestyle as the model minority should. Some Asian American students who academically struggle in elementary and high schools are often left at a disadvantage because their teachers place higher educational expectations on them than other students because of the model minority representation.

As yet another negative consequence of the representations of Asian Americans created by dominant structures of power, Asian Americans have experienced physical acts of prejudice because of the reproduced meaning of Asian Americans as foreign economic threats. The 1980s marked a tumultuous economic time for the U.S., which was dependent on foreign investment from Japan and other nations. Auto plants in Detroit were bought out by Asian companies and moved out of the country, which displaced thousands of U.S. auto-plant workers. This incident sent a message that all Asian Americans (despite the many different Asian ethnicities) were considered to be foreign threats who were not welcome in this country.

Due to the overwhelming reproduction of Asian/Asian American stereotypes, it has been difficult, then, for Asian American communities to redefine their images and cast more complex mainstream representations of their cultures. The question becomes: How can cultural groups ever step outside of the externally created meanings that depict their cultures? Thus, specific cultural groups struggle economically, politically, and socially with external representations of themselves and work hard to redefine themselves.

These four premises illustrate that cultural groups are not singular and self-contained entities; they are fields of forces, as well as constellations of competing representations and meanings from structures that are vying for control over cultures. As intercultural communication scholars Judith Martin and Thomas Nakayama explained in 2000, "culture... is not just a variable, nor benignly socially constructed but a site of struggle where various communication meanings are constructed." Cultures are differentially positioned in relationship to one another within societal structures, material conditions, and power relations, and, as such, culture becomes a field of forces where competing interests vie for dominance and control. Thus, to say that culture is "a site of struggle" is to point to the process whereby competing interests (dominant structures and cultural communities) shape different representations of culture from different **positionalities** of power.

Applications

1. Intercultural Communication in a Globalized World

Saint Jacques, B. (2012). Intercultural communication in a globalized world. In L. A. Samovar, R. E. Porter, & E. R. McDaniel (Eds.), *Intercultural Communication: A Reader* (13th ed.), 45 – 55. Boston, MA: Wadsworth.

Abstract: This essay discusses the impact of globalization on the study of culture and intercultural communication. The essay first critiques pre-globalization era theoretical concepts of culture and proposes a new approach. Earlier cultural concepts, such as Hofstede's model of individualism—collectivism, are dated and no longer reflect the contemporary societal setting. Three considerations are integrated to form the basis for the proposed new theoretical approach to culture. Japan is used as a case study to illustrate how culture is being transformed by the shrinking global community. The concept of identity and how it has been altered by globalization is also discussed in the essay. The author proposes an approach to teaching intercultural communication (ICC) in the globalized society by viewing culture as "ways of thinking, beliefs, and values," and a greater incorporation of language into the teaching of ICC.

Keywords: globalization; impact; culture; intercultural communication; new approaches

2. Monochronic and Polychronic Time

Hall, T. E. (2012). Monochronic and polyhronic time. In L. A. Samovar, R. E. Porter, & E. R. McDaniel (Eds.), *Intercultural Communication: A Reader* (13th ed.), 313 – 320. Boston, MA: Wadsworth.

Abstract: This essay discusses monochronic (M-time) and polychronic (P-time). Specifically, Hall examines the conscious and unconscious ways people perceive and employ these two orientations toward time representing the ends of a continuum that allows for cultural variations and placements along the continuum. Cultures that operate near the M-time end of the time scale organize their lives around time by relying heavily on time-keeping instruments like clocks, calendars, computers, and cell-phone reminders. They emphasize schedules, the segmentation of time, and promptness. Individuals from P-time cultures do many things simultaneously, are more concerned with people and the present moment than with schedules, and believe that they are in command of time rather than being controlled by it. This essay helps you avoid communication problems such as misunderstandings by introducing you to the many forms and manifestations these two interaction patterns may take.

Keywords: M-time; P-time; time orientations; continuum; interaction patterns

3. Dimensionalizing Cultures: The Hofsede Model in Context

Hofstede, G. (2011). Dimensionalizing cultures: The Hofstede model in context. *Online Readings in Psychology and Culture*, 1, 3 – 26.

Abstract: This article describes briefly the Hofstede model of six dimensions of national cultures: Power Distance, Uncertainty Avoidance, Individualism/Collectivism, Masculinity/Femininity, Long/Short Term Orientation, and Indulgence/Restraint. It shows the conceptual and research efforts that preceded it and led up to it, and once it had become a paradigm for comparing cultures, research efforts that followed and built on it. The article stresses that dimensions depend on the level of aggregation; it describes the six entirely different dimensions found in the Hofstede et al. (2010) research into organizational cultures. It warns against confusion with value differences at the individual level. It concludes with a look ahead in what the study of dimensions of national cultures and the position of countries on them may still bring.

Keywords: dimensions; paradigm; organizational cultures; value differences; national cultures

Interactive Activities

1. Individually, please finish reading Text A, Text B, and the application abstracts and work out the meanings of the terms in bold type by consulting the dictionary whenever necessary.

2. In pairs, please summarize the content in 2 to 3 sentences of each sub-heading in the unit outlines of Text A and Text B based on your reading and understanding of the texts.

3. In groups, share your gains, comments and suggestions regarding the three application abstracts. Based on your interests, locate and finish reading the full-length papers of your interested abstracts.

4. Q&A: Questions are encouraged about any uncertain or confused part or parts in the unit and seek answers either from other fellow students or the instructor.

5. Complete the Personal Report of Low-Context and High-Context Communication Scale, a scale designed to measure how you feel about communication in different ways. Take a few moments and complete the self-assessment for Unit 4.

The Chinese culture is usually considered a high-context culture. What are its major merits and demerits in terms of their impacts upon intercultural communication?

6. Developing a strong **thesis statement** is a very important element in paper writing. Usually appearing at the end of the introductory part of a paper, a thesis statement must be on a debatable claim for an argumentative or persuasive piece of academic writing. To be debatable, the thesis must be on something that people can reasonably have different opinions on. Next, a thesis statement clarifies your claim over a debatable or argumentative topic. Finally, a working or effective thesis statement makes a preview of the main points to be covered in the research paper. Now, first, underline and appreciate the thesis statement or thesis statement paragraph in both Text A and Text B. Second, examine the titles and abstracts in the application section and work out a tentative thesis statement based on one of the three abstract. Finally, compare and improve your version of the thesis statement against the original one.

UNIT FIVE

Identity and Intercultural Communication

Readings

Text A Identity and Intercultural Communication

After Judith N. Martin and Thomas K. Nakayama

This essay presents a discussion of identity and its role in intercultural communication. Identity serves as a bridge between culture and communication. It is important because we communicate our identity to others, and we learn who we are through communication. It is through communication—with our family, friends, and others—that we come to understand ourselves and form our identity. Issues of identity are particularly important in intercultural interactions.

Below, we describe a dialectical approach to understanding identity, one that **encompasses** three communication approaches: social science, interpretive, and critical. We then explore the important role language plays in understanding identity and how minority and majority identities develop. We then turn to the development of specific aspects of our social and cultural identity including those related to gender, race or ethnicity, class, and nationality. We describe how these identities are often related to problematic communication—stereotypes, prejudice, and discrimination. We also examine an increasingly important identity—that of multicultural individuals. Finally, we discuss the relationship between identity and communication.

▸ Thinking Dialectically about Identity

Identity is a core issue for most people. It is about who we are and who others think we are. How do we come to understand who we are? And how do we communicate our identity to others? A useful theory is that of **impression management**—how people present themselves and how they guide the impression others form of them. Some scholars suggest that individuals are constantly performing "spin control" campaigns to highlight their strengths and virtues while also attempting "damage control" by minimizing deficiencies. As we will see, individuals cannot control others' impressions completely, as those we interact with also play an important role in how our identities develop and are expressed.

What are the characteristics of identity? In this section we use both the static-dynamic and the personal-contextual dialectics in answering this question.

There are three contemporary communication perspectives on identity (see Table 5.1). The social science perspective, based largely on research in psychology, views the self in a relatively static fashion in relation to the various cultural communities to which a person belongs:

nationality, race, ethnicity, religion, gender, and so on. The interpretive perspective is more dynamic and recognizes the important role of interaction with others as a factor in the development of the self. Finally, the critical perspective views identity even more dynamically—as a result of contexts quite distant from the individual. As you read this chapter, keep in mind that the relationship between identity and intercultural interaction involves both static and dynamic elements and both personal and contextual elements.

Table 5.1 Three Perspectives on Identity and Communication

Social Science	Interpretive	Critical
Identity created by self (by relating to groups)	Identity formed through communication with others	Identity shaped through social, historical forces
Emphasizes individualized, familial, and spiritual self (cross-cultural perspective)	Emphasizes avowal and ascribed dimensions	Emphasizes contexts and resisting ascribed identity

▲ The Social Science Perspective

The social science perspective emphasizes that identity is created in part by the self and in part in relation to group membership. According to this perspective, the self is composed of multiple identities, and these notions of identity are culture bound. How, then, do we come to understand who we are? That depends very much on our cultural background. According to Western psychologists like Erik Erikson, our identities are self-created, formed through identity conflicts and crises, through identity **diffusion** and confusion. Occasionally, we may need a break, a time-out, in the process. Our identities are created not in one smooth, orderly process but in sudden occurrences, with some events providing insights into who we are and long periods intervening during which we may not think much about ourselves or our identities.

Cross-Cultural Perspectives. In the United States, young people are often encouraged to develop a strong sense of identity, to "know who they are," to be independent and self-reliant, which reflects an emphasis on the cultural value of individualism. However, this was not always the case, and even today in many countries there is a very different, more collectivist notion of self. In 2002, Min-Sun Kim, a communication scholar, traced the evolution of the individualistic self. Before 1500, people in Europe as well as in most other civilizations lived in small **cohesive** communities, with a worldview characterized by the interdependence of spiritual and material phenomena. With the beginning of the industrial revolution in the 1600s came the notion of the world as a machine; this mechanistic view extended to living organisms and has had a profound effect on Western thought. It taught people to think of themselves as isolated **egos**—unconnected to the natural world and society in general. Thus, according to Kim, a person in the West came to be understood as "an individual entity with a separate existence independent of place in society." In contrast, people in many other regions of the world have retained the more interdependent notion of the self.

Cross-cultural psychologist Alan Roland identified three universal aspects of identity present

UNIT FIVE
Identity and Intercultural Communication

in all individuals in 1988: (a) an individualized identity, (b) a familial identity, and (c) a spiritual identity. Cultural groups usually emphasize one or two of these dimensions and downplay the other(s). Let's see how this works. The **individualized identity** is the sense of an independent "I," with sharp distinctions between the self and others. This identity is emphasized by most groups in the United States, where young people are encouraged to be independent and self-reliant at a fairly early age—by adolescence.

In contrast, the **familial identity**, evident in many collectivistic cultures, stresses the importance of emotional connectedness to and interdependence with others. For example, in many African and Asian societies, and in some cultural groups in the United States, children are encouraged and expected to form strong, interdependent bonds, first with the family and later with other groups. As one of our students explains, to be Mexican American is to unconditionally love one's family and all it stands for. Mexican-Americans are an incredibly close-knit group of people, especially when it comes to family. We are probably the only culture that can actually recite the names of our fourth cousins by heart. In this respect our families are like clans, they go much further than the immediate family and very deep into extended families. We even have a celebration, Dia de los Muertos (Day of the Dead), that honors our ancestors.

In these societies, educational, occupational, and even marital choices are made by individuals with extensive family guidance. The goal of the developed identity is not to become independent from others but rather to gain an understanding of and **cultivate** one's place in the complex web of interdependence with others.

In addition, the understanding of the familial self may be more connected to others and situation bound. According to studies comparing North Americans' and East Asians' senses of identity, when asked to describe themselves, the North Americans give more abstract, situation-free descriptions ("I am kind," "I am outgoing," "I am quiet in the morning"), whereas East Asians tend to describe their memberships and relationships to others rather than themselves ("I am a mother," "I am the youngest child in my family," "I am a member of a tennis club").

The third dimension is the **spiritual identity**, the inner spiritual reality that is realized and experienced to varying extents by people through a number of outlets. For example, the spiritual self in India is expressed through a structure of gods and goddesses and through rituals and meditation. In Japan, the realization of the spiritual self tends more toward aesthetic modes, such as the tea ceremony and flower arranging. Clearly, identity development does not occur in the same way in every society. The notion of identity in India, Japan, and some Latinos/Latinas and Asian American groups emphasizes the integration of the familial and the spiritual self but very little of the more individualized self.

This is not to say there is not considerable individuality among people in these groups. However, the general identity contrasts dramatically with the predominant mode in most U.S. cultural groups, in which the individualized self is emphasized and there is little attention to the familial self. However, there may be some development of the spiritual self among devout Catholic, Protestant, or Jewish individuals.

Groups play an important part in the development of all these dimensions of self. As we are growing up, we identify with many groups, based on gender, race, ethnicity, class, sexual orientation, religion, and nationality. And depending on our cultural background, we may develop tight or looser bonds with these groups. By comparing ourselves and others with members of these groups, we come to understand who we are. Because we belong to various groups, we develop multiple identities that come into play at different times, depending on the context. For example, in going to church or temple, we may highlight our religious identity. In going to clubs or bars, we may highlight our sexual orientation identity. Women who join social groups exclusive to women (or men who attend social functions just for men) are highlighting their gender identity.

Communication scholar Ting-Toomey argues in her **identity negotiation theory** that cultural variability influences our sense of self and ultimately influences how successful we are in intercultural interactions. Her argument goes like this: Individuals define themselves in relation to groups they belong to due to the basic human need for security and inclusion. At the same time, humans also need **differentiation** from these same groups. Managing relationships to these various groups involves boundary regulation and working through the tension between inclusion and differentiation and can make us feel secure or vulnerable. How we manage this tension influences the coherent sense of self (identity)—individuals who are more secure are more open to interacting with members of other cultures. When people feel good about themselves and the groups to which they belong, they are more successful in intercultural interactions. However, as we will see in the next section, identities are formed not just by the individual but also through interactions with others.

The Interpretive Perspective

The interpretive perspective builds on the notions of identity formation discussed previously but takes a more dynamic turn. That is, it emphasizes that identities are negotiated, co-created, reinforced, and challenged though communication with others; they emerge when messages are exchanged between persons. This means that presenting our identities is not a simple process. Does everyone see you as you see yourself? Probably not. To understand how these images may conflict, the concepts of avowal and ascription are useful.

Avowal is the process by which individuals portray themselves, whereas **ascription** is the process by which others attribute identities to them. Sometimes these processes are congruent. In June 2015, the racial identity of Rachel Dolezal, former president of the local NAACP chapter in Spokane, Washington and former instructor at Eastern Washington University, became a site of contestation. She notes that: "If somebody asked me how I identify, I identify as black. Nothing about whiteness describes who I am." While her avowed racial identity is black, her parents and society identify her as white. When her parents revealed that they are white, the reaction was strong: "Some white people painted Dolezal as mentally unstable, on the grounds that no normal white person would choose to call themselves black. But it was the wave of rage and mockery from the African American community that really stung." Many people felt betrayed by the conflict between her avowed identity and her ascribed identity.

Different identities are emphasized depending on the individuals we are communicating with and the topics of conversation. For example, in a social conversation with someone we are attracted to, our gender or sexual orientation identity is probably more important to us than other identities (ethnicity, nationality). And our communication is probably most successful when the person we are talking with confirms the identity we think is most important at the moment. In this sense, competent intercultural communication affirms the identity that is most salient in any conversation. For example, if you are talking with a professor about a research project, the conversation will be most competent if the interaction confirms the salient identities (professor and student) rather than other identities (e.g., those based on gender, religion, or ethnicity).

How do you feel when someone does not recognize the identity you believe is most salient? For example, suppose your parents treat you as a child (their ascription) and not as an independent adult (your avowal). How might this affect communication? One of our students describes how she feels about the differences between black identity and African American identity:

> I think my identity is multifaceted. In some spaces I am Black. In others I am African American. In very few, I am both. This is both due to the connotations associated with the words and also the location I am in. In social spaces, I identify myself as being black because in my eyes the word "black" is associated with hip hop culture, Black Power, and more recently, Black Lives Matter, topics that I believe appropriate to discuss in social settings. However, the term African American seems more proper. To me it is just a description of a person from a continent I've never stepped foot on. "African American" is an ascribed identity as opposed to my black avowed identity.

Central to the interpretive perspective is the idea that our identities are expressed communicatively—in core symbols, labels, and norms. **Core symbols** (or cultural values) tell us about the fundamental beliefs and the central concepts that define a particular identity. Communication scholar Michael Hecht and his colleagues have identified the contrasting core symbols associated with various ethnic identities. For example, core symbols of African American identity may be positivity, sharing, uniqueness, realism, and assertiveness. Individualism is often cited as a core symbol of European American identity. Core symbols are not only expressed but also created and shaped through communication. Labels are a category of core symbols; they are the terms we use to refer to particular aspects of our own and others' identities—for example, *African American*, *Latino*, *white*, or *European American*.

Finally, some norms of behavior are associated with particular identities. For example, women may express their gender identity by being more concerned about safety than men. They may take more precautions when they go out at night, such as walking in groups. People might express their religious identity by participating in activities such as going to church or Bible study meetings.

The Critical Perspective

Like the interpretive perspective, the critical perspective emphasizes the dynamic nature of identities, but in addition, it emphasizes the contextual and often conflictual elements of identity development. This perspective pays particular attention to the societal structures and institutions that constrain identities and are often the root of injustice and oppression according to Collier in 2005.

Contextual Identity Formation. The driving force behind a critical approach is the attempt to understand identity formation within the contexts of history, economics, politics, and discourse. To grasp this notion, ask yourself, how and why do people identify with particular groups and not others? What choices are available to them?

We are all subject to being pigeonholed into identity categories, or contexts, even before we are born. Many parents ponder a name for their unborn child, who is already part of society through his or her relationship to the parents. Some children have a good start at being, say, Jewish or Chicana before they are even born. We cannot ignore the ethnic, socioeconomic, or racial positions from which we start our identity journeys.

The identities that others may ascribe to us are socially and politically determined. They are not constructed by the self alone. We must ask ourselves what drives the construction of particular kinds of identities. For example, the label "heterosexual" is a relatively recent one, created less than a hundred years ago. Today, people do not hesitate to identify themselves as "heterosexuals." A critical perspective insists on the constructive nature of this process and attempts to identify the social forces and needs that give rise to these identities.

These contextual constraints on identity are also reflected in the experience of a Palestinian woman who describes her feelings of not having a national "identity" as represented by a passport—because of political circumstances far beyond her control:

I am Palestinian but I don't have either a Palestinian passport or an Israeli passport... If I take the Palestinian passport, the Israeli government would prevent me from entering Jerusalem and Jerusalem is a part of my soul. I just can't NOT enter it. And of course I'm not taking an Israeli passport, so... I get frustrated when I talk to people WITH identity, especially Palestinians with Israeli identity. I just get like kind of offended because I think they're more comfortable than me.

Resisting Ascribed Identities. When we **invoke** such discourses about identity, we are pulled into the social forces that feed the discourse. We might resist the position they put us in, and we might try to ascribe other identities to ourselves. Nevertheless, we must begin from that position in carving out a new identity.

French philosopher Louis Althusser used the term **interpellation** in 1971 to refer to this process. He notes that we are pushed into this system of social forces:

By that very precise operation which I have called interpellation or **hailing**, and which can be imagined along the lines of the most commonplace every-day police (or other) hailing: "Hey you there!"... Experience shows that the practical telecommunication of hailing is such that they hardly ever miss their man: verbal call or whistle, the one hailed always recognizes that it is really him who is being hailed. And yet it is a strange phenomenon, and one which cannot be explained solely by "guilt feelings."

This hailing process that Althusser describes operates in intercultural communication interactions. It establishes the foundation from which the interaction occurs. For example, occasionally someone will ask Tom if he is Japanese, a question that puts him in an awkward position. He neither holds Japanese citizenship, nor has he ever lived in Japan. Yet the question probably doesn't mean to address these issues. Rather, the person is asking what it means to be

UNIT FIVE
Identity and Intercultural Communication

"Japanese. " How can Tom adjust his position in relation to this question?

The Dynamic Nature of Identities. The social forces that give rise to particular identities are never stable but are always changing. Therefore, the critical perspective insists on the dynamic nature of identities. For example, the emergence of the European Union has given new meaning to the notion of being "European" as an identity. This larger political context can reshape many identities. For example, the recent influx of refugees into Germany has changed how Germans think of their country, their culture, and their place in the world:

> In the past five years, as the number of people displaced worldwide by conflict and persecution has reached a level not seen since the end of World War Ⅱ, many Germans have expressed pride that their nation—which **unleashed** the violence that prompted the earlier mass flight—has now become a beacon of safety and opportunity for the endangered people around the world. The degree to which many Germans embraced this new identity became exceedingly clear last summer, when Hungary tried to stop the mass of Germany-bound migrants traveling through the country by cutting off their access to trains. Migrants **stranded** outside Budapest's Keleti train station chanted: "Germany! Germany!" And within days, roughly a thousand of them had set out on foot from Hungary and across Austria to Germany, some of them holding posters of the German chancellor, Angela Merkel. Merkel, fearing chaos, should she turn the migrants away, instead sent German trains to pick them up, a decision she later called a "humanitarian imperative. " As migrants arrived at Munich's central station, local residents greeted them with cheers and applause. Some handed out chocolate and balloons. Germans spoke of their strong Willkommenskultur, or "Welcome Culture," and German politicians portrayed the warm reception as a moral achievement, a further step toward redefining modern Germany as a **benevolent** nation that has moved beyond the ignominy of its **ultranationalist** past.

While these refugees may change German culture and identity, Germans are also changing German culture and identity as they demonstrated that many of them embrace their "Welcome Culture. "

Aside from these larger contexts for identity, identities are also dynamic on the individual level because of someone's own experiences. One of our students explains how his personal identity has changed over the past few years:

> I will say I am 100% Chinese, but after I came abroad, studying in the United States for a couple of years, learning a different language, interacting with international students, and **assimilating** into this new environment for quite a while, I feel my self-identity is changed a little, as part of me did have to integrate into this new culture.

It is important to remember that identities—whether national, cultural or personal—are always changing.

For another example, look at the way that identity labels have changed from "colored" to "Negro" to "black" to "Afro-American" to "African American. " Although the labels seem to refer to the same group of people, the political and cultural identities of those so labeled are different. The term "Negro" was replaced by "Black" during the civil rights movement in the 1960s because it stood for racial pride, power, and rejection of the status quo. "Black is beautiful" and "Black power" became slogans during this time. In the late 1980s, Black leaders proposed that "Black" be replaced with "African American," saying that this label would provide African Americans a cultural identification with their heritage and ancestral homeland. The changes in these labels have worked to strengthen group identity and facilitate the struggle for racial equality. Currently, both terms are used—depending on people's preference—and "Black" is preferred by some because it shows commonality with people of African descent who are not U.S. American (e.g., Caribbean Islanders).

Identity Development Issues

People can identify with a multitude of groups: gender, age, religion, nationality, to name only a few. How do we come to develop a sense of identities? As we noted earlier, our identities develop over a period of time and always through interaction with others. How an individual's identity develops depends partly on the relative position or location of the identity within the societal hierarchy. Some identities have a higher position on the social hierarchy. For example, a heterosexual identity has a more privileged position than a homosexual identity; a Christian religious identity is generally more **privileged** than a Jewish or Muslim religious identity in the United States. To distinguish among the various positions, we label the more privileged identities "majority identities" and label the less privileged "minority identities." This terminology refers to the relative dominance or power of the identity position, not the numerical quantity.

Social science researchers have identified various models that describe how minority and majority identities develop. Although the models center on racial and ethnic identities, they may also apply to other identities, such as class, gender, or sexual orientation. It is also important to remember that, as with any model, these represent the experience of many people, but the stages are not set in stone. Identity development is a complex process; not everyone experiences these phases in exactly the same way. Some people spend more time in one phase than do others; individuals may experience the phases in different ways, and not everyone reaches the final phase.

Minority Identity Development

In general, minority identities tend to develop earlier than majority identities. For example, straight people tend to not think about their sexual orientation identity often, whereas gay people are often acutely aware of their sexual orientation identity being different from the majority and develop a sense of sexual orientation identity earlier than people who are straight. Similarly, while whites may develop a strong ethnic identity, they often do not think about their racial identity, whereas members of racial minority groups are aware of their racial identities at an early age. Minority identity development undergoes the following stages:

Stage 1: Unexamined Identity. This stage is characterized by the lack of exploration of identity, be it racial, ethnic, sexual orientation, gender, or whatever. At this stage, individuals may simply lack interest in the identity issue. As one African American woman put it: "Why do I need to learn about who was the first black woman to do this or that? I'm just not too interested." Or minority group members may initially accept the values and attitudes of the majority culture, expressing positive attitudes toward the dominant group and negative views of their own group. Gay young people may try very hard to act "straight" and may even participate in "gay **bashing**."

Stage 2: Conformity. This stage is characterized by the internalization of the values and norms of the dominant group and a strong desire to assimilate into the dominant culture. Individuals in this phase may have negative, self-deprecating attitudes toward both themselves and their group. As one young Jewish woman said: "I tried very hard in high school to not let anyone know I was Jewish. I'd talk about Christmas shopping and Christmas parties with my friends even though my parents didn't allow me to participate at all in any Christmas celebration."

Individuals who criticize members of their own ethnic or racial group may be given negative labels such as "Uncle Tom" for African Americans, "banana" for Asian Americans, "apple" for Native Americans, and "Tio Taco" for Chicanos. Such labels condemn attitudes and behaviors that support the dominant white culture. This stage often continues until they encounter a situation that causes them to question predominant culture attitudes, which initiates the movement to the next stage.

Stage 3: Resistance and Separatism. Many kinds of events can trigger the move to the third stage, including negative ones such as encountering discrimination or name-calling. A period of a growing awareness that not all dominant group values are beneficial to minorities, may also precede this stage.

International students sometimes develop their national identity as a minority identity when they study overseas. Dewi, an Indonesian student, reported that when she first arrived in the United States, she thought little of her national identity (because this was a majority identity in *her* country). She told everyone she thought the United States was the greatest place and really tried hard to use American slang, dress American, and fit in. After several experiences with discrimination, she moved to a more separate stage where she only socialized with other Indonesian or other international students for a time. For writer Ruben Martinez, a defining moment was when he was rather cruelly rejected by a white girl whom he had asked to dance at a high school prom:

I looked around me at the dance floor with new eyes: Mexicans danced with Mexicans, blacks with blacks, whites with whites. Who the hell did I think I was? Still, it would take a while for the gringo-hater in me to bust out. It was only a matter of time before I turned away from my whiteness and became the ethnic rebel. It seemed like it happened overnight, but it was the result of years of **repressed** rage in me.

Sometimes the move to this phase happens because individuals who have been denying their identity meet someone from that group who exhibits a strong identity. This encounter may result in a concern to clarify their own identity. So the young woman who was ashamed of being Jewish and tried hard to act "Christian" met a dynamic young man who was active in his church and had a strong Jewish faith. Through their relationship she gained an appreciation of her own religious background, including the Jewish struggle for survival throughout the centuries. As often happens in this stage, she wholeheartedly endorsed the values and attitude attributed to the minority (Jewish) group and rejected the values and norms associated with the dominant group—she dropped most of her Christian friends and socialized primarily with her Jewish friends.

This stage may be characterized by a blanket **endorsement** of one's group and all the values and attitudes attributed to the group. At the same time, the person may reject the values and norms associated with the dominant group.

Stage 4: Integration. According to this model, the ideal outcome of the identity development process is the final stage—an achieved identity. Individuals who have reached this stage have a strong sense of their own group identity (based on gender, race, ethnicity, sexual orientation, and so on) and an appreciation of other cultural groups. In this stage, they come to realize that racism and other forms of oppression occur, but they try to redirect any anger from the previous stage in more positive ways. The end result is individuals with a confident and secure identity characterized by a desire to **eliminate** all forms of injustice, and not merely oppression aimed at their own group.

Majority Identity Development

In 2003, Rita Hardiman, educator and pioneer in antiracism training, presented a model of **majority identity** development that has similarities to the model for minority group members. Although she intended the model to represent how white people develop a sense of healthy racial identity, it can also be helpful in describing how other majority identities develop—straight sexual orientation, Christian religious identity, male gender identity, middle-class identity, and so on. Again, remember that majority identity, like minority identity, develops through a complex process. And this model—unlike some other identity development models—is prescriptive. In other words, it outlines the way some scholars think a majority identity *should* develop, from accepting societal hierarchies that favor some identities and diminish others to resisting these inequities.

In 2004, Hardiman outlined the following five stages:

Stage 1: Unexamined Identity. This first stage is the same as for minority identities. In this case, individuals may be aware of some physical and cultural differences, but they do not fear the others or think much about their own identity. There is no understanding of the social meaning and value of gender, sexual orientation, religion, and so on. Although young boys may develop a sense of what it means to be a male by watching their fathers or other males, they are not aware of the social consequences of being born male over female. Those with majority identities, unlike those with minority identities, may stay in this stage for a long time.

Stage 2: Acceptance. The second stage represents the internalization, conscious or unconscious, of a racist (or otherwise biased) ideology. This may involve passive or active acceptance. The key point is that individuals are not aware that they have been programmed to accept this worldview.

In the passive acceptance stage, individuals have no conscious identification with being white, straight, male, and so forth. However, they may hold some assumptions based on an acceptance of inequities in the larger society. In general, the social hierarchy is experienced as "normal" for the dominant group, and they may view minority groups as being unduly sensitive and assume that if the minority members really wanted to change their lot in life they could. Here are some possible assumptions.

Individuals in this stage usually take one of two positions with respect to interactions with minorities: (a) They avoid contact somewhat with minority group members or (b) they adopt a patronizing stance toward them. Both positions are possible at the same time.

In contrast, those in the active acceptance stage are conscious of their privileged position and may express their feelings of superiority collectively (e.g., join male-only clubs). Some people never move beyond this phase—whether it is characterized by passive or active acceptance. And if they do, it is usually a result of a number of cumulative events. For example, Judith gradually came to realize that her two nieces, who are sisters—one of whom is African American and one of whom is white—had very different experiences growing up. Both girls lived in middle-class neighborhoods, both were honor students in high school, and both went to Ivy League colleges. However, they often had very different experiences. On more than one occasion, the African American girl was followed by security while shopping; she also was stopped several times by police while driving her mother's sports car. Her white sister never had these experiences. Eventually, awareness of this reality prodded Judith to the next stage.

This model recognizes that it is very difficult to escape the societal hierarchy that influences both minority and majority identity development because of its pervasive, systemic, and interlocking nature. The hierarchy is a by-product of living within and being impacted by the institutional and cultural systems that surround us.

Stage 3: Resistance. The next stage represents a major paradigm shift. It involves a move from blaming minority members for their condition to naming and blaming their own dominant group as a source of problems. This resistance may take the form of passive resistance, with little behavioral change, or active resistance—trying to reduce, eliminate, or challenge the institutional hierarchies that oppress. In reference to one's own identity, this stage is often characterized by embarrassment about one's own privileged position, guilt, shame, and a need to distance oneself from the dominant group. Our student, Kayla, says:

> I was raised as a Christian, so I was never taught to question our beliefs. Since I've left home, I have met gay and lesbian students and I no longer understand why my church has such a problem with homo-sexuality. I get angry and sometimes I speak out when I'm at home and my parents get upset, but I don't want to stand around and let bigots take over my church. I have begun to question my Christian values, as I no longer know if they are compatible with my sense of right and wrong.

Stage 4: Redefinition. In the fourth stage, people begin to refocus or redirect their energy toward redefining their identity in a way that recognizes their privilege and works to eliminate oppression and inequities. They realize that they don't have to accept uncritically the definitions of being white, straight, male, Christian, U.S. American that society has instilled in them. For example, Nick tells us, "As a straight white guy, I often find myself in social situations in which people feel free to make offhand remarks or jokes that are somewhat racist, heterosexist, or sexist. They assume that I would agree with them, since I'm not a minority, gay, or a woman, but I don't. I am happy to be who I am, but this doesn't mean that being a straight white man means I need to be racist, sexist, or homophobic. I am proud to be who I am, but I don't think that means I have to put down others."

Stage 5: Integration. As in the final stage of minority identity development, majority group individuals now are able to internalize their increased consciousness and integrate their majority identities into all other facets of their identity. They not only recognize their identity as white but also appreciate other groups. This integration affects other aspects of social and personal identity, including religion and gender.

Hardiman acknowledged that this model is rather simplistic in explaining the diverse experiences of people. It does not acknowledge the impact of diverse environments and socialization processes that influence how people experience their dominant identities or the realities of interlocking identities.

Systems of privilege are complicated; this is one reason why people can belong to a privileged category and not feel privileged. You may have several identities that are more privileged and several that are less privileged. So, for example, a middle-class white lesbian, benefiting from and yet unaware of the privileges of race or class, may think that her experience of sexual orientation and gender inequality enables her to understand what she needs to know about other forms of privilege and oppression. Or a straight working-class white man may be annoyed at the idea that his sexual orientation, whiteness, and maleness somehow gives him access to privilege. As a member of the working class, he may feel insecure in his job, afraid of being outsourced, downsized, and not at all privileged according to Johnson in 2001.

To make it more complicated, our multiple identities exist all at once in relation to one another. People never see us solely in terms of race or gender or nationality—they see us as a complex of identities. So it makes no sense to talk about the experience of one identity—being white, for example—without looking at other identities. A dialectical perspective helps here in avoiding falling into the trap of thinking we are or are not privileged. Most of us are both.

▶ Social and Cultural Identities

People can identify with a multitude of groups. This section describes some of the major types of groups.

Age Identity

As we age, we also play into cultural notions of how individuals our age should act, look, and behave; that is, we develop an **age identity.** As we grow older, we sometimes look at the clothes displayed in store windows or advertised in newspapers and magazines and feel that we are either too old or too young for that "look." These feelings stem from an understanding of what age means and how we identify with people that age.

Some people feel old at 30; others feel young at 40 or 50. Nothing inherent in age tells us we are young or old. Rather, our notions of age and youth are all based on cultural conventions. The United States is an age-conscious society. One of the first things we teach children is to tell their age. And children will proudly tell their age, until about the mid-20s on, when people rarely mention their age. In contrast, people older than 70 often brag about their age. Certain ages have special significance in some cultures.

UNIT FIVE
Identity and Intercultural Communication

Latino families sometimes celebrate a daughter's 15th birthday with a *quinceañera* party—marking the girl's entry into womanhood. Some Jewish families celebrate with a bat mitzvah ceremony for daughters and a bar mitzvah for sons on their 13th birthday. These same cultural conventions also suggest that it is inappropriate to engage in a romantic relationship with someone who is too old or too young.

Our notions of age often change as we grow older ourselves. When we are quite young, someone in college seems old; when we are in college, we do not feel so old. Yet the relative nature of age is only one part of the identity process. Social constructions of age also play a role. Different generations often have different philosophies, values, and ways of speaking. For example, recent data show that today's college freshmen are more liberal politically and more interested in volunteer work and civic responsibility than were Gen Xers. Scholars who view generations as "cultural groups" say that these characteristics make them similar to the World War I generation—politically curious and assertive and devoted to a sense of personal responsibility.

Different generations often have different philosophies, values, and ways of speaking. For example, recent data show that the millennium generation (or Gen Y, those born between 1982–2001) are more diverse and globally oriented and more knowledgeable about computers and technology than any preceding generation. They are also more optimistic, more committed to contributing to society and more interested in life balance between work and play than the previous, Gen X, group (those born between 1961–1981). This also is reflected in the way they learn and work (multitasking, use of multimedia, etc.).

In 2016, it was predicted that Millennials surpassed Baby Boomers as the largest generation in the United States. Aside from the demographic dominance of this group, Jen Mishory, executive director of a national millennial research and **advocacy** organization, argues against the stereotype that Millennials are lazy. She argues that her generation has had to do more with less, face large student loan debt, contribute to charitable causes, and demonstrate tremendous persistence. She says that: "In the end, the fact remains: We're a generation that does more with less, while thinking about our own futures and trying to build a better tomorrow for those around us." Sometimes these generational differences can lead to conflict in the work-place. For example, young people who entered the job market during the "dot.com" years have little corporate loyalty and think nothing of changing jobs when a better opportunity comes along. This can irritate baby boomer workers, who emphasize the importance of demonstrating corporate loyalty, of "paying one's dues" to the establishment while gradually working one's way "up the corporate ladder." Although not all people in any generation are alike, the attempt to find trends across generations reflects our interest in understanding age identity.

Racial and Ethnic Identities

Racial Identity. Race consciousness, or **racial identity**, is largely a modern phenomenon. In the United States today, the issue of race is both controversial and pervasive. It is the topic of many public discussions, from television talk shows to talk radio. Yet many people feel uncomfortable talking about it or think it should not be an issue in daily life. Perhaps we can better understand the contemporary issues if we look at how the notion of race developed historically in the United States.

Current debates about race have their roots in the 15th and 16th centuries, when European explorers encountered people who looked different from themselves. The debates centered on religious questions of whether there was "one family of man." If so, what rights were to be accorded to those who were different? Debates about which groups were "human" and which were "animal" pervaded popular and legal discourse and provided a rationale for slavery. Later, in the 18th and 19th centuries, the scientific community tried to establish a classification system of race based on genetics and **cranial** capacity. However, these efforts were largely unsuccessful.

Most scientists have abandoned a strict biological basis for classifying racial groups, especially in light of recent genetic research. To date, researchers have found only 55 genes out of almost 3 million that differentiate various groups. Their conclusions about the implications of their research: "All in all, the school of thought which holds that humans, for all their outward variety, are a pretty **homogenous** species received a boost." Rather than adhere to the rather outdated notion of a biological basis for racial categorization, most scholars hold a social science viewpoint—agreeing that racial categories like white and black are constructed in social and historical contexts.

Several arguments refute the physiological basis for race. First, racial categories vary widely throughout the world. In general, distinctions between white and black are fairly rigid in the United States, and many people become uneasy when they are unable to categorize individuals. In contrast, Brazil recognizes a wide variety of intermediate racial categories in addition to white and black. These variations indicate a cultural, rather than a biological, basis for racial classification. Terms like *mulatto* and *Black Irish* demonstrate cultural classifications; terms like *Caucasoid* and *Australoid* are examples of biological classification.

Second, U.S. law uses a variety of definitions to determine racial categories. A 1982 case in Louisiana reopened debates about race as socially created rather than biologically determined. Susie Phipps applied for a passport and discovered that under Louisiana law she was black because she was 1/32 African (her great-grand-mother had been a slave). She then sued to be reclassified as white. Not only did she consider herself white, in as much as she grew up among whites, but was also married to a white man. And because her children were only 1/64 African, they were legally white. Although she lost her lawsuit, the ensuing political and popular discussions persuaded Louisiana lawmakers to change the way the state classified people racially. It is important that the law was changed, but this legal situation does not obscure the fact that social definitions of race continue to exist.

A third example of how racial categories are socially constructed is illustrated by their fluid nature. As more and more southern Europeans immigrated to the United States in the 19th century, the established Anglo and German society tried to classify these newcomers (Irish and Jewish, as well as southern European) as nonwhite. However, this attempt was not successful because, based on the narrower definition, whites might have become demographically disempowered. Instead, the racial line was drawn to include all Europeans, and people from outside of Europe were designated as nonwhite. We intentionally use the term *nonwhite* here to highlight the central role of *whiteness* in defining racial identity in the United States.

Racial categories, then, are based to some extent on physical characteristics, but they are also constructed in fluid social contexts. It probably makes more sense to talk about racial *formation* than racial *categories*, thereby casting race as a complex of social meanings rather than as a fixed and objective concept. How people construct these meanings and think about race influences the ways in which they communicate.

Ethnic Identity. In contrast to racial identity, **ethnic identity** may be seen as a set of ideas about one's own ethnic group membership. It typically includes several dimensions: (a) self-identification, (b) knowledge about the ethnic culture (traditions, customs, values, and behaviors), and (c) feelings about belonging to a particular ethnic group. Ethnic identity often involves a shared sense of origin and history, which may link ethnic groups to distant cultures in Asia, Europe, Latin America, or other locations.

Having an ethnic identity means experiencing a sense of belonging to a particular group and knowing something about the shared experience of group members. For instance, Judith grew up in an ethnic community. She heard her parents and relatives speak German, and her grandparents made several trips back to Germany and talked about their German roots. This experience contributed to her ethnic identity.

For some U.S. residents, ethnicity is a specific and relevant concept. They see themselves as connected to an origin outside the United States—as Mexican American, Japanese American, Welsh American, and so on—or to some region prior to its being absorbed into the United States—Navajo, Hopi, and so on. As one African American student told us, "I have always known my history and the history of my people in this country. I will always be first African American and then American. Who I am is based on my heritage." For others, ethnicity is a vague concept. They see themselves as "American" and reject the notion of **hyphenated Americans.** One of our students explains:

> I don't necessarily identify with my ethnicity. I am Italian American and Irish American but I am three or more generations removed from when either side immigrated to the United States. I also don't look noticeably Italian or Irish. I still tell people that I am half Irish and half Italian, but the only time I really connect and identify with my ethnic heritage is for holidays and for certain traditional meals or styles of cooking.

We will discuss the issues of ethnicity for white people later. What, then, does *American* mean? Who defines it? Is there only one meaning, or are there many different meanings? It is important to determine what definition is being used by those who insist that we should all simply be "Americans." If one's identity is "just American," how is this identity formed, and how does it influence communication with others who see themselves as hyphenated Americans?

Racial Versus Ethnic Identity. Scholars dispute whether racial and ethnic identity are similar or different. Some suggest that ethnic identity is constructed by both selves and others but that racial identity is constructed solely by others. They stress as well that race overrides ethnicity in the way people classify others. The American Anthropological Association has suggested that the U.S. government phase out use of the term *race* in the collection of federal data because the concept has no scientific validity or utility.

On the one hand, discussions about ethnicity tend to assume a "melting pot" perspective on U.S. society. On the other hand, discussions about race as shaped by U.S. history allow us to talk about racism. If we never talk about race, but only about ethnicity, can we consider the effects and influences of racism?

Bounded versus Dominant Identities. One way to sort out the relationship between ethnicity and race is to differentiate between bounded and dominant (or normative) identities. Bounded cultures are characterized by groups that are specific but not dominant. For most white people, it is easy to comprehend the sense of belonging in a bounded group (e.g., an ethnic group). Clearly, for example, being Amish means following the *ordnung* (community rules). Growing up in a German American home, Judith's identity included a clear emphasis on seriousness and very little on communicative expressiveness. This identity differed from that of her Italian American friends at college, who seemed much more expressive.

However, what it means to belong to the dominant, or normative, culture is more elusive. *Normative* means "setting the norm for a society." In the United States, whites clearly are the normative group in that they set the standards for appropriate and effective behavior. Although it can be difficult for white people to define what a normative white identity is, this does not deny its existence or importance. It is often not easy to see what the cultural practices are that link white people together. For example, we seldom think of Thanksgiving or Valentine's Day as white holidays.

Our sense of racial or ethnic identity develops over time, in stages, and through communication with others. These stages seem to reflect our growing understanding of who we are and depend to some extent on the groups we belong to. Many ethnic or racial groups share the experience of oppression. In response, they may generate attitudes and behaviors consistent with a natural internal struggle to develop a strong sense of group identity and self-identity. For many cultural groups, these strong identities ensure their survival.

Characteristics of Whiteness

What does it mean to be white in the United States? What are the characteristics of a white identity? Is there a unique set of characteristics that define whiteness, just as other racial identities have been described?

It may be difficult for most white people to describe exactly what cultural patterns are uniquely white, but scholars have tried to do so. For example, scholar Ruth Frankenburg says that whiteness may be defined not only in terms of race or ethnicity but also as a set of linked dimensions. These dimensions include (a) normative race privilege, (b) a standpoint from which white people look at themselves, others, and society, and (c) a set of cultural practices (often unnoticed and unnamed). More recently, communication scholar Dreama Moon has argued that white identity is a process of becoming white through a process of social pressure and control "utilized in White communities to produce the next generation of 'white-thinking' Whites." Much of this pressure to be "white" in a particular way comes from family and friends, as well as observing public performances of whiteness.

Normative Race Privilege. Historically, whites have been the normative (dominant) group in the United States and, as such, have benefited from privileges that go along with belonging to the dominant group. However, not all whites have power, and not all have equal access to power. In fact, at times during U.S. history, some white communities were not privileged and were viewed as separate, or different, if not inferior. Examples include the Irish and Italians in the early 20th century and German Americans during World War II. And as scholars point out, the memory of marginality outlasts the marginality. For example, memories of discrimination may persist in the minds of some Italian Americans although little discrimination exists today. There also are many white people in the United States who are poor and so lack economic power.

There is an emerging perception that being white no longer means automatic privilege, particularly as demographics change in the United States and as some whites perceive themselves to be in the minority. This has led some whites to feel threatened and "out of place." A Chicago college professor tells the story of how her white students thought that 65% of the population near their university was African American; they perceived themselves to be in the minority and based their estimate on their observations and anecdotes. When she corrected them, they were stunned. In fact, according to the 2000 U.S. Census, the percentage of blacks in Chicago was only 37%. Students' perceptions affected their sense of identity, which, in turn, can affect intercultural communication.

Some white young people today are very aware of their whiteness. Further, they believe that being white is a liability that they are sometimes prejudged as racist and blamed for social conditions they personally did not cause, and that they are denied opportunities that are unfairly given to minority students. One of our white students describes this feeling:

When I was trying to get into college I had to fight for every inch. I didn't have a lot of money to go to school with, so to get a scholarship was of great importance to me. So I went out and bought a book titled *The Big Book of Scholarships*. Ninety percent of the scholarships that this book contained didn't apply to me. They applied to the so-called minorities... I think this country has gone on so long with the notion that white equals wealth or with things like affirmative action, that it has lost sight of the fact that this country is not that way any longer.

In addition, because of corporate downsizing and the movement of jobs overseas in recent decades, increasing numbers of middle-aged white men have not achieved the degree of economic or professional success they had anticipated. They sometimes blame their lack of success on immigrants who will work for less or on the increasing numbers of women and minorities in the workplace. In these cases, whiteness is not invisible; it is a salient feature of the white individuals' identities.

The point is not whether these perceptions are accurate. Rather, the point is that identities are negotiated and challenged through communication. People act on their perceptions, not on some external reality. As the nation becomes increasingly diverse and whites no longer form a majority in some regions, there will be increasing challenges for all of us as we negotiate our cultural identities.

How can whites in the United States incorporate the reality of not belonging to a majority group? Will whites find inclusive and productive ways to manage this identity change? Or will they react in defensive and exclusionary ways? One reaction to feeling outnumbered and being a "new member" of an ethnic minority group is to strengthen one's own ethnic identity. For example, white people may tend to have stronger white identities in those U.S. states that have a higher percentage of nonwhites (e.g., Mississippi, South Carolina, Alabama). In these states, the white population traditionally has struggled to protect its racial privilege in various ways. As other states become increasingly less white, we are beginning to see various moves to protect whiteness.

Although it had been discussed for a while, the U.S. Census Bureau predicted in 2015 that the United States population would become majority-minority in 2044. In other words, non-Hispanic whites would become a minority with less than 50% of the population. Charles Gallagher, a sociologist who studies white identity, notes: "We went from being a privileged group to all of a sudden becoming whites, the new victims... You have this perception out there that whites are no longer in control or the majority. Whites are the new minority group." Although they are not numerically a minority group, their experiences may be shaping what white identity means. Tim Wise, a writer, says: "For the first time since the Great Depression, white Americans have been confronted with a level of economic insecurity that we're not used to. It's not so new for black and brown folks, but for white folks, this is something we haven't seen since the Depression." Fears about the loss of white America drive much of this discussion. In 2009, Hsu as a Vassar College professor noted: "This moment was not the end of white America; it was not the end of anything. It was a bridge, and we crossed it."

A Standpoint from Which to View Society. Opinion polls reveal significant differences in how whites and blacks view many issues, including former U.S. President Obama. For example, a Pew Research Center study conducted one year after President Obama's election found that blacks were more likely to view President Obama as black (55%) rather than mixed race (34%). For whites, the responses were reversed: 53% of whites saw President Obama as mixed race and 24% as black. When asked if opposition to Obama's policies is racially motivated, 52% of blacks thought so, whereas only 17% of whites felt that way. And since the election of President Obama, blacks and whites feel that blacks are better off than five years ago, but a 10 percentage point difference remains.

A Set of Cultural Practices. Is there a specific, unique "white" way of viewing the world? As noted previously, some views held consistently by whites are not necessarily shared by other groups. And some cultural practices and core symbols (e.g., individualism) are expressed primarily by whites and significantly less by members of minority groups. We need to note here that not everyone who is white shares all cultural practices. For example, recent immigrants who are white, but not born in the United States, may share in the privilege accorded to all white people in the United States. However, they might not necessarily share in the viewpoints or the set of cultural practices of whites whose families have been in the United States for many generations. It is important to remember that some whites may identify fairly strongly with their European roots, especially if their families are more recent immigrants and they still have family members in Europe; other whites may not feel any connection to Europe and feel completely "American." These cultural practices are most clearly visible to those who are not white, to those groups who are excluded. For example, in the fairy tale of "Snow White," the celebration of her beauty—emphasizing her beautiful, pure white skin—is often seen as problematic by people who are not white.

▲ Personal Identity

Many issues of identity are closely tied to our notions of self. Each of us has a **personal identity**, which is the sum of all our identities, but it may not be unified or coherent. A dialectical perspective allows us to see identity in a more complex way. We are who we think we are; at the same time, however, contextual and external forces constrain and influence our self-perceptions. We have many identities, and these can conflict. For example, according to communication scholar Victoria Chen, some Chinese American women feel caught between the traditional values of their parents' culture and their own desire to be Americanized. From the parents' point of view, the daughters are never Chinese enough. From the perspective of many people within the dominant culture, though, it is difficult to relate to these Chinese American women simply as "American women, born and reared in this society." The dialectical tension related to issues of identity for these women reveals the strain between feeling obligated to behave in traditional ways at home and yet holding a Western notion of gender equality. A dialectical perspective sees these contradictions as real and presenting challenges in communication and everyday life.

Our personal identities are important to us, and we try to communicate them to others. We are more or less successful depending on how others respond to us. We use the various ways that identity is constructed to portray ourselves as we want others to see us.

▲ Multicultural People

Multicultural people, a group currently dramatically increasing in number, are those who live "on the borders" of two or more cultures. They often struggle to reconcile two very different sets of values, norms, worldviews, and lifestyles. Some are multicultural as a result of being born to parents from different racial, ethnic, religious, or national cultures or they were adopted into families that are racially different from their own family of origin. Others are multicultural because their parents lived overseas and they grew up in cultures different from their own, or because they spent extended time in another culture as an adult, or married someone from another cultural background. Let's start with those who are born into biracial or multiracial families.

Multiracial identity can also be more complex. Korean adoptees who were adopted by white families do not seem to have had an easy reconciliation of these identities. In the Hongdae section of Seoul, the Repulbic of Korea: "The neighborhood is also a popular spot for the approximately 300 to 500 adoptees who have moved to the Repulbic of Korea—primarily from the United States but also from France, Denmark and other nations. Most lack fluency in the language and possess no memories of the country they left when they were young. But they are back, hoping for a sense of connection—to the Repulbic of Korea, to their birth families, to other adoptees." The rejection that they felt in the United States and elsewhere was due to acceptance: "In a 2009 survey of adult adoptees by the Donaldson Adoption Institute, more than 75 percent of the 179

Korean respondents who grew up with two white parents said they thought of themselves as white or wanted to be white when they were children. Most also said they had experienced racial discrimination, including from teachers. Only a minority said they felt welcomed by members of their own ethnic group." Some reported having parents who dismissed the racism that their children experienced or couldn't discuss race and white privilege with their children. In other words, the complexities of interracial families, racial identities, in the context of racism and racial thinking can create complex family relationships as we can see in the case of interracial adoptions. Not all international adoptions end badly, but some do and we should acknowledge the complexity of race and racism as larger contexts for understanding identities and identity development.

In addition to multicultural identities based on race and ethnicity, there are multicultural identities based on religion, sexual orientation, or other identities. For example, children growing up with a Jewish parent and a Christian parent may feel torn between the two and follow some of the same identity development phases as biracial children—where they feel different, forced to choose between one or the other. Teresa says, "My father is Mexican American and my mother is white, so I have a Latino last name. When I was younger, some kids would tease me with racial slurs about Mexicans. My mother totally didn't understand and just said that I should ignore them, but my father understood much better. He faced the same taunting as a child in Indiana." A straight child of gay parents may have similar feelings of needing to negotiate between straight and gay worldviews.

Individuals develop multicultural identities for other reasons. For example, **global nomads** (or **third-culture kids**—TCKs) grow up in many different cultural contexts because their parents move around a lot (e.g., missionaries, international business employees, and military families). According to a recent study, these children have unique challenges and unique opportunities. They move an average of about eight times, experience cultural rules that may be constraining (e.g., in cultures where children have less freedom), and endure periods of family separation. At the same time, they have opportunities not provided to most people—extensive travel, living in new and different places around the world. As adults they settle down and often feel the need to reconnect with other global nomads (easier now through technologies such as the Internet). President Barack Obama is a good example of a global nomad—his father was an African exchange student and his mother a U.S. American college student. He spent his childhood first in Hawaii and then in Indonesia when his mother and his Indonesian stepfather moved there. Like many TCKs, he was separated from his family during high school when he returned to Hawaii to live with his grandparents. His stepsister credits his ability to understand people from many different backgrounds to his many intercultural experiences as a child and adolescent—like many global nomads, these experiences "gave him the ability to...understand people from a wide array of backgrounds. People see themselves in him...because he himself contains multitudes."

Children of foreign-born immigrants may also develop multicultural identities. Foreign-born immigrants in the United States represent one of the fastest-growing segments—almost a third of the current foreign-born population arrived in the United States since 1990. These include refugees from war zones like Syria and Iraq and migrants who come to the United States to escape dire economic conditions. They often struggle to negotiate their identities, torn between family expectations and their new American culture. Melanie, a student of ours, is not a refugee but is an example of a TCK. Having lived in a number of countries, she explains how she feels:

> As a global nomad, I am grateful for all of the experiences I was lucky enough to experience a lot from a young age; however, the downfall for me is that I have a little bit of many cultures and identities. I have never stopped for long enough to learn about one culture or identity because it was constantly changing. I was born in Argentina and my family has kept a lot of Argentine traditions but I know very little about Argentine history and my Spanish has slowly worsened. I grew up in France where I developed my family identity as I was surrounded with family but I didn't associate myself as a "French" person. I lived in New Zealand for 10 years where I learned a lot about the history and social norms but I was missing my family identity.

Tom, another student of ours, explains the complexity of communicating who he is:

> I was born in South Africa and lived there for the first two years of my life. Then my family moved to New Jersey. In the seventh grade, I went across the pond to boarding school in North Yorkshire, England. After I explain where I'm from, people always ask me which country I identify most closely with. Honestly that's a tough question. There are so many aspects and habits in my life which I've taken away with me from every individual culture that I have integrated into what I feel a strong connection to each.

In contrast, Anna, another student, who was born in Russia, does not feel that she is really Russian because of her international experiences:

> I have always strongly disliked the question, "where are you from?" What do you mean by that? Are you asking me where I was born, or where I have lived throughout my life? I could tell you where I was born, but that does not necessarily mean that I feel any connection to that place or that I strongly identify with that particular city. I have always had a tough time truly defining who I am. However, I do believe that identity is not static; it constantly evolves and changes. My identity is made up of the cultures that I have been exposed to throughout my life. Every place that I have lived in has shaped me into the person I am today. The interaction that I have had with individuals from different backgrounds have also influenced my identity. I do not consider myself Russian. In fact, I consider myself Russian-Swedish-American, as strange as that may sound.

All of these students have negotiated their identities in various cultural and national contexts. Multicultural identities can be quite complex, but are becoming increasingly common in an era of globalization.

A final category of multicultural people includes those who have intense intercultural experiences as adults—for example, people who maintain long-term romantic relationships with members of another ethnic or racial group or who spend extensive time living in other cultures. Miguel tells us, "My father is an American, but my mother is from Chile. Because they divorced when I was young and my father returned to the United States, I spent a lot of time traveling back and forth and learning to adapt to two different cultures and languages. I don't feel completely Chilean or American, but I feel like I am both. I have family and friends in both places and I feel connected in different ways."

Social psychologist Peter Adler describes the multicultural person as someone who comes to grips with a multiplicity of realities. This individual's identity is not defined by a sense of belonging; rather, it is a new psychocultural form of consciousness. Milton Bennett describes how individuals can develop an "ethnorelative" perspective based on their attitudes toward cultural difference. The first, and most ethnocentric, stage involves the denial or ignoring of difference. The next stage occurs when people recognize difference but attach negative meaning to it. A third stage occurs when people minimize the effects of difference—for example, with statements like "We're really all the same under the skin" and "After all, we're all God's children." Bennett recognizes that minority and majority individuals may experience these phases differently. In addition, minority individuals usually skip the first phase. They don't have the option to deny difference; they are often reminded by others that they are different.

The remainder of the stages represent a major shift in thinking—a paradigm shift—because positive meanings are associated with difference. In the fourth phase (acceptance), people accept the notion of cultural difference; in the fifth phase (adaptation), they may change their own behavior to adapt to others. The final phase (integration) is similar to Peter Adler's notion of a "multicultural person."

According to Adler, multicultural individuals may become **culture brokers**—people who facilitate cross-cultural interaction and reduce conflict. For example, TCKs/global nomads often develop resilience, tolerance, and worldliness, characteristics essential for successful living in an increasingly diverse and global social and economic world. And, indeed, there are many challenges and opportunities today for multicultural people, who can reach a level of insight and cultural functioning not experienced by others. One of our students, who is Dutch (ethnicity) and Mexican (nationality), describes this:

Being the makeup I am to me means I come from two extremely proud cultures. The Dutch in me gives me a sense of tradition and loyalty. The Mexican side gives me a rich sense of family as well as closeness with not only my immediate family, with my aunts, uncles, and cousins as well. My unique mix makes me very proud of my identity. To me it means that I am proof that two parts of the world can unite in a world that still believes otherwise.

However, Adler also identified potential stresses and tensions associated with multicultural individuals in 1974:

They may confuse the profound with the insignificant, not sure what is really important.

They may feel **multiphrenic**, fragmented.

They may suffer a loss of their own authenticity and feel reduced to a variety of roles.

They may retreat into *existential absurdity*.

Communication scholar Janet Bennett provides insight into how being multicultural can be at once rewarding *and* challenging. She describes two types of multicultural individuals: (a) *encapsulated marginals*, who become trapped by their own marginality and (b) *constructive marginals*, who thrive in their marginality.

Encapsulated marginals have difficulty making decisions, are troubled by ambiguity, and feel pressure from both groups. They try to assimilate but never feel comfortable, never feel "at home." In contrast, constructive marginal people thrive in their marginal existence and, *at the same time*, they recognize the tremendous challenges. They see themselves (rather than others) as choice makers. They recognize the significance of being "in between," and they are able to make commitments within the relativistic framework. Even so, this identity is constantly being negotiated and explored; it is never easy, given society's penchant for superficial categories. Writer Ruben Martinez describes the experience of a constructive marginal:

> And so I can celebrate what I feel to be my cultural success. I've taken the far-flung pieces of myself and fashioned an identity beyond that ridiculous, fraying old border between the United States and Mexico. But my "success" is still marked by anxiety, a white noise that disturbs whatever raceless **Utopia** I might imagine. I feel an uneasy tension between all the colors, hating and loving them all, perceiving and speaking from one and many perspectives simultaneously. The key word here is "tension": nothing, as yet, has been resolved. My body is both real and unreal, its color both confining and liberating.

▲ Identity and Communication

Identity has a profound influence on intercultural communication processes. We can employ some of the dialectics identified in earlier chapters to illuminate this relationship. First, we can use the individual-cultural dynamic to examine the issues that arise when we encounter people whose identities we don't know. In intercultural communication interactions, mistaken identities are often exacerbated and can create communication problems.

Sometimes we assume knowledge about another person's identity based on his or her membership in a particular cultural group. When we do so, we are ignoring the individual aspect. Taking a dialectical perspective can help us recognize and balance both the individual and the cultural aspects of another's identity. This perspective can guide the ways that we communicate with that person (and conceivably with others). "The question here is one of identity: Who am I perceived to be when I communicate with others? ... My identity is very much tied to the ways in which others speak to me and the ways in which society represents my interests" according to Nakayama in 2000.

Think about the assumptions you might make about others based on their physical appearance. What do you "know" about people if you know only that they are from, say, the South, or Australia, or Pakistan? Perhaps it is easier to think about the times that people have made erroneous assumptions about you based on limited information—assumptions that you became aware of in the process of communication. Focusing solely on someone's nationality, place of origin, education, religion, and the like, can lead to mistaken conclusions about the person's identity.

Another way to understand how we communicate our identities comes from the study of performance. Although we can look at someone's individual performance of identity to better understand how they understand who they think they are, we can also look at cultural performance to understand cultural identities.

One part of U.S. history often hidden is the horrific practice of **lynching**. Yet we must acknowledge that lynching was a widespread and common practice in U.S. culture, and we can often be confused when we see many of the perpetrators smiling in these photos because it seems incomprehensible that they were not horrified by this event.

Performance studies scholar Kirk Fuoss suggests that a performance perspective can help us better understand how people can participate in these atrocities like lynchings. For example, Fuoss argues that lynching in the United States functioned as a cultural performance to reinforce a particular kind of racial order for those who participated in or heard about the lynching. Lynchings took place outside of the legal system, and therefore a belief in the evilness of the victim substituted for a proof or evidence of guilt. This inversion of right and wrong served to relieve the group identity of the lynchers from their own evil behavior. These murders reflect aspects of our culture that have deep historical roots. By examining these performative acts, we can begin to see what they communicate to others and the kinds of social order they encourage. Thus, lynchings are a public act that serve to communicate the positions of various cultural groups in society. It is important to remember that performances not only are artistic and interesting but can also be horrific. In both cases, performances of identity can offer insights into our culture.

Now let's turn to the static-dynamic dialectic. The problem of **erroneous** assumptions has increased during the information age, due to the torrent of information about the world and the dynamic nature of the world in which we live. We are bombarded daily with information from around the globe about places and people. This glut of information and intercultural contacts has heightened the importance of developing a more complex view of identity.

Given the many identities that we all negotiate for ourselves in our everyday interactions, it becomes clear how our identities and those of others make intercultural communication problematic. We need to think of these identities as both static and dynamic. We live in an era of information overload, and the wide array of communication media only serves to increase the identities we must negotiate. Consider the relationships that develop via e-mail, for example, some people even create new identities as a result of online interactions. We change who we are depending on the people we communicate with and the manner of our communication. Yet we also expect some static characteristics from the people with whom we communicate. We expect others to express certain fixed qualities; these help account for why we tend to like or dislike them and how we can establish particular communication patterns with them. The tensions that we feel as we change identities from e-mail to telephone to mail to fax and other communication media demonstrate the dynamic and static characters of identities.

Finally, we can focus on the personal-contextual dialectic of identity and communication. Although some dimensions of our identities are personal and remain fairly consistent, we cannot overlook the contextual constraints on our identity.

UNIT FIVE
Identity and Intercultural Communication

Text B Ideology, Identity, and Intercultural Communication: An Analysis of Differing Academic Conceptions of Cultural Identity

After Young Yun Kim

Introduction

Cultural identity has occupied a central place in social sciences, particularly in communication and social psychology. A **substantial** amount of work has addressed issues of cultural identity directly or indirectly, offering a wide array of views on cultural identity in intercultural contexts, and how it should be best investigated. The varying, and sometimes divergent, academic conceptions are closely linked to the ideological shift in recent decades from the traditional "melting pot" perspective on intergroup relations in the United States toward a more pluralistic perspective on ethnicity, race, and culture. This ideological change is reflected in a clear **pluralistic** turn in academic inquiry into cultural identity, along with an increasing appearance of "critical" scholarship adding its voice to, and challenging, the mainstream "disciplinary" social scientific conceptions of cultural identity. Some of the more emerging identity conceptions of cultural identity are examined in this article. They are compared according to respective implicitly or explicitly articulated underlying assumptions. The aim in this analysis is to find out and explain how investigators vary widely, and sometimes intensely, as to what cultural identity is, what it means in the context of intercultural-intergroup relations, and how it is to be researched. The analysis will reveal a close correspondence of differing academic conceptions of cultural identity to the societal trend of ideological turn since the 1970s toward pluralism.

Working Definitions

Given the wide range of differing conceptual and methodological approaches being examined, the term cultural identity is employed broadly to include related concepts such as subcultural, national, ethno-linguistic, and racial identity. Cultural identity also refers to both a sociological or demographic classification, as well as an individual's psychological identification with a particular group. Both sociological and psychological meanings of cultural identity are regarded as two inseparable relevant items of the same phenomenon. Likewise, the term intercultural communication is used to represent various related terms, such as interethnic, interracial, and intergroup communication, that refer to encounters in which individual participants differ, and/or perceive themselves to be different, in group-based experiential backgrounds.

Similarly, the term ideology is also used in this work as a multidimensional concept. At the macro-societal level, ideology is employed to mean what Billig referred to as "lived ideology," or "a **latent** consciousness or philosophy" that is largely shared by people within a society as "a society's way of life" or "what passes for common sense within a society." At the individual level, ideology refers to a set of intellectual beliefs of thinking individuals that are stimulated, substantiated, and constrained by the shared beliefs of the society at large. Here, individuals are regarded as formulating and expressing their opinions by invoking socially shared beliefs as their own. Even in making remarks that are self-serving or internally contradictory, individuals are assumed to consider their argument reasonable or even persuasive in the eyes of a rational audience.

Analytic Framework for Ideological Messages

In examining ideological messages, either implied or advocated in academic writings, the author utilizes four interconnected positions with respect to culture and intercultural relations: assimilationism, pluralism, integrationism, and separatism. These four positions have been identified in an earlier qualitative-interpretive analysis, based on a qualitative-interpretive analysis of a variety of data that includes publicly communicated messages concerning ethnicity, race, and culture made by political and civic leaders, activists, academicians, and ordinary citizens. Some messages are naturally occurring while others are in the form of personal reflections and testimonials. Together, the four ideological positions represent the diverse and often divergent opinions voiced in contemporary American society and beyond, **criss-crossing** many conventional social categories such as ethnicity, race, and political party affiliation.

Assimilationism is best expressed in the saying, E. Pluris Unum—the principle behind the American ethos that seeks to **transcend** a tribal, ancestral, and territorial condition. Rooted in the political philosophy of classical liberalism, assimilationism supports individualism, a cultural mindset that celebrates individual identity, self-reliance, and personal responsibility. This mindset is extended to immigrants and cultural minorities in the form of a degree of "Anglo-conformity" in public spheres of life, consistent with the old folk wisdom, "When in Rome, do as Romans do." In contrast, pluralism stands for an ideological position that is born out of the inevitable gap between the ideals of assimilationism and the reality of everyday life not measuring up to the ideals. The seed for the contradiction is the awareness that the ideals of classical liberalism are not always applied to those of non-dominant group backgrounds. A natural response to such discrepancies has been a movement that challenges the status quo, replacing individualistic beliefs and the melting-pot metaphor with contrary claims of group identity and newer metaphors such as "mosaic," "quilt," and "salad bowl" that emphasize distinctiveness of each group.

Straddled between the assimilationism-pluralism ideological poles is integrationism, which emphasizes the need to moderate the often tortured reality of identity politics and to search for some kind of reconciliation. Integrationist voices often escape media attention or get lost in the midst of more conspicuous messages of committed ideologues. This is a position that sociologist Wolfe asserted in 1998 as occupying "the vital center," the "middle" America. It reflects the struggle of mainstream Americans to seek mutual accommodation and balance, as well as their ambivalence and contradiction. Integrationists may, for example, support bilingual programs, but only if they are short-lived and not used as a political instrument of power demanded by every group for its own separate slice of the political pie.

The full range of American public discourse on interethnic relations further includes the marginal, but persistent, voices of separatism, often characterized as views of so-called extremists. Whereas messages of assimilationism, pluralism, and integrationism commonly adhere to the societal goal of interethnic integration, extremist messages advocate, or at least suggest, a preference for a maximum ingroup-outgroup distance. Often, the rigidity with which cultural identity boundaries are drawn turns Americans into "us-against-them" posturing. In some cases, the claims of equal and distinct identity tends to manifest itself in tendencies of collective self-glorification and **imputation** of other groups, and, at times, even violence and terror. Although not always explicit, separatist views can be inferred from the inflammatory rhetorical devices employed to condemn or scapegoat an outgroup or position the ingroup as innocent "victims."

These four ideological messages—assimilationism, pluralism, integrationism, and separatism—are not mutually exclusive categories. Rather, they form an ideological circle, in which each position defines, and is defined by, the other. The circle highlights the ideological debates that play out in everyday public discourse in the United States and beyond. The vision and principles embodied in E. Pluribus Unum continue to be voiced in the form of assimilationism, while being vigorously challenged by the counter-themes of pluralism advocating the primacy of group identity, along with the **compromising** efforts to promote ideological balance and moderation in integrationism, as well as separatism of the extreme right and the extreme left, closing the circle.

Inquiry in Cultural Identity

Systematic investigations of cultural identity can be traced back to psychologist Erickson's groundbreaking theoretical work in 1950 and 1968. Erickson described the process of identity development as one in which the two identities of the individual and of the group are merged into one. Erickson placed cultural identity at the core of the individual and yet also in the core of his or her "common culture." Erikson's early identity conception has been echoed in subsequent academic writings about cultural identity. For de Vos, for example, cultural identity provides "a sense of common origin, as well as common beliefs and values, or common values" and serves as the basis of "self-defining in-groups." For Yinger, ethnic attachment is a "genuine culture" that forms the person's "basic identity" and offers "a sense of historical continuity and embeddedness and a larger existence in a collectivity of one's group."

Cultural Identity as Social and Individual Concepts. Given the inseparability of the personal and the social in an individual's identity, cultural identity has been approached at both levels. Cultural anthropologists typically view culture and ethnicity as a kind of temporal continuity or common tradition linking its members to a common future, which is fostered by the communal life patterns and practices associated with language, behavior, norms, beliefs, myths, and values, as well as the forms and practices of social institutions. In sociological research, culture is commonly treated as a social category that is an element of ethnicity, defined by membership that is differentiated from other groups by a set of objective characteristics, qualities, or conditions such as national and/or geographical origin, language, religion, and race. This is the way, for instance, sociologists such as Glazer and Moynihan investigated the phenomenon of "ethnic stratification" in the United States.

Psychological studies, on the other hand, typically approach cultural identity in terms of "the subjective orientation of an individual toward his or her ethnic origins" as Alba put forward in 1990. Terms such as cultural identity, ethno-linguistic identity, or ethnic identification are often exchangeably used to replace ethnicity per se in most social psychological studies of intergroup behavior. From the perspective of the influential social identity theory, cultural identity is seen as "that part of an individual's self-concept which derives from his knowledge of his membership in a social group (or groups) together with the value and emotional significance attached to that membership" according to Tajfel in 1978. The social identity theory and many experimental studies based on this theory further illuminate the interplay of the two dimensions of personhood, the personal and the social. That is, identification with a social group is rooted in the basic human tendency of cognitive categorization, and the membership in, and identification with, an ethnic group renders the individual an emotionally significant aspect of the individual's self-concept.

The Pluralistic Turn and Activism in Identity Research. Increasingly, collective group interests have become of concern to the individual, above and beyond their implications for personal self-interest. As Turner, Hogg, Oakes, Reicher, and Wetherell observed in 1987, cultural identity, in effect, has been deemed by many social researchers an extension of the self, indicating "a shift towards the perception of self as an interchangeable exemplar of some social category and away from the perception of self as a unique person."

The emphasis psychologists have placed on group-level cultural identity has been a dominant voice in academic discourse in recent decades. Idealized or essentialist conceptions of cultural identity parallel the ideological shift toward greater pluralism in the ideological landscape of the United States, beginning with the "new ethnicity" movement prompted by the civil rights movement in the 1960s in the United States. In their early work in 1963, Glazer and Moynihan concluded a sociological analysis by stating: "The point about the melting pot is that it did not happen." In 1971, Novak argued against assimilation and advocated "equal ethnicity for all." Novak pointed to the feelings of alienation held by one large ethnic group, Poles, who had been drawn to "ethnic power" movements in the competition for jobs, respect, and attention. In this pluralistic turn in cultural identity, the primacy of individualism and individual identity has been challenged by contrary claims of group identity and the associated attempts to elevate group distinctiveness over a larger, societal identity.

Side by side with the pluralistic turn, there has been an increasing trend of departure in research addressing issues of cultural identity from the traditional representational stance of value-neutrality to the primacy of political advocacy and other forms of practice. This politicization of academic inquiry has been largely motivated by the increasing number of traditional social scientists who find the value-neutral stance of the traditional scientific approach less than satisfying. Arguments have been made by some social scientists for a redistribution of power and resources to overcome inequalities in group status, and for a greater diversity of the university curriculum by replacing it with one "that would focus on the achievements of marginalized peoples and on the sins of the nation's founders" according to Traub in 1998.

The shift in emphasis from realism-based "disciplinary" theory to more idealistic social activism has been fueled by non-traditional scholars of various postmodern philosophical schools such as "critical theory," "cultural studies," and "muted group and standpoint theory," among others. Vigorous arguments have been mounted to gear research directly to "emancipatory" political goals of eliminating "white racism" at home and countering Western/American "imperialism" abroad. Indeed, pressure has been felt by many traditional researchers who find the field too political, so much so that a given theory, along with the credibility of the theorist, appears to be dismissed by some, not based on the validity of the knowledge claim in representing the reality in question, but simply based on the implied question, "Whose side are you on?"

Ideology and Basic Themes in Academic Conceptions of Cultural Identity

Intended or not, then, social researchers have been participants in the ideological polemics of American society and elsewhere. A close examination of academic writings across disciplines reveals five basic themes of cultural identity generally reflecting or supporting one or more of the four ideological positions in Kim's ideological circle described 2006: (a) cultural identity as an adaptive and evolving entity of an individual; (b) cultural identity as a flexible and negotiable entity of an individual; (c) cultural identity as a discrete social category and an individual choice; (d) cultural identity as a flexible and negotiable entity of an individual; and (e) cultural identity as a discrete and non-negotiable social category and group right.

Cultural Identity as an Adaptive and Evolving Entity of an Individual. Social scientific theories since the 1930s have been predicated on the premise that adaptation of immigrants and other cultural minorities is an important and desirable goal for the individual as well as for the society as a whole. This **affirmative** view of cross-cultural adaptation is consistent with the widely held assimilationist view that calls for convergence and fusion among alien or minority cultures into a coherent system of ideas and practices of the society at large.

Numerous empirical studies document the assimilative trend. Sociological studies have investigated minority-majority relations in which minority groups are structurally integrated into the political, social, and economic systems of the society at large. The assimilative trend is even more definitively evidenced in cross-generational studies, including Page's study of the Japanese and their children in Brazil in 1994. According to Page, the Japanese first immigrated to Brazil in 1908 as contract workers for coffee plantations and strongly resisted assimilation, and yet the present third-generation Japanese-Brazilians are on the whole fully integrated into Brazilian society, entering into racially mixed marriages as freely as other Brazilians. In 1995, Lind documented that the European immigrant groups in the United States began as distinct groups at the beginning of the twentieth century and have almost completely assimilated. According to Lind, four-fifths of Italian-Americans, half of American Jews, one-third of Hispanics, and one-half of Asian-Americans have married outside their officially designated categories since 1950. Lind further reports that the number of children born to black-white marriages quintupled between 1968 and 1988, and a growing number of mixed-race Americans are now lobbying for their own "multiracial" category.

The assimilative trend is further documented in a study by the American Jewish Committee, which shows a significant increase in the members' merging into non-Jewish organizations and a substantial decrease in their Jewish identification. Masuda, Matsumoto, and Meredith similarly demonstrate that the cultural identity of Japanese-Americans in the United States gradually has decreased across the generations. Triandis, Kashima, Shimada, and Villareal in 1986 and Suro in 1998 independently reported that long-term Hispanics showed diminished Hispanic "cultural scripts" in their judgments and increased social interactions with non-Hispanics. Namazi in 1984 likewise observed an assimilative trend among Mexican, Cuban, and Middle Eastern immigrants. In Canada, McCauley in 1991 reported decreasing traditional forms of behavior in the French and English Canadian populations of Penetanguishene in southern Ontario. In a study of language maintenance and shift, Morgan in 1987 reported that Haitian migrants in the Dominican Republic have shifted, over time, from their native language, Creole, to the host language, Spanish.

Emerging from these and many other empirical findings is the nature of cultural identity that is, over time, dynamic and evolving, and not static and categorical. This basic reality of assimilation is explained in Kim's integrative communication theory of cross-cultural adaptation in 1988 and 2005. Defining adaptation as a natural process of individuals striving to establish a relatively stable, reciprocal, and functional relationship with the environment, the theory explains that, through extensive, intensive, and cumulative experiences of intercultural communication, an individual's original cultural identity undergoes a gradual transformation. This identity transformation is described as an emergence of an "intercultural identity," that is increasingly more "universalized" and "individuated" in self-other orientation, one that is more flexible and less rigidly bound by group categories.

While consistent with the "melting-pot" view of cultural identity, Kim's theory also addresses pluralists' concerns for the maintenance of original cultural identity. It does so by emphasizing that intercultural identity development does not come about without "costs." The adaptation process is explained in terms of the "stress-adaptation-growth dynamic," a process filled with ambivalence and internal conflict between one's loyalty to the original identity and a necessity to **embrace** a new one. Yet, according to the theory, it is the stressful experience that "pushes" individuals to restructure their existing internal conditions to regain an internal equilibrium. This functional interrelatedness of stress and adaptation describes the process of organizing and reorganizing oneself, bringing about psychological "growth" at a higher level of self-integration. Furthermore, the theory disputes the pluralist view that the long-term identity evolution toward assimilation necessarily entails "giving up" or "discarding" the original identity. The author thereby rejects the **dichotomous** view that individuals have to choose either one or the other, and proposes the concept, intercultural identity, as a viable self-other orientation that facilitates social integration and discourages unwarranted divisiveness along group lines.

Cultural Identity as a Flexible and Negotiable Entity of an Individual. A number of intercultural communication theories offer conceptions of cultural identity that can be characterized as integrationist in ideological position. In Imahori and Cupach's identity management theory in 2005, for example, identity is conceived categorically as a given society's (or sub-society's) way of life embodied in each individual as an interpretive frame for experience, provides expectations for behavior and motivates individuals' behavior. At the same time, this theory presents a more complex and refined identity conception that recognizes that individuals have multiple identities, of which cultural (as well as relational) identities are central to interpersonal relationship development with culturally dissimilar others. The central argument made in this theory points to the importance and necessity of flexible "identity management" in dealing with others whose cultural identities differ from one's own. This, according to Imahori and Cupach, is because aspects of individuals' identities are revealed through the presentation of "face" (e.g., situated identities individuals claim) and the ability to maintain face in interactions is one indicator of individuals' interpersonal communication competence in both intra-cultural and intercultural contexts.

Similarly categorical, but flexible, identity conceptions are offered in Ting-Toomey's identity negotiation theory in 1993 and 2005, that an individual's ability to negotiate one's cultural identity (or regulate one's identity boundary) is at the center of "communicative resourcefulness." Also, Hecht, Warren, Jung, and Krieger in laying the groundwork for a communication theory of cultural identity, conceptualize cultural identity as one of the four levels of "identity frames" that serve as the "interpretive context" of a communication context, identified as: personal (individual characteristics), enacted (emergent in social behavior and symbols), relational (emerging in relationships with others and are "jointly negotiated"), and communal (something held by a group of people which, in turn, bonds the group together). The notion that cultural identity is not fixed, but a flexible and individually variable entity also underlies Kim's contextual theory of interethnic communication. In this multidimensional theory focusing on the "associative" and "dissociative" intercultural communication behavior of individuals, Kim incorporates cultural identity into a broader identity orientation of a communicator, and identifies its two main factors, "identity inclusivity/exclusivity" and "identity security/insecurity," as influencing the communicator's associative/dissociative behavior when dealing with culturally and ethnically dissimilar others.

Cultural Identity as a Discrete Category and an Individual Choice. Whereas the conceptions described so far highlight, implicitly or explicitly, the evolving or flexible and negotiable nature of cultural identity, other conceptions emphasize that cultural identity is a discrete social category, but that individuals choose to identify themselves with one or more categories through an act of voluntary identification. Phinney and Rosenthal in 1992, for instance, described "cultural identity development" in minority adolescents by emphasizing the importance of achieving a secure sense of themselves as cultural group members and a "commitment" to one's cultural identity. Not achieving such a commitment to one's own group is viewed as resulting in significant detriment to the individual's psychological and social functioning. Phinney in 1993 also discussed the possibility for some minority adolescents to develop a "bicultural identity." Suggested in this conception of cultural and bicultural identity development is a mixture of integrationist and pluralistic ideological messages. The main insight one can draw from this theory is the paramount importance for individuals associated with a minority culture and cultural group to develop a clear sense of commitment to that group. At the same time, it allows for the possibility of moving beyond one's original identity by observing that, for some adolescents, a secure cultural identity can be one that integrates at least two cultural identities.

Integrationist-pluralist conceptions of cultural identity have been offered by many other social researchers. Stonequist argued in 1964 that immigrants would follow one of three distinct paths mainly as a function of individual choice: (a) assimilation into the dominant group; (b) assimilation into the "subordinate" group; or (c) some form of accommodation and reconciliation of the two societies. Similarly, Berry's psychological model of acculturation is built on two key questions concerning the subjective identity orientation: "Are cultural identity and customs of value to be retained?" and "Are positive relations with the larger society of value and to be sought?" By combining the response types (yes, no) to these two questions, the model generates four acculturation modes: (a) "integration" (yes, yes); (b) "assimilation" (no, yes); (c) "separation" (yes, no); and (d) "marginality" (no, no). These theories are constructed on the premise that, although cultural identity is a discrete category, individuals do have some choice in forming their own cultural identity.

Cultural Identity as a Distinct System of Communal Practices. To many ethnographic researchers, cultural identity is conceived as a communally shared system of communicative practices that is unique to the community and enduring over time, a phenomenon that cannot and should not be understood either as a discrete variable or an individual choice.

Rooted in the phenomenological-hermeneutic tradition and applying Geertz's framework of the interpretation of culture, Philipsen and his associates developed in 2005 an interpretive theory of cultural communication. This theory offers a foundational framework for ethnographic studies that are aimed at identifying, describing, and illuminating the essential cultural features of communication that differentiate one community from another. An extensive body of original field studies grounded in this perspective have contributed to a deepening understanding of the conversation patterns and other communication practices unique to a given cultural or subcultural community. Among the notable works are an examination of the cultural meaning of the word "communication" in some American speech, recognizable Indian ways of speaking in Native American communities, Russian "cultural pragmatics" in the context of Russian-American encounters, Finnish silence and third-party introduction, and interpersonal communication and relationship patterns in Columbia, to name only a few.

Directly or indirectly, ethnographic descriptions of cultural identities provided in studies end to emphasize the enduring and communal nature of cultural identity—the shared life patterns, practices, and symbols connoting a common tradition and common future. In emphasizing distinctiveness and consistency of cultural communication practices, they suggest a pluralistic "we-and-they" ideological perspective, one that is largely silent on individual variations in identity orientations.

Cultural Identity as a Discrete and Non-negotiable Social Category and Group Right. The most explicit and unambiguous pluralistic messages have been presented by "critical" scholars, including some whose writings connote a sense of separatism. Critical scholarship has been a salient and productive intellectual force in intercultural communication in recent years. The critical inquiry is by no means internally homogeneous, with different conceptions and competing lines of thought variously represented in "postimperialism," "**postcolonialism**," "muted group and standpoint theory," "critical pragmatism," and "cultural studies," among others.

Nevertheless, this author observes some ideologically-grounded common threads running through many critical conceptions of cultural identity, in varying degrees. Among them is the argument that authors of social scientific theories fail to address the predicaments in which members of traditionally underprivileged groups find themselves as "victims" of systematic oppression, thereby serving to reproduce the status quo of the dominant cultural ideology according to Hall in 1989. In introducing an anthology of essays presented largely from a critical perspective, for example, Gonzalez, Houston, and Chen stated in 1994 their goal of presenting the perspective of the authors' own cultural experience "instead of writing to accommodate the voice that is culturally desirable by the mainstream Anglo standards." Critical researchers tend to be united in their opposition to the traditional normative-representational-disciplinary social research. Critical researchers see this social science tradition as serving to reproduce the status quo of the dominant ideological construct, assimilationism. Young in 1996, for example, even went so far as to characterize social science research as a "universal" science that serves as "the beholders of cultural individualism" of European societies whose work "has led to a theory of politics about individual power" neglecting the "battles of cultural politics."

Reflecting these pluralistic and, to a degree, separatist ideological positions are the conceptions of cultural identity that have been articulated by a number of intercultural communication researchers. Hedge in 1998, based on interviews with 10 Asian Indian women in the United States, characterizes the adaptation experiences of these women in light of their "struggle" and "displacement." These experiences are attributed by Hedge to the "contradictions" between their internal identity and external "world in which hegemonic structures systematically marginalize certain types of difference." A similarly suggested opposition to assimilation of "members of marginalized communities" is claimed by Flores in 2001. From a "Chicana feminist" perspective, Flores appears to dismiss assimilation as a "myth" and, instead, argues that members of "marginalized communities," including "those of us in academia," produce "oppositional readings of dominant or mainstream texts" as a "strategy of resistance."

A related common thrust in critical scholarship is the conception of cultural identity as a discreet, largely monolithic, and non-negotiable social category. In 1986, Tsuda's went close to a separatist ideological perspective when he criticizes Western ideological domination as the genesis of "distorted intercultural communication" around the world. Tsuda argued, in particular, that the dominance of the English language imposes an overt restriction on non-Western peoples' freedom of expression and damages their identity. Likewise, Young presented his criticism of Western "cultural imperialism" in 1996 by depicting today's global reality as one of power asymmetry between communicators rooted in "oppressive" and "imperialistic" Western cultural-institutional systems. Characterizing his view as a "moderation" or "middle-path between imperial universalism and separatist cultural relativism." Young offers a vision of "true intercultural communication" in which "there is joint interest, a common interest, so that one is eager to give and the other to take."

On the whole, critical scholarship gives little attention to the possibilities of identity adaptation, transformation, flexibility, negotiation, and individual variations or choices. At least one possible exception to this observation is co-cultural theory. In 2005, Orbe and Spellers framed this theory as a critical theory designed to explain how individual members of a traditionally "muted social group" orient themselves to members of a dominant group. Within this framework, however, Orbe and Spellers went on suggesting individual variations and choices when they offer a theoretical typology that explicates specific "co-cultural communication strategies"—from "avoiding," "mirroring," "embracing stereotypes," and "**censoring** self," to "educating others," "bargaining," "attacking," and "sabotaging others."

▶ Synthesis

Though far from being complete or precise, the present analysis has been an attempt to identify common themes underlying various academic conceptions of cultural identity and the ideological underpinnings thereof. Together, the five themes—from the most dynamic, adaptive, and transformative to the most categorical and non-negotiable—illustrate some of the points of contention as well as of convergence in the on-going debates with respect to the nature of cultural identity and its role in intercultural communication within and across societies. Intended or not, and implicit or explicit, the ideological messages emanating from the literature are consistent with or support one or more of the four positions: assimilationism, integrationism, pluralism, and separatism.

Through this analysis, the author has come to a tentative understanding of the identity polemics in social research, both within and outside the field of intercultural communication, as being fundamentally rooted in two very different versions of what an ideal society or an ideal intercultural relation should be and how cultural (along with other) differences must be managed. At the assimilationist and integrative side of the debate are views that are built on the premise of the primacy of individual identity, a universalized vision of citizenship, and mutual accommodation. At the pluralistic and separatist side, arguments are made to open ourselves to possibilities of constructing a society that keeps faith with the principle of Pluribus, the primacy of group identity as a basic and profound right of individuals.

Philosophical-Methodological Challenges

The ideological divergence described above is most acute along the lines of traditional representational scholarship and critical scholarship. The main research aim for traditional social scientific research is accurately describing and explaining a given reality as is, regardless of particular opinions of individual investigators. Although varied along (neo)posist, systems, and phenomenological-interpretive in methodological details, there is a general agreement as to the importance of maximally removing from the conduct of research the researcher's own social or political agenda. In this broad philosophical-methodological framework, social scientists have made a range of knowledge claims about cultural identity that emphasize different degrees of complexity, flexibility, and individual variations. In addition, critical researchers' advocacy of pluralistic ideals is reflected in the conception of cultural identity as largely ascription-based and monolithic entity. Some of the writings even suggest a sense of "cultural identity at any cost"—an implicit message that gives cultural identity a non-negotiable moral and political imperative. This pluralist-separatist moral presupposition tends to overlook the potential "dark side" of a rigid, categorical adherence to cultural identity, that is, the tendencies of collective ingroup glorification and outgroup denigration.

As fellow investigators striving to better understand the nature of cultural identity, both traditional social scientists and critical researchers are confronted with the fundamental question about what constitutes an acceptable and legitimate knowledge claim. Philosophical-methodological divergence, indeed, has presented an intellectual barrier that cannot be easily reconciled and bridged. Efforts have been made by some to either merge, or embrace the inevitable tension in a dialectic relationship between oppositional paradigms. It is yet to be seen whether or not the fundamental philosophical-methodological differences can be bridged or reconciled. For now, there is clearly a need for intercultural communication researchers to acquire deeper knowledge of differing philosophical-methodological systems. It is through expanded methodological literacy that divergent perspectives may be better understood and even appreciated, so as to be able to compare and contrast differing perspectives and to seek consensus regarding some basic requisite criteria for assessing the soundness of all knowledge claims and research practices. As well, all researchers of all methodological-ideological orientations can benefit from engaging in rigorous self-reflection and cross-examination, so as to form a clearer understanding of the varied methodological-ideological underpinnings in their own work and each other's work.

Conclusion

We live in the post-9/11 era of clashing identities. Tightly knit communications technologies and transportation systems continue to bring together differing languages, religions, cultures, races, and nationalities closer than ever before in a web of interdependence, conflict, and a common fate. **Paradoxically**, the very forces that diminish physical, social, and cultural boundaries exacerbate group rivalries, rendering a deeply fractious and unsettling landscape of today's world. The seemingly innocent banner of cultural identity is now a compelling sore spot galvanizing many into "us-against-them" posturing. Some of the most passionate domestic and international conflicts headlining the daily media involve differing cultural identities. From long-festering prejudices, discriminations, and hatreds to the more recent acts of violent rage and terror, we are seeing in all corners of the world so many angry words, hurt, and destruction.

Although the future is fundamentally uncertain, one thing is clear. For the foreseeable future, issues pertaining to cultural identity will continue to be a **salient** and politicized phenomenon. In this global context, this author proposes some basic questions to be considered by other researchers seeking to make knowledge claims about cultural identity. Is rigid adherence to the ethnicity of our youth feasible or desirable? At what point do we cross the line from rightful and constructive claims for group identity to disastrous collisions with undue prejudice directed against one another? How can a society of multiple cultural identities such as the United States support and give confidence to all groups, while upholding the communal values and responsibilities that transcend allegiance to each group?

Applications

1. Cultural Identity and Intercultural Communication

Collier, J. M. (2015). Cultural identity and intercultural communication. In L.A.Samovar, R.E. Porter, E.R.McDaniel, & C.S.Roy (Eds.), *Intercultural communication: A reader* (14th ed.), 53–60. Boston, MA: Cengage Learning.

Abstract: This article presents an approach to culture that focuses on how individuals enact or take on one or more cultural identities. Questions that are answered here include the following: (1) What is a cultural identity? (2) How are multiple cultural identities created and negotiated with others? (3) How can knowledge of the cultural identity approach help you become more competent when dealing with persons who are taking on an identity different from yours? (4) What are the benefits of such an approach to intercultural communication research, training, and practice?

Keywords: approach; individual; cultural identity; create and negotiate; competent

2. Cultural Identity and Intercultural Communication: An Interdisciplinary Research Approach

Noronha, M., & Chaplin, I. (2014). Cultural identity and intercultural communication: An interdisciplinary research approach. *Clinical Anatomy*, 1, 211–225.

Abstract: The research on which this paper is based provides evidence that blending has indeed occurred in the creation and negotiation of Macao's cultural identity. However, the authors argue that more interdisciplinary research is needed to examine cultural changes which are occurring in the Asia region and identify the role that the study of discourse and intercultural communication might play in the preservation and perpetuation of Macao's unique cultural identity. In this paper, the importance of English as a research tool is acknowledged with reference to the literature on intercultural communication. The authors however emphasize the need for an interdisciplinary approach to research on cultural change, ethnicity, migration, and second language acquisition, influencing discourse and intercultural communication.

Keywords: blending; Macao; cultural identity; discourse and intercultural communication; preservation and perpetuation

3. On Identity: An Alternative View

Chen, G. M. (2009). On Identity: An alternative view. *China Media Research*, 4, 109–118.

Abstract: "Identity" has become a magic word in the disciplines of social sciences and humanities, in which, due to the impact of globalization, scholars examine the concept from different perspectives, including personal, intergroup, cultural, critical, and postcolonial approaches. Unfortunately, the plethora of research seems to further obscure the meaning and nature of identity, and worse, advocates of the importance of establishing, authenticating, or negotiating one's own identity seems to encourage people to tightly hold their own identity. Like a cocoon, this can weave a stronghold, preventing a person from penetrating into the identity of others. Facing this dilemma on the research of identity, this paper offers a critical overview of this line of study and proposes a different view on the nature of the self and identity from the Asian cultural perspective, specifically from the Taoist view.

Keywords: Identity, identity theory, self, social identity theory, Taoism

Interactive Activities

1. Individually, please finish reading Text A, Text B, and the application abstracts and work out the meanings of the terms in bold type by consulting the dictionary whenever necessary.

2. In pairs, please summarize the content in 2 to 3 sentences of each sub-heading in the unit outlines of Text A and Text B based on your reading and understanding of the texts.

3. In groups, share your gains, comments and suggestions regarding the three application abstracts. Based on your interests, locate and finish reading the full-length papers of your interested abstracts.

4. Q&A: Questions are encouraged about any uncertain or confused part or parts in the unit and seek answers either from other fellow students or the instructor.

Based on your understanding of identity, ideology, and communication in Text A and Text B, what suggestions do you want to make concerning the effective and appropriate expressions of the Chinese identity and ideology for smooth and meaningful intercultural communication?

5. Complete the Personal Report of Individualism and Collectivism Scale, a scale designed to measure how you act within your relationships with others. Take a few moments and complete the self-assessment for Unit 5.

6. When writing a research paper, it is critical to know the **citation format** for in-text citations and entries for the reference lists. There are two basic approaches to citation: 1) in-text citations + a list of references at the end of the paper; and 2) endnotes or footnotes +/− a bibliography at the end of the paper. Scholars writing in the sciences and social sciences typically use in-text citations, while scholars in the humanities utilize endnotes or footnotes. Generally speaking, there are three main citation styles: American Psychological Association (APA), Modern Language Association (MLA), and Chicago. APA style is most appropriate for research papers related to the field of social sciences, MLA for research papers related to the field of liberal arts and humanities, and Chicago style is meant for doing citations in history courses. Below are sample entries for the three styles:

Frank, Harry. (2011). Wolves, dogs, rearing and reinforcement: Complex interactions underlying species differences in training and problem-solving performance. *Behavior Genetics*, 41(6), 830–839. (APA)

Frank, H. "Wolves, Dogs, Rearing and Reinforcement: Complex Interactions Underlying Species Differences in Training and Problem-Solving Performance." *Behavior Genetics* 41.6 (2011): 830–39. Print. (MLA)

Frank, H. 2011. "Wolves, Dogs, Rearing and Reinforcement: Complex Interactions Underlying Species Differences in Training and Problem-Solving Performance." *Behavior Genetics* 41 (6): 830–839. (Chicago)

Now, please check the citations of the three abstract and try to change them from APA style to either MLA or Chicago style for practice.

UNIT SIX

Verbal Intercultural Communication

Readings

Text A Verbal Communication:
How Can I Reduce Cultural Misunderstandings
in My Verbal Communication?

After John R. Baldwin, Robin R. Means Coleman, Alberto González, & Suchitra Shenoy-Packer

Introduction

Verbal codes refer to spoken or written language. A verbal code comprises a set of rules governing the use of words in creating a message, along with the words themselves. We acquire or learn the rules and contents of our native language (or languages) as we grow up; thus, we can express our thoughts, emotions, desires, and needs easily in our first language. The study of language begins with identifying its components and how they are put together.

Language refers to a system of verbal, non-verbal, and visual symbols that a group pieces together to share meaning. There are often forceful politics surrounding language, because making one language a "national language" gives those who speak that language prestige and power over others who do not speak the language well, or even who speak it with a different dialect or pronunciation that has become dominant. For example, in Québec, Canada, language politics between French and English have been longstanding. One recent policy there requires that all advertising, including in Chinese businesses and restaurants, post French as the largest language on signs and advertising.

In any language community, there are multiple ways of speaking (speech codes)—but people in different situations have different "communicative resources." For example, students in a classroom are guided by culture as to how (or if) to ask the teacher questions in class or challenge a teacher's mistake. Language also structures the interaction, so that certain people have the right to do some things and others to do other things. These rights are accepted and consented to by people in the situation, but sometimes challenged. In sum, language is not something we simply participate in as individuals—it is structured by history, social situations, social relations, and hierarchies.

Systems of Language and Culture: Why Is Talking across Cultures So Difficult?

The Components of Human Language

While studying human language, linguists focus on different aspects of the language system:

sound, structure, and meaning. In 2013 Lustig and Koester identified five interrelated components of language: phonology, morphology, syntax, semantics, and pragmatics. Collectively, knowledge of each aspect of the language system provides us with a holistic understanding of the nature of human language.

Phonology explores how sounds are organized in a language. The smallest sound unit of a language is called a phoneme. The phonological rules of a language determine how sounds are combined to form words. For example, the **phonemes** [k] and [au] can be arranged to form the word "cow" [kau] in English. Mastery of any language requires the speaker to be able to identify and pronounce different sounds accurately. This may prove difficult for second language speakers, particularly those whose native language does not have a similar sound system to the new language.

Morphology refers to the combination of basic units of meaning, morphemes, to create words. For example, the word "happy" consists of one **morpheme**, meaning to feel cheerful. The word "unhappy" contains two morphemes: happy and the prefix "un" meaning "not" or the "opposite." Used together, they refer to a feeling akin to sadness. Morphemes, and the ways in which they are combined, differ across cultures. In the English language, prefixes or suffixes constitute morphemes as well as individual words, whereas in tonal languages such as Chinese, tones are morphemes and the meaning of units depends on the tone with which the word is pronounced.

Syntax concerns the grammatical and structural rules of language. We combine words into sentences according to grammatical rules in order to communicate. In English and other languages of the Indo-European family, people change the tense of a verb by adding a suffix or prefix or changing the morpheme, to describe past, present, and future events. In German, prepositions are often placed at the end of a sentence, whereas in French they are placed before nouns or noun phrases. Every language has a set of grammatical rules that govern the sequencing of words. Mastery of another language means knowing those grammatical rules in addition to building a stock of vocabulary.

Semantics refers to the study of the meanings of words, and the relationships between words and the things to which they refer. A command of vocabulary is an essential part of linguistic proficiency in any language. When we learn a second language, we devote much time to memorizing words and their meanings, concrete or abstract. However, just memorizing words and their dictionary meanings is often insufficient for successful intercultural communication, because meaning often resides in a context.

Pragmatics is concerned with the impact of language on human perception and behavior. It focuses on how language is used in a social context. Pragmatic analysis of language goes beyond its structural features and concentrates on the social and cultural appropriateness of language use in a particular context. For example, a fairly direct communication style is preferred for resolving interpersonal conflicts in South Africa or Germany; a more indirect approach tends to be favored in the Republic of Korea, where the preservation of harmony is strongly valued.

Systems of Meaning

Semantics language researchers discuss several aspects of language that are beyond the scope of our discussion, such as writing systems, sounds that different languages make, or grammar and word order. Two main areas of language are relevant in the study of cultural communication semantics and discourse. **Semantics** is the area of language study that considers what words mean. Words have **denotation**—the relatively objective dictionary type of definition of a word, and **connotation**—the feelings (personal or social) that individuals associate with a word. Meaning comes in part from the personal experiences we have with a word. When we are little, we see a dog on the street and someone says either "puppy!" or "*viralata*!" We associate the sound or image with something we see ("reality")—either face-to-face or in a mediated text—and we get a sense of how we should feel about it. "Puppies" are cuddly and cute and want to be petted; "*viralatas*" should be avoided and left alone.

Through interaction, then, we create meanings, and these meanings differ from culture to culture. For example, the word "friend" translates into "amigo" in Spanish and Portuguese—but people who speak these as first languages often have different expectations and meanings for what a friend is and does than those who speak U.S. American English. In the mobile American culture, a friend may be someone one sees after a long absence and feels as if the relationship continues right where it left off. But in other cultures, friendship implies a deep sense of obligation and continued communication. At the same time, social ideologies also frame language, through the reproduction of mediated messages, politics and so on.

Some argue that meanings of words are not simply neutral, but are loaded with power implications. Groups struggle to define certain words, illustrating the notion of **discourse**. Discourse, in this sense, refers to the sets of ideas surrounding a concept. In 1978 Michel Foucault talked about the history (what he calls the archeology) of words, noting how cultures and societies create notions such as mental illness, sexuality, and crime in a way that keeps certain sets of ideas in power. These meanings change over time, such as the notion of "race" in U.S. American culture, but they change through group striving, as people with different ideologies fight to make their meanings central.

What you say is what you get: the **Sapir-Whorf hypothesis** posits that, in a way, language creates social reality through language structure, such as the fact that different languages make different verb tenses, word order, or words available to describe certain things(See Figure 6.1). In 1991 Harry Hoijer cited examples from Navajo, Hopi, and other languages in which people from different cultures have wider or narrower sets of names for color spectrum. In 1989 Thomas Steinfatt analyzed the evidence on both sides and concludes that, while language may not create a "reality" for people, it does lead people in a culture to tend to think about certain things rather than others.

Figure 6.1 The Sapir-Whorf Hypothesis and Verbal Communication

Speech Acts and Cultural Communication

Another important area for intercultural communication is what we do with words—the pragmatic aspect of language. For example, someone tells you, "You look great." The words contain a second-person singular pronoun, "you," a linking verb suggesting how something appears, "look," and an adjective with a positive feeling behind it, "great." In one situation, this could be a compliment, but, if you have just spent all night studying and have not cleaned up before class, it could be sarcasm. It could be flattery, to your bosses' wife, or a lie, to avoid hurting someone's feelings.

This example shows us that there are many things we can do with a phrase, just as there are many ways to accomplish the same sort of act. **Speech acts theory** outlines the types of actions we perform with utterances. We follow basic rules when we communicate, as long as we are trying to cooperate with others in conversation. If we are competent, we will stay on topic, give sufficient detail but not more than is necessary, speak things we believe to be true, and speak in a way that is relatively clear according to Grice in 1957. There are different types of action we can do with words—we can make statements (observations), express our feelings or opinions (**compliment**, curse, greet), try to influence others (hint, question, command), commit to a future act (promise, threat, vow), or change the state of things with our words (fire someone, decree something—acts that can usually only be done by people in authority). And each of these follows a set of hidden rules about what constitutes an act (an apology must be about a negative event over which a person has control and feels sincerely sorry for) or who can do it (only someone with authority can make a "pronouncement"). We probably follow all of these rules without thinking about them.

Speech acts theory helps us understand cultural language difficulties. What counts as enough detail in one culture may not be the same in another culture. In one culture, someone might make a request using indirect language, which would violate unstated expectations for clarity in another culture; and the intended purpose of a message is often not what is received. We experience this in our daily lives. In 1991 Deborah Tannen outlined sex-based differences in the workplace: a woman might give an order that looks and sounds like a suggestion ("you might try..."), and men might misunderstand it, with the result that women's requests are often not fulfilled by men. In 1997 Shoshana Blum-Kulka illustrated such forms of indirectness in requests by analyzing a scene at an Israeli dinner table, where the father is hungry and seeks permission to make himself some food, but the mother perceives it as a complaint about what is offered, so defends her choice of rice for dinner.

In intercultural communication, people often mistake the force of a statement for what it actually looks like. Many newcomers to the United States get frustrated when people ask, "How's it going?" when they do not really want to know. While "How's it going?" can be a heartfelt request for information in the U.S., it usually serves as a greeting, and the speaker does not expect a response. In cultures that prefer indirectness, like Japan, a statement in a negotiation session like "We'll think about it" sounds like a promise for future consideration but may be a polite way to say "no."

Getting Things Done with Language

We can see culture's impact on how we accomplish many different communication acts. These include things like making and responding to apologies, making requests, showing friendship, giving criticism, and gaining agreement on a project. Each area has produced rich research in cross-cultural and intercultural communication, but we will consider just four areas.

Directives. As noted earlier, **directives** (attempts to influence the behavior of or persuade another) can range from subtle hints to overt commands. In 1994 Kristine Fitch found that attempts to persuade in Colombia were informed by two dimensions: *hierarchia* (hierarchy) and *confianza* (trust, relatedness), similar to power and solidarity already mentioned, people in Colombia might use a go-between or **intermediary** to persuade someone across status lines. People in Colorado (U.S.) tend to use politeness behaviors, giving the target of persuasion a way to avoid the imposition. Someone might say, "Hey, if you're not busy, would you be able to give me a ride?" so that the other person could reply that she or he is busy. Min-Sun Kim and Steven Wilson found in 1994 that U.S. Americans and People of the Republic of Korea both felt that direct requests were the clearest way to get someone to do something, but that the U.S. Americans felt such a form to be the most effective, and People of the Republic of Korea, the least effective.

Criticism. In a study of criticism, Chinese and U.S. American participants gave their most likely responses to situations that might yield a complaint or criticism, such as being late for an appointment, invasion of privacy by a parent, or a server's mistake at a restaurant. There were no important differences in the frequencies of options such as saying nothing or using accusing questions to criticize; but analysis of open-ended data showed that U.S. American questions about a behavior were often phrased to assume guilt on the part of the other person, where the Chinese questions were framed more to ask if the other was aware of the sender's perceptions and resulting disappointment according to Chen et al. in 2011. Findings from conversational data suggest that some cultures prefer to soften criticism or not offer it—but for different reasons. Japanese people might avoid criticism and strong emotional displays in many cases because it shows lack of *omoiyari*—the ability to sense the pain or pleasure of another. The Japanese often do not want the other person to feel bad. Malays might engage in self-silencing to avoid having the other think badly of them. Polish speakers, however, are more likely to say things like, "Where did you get such an idea from? You are wrong!" In fact, the ability to openly express one's perception of "disagreement, exasperation, and impatience" with the other is a sign of the feeling of openness one feels one should have in relationships.

Apologies. In response to an embarrassing situation, should someone make a joke, give an explanation or defense, or make an apology of some sort? In 1994 Todd Imahori and William Cupach had student participants describe an embarrassing predicament of their choice. The Japanese students were more likely to describe something that had happened with someone from their in-group, and the U.S. Americans, someone from an out-group. The Japanese were more likely to feel a sense of **shame**, in the sense of negative reflection upon their group for the embarrassing situation, but the U.S. Americans, **guilt**, or a sense of personal responsibility. While people in both cultures preferred to avoid mentioning the wrong and an "apology" as the primary responses, in some situations, Americans were much more likely to use humor to lighten the situation, whereas Japanese were more likely to use **remediation**—that is, to do something concrete to make up to the injured party for the embarrassment.

Compliments. Finally, Farhad Sharifian in 2008 described how Persian speakers, even when they are speaking English as a second language, give and receive compliments. The Persian notion of *adah*, a form of politeness in which one seeks to give compliments, suggests one should give many, but sincere, compliments on various aspect of the other person's life. While one may give lots of compliments, however, a contrasting notion of *shekastehnafsi*—modesty—leads one to downplay one's own accomplishments. In response to a prompt that one had done a great job, one participant responded with, "I owe this achievement to your efforts. If it hadn't been for your help, I would never have achieved this." Another study classifies the various types of compliments given in Pidgin English in Cameroon, such as direct appraisals ("What a beautiful blouse you have!"), or interrogative appraisals ("Where do you do your hair?"). The author suggests that the compliments, shared between people of different ethnic or tribal groups but shared in a common trade language of Pidgin, serve to build solidarity between speakers, as long as they are perceived as genuine.

UNIT SIX
Verbal Intercultural Communication

Explaining the Details: Seeking Ways to Explain Differences across Cultures

As we have seen, there are many different ways to make an argument, negotiate, joke, request, compliment, promise (or threat), show respect, or give instructions. Even with fluency in the logistics of a language, if we do not master the pragmatics of the culture, we will be incompetent. There are too many types of specific differences to explain here, but here we will explain several approaches researchers have used to try to explain cultural difference in language use.

Relational Orientations. Many scholars have defined relational orientations in two primary dimensions of interaction: power and solidarity. Power refers to the level of control over another's thoughts, feelings, or behavior. This includes communication in which one person imposes upon or yields to another. In any culture, different situations or relationships have more of a hierarchical difference, which impacts our communication. We communicate differently with our friends than with our employer, and differently with our employer than we might if we met the Queen or the Prime Minister. Another dimension of interaction is **solidarity**, the degree of familiarity and/or intimacy we have with another person. We tend to react differently—more formally or less rudely—to someone who is a stranger than to an acquaintance, a friend, or a close friend.

The two dimensions interact. In some cases, we might have a closer level of intimacy with a supervisor, even though she is also hierarchically above us in the organizational structure; but we might act more cordially to a stranger who is our age than one with a higher status. In 1994 Deborah Tannen noted that some cultures, like the United States, associate power with asymmetry, hierarchy, and distance, and see it as the opposite of solidarity; it is difficult to be in a close relationship with a boss or status superior. Other cultures, such as one might find in Indonesia or Japan, imagine relationships that bind people together hierarchically, but also with a strong sense of solidarity. These dimensions exist in all cultures, though individual, cultural, and structural influences shape them in actual communication.

Face Theory. As we consider these various types of action that one can accomplish with communication, we see both cultural differences and cultural similarities. Researchers have proposed several frameworks to try to make sense of a wide variety of communication behavior (verbal and non-verbal). Some seek explanations that apply across all cultures. Many authors use notions of face and politeness theory. In 1959 Irving Goffman argued that we are often concerned about what he calls **face**—the image we seek to have of ourselves in interaction. We are like actors on a stage, with props, lines, and performances; but sometimes, we let others **"backstage"** to see more of what we are really like. In 1967 Goffman argued that in interaction, we work together with others to protect and repair loss of face, because face-loss can interrupt the flow of interaction. Once face has been damaged, conversation often stops while someone makes a joke, an apology, a threat, or some other remedy, and that remedy is accepted by others—unless the most face-saving move is to say nothing, such as we do when people pass audible gas publicly in cultures where this is disapproved of.

Penelope Brown and Stephen Levinson found evidence in 1987 that in all cultures, people seek to preserve the idea that they are free and autonomous (**negative face**) as well as the idea that they are competent and qualified for some task; people also like to feel included or liked by others (the last two notions are aspects of **positive face**). We see an example of how cultural dimensions might be explained and predicted using notions of face in the Imahori and Cupach's study in 1994.

Cultural Scripts. Other researchers, rather than try to predict behaviors, use observation and talk to people to learn the communication **scripts** used in a culture. These are cultural rules regarding expected behavior that include expectations of who does what, and any expected sequence of actions in a communication routine. In 1997 Cliff Goddard and Anna Wierzbicka, using a script approach, described what they call a "natural semantic **metalanguage**" that uses simple words, like *people*, *something*, *say*, *think*, *know*, *good*, and *bad*, to describe a behavior in a particular culture. They use this approach to describe what they call *halus* speech—a speech form in Malaysia in which people talk carefully with people outside of the immediate family. The cultural logic is that:

When people hear someone saying something sometimes they think something like this:
"This person knows how to say things well to other people; this is good."
Sometimes they think something like this:
"This person doesn't know how to say things well to other people; this is bad."

In a similar way, Donal Carbaugh in 2005 unpacked a negative live-audience reaction to Phil Donahue, as he tries to goad Russian youth into talking about the "problem" of premarital sex in Russia. Carbaugh concludes that, while "public talk" and turning issues into problems is a mainstay of American talkshow television, with sex being treated very **rationally**, the Russians perceive sex to be a deeply emotional topic and do not perceive public television as the correct place to air public problems.

Dimensions of Difference. Instead of theories and frameworks, many authors summarize types of differences one might expect between cultures. These provide a simple way to think of how cultures can differ, as long as we realize that: (a) most cultures will sit between the "extremes" on any set of terms and contain elements of both aspects of a dimension; (b) there will be differences within each culture based on age, social class, task at hand and so on; and (c) cultures balance change and tradition in the face of globalization.

Direct versus Indirect. As we have already seen, people in some cultures—depending on the relationship between individuals, the urgency of the topic, and other factors—can be very direct, even "in your face." People in some cultures can be direct and forthright in their speech. People in other cultures can be quite indirect, such as in organizational communication in Japan or Korea (though young Korean friends might make a request or joke quite directly to each other). For example, Egyptians in many cases use *musayara* speech, marked by deference, commonality, and avoidance of conflict.

Formal versus Informal. All cultures have situations that are more or less formal, though in some cultures, there are *more* occasions for formality than others. For example, in midwestern U.S. American classrooms, students are more informal, some even calling professors by first name. In other cultures, communication in business or education situations or with status superiors demands formality.

Differentiated and Undifferentiated Codes. Language is differentiated when there are different **registers**, or forms and levels of formality of speech for people in different societal groups, such as based on social status. Romance languages are more differentiated than English, with both formal and informal forms for singular "you" (Spanish: tú, usted)—though the specific rules for going from tú to usted vary from culture to culture, even within a single Spanish-speaking country. Korean, on the other hand, has multiple levels of formality in language, and even "honorific verbs" to describe things such as eating or sleeping for those very high in status. A reporter for *Seoulbeats* demonstrates how these levels of formality apply even in K-pop, a **contemporary** form of popular music from Korea.

Instrumental and Affective Styles. People in some cultures may be more direct and goal oriented, preferring efficient linguistic forms, while other cultures may have a preference for more emotional and expressive communication. This combines elements we discuss in unit 4, such as being versus doing, or instrumental versus expressive.

Exaggerated, Exacting, Succinct Styles. An **exaggerated style** may use language more to embellish upon reality than to describe it, as a major function of communication is to reveal the speaker's ability to use language creatively. For example, many U.S. African American males might employ boasting, rapping (romantic come-ons), and verbal games like "the dozens." An **exacting style** emphasizes saying what one means, giving the detail necessary—with a focus on efficiency similar to the instrumental style noted earlier. The **succinct style** reflects a cultural or personal preference for fewer words. The instrumental/exacting communication is speaker-focused, with the speaker providing the detail she or he feels the other needs, where a succinct style is listener-focused, leaving the listener to fill in the gaps, such as in the traditional notion of British understatement or some Asian forms that include more silence and subtlety in communication.

▲ Discursive Elements of Cultures: What Happens When Joining the Language Elements?

We often interact with friends and relatives for easily identifiable reasons. We engage in conversation to exchange information and to express our feelings and judgments. However, there are times when our interactions with others have meaning beyond the immediate context and are explained by broader patterns of communication. For example, when sports fans arise for their national anthem before a game, they participate in a public ritual. The song is an expression of national pride and is a deliberate reminder of national greatness and national ideals. When fans stand, sing, remove their hats and show other signs of respect, they publicly confirm their loyalty to the state. The anthem along with other verbal (for example, a formal pledge of allegiance) and non-verbal (a flag) symbols, compose a set of meanings—or a discourse—that guides understanding and action.

These broader patterns of communication are **discursive** elements of language. Cultural myth, conversational episodes, social dramas, and metaphor are examples of discursive elements of cultures that are examined in this section. Being prepared for successful civic action requires having an understanding of the discursive elements that guide communities.

Cultural Myth

Cultural myth is a narrative that is popularly told to teach preferred ways of behaving, such as a familiar story that recommends particular values and responses to situations. An example might be the U.S. American myth of the "American Dream," traditionally a view that anyone can work hard to achieve a better life (expressed in terms of monetary wealth/security and material goods). Myths may have origins in historical events or may be anchored in values that have evolved over time. A myth is told that Buddha called all the animals to him as he ended his earthly stay. Only 12 animals answered the call, so Buddha rewarded the rat, ox, tiger, rabbit, dragon, snake, horse, sheep, monkey, rooster, dog, and bear by giving each animal its own year. People born during the year of a particular animal have the characteristics of that animal, thus giving honor to each animal. As a cultural myth, the story allows parents to recommend to their children socially valued behaviors. Though the 12 animals are assigned different traits, all have traits that point toward passion, focus, and hard work.

Myths are conveyed through a variety of methods, including popular culture. For example, the U.S. song "The Ballad of Davy Crockett", found on a popular children's CD titled *For Our Children* by Stern & Kleiner in 1999, tells the story of Davy, who was "born on a mountaintop in Tennessee" and who was so skilled in the woods that he "kilt him a bar [killed him a bear] when he was only three." In addition to conquering the land, he fought different Native tribes and got elected to the U.S. Congress. He "saw his duty clear" and went off to fight with the Texas Revolution at the Alamo, where he met his demise in 1836. The actual Davy Crockett dropped out of school, ran away from home and angrily left Tennessee after losing an election. So why is Crockett commemorated in this song? The song emphasizes aspects of a U.S. American character that are deeply rooted in American folklore. Crockett, as the "King of the wild frontier," reinforces the goodness of turning natural resources to human use—by force if necessary. He reinforces the goodness of individualism and single-minded determination and he legitimizes the superiority of Euro-American Protestantism over other beliefs. Additional stories of characters such as Paul Bunyan and Babe the Blue Ox serve much the same purpose.

In contrast, Cherokee storyteller Gayle Ross described in 1986 how the Cherokee obtained the first sacred fire. In *The First Fire*, various animals volunteered to bring fire from a burning log that lay across the water on an island. The council first chose several birds to go to bring the fire, because they were the fastest: the raven, screech owl and the hooting owl. But the birds could not get through the thick smoke of the fire. Then the bear and the snake were chosen because they were brave and strong. But they failed as well. Finally, the tiny water spider asked to go and everyone laughed. How could the tiny spider hope to succeed when the biggest, bravest and fastest animals had failed? The water spider was allowed to try anyway. It spun a bowl in which to put a piece of coal from the fire and soon it returned to light the sacred fire of the Cherokee. The lesson is that often the "smallest and meekest" have a role in finding solutions to problems. This cultural myth emphasizes the goodness of a collectivist orientation. Action is determined through group decision-making. Instead of each animal acting individually, the council decided which animal would try to bring the fire. In the end, the least dominant animal succeeded through intelligence and patience. *The First Fire* and "The Ballad of Davy Crockett" express different cultural values and recommend different approaches for acting in the world.

Conversational Episodes

A conversational episode (CE) or communication ritual is a routine portion of conversation that has an expected beginning and end, like ordering a meal at a restaurant, or friends exchanging details about what they did last night. Though usually brief, exchanges are important and guided by tradition. As language philosopher Judith Butler wrote in 1997, the episode "exceeds itself in past and future directions." In this sense, CEs are performances of cultural knowledge. When a Spanish-speaking individual is introduced to another, the common reply is "*mucho gusto*" or "nice to meet you." In Morocco, it is nearly impossible to greet someone without invoking Allah. In a CE, something specific gets accomplished: a joke is told, a bet is made, a greeting is given, much as in speech acts earlier though the CE involves more than one turn, as opposed to a hint or a threat. So, "*mucho gusto*" would be a speech act, but it would occur within an episode, typically upon first meeting someone, and would be followed with an expected follow-up, like, "*el gusto es mio*" ("the pleasure is mine"). In a different example, during the first three days of the Chinese New Year, people commonly use the expression "*gong xi fa cai*" (may you have a happy and prosperous new year) and avoid negative topics. If a speaker makes a disparaging remark and invites bad luck, the hearer replies, "*Tou heu soey dzoi geng gwa*" (spit out your saliva and speak once more) according to Fong in 2012. Some writers speak of different **discourses** as expectations and patterns of speech that occur in different situations, such as courtroom discourse, television interview discourse, or informal conversation. Who shares what in each situation is shaped by social roles, norms, and hierarchies, like other aspects of language.

Social Dramas

A **social drama** is a conflict that arises in a community after a social norm is violated. The violation becomes a social drama when discussion about it calls into question that social norm, and the resolution of the conflict validates, strengthens, or weakens the norm for members of the community. Social dramas can occur on an international scale, on a national scale, or at local levels. Yet even the local-level dramas can be intercultural in nature.

In 2010, the City Council in Toledo, Ohio, drafted a resolution calling for the federal government to undertake comprehensive reform of immigration policy as a response to controversial immigration laws passed in Arizona. The resolution was introduced by the lone Latino on the City Council. In this case, the drama centers around the response of the city leader, the mayor of the city. Through his response, we can see the four phases of a social drama:

Breach of the code—this is violation of an accepted rule or law.

Crisis—this is the talk or discussion in response to the breach.

Redress—this is the method for resolving the breach. Redress can be formal (a trial) or informal (public opinion). Redress can result in **reintegration**.

Reintegration is forgiveness and inclusion back into the community. **Dissensus** means there is ongoing disagreement about the breach and its implications for the community.

Our verbal communication often is about community or national and international controversies. Our opinions become part of a larger dialogue on acceptable or reprehensible conduct. As we discuss topics with others and give our judgment on our own actions or the actions performed on our behalf (and perhaps change our judgment), we examine and prioritize our individual and cultural values. Thus, not only do social dramas shape our individual cultures, but as they arise in discussion, they become part of our intercultural dialogue.

Cultural Metaphor

A **metaphor** is an association of two items. A characteristic of the more familiar item is associated with the less known item. If we talk about "saving time," we are treating time in terms of something tangible that can be saved, like money. Metaphors can have many different origins. For example, "*zubda*" is an Arabic word for "the best butter or cream." *Zubda* refers to the best of what has been mixed or churned. So imagine a music CD called *The Zubda of Shakira*, which would mean "the best of Shakira" or "the essential Shakira."

Metaphors and metaphorical expressions in talk and literature have fascinated critics since Aristotle. In 2003 George Lakoff and Mark Johnson, a linguist and a philosopher, went so far as to say that we "live by" metaphors—they structure the very way that we think. For example, we will treat immigrants differently if we think of them as a "scaffolding for our construction economy" as opposed to a "drain on society resources." An especially helpful notion is the **metaphorical archetype**—a comparison of items that has many expressions (a "family" of metaphors, metaphorically speaking) and is deeply ingrained in a culture. The metaphorical archetype is instantly recognized when it is used, and so assumed that it is rarely questioned. The archetypal metaphor found in President Barack Obama's 2008 campaign speeches was the metaphor of the "journey." Expressions such as "the journey that led me here," "path of upward mobility," and "the road to change" allow Obama to connect to the larger narrative of America's forward motion.

Metaphors of travel and motion are not hard to come across in ordinary North American speech. Expressions such as "I see where you're going with that," and "just follow me for a second" connect motion with argument and reasoning. Other metaphors such as "being concrete," "getting to the bottom line," "getting to the point," and "the weight of evidence" all suggest a linear ("now it's time to connect the dots") orientation. The dominant U.S. culture preference for linearity (time's arrow) contrasts with Native American metaphors of **circularity** and looking backward. Another cultural difference can be seen in archetypes or metaphors for animals. All cultures use animals for different metaphoric purpose, but sometimes the meanings and feelings differ. For example, in U.S. American culture, if we call someone a "rat," that person is "contemptible... sneaky, disloyal, and hated." But in many cultures, such as India, ancient Egypt and Rome, the rat is revered.

As critical observers and participants in cultures, we are reminded that discursive elements of cultures serve a variety of purposes. The words and expressions that existed before us may have become popular to further marginalize a specific population or region or to privilege a particular cultural value or view of something, like success, beauty, or human nature. We should not automatically accept the verbal options given to us. We should always reflect upon who is served or under-served by a particular narrative, metaphor, or conversational episode. Typically, we view the breach of a code as negative. But we should ask: did that code need to be violated to advance social justice? Is dissensus the right outcome to achieve social justice?

Theories of Conversation and Culture: What Happens When We Actually Talk to Each Other?

We have looked at what happens within each culture, either in terms of forms of languages (apologies, compliments) or in terms of larger levels of discourse and meaning (metaphors, rituals). But what happens when people from different cultures communicate? To the extent that differences in expectations for different behaviors are beyond our awareness, when someone else requests, criticizes, compliments, or greets in a way we do not expect, we will give meaning to their behavior based on our own cultural norms. In many cases, this can lead to a negative evaluation or simply to misunderstanding. Here we introduce one theory that has gained much attention, and then address issues of dominance and power in intergroup communication.

Communication Accommodation Theory

Often people with different speaking styles communicate with each other, even from within the same nation. Basil Bernstein stated in 1966 that the social situation, including communicative context (for example, a job interview versus a party) and social relationships (for example, peers versus status unequals), dictates the forms of speaking used in a particular situation. Bernstein suggested that in all cultures, there are different types of codes. A **restricted code** is a code used by people who know each other well, such as jargon or argot. **Jargon** refers to a vocabulary used by people within a specific profession or area (such as rugby players or mine workers), while **argot** refers to language used by those in a particular underclass, often to differentiate themselves from a dominant culture (e.g., prostitutes, prisoners). However, as people get to know each other better, even good friends can develop this sort of linguistic shorthand, speaking in terms or references that others do not understand. In an **elaborated code**, people spell out the details of meaning in the words in a way that those outside of the group can understand them. This switching back and forth between codes is called **code-switching**. Effective communicators should be able to speak in restricted codes appropriate to their context, but also know how to switch to elaborated code (for example, to include outsiders)—to change their vocabulary, level of formality, and so on, to match the audience and social occasion.

Based on the notions of different codes within a community, as well as code-switching and other theoretical ideas, Howard Giles and his colleagues introduced **communication accommodation theory**. This theory predicts how people adjust their communication in certain situations, the factors that lead to such changes, and the outcomes of different types of changes.

In the U.S. television series, *Lost*, through a series of flashbacks and present communication, we observe the speech of Jin Kwon, a Korean man, the son of a fisherman, but hired by a wealthy restaurant owner. In some cases, his communication is respectful, indirect, deferential; in others, it is direct, friendly or aggressive, and non-verbally more expressive. In some cases, he might change his behavior to be more like that of the person with whom he is speaking (**convergence**), and in others, he might make no changes in his behavior (**maintenance**) or even highlight his own style to mark it as different from that of the other group (**divergence**). Jin can change his behavior in terms of non-verbal behavior (distance, posture, touch, etc.), paralinguistic behavior (tone of voice, rate of speech, volume, etc.), and verbal behavior (word choice, complexity of grammar, topic of conversation, turn-taking, etc.). Many things influence shifts in his speech, such as the status and power of the other communicator, the situation, who is present, communication goals (for example, to seem friendly, or to show status or threat), the strength of his own language in the community, and his communication abilities.

Communication and Sites of Dominance

Convergence can often go wrong. Giles and Noels explained in 2002 that, although converging is usually well received, we can **over-accommodate**, or converge too much or in ineffective ways, by adjusting in ways we might think are appropriate, but are based on stereotypes of the other. People often speak louder and more slowly to a foreigner, thinking that they will thus be more understandable. Over-accommodation also works in situations of dominance. For example, younger people often inappropriately adjust their communication when talking with elderly people. Often called **secondary baby talk**, this includes a higher pitch in voice, simpler vocabulary, and use of plural first-person ("we"—"Would we like to put our coat on? It's very cold outside"). While some older people find this type of communication comforting, especially from health workers, some feel it speaks down to them and treats them as no longer competent. A similar feeling might be experienced by Blacks in the United States when Whites use **hyper-explanation**. This inappropriate form of adjustment also includes use of simpler grammar, repetition, and clearer enunciation. But Harry Waters suggested in 1992 that it is a behavior some Whites engage in while talking with Blacks (or other minority members)—perhaps based on real communication differences or perhaps based on stereotypes, but certainly leaving hurt feelings or resentment on the part of the Black listeners.

Writers have outlined the ways in which word choice, turn-taking and length, or topic selection may also serve to exclude others, often without us even being aware of it. Don Zimmerman and Candace West found in 1975 that while women "overlapped" speech turns in talking to men, often with "continuers" ("mm hmm," "yes") that continued the turn of the male, men were more often likely to interrupt women, often taking the turn away from them. And when women did interrupt men, the men did not yield the turn to women, while women did yield the turn to men. Jennifer Coates, observing storytelling, found that men and boys often framed themselves as heroes, as being rebels or rule-breakers. In analysis of family communication, she found that there is "systematic" work done by all family members in many families to frame the father as either the primary story teller or the one to whom children tell their stories. Coates concludes, "Family talk can be seen to construct and maintain political order within families ... to conform roles and power structures within families," giving men more power in most mixed-gender storytelling over women. We can see that each aspect of verbal communication could be used in ways to impose power over others, often based on group identity, cultural difference, maintenance of group power, or, simply put, prejudice.

Summary

Our focus in this unit has been on various aspects of verbal communication as these relate to culture and intercultural communication. We considered elements that make up the language system—from the smallest parts of sound (phonemes) to language woven into myth, ritual, and practice. We considered perspectives of language and culture, such as whether linguistic relativity is a valid concept, that is, whether the language that a culture speaks creates the reality that the speakers of that language inhabit. We gave special attention to the use of language in building myth, communication episodes, and social dramas.

Beyond lists of dimensions of language variation (e.g., formal to informal), we provided some overarching ideas to explain how these might vary across cultures, such as speech acts and face theory. We considered explanations of what happens when people of different groups or cultures speak to each other, through the notion of communication accommodation. Finally, we suggested ways that people use verbal language, perhaps without intention, to reinforce power structures and social discourses, such as discourses of traditional gender roles or ideas of group stereotypes.

An understanding of the elements of language and how they can differ among cultures is useful as we engage ourselves with a multicultural world. Realizing how adjusting our language to others can often be helpful may help us to be aware of our own communication behavior when interacting with others. And, while our focus has been on how language might oppress others with or without intention, we can use this knowledge to speak more respectfully with others. Indeed, many scholars today are using this knowledge to give those who are in groups that dominant culture subordinates new ways of speaking that provide more equality of power among communicators.

Text B   Verbal Communication across Cultures

After Tae-Seop Lim

Introduction

The study of cultural differences in verbal communication has undergone three stages of development. The first stage was the birth of linguistic relativism and its challenge to absolutism or linguistic **universalism**. There was no denying that verbal communication behaviors were different across cultures. The debate was over the nature and scope of the differences. Universalists would argue the differences are not fundamental, and the similarities are more striking, whereas relativists would claim the differences are essential since they are based upon different world-views and thought patterns. Universalism or absolutism is rooted in the modernistic tradition and a strong faith in the Western culture as a model culture. Relativism rejects the possibility of universal theories of communication. Even a mild version of Whorfian **Hypotheses**, linguistic relativism requires fundamentally different theories for cultures with structurally different languages. The controversy has not been resolved after a century of debate.

The second stage was as theoretical as, but much less philosophical or ideological than the previous stage. As sociolinguistic research developed, researchers began to show strong interests in comparing linguistic behaviors or rules of communication across different groups such as gender and social classes. In Britain, Bernstein compared linguistic codes used by children from the working class families with those used by children from the middle class. He **attributed** the differences to the structural differences in the family communication system between the two classes. In the U.S., Lakoff in 1975 compared languages used by males and females, attributing the differences to the different social expectations stemming from power disparity between two sexes. The development in sociolinguistics inspired Hall, a cultural anthropologist, to extend the findings, particularly Bernstein's work on linguistic code, to the study of culture in 1976. Both Bernstein and Hall were less interested in the absolutist-relativist debate than finding different rules operating in different speech communities.

The third stage has been much more practical and business-oriented. As the Western researchers realized that the rest of the world is operating on a fundamentally different system, they began to put cultural divides between them and the rest, putting the two worlds at the opposite extremes. A variety of dichotomies have been developed including Hofstede's cultural dimensions in 1980, which prompted researchers to explore how these opposite cultural dimensions influence individuals' verbal communication behaviors. At this stage, researchers are not concerned with the absolutism-relativism debate or any other ideological issue of language. However, knowingly or unknowingly, researchers display their subscription to the relativist position. In fact, they sometimes tend to exaggerate the cultural differences more than their data support.

In this essay, I discuss major findings generated through these three stages of research. As the first stage was devoted mostly to establishing linguistic relativism, my discussion will begin with the main researchers in the second stage.

▲ Cultural Differences in Verbal Communication

Edward T. Hall and High-Context and Low-Context Communication

Hall is one of the first researchers who systematically studied cultural differences in communication style. In verbal as well as written communication, following him, people inevitably utilize the context to communicate properly in the given situation. He distinguishes between high-context and low-context communication or message, according to the degree to which the information is subject to the context for meaningful understanding. In a high-context communication, most information is either in the physical context or internalized in the person, while very little is in the coded, explicit, transmitted part of the message. In a low-context communication, the mass of the information is vested in the explicit code according to Hall in 1976. Many Western cultures including North America are located toward the lower end of contextual communication, whereas most Eastern cultures belong to the higher end. However, Japan is known to have double sides: High-contextual private communication and low-contextual public communication. In the low context culture, communicators do not mind their partner's verbalization of already shared assumptions or context. Communication often requires reviewing the context to make sure that both parties are on the same page. In the high-context culture, on the contrary, reiterating shared or even assumed-to-be-shared contexts makes the other feel ignored, belittled, or pushed away.

Hall's high-low context communication is comparable to Bernstein's theory of code. In 1971 Bernstein, while studying the linguistic proficiency of the children from working class families, found that they used a linguistic code that is different from (or inferior to) the well-formed code used by the children raised in middle class families. The working class children spoke fast and fluently, taking not much time to think about what to say. However, they used a limited range of syntactic alternatives, simple and repetitive structural organization, and small vocabulary. They often used incomplete, short, and discontinuous sentences. Speaker's intention was not elaborated and left implicit. All in all, their communication was context-bound, and requires a lot of shared assumptions. The middle class children, in contrast, used a context-free language style that required no shared assumptions, taking very little for granted. Speaker's intention was explicit and well **elaborated**. A wide range of syntactic alternatives, flexible structural organizations, large vocabulary, and continuous, lengthy, and often complex sentences were used. They maintained proper pace, often taking time to think about what to say.

In 1971 Bernstein named the language style used by the middle class children the elaborate code, and the one used by the working class children the restricted code. Bernstein attributed the difference in code to the different family communication systems between the middle and working classes. Working class families were mostly positional families where the members were regarded as the occupants of certain family roles. This type of families therefore used a closed-communication system, in which what and how one could say were predetermined by their relative positions. The middle class families were mostly person-oriented families in which the members were regarded as unique persons. Thus, the family communication system was open, allowing anyone to say whatever and in whichever way they wanted to say.

Bernstein's work underwent a heavy criticism since it implied the working class language was inferior to the middle class language. Facing the charge of being a classist, Bernstein reoriented his theoretical focus from the desirability of the family communication system to the identity management of speech communities. Working class children used the **restricted** code not because their family communication system was inferior, but because their community was communal that emphasizes commonness, shared experiences and assumptions, high solidarity, and we-ness. In a closely-knit community, elaboration is not only unnecessary but also useless. To them, meanings are particular so that no matter how well you elaborate, the other may not understand you unless he/she shares the assumptions and experiences. The middle class lives in a community that values independence and individuality. Since this type of community subscribes to the principle of universal meaning, the belief that a meaning can be shared with anyone if it is well elaborated, speakers are expected to practice a context-free language style. Bernstein has never tried to apply his theory to differences across geographical cultures. However, his theory of code has conceptual affinity to one of the most frequently applied **dichotomies** in intercultural communication, high/low-context communication. In addition, his renewed theory, the identity management of a speech community by means of code-choice, influenced several generations of intercultural communication researchers, which I will discuss in the later part of this unit.

Address Terms, Power, and Intimacy

Different societies have different systems of structuring a relationship. **Egalitarian** societies precede the horizontal relationship (or intimacy or solidarity) to the vertical relationship (or power **disparity**). Brown and Gilman's work in 1960 is one of the earlier efforts to explain systematically how address terms and pronoun uses reflect the relational ideology of the given society. They differentiate between V-type and T-type pronouns. T-type pronouns are the descendants of Latin *TU*, which was a singular second person pronoun used to refer to addressees who are equal to or lower than the speaker. V-type pronouns are varieties of Latin *VOS*, which was originally a plural second person pronoun, but widely used to address a single person who was superior to the speaker.

In 1960 Brown and Gilman identify two different relational semantics: the power semantic of the traditional society and the solidarity semantic of the modern egalitarian society. The power semantic dictates the powerless to use *V* towards the powerful, who in turn use *T* to the powerless. It also encourages the equals among the upper class (nobles) to use *V* reciprocally and those of the lower class (commons) to **reciprocate** *T*. The egalitarian movement after the Great Enlightenment broke the class barrier and brought about the solidarity semantic, under which a mutual use of *T* signals a close relationship while a mutual use of *V* manifests a distant relationship. Brown and Gilman observe in 1960 that the solidarity semantic varies across cultures. German *T* is used more frequently within the family including more powerful and more remote members. French *T* is used to express the camaraderie of co-workers or fellow students. Italians combined French and German uses of *T*.

In 1972 Ervin-Tripp, based on Brown and Gilman's study in 1960, proposed flow-chart models of selecting appropriate address terms of several languages. In the U.S., individuals consider relational distance, power difference, kinship, gender, and age to reach a final decision. The Bisayan (Philippines) emphasizes relative rank, age difference, and friendship. To Koreans, relative rank precedes age and **solidarity**. In Yiddish, older ones receive deference despite familiarity. Irvin-Tripp's comparative study of the rules of selecting address terms shows that outsides Western Europe and North America, the power semantic still overpowers the solidarity semantic.

Japanese culture has a rich system of marking status difference. In 1981 Ishikawa et al.'s flow chart analysis of Japanese address system identified six different categories of address terms: kin terms, names, professional titles, post-designating terms (job title), pronouns, and **fictives** (symbolically used kin terms). Age, sex, and role relationships, which are hierarchical in nature, function as the key determinants of address terms. The complexity of the address terms and the hierarchical nature of selection reflect that the power semantic is overpowering the solidarity semantic in this culture. Chinese address system is also dominated by the power semantic. Kinship terms, age, and seniority play important roles. The use of professional or job titles is preferred over using names. Bates and Benigni reported in 1975 that age and social class play important roles in selecting address terms in Italian. Particularly, age differences bring about differences in status, which trigger non-reciprocal power semantic.

Language and Connectedness

Studies in sociolinguistics, language, and business communication have consistently reported individuals' group-identity influences their use of language. Goldstein and Tamura found in 1975 that, compared to Americans, Japanese are much more group-oriented. Japanese children gradually learn that family members are so interconnected that a family eventually forms a single linguistic unit. A child is not separated from their parents or siblings. To make oneself humble, they need to make their family members humble, too. Therefore, Japanese parents often refer to their children as "this humble child," which is an act of politeness towards outsiders. Koreans are not much different in this respect. They prefer to use "we," "our," and "us" instead of "I," "my," and "me" when they actually refer to oneself. Koreans use "our house" and "our wife" when they actually mean "my house" and "my wife." Since a wife cannot be shared even if a house can be, "our wife" does not make much sense as it is. However, considering it is only used to those outside of the marriage (not to brothers or parents) and often replaced by "the woman of our house," it must also have been invented to emphasize the unity of a nuclear family.

Some Western researchers, who use collectivism and holism interchangeably (e.g., Hofstede 1980), might argue that the group-orientedness displayed in Asian languages signals their emphasis on the collective identity. However, the "we-ness" in these languages reflects the holistic worldview rather than the collective identity. A collective identity is a sense of belonging to a collective, which comes and goes even if it can be strong at times. The holistic worldview that posters **holistic** cognition is a culture's fundamental understanding that the universe is composed of layers of organic wholes that are semi-permanent. The highest end of the whole is the universe itself and the lowest end is one's self. A family is a not a collection of separate selves, but an organic whole where individual selves are dissolved into. Thus, as a self is one unit, the family is a unit of a different order.

Members of the holistic culture tend to avoid separating others from themselves. Consequently, they have developed the speech habit not to use explicitly such identity markers as "I," "you," "we," and "they." The Korean and Japanese languages have developed into extreme sub-drop (or subject-drop) languages, which drop not only I or you, but any subject of a sentence. The Chinese, Persian, and Slavic languages also drop more often than not the pronouns when they are the subject of the sentence. Subject drop languages sometimes cause misunderstandings due to the lack of clarity. However, the users seem to be willing to lose efficiency in exchange for being appropriate.

Speech Acts and Conversational Analysis

The research in pragmatics, particularly the study on speech acts and conversational analysis, has produced a number of significant findings of cultural differences. A speech act is designed to accomplish a certain action goal of the speaker through its **illocutionary** and **perlocutionary** forces. For example, a request or order is intended to make the listener help accomplish what the speaker wants. An apology carries the speaker's regret so that the listener may know that speaker wishes to take responsibility for the possible offense. In a conversation, there are rules of preferred sequence, interaction order, or adjacency pair, which constraint the type of speech act to follow (as a response to) a given speech act. For an instance, a request or order is usually followed by an acceptance or rejection, while an apology is paired with acceptance-forgiveness or further accusation. Different cultures approach speech acts differently in several respects.

First of all, holistic cultures such as Asian, African, and Latin American cultures care more about a higher level of goals, while individualistic cultures focus more on a lower level of goals. Individuals engage themselves in a conversation with multiple goals. The lower level goal includes specific speech act goals comprising both illocutionary and perlocutionary forces. If one gains compliance from the other through a request, the other's initial acceptance of the request makes up the acceptance of the illocutionary force, and the other's follow-up actions to complete the compliance constitutes the acceptance of the perlocutionary force. The speech act goal of request comprises both the initial acceptance and the follow-up completion. The higher level of goal is not necessarily related to the specific speech act performed, but concerned with enduring needs and priorities such as maintaining one's own image or relationship with the other. When individuals attempt to gain compliance through a request, they need to select an appropriate strategy within the constraint of the higher level of goal. The tension between the lower and higher levels of goal is well-addressed by Brown and Levinson's model of politeness strategies in 1987. The lower level of goal is referred to as a local goal or action goal, and the higher level of goal as a global or relational goal. In the holistic society, the relationship takes priority over the contract. Therefore, holistic people care more about the relational or global goal over the specific speech act goal or local goal.

In any cultures, greetings and partings are not simply acts of acknowledging the other's presence or bidding a farewell; rather, they function to reinforce or strengthen the current relationship. However, the greeting and parting rituals are much more important in the relationship-oriented cultures than the deal-oriented culture. In the U.S., people tend to greet each other once for a given day, and when they are engaged in a conversation with another person, they tend not to greet a person who passes by. However, people in the holistic culture tend to greet each other every time they run into the other although the length and intensity of greeting might vary. They usually break a conversation with another person to greet a third person whom one or both of them know. Between friends, the greeting does not simply end as greeting but develops into a lengthy conversation full of questions asking each other's personal life. Expression of warmth and concern for the other is essential to the speech of greeting.

Chinese greeting expresses one's concern for the other's welfare by asking "Have you eaten?" or "What are you doing" or "Where are you going?" Partings are similar. Holistic people invest much more time and effort in parting. They may take a short walk together while parting, and asking each other to give their warmest regards to each other's family. In these cultures, a parting often includes a plan for a future get-together.

Most holistic cultures are sensitive to the status differences. Greeting and partings, therefore, need to reinforce the existing power relationships. Non-verbal behaviors such as bowing play important role in Japan and Korea. But verbal elements are also involved. Nonreciprocal use of T-type and V-type address terms reinforce the status difference. It is also common in these cultures that the subordinate ask about the health and general wellbeing of the superior, who in turn ask about the specific events or changes that happened to the subordinate recently. In 1996 Qian related Chinese greetings and partings to politeness, which reinforces the Confucian values on the relationships that are holistic and complementary. Thus, attending to the other's status is essential in Chinese greetings and partings.

In individualistic societies, people are always ready to say "thank you" to anyone doing a favor to them. Thanking is almost a routine behavior expected whenever a certain social exchange occurs in Northern America. In the holistic society, the "nominal" thanking does not occur as frequently. Sometimes, the person who is thanked resents the thanking because it effectively drives the person out of the whole where the thank-giver belongs. If both belong to the same whole, then there is no necessity to offer a routine thanking since both are one. Japanese often issues an apology when the other person does a favor. A routine apology can acknowledge the trouble the other person has gone through, not driving him or her away from the beneficiary. Lee and Park reported in 2011 that Koreans also prefer apologies to thanking as a proper response when they do a favor to others.

This does not mean that holists do not thank each other. They actually thank their neighbors, friends, parents, and teachers. When they express their thanks, they really mean it. Therefore, thanking does not end with a simple verbal expression. It usually accompanies special facial or bodily expressions of happiness, sincerity, affection, and so on. Often times thanking comes with a present. These show that thanking in the holistic society is not a routine and habitual reaction to the favor or service one has received. It is expression of their feeling of indebtedness. In 2008 and 2010, Ohashi analyzed Japanese ritual of *o-rei*, through which the **beneficiary** and the giver cooperatively achieve a symbolic settlement of a state of debt-credit equilibrium after a considerable favor or gift has been offered outside a family circle. The beneficiary bows with an utterance acknowledging his or her debt, and the giver reciprocates a bow with "no, no", which plays down his or her credit. *Orei* does not free the beneficiary from debt, but is a symbolic settlement that is necessary to care for each other's debt-sensitive face.

Whereas holists take thanking seriously, they tend to take apologizing much less seriously than individualists. Westerners are hesitant to admit that they are at fault because, under the contractual individualism, admitting one's wrongdoing may incur some legal or practical responsibilities. Americans rarely say, "I am sorry" or "I apologize." A vast majority of inconveniences they cause is dealt with by an "Excuse me." Politicians developed such an evasive expression as "it was unfortunate" or the term, "regretful acknowledgement" to evade the situation that requires an apology.

In the East, apology is perceived much more positively and personally, not legally. The holistic atmosphere calls for forgiveness when an apology has been issued, and healing follows. Thus, the consequence of apologizing in the holistic society is not incurring responsibility, but improving the relationship as well as one's own image. Under the Taoist and Confucian tradition, people are believed to be incomplete, and individuals' effort to improve themselves through self-critical reflection is commended. Thus, a person who admits his or her fault is thought to be mature and reflective. Mutual apologizing and both parties' claiming for their own fault can be frequently observed in these cultures, because an apology in this cultures is a sign of care and concern for the other person according to Sugimoto in 1997.

Compliments are also understood and performed differently across cultures. In English, a compliment is understood as a polite expression promoting solidarity rather than a real positive evaluation or praise. Some cultures have this type of positive politeness devices, but some other cultures do not. Japanese use *oseji* to refer to a polite act of praise, but the Korean language does not have any word for ritualized or polite form of praise. Koreans, therefore, do not distinguish compliments from a favorable judgment or an overt expression of approval.

As different cultures have different values, compliments target different aspects of a person. While a person's appearance is one of the most frequently complimented targets in America, one's ability and accomplishments are more frequently complimented in Japan. In responding to a compliment, Americans tend to agree with it although they do not simply accept it. Asians including Japanese, Koreans, Chinese and Indians tend to disagree or reject the compliment much more frequently to present themselves more to be moderate and humble. Tang and Zhang find in 2009 that Chinese students, compared to Australian **counterpart**, use fewer accepting and more evading or rejecting responses. Compared to Asians, Europeans such as Germans, Briton, and Spaniards tend to accept the compliment more readily.

In Asia, particularly in Korea, compliments are given mostly to equals. No matter how positive they may be, compliments still carry one's evaluation of the other's desirability. In cultures where status overpowers intimacy, the subordinate is not supposed to judge their superior. Thus, offering a compliment to or making an overt positive judgment of a superior is much more face-threatening than doing the same act to equals. The superior might take it as a flattery which is considered very negative in these societies or a bold action taken by an ill-advised youth.

Requests have been studied in relation to politeness and indirectness. Since direct requests or orders may offend the other by limiting his or her freedom, people often use indirect requests. For example, people may say, "Can I borrow a cup of flour?" instead of saying, "Give me a cup of flour, please." "Do you have a cup of flour I can borrow?" or "I ran out of flour!" can also be used. These utterances do not look like a request on the surface, but they are considered requests through the conventions. Brown and Levinson's work in 1987 on politeness strategies offers a systematic theory on selecting a proper speech act when a speaker needs to threaten the other's desire for self-determination.

All cultures use conventional indirectness. However, few specific forms are equivalent across cultures. The degrees of indirectness (or social meanings) carried by similar (or somewhat equivalent) category are different from culture to culture, and relative frequencies of using (or preference for) different strategies vary across cultures. An English politeness marker, "please," does not find its cross cultural match easily. French *s'il vous plait* is a close match, but German *bitte* has much more complex usage. Chinese *qing* and Japanese *kudasai* do not have such implication as "if you please." They simply carry the meaning that the speaker is asking for a favor.

When making requests, English speakers are known to be more indirect than most other language speakers. This indirectness should not be confused with indirectness in expressing one's own opinion or decision. Asians are much more indirect when they express their own feelings or preferences. However, in making requests, Britons and Americans are much more indirect. The reason is not that they are politer than others, but that the English language lacks the grammatical features to **compensate** for threats to face other than indirectness. Most Asian and African languages have honorific system built in the grammar. Most other European languages have at least V-type pronouns that can carry a certain degree of respect. However, English has no such grammatical scheme. Thus, politeness in English is heavily dependent upon indirectness devises such as convention-al indirectness and off-record strategies. This nature of English politeness leads Brown and Levinson, two British scholars, to propose in 1987 a model of politeness strategies revolving around the degree of indirectness.

Koreans and Japanese can go bald-on-record without any effort to mitigate face-threat if they choose a proper level of honorifics. Indirectness plays much more important roles between equals or towards subordinates, since honorifics are not applicable to them. Therefore, when translated to English, Asian requests may sound impolite because they are not indirect enough. Asians who are used to making direct requests in their honorifics-rich languages often make mistakes issuing the same kind of requests in English when they are traveling abroad. Native English-speaking sojourners in the Far East Asia often make the opposite mistakes.

The holistic people, as a recipient of a request, sometimes prefer a direct one to an indirect one. Individualists expect people to take care of themselves, so they do not want to be dependent upon others or bothered by others. However, holists believe that helping each other is a necessity. Thus, they are ready to help others and equally ready to owe. A direct request has two positive implications in the holistic society. First, the speaker is optimistic that the other will help, which implies that the speaker includes the other in the whole that he or she belongs to. Second, through a direct request, speakers signal they will "owe one" to the other, which means that they see the relationship as a relationship in which parties are mutually obliged to help one another.

The use of direct requests signaling relational closeness and willingness to **incur** debt is not limited to the Eastern culture. Félix-Brasdefer report in 2005 that contrary to Brown and Levinson's and Leech's predictions in 1987 and 1983 respectively, in Mexico, direct requests are situation-dependent and expected behavior in a solidarity politeness system. Also in German and Polish cultures, directness is not necessarily considered impolite, but is often seen as a way of expressing closeness and **affiliation**.

Rejecting the other's request is face-threatening in any culture. Particularly, in the holistic society where relationships are abundant, outright rejection is unimaginable unless the relationship is rock solid like family or "bosom buddy" relationships. Holists, therefore, attempt avoid saying "no" as much as possible. Japanese often use "it's hard" to mean "I can't help you." Koreans might nod or say unenthusiastic "yes" to mean "I know I have to help you. But, I may not be able to do so." Non-verbal cues in these cases transmit much more information than verbal messages.

Values of Speech, Silence and Argumentativeness

The Western society has a stronger faith in verbal communication. From early on, rhetoric and oratory have been studied and practiced. **Articulation** and eloquence have been believed to reflect the knowledgeability of the speaker, which is closely related to the credibility. The Greco-Roman philosophy and the Christian faith in words have contributed greatly to this tradition. The rest of the world does not put as much faith in speech. The Eastern society, influenced heavily by Taoism, Confucianism, and Buddhism, does not give much credit to speech. Laozi teaches, "No amount of words can fathom it: Better look for it within you" and "To talk little is natural. High winds do not last all morning." Although Confucius himself was an articulate and eloquent communicator, he had a strong faith in simplicity in manners and slowness of speech. He taught, "Fine words and an **insinuating** appearance are seldom associated with true virtue," which is directly opposite to the Greco-Roman tradition. Zen Buddhism goes even further to diminish the value of speech with the episode of "the flower sermon." In one occasion, Buddha had no words but held a lotus flower silently before his disciples, which confused greatly all of them except one who smiled at the flower. Then, Buddha gave the flower to this disciple, and said, "What can be said I have said to you, and what cannot be said, I have given to him." To Buddhists, the deepest truth cannot be communicated verbally.

The Eastern culture takes a holistic approach to communication. The words are only part of, and are inseparable from, the total communication. The total communication is more than Hall's concept of context in 1976, which basically limited to shared information stemming from the generic cultural knowledge and the specific interaction history. Total communication includes the behavioral elements that co-occur with verbalization on the part of the speaker, and the unique abilities or experiences on the part of the hearer.

For speakers, whether their words are being fulfilled by their actions is crucial. If their behavior betrays their words, then the words carry no meaning other than they should not be taken seriously. Koreans call such a person "flighty." For hearers, the ability to figure out the meaning, incorporating all available information and knowledge, is crucial. The burden of successful communication is not on the speaker but on the hearer. Those who are often slow to get the meaning of others are called "slow."

The reliance on total communication stems from the particularistic culture, or one with the belief in relativity. The holistic worldview in the East gave birth to the belief that one's situation varies based upon the position or role he or she is taking in the system of a whole. Zhuangzi, an ancient Taoist scholar, **expounds** it well. The universe is a whole without division. However, the development of human language that is fundamentally categorical has led people to cut up the world. When humans invent a category, the thing categorized stands apart from all other categories. Dependent upon what category one belongs to in the holistic network, one tends to see things differently, which subscribe to the principle of particularity of meaning.

Faith in relativism and **particularistic** nature of communication discourages Asians from making excessive efforts to make themselves understood against all the differences—unless others are in my shoes, they would not understand me; or if they are like me, they will know what I want to say even if I do not say anything. This belief in particular meanings lead Asians to keep silence whenever they feel uncomfortable to verbalize. In the East, silence then is not absence of communication, but a legitimate speech act. Silence carries a variety of meanings: agreement, disagreement, obedience, challenge, avoidance, space-giving, and so on.

Westerners become uneasy when silence prolongs between two acquaintances closely at presence to each other. In the East, two friends can sit side-by-side for hours not talking to each other. To Japanese, silence is a marker of close relationships, so that they become quieter as they become closer. Silence is understood as an eloquent speech act in many other cultures than the Eastern culture, including Akan, Igbo, Western Apache, Hebrew, and Greek. Particularly among Akan of Ghana, silence serves to regulate the social relationships among individuals according to position, status, gender, and age. Its major function is to show **reverence**, love, or awe. Among Akan people, like in the East, silence may signal agreement, a lack of interest, or a manifestation of injured feelings or contempt.

In contrast, argumentativeness, the willingness to engage in constructive persuasive debate, and **assertiveness**, the tendency to claim one's own rights without hampering others' rights, are higher in the European and North American cultures. The rhetorical sensitivity and individualistic tendency encourage Westerners to express their position clearly and eloquently.

Expressiveness and Emotion

The colorfulness of speech is another aspect that varies across cultures. Volubility and rich language are characteristic for everyday discussions in the cultures of Middle East. For the Arab culture, emphasis is on form over function, affect over accuracy, and image over meaning. While most cultures view language as a means for transferring meanings, Arabs see the role of their language as an art form and religious phenomenon, and tool of expressing their identity.

In 1995 Zaharna attributes the Arabic expressiveness partly to its oral dominant culture. The literate dominant society tends to rely on the factual accuracy of a message than its emotional resonance, and favor analytic reasoning over intuitive judgment. This contrasts to the logic of oral cultures, where a single anecdote can constitute adequate evidence for a conclusion and a specific person or act can embody the beliefs and ideals of the entire community. Speakers in oral cultures depend heavily on the involvement of their audience, which leads them to invent devices that can enhance audience rapport: repetition, formulaic expression, humor, exaggeration, parallelism, phonological elaboration, special vocabulary, puns, metaphor, and **hedge**.

Within the American society, African Americans are known to be much more colorful, intense, expressive, and emotional. European Americans have faith in individualism that guarantees others' respect for one's own opinion. Since these people just look for others' affirmation of their essential worth and dignity, they do not attempt to force others to agree with them. In African American culture, one's sense of selfhood is rooted in one's community. African American, therefore, does not seek individual dignity or respect, but desire the community's confirmation of one's authentic self, that is, audience involvement and **rapport**. In this respect, African Americans share a similar motivation with Arabs.

The mainstream American culture is much less expressive or emotional compared to the African American culture or the Arabic culture. Even less expressive or emotional a culture is Japan that has a strong rule of emotional display. The Japanese culture is often called the culture of considerateness: People are raised to suppress their individual desires or emotions not to bother others who value serenity.

▶ Conclusion

This essay has reviewed the development of the research on the cultural differences and similarities in verbal communication. Researchers over the past five to six decades have accumulated enough data to claim that people across cultures use different linguistic practices and communication styles. However, these differences are not distinct and pervasive enough to support rigid cultural dichotomies. One may say, "Japanese love to go low-context;" however, labeling the Eastern culture a high-context culture, opposite to the Western low-context culture, is an over-simplification. Cultures are different but they are not divided. **Disjunctive** approaches hinder intercultural communication by instilling stereotypes in people's mind.

On the other hand, overemphasizing the similarities, ignoring the differences, inevitably fosters ethnocentrism. Universalists tend to think their way is the most natural and right, and any deviation from it is a sign of primitiveness. The attempt to "manufacture" universal theories is to be misguided by the researcher's own cultural bias no matter how many others cultures are accounted for. For instance, Brown and Levinson's politeness theory in 1987 explores more than a dozen of languages other than English. The theory, however, has encountered a number of problems in explaining the majority of non-Western cultures. The cultural awareness should go both ways: We are different, yet we have a lot in common.

Applications

1. Verbal Communication Styles and Culture
Liu, M. (2016). Verbal communication styles and culture. *Oxford Research Encyclopedia of Communication*, 1-18. London: Oxford University Press.

Abstract: The differentiation between high-context and low-context communication by Edward T. Hall, in 1976 is used to understand human communication styles, verbally and non-verbally. Communication styles can be direct and indirect (whether messages reveal or camouflage the speaker's true intentions), self-enhancing and self-effacing (whether messages promote or deemphasize positive aspects of the self), and elaborate and understated (whether rich expressions or extensive use of silence, pauses, and understatements characterize the communication). These stylistic differences can be attributed to the different language structures and compositional styles in different cultures, as many studies supporting the Sapir-Whorf hypothesis have shown, which can become, in turn, a major source of misunderstanding, distrust, and conflict in intercultural communication. Understanding differences in communication styles and where these differences come from allows us to revise the interpretive frameworks we tend to use to evaluate culturally different others and is a crucial step toward gaining a greater understanding of ourselves and others.

Keywords: communication styles; cultural values; thinking styles; high-and low-context; communication accommodation

2. Translation as Intercultural Communication

Katan, D. (2011). Translation as intercultural communication. In M. Baker, & G. Saldanha (Eds.), *Routledge Encyclopedia of Translation Studies*, 74 – 91. New York, NY: Routledge.

Abstract: Translation as intercultural communication requires treating the text itself as only one of the cues of meaning. Other, "silent," "hidden" and "unconscious" factors, which when shared may be termed cultural, determine how a text will be understood. In translating, a new text will be created which will be read according to a different map or model of the world, through a series of different set of perception filters. Hence the need to mediate. The translator should be able to model the various worlds, through, for example, the Logical Levels model, and by switching perceptual positions gain a more complete picture of "What it is that is, could or should be, going on."

Keywords: translation; intercultural communication; cultural factors; perception filters; logical levels model

3. Incorporating Cross-Cultural Communication in ELT: A Pedagogical Approach

Suneetha, Y., Sundaravalli, G. M. (2011). Incorporating cross-cultural communication in ELT: A pedagogical approach. In R. Jaidew, M. L. Sadorra, W. J. Onn, L. M. Cherk, & B. P. Lorente (Eds.), *Global Perspectives, Local Initiatives: Reflections and Practices in ELT*, 123 – 132. Singapore: Center for English Language Communication, National University of Singapore.

Abstract: Cross-cultural communication has become ever more significant through the globalization of markets, affairs of nation-states and technologies. Consequently, the cultural quotient (CQ) is becoming increasingly important, especially in the context of the changing dynamics of work culture around the world. This paper makes a case for the need to pay attention to intercultural communication and discusses some specific approaches and strategies in the teaching of intercultural communication in the classroom. These approaches include addressing issues like learning to honor one's own culture and sharing it with others while developing a capacity to be open to other cultures. Other strategies include progressing from an ethnocentric to an ethno-relative state of understanding and acceptance of cultural differences and increasing one's ability to communicate with non-native speakers. Specifically, classroom practices and strategies suggested include intercultural explorations, use of texts, films, short stories and other multi-media resources, contrastive case studies of cultures, group encounters and role plays.

Keywords: cross-cultural communication; globalization; cultural quotient; teaching approaches and strategies; suggestions

Interactive Activities

1. Individually, please finish reading Text A, Text B, and the application abstracts and work out the meanings of the terms in bold type by consulting the dictionary whenever necessary.

2. In pairs, please summarize the content in 2 to 3 sentences of each sub-heading in the unit outlines of Text A and Text B based on your reading and understanding of the texts.

3. In groups, share your gains, comments and suggestions regarding the three application abstracts. Based on your interests, locate and finish reading the full-length papers of your interested abstracts.

4. Q&A: Questions are encouraged about any uncertain or confused part or parts in the unit and seek answers either from other fellow students or the instructor.

There is an urgent need for bilingual and bicultural talents in China today. Based on your language acquisition experiences in both Chinese and English, please share a specific, successful story on reaching the objective of becoming both bilingual and bicultural.

5. Complete the Personal Report of the Scale of Anti-Asian American Stereotypes, a scale designed to measure how you view Asian Americans. Take a few moments and complete the self-assessment for Unit 6.

6. To ensure satisfactory learning outcomes, please work out a detailed **outline critique** including the citation information in either APA or MLA, summary of the main ideas, critical comments, and provoking questions of either Text A or Text B. A sample is provided below.

Sample Outline Critique

Citation:
MLA style:
Tian, Dexin, and Chin-Chung Chao. "Strategies under Pressure: U.S.A-China Copyright Dispute." *Journal of Science and Technology Policy in China* 2 (2011): 219 – 37.
APA style:

Tian, D. X., & Chao, C. C. (2011). Strategies under pressure: U.S.A-China copyright dispute. *Journal of Science and Technology Policy in China*, 2(3), 219–237.

Summary:

This paper aims to explore the Chinese and U.S. efforts in keeping the balance of innovation and copyright protection, with an emphasis on China's strategies under Western, especially U.S. pressure. Under the theoretical guidance of strategies and tactics and via the research method of thematic analysis, the research findings are twofold. First, both the U.S.A and China used strategies for the calculation and manipulation of power in the enactment and implementation of their copyright laws. Second, in order to defend their own interests and obtain national advantages, both countries made full use of various tactics. It is promising for the large developing countries like China to implement and enforce their copyright law and other IPR regulations more effectively under global bargaining and collaborating.

Critique/Comments:

Strong Points: This is an interesting and valuable study. The authors have achieved their research findings based on thorough and extensive literature review and first-hand data from in-depth interviews. The theoretical frameworks prove helpful and the research results appear trustworthy, insightful, and instructional. Moreover, the research findings are also applicable to many other IPR disputes between developed and developing trade partners.

Weak Points: The study results are based on a snow-ball sampling of 45 participants as copyright holders and consumers just from China. It would have been better if the study had either broadened the sample size and diversity of participants from both China and the U.S.A or included quantitative methods as well to further clarify the relationships between innovation and copyright protection with empirical results.

Thought-Provoking Questions:

1.
2.
3.

UNIT SEVEN

Non-verbal Intercultural Communication

Readings

Text A The Non-verbal Code

After James W. Neuliep

Many linguists, psychologists, and sociologists believe that human language evolved from a system of nonlinguistic (non-verbal) communication. To these scholars, language and communication are not the same. Humans possess a host of nonlinguistic ways to communicate with each other through the use of their hands, arms, face, and personal space. When we combine verbal and non-verbal language, we create an intricate communication system through which humans come to know and understand each other. All animals communicate non-linguistically—that is non-verbally—through sight, sound, smell, or touch. **Moths**, for example, communicate by smell and color. Through smell, some species of male moths can detect female moths miles away. Elephants communicate with low-frequency sound waves undetectable by humans. Felines are well-known for rubbing their scent on (marking) people and objects to communicate their ownership of such property. This kind of animal or nonlinguistic communication is probably innate and invariant within a particular species. Most scholars also recognize that a significant portion of our non-verbal behavior, such as the expression of emotion, is innate and varies little across cultures. Like verbal language, however, much of our non-verbal communication is learned and varies across cultures.

This text investigates non-verbal communication and how it differs across cultures. It begins with some definitions of non-verbal communication and a discussion of how verbal and non-verbal codes differ. The chapter then outlines the various channels of non-verbal communication and how cultures differ regarding their use. These channels are kinesics, paralanguage, proxemics, haptics, olfactics, physical appearance and dress, and chronemics. The chapter closes with a discussion of non-verbal expectancy violation theory.

▶ Definitions of Non-verbal Communication

The study of non-verbal communication focuses on the messages people send to each other that do not contain words, such as messages sent through body motions; vocal qualities; and the use of time, space, artifacts, dress, and even smell. Communication with the body, called **kinesics**, consists of the use of the hands, arms, legs, and face to send messages. **Paralanguage**, or the use of the voice, refers to vocal characteristics such as volume, pitch, rate, and so forth. Through paralanguage, people communicate their emotional state, veracity, and sincerity. Most of us can identify when speakers are confident or nervous through their vocal pitch, rate, and pace. Through **chronemics**, the use of time, people can communicate status and punctuality. We saw earlier that cultures differ widely in their monochronic or polychronic orientation. By studying space or **proxemics**, we can learn how people express intimacy and power. In the United States, for example, people tend to prefer an "arm's length" distance from others during communication. Through smell, called **olfactics**, a person's ethnicity, social class, and status are communicated. Many cultures establish norms for acceptable and unacceptable scents associated with the human body. To other cultures, for example, people raised in the United States seem obsessed with deodorants, perfumes, soaps, and shampoos that mask natural body odors.

Linguist Deborah Tannen estimates that as much as 90 percent of all human communication is non-verbal, although other scholars argue that the percentage is much lower. During intercultural communication, verbal and non-verbal messages are sent simultaneously. Verbal communication represents the literal content of a message, whereas the non-verbal component communicates the style or how the message is to be interpreted. Hence, the non-verbal code often complements, accents, substitutes, repeats, or even contradicts the verbal message. For example, a speaker might complement the verbal message "This dinner is delicious!" with a smile and increased vocal volume. Politicians often accent their speeches by pounding their fists on podiums. When asked how many minutes are left to complete an exam, the professor might simply raise five fingers to substitute for the words "five minutes." Persons often repeat their verbal message "Yes" with affirmative head nodding.

Sometimes, however, a person's verbal and non-verbal messages contradict each other. When this happens, we usually believe the non-verbal message. For example, your roommate has been very quiet and reserved for a couple of days. Finally, you ask what is wrong. Your roommate replies with a long sigh and says, "Oh...nothing." Which do you believe, the verbal or the non-verbal message? Most people believe the non-verbal message because, unlike the verbal message, which requires conscious effort to encode, non-verbal messages are often less conscious and therefore are perceived as more honest. Psychologist David McNeill argues that our non-verbal behavior is partly unconscious and represents a sort of visual metaphor or analogue of conscious thought. He states that gestures and other body motions are primitive forms of speech. Whereas verbal language takes thought and puts it into linear digital form—that is, a sentence—gestures and body movements show the instantaneous thought itself as an analogue of the thought. This is why verbal communication is often called digital communication and non-verbal communication is called **analogic** communication. Because we have less control over our non-verbal behavior, it tends to be perceived as more honest than our verbal behavior.

In addition to complementing, accenting, substituting, repeating, and contradicting verbal communication, non-verbal communication also regulates and manages our conversations with others. Professors delivering lectures can monitor the reactions of their students through their eye contact, body posture, and other non-verbal behaviors (for example, yawning) and adapt their lectures accordingly. Students who raise their hands are signaling the professor that they have questions or comments. Such behavior manages the flow of communication in the classroom. Individually, we can regulate the flow and pace of a conversation by engaging in direct eye contact, affirmative head nodding, and stance, thus signaling our conversational partner to continue or stop the communication.

▶ The Relationship between Verbal and Non-verbal Codes

By comparing and contrasting the human verbal and non-verbal codes, many linguists have concluded that verbal language evolved from its nonlinguistic predecessor. Noam Chomsky argues that verbal language is an advanced and refined form of an inherited nonlinguistic (non-verbal) system. A key distinction between the two is that the verbal language system is based primarily on symbols, whereas the non-verbal system is signal based. The difference between a symbol and a signal is that a symbol is an arbitrarily selected and learned stimulus representing something else. A sign, or signal, however, is a natural and constituent part of that which it represents. For example, when we hear thunder in the distance, it signals us that a storm is approaching. The thunder is a sign of a storm. But the thunder is also an intrinsic part of the storm. Sweating, for example, signals that one may be hot, but sweating is a natural part of being hot, as is shivering of being cold. Humans do not learn to sweat or shiver. Unlike signals, symbols have no natural relationship with that which they represent; therefore, they are arbitrary abstractions and must be learned. For example, the symbol *cat* has no intrinsic connection with a feline animal. Speakers of any language learn to associate symbols with referents.

Another difference between the verbal and non-verbal code is that the non-verbal signal system is much more restrictive in sending capacity than the verbal code. For example, it is virtually impossible to communicate about the past or future through non-verbal communication. You might be able to signal a friend of impending danger by waving your hands, but you cannot warn your friend of danger that might occur tomorrow or recall danger that occurred yesterday with non-verbal signals. In addition, communication of negation is practically impossible with the non-verbal code system. Try communicating to a friend non-verbally that you are not going to the grocery store tomorrow. The same task is relatively easy through the linguistic system, however.

Formal versus Informal Code Systems

In the previous unit, verbal language was defined as a systematic set of sounds combined with a set of rules for the sole purpose of communication. All verbal languages have a formal set of sounds, syntax, and semantics. The degree of formality of verbal language is not found in the non-verbal code, however. The alphabets of most verbal languages in the world represent about forty sounds. No such formalized alphabet exists for non-verbal codes. Different types of non-verbal behavior can be categorized, but these categories are much more loosely defined than in the verbal code. All verbal languages have a set of rules, called grammar or syntax that prescribes how to combine the various sounds of the language into meaningful units, such as words and sentences. Although there are rules governing the use of non-verbal communication, a formal grammar or syntax does not exist. Nowhere is there a book or guide prescribing exactly what non-verbal behavior should be used when and where. There is no doubt that certain social contexts prescribe certain non-verbal behaviors, such as a handshake when greeting someone in the United States, but no systematic rule book on the same level of formality as an English grammar book exists for non-verbal communication. The rules for non-verbal communication are learned informally through socialization and vary considerably, even **intraculturally**. Finally, the verbal code, when used with the correct syntax, takes on denotative meaning. When using verbal language, if we hear a word that we do not understand, we can quickly go to a dictionary that will define the word for us. The dictionary tells us what the language means. No such device exists for our non-verbal communication. If someone touches us, or stands too close, or engages in prolonged eye contact, we can only surmise its meaning. Popular psychology notwithstanding, we have no dictionary for non-verbal communication. To be sure, non-verbal communication is meaningful, perhaps even more meaningful than verbal communication, but the denotative meaning of the non-verbal act must be inferred.

Channels of Non-verbal Communication

The closest thing the non-verbal code has to an alphabet is a gross classification system of the various channels though which non-verbal communication is sent. These channels are kinesics, paralanguage, proxemics, haptics, olfactics, physical appearance and dress, and chronemics. As we will see later in this chapter, some non-verbal expressions, particularly some facial expressions of emotion, seem to be universal, but much of our non-verbal behavior is learned and is therefore culturally unique.

Kinesics

Kinesic behavior, or body movement, includes gestures, hand and arm movements, leg movements, facial expressions, eye gaze and blinking, and stance or posture. Although just about any part of the body can be used for communicating non-verbally, the face, hands, and arms are the primary kinesic channels through which non-verbal messages are sent. Relative to other body parts, they have a high sending capacity, especially the face.

The most widely recognized system for classifying kinesic channels was developed by Paul Ekman and Wallace Friesen. Together, they organized kinesic behavior into five broad categories: (a) **emblems**, (b) illustrators, (c) affect displays, (d) regulators, and (e) adaptors. The meaning behind most of these kinesic behaviors varies across cultures.

Emblems and Illustrators. Emblems are primarily (though not exclusively) hand gestures that have a direct literal verbal translation. In the United States, the hand gesture used to represent "peace" is an example of a widely recognized emblem. Dane Archer asserts that emblems are a rich channel of communication. Moreover, he maintains that emblems are often subtle yet filled with precise meaning. People in different cultures use different emblems, yet within any culture there is usually a high level of agreement on a particular emblem's meaning. To a stranger, however, a culture's favorite emblem is probably meaningless.

Whereas emblems are primarily hand gestures that have a direct verbal translation, **illustrators** are typically hand and arm movements that accompany speech or function to accent or complement what is being said. Pounding your fist on the podium during a speech is an illustrator. Illustrators serve a **meta-communicative** function—that is, they are messages about messages. They are non-verbal messages that tell us how to interpret verbal messages. Shaking your fist at someone while expressing anger is an illustrator.

For the most part, emblems and illustrators are not taught in school but are learned informally through a child's socialization in his or her culture. By six months, babies in all cultures begin to use gestures to communicate to their parents.

Dane Archer maintains that emblems and illustrators are at least 2,500 years old and can be seen in the ancient artwork of various cultures. Archer asserts that the systematic study of gestures began about 400 years ago, during Shakespeare's time. Although cultures differ widely in their use of emblems and illustrators, people in most cultures tend to use them for the same kinds of communication situations. For example, most cultures use emblems and illustrators during greetings and departures, to insult or to utter obscenities to others, to indicate fight or flight, and to designate friendly or romantic relationships.

Greeting rituals are an important component in any person's communicative **repertoire**. To know the greetings of different cultures when interacting outside your own culture is a first step toward developing intercultural communication competence. In high-context and collectivistic cultures, greeting rituals often differ according to one's social status. Moreover, in some cultures, men and women have different rules for how to greet someone. Bowing is the customary greeting in Korea and other Asian cultures, such as Japan and Vietnam. When Koreans greet elders, professors, persons of power, and persons of higher status than themselves, they bow lower and longer and divert eye contact. When businesspeople or friends meet, the bow is generally shorter and quicker. In Japan, the appropriate bow is with the hands sliding down toward the knees, back and neck stiff, and eyes averted. As in other Asian cultures, bowing recognizes social stratification. Social subordinates should bow lower and longer than their superiors. Persons of equal status match bows unless one is younger, in which case the younger person should bow a shade lower and longer. The eyes should always be lowered.

In addition to bowing as a greeting, Japanese businesspeople typically exchange business cards. The exchange is indispensable in order to **commence** formal communication with each other. The business card communicates the group to which the person belongs and the rank of the person. Great care and time should be spent examining another's card, and only when a meeting is finished can the card be put away into a shirt or coat pocket (but never into a pants pocket, as that shows disrespect). When receiving the card of a Japanese businessperson, one should take the card with both hands, as a sign of respect.

Micro-cultural groups in the United States have unique greetings as well. Moellendorf notes that although most Amish generally will not initiate greetings with strangers or non-Amish persons, many Amish will respond to an outsider's wave by pointing their index finger toward the sky. The raised finger points to heaven and shows respect to non-Amish while revealing the Amish people's strong religious beliefs.

As in the United States, the handshake is a common gesture/illustrator during a greeting in most parts of developed Kenya. In this case, however, when greeting a person of higher status, such as a teacher, the person of lower status should take the left hand (the hand not being used in the hand-shake) and grasp his or her own right arm somewhere in the proximity of the forearm during the shake. According to Axtell, the handshake is a common greeting in China as well. The traditional Chinese greeting is to cup one's hands (left over right), place them about chest high, and raise them while bowing. According to Bishop, when greeting a holy man or priest, East Indians bow slightly or kneel with their hands pressed together palm to palm in front of their chests. This shows ultimate respect for the higher castes. Harris and Moran report that when greeting male friends in Saudi Arabia, Saudi men kiss both cheeks of the friend. They prefer to get very close during the greeting. The cheek-kissing ritual is practiced in other Middle Eastern cultures as well. The Arab handshake feels loose compared with the firm handshake practiced in many Western cultures. In traditional Sri Lanka greetings, the hands are placed together, palms touching at the chin level, and the person bows slightly and says "*Namaste*," which means "I salute the Godlike qualities in you."

Archer has observed that many cultures have emblems and illustrators for insulting others and for communicating obscenities. According to Archer, some cultures may have as many as six or seven obscene gestures, whereas some northern European cultures, such as the Netherlands and Norway, do not have any native obscene gestures. Giving someone "the finger" (making a fist with the hand and extending the middle finger upward) is a widely recognized obscene gesture in many parts of the world, including the United States, Mexico, and much of Europe. Forming a "V" with the index finger and middle fingers with the palm facing in is vulgar in Australia and England, communicating the same intent as "the finger." Creating the very same gesture with the palm facing out is completely acceptable, however, and represents "V for victory." In the Ladino culture of Guatemala, a hand gesture called the *la mano caliente* ("the hot hand") is equivalent to "the finger" and is created by placing the thumb between the first and middle fingers then squeezing the hand to make a fist [see Figure 7.1(a)]. This gesture is considered obscene in other Central and South American cultures as well. In the Ladino culture, however, this gesture is very offensive, and anyone using it should be prepared to fight. If a person were to use the *mano caliente* to a military or police officer, the offender could expect to spend time in jail or do hard labor in the army. The same hand gesture is used in Hmong culture to belittle or insult someone. In the Hmong culture, only males use this gesture. In Jamaica, this gesture is called "the fig" and is considered obscene there also.

In Peru, making a pistol gesture with each hand and then pointing the "pistols" at someone from about waist level is considered obscene and may provoke a fight [see Figure 7.1(b)]. In Iran, putting an open hand directly in front of and horizontal to one's face with the palm facing in and rubbing the hand down over the face from about the eyes to the chin, almost as if stroking a beard, is considered **obscene** [see Figure 7.1(c)]. An obscene gesture recognized in many European cultures, especially France, is taking either hand, palm down, and putting it on the biceps of the opposite arm while quickly raising the opposite arm and making a fist in one fluid motion [see Figure 7.1(d)]. This gesture is basically equivalent to "the Finger" and to the verbal **designate** "Up yours."

UNIT SEVEN
Non-verbal Intercultural Communication

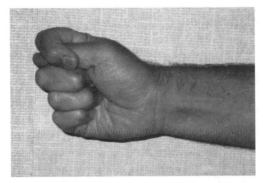
(a) An Offensive Gesture in the Latino Culture of Guatemala

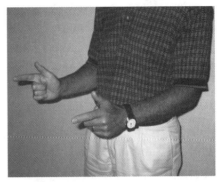
(b) A Highly Offensive Gesture in Peru

(c) The Iranian Equivalent to "the Finger"

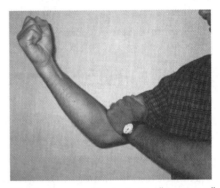
(d) The European Equivalent to "the Finger"

Figure 7.1 Non-verbal Codes Using Hands

Archer contends that gestures communicating "I am afraid" or "I want to fight you" (that is, fight or flight) are uncommon in the United States but occur with some regularity across cultures. In Mexico and Nepal, placing a hand with the palm up, fingers extended upward while moving in and out touching the thumb is an invitation to fight. In Japan, putting the index fingers on the temples of the head, as in making horns, is a sign that one is angry. In China, pretending to pull up one's sleeve with the hand of the opposite arm designates that one is ready to fight. In Hmong culture, clapping one's hands during an argument is a signal to the opponent that it is time to fight. The gesture is usually reserved for very intense situations in which someone intends to harm the other.

Most cultures use emblems and illustrators to designate friendly and/or romantic relationships. In the United States, for example, crossing the index and middle fingers of the same hand designates closeness and communicates, "We're close" or "We're tight." In China, clasping the index fingers from each hand together signals love or romance. In Thailand, pressing the palms of both hands together and placing them against a cheek (as in a "Sleeping Beauty" gesture) is indicative of romance. Tapping the tips of the index fingers together in Japan, or extending both index fingers parallel at waist level in Mexico, communicates that someone is in love.

Affect Displays: Facial Expressions of Emotion. Knapp and Hall point out that perhaps more than any other part of the body, the face has the highest non-verbal sending capacity. Through facial expressions, we can communicate our personality; open and close channels of communication; complement or qualify other non-verbal behavior; and, perhaps more than anything, communicate emotional states.

Many linguists believe that our verbal language evolved from a system of nonlinguistic communication that was inherited from our animal past. If this is a valid assumption, then we should expect that some forms of our non-verbal communication would be invariant across cultures. Current evidence suggests that some facial expressions of emotion, called affect displays, are universal. Paul Ekman alleges that humans can make more than 10,000 facial expressions, and that 2,000 to 3,000 of them have to do with emotion. Ekman is careful to point out that by studying faces, we cannot tell what people are thinking, only what they are feeling about what they are thinking. Initially, Ekman believed that affect displays, like so many other forms of communication, were the result of learning and were culturally unique. He originally agreed with sociologist Ray Birdwhistell, who wrote,

> Just as there are no universal words, no sound complexes, which carry the same meaning the world over, there are no body movements, facial expressions, or gestures which provoke identical responses the world over.

In contrast to Birdwhistell, other scholars hypothesized that because they were inherited, human non-verbal expressions would be similar, if not universal, the world over. The basis of this argument can be found in the writings of evolutionary scholar Charles Darwin, who wrote,

> We can thus also understand the fact that the young and the old of widely different races, both with man and animals, express the same state of mind by the same movements... I have **endeavored** to show in considerable detail that all the chief expressions exhibited by man are the same throughout the world. This fact is interesting, as it affords a new argument in favor of the several races being descended from a single parent-stock, which must have been almost completely human in structure, and to a large extent in mind, before the period at which the races diverged from each other.

The late Harvard University professor Stephen Jay Gould, well known for his stance on evolution, agrees with Darwin and argues that although universal facial expressions may have been functional for the animals from whom we inherited them, they are not functional for us today. Take, for example, a facial expression of anger, in which a person snarls, grits his or her teeth, and displays the **canine** teeth. This facial expression is remarkably similar to expressions of anger in several animal species. The fact that there is no need for us to display our teeth in order to express anger (we can simply say how angry we are) suggests that such a gesture must have been inherited.

Ekman was determined to find whether certain elements of facial behavior are universal or culturally specific. He and his colleagues believed that there may be distinctive movements of the face for the primary emotions of surprise, fear, anger, disgust, happiness, and sadness that are probably universal. They further argued that while people from divergent cultures may express emotions similarly, what stimulates the emotion and the intensity with which it is expressed is probably culturally specific. In other words, although Germans and Japanese may express fear, surprise, anger, happiness, disgust, and sadness similarly in terms of muscular facial expressions, what **elicits** fear in Germans may be different from what elicits fear in Japanese. Moreover, cultures may differ in how they manage and regulate facial expressions of emotion, particularly in the presence of others.

Ekman and Friesen (among others) have conducted numerous studies testing their hypotheses. In one study, Ekman, Friesen, and a number of their associates had more than 500 participants from ten different countries look at slides of people expressing the six emotions of fear, anger, happiness, disgust, sadness, and surprise. The participants in the study came from a variety of cultures the world over: Estonia, Italy, Germany, Japan, China, Scotland, Sumatra, Turkey, Greece, and the United States. Participants were shown photographs of Caucasians in posed facial expressions of the six different emotions, one at a time for ten seconds each, and were instructed to indicate which of the six emotions was presented. The participants were also asked to rate the intensity of the presented emotion on a scale of 1 to 8. The results showed that in the overwhelming number of trials, the emotion rated strongest by the largest number of observers in each culture was the predicted emotion. Where cultures differed was in their ratings of intensity of the emotion. Ekman reasoned that perhaps people judge a foreigner's expressions to be less intense than expressions shown by members of their own culture, or that attributions of less intense emotions to foreigners might be due more to uncertainty about the emotional state of a person from an unfamiliar culture. In interpreting these results, Izard claims that there appears to be an evolutionary and biological relationship between facial expressions and certain emotional states, but that this connection can be uncoupled by the human capacity to exercise voluntary control over innate emotional expressions.

Although Ekman's studies provide evidence that facial expressions of primary emotions appear to be universal, other data suggest that cultural influences, such as individualism and collectivism, play a role in the expression of emotion. Stephan and De Vargas found that persons from individualistic cultures express emotions affirming independent self-conceptions, such as self-actualized, capable, self-satisfied, and proud of oneself. They also found that persons from collectivistic cultures were less comfortable expressing negative emotions than persons from individualistic cultures.

In related research, Schimmack found that persons from individualistic cultures are better able to recognize happiness than collectivists, and that persons from high-uncertainty-avoidant cultures were less accurate in the recognition of facial expressions of fear and sadness than persons with low uncertainty avoidance. Matsumoto alleges that high-uncertainty-avoidant cultures create social institutions to deal with fear and therefore recognize this emotion less well. Along similar lines, Pittam, Kroonenberg, Gallois, and Iwawaki found that Australians were rated as more expressive by Japanese, and that Japanese may conceptualize emotions as less intense.

Cross-Racial Recognition of Faces. Most of us have heard statements such as "I can't tell one Japanese from another ... they all look alike!" Although this statement smacks of racism and ignorance, scientific evidence indicates that own-race identifications tend to be more accurate, by as much as 10 percent to 15 percent, than cross-race identifications. Own-race identifications are those in which we identify someone of the same race as our own. Cross-race identifications are those in which we identify people from a race different from our own. Legal scholars have expressed a concern over an own-race recognition bias in eyewitness identification for some time. In fact, Feingold argued nearly ninety years ago that it is well known that, other things being equal, individuals of a given race are distinguishable from each other in proportion to our familiarity, to our contact with the race as a whole. Thus, to the uninitiated American, all **Asiatics** look alike, whereas to the Asiatic, all White people look alike.

Experts in the field of eyewitness memory and about half of potential jurors endorse the belief that cross-racial identifications are less reliable than same-race identifications. This **presumption** is based on the belief in the existence of an own-race bias—that is, that people recognize people of their own race better than people of another race. Brigham and Malpass note that the own-race recognition bias has been demonstrated among Whites, Blacks, Asians, Latinos, and Hispanics. Explanations for this phenomenon vary. Some evidence shows that persons who have close friends of the other race show less of an own-race recognition bias. Moreover, Ferman and Entwistle found that children living in mixed-race environments show less of an own-race recognition bias than children living in a segregated environment. Conversely, other research indicates that the own-race recognition bias is not reduced by frequent contact with the other race and that prejudiced persons are no more likely to exhibit an own-race recognition bias than nonprejudiced persons. There is some evidence indicating that persons who view other-race faces tend to focus on the constituent (individual) features of the face, whereas observers of same-race faces focus on **configural** features of the face.

Regulators. Non-verbal regulators are those behaviors and actions that govern, direct, and/or manage conversation. During conversations in the United States, for example, direct eye contact and affirmative head nodding typically communicate agreement or that a conversant understands what is being communicated. How close one stands to another during a conversation can also signal to the conversant whether to continue the communication. Rules for direct eye contact and distance during communication vary considerably across cultures. In many Asian cultures, such as the Republic of Korea, Vietnam, and Japan, direct eye contact is prohibited between persons of differing status. In these cultures, the person of lower status avoids making direct eye contact with his or her superior as a sign of respect. Direct eye contact in these cultures can communicate insolence or signal a challenge to the person of higher status. In the Republic of Korea, when people of higher status hand something to a person of lower status (for example, a professor handing something to a student), the person of lower status accepts whatever is handed with both hands, gives a slight nod of the head, and averts eye contact during the act, all as a sign of recognizing the status differential.

Communicator distance during conversation can also govern the flow of communication. According to Almaney and Alwan, in some Middle Eastern cultures, people stand very close together during interaction to smell each other's breath. To smell one another is considered desirable. In fact, to deny someone your breath communicates shame. Harris and Moran point out that in many Arab cultures, men hold hands as they converse to demonstrate their trust in each other. During conversation, a raising of the eyebrows or a clicking of the tongue signifies a negative response and a disruption in the flow of communication.

Adaptors. Adaptors are kinesic actions that satisfy physiological or psychological needs. Scratching an itch satisfies a physiological need, whereas tapping the tip of your pen on the desk while waiting for the professor to deliver a final exam satisfies a psychological need. Very little, if any, cross-cultural research on adaptors has been conducted. For the most part, adaptors are not learned and probably do not vary much across cultures.

Paralanguage

Paralanguage refers to vocal qualities that usually, though not necessarily, accompany speech. Knapp and Hall divide paralanguage into two broad categories: voice qualities and vocalizations. Paralinguistic voice qualities include pitch, rhythm, tempo, articulation, and resonance of the voice. Paralinguistic vocalizations include laughing, crying, sighing, belching, swallowing, clearing of the throat, snoring, and so forth. Other paralinguistic vocalizations are intensity and **nonfluencies**, such as "um," "ah," and "uh." Silence is also considered within the domain of paralanguage.

Often, paralinguistic qualities, vocalizations, and nonfluencies reveal a speaker's emotional state and/or veracity. Audiences can discern when speakers are nervous or confident by listening to their tone of voice, rhythm, pace, and number of nonfluencies. Parents often detect a child's deception not so much by what the child says but by how it is said. Through paralanguage we can tell whether speakers are being genuine, cynical, or sarcastic. Moreover, a person's geographical origin can be determined by listening closely to his or her paralanguage.

In all spoken languages, vocal sounds are carried by vowels; it is impossible to speak words without them. Consonants, on the other hand, function to stop and start sound. Linguist Peter Ladefoged has observed that although there are perhaps as many as nine hundred consonants and two hundred vowels in all the world's languages, many languages tend to use only five vowel sounds. In fact, one in five languages uses the same vowel sounds as used in Spanish and English—*a*, *e*, *i*, *o*, and *u*—although there are variations on their pronunciation. According to Ladefoged, although there are literally thousands of speech sounds that any human is capable of making, only a few hundred sounds have ever been observed among the world's spoken languages. The average language uses only about forty sounds, and all babies are capable of making all of them. All babies, the world over, make the same sounds during infancy. Linguists believe that these sounds are the building blocks by which infants construct mature sounds. Although infants have not yet learned the specific language of their culture and have not yet spoken a single word, they practice the sounds of all human languages. All babies regularly produce a small subset of universal syllable types that occur in all of the world's languages. This is strong evidence that human language was not invented by humans but rather evolved. To be sure, unusual sounds show up in some languages. Clicking sounds, for example, can be heard in South Africa's Zulu and Xhosa languages, and nasal sounds are heard in Eskimo languages. And although these sounds may be unique components of these languages, all human babies, regardless of culture, can be heard making them at some time prior to learning their culture's formal verbal language.

Some languages, called tonal languages, rely on vocalized tones to communicate meaning. In these languages, a rising or falling tone changes the meaning of a word. Thai is a **pentatonal** language that uses five tones: monotone, low, falling, high, and rising. Modern Vietnamese is a monosyllabic language, meaning that all words are only one syllable long. Like the Thai language, Vietnamese is tonal, and the meaning of the syllable changes with tone. The Chinese language is tonal also. Mandarin Chinese, the most common language in China, is based on four or five tones. Every syllable in Mandarin has its definite tone. The first tone, called *yinping*, is a high-pitched tone without variation from beginning to end. The syllable is spoken with an even tone, using the highest pitch of the speaker's voice. The second tone, *yangping*, starts from a lower pitch and ends high. The syllable is spoken with a rising tone, not unlike speakers of English asking a question. The third tone, *shangsheng*, is perhaps the most difficult to master. It begins as a middle-level tone, goes down, bounds up, and ends with a relatively higher pitch. The fourth tone, *qusheng*, is a falling tone that starts high and ends at the lowest range of the speaker's voice. The fifth tone, *qingsheng*, is often left out of descriptions of Mandarin. This tone is spoken very quickly and lightly, as if it has no one. *Qingsheng* is often called the neutral tone.

To be sure, English and other languages have inflections—that is, a change in pitch on certain words and sentences. English speakers can communicate anger or sadness by changing the pitch of their voice. Without the appropriate inflection, the meaning of an English speaker's sentence can be misinterpreted. In Chinese, however, tones completely change the meaning of a word. Take, for example, the word *ma*. In the first tone, *ma* is "mother." In the second tone, *ma* becomes "hemp" or "grass." In the third tone, *ma* becomes "horse," and in the fourth tone, *ma* becomes "to scold" or "to nag." In Mandarin Chinese, the meanings of words are strictly based on the tones, which remain constant in whispering, yelling, or even singing. Mandarin tones are relative to the natural pitch of the speaker. A deep-voiced man's high note may be much lower than the high note of a woman.

As with any other form of communication, some paralinguistic devices are learned and vary across cultures. People from the Republic of Korea are taught to avoid talking or laughing loudly in any situation; such behavior is seen as rude and unbecoming since it tends to draw attention. Many of them, especially women, cover their mouths when laughing.

In their study of paralanguage, Zukerman and Miyake introduce the idea of a vocal attractiveness stereotype. They contend that, like one's physical attractiveness, individuals perceived to be vocally attractive elicit more favorable impressions than those not perceived to be vocally attractive. The results of their study indicate that attractive voices are those that are relatively loud, resonant, and articulate. Unattractive voices are squeaky, nasal, monotone, and off-pitched. Zukerman and Miyake found some sex differences in vocal attractiveness. For example, **throatiness** was perceived more negatively among female voices than among male voices.

Silence is a part of the paralinguistic channel. Hasegawa and Gudykunst maintain that silence is the lack of verbal communication or the absence of sound. Hasegawa and Gudykunst assert that culture influences the meaning and use of style. In their research, they compared the use of silence among Japanese and Americans and found that, in the United States, silence is defined as pause, break, empty space, or lack of verbal communication. Hasegawa and

Gudykunst maintain that silence generally is not a part of Americans' everyday communication routines. They argue that although silence is acceptable among intimate others, when meeting strangers, Americans are very conscious of silence and find it quite awkward. In Japan, however, silence is a space or pause during verbal communication that has important meaning. Pauses, or silence, are to be interpreted carefully. Stylistically, Japanese are taught to be indirect and sometimes ambiguous to maintain harmony. Silence, then, can be used to avoid directness, such as bluntly saying "no" to a request.

Charles Braithwaite has studied silence across cultures and argues that silence is a central non-verbal component of any speech community. He argues that some communicative functions of silence may be universal and do not vary across cultures. For example, Braithwaite maintains that among Native American groups, Japanese, Japanese-Americans in Hawaii, and people in rural Appalachia, the use of silence as a communicative act is associated with communication situations where the status of the interactants is uncertain, unpredictable, or ambiguous. In addition, Braithwaite argues that silence as a communicative act is associated with communication situations where there is a known and unequal distribution of power among interactants. In other words, when interactants consciously recognize their differential status, they consciously use silence. Braithwaite cites evidence of this in many cultures, including the Anang of southwestern Nigeria, the Wolof of Senegal, the Maori of New Zealand, the Malagasy in Madagascar, urban African-American women, and some working-class White Americans.

Proxemics

Proxemics refers to the perception and use of space, including **territoriality** and personal space. Territoriality refers to physical geographical space; personal space refers to perceptual or psychological space—sometimes thought of as the "bubble" of space that humans carry with them in their day-to-day activities. In cultures whose population density is high, personal space and territoriality are highly valued. Privacy in densely populated locations is often accomplished psychologically rather than physiologically. In Calcutta, India, for example, there are nearly eighty thousand persons per square mile. There is literally not enough room in the city to claim any personal space. Touching and bumping into others while walking through the streets of Calcutta is quite common and to be expected.

Socioeconomic factors can also affect a culture's perception of space. Cramped and insufficient housing is common in much of Sri Lanka. In the 1980s most housing units were quite small. Thirty-three percent of the homes had only one room, 33 percent had two rooms, and only 20 percent had three rooms. Moreover, the average number of persons per home was five. (Overcrowding in Sri Lanka is declining, however, since the government initiated intensive housing programs in the 1990s).

The Moroccan perception of space reflects the culture's valuing of community. Personal space during a conversation is typically less than an arm's length. In mosques, worshipers line up shoulder to shoulder to pray. Houses typically have very little space between them as well. Because Kenyan culture values harmony and sharing, Kenyans tend to be less aware of personal territory than people in the United States. For example, many Kenyans do not designate specific rooms in the home for specific activities, such as a living room or a dining room. In addition, the personal space distance between interactants is much closer than in the United States. Saudi Arabians, too, are known to have closer personal space than Americans. Saudis typically enjoy getting very close, face to face, and engaging in direct eye contact. Many other studies support the link between culture and proxemic behavior in comparing Americans with Arabs, Latin Americans, Pakistanis, Germans, Italians, Japanese, and Venezuelans. These examples suggest that culture plays a decisive role in how spatial distances are maintained during communication. Other variables besides culture can affect proxemic distances, however, such as the age and sex of the interactants, the nature of the relationship, the environment, and ethnicity. Several studies have documented that in most cultures, the need for personal space increases with age. In addition, the use of space as influenced by sex seems to vary significantly by culture.

Haptics

Haptics, or tactile communication, refers to the use of touch. Mark Knapp argues that touch may be the most primitive form of communication. In the United States, much research has been conducted to examine the impact of touching during the first few years of life. Haptic communication varies widely across cultures, and the amount and kind of touch varies with the age, sex, situation, and relationship of the people involved. In his theorizing about culture and non-verbal communication, Edward T. Hall distinguishes between contact and noncontact cultures. Contact cultures are those that tend to encourage touching and engage in touching more frequently than either moderate-contact or noncontact cultures, in which touching occurs less frequently and is generally discouraged. Many South and Central American cultures are considered contact countries, as are many southern European countries. The United States is regarded as a moderate-contact culture, whereas many Asian countries are considered noncontact. Many Asian cultures have established norms that forbid public displays of affection and intimacy that involve touch. One of the five central tenets of Confucian philosophy is the division between the sexes. Because Confucianism is so central to many Asian cultures, engaging in touch with the opposite sex is considered uncivil. In their field study of touch patterns among cross-sex couples, McDaniel and Andersen observed the touch behavior of couples in airports. They found that couples from the United States touched most, followed by (in order of most to least touching) couples from Northern Europe, Caribbean/Latins, Southeast Asia, and Northeast Asia. Psychologist Sidney Jourard conducted a study that counted the frequency of body contact between couples as they sat in cafés in different cities and countries. He found that the average number of touches per hour in San Juan, Puerto Rico, was 180; in Paris, 110; in Gainesville, Florida, 2; and in London, 0.

Because we are often taught not to touch others, some people develop touch avoidance. These people feel uncomfortable in situations requiring touch and generally avoid touching when possible. In her study of Americans, Japanese, Puerto Ricans, and Koreans, Beth Casteel found no touch avoidance differences in same-sex dyads for the Japanese and Americans, in that both were significantly more touch-avoidant than same-sex dyads in Puerto Rico and Korea. In opposite-sex dyads, however, Japanese and Koreans showed much higher levels of touch avoidance than Americans and Puerto Ricans. Casteel concluded that the Japanese and Americans allow women to touch other women, but men should not touch men. Koreans and Puerto Ricans are just the reverse.

In their comparison of high-contact cultures of southern Europe and low-contact cultures of northern Europe, psychologists Remland, Jones, and Brinkman found that more touch was observed among Italian and Greek dyads than among English, French, and Dutch dyads. The people of northern Italy have few inhibitions about personal space and touch. Heterosexual men are often seen kissing each other on both cheeks and walking together arm in arm, as are women. East Indians are very expressive with touch. To touch the feet of elders is a sign of respect. Indians demonstrate their trust for one another by holding hands briefly during a conversation or religious activity. When a Hindu priest blesses others at religious gatherings, he gently touches the palms of their outstretched hands. Saudi Arabians tend to value touching also. Saudi businessmen often hold hands as a sign of trust, a form of touch behavior that some Americans often misunderstand. Saudi women, however, are never to be touched in public.

Most cultures prohibit some forms of touch. Harris and Moran observe that in Thailand, Sri Lanka, and some other cultures, the head is considered sacred and should not be touched by others. Americans sometimes make the mistake of patting children of other cultures on the top of the head as a sign of affection or endearment. In some cultures, this is seen as a serious breach of etiquette.

In many African and Middle Eastern cultures, the use of the left hand is forbidden in certain social situations. In Kenya, Indonesia, and Pakistan, for example, the left hand should not be used in eating or serving food. Harris and Moran report that in Kenya, the left hand is considered weak and unimportant. Sometimes, Kenyans intentionally use the left hand when serving food to someone they disrespect. In other cultures, such as Iraq and Iran, the left hand is used for cleaning and bodily functions and should never be used to give or receive gifts or other objects.

Like proxemics, the nature of touch is often mediated by more than culture. The relationship between the interactants, the location and duration of touch, the relative pressure of the touch, the environment in which the touch occurs (public or private), and whether the touch is intentional or accidental influence touch across cultures.

Olfactics

Probably the least understood, yet most fascinating, of all human sensations is **olfactics**—that is, our sense of smell. Our lack of understanding is certainly not because we lack a sense of smell. According to Gibbons, humans can detect as many as ten thousand different compounds by smell. Moreover, approximately 1 percent of our genes are devoted to detecting odors. Although this may not seem like much, humans have more olfactory genes than any other type of gene identified in human and mammalian DNA. Gibbons suggests that our lack of understanding may be because we lack a vocabulary for smell and are discouraged from talking about smell. Particularly in the United States, we have become obsessed with masking certain smells, especially those of the human body. According to Gibbons, the biggest users of fragrance in the world are U.S.-based companies like Procter & Gamble, Lever Bros., and Colgate. Some brands of soap use more than 2 million pounds of fragrance a year. In many Western cultures, body odor is regarded as unpleasant and distasteful, and we go to great efforts to mask or remove it.

David Stoddart asserts that in addition to their ability to detect odors, humans are even more adept at producing odors. According to Stoddart, evidence from anatomy, chemistry, and psychology indicates that humans are the most highly scented of all the apes. Human scent comes from two types of glands that lie beneath the skin, the sebaceous **glands** and the apocrine glands. Sebaceous glands are all over the body wherever there are hair follicles. They produce an odorous oily fluid whose original purpose was to protect hair. The apocrine glands are a type of sweat gland. They are most dense in our armpits but are also found in the pubic and anal regions, the face, the scalp, and the umbilical region of the abdomen (the belly button). Women appear to have more apocrine glands than men, but some evidence suggests that their glands are less active than those in men. The most distasteful odors come from the apocrine glands, which are activated when we are frightened, excited, or aroused. Human **saliva** and urine also produce human scent.

According to Kohl and Francoeur, research has repeatedly shown that women perceive odors differently at various phases of their menstrual cycles. They tend to be the most sensitive to odors during ovulation. Other studies indicate that when in close proximity to each other over time, as in dormitory living, women synchronize their menstrual cycles. Scientists believe that axillary organ secretions function as odor cues to stimulate their cycles.

Kohl and Francoeur suggest that although preferences for certain smells seem to vary across cultures, there appears to be a universal preference for some kinds of scents that may have biological and evolutionary roots. These preferences are probably mediated by culture to some extent, however. For example, the finest perfumes in the world contain olfactory hints of urine. Scientists allege that these scents function as sex attractants. We know, for example, that sex-attractant pheromones are expelled from the body in urine. These two kinds of smell may mirror those of our humanoid ancestors and unconsciously stimulate the deepest parts of the brain.

In addition to functioning as a sex attractant, smell is also used politically for marking social class distinctions. Classen, Howes, and Synnott contend that smell plays a significant role in the construction of power relations in many societies. Le Guerer comments, for example, that idiomatic expressions often employ smell-related terms to voice antagonism toward others. People refer to persons they dislike as "stinkers." When we are suspicious of someone, we say we "smell a rat." When something seems wrong or amiss, we comment that "it doesn't smell right" or "smells fishy." Dishonest politicians may "reek of hypocrisy."

Anthony Synnott claims that odor is often used to categorize groups of people into status, power, and moral classes. To be sure, the smells themselves are not intrinsically moral or immoral, but the qualities or thoughts attributed to the specific scents are what give them their moral significance. Synott argues that a person's scent is not only an individual emission and a moral statement, but also a perceived social attribute that is significant especially for members of subordinate groups, who are often labeled "smelly." Such labels often foster racial, ethnic, and religious prejudice and hatred. Subordinate and micro-cultural groups are often described as possessing negative olfactory characteristics. In fact, Synnott argues that perceived foul odors legitimize inequalities and are one of the criteria by which a negative identity is imposed on a particular class or race. Many cultures establish norms for acceptable and unacceptable scents associated with the human body. When individuals or groups of people fail to fit into the realm of acceptability, their odor signals that something is "wrong" with them, either physically or mentally. Kohl and Francoeur note that the American Puritan tradition of "cleanliness is next to godliness" may explain the American obsession with deodorants, perfumes, soaps, and shampoos. Muslims believe that cleanliness of the body and purity of the soul are related.

Social class distinctions based on smells are the cultural product of education, religion, parenting, and social pressure from peers. With the exception of those scents that appeal to everyone, people are conditioned to find certain scents attractive and others dirty or foul. Moreover, such distinctions sustain social barriers between groups and even justify a dominant group's persecution of subordinate groups. In the Middle Ages, wealthy people bought perfumes to diminish the scent of the lower classes. Nineteenth-century Japanese described European traders as *bata-kusai*—"**stinks** of butter." Adolf Hitler's hatred of Jews was based partially on olfactics; he claimed that their foul odor was representative of their "moral mildew" and reflected their outer and inner foulness, and therefore their immorality. Gibbons reports that during World War I and World War II, German and English soldiers claimed they could identify the enemy by their smell. Similar claims have been made by North Vietnamese and U.S. troops. Baker reports that in U.S. history, Thomas Jefferson is purported to have said that Blacks have "a very strong and disagreeable odor." Dollard claims that many White racists used the "disagreeable scent" of Blacks as a final proof of the impossibility of close association between the races. In 1912, sociologist Georg Simmel wrote, "It would appear impossible for the black people ever to be accepted into high society in North America because of his bodily odor." Indeed, Simmel concluded that "the moral ideal of harmony and equality between the different classes and races runs up against the brick wall of an invincible disgust inspired by the sense of smell."

Classen, Howes, and Synnott maintain that more than any other group, women are stereotyped and classified by their scent. Historically, in many cultures, women were considered the fragrant sex, unless they were prostitutes or **suffragettes** or challenged the male-dominated social order. The role of fragrance was primarily to entice men. In general, the Western cultural axiom has been that, unless perfumed, women stink. Jonathan Swift's poem *The Lady's Dressing Room* expresses this belief:

His foul imagination links

Each Dame he sees with all her Stinks;

And, if unsavory Odours fly,

Conceives a Lady standing by.

Although it may be the least studied of all the senses, social scientists are discovering that olfactory sensation is a potent influence on social interaction. Survey data indicate that a significant percentage of adults are conscious of and influenced by smells in their environment. In their poll of more than 350 American adults, the Olfactory Research Fund found that 64 percent of respondents indicated that smell greatly influenced the quality of their lives. Specifically, 76 percent of the respondents reported that the sense of smell was "very important" in their daily relationships with persons of the opposite sex, and 20 percent indicated that it was "somewhat important." Seventy-four percent indicated that smell was "very important," and 22 percent said that it was "somewhat important" in their relationships with their spouses. Although the percentages dropped somewhat, 36 percent of the respondents indicated that smell was "important" in their relationships with friends, and 40 percent agreed that smell was "very important" in their relationships with co-workers. Eighty percent of the respondents reported using environmental fragrances, such as potpourri, room sprays, and scented candles. Well over 60 percent of respondents believed that particular aromas enhance the quality of life, relieve stress, and help retrieve memories. Of those respondents who used cologne, perfume, or aftershave, 83 percent said they did so because they liked the scent, 68 percent said it made them feel better about themselves, 56 percent said it enhanced their sense of well-being, 51 percent said they used fragrances to make themselves more romantically attractive to others, and 46 percent said they used fragrances to make a fashion statement.

  This emphasis on smell is often motivated by the pivotal role olfactics play in the maintenance of social relationships. Todrank, Byrnes, Wrzesniewski, and Rozin assert that most cultures assign meaning to odors that is often displaced onto the people wearing them. This is especially evident in relationships with members of the opposite sex. Although it is widely recognized that odors play a determinant role in the mating practices of many animal species, Kohl and Francoeur argue that odors are also an important ingredient in human mating and bonding and cite empirical evidence showing that odors hasten puberty, mediate women's menstrual cycles, and even influence sexual orientation. Extant research indicates that odors help people identify their family members, facilitate the bond between parents and children, and influence how often and with whom individuals mate.

  Kate Fox is a social anthropologist and the Director of the Social Issues Research Center in Oxford, England. Fox has studied cultural differences inolfactics, with a special emphasis on non-Western cultures. Fox maintains that, unlike most Western cultures, smell is "the emperor of the senses" in many cultures. For example, Fox describes the importance of smell among the Ongee people of the Andaman Islands, a group of islands off the southeast coast of India. According to Fox, much of Ongee cultural life revolves around smell. For example, their calendar is based on the smell of flowers that bloom at different times of the year. One's personal identity is defined by smell. Fox writes that to refer to oneself, an Ongee touches the tip of his or her nose, which is a gesture meaning both "me" and "my smell." Fox also reports that during greetings, Ongee routinely ask "How is your nose?" rather than "How are you?" Ongee etiquette prescribes that if a person responds that he or she feels "heavy with smell," the greeter should inhale deeply to remove the excess smell. Conversely, if the greeted person indicates that he or she is short of smell energy, Ongee etiquette prescribes that the greeter contribute some extra scent by blowing on him or her.

  Fox also describes smell rituals among the Bororo peoples of Brazil and the Serer Ndut of Senegal (Western Africa). Among the Bororo, personal body smell indicates the life force of the individual, whereas one's breath odor indicates the state of one's soul. The Ndut believe that individuals possess a physical smell, defined by one's body and breath odor, and a spiritual smell.

The spiritual smell is thought to be a reincarnated smell. For example, the Ndut can tell which ancestor has been reincarnated by associating the smell of a child to that of a deceased person.

In her olfactic research, Fox has discovered that among those cultures where smell is so closely associated with one's personal identity, the exchange or mixing of odors among people is carefully prescribed. For example, among the Amazonian Desana, members of a particular tribal group are thought to share a similar odor. Marriage is only allowed between people of different odors; that is, between members of different tribal groups. Similarly, among the Batek Negrito of the Malay Peninsula, people of similar odor groups are prohibited from even sitting too close to one another. The Batek Negrito believe that the prolonged mixing of similar odors causes illness in the people themselves and any children they may conceive.

Fox also writes that Western smell preferences are not universal. For example, the Dassanetch, a tribal cattle-raising group in Ethiopia, believe that the smell of cows is the most pleasing of all smells. Dassanetch men routinely wash their hands in cattle urine and smear their bodies with cattle manure. Such smells are associated with status and fertility. The Dogon people of Mali find the scent of onions very attractive, especially for young men and women, who rub fried onions all over their bodies.

Physical Appearance and Dress

Often, we can identify a person's culture by his or her physical appearance and dress. Communication with another is often preceded by visual observations of the other's physical appearance. Moreover, in most cultures, people consciously manipulate their physical appearance to communicate their identity. Most cultures have strict rules for how their members should present themselves. To violate a culture's prescriptions for appearance may result in negative sanctions. In many cultures, a person's physical appearance and dress communicate the person's age, sex, and status within the culture.

In virtually every culture, men and women dress differently, and in many cultures, the differences begin at birth. In the United States, for example, male infants are traditionally dressed in blue and female infants are dressed in pink. In the Masai culture of Kenya, the distinction between young girls and women is communicated through body artifacts. According to Vandehey, Buerger, and Krueger, Masai women wear specific necklaces and earrings to designate their marital status. For a married woman to be seen without her earrings may bring harsh physical punishment from her husband. Masai men wear earrings and arm rings that designate social status. The specific earring distinguishes the man as an elder or warrior. Other body ornaments communicate whether a Masai (male or female) has been circumcised.

Harris and Moran observe that in India, businessmen wear a *dhoti*, a single piece of white cloth about five yards long and three feet wide that wraps around their lower body. Long shirts are worn on the upper part of the body. Most Indian women wear a *sari* and blouse. A *sari* consists of several yards of lightweight cloth draped so that one end forms a skirt and the other a head and shoulder covering. It is not acceptable for women to show skin above the knees or a large portion of the back. Wearing clothes that are in any way revealing is discouraged because it may unintentionally communicate "a loose woman."

In Japan, the kimono—a long robe with wide sleeves—is the traditional clothing for both men and women; it is traditionally worn with a broad sash, or *obi*, as an outer garment. The specific design of the kimono varies according to one's sex, age, marital status, the time of year, and the occasion. In the ancient past, there was no distinction between a man's and a woman's kimono. Today, there are several types of kimonos worn by men, women, and children. Men typically wear kimonos of blue, black, brown, gray, or white. Women's kimonos are the most elaborate and varied in style and design. The fabric, cut, color, sleeve length, and the details of the *obi* vary according to a woman's age, social status, marital status, and the season. During the summer months, women wear *yukatas*, or lightweight cotton kimonos. Many Japanese hotels provide *yukatas* for guests to wear in their rooms. In Japan, on "7-5-3 Day" (November 15), boys who are three or five years old and girls who are three or seven years old dress up in kimonos to pray at the temples. There is also a special day for all girls and all boys to go to the temple: March 3 is Girls' Day and May 5 is Boys' Day. Kimonos are worn on these days as well.

▶ Non-verbal Expectancy Violations Theory

Judee Burgoon has formalized a theory of non-verbal communication called the non-verbal expectancy violation theory (NEV). The basic premise of the theory is that people hold expectancies about the appropriateness of the non-verbal behaviors of others. These expectations are learned and culturally driven. For example, in the United States, people expect to shake hands when they are introduced to someone. Burgoon posits that occasionally people violate non-verbal expectations. When this happens, the violation produces arousal, which can be physiological or cognitive and either positive or negative. Burgoon maintains that once a violation has been committed and arousal is triggered, the recipient evaluates the violation and the violator. Violations initiated by highly attractive sources may be evaluated positively, whereas those initiated by unattractive sources may be evaluated negatively. The very same violation may produce very different evaluations, depending on who committed it. The evaluation of the violation depends on (a) the evaluation of the communicator, (b) implicit messages associated with the violation, and (c) evaluations of the act itself. In presenting the theory, Burgoon outlines several key assumptions (see Table 7.1).

Burgoon bases Assumption 1 on literature from anthropology, sociology, and psychology, indicating that humans are a social species with a biological/survival instinct to be with other humans. Conversely, humans cannot tolerate extended physical contact with, or excessive closeness with, others; that is, humans have a basic need to insulate themselves from others and a need for privacy. Although this first assumption appears to be universal, the degree to which a person feels the need to be with others or insulated from them is probably culturally driven. Individualists may be more comfortable alone in the same situations in which a collectivist feels uncomfortable. Moreover, the way in which a person satisfies the need for privacy or affiliation certainly varies across cultures. In the United States and Germany, for example, privacy is often satisfied by physical separation from others (for example, closed doors), whereas in densely populated cultures such as India, privacy may be fulfilled psychologically.

UNIT SEVEN
Non-verbal Intercultural Communication

Table 7.1 Fundamental Assumptions of the Non-verbal Expectancy Violation Theory

> **Assumption 1**: Humans have two competing needs, a need for affiliation and a need for personal space (or distance). These two needs cannot be satisfied at once.
>
> **Assumption 2**: The desire for affiliation may be elicited or magnified by the presence of rewards in the communication context. The rewards may be biological or social.
>
> **Assumption 3**: The greater the degree to which a person or situation is defined as rewarding, the greater the tendency for others to approach that person or situation; the greater the degree to which a person or situation is defined as punishing, the greater the tendency for others to avoid that person or situation.
>
> **Assumption 4**: Hunmans are able to perceive gradations in distance.
>
> **Assumption 5**: Human interaction patterns, including personal space or distance patterns, are normative.
>
> **Assumption 6**: Humans may develop idiosyncratic behavior patterns that differ from the social norms.
>
> **Assumption 7**: In any commuication context, the norms are a function of three classes of factors: (a) characteristics of the interactants, (b) features of the interaction itself, and (c) features of the immediate physical environment.
>
> **Assumption 8**: Interactants develop expectations about the communication behavior of others. Consequently, they are able to recognize or at least respond differently to normative versus deviant behaviors on the part of others.
>
> **Assumption 9**: Deviations from expectations have arousal value.
>
> **Assumption 10**: Interactants make evaluations of others.
>
> **Assumption 11**: Evaluations are influenced by the degree to which the other is perceived as rewarding such that a positively valued message is only rewarding if the source is highly regarded and a negatively valued message is only punishing if the source is not highly regarded.

Assumption 2 indicates that affiliation for others is triggered by rewards within the communicative context. These rewards may be biological (food, sex, safety) or social (belonging, esteem, status). Biological needs are no doubt universal, but social needs are often learned and vary across cultures. Belonging needs are felt much more strongly in collectivistic cultures than in individualistic ones. Conversely, esteem needs are more strongly felt in individualistic cultures than in collectivistic ones. Assumption 3 extends Assumption 2 by stating that humans are attracted torewarding situations and repelled by punishing situations. This phenomenon is probably universal, but it should be noted that what people deem rewarding and punishing varies across cultures.

Assumption 4 asserts that humans have the perceptual ability to discern differences in spatial relationships. We can tell when someone is standing close to us or far away from us. Assumption 5 deals with the establishment of normative non-verbal behaviors. Normative behavior is that which is usual or typical, or that follows a regular pattern. For example, the lecture style of your professor is probably consistent day after day. The professor has established a normative way of delivering his or her material. Many normative behaviors are established by society and culture. In the United States, for example, saying "good-bye" is a normative way of terminating a telephone conversation.

Assumption 6 recognizes that even though most of us follow similar normative rules and regulations for our verbal and non-verbal behavior, we also develop our own personal style of interaction that is unique in some way. Assumption 7 states that norms operate as a function of the interactants, the interaction, and the environment. Characteristics of the interactants might include their sex, age, personality, and race. Characteristics of the interaction itself might include status differences or degree of intimacy between the interactants. Finally, characteristics of the environment may include the physical features of the setting, such as furniture arrangement, lighting, or even temperature.

Assumption 8 deals with the notion of expectancies, a key element of the theory. Burgoon argues that during interaction, interactants develop expectancies and preferences about the behaviors of others. These expectancies are anticipations of others' behavior that are perceived to be appropriate for the situation. Typically, expectancies are based on a combination of societal and cultural norms. For example, students expect that their professors will behave in an appropriate and consistent manner. In certain cases, however, students might expect idiosyncratic deviations from the norms for particular professors (for example, a certain professor frequently tells jokes in class).

Assumption 9 focuses on two other key ingredients in the theory, violation of expectancies and arousal. Burgoon subscribes to the notion that when a person's non-verbal expectancies are violated, the person becomes aroused. The violation tends to stimulate the receiver/communicator's attention and to arouse either adaptive or defensive reactions. For example, we learned earlier in this chapter that in some cultures (for example, Korea), touching the top of a child's head is prohibited. To do so would be a violation of expectancy, and the child or the parents might respond negatively or defensively. In some situations, however, some violations are perceived positively. A shaman may be allowed to touch the top of a child's head, and such behavior may be perceived positively.

Assumption 10 states that people make value judgments about others. Assumption 11 extends this notion by specifying how evaluations are made. Burgoon contends that the first factor influencing the positive or negative evaluation of a violation is the communicator reward valence—that is, how much the violator is perceived as someone with whom it is desirable to interact. Thus, communicator reward valence is based on communicator and relationship characteristics (age, sex, personality, status, reputation, **anticipated** future interaction) and interactional behaviors (style, positive feedback). Communicator reward valence influences how one will evaluate the violation of expectancies. Burgoon's theory holds that more favorable evaluations will be given when the violation is committed by a high-reward person than when it is committed by a low-reward person. If someone to whom you are attracted stands very close to you at a party, much closer than is normative, you may interpret this violation positively as a sign of mutual attraction or affiliation. Conversely, if someone by whom you are repulsed stands too close to you at a party, you may evaluate this violation quite negatively.

Burgoon asserts that positively evaluated violations produce favorable communication patterns and consequences, whereas negatively evaluated violations produce unfavorable communication patterns. In addition, Burgoon contends that even extreme violations, if committed by a high-reward person, can be evaluated positively and produce reciprocal communication patterns. Although a significant number of studies support the assumptions of Burgoon's theory, very few, if any, have investigated its cross-cultural applicability.

UNIT SEVEN
Non-verbal Intercultural Communication

▶ Cultural Contexts and Non-verbal Expectancies

As we have seen throughout this book, the cultures of Japan and the United States differ significantly. Japan is a collectivistic, high-context culture, whereas the United States is an individualistic, low-context culture. Individualistic cultures stress the importance of an individual's unique identity. Emphasis is placed on individual goals over group goals. From an early age, American children are taught that they are individuals with unique abilities and talents. People are rewarded for being "the best," "the one and only," and "number one" in whatever they do. The goal of Americans is to be the best that they can be and to strive for the top. A well-known cliché in the United States goes that "the **squeaky** wheel gets the grease," meaning that in order to get attention or to have one's needs met, one must draw attention to oneself.

In contrast, collectivistic cultures place precedence on group goals over individual goals. Collectivist cultures emphasize values that serve the ingroup by subordinating personal goals for the sake of the ingroup. Group activities are dominant and pervasive. Responsibility is shared, and accountability is collective. Japan has an unofficial motto that reads, "*Deru kugi wa utareru*," or "The tallest nail gets hammered down." Children are taught at a young age that their identity is based on their relationship within the group (family or business). Group leadership, rather than individual initiative, is valued. However, especially among Japanese youth, a new sense of individualism is growing in Japan.

A high-context culture, such as Japan, is one whose members are highly sensitive to the perceptual, socio-relational, and environmental contexts for information. High-context cultures have a restricted code system (language). Members do not rely on verbal communication as their main source of information. Silence and non-verbal behavior are most informative. Statements or actions of affection are rare. Members are quite adept at decoding non-verbal behavior. Japanese, for example, expect others (that is, Japanese) to understand the unarticulated communication. Cultural members are expected to know how to perform in various situations where the guidelines are implicit.

Members of a low context culture, such as the United States, are less sensitive to the perceptual, socio-relational, and environmental contexts. That is not to say that they ignore the environment—they are simply less aware of it than are members of a high-context culture. A low-context communication is one in which the mass of information is found in the explicit code. Hence, low-context cultures have an elaborated code system. Verbal messages are extremely important when information to be shared with others is coded in the verbal message. Members of low-context cultures do not perceive the environment as a source of information. Guidelines and expectations are frequently explained explicitly. In addition to high-context/low-context distinctions between the two countries, Japan is considered a low-contact culture, whereas the United States is considered a moderate contact culture.

Many of the communicative behaviors of high/low context, individualistic/collectivistic, and high-/low-contact cultures are different, and the interactants will inevitably violate each other's expectations regarding appropriate non-verbal behavior.

▶ An Intercultural Conversation: Violation of Non-verbal Expectancies

In the following two scenarios, Jim, Akira, and Mitsuko interact. Akira and Mitsuko are exchange students from Japan who are spending a semester studying at an American college. Jim is an American student at the same college. Notice how each violates the others' expectations without realizing it. When reading the scenes, keep in mind the different cultural orientations and the assumptions of non-verbal expectancy violation theory.

Jim and Akira are at a party.

1. Jim: (Nudges Akira and says loudly) This is a great party, eh?
2. Akira: (Is startled—stands back—tries to put some distance between himself and Jim) Yes, thank you.
3. Jim: (Leaning forward toward Akira, with direct eye contact) If you want to meet some girls, I could introduce you.
4. Akira: (Shocked by such an offer, he backs away) But I don't know them. They might be upset.
5. Jim: Well, how else are you going to meet them?
6. Akira: (Uncomfortable) Maybe during a class or something.

Mitsuko, another Japanese exchange student, approaches Jim and Akira. She knows Akira, but not Jim.

7. Mitsuko: Hello, Akira. (Bows slightly and looks down)
8. Akira: Ah, Mitsuko, this is my friend Jim.
9. Jim: Hi! (Forward leaning into her space)
10. Mitsuko: Hi, Jim. (Bows slightly and does not make direct eye contact)
11. Jim: Are you two friends? (Wonders why she won't look at him, thinks to himself, "Well, I'm not one of them. She probably thinks I'm ugly.")
12. Akira: Yes, we know each other.

A long pause ensues.

13. Jim: (Thinks to himself, "This is going nowhere—I've got to think of something to say." He speaks rather loudly.)

Great party, hey guys?

Akira and Mitsuko both jump back.

14. Akira: (Thinks to himself, "This guy is too weird!") Yeah, this is fun.

During this scenario, Jim violates Akira's kinesic, proxemic, paralinguistic, and haptic expectations. Several of the axioms and propositions from Burgoon's NEV theory can be applied to this interaction. Notice in Lines 1 through 4 that Akira perceives that Jim is standing too close, talking too loud, and thus backs away. From Akira's point of view, Jim violated his proxemic and paralinguistic expectations. In Line 1 Jim touches Akira, which probably violated Akira's non-verbal expectations regarding haptics. From Jim's vantage point, Akira violated his expectations as well, by not looking at him and not responding to his offer that he introduces him to women.

According to NEV theory, violations have arousal value (Assumption 9). Throughout the dialogue we can see how Akira and Jim became aroused (shocked, uncomfortable, startled, annoyed) by each other's violations. Both Mitsuko and Akira jump when Jim yells, "Great party, hey guys?" In Lines 13 and 14 we can see how Burgoon's Assumption 10 applies in that the arousal leads to evaluations ("This is going nowhere," "This guy is too weird"). In this case, the evaluations are negative.

According to the theory, the greater the degree to which a person is perceived as rewarding, the greater the tendency for others to approach that person. Likewise, the greater the degree to which a person is perceived as punishing, the greater the tendency for others to avoid that person. Unfortunately for Akira, because he is in a "foreign" country, he will be the more likely of the two to change his behavior to conform to the expectations of others.

Summary

Many social scientists believe that our verbal language evolved from a system of nonlinguistic communication that we inherited from our animal predecessors. As humans we possess a host of nonlinguistic ways to communicate with each other through the use of kinesics, proxemics, paralanguage, haptics, olfactics, and physical appearance. Our non-verbal communication, when combined with verbal language, creates a very complicated communication system through which humans come to know and understand each other.

Our non-verbal behavior is innate and learned. Many of our unconscious behaviors, such as the expression of emotions, are universal. People from all cultures express anger, happiness, and sadness the very same way. Yet other forms of non-verbal communication, such as gestures, are unique **manifestations** of our culture's distinctive cosmos. We learn how to communicate with our bodies (kinesics) through the use of space (proxemics), by touching others (haptics), with our voice (paralanguage), with smell (olfactics), and through the way we dress and present ourselves. Sometimes, our non-verbal behaviors violate the expectations of others. Sometimes, we stand too close or touch too much. When this happens, the other person evaluates the violation as positive or negative depending on whether we are perceived as attractive or unattractive. If we are thought of as attractive, our violation may be welcome. If we are perceived as unattractive, the same violation may be evaluated quite negatively.

Text B A Cultural Look at Non-verbal Cues

After Valerie Manusov

Introduction

Scholarship on non-verbal signs or cues as relevant to this unit can be categorized as cultural, cross-cultural, or intercultural. Studies that are classified as cultural tend to take a more qualitative and in-depth approach that describes patterns of behaviors and meanings associated with the behaviors or other cues within a cultural context. The culture may be a national one (e.g., Japanese) or one that represents an identifiable cultural collective (e.g., Cherokee), or it may be a group within a larger culture or region based on, for example, ethnicity, age, location, gender, or occupation (e.g., youth in Armenia). This research often comes from an Ethnography of Communication tradition and refers typically to the study of speech communities and their cultural codes. Studies that are classified as cross-cultural compare two or more cultural groups (e.g., Lao to Thai or Latino-Americans to African-Americans) and their potentially differential use of the same cues (e.g., proximity norms, touch behavior) or, less often, the meaning for those cues. Intercultural work is defined as research centering on people from different cultural groups talking with one another and investigates the ways in which the behavior of members of the groups is aligned or distinct and/or whether the interactants interpret what goes on between them in the same or different ways that may influence the interaction.

In this text, I overview the types of work that have been done looking at culture and non-verbal cues and try to provide some useful ways to organize different bodies of scholarship. I also emphasize places in which the innate nature of non-verbal cues is superseded by, interacts with, and exists outside of cultural patterns. I start with the communicative functions that appear to be enacted differently across cultures through non-verbal means. I next discuss some of the ways in which latent values as described in cultural dimensions have been found to differentiate culture members' cues from one another. Finally, I offer a brief discussion of some of the scholarship that suggests specifically what may occur—often creating problems—when people from different cultures interact with one another. This review is necessarily incomplete, but hopefully it will guide the reader to exemplars that help speak to the full body of scholarship as well as provide some new means for organizing this work.

The Functions of Non-verbal Behavior

As can be seen, an array of cues can take on sign value and/or be part of the rule system in a culture, often reflecting what is important within that culture and what worldview it holds. But it is useful to go beyond the cues to deeper processes. One of the largest bodies of research by non-verbal scholars—usually outside the intercultural context—identifies the functions that non-verbal behavior serves for people. Functions can be defined as "the communication-related activities" that our behavior helps us with, and they include such things as persuading another, impression formation, and expressing emotions. Several reviews of these functions have been written. Within the intercultural literature, however, certain functions appear as particularly noteworthy, although the research itself seldom references itself this way. The primary functions that are revealed as important within this scholarship are emotional expression, coordinating interaction, relational messages, and identity management.

Emotional Expression

Perhaps more than any other area of scholarship, the ways in which people express and interpret emotions within and across cultures have been scrutinized. Early work focused on finding out whether people across highly disparate cultures could identify (and in some cases express) emotions in the same way. Although controversial for its methodology, Ekman and his colleagues found support for several basic emotions (usually anger, disgust, fear, joy, sadness, and surprise) that people across groups can recognize in others' faces and, particularly when done in the absence of others, that people have similar expressions for some of those emotions. Cross-cultural recognition of the basic emotions from vocal cues has also been found.

More **germane** perhaps to this text, however, was the observation that, in some cases overriding biologically-based expressions, cultures create a set of rules for how to enact emotions. *Cultural Display Rules* refer to the ways in which a particular group defines "appropriate" and normative emotional expression, including whether or not to show an experienced emotion. In a project testing a categorization of display rules (the Display Rule Assessment Inventory), Matsumoto, Yoo, Hirayama, and Petrova found in 2005 that, of the groups they studied, their Japanese participants were least likely to show anger and contempt, with U.S. Americans showing the most happiness.

Wikan studied a particular display rule within the Balinese culture in 1990. In detail, the author looked closely at one cue (a smile when talking about a loved one's death) used by one woman, Suriati. According to Streeck in 2002, "Wikan's analysis exhibits a pervasive dilemma of Balinese interpersonal life. The dilemma is that, according to the assumptions of their culture, the Balinese are inscrutable to one another. The culture puts premium on keeping a 'bright face' ... Accordingly, they must constantly reassure one another that they are not angry—which they do by keeping a bright face." Streeck argues that similar smile-based display rules exist in other cultures, although their value bases for the smiles are different, and cites Hochschild's work in 1983 on emotional labor and her example of U.S. flight attendants' smiles as a cultural commodity, a behavior required of the employees and sold to the customers as part of the airlines' service.

Coordinating Interaction

Having a conversation with another requires knowledge and implementation of a range of cues that signal the beginning of a conversation, changes in topic, when to avoid talk, and the like. These cues allow for the coordination of interaction (also referred to as conversation management) between people, one of the fundamental social functions of non-verbal cues. Research on culture and non-verbal cues related to this function has looked frequently at differences in greeting behavior. This may be because, as Hassanain contended in 1994 that "[m]odes of greeting rituals represent the fabric and the conceptual aspect of the daily life of the individuals and [are] the mirror that reflects the interactional social life of any given speech community". Singh, McKay, and Singh noted in 1998 that, as body contact is often not appropriate in Sri Lanka and India, people greet one another by holding their hands together and using a slight head nod. For Saudis, the value of communion is at the basis of their greeting rituals.

Detailed looks at non-verbal cues-in-talk have found additional ways in which non-verbal cues work as part of conversation management as influenced by culture. Yang argued in 2010 that the Mandarin Chinese concept of *mianzi*-saving (face-saving) for both self and other is revealed in non-verbal interaction cues. Yang also found that looking at non-verbal aspects of coordinating interaction reveals gender-based rules of conduct for Mandarin-speaking Chinese, with female speakers unique in using gestures that shield the mouth and clapping while expressing joy, and males showing a tendency to put their chins up and point their index-finger when implying blame. In 2012 in a different vein, Zhang and Kalinowski compared non-verbal responses to another's stuttering and found that their Chinese participants were more likely than their African-American or European-American participants to avert gaze from speakers' eyes and mouths, although gaze aversion from the others' eyes was common to all groups.

Some groups rely more on non-verbal cues within interaction than do others (see, also, the section on high-context and low-context). Mejia-Arauz, Roberts and Rogoff reviewed in 2012 literature on indigenous communities in North and Central America and found consistently that the communities are particularly reliant on non-verbal means of communicating. Indeed, the authors work to conceptualize this practice by referencing non-verbal conversations, which they define as the "articulate complex rounds of back-and-forth communication with multiple turns where the main exchange is non-verbal." The authors provided data that support the conclusion that children in these communities learn such patterns early in their lives. Mejia-Arauz et al. argue that this early learning reflects Mesoamerican groups' value of balancing across non-verbal conversations and talk as a way to accomplish shared activities. The authors suggested that the specific value of *respecto* (mutual consideration and support) may explain these patterns.

Relational Messages

Non-verbal cues are also used regularly to "speak to" the relationship people have with one another, a process involving what have been called relational messages. Within the intercultural literature, the relational message studied most frequently is status, perhaps because status differential is one way in which cultures have been distinguished from one another according to Gudykunst in 1997. Bente, Leuschner, Al Issa and Bascovich, however, were interested in pan-cultural or trans-cultural status displays. Comparing Germans, Arabs, and U.S. Americans, the researchers found that that many non-verbal cues of status were the same across the groups. Interestingly, however, differences arose in the group members' evaluation of the cues, suggesting that, in this case, the meaning more than the behavior was culturally-influenced. Consistent with this finding, Kowner and Wiseman observed in 2003 that the same cues were perceived by Japanese and U.S. Americans to connote status, but the **magnitude** to which they were perceived as being used as such varied, with their Japanese respondents noting greater differences in the behaviors of high and low status people. Rule et al. also provided evidence in 2010 that cultures differ based on how much warmth is connected to status or power.

Other forms of relationship-based variables have also been highlighted in the intercultural context. In 2010, Bello, Brandau-Brown, Zhang, and Ragsdale compared 200 people from China and the U.S., who were asked how they showed appreciation to others. They found that those from China strongly preferred non-verbal means of letting another know they appreciated them, with those from the U.S. reporting that they used verbal and non-verbal means in equal parts. Moreover, the U.S. respondents reported showing appreciation more often overall than did those from China, reflecting a greater cultural value on expression. People can reveal their regard for others in many ways, including time spent together (i.e., chronemics). In 1991, Witte studied

Arab health care workers and found that, in order to be effective in their work, they learn that they must take time to establish relationships and build rapport with patients and families before proceeding with medical consultation.

Identity Management

An additional function of non-verbal cues relevant to the cultural/intercultural context has to do with signs that reflect on people's group or cultural membership (i.e., their social identity). As part of self-presentation, identity management references in what ways we "display" aspects of our identity to others, including our cultural identity/ties. According to Keating in 2006, "[a] cross cultures and millennia, face and body parts have been dressed, painted, pierced, shaved, plucked, injected, molded, stretched, cut and sewn to manage images of self and identity." Keating also asserts that "[t]hese (pre)occupations often reflect cultural values" and cites the TV show *Extreme Makeover* as reflective of a U.S. American ethos of (a certain) beauty at any cost. She likewise references Chinese plastic surgeons who are called upon to increase people's height, as, like in the U.S., height in China often equates with greater status or power that, in turn, engenders higher salaries, for men at least.

Vocal accents are one of the primary ways that people recognize a person's cultural or social identity. But Marsh et al. contended in 2003 that people also have facial "accents" that signify our group membership. They asked their participants to judge the nationality of people's faces and found that they could do so when the posers were displaying an emotional expression rather a neutral one, leading the authors to argue that the decoders could see facial markers that were more common to one culture than another.

Cultural Dimensions

Grouping scholarship on culture and non-verbal communication into the functions that the cues serve for members of those cultures is not often done. As with much work in intercultural scholarship, the most easily identifiable scholarship tends to focus on the factors or dimensions of culture and how they affect the non-verbal behavior of cultural members. Although a dimensional approach has been critiqued for being too simplistic and static according to Gudykunst et al. in 1996, it remains a commonly used and oft-recommended construct by Ting-Toomey in 2010. Some of these dimensions (e.g., high and low contact and high and low context) are particularly likely to mark cultural differences in non-verbal cues, as the dimensions themselves implicate non-verbal action (i.e., to be a high contact culture means that people are more likely to touch and have close proxemic distances). Others (e.g., status differential) are less inherently tied to non-verbal cues, although non-verbal cues have been discussed outside of the cultural context as important means by which that dimension may be reflected.

Although taking a dimensional approach to culture is somewhat controversial, it offers some advantages. Specifically for the purposes of culture's tie to non-verbal cues, cultural dimensions tend to reflect underlying values and beliefs of a culture (e.g., collectivism suggests that harmony is a deep cultural value). In doing so, they provide a way to understand why certain cultural differences exist and why they show up in a culture in the way that they do.

Importantly, although "the dimensions of cultural variability afford broad predictions of cultural similarity and difference, each dimension is manifested in a unique way within each culture" according to Gudykunst in 1997. Whereas there are other ways to identify the larger world views and attitudes of a culture, specifically in culture-based studies that work to provide rich background for making sense of a group's ways of behaving and making sense of non-verbal elements, research that uses dimensions as the basis of predicted differences provide at least a surface-level story for such differences. This section therefore reviews some of the cultural dimensions where scholarship has been done looking at non-verbal similarities and differences between cultures.

Individualism/Collectivism

Perhaps more than any other defining dimension of culture, the degree to which a culture can be identified as more individualistic (oriented toward the individual's needs) or collectivist (oriented toward the group's needs) has been at the basis of many cross-cultural studies of non-verbal behavior. Following Hofstede and Triandis, a range of scholars have looked for ways in which different cultural orientations on this dimension show up in varying behaviors across cultures. Most notably, Matsumoto developed in 1991 a theory about the role of orientation in explaining differences in expressiveness. He argued that individualistic cultures tend to promote self-expression; as such, people within them tend to be more overtly expressive of a wide range of emotions, usually through non-verbal means. More specifically, politeness norms within these cultures tend to encourage the (sometimes false) displays of positivity. People in collectivist cultures are taught to note the effect of their behavior on the group, and the suppression of negative emotional displays is more likely to be part of the rules people follow, at least with those within their cultural (in) group. The same pressure does not apply with those outside of their group, however. Consistent with the theory, Matsumoto, Yoo, and Fontaine found that, compared to individualistic cultures, collectivistic cultures enforce a display rule of less emotional expressivity overall.

Interestingly, the connection between individualist/collectivist orientation and emotional display preference carries into the online environment. Park, Baek, and Cha used in 2014 "big data" analyzing to look at whether emoticon use is related to the orientation of the user's nationality. Using Twitter data from 78 countries, the authors saw a pattern of favoring horizontal and open-mouthed emoticons by people from cultures labeled as individualistic, with vertical and eye-oriented emoticons used more often by people in countries labeled collectivist. It is not only expressiveness that has been found to differ between individualist and collectivist cultures, however. Choi, for example, found that collectivist mothers (from Korea) are more likely to value listening than are individualist mothers (from Canada). Andersen and Wang asserted in 2006 that individualism likewise affects U.S. Americans' dance style.

High-Context and Low-Context

In addition to introducing cultural differences in the use of space and time, Edward T. Hall referenced the idea of context in 1966, which underlies a second cultural dimension. For Hall, high-context cultures are particularly "non-verbal" in that less of their social meaning is encoded in what they say to one another; instead people rely on what they know about a person and on information in the environment, including that expressed non-verbally. Singh et al. also noted in 1998 communication within high-context cultures is more indirect. Given that cues available in the larger context, such as each interactant's status, become a primary way of understanding behavior and determining what social actions are appropriate, being able to understand the system of cue reliance in one's own culture is part of an individual's mental health.

Myriad studies have been produced to test the observable differences of people from high-context and low-context cultures. In high-context cultures, such as China and Malaysia, for instance, knowing cultural rules and meanings is imperative. In Japan, another high-context culture, people tend to look carefully at another's eyes for unspoken information about what she or he is feeling. Such differences show up in the media as well: In their study of political advertisements, Tak, Kaid and Khang found in 2007 that the Korean (a high-context culture) ads were more subdued and subtle than were the U.S. (a low-context culture) ads. Singh et al. likewise discussed in 1998 how silence is used differently based on whether or not a culture is more context-oriented. "In low-context cultures, silence is a linguistic space to be filled; in high-context cultures, silence is an active part of communication."

High-Contact and Low-Contact

In addition to high-context and low-context, Hall's work in 1966 also delineates cultures into contact and noncontact groups, with those in contact cultures more likely to engage in touch and have smaller proxemic zones, two cues in a set of behaviors referred to elsewhere as immediacy cues. Indeed, Andersen argued in 2008 that cultures should be differentiated on their *immediacy* orientation rather than as high-contact or low-contact, as immediacy **supercedes** the cues associated with contact. But "contact" is used more commonly in the cultural/intercultural literature at present, even as its use as a cultural determinant is contested. Moreover, being low-contact can be tied more specifically to touch avoidance, and in general, research across regions suggests that "Asia is the most touch avoidant in the world, and countries in the Mediterranean region are the most touch oriented." In 1966 Hall originally categorized North and Central American cultures as low-contact, but more recent research found support that they, along with Great Britain, are contact cultures.

Interestingly, there may be a link between nature and nurture when it comes to a culture being high-contact or low-contact, but with a twist. Several scholars have found that cultures being contact or not often depends at least in part on the latitude where they exist. Andersen, Lustig, and Andersen in 1990, found that, globally, cultures in cooler zones tended to be cooler interpersonally as well, which led to less contact. This occurred even within a single nation, with warmer parts of a country associated with warmer temperament and more contact than in colder regions. Some of the possible reasons for this climate-based difference include greater time interacting with others in warm temperature cultures and increased structure of or formality in colder climate cultures, seen as necessary for dealing with the lower temperatures.

Given that cultures differ on how much contact they expect and engage in, it makes sense that people from diverse cultures would also interpret contact behaviors differently. In 2004, Albert and Ah Hah asked teachers and students from Anglo and Latino countries to respond to various scenarios in which the actors touched one another (they also looked at interpretations—or attributions—made for silence). Among other things, the authors found Latinos were particularly likely to evaluate a man being hit in the face in one scenario as an insult when compared to their U.S. Anglo counterparts. The authors suggested this difference may be due to the dimension of masculinity-femininity according to Hofstede in 1991, with the U.S. Latinos' culture reflecting more masculinity, wherein being hit shows weakness and can be used to emasculate another.

▶ Implications of Non-verbal Differences in Intercultural and Multicultural Contexts

Whereas I have only been able to scratch the surface of the extensive literature on "cultured" non-verbal cues, my hope is that the discussion in this unit points toward some primary areas of scholarship relevant to intercultural communication. I also believe that the literature suggests some the potential challenges (and benefits) of communicating with others who are culturally different from us. I end this unit, then, with some places where scholarship speaks to areas for investigating—and potentially improving—intercultural discourse.

A large area, of course, is the recognition that, despite some cues being used and understood universally, and the underlying biological and evolutionary consistency we share, culture tends to shape the rules, use, and interpretation of its members' non-verbal cues. If we do not see non-verbal cues as cultured we risk judging and interpreting others erroneously from our own cultural perspective. Vargas-Urpi wrote in 2013 about difficulties for Chinese immigrants living in Catalonia, noting that interpreters for the immigrants have been challenged to understand the Chinese pattern of gaze aversion and smiling to cover negative emotions. Rule et al. offered that in 2010 people may tend to judge another's behavior from their own (cultural) perspective rather than take the other's into account as they may be influenced by people's tendency toward self-projection. To help, Albert and Ah Hah suggested the following in 2004: "To interact effectively with members of another culture, it is helpful if individuals learn to make "isomorphic attributions" to those made by members of the other culture ... The explanations of social behavior that individuals provide about the behavior of the other must be similar to the attributions that the other makes about his or her own behavior; otherwise, the message received will not be the message the other is attempting to convey."

Doing so is challenging, however, as in some ways we seem hard-wired into understanding the world once we are enculturated to see it a certain way. Condon and Yousef, for instance, state that "[t]he fusion of individualism and equality is so valued and so basic that many Americans find it most difficult to relate to contrasting values in other cultures where interdependence greatly determines a person's sense of self". Moreover, it may be easier for us to interpret our own culture's (in-group) communication than that of another's (out-group), but this advantage has been strongly contested. We may also prefer our own cues. In 2013 Endrass, Andre, Rehm, and Nakano used computational models to create prototypical behaviors of people from German and Japanese cultures. Overall, they found that people from each culture, at least in part, preferred the behaviors that resembled their own background.

　　These preferences or tendencies often lead to discriminatory behavior, including subtle cues such as spending more time in an interview when the interviewee is of the same race or being more engaged non-verbally with cultural members who we believe come from cultures that are more like our own. Such behavior patterns are often outside of our awareness and can have significant consequences. Importantly, time spent in another culture can help people become more competent at recognizing others' behaviors according to the users' system—this points to the importance of sojourning in increasing cultural awareness. As we work to create additional scholarship on similarities and differences across cultural members' use of non-verbal cues, these **dynamics** are important to consider.

Applications

1. Different Aspects of Intercultural Non-verbal Communication: A Study
Kaushal, S. (2014). Different aspects of intercultural non-verbal communication: A study. *Asian Journal of Advanced Basic Science*, 2, 31–39.
Abstract: Out of a number of forms, there are two very important kinds of communication, verbal and non-verbal and the relation between them is inseparable. Non-verbal communication keeps the major portion of the periphery occupied and in absence of it communication can never happen. There is a very common perception among people that for understanding any oral message we have to concentrate and subsequently be able to understand the non-verbal elements, but in reality non-verbal communication is not as easy to understand as it seems to be. Often it is misinterpreted and because of that wrong message is understood by the receiver. Another widely accepted fact states that by focusing upon the body language of a person we can predict how he/she feels about any situation. But all that varies from context to context, from culture to culture. This paper focuses mostly upon the basic understanding required to be taken into consideration while understanding non-verbal elements along with verbal elements in different cultural settings.
Keywords: intercultural communication; NVC in politics; factors affecting cross-cultural communication; NVC in gender; cultural settings.

2. Verbal and Non-verbal Communication: Distinguishing Symbolic, Spontaneous, and Pseudo-Spontaneous Non-verbal Behavior
Buck, R., & VanLear, A. C. (2002). Verbal and non-verbal communication: Distinguishing symbolic, spontaneous, and pseudo-spontaneous non-verbal behavior. *Journal of Communication*, 3, 522–541.
Abstract: Verbal and non-verbal communication are seen in terms of interacting streams of

spontaneous and symbolic communication, and posed "pseudo-spontaneous" displays. Spontaneous communication is defined as the non-intentional communication of motivational-emotional states based upon biologically shared non-propositional signal systems, with information transmitted via displays. Symbolic communication is the intentional communication, using learned, socially shared signal systems, of propositional information transmitted via symbols. Pseudo-spontaneous communication involves the intentional and strategic manipulation of displays. An original meta-analysis demonstrates that, like verbal symbolic communication, non-verbal analogic (pantomimic) communication is related to left hemisphere cerebral processing. In contrast, spontaneous communication is related to the right hemisphere.

Keywords: non-verbal communication; interacting stream; display; meta-analysis; gemisphere

3. Verbal and Non-verbal Communication Cues in Daily Conversations and Dating

Fichten, S. C., Tagalakis, V, Judd, D., Wright, J. & Amsel, R. (2001). Verbal and non-verbal communication cues in daily conversations and dating. *The Journal of Social Psychology*, 6, 751-769.

Abstract: Effective social interaction assumes the ability to communicate one's own level of interest and to gauge the other person's state accurately. In this investigation of beliefs about communication cues that convey interest and lack of interest, the responses of 50 male and 34 female Canadian adults to a structured interview concerned with expressing and interpreting others' verbal and non-verbal communication were examined. Cues were grouped as follows: verbal, non-verbal visual, non-verbal touch, and non-verbal paralinguistic cues, unclassifiable behaviors, and intangible signals. Subjects reported decoding more non-verbal cues than they expressed. This trend was reversed for verbal cues, suggesting that subjects paid particular attention to their own verbal cues and to others' non-verbal behaviors. Intimate and non-intimate interactions were characterized by different balances between interest and lack-of-interest cues. Communication cues with ambiguous meanings were noted, and cues that comprised interest and lack-of-interest schemata in both dating and daily conversation contexts were identified.

Keywords: social interaction; communication cues; verbal and non-verbal communication; intimate and non-intimate interactions; dating and daily conversation

Interactive Activities

1. Individually, please finish reading Text A, Text B, and the application abstracts and work out the meanings of the terms in bold type by consulting the dictionary whenever necessary.

2. In pairs, please summarize the content in 2 to 3 sentences of each sub-heading in the unit outlines of Text A and Text B based on your reading and understanding of the texts.

3. In groups, share your gains, comments and suggestions regarding the three application abstracts. Based on your interests, locate and finish reading the full-length papers of your interested abstracts.

4. Q&A: Questions are encouraged about any uncertain or confused part or parts in the unit and seek answers either from other fellow students or the instructor.

To facilitate the implementation of intercultural communication along the "One Best, One Road" initiative, please make a table comparing and contrasting a series of main non-verbal cues in the Chinese culture and other cultures in the Middle East.

5. Complete the Personal Report of Olfactory Perception and Sensitivity, an instrument designed to assess your level of olfactory perception and sensitivity. Take a few moments and complete the self-assessment for Unit 7.

6. Based on your understanding of verbal and non-verbal intercultural communication in Unit 6 and Unit 7, work out **a literature review paper** related to your problem statement. The paper is designed to develop an argument that justifies completing new research on the problem you have selected. Let the paper take the following form:

Introduction: Justify the selection of this topic in the study of intercultural communication and overview the remaining points of the paper.

Problem: State the problem and provide any necessary context to understand it.

Theoretic Expectations: Describe what is conceptually expected with the concepts or variables involved and review how any relevant theory may explain these effects.

Review of Literature: Examine the relevant literature for each main concept or variable you have selected either separately or together, depending on the nature of past research by including these elements: (a) identification of the concepts or variables to be reviewed; (b) summary of the relevant research findings on the concepts or variables with appropriate criticism to help you justify the completion of a new or different research on the topic; and (c) assessment of relevant materials that remain unknown about the topic by demonstrating a gap in knowledge that invites the new research suggested by the problem statement.

Future Research Priorities: Indicate what research should be completed and identify the specific reasons for inviting the new research.

Conclusion: Summary of paper and bottom line statement of the notion suggested in it.

Write the paper very well. Work from an outline. Turn in two copies. Staple this form to the front of your paper. Use the APA form and cite everything you use.

UNIT EIGHT

Eastern and Western Theorizing about Intercultural Communication

Readings

Text A Theorizing about Intercultural Communication: An Introduction

After William B. Gudykunst, Carmen M. Lee, Tsukasa Nishida, and Naoto Ogawa

▶ Introduction

Theorizing about intercultural communication has made tremendous progress in the last 20 years. When two of the authors completed their doctorates, there were no theories of intercultural communication. Initial attempts to theorize about interpersonal communication between people from different cultures were included in the first thematic volume of the *International and Intercultural Communication Annual* published by Gudykunst in 1983. By the time the second volume of the *Annual* on theory was published by Kim and Gudykunst in 1988, theorizing about intercultural communication had increased in **sophistication** supported by lines of research. There was another leap in the quality of theorizing when the most recent volume of the *Annual* on theory was published by Wiseman in 1995.

There are several approaches to incorporating culture into communication theories. First, culture can be integrated with the communication process in theories of communication. In other words, culture is linked to communication within the theory. Second, theories can be designed to describe or explain how communication varies across cultures. Third, theories can be generated to describe or explain communication between people from different cultures. By far, the most theorizing exists in the third category.

Many of the theorists who attempt to describe or explain communication between members of different cultures focus on intergroup communication generally rather than intercultural communication specifically. Theorists using an intergroup approach tend to assume that culture is one of the many group memberships influencing communication. These theorists also tend to assume that the processes occurring in intercultural, interethnic, and intergenerational communication, among others, are similar. We divide the intergroup and intercultural theories into five categories that are not mutually exclusive: theories focusing on effective outcomes, theories focusing on accommodation and adaptation, theories focusing on identity management, theories focusing on communication networks, and theories focusing on adjustment and adaptation to new cultural environments.

Whatever the approach that is used to develop theories, the theories are based upon a set of

meta-theoretical assumptions. In 1989 Gudykunst and Nishida used Burrell and Morgan's distinction between objectivist and subjectivist approaches to theory (see Table 8.1) to compare theories in intercultural communication. **Objectivists**, for example, see a "real world" external to individuals, look for regularities in behavior, and see communication as "determined" by situations and environments. **Subjectivists**, in contrast, contend that there is no "real world" external to individuals, try to understand individual communicators' perspectives, and view communication as a function of "free will." Gudykunst and Nishida contend that extreme objectivist or subjectivist perspectives are not defensible. They argue that both approaches are necessary to understand intercultural communication, and that the ideal is eventually to integrate the two perspectives.

The goals of theories in the objectivist and subjectivist perspectives tend to be different. Objectivists, for example, argue that theories should explain and predict the phenomena under study. Subjectivists, however, argue that theories should describe the phenomena under study. Both types of theorists might agree that theories should be heuristic; that is, they should generate future research. When evaluating theories, we must grant the theorists' assumptions and examine the theories for logical consistency and heuristic value. Theories rarely are designed to describe or explain the same thing. Unless they are, they are not directly comparable.

It is important to understand the meta-theoretical assumptions that theorists make. The theoretical propositions in theories should be logically consistent with the meta-theoretical assumptions on which the theories are based. The methods used to test theories also should be consistent with the meta-theoretical assumptions. We can question a theory's meta-theoretical assumptions, but when we evaluate the theory we must grant the assumptions and not impose other meta-theoretical assumptions in our critiques.

Table 8.1 Assumptions about Theory

Subjective Approach (Human Action/Interaction)	Objectivist Approach (Causal Process)
ONTOLOGY	
Nominalism: There is no "real" world external to individual; "names," "concepts," and "labels" are artificial and are used to construct reality.	Realism: There is a "real" world external to individual; things exist, even if they are not perceived and labeled.
EPISTEMOLOGY	
Antipositivism: Communication can only be understood from the perspective of the individuals communicating; no search for underlying regularities.	Positivism: Attempts to explain and predict patterns of communication by looking for regularities and/or causal relationships.
HUMAN NATURE	
Voluntarism: Communicators are completely "autonomous" and have "free will." traits.	Determinism: Communication is "determined" by the situation, environment in which it occurs or by individuals' traits.
METHOLOGY	
Ideographic: To understand communication, "firsthand knowledge" must be obtained; analysis of subjective accounts.	Nomothetic: Research should be based on systematic protocols and "scientific" rigor.

UNIT EIGHT
Eastern and Western Theorizing about Intercultural Communication

In evaluating theories, we also need to look at logical consistency. Are the meta-theoretical assumptions and the theoretical statements logically consistent? Are the theoretical statements logically consistent with each other? We also must pay attention to scope and boundary conditions that theorists specify when we evaluate their theories. Do theorists, for example, limit their theories to certain types of situations (e.g., initial interactions between strangers)?

If theorists limit their theories to initial interactions, then data in romantic relationships that are inconsistent with the theory do not call the theory into question. Theories should not be criticized because they do not explain something beyond the scope theorists specify for their theories. Theorists may limit complete theories to specific conditions or limit certain theoretical claims to only specific conditions. If a theorist claims that a statement holds only for people who feel secure in their identities, then data from respondents who do not feel secure do not test the theoretical claim.

Our purpose in this paper is to overview the theories in intercultural communication. Our goal is to put the theories in context. By understanding the variability in the approaches used to construct theories, readers will be in a good position to understand and question the choices the theorists make. We divide the theories into seven categories that are not necessarily mutually **exclusive**: (a) theories that integrate culture with communication processes, (b) theories explaining cultural variability in communication, (c) intergroup/intercultural theories focusing on effective outcomes, (d) intergroup/intercultural theories focusing on accommodation or adaptation, (e) intergroup/intercultural theories focusing on identity management or negotiation, (f) intergroup/intercultural theories focusing on communication networks, and (g) intercultural theories focusing on acculturation or adjustment. Both objectivistic and subjectivistic theories are included. The majority of the theories that have been developed, however, are objectivistic. Very few of the theorists attempt to integrate objectivistic and subjectivistic assumptions.

▶ Theories in Which Culture and Communication Are Integrated

Several theorists have integrated culture with communication processes. We briefly overview the three major approaches: (a) constructivist theory by Applegate and Sypher in 1983 and 1988); (b) coordinated management of meaning by Cronen et al. in 1988), and (c) cultural communication by Philipsen in 1992.

Constructivist Theory

Applegate and Sypher integrated culture with constructivist theory. They make several assumptions, including that "theory should be interpretive," "dense and detailed accounts of everyday interaction... are needed," "the focus of study should be the relationship between culture and communication," "value judgments should be made," and "theory and training should be linked closely."

Applegate and Sypher pointed out in 1988 that communication occurs when individuals have "a mutually recognized interaction to share, exchange messages" in constructivist theory. This process is goal driven and individuals do what they think will help them accomplish their goals.

Applegate and Sypher view complex message behavior (a function of the number of goals and situational factors incorporated in messages) as leading to "person-centered" communication (which involves the degree to which individuals adapt to their interactional partners). Individuals' constructs generate "communication and goal-relevant beliefs" that influence their definition of the situation and guide their "strategic behavior."

Applegate and Sypher believed in 1988 that "culture defines the logic of communication" and that different cultures emphasize different goals and ways to achieve these goals. They go on to argue that "cultural communication theories specify how to place and organize events within larger contexts of meaning and elaboration." Hong et al. argued in 2003 that construct activation is a major factor influencing cultural differences in social perception (they also review evidence for a dynamic constructivism approach). Applegate and Sypher concluded that intercultural communication training "should focus on developing flexible and integrative strategic means for accomplishing goals."

Coordinated Management of Meaning

In 1988 Cronen et al. examined the role of culture in the coordinated management of meaning. They isolate three goals of CMM: (a) "CMM seeks to understand who we are, what it means to live a life, and how that is related to particular instances of communication;" (b) "CMM seeks to render cultures comparable while acknowledging their incommensurability;" and (c) "CMM seeks to generate an illuminating critique of cultural practices, including the researcher's own."

In 1988 Cronen et al. isolated several propositions regarding CMM. To illustrate, they argue that "all communication is both idiosyncratic and social," "human communication is inherently imperfect," "moral orders emerge as aspects of communication," and "diversity is essential to elaboration and transformation through communication."

Cronen et al. have proposed three **corollaries** involving culture: "cultures are patterns of coevolving structures and actions," "cultures are polyphonic," and "research activity is part of social practice." They believe that it is necessary to describe the cultural context if we are going to understand communication within cultures and/or across cultures. It also is necessary to understand the individuals' interpretations of their communication.

CMM tends to be viewed as a "rules" theory that is based on U.S. pragmatism. CMM is used to analyze rules that are used as social episodes (e.g., communication that occurs at the dinner table). The description of the episodes generates "a critical focus" on the situation being described.

Cultural Communication

In 1981 Philipsen laid out the groundwork of cultural communication. Philipsen argues that:
> The function of communication in cultural communication is to maintain a healthy balance between the forces of individualism and community, to provide a sense of shared identity which nonetheless preserves individual dignity, freedom, and creativity. This function is performed through maintaining equilibrium between the two sub-processes of

cultural communication, (a) the creation, and (b) the affirmation, of shared identity. Cultural communication, therefore, involves the negotiation of cultural codes through communal conversations. Communal conversations are communicative processes through which individuals negotiate how they will "conduct their lives together."

Philipsen proposed speech code theory in 1992: a theory of "culturally distinctive codes of communication conduct." Speech code theory posits that communal conversations imply distinctive codes of communication. He suggests that "a speech code refers to a historically enacted, socially constructed system of terms, meanings, premises, and rules pertaining to communicative conduct."

Philipsen isolated two principles of cultural communication in 2002. Principle One states that "every communal conversation bears traces of culturally distinctive means and meanings of communicative conduct." Philipsen believes that the notion that members of groups engage in communal conversations is a universal of human life, but that each communal conversation has culture-specific aspects. The second principle of cultural communication is that "communication is a **heuristic** and performative resource for performing the cultural function in the lives of individuals and communities." The communal function involves "how individuals are to live as members of a community." Communication is "heuristic" because it is through communication that babies and newcomers to the community learn the specific means and meanings in the community. Communication is "performative" because it allows individuals to participate in the communal conversation.

Theories of Cultural Variability in Communication

A few theorists have attempted to explain cross-cultural differences in communication using cultural-level and/or individual-level dimensions. These theories include: face-negotiation theory, conversational constraints theory, and expectancy violations theory. EVT, however, is not a formal theory of cross-cultural communication. Rather, the focus is on cross-cultural variability of a theory designed in the United States. Each of these theories draws on Hofstede's dimensions of cultural variability in 1980, 1991, and 2001. We provide a brief introduction to these dimensions here.

Hofstede's Dimensions of Cultural Variability

Hofstede isolated four dimensions of cultural variability: individualism—collectivism, low uncertainty avoidance—high uncertainty avoidance, low power distance—high power distance, and **masculinity**—**femininity**. Both ends of each dimension exist in all cultures, but one end tends to predominate in a culture. Individual members of cultures learn the predominate tendencies in their cultures to various degrees. It, therefore, is necessary to take both cultural-level and individual-level factors into consideration when explaining similarities and differences in communication across cultures.

Individuals' goals are emphasized more than groups' goals in individualistic cultures. Groups' goals, in contrast, take precedence over individuals' goals in collectivistic cultures. In individualistic cultures, "people are supposed to look after themselves and their immediate family only," and in collectivistic cultures, "people belong to ingroups or collectivities which are supposed to look after them in exchange for loyalty" according to Hofstede and Bond in 1984.

Triandis argued in 1995 that the relative importance of ingroups is the major factor that differentiates individualistic and collectivistic cultures. Ingroups are groups that are important to their members and groups for which individuals will make sacrifices. Members of individualistic cultures have many specific ingroups that might influence their behavior in any particular social situation. Since there are many ingroups, specific ingroups exert relatively little influence on individuals' behavior. Members of collectivistic cultures have only a few general ingroups that influence their behavior across situations.

Cultural individualism—collectivism influences communication in a culture through the cultural norms and rules associated with the major cultural tendency (e.g., the U.S. tends to have individualistic norms/rules, Asian cultures tend to have collectivistic norms/rules). Cultural individualism—collectivism also indirectly influences communication through the characteristics individuals learn when they are socialized. There are at least three characteristics of individuals that mediate the influence of cultural individualism—collectivism on communication: their personalities, their individual values, and their self **construals** according to Gudykunst and Lee in 2002.

Individualism—collectivism provides an explanatory framework for understanding cultural similarities and differences in self-ingroup behavior. Hall's differentiation between low-context and high-context communication in 1976 can be used to explain cultural differences in communication. High-context communication occurs when "most of the information is either in the physical context or internalized in the person, while very little is in the coded, explicit, transmitted part of the message." Low-context communication, in contrast, occurs when "the mass of information is vested in the explicit code." Low-context and high-context communication are used in all cultures. One form, however, tends to predominate. Members of individualistic cultures tend to use low-context communication and communicate in a direct fashion. Members of collectivistic cultures, in contrast, tend to use high-context messages when maintaining ingroup harmony is important and communicate in an indirect fashion according to Gudykunst and Ting-Toomey in 1988.

High uncertainty avoidance cultures tend to have clear norms and rules to guide behavior for virtually all situations. Norms and rules in low uncertainty avoidance cultures are not as clear-cut and rigid as those in high uncertainty avoidance cultures. In high uncertainty avoidance cultures, **aggressive** behavior is acceptable, but individuals prefer to contain aggression by avoiding conflict and competition. There also is a strong desire for consensus in high uncertainty avoidance cultures, and deviant behavior is not acceptable. Tolerance for ambiguity and uncertainty orientation are two individual-level factors that mediate the influence of cultural uncertainty avoidance on communication.

Power distance is "the extent to which the less powerful embers of institutions and organizations accept that power is distributed unequally" in the words of Hofstede and Bond in 1984. Members of high power distance cultures accept as part of society (e.g., superiors consider their subordinates to be different from themselves and vice versa). Members of high power distance cultures see power as a basic factor in society, and stress coercive or referent power. Members of low distance cultures, in contrast, believe power should be used only when it is legitimate and prefer expert or legitimate power. **Egalitarianism** and social dominance orientation are two individual-level factors that mediate the influence of cultural power distance on communication.

The major differentiation between masculine and feminine cultures is how gender-roles are distributed in a culture according to Hofstede in 1991 as follows:

> *Masculinity* pertains to societies in which social gender roles are clearly distinct (i.e., men are supposed to be assertive, tough, and focused on material success whereas women are supposed to be more modest, concerned with the quality of life); *femininity* pertains to societies in which social gender roles overlap (i.e., both men and women are supposed to be modest, tender, and concerned with the quality of life).

Members of cultures high in masculinity value performance, ambition, things, power, and assertiveness. Members of cultures high in femininity value quality of life, service, caring for others, and being nurturing. Psychological sex-roles are individual-level factors that mediate the influence of cultural masculinity—femininity on communication.

Face-Negotiation Theory

Cultural norms and values influence and shape how members of cultures manage face and how they manage conflict situations. Originally a theory focusing on conflict, face-negotiation theory (FNT) has been expanded to integrate cultural-level dimensions and individual-level attributes to explain face concerns, conflict styles, and facework behaviors.

Ting-Toomey argued in 1985 that conflict is a face-negotiation process whereby individuals engaged in conflict have their situated identities or "faces" threatened or questioned. Face is "a claimed sense of favorable social self-worth that a person wants others to have of her or him." Although mentioned only briefly in the 1988 version of the theory, the concept of face is an integral part of the most recent version of the theory.

Ting-Toomey and Kurogi argued in 1998 that members of collectivistic cultures use other-oriented face-saving strategies more than members of individualistic cultures. Conversely, members of individualistic cultures use more self-oriented face-saving strategies more than members of collectivistic cultures. Members of low power distance cultures defend and assert their personal rights more than members of high power distance cultures. Members of high power distance cultures, in contrast, perform their ascribed duties responsibly more than members of low power distance cultures. Members of low power distance cultures tend to minimize the respect-deference distance via information-based interactions more than members of high power distance cultures. Members of high power distance cultures are concerned with vertical facework interactions more than members of low power distance cultures.

Ting-Toomey and Kurogi contended that members of collectivistic cultures use relational, process-oriented conflict strategies more than members of individualistic cultures. Members of individualistic cultures, in contrast, tend to use more substantive, outcome-oriented conflict strategies than members of collectivistic cultures. High-status members of high power distance cultures tend to use verbally indirect facework strategies more than low-status members of high power distance cultures. High-status members of low power distance cultures tend to use verbally direct strategies more than high-status members of high power distance cultures.

Ting-Toomey and Kurogi also linked individual-level mediators of the dimensions of cultural variability to face behaviors and conflict styles. Emphasizing self-face leads to using dominating/competing conflict styles and substantive conflict resolution modes. Emphasizing other-face leads to using avoiding/obliging conflict styles and relational conflict resolution modes. Independent self construal types tend to use dominating/competing conflict styles and substantive conflict resolution modes. Interdependent self construal types tend to use avoiding/obliging conflict styles and relational conflict resolution modes. **Bi-construal** types (high on both self construals) use substantive and relational conflict resolution modes, and ambivalent types (low on both self construals) tend not to use either.

Conversational Constraints Theory

Conversations are goal-directed and require coordination between communicators in CCT. Kim isolated two types of conversational constraints in 1993: social-relational and task-oriented. Social-relational constraints emphasize concern for others that focuses on avoiding hurting hearers' feelings and minimizing imposition on hearers. The task-oriented constraint emphasizes a concern for clarity.

In 1993 Kim explained cross-cultural differences in the selection of communicative strategies. Members of collectivistic cultures view face-supporting behavior (e.g., avoiding hurting the hearers' feelings, minimizing imposition, and avoiding negative evaluation by the hearer) as more important than members of individualistic cultures when pursuing goals. Members of individualistic cultures, in contrast, view clarity as more important than members of collectivistic cultures when pursuing goals.

Kim argued in 1995 that individuals who activate interdependent selfconstruals view not hurting hearers' feelings and minimizing impositions on hearers in the pursuit of their goals as more important than individuals who activate independent self construals. Individuals who activate independent self construals view clarity as more important in pursuing goals than individuals who activate interdependent self construals. Individuals who activate both self construals are concerned with relational and clarity constraints. Kim also argued that the more individuals need approval, the more important they view being concerned with hearers' feelings and minimizing impositions on hearers. The more individuals need to be dominant, the more importance they place on clarity. The more masculine individuals' psychological sex-roles, the more importance they place on clarity. The more feminine individuals' psychological sex-roles, the more importance they place on not hurting hearers' feelings and hearers.

Expectancy Violation Theory

Every culture has guidelines for human conduct that provide expectations for how others will behave as noted by Burgoon in 1978. Expectancy violation theory (EVT) frames interpersonal communication within the context of expectations held by individuals and how individuals respond

UNIT EIGHT
Eastern and Western Theorizing about Intercultural Communication

to violations of those expectations. Expectancies are based on social norms and rules as well as individual-specific patterns of typical behavior. Individual deviation in expected behavior causes arousal or alertness in others. Whether or not deviant behavior is interpreted as positive or negative depends on communicators' **valences**. Communicators valances refer to characteristics of individuals (e.g., how attractive and familiar they are perceived to be). Burgoon argued that "communicator's positive or negative characteristics are posited to moderate how violations are interpreted and evaluated."

Burgoon contends in 1992 that the "content" of each culture's expectancies vary along Hofstede's (1980) dimensions of cultural variability. Specifically, members of collectivistic cultures expect greater verbal indirectness, politeness, and non-immediacy than members of individualistic cultures. Uncertainty avoidance is linked to expectancies to the extent that communication behavior is regulated by rules. Low uncertainty cultures have fewer rules and norms regulating behavior than high uncertainty avoidance cultures. Members of high uncertainty avoidance cultures tend to be more intolerant of deviant behavior than members of low uncertainty avoidance cultures. Power distance influences how violations of high status and low status are interpreted by Burgoon in 1995. A violation (e.g., non-verbal proxemic violation) by a high-status person in a high power distance culture, for example, would be perceived as a violation of ascribed role behavior, and such an action would inevitably produce stress and anxiety, a negative outcome.

▲ Theories Focusing on Effective Outcomes

One goal of theorizing is to explain specific outcomes. One outcome that intercultural theorists have used in developing theories is effective communication and effective group decisions. Four theories fit in this category: (a) cultural convergence theory by Barnett and Kincaid in 1983; (b) anxiety/uncertainty management theory by Gudykunst in 1995; (c) effective group decision making theory by Oetzel in 1995; and (d) the integrated theory of interethnic communication by Kim in 1997 and 2004.

Cultural Convergence

Cultural convergence theory is based upon Kincaid's convergence model of communication. Kincaid defined communication in 1979 as "a process in which two or more individuals or groups share information in order to reach a mutual understanding of each other and the world in which they live." He argued that mutual understanding can be approached, but never perfectly achieved. "By means of several iterations of information exchange, two or more individuals may converge towards a more mutual understanding of each other's meaning."

In 1983 Barnett and Kincaid used the convergence model of communication to develop a mathematical theory of the effects of communication on cultural differences. They argue that "the laws of thermodynamics predict that all participants in a closed system will converge over time on the mean collective pattern of thought if communication is allowed to continue indefinitely." Information that is introduced from outside the system can delay convergence or reverse it (i.e., lead to divergence). They present a mathematical model that predicts the convergence of the collective cognitive states of members of two cultures whose members are interacting. Kincaid's convergence model in 1979 applies to individual-level communication, and Barnett and Kincaid's mathematical theory applies to group-level (e.g., culture) phenomena.

In 1988 Kincaid presented the theory in verbal form. Kincaid summarized the theory in two theorems and three hypotheses. Theorem 1, for example, states that, "In a relatively closed social system in which communication among members is unrestricted, the system as a whole will tend to **converge** over time toward a state of greater cultural **uniformity**." The system will tend to diverge toward diversity when communication is restricted (theorem 2). The hypotheses apply the theorems to the case of immigrant groups and native/host cultures.

Anxiety/Uncertainty Management

In 1985 Gudykunst extended Berger and Calabrese's uncertainty reduction theory (URT) in 1975 to intergroup encounters as the first step in developing anxiety/uncertainty management (AUM) theory. In 1988 Gudykunst and Hammer used uncertainty (e.g., the inability to predict or explain others' attitudes, behavior, feelings) and anxiety (e.g., feelings of being uneasy, tense, worried, or apprehensive) to explain intercultural adjustment (see adjustment section below).

Gudykunst proposed a general theory using uncertainty and anxiety reduction to explain effective interpersonal and intergroup communication (i.e., minimize misunderstandings; this theory was not referred to as AUM). Intercultural communication is one type of intergroup communication in AUM theory. Gudykunst used Simmel's notion of "the stranger" in 1950 (e.g., individuals who are present in a situation, but are not members of the ingroup) as a central organizing concept. In 1990 Gudykunst applied the axioms of the 1988 version of the theory to diplomacy, a special case of intergroup communication.

In 1993 Gudykunst expanded the theory using a competency framework. Gudykunst specified the meta-theoretical assumptions of the theory in this version. The assumptions underlying the theory avoid the extreme objectivist or subjectivist positions (e.g., he assumes that individuals' communication is influenced by their cultures and group memberships, but they also can choose how they communicate when they are mindful). This suggests that under some conditions objectivist assumptions hold and other conditions subjectivist assumptions hold. Further, Gudykunst expanded the number of axioms in the theory to make the theory easier to understand and easier to apply. This version of the theory also incorporates minimum and maximum thresholds for uncertainty and anxiety. Finally, Gudykunst integrated Langer's notion of mindfulness as a moderating process between AUM and effective communication in this version.

In 1995 Gudykunst argued that there are "basic" and "superficial" causes of effective communication. He contends that anxiety and uncertainty management (including mindfulness) are the basic causes of effective communication, and the effect of other "superficial" variables (e.g., ability to empathize, attraction to strangers) on effective communication is mediated through anxiety and uncertainty management. The extent to which individuals are mindful of their behavior moderates the influence of their anxiety and uncertainty management on their communication effectiveness. Gudykunst suggested that dialectical processes are involved in AUM (e.g., the uncertainty dialectic involves novelty and predictability), but these processes have not been elaborated.

Effective Decision Making

Oetzel proposed a theory of effective decision making in intercultural groups in 1995. Oetze ingegrated Hirokawa and Rost's **vigilant** interaction theory (VIT) in 1992 and Ting-Toomey's cross-cultural theory of face negotiation and conflict management in 1988.

In 1992 Hirokawar and Rost assumed that the way members of groups talk about things (e.g., problems) associated with group decisions influences how they think about things associated with the decisions they must make. How group members think about things associated with the decision they make influences the quality of their decisions. A group's final decision is a result of "a series of interrelated sub-decisions." Oetzel suggested that VIT may be limited to mono-cultural groups in the United States because different outcomes are emphasized in individualistic and collectivistic cultures. He, therefore, defines decision effectiveness in terms of quality appropriateness.

Oetzel's theory contains 14 propositions. The initial set of propositions focuses on homogeneous (e.g., monocultural) and heterogeneous (e.g., intercultural) groups. He contends that when members of homogeneous groups activate independent self construals, they emphasize task outcomes; when they activate interdependent self construals, they emphasize relational outcomes. Members of homogeneous groups who activate independent construals are less likely to reach consensus and will have more conflict and manage it less cooperatively than members of homogeneous groups who activate interdependent self construals. Member contributions tend to be more equal in homogeneous groups and members are more committed to the group than members in heterogeneous groups.

Oetzel contended in 1995 that when most members activate independent self construals, they tend to use dominating conflict strategies. When most members activate interdependent self construals, in contrast, they tend to use avoiding, compromising, or obliging conflict strategies. Groups that use cooperative styles to manage conflict make more effective decisions than groups that use competing or avoiding styles. Groups in which members activate personal identities make better decisions than groups in which members activate social identities.

Oetzel's theory suggests that the more equal members' contributions and the more group members are committed to the group and its decision, the more effective the decisions. Consensus decisions are more effective than majority or compromise decisions. Finally, Oetzel believes that the "fundamental requisites" of VIT apply to intercultural groups: Groups that understand the problem, establish "good" criteria, develop many alternatives, and examine the positive/negative consequences of the alternatives make more effective decisions than those that do not.

An Integrated Theory of Interethnic Communication

In 1997 Kim laid the groundwork for the integrated theory of interethnic communication. She uses general systems theory (open systems) as an organizing framework. Her organizing scheme consists of a set of four circles: a circle with behavior in the center surrounded by three circles representing contexts (from center to outer circles): (a) behavior (encoding/decoding), (b) communicator, (c) situation, and (d) environment.

In 1997 Kim organized various aspects of encoding and decoding using an **associative/ disassociative** behavior continuum. She argues that "behaviors that are closer to the associative end of this continuum facilitate the communication process by increasing the likelihood of mutual understanding, cooperation ... behaviors at the disassociative end tend to contribute to misunderstanding, competition." To illustrate, associative decoding behaviors include processes like particularization, decategorization, personalization, and mindfulness. Disassociative decoding behaviors include processes like categorization, stereotyping, communicative distance, and making the ultimate attribution error. Associative encoding behaviors include processes like convergence, person-centered messages, and personalized communication. Disassociative encoding behaviors include processes like divergence, prejudiced talk, and the use of **slander**.

Kim examines the communicator in terms of "relatively stable psychological attributes." She includes such factors as cognitive structures (e.g., cognitive complexity, category width), identity strength (e.g., ethnic identity, ethnolinguistic identity, ingroup loyalty), group biases (e.g., ingroup favoritism, ethnocentrism), and related concepts (e.g., intercultural identity, moral inclusion).

Kim views the situation as defined by the physical setting. She isolates interethnic heterogeneity, interethnic salience, and interaction goals (e.g., goals) as critical factors of the situation. The environment includes national and international forces that influence interethnic communication such as institutional equity/inequity (e.g., history of subjugation, ethnic stratification), ethnic group strength (e.g., ethnolinguistic vitality), and interethnic contact (e.g., interaction potential of environment).

Kim argues that the organizing model provides a framework for integrating research in a variety of disciplines. It also serves as "a framework for pragmatic action ... For instance, we can infer from the model that, by changing certain existing conditions in the environment, we can help facilitate associative communicative behaviors."

▶ Theories Focusing on Accommodation or Adaptation

Another goal on which theorists focus is how communicators accommodate or adapt to each other. There are three theories that fit this category: (a) communication accommodation theory by Gallois, Giles, Jones, Cargile, & Ota in 1995; (b) intercultural adaptation theory by Ellingsworth in 1988); and (c) co-cultural theory by Orbe in 1998.

Communication Accommodation

Communication accommodation theory (CAT) originated in Giles' work in 1973 on accent mobility. CAT began as speech accommodation theory. SAT proposed that speakers use linguistic strategies to gain approval or to show distinctiveness in their interactions with others. The main strategies communicators use based on these motivations are speech convergence or divergence. These are "linguistic moves" to decrease or increase communicative distances, respectively.

Giles et al. expanded SAT in 1987 in terms of the range of phenomena covered and relabeled it CAT. Coupland et al. adapted CAT in 1988 to intergenerational communication and incorporated additional modifications to the theory (e.g., conceptualizing speaker strategies as based on an "addressee focus" and incorporating addressees' attributions about speakers' behavior). In 1998 Gallois et al. adapted Coupland et al.'s model to intercultural communication of 1988. This modification integrated predictions from ethnolinguistic identity theory, and emphasized the influence of situations on intercultural communication. In 1995 Gallois et al. updated the 1988 version of the theory incorporating research that had been conducted and cross-cultural variability in accommodative processes.

CAT begins with the "sociohistorical context" of the interaction. This includes the relations between the groups having contact and the social norms regarding contact (intercultural contact is one type of intergroup contact in CAT). This component also includes cultural variability.

The second component of CAT is the communicators' "accommodative orientation;" their tendencies to perceive encounters with outgroup members in interpersonal terms, intergroup terms, or a combination of the two. There are three aspects to accommodative orientations: (a) "intrapersonal factors" (e.g., social and personal identities), (b) "intergroup factors" (e.g., factors that reflect communicators' orientations to outgroups, such as perceived ingroup vitality), and "initial orientations" (e.g., perceived potential for conflict; long-term accommodative motivation toward outgroups).

The perceived relations between groups influences communicators' tendencies to perceive encounters as interpersonal or intergroup. Similarly, members of dominant groups who have insecure social identities and perceive threats from outgroups tend to perceive convergence by members of subordinate groups negatively. Also, individuals who are dependent on their groups and feel solidarity with them tend to see encounters in intergroup terms and tend to emphasize linguistic markers of their groups.

The third component in CAT is the "immediate situation." There are five aspects to the immediate situation: (a) "socio-psychological states" (e.g., communicators' interpersonal or intergroup orientation in the situation), (b) "goals and addressee focus" (e.g., motivations in the encounter, conversational needs, relational needs), (c) "sociolinguistic strategies" (e.g., approximation, discourse management), (d) "behavior and tactics" (e.g., language, accent, topic), and (e) "labeling and attributions." The five aspects of the immediate situation are interrelated.

The final component of CAT is "evaluation and future intentions." The propositions here focus on communicators' perceptions of their interlocutors' behavior in the interaction. Convergent behavior that is perceived to be based on "benevolent intent," for example, tends to be evaluated positively. When **interlocutors** who are perceived to be typical group members are evaluated positively, individuals are motivated to communicate with the interlocutors and other members of their groups in the future.

Intercultural Adaptation

Ellingsworth assumed in 1983 that all communication involves some degree of cultural variability. He, therefore, argues that explaining intercultural communication needs to start from interpersonal communication and cultural factors need to be incorporated. Ellingsworth's theory in 1983 is designed to explain how communicators adapt to each other in "purpose-related encounters." He isolates eight "laws" (i.e., "ongoing relationships by which units affect one another."). Examples of Ellingsworth's laws are "Adaptation of communication style affects invocation of culture-based belief differences." And "the burden of adaptive behavior is affected by the extent to which setting favors one or the other participant."

Ellingsworth argued in 1983 that functionally adapting communication and equity in adaptation facilitate task completion. Nonfunctional adaptive communication leads to **invocation** of cultural differences and slowing task completion. When communicators have to cooperate there is equity in adapting communication. Using persuasive strategies leads to adapting communication. When the situation favors one communicator or one communicator has more power, the other communicator has the burden to adapt. The more adaptive behavior in which communicators engage, the more their cultural beliefs will change. Ellingsworth updated the theory in 1988 by expanding discussion of the laws and propositions in the theory. The theory, however, remains essentially the same.

Co-cultural Theory

In 1998 Orbe used a phenomenological approach to develop co-cultural theory. Co-cultural theory is based in muted group theory (e.g., social hierarchies in society privilege some groups over others) and standpoint theory (e.g., specific positions in society provide subjective ways that individuals look at the world). Co-cultures include, but are not limited to, nonwhites, women, people with disabilities, homosexuals, and those in the lower social classes.

Orbe pointed out in 1998 that "in its most general form, co-cultural communication refers to interactions among underrepresented and dominant group members". The focus of co-cultural theory is providing a framework "by which co-cultural group members negotiate attempts by others to render their voices muted within dominant societal structures". Two premises guide co-cultural theory: (a) co-cultural group members are marginalized in the dominant societal structures, and (b) co-cultural group members use certain communication styles to achieve success when confronting the "oppressive dominant structures."

Orbe argues that co-cultural group members generally have one of three goals for their interactions with dominant group members: (a) assimilation (e.g., become part of the mainstream culture), (b) accommodation (e.g., try to get the dominant group members to accept co-cultural group members), and (c) separation (e.g., rejecting the possibility of common bonds with dominant group members). Other factors that influence co-cultural group members' communication are "field of experience" (e.g., past experiences), "abilities" (e.g., individuals' abilities to enact different practices), the "situational context" (e.g., where are they communicating with dominant group members?), "perceived costs and rewards" (e.g., the pros and cons of certain practices), and the "communication approach" (i.e., being aggressive, assertive or nonassertive).

Orbe isolates practices co-cultural group members use in their interaction with dominant group members. The practices used are a function of the co-cultural group members' goals and communication approaches. The combination of these yield nine communication orientations in which different practice tend to be used: (a) nonassertive separation involves practices of "avoiding" and "maintaining interpersonal barriers"; (b) nonassertive accommodation involves practices of "increasing visibility" and "dispelling stereotypes"; (c) nonassertive assimilation involves practices of "emphasizing commonalities," "developing positive face," "censoring self," and "averting controversy"; (d) assertive separation involves practices of "communicating oneself," "intragroup networking," "exemplifying strengths," and "embracing stereotypes"; (e) assertive accommodation involves practices of "communicating self," "intragroup networking," "utilizing liaisons," and "educating others"; (f) assertive assimilation involves practices of "extensive preparation," "overcompensating," "manipulating stereotypes," and "bargaining"; (g) aggressive separation involves practices of "attacking" and "sabotaging others"; (h) aggressive accommodation involves practices of "confronting" and "gaining advantage"; and (i) aggressive assimilation involves practices of "dissociating," "mirroring," "strategic distancing," and "ridiculing self." The above can be summarized in the Table 8.2 below.

Table 8.2　Orbe's Co-cultural Communication Orientations

Communication Orientation	Separation	Accommodation	Assimilation
Nonassertive	Avoiding Maintaining interpersonal barriers	Increasing visibility Dispelling stereotypes	Emphasiziting commonalities, Developing positive face Censoring self Averting controversy
Assertive	Communicating oneself Intragroup networking Exemplifying strengths Embracing stereotypes	Conmmnicating self Intragroup networking Utilizing liaisons Educating others	Extensive preparation Overcompensating Manipulating stereotypes Bargaining
Aggressive	Attacking Sabotaging others	Confronting Gaining advantage	Dissociating Mirroring Strategic Distancing Ridiculing self

▶ Theories Focusing on Identity Negotiation or Management

Another goal that theorists use as a focus of their work is negotiating identities in intercultural interactions. These theories address adaptation of identities, not specific communication behaviors (as in the preceding section). Four theories focus on identity: (a) cultural identity theory by Collier and Thomas in 1988; (b) identity management theory by Cupach and Imahori in 1993; (c) identity negotiation theory by Ting-Toomey in 1993; and (d) the communication theory of identity by Hecht in 1993.

Cultural Identity

In 1988 Collier and Thomas presented an "interpretive" theory of how cultural identities are managed in intercultural interactions. Their theory is stated in six assumptions, five axioms, and one theorem. The assumptions are: (a) individuals "negotiate multiple identities in discourse"; (b) intercultural communication occurs "by the discursive assumption and avowal of differing cultural identities"; (c) intercultural communication competence involves managing meanings coherently, and engaging in rule-following (i.e., appropriate) and outcomes that are positive (i.e., effective); (d) intercultural communication competence involves negotiating "mutual meanings, rules, and positive outcomes"; (e) intercultural communication competence involves validating cultural identities (i.e., "identification with and perceived acceptance into a group that has shared systems of symbols and meanings as well as norms/rules for conduct"; and (f) cultural identities vary as a function of scope (e.g., how general identities are), salience (e.g., how important identities are), and intensity (e.g., how strongly identities are communicated to others).

Given the six assumptions, Collier and Thomas developed five axioms in 1988. The first axiom states that "the more that norms and meanings differ in discourse, the more intercultural the contact." The second axiom suggests that the more individuals have intercultural communication competence, the better they are able to develop and maintain intercultural relationships. The third axiom is similar to the first and states that "the more that cultural identities differ in the discourse, the more intercultural the contact."

The fourth axiom suggests that the more one person's ascribed cultural identity for the other person matches the other person's avowed cultural identity, the more the intercultural competence. The final axiom states that "linguistic references to cultural identity systematically **covary** with socio-contextual factors such as participants, type of episode, and topic." The theorem claims that the more cultural identities are avowed, the more important they are relative to other identities.

Identity Management

Cupach and Imahori's identity management theory (IMT) in 1993 is based on interpersonal communication competence. IMT is based on Goffman's work in 1967 on self-presentation and facework.

Cupach and Imahori view identity as providing "an interpretive frame for experience." Identities provide expectations for behavior and motivate individuals' behavior. Individuals have multiple identities, but Cupach and Imahori view cultural and relational identities (e.g., identities within specific relationships) as central to identity management. Following Collier and Thomas, Cupach and Imahori view identities as varying as a function of scope (e.g., number of individuals who share identity), salience (e.g., importance of identity), and intensity (e.g., strength with which identity is communicated to others). Intercultural communication occurs when interlocutors have different cultural identities and intracultural communication occurs when interlocutors share cultural identities.

Cupach and Imahori argue that aspects of individuals' identities are revealed through the presentation of face (e.g., situated identities individuals claim). They contend "the maintenance of face is a natural and inevitable condition of human interaction." In IMT, "interpersonal communication competence should include the ability of an individual to successfully negotiate mutually acceptable identities in interaction." The ability to maintain face in interactions is one indicator of individuals' interpersonal communication competence. Cupach and Imahori believe this extends to intercultural communication competence as well.

Cupach and Imahori argue that since individuals often do not know much about others' cultures, they manage face in intercultural encounters using stereotypes. Stereotyping, however, is face-threatening because it is based on externally imposed identities. The result is a dialectic tension regarding three aspects of face: (a) fellowship face versus autonomy face, (b) competence face versus autonomy face, and (c) autonomy face versus fellowship or competence face. Intercultural communication competence involves successfully managing face, which involves managing these three dialectical tensions.

Cupach and Imahori contend that competence in developing intercultural relationships goes through three phases. The first phase involves "trail-and-error" processes of finding identities on which communicators share some similarities. The second phase involves enmeshment of the identities of the participants into "a mutually acceptable and convergent relational identity, in spite of the fact that their cultural identities are still divergent." The third phase involves renegotiating identities. "Competent intercultural interlocutors use their narrowly defined but emerging relational identity from the second phase as the basis for renegotiating their separate cultural identities." Cupach and Imahori argue that the three phases are "cyclical" and individuals in intercultural relationships may go through the three phases for each aspect of their identities that are relevant to their relationships.

Identity Negotiation

Ting-Toomey argued in 1993 that intercultural communication competence is "the effective identity negotiation process between two interactants in a novel communication episode." She makes several assumptions in constructing identity negotiation theory (INT): cultural variability influences the sense of self, self-identification involves security and vulnerability, identity boundary regulation motivates behavior, identity boundary regulation involves a tension between inclusion and differentiation, managing the inclusion differentiation dialectic influences the coherent sense of self, and a coherent sense of self influences individuals' communication resourcefulness (i.e., the knowledge and ability to apply cognitive, affective, and behavioral resources appropriately, effectively, and creatively in diverse interaction situations).

Ting-Toomey argues that the more secure individuals' self-identifications are, the more they are open to interacting with members of other cultures. The more vulnerable individuals feel, the more anxiety they experience in these interactions. Individuals' vulnerability is affected by their need for security. The more individuals need inclusion, the more they value ingroup and relational boundaries. The more individuals need differentiation, the more distance they place between the self and others.

Individuals' resourcefulness in negotiating identities is affected by effectively managing the security-vulnerability and inclusion-differentiation dialectics. The more secure individuals' self-identifications, the greater their identity coherence and global self-esteem. The greater individuals' self-esteem and the greater their membership collective esteem, the more resourceful they are when interacting with strangers.

Individuals' motivation to communicate with strangers influences the degree to which they seek out communication resources. The greater individuals' cognitive, affective, and behavioral resourcefulness, the more effective they are in identity negotiation. The more diverse individuals' communication resources are, the more effective they are in interactive identity confirmation, coordination, and attunement. Finally, the more diverse individuals' communication resources, the more flexible they are in "co-creating interactive goals" and "developing mutual identity meanings and comprehensibility" according to Ting-Toomey in 1993.

A Communication Theory of Identity

In 1993 Hecht laid the foundation for the theory. He argues that there are "polarities or contradictions in all social life … elements of these polarities are present in all interactions." Hecht argues that identity is a "communicative process" and must be studied in the context of exchanged messages. He starts from several assumptions:

(a) Identities have individual, social, and communal properties;

(b) Identities are both enduring and changing;

(c) Identities are affective, cognitive, behavioral, and spiritual;

(d) Identities have both content and relationship levels of interpretation;

(e) Identities involve both subjective and ascribed meanings;

(f) Identities are codes that are expressed in conversations and define membership in communities;

(g) Identities have semantic properties that are expressed in core symbols, meaning, and labels;

(h) Identities prescribe modes of appropriateand effective communication.

Hecht contends that these assumptions are consistent with dialectical theory.

Hecht argues that there are four identity frames: personal, enacted, relational, and communal. Frames "are means of interpreting reality that provide a perspective for understanding the social world." Identity as a personal frame involves the characteristics of individuals. He makes three assumptions about the personal frame: (a) "Identities are hierarchically ordered meanings," (b) "Identities are meanings ascribed to the self by others," and (c) "Identities are a source of expectation and motivation."

Hecht argues that identities are enacted in interactions with others. He contends that "not all messages are about identity, but identity is part of all messages." There are three assumptions about identity enactment: "Identities are emergent," "Identities are enacted in social behavior and symbols," and "Identities are hierarchically order[ed] social roles."

Hecht sees identities as emerging in relationships with others and part of the relationships because they are "jointly negotiated." He isolates three relationship frame assumptions: "Identities emerge in relationship to other people," "Identities are enacted in relationships," and "Relationships develop identities as social entities."

Hecht also views identities in a communal frame: "something held by a group of people which, in turn, bonds the group together." He isolates one proposition: "Identities emerge out of groups and networks."

Theories Focusing on Communication Networks

Network theories are based on the assumption that individuals' behavior is influenced by relationships between individuals rather than the characteristics of the individuals. "In network theory, the main focus is on positions and social relationships, rather than beliefs or internalized norms. Also, the focus is on series of interconnecting relationships, rather than static, bounded groups," as Yum stated in 1988. These theories focus on explaining linkages between people from different cultures. Three theories focus on networks: (a) outgroup communication competence theory by Kim in 1986; (b) intracultural versus intercultural networks theory by Yum in 1988; and (c) networks and acculturation theory by Smith in 1999.

Networks and Outgroup Communication Competence

In 1986 Kim used a personal network approach to explain outgroup communication competence. Personal networks emphasize the links between individuals. She argues that "one of the most important aspects of a personal network is ego's conscious and unconscious reliance on the network members for perceiving and interpreting various attributes and actions of others (and of self)."

Kim assumes that having outgroup members in individuals' personal networks and the nature of these outgroup ties influence their outgroup communication competence. Theorem 1 states that "a higher level of heterogeneity of a personal network is associated with a higher level of ego's overall outgroup communication competence." This theorem suggests that having outgroup members in individuals' personal networks facilitates outgroup communication competence.

Theorem 2 in Kim's theory proposes that "a higher level of centrality of outgroup members in a personal network is associated with a higher level of the ego's outgroup communication competence." This theorem suggests that having outgroup members in central positions in individuals' personal networks facilitates outgroup communication competence.

Theorem 3 contends that "a higher level of an ego's tie strength with outgroup members is associated with a higher level of his/her ego's outgroup communication competence." This theorem suggests that the more frequent the contact and the closer the ties individuals have with outgroup members, the more their outgroup communication competence.

Intracultural versus Intercultural Networks

Yum's theory in 1988 is designed to explain the differences in individuals' intracultural and intercultural networks. She begins with the assumption that there is more variance in behavior between cultures than within cultures. There are six theorems in Yum's theory.

Yum's first theorem posits that intercultural networks tend to be radial (e.g., individuals are linked to others who are not linked to each other) and **intracultural** networks tend to be interlocking (e.g., individuals are linked to others who are linked to each other). Theorem 2 predicts that intracultural networks are more dense (e.g., the ratio of actual direct links to number of possible links) than intercultural networks.

Yum's third theorem proposes that intracultural networks are more multiplex (e.g., multiple messages flow through linkages) than intercultural networks. Theorem 4 states that "intercultural network ties are more likely to be weak ties than strong ties." Strong ties involve frequent and close contact (e.g., friendships). Links between acquaintances and people with whom individuals have intermittent role relationships (e.g., hair dressers) tend to be weak ties.

Theorem 5 in Yum's theory states that "the roles of liaison and bridge will be more prevalent and more important for network connectedness in intercultural networks than in intracultural networks." Liaisons are individuals who link cliques (e.g., a group of connected individuals) but are not members of any of the cliques. Bridges are individuals who link cliques and are members of one of the cliques. Both are "intermediaries" and can form indirect linkages between members of different groups.

Yum's final theorem suggests that "**transivity** will play a much smaller role in creating intercultural networks than intracultural networks." Transivity occurs when "my friend's friends are my friends." Since intercultural networks tend to be **uniplex** and involve weak ties, they do facilitate forming networks with friends of outgroup members in the network.

Networks and Acculturation

Smith's theory in 1999 links social networks to immigrant acculturation. The theory consists of seven assumptions about the nature of networks, and seven propositions. The first proposition suggests that immigrants tend to be linked to those individuals who define their identities (e.g., other immigrants from their cultures or host nationals). The second proposition claims that the way immigrants experience their social networks is influenced by their native cultures.

Smith's third proposition suggests that the more host nationals are in immigrants' social networks, the more likely immigrants are to acculturate. The fourth proposition claims that as immigrants become integrated into host communities, their social networks change. Proposition 5 contends that factors like where immigrants live and their social class influence their abilities to form intercultural networks and acculturate.

Smith's sixth proposition states that dense networks (e.g., links connected to each other) decrease immigrants' abilities to obtain the resources needed for acculturation. The final proposition contends that "intercultural networks will be less dense, with more radial ties in cultures reflecting a contextual-based relationship norm than those found in cultures reflecting a person-based relationship norm."

Theories Focusing on Acculturation and Adjustment

The acculturation of immigrants and the adjustment of sojourners have been of interest to scholars for over 50 years. Only in recent years, however, have formal theories focusing on communication been proposed. Five theories are examined in this section: (a) communication acculturation theory by Kim in 1988 and 2001; (b) interactive acculturation model by Bourhis et al. in 1997; (c) anxiety/uncertainty management theory of adjustment by Gudykunst in 1998; (d) communication in assimilation, deviance, and alienation states theory by McGuire and McDermott in 1988; and (e) a schema theory of adaptation by Nishida in 1999. The first two focus on the acculturation of immigrants and the other three focus on the adjustment of sojourners.

Cross-Cultural Adaptation

Kim has been developing her theory of communication and acculturation for over 20 years. The first version of the theory appeared in a causal model of Korean immigrants' **acculturation** to Chicago according to Kim in 1977. She has refined the theory several times using an open-system perspective. One of the major changes incorporated into the theory is adding the "stress, adaptation, and growth dynamics" that immigrants go through, and focusing on immigrants becoming "intercultural." In addition, the current version of the theory attempts to portray "cross-cultural adaptation as a collaborative effort, in which a stranger and the receiving environment are engaged in a joint effort."

The current version of Kim's theory in 2001 contains assumptions based on open-systems theory, axioms, and theorems. The axioms are "law like" statements about relationships between units in the theory. Theorems are derived from the axioms. The first five axioms are broad principles of cross-cultural adaptation: acculturation and **deculturation** are part of the cross-cultural adaptation process; the stress-adaptation-growth dynamic underlies the adaptation process; intercultural transformations are a function of the stress-adaptation-growth dynamic; the severity of the stress-adaptation-growth dynamic decreases as strangers go through intercultural transformations; and functional fitness and psychological health result from intercultural transformations. The final five axioms deal with the reciprocal relationship between intercultural transformations and host communication competence, host communication activities, ethnic communication activities, environmental conditions, and strangers' predispositions.

The first three theorems posit relationships between host communication competence and host communication activities (+), ethnic communication activities (−), and intercultural transformations (+). Host interpersonal and mass communication activities are related to ethnic communication activities (−), and intercultural transformations (+). Ethnic interpersonal and mass communication activities are related negatively to intercultural transformations.

The next three theorems relate host receptivity and conformity pressure to host communication competence (+), host communication activities (+), and ethnic communication activities (－). Ethnic group strength is related to host communication competence (－), host communication activities (－), and ethnic communication activities (＋). Ethnic proximity is related to host communication competence (＋), host communication activities (＋), and ethnic communication activities (－).

Strangers' preparedness for change is related to host communication competence (＋), host communication activities (＋), and ethnic communication activities (＋). Strangers' adaptive personalities are related to host communication competence (＋), host communication activities (＋), and ethnic communication activities (－).

Interactive Acculturation Model

Bourhis et al.'s interactive acculturation model (IAM) in 1997 suggests that relational outcomes between host nationals and immigrant groups are a function of the "acculturation orientations of both the host majority and immigrant groups as influenced by state integration policies." They begin by adapting Berry's model of immigrant acculturation in 1980 and 1990.

Berry's model in 1980 is based on immigrants' responses to two issues: (a) "do they want to maintain their native cultural identities?", (b) "do they want to maintain good relations with members of the host culture.?" If the answer is "yes" on both issues, they use an "integration" orientation with respect to the host culture. If they answer "yes" to having relations with hosts and "no" to maintaining their cultural identities, immigrants have an "assimilation" orientation toward the host culture. If immigrants answer "yes" to maintaining their native cultural identities and "no" to having good relations with hosts, they have a "separation" orientation toward the host culture. If they answer "no" to both issues, they have a marginal orientation toward the host culture. In 1997 Bourhis et al. divided the marginal orientation into "anomie" (e.g., cultural alienation) and "individualism" (e.g., they define themselves and hosts as individuals rather than as members of groups).

Bourhis et al. developed a similar model for hosts' acculturation orientation in 1997. The model is based on responses on two questions: "(a) Do you find it acceptable that immigrants maintain their cultural heritage? (b) Do you accept that immigrants adapt to the culture of your host culture?" If hosts answer "yes" to both questions, they have an "integration" orientation toward immigrants. If they answer "no" to question 1 and "yes" to question 2, they have an "assimilation" orientation. If hosts answer "yes" to question 1 and "no" to question 2, the "segregation" orientation. If hosts answer "no" to both questions, they have an "exclusion" or "individualism" orientation.

In 1997 Bourhis et al. combined the two models to form the IAM. They use the IAM to predict whether there are "consensual," "problematic," or "conflictual" relational outcomes between hosts and immigrants. To illustrate, "the most consensual relational outcomes are predicted in three cells of the model, namely when both host community members and immigrant group members share either the integration, assimilation, or individualism acculturation orientations."

UNIT EIGHT
Eastern and Western Theorizing about Intercultural Communication

Anxiety/Uncertainty Management

Defining strangers is a figure-ground phenomenon. The effective communication version of ADM theory is written from the perspective of individuals communicating with strangers (e.g., others approaching individuals' ingroups). The adjustment version of the theory is written from the perspective of strangers (e.g., sojourners) entering new cultures and interacting with host nationals.

The original version of ADM theory was a theory of adjustment by Gudykunst and Hammer in 1988. Gudykunst included axioms comparable to the 1995 version of the effective communication version, plus two additional axioms focusing specifically on adjustment (i.e., pluralistic tendencies in host culture decreases and permanence of stay increases strangers' anxiety).

When strangers enter a new culture they have uncertainty about host nationals' attitudes, feelings, beliefs, values, and behaviors. Strangers need to be able to predict which of several alternative behavior patterns hosts will employ. When strangers communicate with hosts, they also experience anxiety. Anxiety is the tension, feelings of being uneasy, tension, or apprehension strangers have about what will happen when they communicate with hosts. The anxiety strangers experience when they communicate with hosts is based on negative expectations.

To adjust to other cultures, strangers do not want to try to reduce their anxiety and uncertainty totally according to Gudykunst in 1995. At the same time, strangers cannot communicate effectively with hosts if their uncertainty and anxiety are too high. If uncertainty is too high, strangers cannot accurately interpret hosts' messages or make accurate predictions about hosts' behaviors. When anxiety is too high, strangers communicate on automatic pilot and interpret hosts' behaviors using their own cultural frames of reference. Also, when anxiety is too high, the way strangers process information is very simple, thereby limiting their ability to predict hosts' behaviors. When uncertainty is too low, strangers become overconfident that they understand hosts' behaviors and do not question whether their predictions are accurate. When anxiety is too low, strangers are not motivated to communicate with hosts.

If strangers' anxiety is high, they must mindfully manage their anxiety to communicate effectively and adjust to the host cultures. Managing anxiety requires that strangers become mindful (e.g., create new categories, be open to new information, be aware of alternative perspectives). When strangers have managed their anxiety, they need to try to develop accurate predictions and explanations for hosts' behaviors. When strangers communicate on automatic pilot, they predict and interpret hosts' behaviors using their own frames of reference. When strangers are mindful, in contrast, they are open to new information and aware of alternative perspectives (e.g., hosts' perspectives) and they, therefore, can make accurate predictions.

Lieberson argued in 1985 that it is necessary to isolate "basic" and "superficial" causes of the phenomenon being explained. In ADM theory, managing uncertainty and anxiety are the basic causes of strangers' intercultural adjustment. The amount of uncertainty and anxiety strangers experience in their interactions with hosts is a function of many superficial causes (e.g., self-concepts, motivation, reactions to hosts, social categorization, situational processes, connections with hosts). Research supports the theoretical argument that the superficial causes of adjustment (e.g., ability to adapt behavior) are linked to adjustment through uncertainty and anxiety).

Assimilation, Deviance, and Alienation

McGuire and McDermott argued in 1988 that assimilation and adaptation are not permanent outcomes of the adaptation process, rather they are temporary outcomes of the communication process. The reason is that everyone, no matter how well integrated into their cultures, deviates from social norms and rules at some point. They contend that "individuals (or groups) have achieved the assimilation state when their perceptions are receiving positive reinforcement from others' communications ... The group accomplishes an assimilation state when an individual conforms to expected norms."

McGuire and McDermott contended in 1988 that the hosts' response to immigrants' deviation from cultural norms is neglectful communication. Neglectful communication involves negative messages or the absence of messages. When immigrants are not deviant or engage in assimilative communication (e.g., interact with hosts, increase fluency in host languages), host nationals respond with assimilative communication (e.g., praise immigrants' behavior, being available to interact with immigrants).

When immigrants are in a deviancestate they experience tension with their new cultures. Host nationals tend to respond with neglectful communication (e.g., low level of communication, negative feedback). One possible response to host nationals' neglectful communication is for immigrants to become alienated from the host cultures. Alienation involves feelings of "normlessness and social isolation," according to McGuire and McDermott. Immigrants, therefore, may feel that they cannot accomplish their goals and are being excluded from the host cultures. This does not, however, necessarily "involve hostility, aggression or conflict."

The way host nationals respond to immigrants when immigrants feel alienated influences whether immigrants stay in an alienated state. If host nationals respond in a way to strengthen alienation (e.g., refusing to interact with immigrants, being obscene, ridiculing immigrants), immigrants are likely to withdraw from host cultures, be hostile toward the host cultures, or refuse to use the host languages.

McGuire and McDermott argue that the way host nationals and immigrants respond to neglectful communication is similar. They conclude that "changes in the amount or kind of deviance or amount or kind of neglectful communication will push an individual toward or into either the alienation or the assimilation state ... Alienation or assimilation, therefore, of a group or an individual is an outcome of the relationship between deviant behavior and neglectful communication."

A Schema Theory of Adaptation

In 1999 Nishida used schema theory to develop a theory of sojourner adaptation to new cultural environments. She defines schemas as "generalized collections of knowledge of past experiences which are organized into related knowledge groups and are used to guide our behaviors in familiar situations." Nishida contends that sojourners' failures to understand host nationals' behavior is due to sojourners' lack of schemas used in the host culture.

When sojourners do not have the schemas used in the host culture, they tend to focus on "data-driven processing which requires effort and attention." Data-driven processing is affected by sojourners' self-schemas. In other words, sojourners pay attention to information that is important to them (as opposed to what is important to host nationals). Nishida argues that sojourners "actively try to reorganize their native-culture schemas or to generate new schemas in order to adapt to the host culture environment."

Conclusion

As indicated earlier, theorizing about intercultural communication has improved tremendously in recent years. There are, however, still several issues that need to be addressed in future theorizing on intercultural communication.

First, the vast majority of the theories proposed to date are objectivistic in nature. Only a few of the theorists included here claim to have developed **subjectivistic** theories. Some objectivistic theories include subjectivistic components (e.g., mindfulness in AUM), but the general trend is for the two types of theorizing not to be integrated. Clearly, there is a need for more subjectivistic theorizing and for integrating subjectivistic and objectivistic theories.

Second, the vast majority of the theorists were born in the United States. Researchers born in other cultures, however, have developed several of the theories discussed. There may be theories of intercultural communication published in languages other than English of which we are not aware. The lack of theories from outside the United States may be a malfunction of the role of theory in scholarship in different cultures (e.g., developing theories is not emphasized in many cultures). There is, nevertheless, a need for indigenous theories developed by scholars outside the United States.

Third, the issue of power is not incorporated in very many of the theories constructed to date. Clearly, power plays a role in many, but not all, intercultural and intergroup encounters. In 1999 Reid and Ng described the relationships among language, power, and intergroup relations. Power needs to be incorporated in theories of intercultural communication. In 1994 Berger examined power in interpersonal communication, and his analysis provides one starting point for looking at power in intercultural communication.

Fourth, many of the theories proposed to date are compatible with each other, with different scopes and boundary conditions. This allows for the possibility of integration. Gallois et al. indicated in 1995 that CAT could incorporate other theoretical positions but do not present specifics. Similarly, Cupach and Imahori's theory in 1993 appears to be theoretically compatible with Collier and Thomas' theory in 1988. Gudykunst suggested in 1995 that dialectical theory can be integrated with AUM. We believe that integrating theories, especially objectivistic and subjectivistic theories, will increase our ability to understand intercultural communication.

Finally, there is little or no published research supporting some of the theories presented in this article. Given the state of theorizing in intercultural communication, conducting **atheoretical** research is unwarranted. Research designed to test theories is needed to advance the state of our understanding of intercultural communication, not more atheoretical research.

Text B Theorizing Culture and Communication in the Asian Context: An Assumptive Foundation

After Yoshitaka Miike

 Introduction

Throughout the 20th century, the field of communication studies has been one-sidedly dominated by U.S. Eurocentric anthropo-centered, individualistic, efficiency-oriented, positivistic theory and research as Ishii noted in 2001. Conventional academic views of communication have been **skewed** by Western frames of reference. They have not represented a sample of all possible conceptual positions from which the knowledge of communication can be adequately constructed. The world in the 21st century, therefore, needs a plurality of human communication theories, and not any single nation's theory preserving hegemonic rule. Now that this new multilingual and multicultural millennium has arrived, communication researchers today are more than ever before urged to generate theoretical perspectives and paradigms that can resonate with the diversity of human experiences in communication.

In order to expand and enrich current U.S. Eurocentric conceptions of humans communicating, non-Western scholars in the discipline of communication ought to rethink the nature of communication theory from indigenous and comparative perspectives. More specifically, in 1986 Dissanayake pinpointed two main reasons why the study of indigenous and comparative communication theories is of great value. First, it helps to widen the field of discourse and facilitate the emergence of new insights from various cultures that make it possible to better comprehend and conceptualize the act of communication. Second, since theory has a vital link with research, it promotes more productive and relevant communication research in non-Western societies rather than encourages a blindly servile adherence to Western communication research principles.

The major purpose of the present essay is to lay an assumptive foundation from which theoretical perspectives indigenous to Asia will hopefully be designed and developed in comparison with those borrowed from the United States. Toward this end, the essay first delimits what is Asiacentric communication scholarship in relation to U.S. Eurocentric communication scholarship. Second, touching on three central themes in Asian communicative life, it maps out three sets of philosophical assumptions for an Asiacentric theoretical paradigm. Third, in accordance with the philosophical assumptions outlined, it sketches out three core assumptions of human communication for an Asiacentric theoretical approach. In terms of the assumptive foundation proposed, the essay finally discusses possibilities and challenges of Asiacentric communication scholarship in order to theorize culture and communication in the Asian context.

What is Asiacentric Communication Scholarship?

In this first section, I make clear what Asiacentric communication scholarship is in relation to U.S. Eurocentric communication scholarship. For the purpose of the present discussion, I would tentatively define Asiacentric communication scholarship as a theoretical system or a school of thought in communication whose concepts, **postulates**, and resources are rooted in, or derived from, the cumulative wisdom of diverse Asian cultural traditions. There are three important implications of this definition for theorizing culture and communication from Asiacentric perspectives.

First, Asiacentric communication scholarship does not simply refer to a body of knowledge, either theoretical or empirical, about Asian cultural systems of communication. In 1988 Ho, a pioneering advocate of Asian indigenous psychologies, emphatically asserted as follows:

> An Asian psychology with an Asian identity must reflect the Asian intellectual tradition, which is distinct from the Western in its conceptions of human nature, the goal and meaning of life, relationships between the human person and other humans, the family, society, nature, the cosmos, and the divine.

In a similar vein, Asiacentric communication scholarship proposes and promotes non-Western approaches to codes, contexts, and complexities of communication that reflect and respond to the cultural ethos of Eastern peoples.

Asiacentric communication scholarship, therefore, differs from U.S. Eurocentric communication scholarship that deals with Asian modes of communication in Western terms. Ho stated in 1993 that there may be no particular Asianness about a psychology of Asian peoples. Likewise, a body of knowledge about Asian cultural styles of communication generated through U.S. Eurocentric theoretical perspectives and research procedures is U.S. Eurocentric communication scholarship *about* Asian cultural patterns of communication. What is sought after at this juncture is a body of knowledge that accounts for Asian cultural values and communicative behaviors gained through indigenous theoretical insights drawn from the intellectual traditions of Asia.

Second, Asiacentric communication scholarship embraces the diversity of Asia and does not purport to reinforce a monolithic concept of Asia. Jensen noted in 1992 that sharp differences in cultural traditions certainly exist throughout Asia where there are multiple strands which have evolved over time due to various religious, philosophical, political, economic, and geographical factors. Garrett echoed in 1991 that "as we move through space and time, from early China to contemporary Korea, the intellectual **milieux**, major religions, political systems, social and family structures, economic organizations, and languages and writing systems vary tremendously." It is, therefore, very important to remember the diversity of Asia in all discussions of communication across national borders and cultural boundaries.

Unlike U.S. Eurocentric communication scholarship that often depicts Asia as a **homogeneous** entity, Asiacentric communication scholarship ought to embrace, rather than neglect, the diversity of Asia. This does not mean, however, that Asiacentric scholarship cannot have core assumptions that cut across Asian nations and cultures because the existence of the diversity of Asia does not imply the non-existence of a sufficiently identifiable core of Asian traditions. According to Wong, Manvi, and Wong in 1995, Asiacentric scholarship can expound on a common core of Asian beliefs, values, and worldviews which encompass a number of religions and philosophies (e.g., Buddhism, Confucianism, Hinduism, and Taoism) and overlap in their influence on particular countries and regions. Wong, Manvi, and Wong further clarified the goal of Asiacentrism:

> Asiacentrism must thus attempt to explore the possibility of **articulating** a post-Orientalist Asian perspective, grounded in an awareness of the dynamics of a post-colonial world... What is being implied here is not a reiteration of a view that overestimates the unity of Asia in order to construct a monolithic concept of Asia.

Third, Asiacentric communication scholarship endeavors to complement, rather than to reject, U.S. Eurocentric communication scholarship. The afore-mentioned definition does not implicitly suggest that Asiacentric communication scholarship should completely ignore and reject U.S. Eurocentric communication scholarship. Rather, it should seek to understand the limitations or weaknesses of U.S. Eurocentric communication scholarship and strive to complement them by providing "alternative" possibilities of viewing culture and communication. As Goonasekera and Kuo articulated in 2000, "the search for an Asian perspective therefore does not imply the outright rejection of Western theories. What is at issue is the uncritical acceptance of Western models and the neglect of the cumulative wisdom embodied in Asian literature."

In 2001 Ishii identified four theoretical weaknesses of U.S. Eurocentric communication scholarship: (a) it has been white-centric and reluctant to study and accept Eastern thought, philosophy, and assumptions concerning communication studies; (b) it has been uncritically dominated by the Cartesian philosophy based on mind-matter dualism, mechanistic views of human beings and natural beings, and the linear progressivism of science and technology; (c) it has been based on, and supported by, the values of independence and individualism, although there can be no such thing as a completely independent and individual being in the universe; and (d) it has been speaker-centered and persuasion-oriented without paying due attention to relational aspects of communication.

In 1988 Chu observes two methodological problems of U.S. Eurocentric communication scholarship. First, many researchers in U.S. Eurocentric communication scholarship are tempted to follow work done by the more creative pioneers because they do not want to "reinvent the wheel," but want to make sure that their **empirical** research is "cumulative." Unfortunately, according to Chu in 1988, this "sometimes leads to a faddish tendency, abetted further by the 'publish or perish' tradition in the [U.S.] American academic world for quick publication." Second, the heavy reliance on quantitative methodology and statistical analysis in U.S. Eurocentric communication scholarship sets a limit on what one can investigate. Chu confessed in 1988:

> We tend to tackle only those research problems that can be handled by quantitative measures and statistical tests. We often let methodology determine our choice of research topics. This tendency is sometimes referred to as "the tail wagging the dog." The result is that communication research in the Western perspective tends to become repetitive and lacks a clear focus, tackling the problems that may seem to be trivial or irrelevant, although methodologically rigorous.

In order to enlarge the intellectual horizons of culture and communication studies, it is indeed imperative for professionals in Asiacentric communication scholarship to be keenly aware of the above-discussed four theoretical weaknesses and two methodological problems of U.S.

Eurocentric communication scholarship.

▶ Theoretical Assumptions for an Asiacentric Paradigm

In an attempt to propose a conceptual framework in Asian psychology, Ho looked at three Asian cultures (i.e., Chinese, Filipino, and Japanese cultures) in 1993 from which more indigenous key concepts have been derived than from other Asian cultures and discovers three common themes—reciprocity, other-directedness, and harmony. Following his lead, I reread the existing literature on Eastern cultural practices of communication and reviewed Asian conceptualizations of communication theory. From my close rereading emerged three central themes that seemed to be particularly helpful in establishing an Asiacentric paradigm of communication theory: (a) relationality, (b) **circularity**, and (c) harmony.

Irwin duly wrote in 1996 that Asia has no absolute boundaries even though "Asia" designates a certain geographical area in the world where Asianness predominates, and that "what is included in, and thus excluded from, Asia, is often a matter of personal preference or a decision taken according to the purpose of the argument." The reviewed literature focuses primarily on China, India, Japan, and Korea. Asia in the present essay is therefore confined to these four countries. Nonetheless, the proposed Asiacentric assumptions might be applicable to culture and communication scholarship in other Asian nations and regions.

In this second portion, touching on the above three themes in Asian communicative life, I first stipulate three sets of philosophical assumptions—**ontological**, **epistemological**, and **axiological**. Second, coupled with the philosophical assumptions uncovered, I lay out three core assumptions of human communication while making brief mention of several Eastern models of culture and communication. The following assumptions altogether constitute the "tentative" theoretical position of an Asiacentric paradigm of communication theory. It should be kept in mind that the Asiacentric assumptions proposed below are not cultural premises that have been internalized in the minds of all or real Asians. They are formulated for the "specific" purpose of successfully highlighting the meaningfulness of Asian cultural values and communicative behaviors.

Asiacentric Philosophical Assumptions

The ontological assumption for an Asiacentric paradigm is that everyone and everything are interrelated across space and time. This ontological assumption is comprised of the two themes of relationality and circularity. As Kincaid correctly pointed out in 1987, Western ontology has been traditionally dominated by the theme of individualism where the independent self is the figure, and interdependent relationships are the background. The reverse figure-background ontology is more applicable in the East. Oliver aptly explicated it in 1976 as follows:

In India, the **relatedness** of everything that is or that occurs has been basic, with the result that a principal study has been the nature and consequences of relationships... In China the major concern has been societal relatedness—the nature and the means of human intercourse ...

The Asian sense of self is more deep-rooted in the web of human relationships than the

Western sense of ego. In Eastern ways of thinking, humans exist not as independent individuals but as interdependent and interrelated beings. Humans are also enormously influenced by their relationships with political systems, economic power, historical interpretations, religious beliefs, and natural environments. Nature beyond human control is imbricated with the human-made world under human control. It goes without saying that their interconnectedness has far-reaching impacts on humans.

The theme of circularity here refers to transcendence in space and time. It provides a sense of relatedness of the present to the past and the future, and a sense of relatedness of the life world to the whole of nature. Humans exist between their past ancestries and their future descendants. In this regard, they have a crucial role in connecting the past to the future. In the Buddhist worldview of **reincarnation**, moreover, there is a chance that humans will become animals or insects in the birth-death-rebirth cycle. It can be said, then, that they might be related even with animals or insects. Any creature on the earth could be their ancestor. Space is in nature one though humans are prone to think and feel as if it was linearly divided, separated, and controlled. All continents are linked in the sea, and the earth is located in the cosmic space where other planets exist, and possibly other beings live. Any space on the earth is part of a larger circular space.

From a Zen Buddhist viewpoint, Nordstrom went so far as to say in 1979 that "when any two beings communicate, they prove that the whole universe communicates with all aspects of itself, since any time there is communication, there is the vivid experience of the non-separateness of everything." His enlightening statement is perfectly in associated with the proposed "trans-spatial, trans-temporal" Asiacentric ontological assumption.

The epistemological assumption for an Asiacentric paradigm is that everyone and everything become meaningful in relation to others. The foregoing ontological assumption naturally leads to this epistemological assumption. Indian philosophers teach us that since all things, events, phenomena, and beings are united to one another at a higher ontological level, they can be meaningfully understood only in relation to one another according to Dissanayake in 1983. In Chinese epistemology, likewise, genuine knowledge is believed to result from interaction and interrelation between the individual mind and the world. It is not an isolated phenomenon totally independent of individual life and society, nor is it a construction related merely to the basic functioning of the mind.

Dualism and dichotomy are hallmarks of Western thought despite the fact that there are a number of self-criticisms on their weaknesses within the West. In Eastern thought, "because the universe is seen as a harmonious organism, there is a corresponding lack of dualism in epistemological patterns ... The ultimate purpose of knowledge is to transcend the apparent contrasts and 'see' the interconnectedness of all things," as Kim noted in 2000. In passing, the Chinese tendency to polarize is distinctly different from the Western propensity to dichotomize in the sense that it does not uphold one extreme at the expense of the other and advocates a balanced and complementary unity of the two so as to achieve ultimate harmony in the whole.

According to the Buddhist concept of dependent co-origination, it cannot be maintained that a cause produces some object or event. It can be only said that an object or event arises infunctional dependence on such and such a thing. Dissanayake further illustrated in 1983: "The relationship between the cause and effect is one of mutual dependence. Therefore, to refer to them as 'cause' and 'effect' would be misleading because that would presuppose the clear priority of the causes." This Buddhist line of thinking is definitely in tune with the suggested "non-dualistic, non-dichotomous" Asia-centric epistemological assumption.

The axiological assumption for an Asiacentric paradigm is that harmony is vital to the survival of everyone and everything. This axiological assumption springs from the theme of harmony and is **intertwined** with the above-described two other assumptions. In Eastern cultural and communicative life, "harmony, achieving oneness with other human beings, and indeed with nature and all of life, is a historic *summum bonum*, a central value to cherish," according to Jensen in 1992. In 1971 Oliver **succinctly** commented that "in China the goal generally was a harmonious society, in India a harmonious relationship of the individual with the course of nature—which was also the goal of the Chinese Taoists." The countries of East and South Asia embrace religious traditions that feature harmony as the ultimate good. Harmony is "The Way" for Confucianism, Hinduism, Shintoism, and Taoism.

This Eastern axiology of harmony marks a sharp contrast to the Western axiology of control. Servaes assumed in 2000 that the doing orientation of Westerners and the being orientation of Asians dictate different attitudes toward nature and technology. Westerners want to command and control them, while Asians try to achieve harmonious relationships with them. In 1998 Stewart, Danielian, and Foster took notice of this obvious disparity between Eastern and Western axiological underpinnings. The world within the minds of many Westerners is material rather than spiritual and should be exploited for the benefit of humanity. On the contrary, the traditional worldview that reflects the ethos of Asian peoples holds that humanity is inseparable from the environment. It tells us that we should strive for harmony with nature and the physical world rather than attempt to control these forces.

It is philosophically and religiously prioritized in Asia to achieve harmony between humans, between humans and things, between humans and nature, between the past and the present, between the present and the future, and between one space and another. This priority in the East appears to be extremely valuable in the present age when the dominant notion of unrestrained individual freedom at the expense of the natural environment and harmony in interpersonal relationships is increasingly being challenged in the West. Human beings, who have become excessively anthropo-centered and materialistic as a result of the recent progress in science and technology, are now destined to coexist by interacting harmoniously with supernatural beings and natural beings as well as other human beings according to Ishii in 2001.

Asiacentric Communicative Assumptions

The first core assumption of human communication for an Asiacentric paradigm is that communication takes place in contexts of multiple relationships across space and time. The Asiacentric ontological assumption places the utmost **premium** on communication contexts. It is commonly said that communication takes place not in a vacuum but in a context. Nevertheless, a glance at most U.S. Eurocentric models of human communication reveals that conceptualizations of communication contexts are not in-depth and clear-cut ones in spite of the fact that communicator attributes and message encoding and decoding processes are well-documented and carefully elucidated. Yum contended in 1989 as follows:

> Many communication theories that are based upon the individual as the unit of analysis have tended to account for human communication behavior in term of personality characteristics or individual socioeconomic positions. Such theories imply that the individual behaves in a context-free world as if internal predispositions alone can explain one's course of action. On the other hand, other theories imply that the message itself is the most important component in creating certain communication effects... This overemphasis on the individual [and the message] at the expense of the social context in communication theories may be due to the Western culture's emphasis on individualism... [U.S.] American approach to the world is characterized by individual-centeredness and independence in comparison to an East Asian approach of situation-centeredness and mutual dependence. The fundamental value orientation of individualism is expressed in theorizing communication phenomena as well.

Contexts should garner increasing attention among conceptual theorists in human communication because they make it possible for the whole communication process to function. In 1972 Kleinjans called for the study of historical interpretations and socio-economic conditions which form the context for communicating with Asia. It is high time for Asiacentric communication experts to scrutinize political systems, religious beliefs, historical events, and philosophical thoughts that are integral to a culture and to conceptualize them as communication contexts. It is also imperative that they delve into how such various contexts influence one another.

Another important point to be made with reference to this first Asiacentric communicative assumption is that communication contexts need to be conceived as "transspatial" and "transtemporal." Transspatiality and transtemporality in ontological relatedness are not found in most U.S. Eurocentric conceptualizations of communication contexts. In this connection, Asiacentric communication professionals are particularly expected to conceptualize religious belief systems as communication contexts of spatial and temporal circularity. As Dissanayake posited in 1983, since in the East, religion and traditional culture are closely **interwoven** in a way that is uncommon in the West. Religion serves as an excellent window through which to view postulates and presuppositions that guide and govern Asian communicative behavior.

Ishii's Japanese model of communication in 1998 contexts based on the Buddhist concept of *en* (predestined connection) is one of the few Eastern communication models that captures transspatiality and transtemporality in ontological relatedness. It is in stark contrast to the typical Western model of communication in that religious belief contexts of multiple relationships across space and time are the figure, whereas the communicators who are mysteriously interrelated and interdependent are the background. Chen's Chinese model of human relationship development in 1998 based on the *I Ching* is also worthy of great attention. The eight stages and the cyclic process of human relationship development in Chinese communication delineated in his model are grounded on the *I Ching* ontological assumptions of spatial and temporal circularity.

The second core assumption of human communication for an Asiacentric paradigm is that the

UNIT EIGHT
Eastern and Western Theorizing about Intercultural Communication

communicator is perceptually and behaviorally both active and passive in a variety of contexts. What the Asiacentric epistemological assumption brings into focus in human communication is that the communicator's perception and behavior are not independent of her or his relationships with her or his surroundings, namely, communication contexts. This suggests that communication specialists cannot identify and analyze human agency in communication processes without taking multiple communication contexts into full consideration. To put it in another way, they cannot specify and evaluate the activeness and passiveness of humans communicating until they clarify the contexts and complexities of communication.

This second Asiacentric communicative assumption is also intended to stress at least two levels (i.e., sense-making and behavioral levels) on which the communicator's activeness and passiveness are comprehended. The sensemaking level refers to whether the communicator is **intrapersonally** active or passive in making sense of her or his perceptual world. The behavioral level indicates whether or not the communicator is outwardly active or passive in participating in communicative interactions verbally and/or non-verbally.

People from Asian cultures are oftentimes one-sidedly labeled by U.S. Eurocentric cross-cultural communication researchers as "passive communicators." And in most cases, the implication of this statement is that Asians are less communicatively competent and need to be trained so as to communicate internationally and interculturally. Those investigators do not usually direct any attention to political-ideological contexts of international and intercultural communication and to the sense-making and behavioral levels. Asians are, in fact, extremely active on the sense-making level when they accept or reject various communication contexts such as *en-*belief systems.

Asante and Vora argued in 1983 that one of the U.S. Eurocentric theoretical perspectives in communication is "the emphasis and reliance on overt behavior to measure effectiveness of a communication effort," and that "the philosophy is that the end results are the primary measure of success". They poignantly question:

Isn't it possible that the behavior may have occurred despite poor communication or may not have materialized in spite of effective communication? ... The emergent behavior (action or lack of it) may be affected by many variables, such as immediate issues, technological infeasibility, and resistance to change.

It could be **speculated** that whereas Westerners have a general propensity to be more outwardly and behaviorally active in communicative interactions, Easterners are, by and large, **predisposed** to be more inwardly and perceptually active in communicative interactions. This focal point of difference possibly leads Asiacentric and U.S. Eurocentric communication experts to construct complementary models of communication. According to Dissanayake, for example, the proponents of the Indian indigenous model detect that "what is important in human communication is to find out how a receiver makes sense of verbal stimuli received and engages in a search for meaning. And this search is an inward one."

The third core assumption of human communication for an Asiacentric paradigm is that mutual adaptation is of central importance in harmonious communication processes. This assumption is coupled with the Asiacentric axiological assumption. There is no denying that mutual adaptation is the key to harmonious communication and relationships. Most communication professionals agree with Howell who maintains that communication is a joint venture where both participants adjust continually to what happens from moment to moment. Not so many theorists, nonetheless, put this adaptation postulate at the center when they theorize human communication. Howell's model of communication is probably one of the few Western models that substantially illuminates and illustrates message adjustment processes and practices.

Ishii's *enryo-sasshi* model of Japanese interpersonal communication in 1984 is one of the first non-Western attempts to explore and explain the mechanism of how the communicators adjust their messages to maintain interpersonal and situational harmony. His model captures the mutually adjusting functions of *enryo* and *sasshi* as crucial abilities for successful and smooth communication. The speaker, depending on the listener and the communicative situation, simplifies and economizes messages (*enryo*) rather than elaborating on them. Messages are then usually "safe" and "vague." The listener is expected to engage in empathic guesswork so as to expand and develop the messages (*sasshi*) and decipher their intended meanings. In order to make this *enryo-sasshi* communication successful, the extent of *enryo* on the part of the speaker meshes with that of *sasshi* on the part of the listener according to Miike in 1997.

Another non-Western contribution in this line of theorization is Kume's *mawashi* decision-making model of Japanese group and organizational communication in 1997. *Mawashi*, which originates from the traditional village meeting in Japan, can be defined as "a way of reaching consensus by passing around views almost endlessly among members of a group." In *mawashi* communication processes, where intrapersonal reflection is far more important than interpersonal self-assertiveness, each group member's opinion is supposed to be mutually shared and adjusted toward unanimous agreement. This *mawashi* decision-making style, which is time-consuming and one-sidedly criticized by Westerners for that reason, in effect reflects **egalitarian** values in "vertical" Japanese society.

It is quite certain that Westerners also employ *enryo-sasshi* and *mawashi* communication styles. However, similar theoretical models have not yet enjoyed much research attention among U.S. Eurocentric communication scholars. Such relational, reciprocal models of communication based on Asian cultural concepts of other-directedness may be applied cross-culturally to re-observe and/or re-evaluate human communication phenomena in Western (co-)cultures. The two Japanese models above only highlight the impact of reciprocity on communication processes within limited spatial and temporal contingencies. Asiacentric communication specialists can theorize **reciprocal** aspects of adaptive communication from "extended" perspectives on space and time, which are undoubtedly blind spots of U.S. Eurocentric thinking on communication. The Asian sense of indebtedness and obligation, for instance, usually goes beyond here-and-now reciprocity and greatly affects adaptation in human communication. Indebtedness is expected to be paid in Asian societies, and this obligation has no time limitation, as Ho stated in 1982.

Incorporating this third communicative assumption into the core Asiacentric assumptions has implications for theorizing communication competence because mutual adaptation has a great deal to do with otherness. Bruneau held in 1998: "Competency in the United States is often based in assessment made as to one's performance, efficiency, quality and quantity of productivity, and relating to the end-results of effort. " He criticized severely in 1998 as follows:

> [The] United States [communication] scholarship has initially fostered the idea of competency-based communication mainly from an individualistic, ego-centric, geo-centric, rational, goal-oriented or purposive, compliance-gaining perspective. The U.S. approach has neglected affective communication variables except for scarce or token mention.

Bruncau continued in 1998:

> The lack of allocentric (other-directed) thinking (mainly feminine) or the use of empathic processes... is especially absent. What this means is that the current thought about ICC [intercultural communication competency] does not fit the thought patterns of not only most of the peoples of the world, it excludes a feminine perspective.

Possibilities and Challenges of an Asiacentric Paradigm

In the previous pages, I defined and delimited Asiacentric communication scholarship and laid out philosophical and communicative assumptions for the development of an Asiacentric paradigm. In the following pages, based on the preceding discussion, I address possibilities and challenges that lie ahead for Asiacentric communication researchers in their efforts to theorize culture and communication in the Asian context.

Possibilities for an Asiacentric Paradigm

Theory building is not just a matter of scholars' thought processes but also a matter of their choices of research materials and methods. It is undoubtedly swayed by the use of research materials and methods that scholars are socialized to consider as useful and helpful. Participating in alternative theorizing activities, therefore, partially means engaging in alternative research topics, materials, and methods. By the same token, modifying theoretical orientations inevitably leads to changing research orientations. With this inseparability of theorizing activities and research attitudes in mind, I will propose three lines of future inquiry for an Asiacentric paradigm of communication theory.

First, Asiacentric communication professionals can take full advantage of indigenous literature in Asia and in Asian languages and **conceptualize** communication contexts of multiple relationships across space and time. China has her own over 5000-year history of the Asian heritage. India embraces age-old, profound religions and philosophies. Histories, religions, and philosophies in Asia are "rich storehouses" for conceptualizing Asiacentric models of communication contexts such as Ishii in 1998 and Chen in 1998. U.S. or Eurocentric communication scholarship almost always ignores the relevant literature in other languages and countries. Asiacentric communication scholarship ought to fill this void by making use of academic resources in Asia and in Asian languages.

It is hoped that Asiacentric conceptualizations of communication contexts will probe into deep structures of communication. As Yum pointed out in 2000, most U.S. Eurocentric cross-cultural studies of communication simply discern and describe cultural patterns in other countries and then compare and contrast them to those of the United States, rarely going beneath the surface to explore the source of such differences. Encouraging the study of deep structures of communication, Saral identified its parameters in 1983 including "philosophical contexts and metaphysical assumptions about the origin, purpose, and meaning of life and nature and quality of the relationship of human beings with other livings as well as non-living systems believed to be existing in the universe."

Second, Asiacentric communication theorists can explore more and more indigenous concepts in Asian languages in order to better understand the complexities of Asian communication and properly evaluate the activeness and passiveness of the Asian communicator. As can be seen in Chen's attempt to build a harmony theory of Chinese communication in 2001, each **indigenous** concept can eventually be connected with one another in a systematic way in order to paint a bigger picture of Asian communication and a more holistic profile of the Asian communicator. Whereas U.S. Eurocentric communication scholarship continues to define Asian cultural identities and modes of communication through pseudo-etic concepts in the English language, Asiacentric communication scholarship should creatively redefine them through emic concepts in Asian languages.

Dissanayake mentioned in 1986 that it is of vital importance for Eastern communication scholars to set out to broaden the domain of inquiry by exploring indigenous theoretical concepts that have been formulated in non-Western societies as a means of promoting a greater degree of understanding of the nature of human interaction. Ho supported Dissanayake's hope in 1982: "Asian cultures abound with concepts that are pregnant with sociological and psychological meanings, and that they constitute a vast, yet underdeveloped asset which, when more fully exploited, hold great promise for the advancement of behavioral science."

Third, Asiacentric communication researchers can turn their attention to the rich histories of Asia and obtain insights into **allocentric** or integrative ways of adapting mutually toward harmonious communication. Investigations into historical events and incidents within and between Asian countries and cultures will yield insights of enormous value to Asiacentric communication professionals. Such insights will enhance their ability to envision mutual adaptation taking place within harmonious communication processes. Thoroughgoing analyses of writings or autobiographies of great Asian thinkers who ventured to synthesize the seemingly incompatible cultural traditions of the East and the West may also disclose the essence of allocentrism and the transspatial/transtemporal principle of reciprocity in harmonious communication practices.

U.S. Eurocentric communication scholarship is inclined to deal only with the present-day issues of communication and culture as Ishii noted in 1997. Likewise, unfortunately, communication scientists in Asian nations seem to follow this U.S. present-centered focus of theorizing and researching. In 1986 Chu reminded Asiacentric communication specialists of the importance of studying the past:

Chinese civilization and Asian civilization are both characterized by their long histories. An exploration into the past will provide rich insights for theory construction and development, and will contribute to theoretical methodological breakthroughs. As most Asian communication researchers are both bilingual and bicultural, they occupy a unique position to make such contributions.

Challenges for an Asiacentric Paradigm

While research possibilities are immense within an Asiacentric paradigm, there are also challenges that Asiacentric communication scholars should take up. In 1988 Chu specified two of such challenges. The first challenge for an Asia-centric communication paradigm is the dilemma between "the great traditions" and "the little traditions." Asiacentric communication theorists must think about how to bridge the gap between the philosophical wisdom of the great masters such as Confucius (the great traditions) and the values, beliefs, and ways of life of the common people (the little traditions). Chu (1988) cautions that they may devote their effort to a highly philosophical discourse about Buddhism, Confucianism, or Taoism, but forget to ask to what extent the common people understand these philosophies and in what ways they are influenced by them.

The second challenge of an Asiacentric communication paradigm is observability in real life. Asiacentric communication researchers ought to consider how to test or observe their theoretical explications in real life. Chu insisted in 1988:

> The term "testable" sounds Western and may imply the use of quantitative measures and statistical testing. This is not what I mean. All I am suggesting is that behavioral implications of the theoretical propositions must be observable in real life, so that we cantell whether the propositions are true or not. Otherwise, our theory will become philosophy, or polemics, and dogmatic ideology.

What would be the forms and functions of Asiacentric empirical communication research? In order to answer this question, Asiacentric communication experts should ultimately challenge conventional U.S. Eurocentric views as to what is theory, how theory should be built, what should be the relationship between theory and research, and whether theory should be evaluated in terms of validity or utility according to Miike in 2000.

The third challenge of an Asiacentric communication paradigm is the paradox of cultural specificity and universal relevance. Wang and Shen **posited** in 2000 that generalizations which at least imply the potential for universality are inevitable for theories, and that a theory whose relevance or validity is confined to a certain group of people or to a specific geographical region is, by this criterion, not yet a theory. Whether such a conception of theory is agreeable or not, their thesis is understandable. Certainly, Asian communication theories should bear some universal relevance beyond Asia or any particular Asian culture. Otherwise, they cannot contribute to the enlargement of theoretical boundaries of communication research elsewhere. In other words, Asian theories of culture and communication must be of distinctly Asian flavors but transspatial and transtemporal. Goonasekera and Kuo put this point well in 2000: "To be Asian it has to be **particularistic**; to be theoretical it has to be universalistic. Herein lies the **paradox**, and the challenge an Asian theory of communication needs to face and resolve."

Concluding Remarks

This essay has been a modest attempt to lay an assumptive foundation in order to theorize culture and communication from Asiacentric perspectives. The essay began by defining Asiacentric communication scholarship in relation to U.S. Eurocentric communication scholarship and by explaining three implications of the definition. It then mapped out three philosophical assumptions and three communicative assumptions for the development of an Asiacentric paradigm of communication theory. The essay ended with some discussion on possibilities and challenges of Asiacentric communication scholarship in quest of an alternative approach to culture and communication studies. Admittedly, some of the Asiacentric assumptions are not diametrically opposed to the U.S. Eurocentric ones. Rather, they need to be re-recognized and re-emphasized because they do not appear to be vitalized and validated enough in U.S. Eurocentric communication scholarship.

Most popular models and methods in communication research today have evolved in the West and, as such, reflect the biases of Western thought and worldview. They are culture-bound expressions of the Western idea and most applicable in the context of Western philosophy and **metaphysics**. One of the crucial limitations of culture and communication studies has been that almost all of the known research has been carried out by Western scholars or non-Western scholars trained in the Western paradigms. "In order for research to be truly 'intercultural,'" as Saral suggested in 1979, "a way must be found for the researchers from various cultures to do independent research on the subject and contribute to the growing body of knowledge."

The communication discipline in the new millennium must be multilingual and multicultural in the genuine sense so as to respond to diverse human experiences in both local and global spheres of communication. The future of communication research depends in large part on how much non-Western professionals will be able to step out of the U.S. Eurocentric academic worldview to theorize culture and communication from alternative standpoints. Indigenous communication theories need to be developed from within cultures around the world and should be actively exported to the United States. U.S. Eurocentric theories of communication ought to be informed by world theories of communication. Given such a scholarly milieu, "for an Asian researcher to fail to recognize, and to take advantage of, their rich cultural heritage is to throw away the most valuable assets in making a significant contribution to the field of communication study," according to Wang and Shen in 2000.

Applications

1. On the Integration of Theoretical Framework into Research Paper Writing
Tian, D. X., & Wu, W. F. (2020). On the integration of theoretical framework into research paper writing. *Test Engineering & Management*, 83(May-June), 20949-20961.
Abstract: This paper aims at exploring the major problems, philosophical causes and illustrative process of integrating theoretical frameworks into research paper writing. Based on a thematic analysis of 850 graduate students' theses randomly selected from two universities in P. R. China

and the transcripts of 93 in-depth interviews of graduate students in the two universities, the paper has discovered three major problems in terms of the lack of literature review and theoretical framework, little theoretical guidance in data analysis, and missing link between the researches and their relevant philosophical foundations. As the root causes, the inexperienced graduate students are lacking in both the awareness of the significant roles of theoretical frameworks and necessary training to integrate theoretical frameworks into their research projects. To root out the problems, an elaboration of the differences between qualitative and quantitative research paradigms in terms of their respective philosophical assumptions and research enquiries has been provided. Meanwhile, the theoretical frameworks of two sample papers have been analyzed to illustrate the steps of theoretical framework integration.

Keywords: graduate students' thesis; integration; theoretical frameworks; qualitative and quantitative research; paper writing

2. Construction of a Water and Game Theory for Intercultural Communication

Tian, D. X. (2020). Construction of a water and game theory for intercultural communication. *The International Communication Gazette*, 5, 1-23.

Abstract: Through the theoretical lenses of cultural gaming and paradigmatic assumptions of Eastern and Western cultures, this article looks into the interrelationships between game intentions and communication strategies. Through a thematic analysis of the Chinese traditional cultural classics from the pre-Qin (221 BCE - 206 BCE) to the Republic of China (1912—1949) from the Chinese Text Project, three featured themes of water including the best and the softest, carrying boats and capsizing boats, and the most violent and the strongest have emerged in correspondence to the positive zero sum, zero sum, and negative zero sum game intentions. Thus, a water and game theory for intercultural communication has been constructed. The theory is applicable to managing intercultural communication barriers, esp. systematic misunderstanding between individuals from China and the West, between Chinese enterprises and their counterparts in other countries, and between China and other countries on various intercultural communication occasions.

Keywords: construction; game; intercultural communication barriers; theory; water

3. Non-Western Theory in Western Research: An Asiacentric Agenda for Asian Communication Studies

Miike, Y. (2006). Non-Western theory in Western research: An Asiacentric agenda for Asian communication studies. *The Review of Communication*, 6(1-2), 4-31.

Abstract: The purpose of the present article is aimed to review Kim's book along with the two edited volumes of Kincaid and Dissanayake, assess past Asian contributions to communication theory, and suggest future directions for Asian communication research. The article argues especially for the necessity of Asiacentricity in theoretical investigations on Asian cultures and communication. Asiacentricity is the meta-theoretical notion that insists on placing Asian values and ideals at the center of inquiry in order to see Asian phenomena from the standpoint of Asians as subjects and agents. Asiacentric studies of Asian communication hence demand that Asian communication should be researched from Asian theoretical perspectives. Based on this paradigmatic position, the article charts a five-pronged Asiacentric agenda. Future Asian communication studies should: ① derive theoretical insights from Asian cultures; ② expand the geographical focus of study; ③ compare and contrast Asian cultures; ④ pluralize and historicize theoretical lenses; and ⑤ confront meta-theoretical and methodological questions.

Keywords: Asian contributions; communication theory; future directions; Asian values and ideals; Asiacentric agenda

Interactive Activities

1. Individually, please finish reading Text A, Text B, and the application abstracts and work out the meanings of the terms in bold type by consulting the dictionary whenever necessary.

2. In pairs, please summarize the content in 2 to 3 sentences of each sub-heading in the unit outlines of Text A and Text B based on your reading and understanding of the texts.

3. In groups, share your gains, comments and suggestions regarding the three application abstracts. Based on your interests, locate and finish reading the full-length papers of your interested abstracts.

4. Q&A: Questions are encouraged about any uncertain or confused part or parts in the unit and seek answers either from other fellow students or the instructor.

Engels said: "if a nation aspires to stand at the peak of science, it can't be without theoretical thinking for a moment." What would you do to make your own contributions in theory construction in your academic field?

5. Complete the Personal Report of the Socio-communicative Orientation, an instrument designed to assess the degree to which you believe in each of the 20 personality traits in a questionnaire. Take a few moments and complete the self-assessment for Unit 8.

6. To make full use of a theory, it is necessary and important to tell a theory from **a theoretical framework** and a conceptual definition from an operational one. First, a theory is an organized body of concepts and principles intended to explain a particular phenomenon by providing researchers with a lens to view and understand the world. Second, a theoretical framework refers to a set of concepts drawn from one theory or a series of theories to shed light on a particular phenomenon or research problem. Finally, a conceptual definition of a theory tells the reader what a concept means and what your constructs are by explaining how they are related to other constructs, while an operational definition tells the reader how to measure it by outlining a metric for clarifying or quantifying the term. For example, a conceptual definition of "culture shock" is "a multifaceted experience that results from the numerous stressors that occur when coming into contact with a different culture." An operational definition can be illustrated by the four-stage model which includes elation, depression, recovery, and acculturation. The four stages provide researchers with a theoretical framework of four dimensions or aspects to explore the research problem. Now, please locate the full-length paper of one of the three abstracts in the course package and appreciate the adopted theoretical framework in the paper.

UNIT NINE

Research Methods of Intercultural Communication

Readings

Text A Methods for Intercultural Communication Research

After John Oetzel, Saumya Pant, and Nagesh Rao

▲ Introduction

Our worldview shapes what is "interesting" to a particular audience, what is considered a problem, what problem is interesting to study, and whether the goal of studying a problem is to analyze the problem, to analyze and solve the problem, or to analyze, solve, and implement the solution. Our worldview defines if an issue is a problem or not and if we need to come up with a solution. For example, behaviors associated with attention deficit **hyperactivity** disorder (ADHD) are seen as a problem in the United States, and there are medications to solve the problem. In India, the same set of behaviors among children is seen as what children tend to do, as normal and not as a problem.

Our worldview not only shapes what we see as an interesting problem to study but also the methodology we use to study the problem. The purpose of this article is to describe and explore the integration of three main methodological perspectives in studying intercultural communication issues: social scientific, interpretive, and critical. First, the ontological, epistemological, and axiological assumptions underlying each of these methodological perspectives are explored. Then, for each methodological perspective, common methods and types of data collected and some exemplars are identified. Finally, we offer traditional integration of the three approaches and also alternate methodological perspectives to study intercultural issues from a non-Western lens.

▲ Ontology, Epistemology, and Axiology

Ontology is the study of the researcher's orientation to reality. In the social scientific perspective, the researcher views the world objectively in that there is a world outside of us that can be systematically studied. Researchers from this perspective use a deductive approach and are keen to explain and predict phenomena. Social scientific ontology provides clarity and direction due to its rigorous questioning of plausibility and reduction of subjectivity. In contrast and as a reaction to the social scientific perspective, **interpretive** researchers argue that the observer and the observed are subjective and the most important lessons are in how they co-create meaning. If the social scientists take a deterministic view of human behavior, interpretivists thrive in a person's free will. Critical theorists focus particularly on social injustices and inequalities in life.

Researchers in this area explore how social structures create power inequalities and injustices. Thus, they believe that power differences are at the base of social transactions according to Scotland in 2012. Any ontological investigation for a critical theorist will thus have to help unearth these inequities.

Epistemology looks at how we come to know a chosen phenomenon and thus how researchers study this phenomenon. Social scientists, interested in assessing objective reality (or at least reduced subjectivity), use a scientific method to collect empirical evidence. They focus particularly on causal relationships between phenomena and generally use quantitative approaches to collect data. The basis of their assessment and data collection is the premise that objects have an existence independent of the knower. Interpretivists, who are interested in situational and contextual meaning, generally use qualitative methods to assess participants' sense of reality. They are not exploring one truth, but the play of multiple truths simultaneously. They do so by studying individual interactions and the historical and cultural contexts in which these individuals interact. Critical researchers use a variety of qualitative methods to explore, for example, how language is used to create power imbalances or how mass media is used to avoid critical thinking. Critical scholars are particularly sensitive to the overdependence on empirical and social scientific evidence. They do so as critical investigations are premised on the fact that social/positional power determines what is considered knowledge.

Axiology explores the values that guide a researcher's questions, the methods used to collect and analyze data, the interpretation of the data, and the implications of the findings. Social scientists study phenomena to find the truth, which, in turn, guides specific types of action. They are focused on exploring what is referred to as the value axiom, or how much a phenomenon being studied fulfills the requirements of the concept to which it belongs as Kelleher stated in 2013. Both interpretivists and critical theorists are interested in describing what exists, how the participants in the community interpret phenomena, with critical theorists particularly interested in reducing class imbalances and other forms of oppression. Interpretivists are axiologically determined to encourage the fact that observations drawn can always be disagreed upon and reopened to interpretation. With respect to control, social scientists wish to control as many variables as possible, narrowing down the causal pattern to the variables under study. Interpretivists seek active participation in the study to understand how they view reality. Critical theorists are particularly aware of the community members' need to take control of their own situations. With this brief overview in mind, we now explain the methodological approaches of the social scientific, interpretive, and critical perspectives; the types of data collected; some exemplars for each perspective; and some general concerns about each of the methods.

▲ Social Science Methods

Social science research methods address questions related to both cross-cultural and intercultural communication. Much of the foundational work on intercultural communication research is based on comparisons of two or more cultures. Both forms of communication research try to enhance the comprehension of communication that are mediated by and through cultural context. These comparisons helped to identify how the normative and subjective aspects of culture vary across cultures and presumably provided information about what to expect when interacting with members from different cultures. This type of research is classified as cross-cultural. In contrast, intercultural communication is the exchange of messages between people from different cultural groups according to Gudykunst in 2003. Regardless of the interest in cross-cultural or intercultural communication, the social scientific perspective seeks to understand and predict the effect of culture on communication variables and the subsequent effect of communication on various outcomes. Thus, the methods of study are similar. This section reviews the three most prominent social scientific methods providing an example of each. Additionally, the types of data generated and methodological concerns are discussed.

Methods

There are three methods used by most social scientific researchers to study cross-cultural and intercultural research: (a) survey questionnaire, (b) experimental design, and (c) content analysis. The survey questionnaire is by far the most frequently used research method. It is typically a self-administered and self-report instrument that is distributed to large samples in multiple cultures. Most cross-cultural comparisons utilize self-report questionnaires because of the difficulty of collecting data from large samples in multiple cultures using other methods. Finally, self-report questionnaires are relatively easy to construct. Numerous cross-culturally valid scales exist, and methodological difficulties have been clearly identified. While not easy to overcome, methodological difficulties of survey questionnaires are manageable (see below for more detail). Survey questionnaires provide detailed description of cultural associations of communication behavior and outcomes and allow for comparisons to other cultures.

In 2014 Hanasono, Chen, and Wilson made a study of perceived discrimination, social support, and coping among racial minority university students, which is an example of survey research. The authors surveyed 345 students, half international students and half U.S. students, about their acculturation, experiences with discrimination, support, and coping needs. They found that the level of acculturation helped to explain students' need for support and how they coped with discrimination.

Experimental designs are highly regarded social scientific research because of the control of variables, which enables causal relationships to be examined. Culture is not a variable that lends itself well to experimental **manipulation**, and thus experimental designs are relatively rare in this line of research. Rather than experimental controlling culture, researchers typically use quasi-experimental designs manipulating the composition of groups or dyads to be intra-cultural or intercultural. These experiments collect a combination of self-report information (e.g., cultural and individual variables) as well as videotaped interaction. Additionally, some researchers have used experimental conditions on survey questionnaires. These studies utilize stimulus variables (e.g., contextual features) that ask participants to respond to specific situations.

A third method used in social scientific research is content analysis of media sources. This method is utilized to identify patterns prevalent in the media. Additionally, some researchers survey participants for their reactions about media patterns. Content analysis, while time consuming, is convenient and inexpensive since the only access needed is a recording or transcript of the artifact of study. It involves the use of a coding scheme to provide an "objective" description of the media and thus insights into cultural values and behaviors. The categorizations are then compared across cultures. When these categorizations are compared, it is done on the basis of frames, which are defined as a "schema of interpretation, collection of anecdotes, and stereotypes." Once these frames are determined, the way in which individuals deal with their realities within and across cultures can be studied.

An example of such content analysis was the study of the coverage of the Fukushima nuclear accident in Japan in two Belgian newspapers: *Le Soir* and *De Standard* by Perko et al. in 2011. The time period of the study was from March 11, 2011, to May 11, 2011. Every article was coded by two independent coders. The authors had begun their study with a question as to how the framing of the question of nuclear power would appear in the two Belgian newspapers. They arrived at the conclusion that the reporting was mostly neutral. Further, since the Fukushima nuclear accident was in a country quite remote, the articles did not frame the issue as an example of a possible threat to their own country from nuclear power plants.

Data Analysis and Methodological Concerns

Data from these three methods are quantified to allow for statistical analysis. All forms of data must be reduced to categories that are independent from one another (exhaustive and exclusive categories). These can include frequency counts of behaviors, sequence of behaviors, and self-report information on numerical scales. Data are then analyzed with statistical software to determine associations between cultural (independent) and communication (dependent) variables (outcomes are dependent variables with culture and/or communication as independent). The nature of analysis depends on the numerical measurement of the variables, but frequent tests include t-tests, analysis of **variance**, **correlation**, and **regression**. Additionally, complex modeling of dependent variables can be undertaken using, for example, structural equation modeling and hierarchical linear modeling. The key concern with the statistical tests is accounting for variance in the dependent variables. The more variance explained means the "more important" a cultural factor is for communication behavior. Because of the vast number of factors that explain human behavior, intercultural researchers believe that as little as 5% - 10% of variance explained is meaningful.

There are four concerns for data analysis in social scientific research: (a) reliability, (b) measurement validity, (c) internal validity, and (d) external validity. Reliability is reproducibility. For the aforementioned methods, two types of reliability are relevant. First, internal consistency of measures is usually measured with Cronbach's alpha. Second, when completing content or interaction analysis, **intercoder** reliability (agreement between two or more coders) is important and measured with Cohen's K or Scott's pi (or the like). Reliability means a researcher has consistent measures, whereas validity focuses on accurate information.

Validity is a combination of measurement, internal, and external validity (depending on the goals in the study). Measurement validity focuses on the accuracy with which a scale (or coding scheme) is measuring what is supposed to be measured. Internal validity is the strength to which a researcher can conclude that the independent variable is associated with the dependent variable as hypothesized. Internal validity is established by eliminating rival explanations for statistical associations through statistical or experimental control of confounding (or nuisance) variables. External validity is the degree to which a study's results can be generalized to the larger populations from which a sample was drawn. In intercultural research, researchers are more concerned with measurement and internal validity than external validity.

While these general methodological concerns are true for all social science research, there are also unique concerns with cross-cultural/intercultural communication research. In 2003 Gudykunst outlined a number of concerns with cross-cultural research, but chief among the methodological issues is establishing equivalence. In order to make cross-cultural comparisons (and have valid measures for intercultural research), researchers need to ensure that the constructs and measures are equivalent on five levels. First, constructs must be functionally equivalent; that is, the construct must work the same way in the cultures under study. Second, constructs must be conceptually equivalent; that is, the construct must have the same meaning within the cognitive system of the members of cultures being examined. Third, linguistic equivalence for constructs refers having language that is equivalent. Linguistic equivalence is often established through translating and back-translating of measures. Fourth, metric equivalence is established by ensuring that participants in different cultures do not respond to numerical scales in different ways (e.g., one cultural group may not use the extreme scores in a scale). Finally, researchers need to take care and establish that there is sample equivalence in the two cultural groups. The samples need to be comparable (e.g., similar age, gender, education, etc.). Fletcher and colleagues explore the steps needed to statistically ensure equivalence in measurement across multiple cultures in 2014. Establishing equivalence on these issues helps to eliminate rival explanations and further ensures that differences found are due to cultural differences. In addition to such methodological rigor, scholars from other orientations argue that it is also imperative for the researcher to be reflexive and aware of theoretical and methodological centeredness that can come from such systematic rigor according to Asante, Miike, and Yin in 2008.

Interpretive Methods

Interpretive scholars are interested in unearthing multiple simultaneous truths, believe in a person's free will, acknowledge that the known and the knower cannot be separated, and believe that interpretation is based on one's persuasive abilities. Striving for meaning, interpretive scholars generally use a variety of qualitative methods to study specific intercultural phenomena. As a result of this, interpretivists examine theoretical limits by comparing results from multiple forms of research about the same phenomenon. For this article, we focus on ethnography of communication and interpretive interviews as these are two common approaches. We then discuss the general methodological issues in collecting and analyzing interpretive data.

Methods

Ethnography of communication (EOC) is a method to study the relationship between language and culture through extensive field experience. The concept of the ethnography of communication was developed by Dell Hymes in 2002. It can be defined as the discovery and explication of the rules for contextually appropriate behavior in a community or group or what the individual needs to know to be a functional member of the community. EOC applies ethnographic methods to understand the communication patterns of a speech community. A speech community is a group of speakers who share common speech codes and use these codes based on a specific situation. From the presence or absence of certain speech codes, one can interpret the culture of a community with its shared values, beliefs, and attitudes. In his classic study in 1975, Philipsen explored the communication patterns of white males in a predominantly blue-collar neighborhood called "Teamsterville" in South Chicago. Philipsen lived in the community for several years and worked and interacted as a member of the community while also conducting his research. Results from this study explained when talk was appropriate, at what levels, and when action was more appropriate than talk. When two men were of similar backgrounds, of more or less equal status, and were close friends, they could talk to each other. There was less talk when the relationship was asymmetrical (e.g., father-son and husband-wife). The least amount of talk occurred when a "Teamsterville" was responding to an insult or trying to assert his power over someone. It is in these instances that action was more appropriate than words. If a man did talk during this interaction, he was seen as not masculine enough. Another interesting study was conducted by Radford et al. in 2011. The study focused on applying EOC to the case of virtual reference context. Here, the researchers focused on the interactions that constitute the context in which the participants make verbal statements and coordinate them with other statements in order to closely analyze the relational barriers and relational facilitators. The interactions spanned a 23-month time period (July 2004 – May 2006), and the transcripts of 746 live chats of this period were studied. The researchers were able to conclude from their study that when professional librarians chatted, they were more formal, less free with accepted online abbreviations, whereas students were more comfortable with using abbreviations and other turns of phrases. One of the conclusions the researchers drew was that if the librarians used more informal language they would appear more friendly and approachable.

Interpretive interviews are a second common approach. The purpose of the interpretive interview is to uncover insider meanings and understandings from the perspective of the participants according to Denzin in 2001. To Denzin, the characteristic of interpretive interviews is that they allow us to understand the society in which we live, which is referred to as an interview society. Typically, these interviews are one-on-one and face-to-face interviews designed to elicit in-depth information. The interviews can focus on narratives, topics, perspectives, and opinions and often are conducted in a semi-structured manner (although unstructured interviews are sometimes conducted). One of the reasons why the semi-structured and/or narrative form is used is to allow for deeper and embedded meanings that might elude a more inquiry-based approach. An example of interpretive interviews is Baig, Ting-Toomey, and Dorjee's study of meaning construction of the South Asian Indian term *izzat* (face) in intergenerational contexts in 2014. The authors interviewed six younger (aged 31 – 40) and six older (aged 55 – 72) South Asian Indian American women about face concerns in their intergenerational family communication situations. The authors found that family *izzat* is of primary importance in these contexts and that the motif of respect is central to the meaning of *izzat*. They also identified differences in the younger and older facework strategies.

Data Analysis and Methodological Concerns

The primary focus of analyzing interpretive research data is rather nicely summarized by Carbaugh in 2007:

> It is important to emphasize the interpretive task before the analyst: while engaging in a communication practice, an analyst seeks to understand what range of meanings is active in that practice, when it is getting done. The analyst sets out to interpret this practice, what is being presumed by participants for it to be what it is, that is, to understand the meta-cultural commentary imminent in it. What all does this practice have to say?

Thus, the interpretive scholar analyzes data in order to describe and interpret.

Carbaugh identified two concerns in analyzing interpretive data—the framework used to analyze the semantic content of cultural discourse and the vocabulary used to formulate these contents. A researcher's analysis of the content of the communication exchange also includes a meta-analysis of the subject, the object, the context, the history, and the stories revolving around the exchange. Carbaugh noted that "these cultural meanings—about personhood, relationships, action, emotion, and dwelling, respectively—are formulated in cultural discourse analyses as **radiants** of cultural meaning." These radiants of cultural meanings focus on personhood and identity, relating and relationships, meanings about acting, action and practice, meanings about emotions and feelings, and meanings about place or context.

Reliability and validity are explicated differently in interpretive research compared to social science research. If social scientific scholars are interested in consistency for reliability, interpretive scholars see reliability as the quality of the information obtained; does the data give us a richer, clearer understanding of the phenomena? In 1985 Lincoln and Guba used the term "dependability" in place of reliability to assess the quality of a research project. For validity, it is important to assess the quality based on the specific paradigm used to conduct the qualitative research. Further, while many scholars argue that validity is not a critical concept for interpretive research, Lincoln and Guba explained in 1985 that the "trustworthiness" of data is similar to validity in social science research. Do the community of scholars conducting interpretive research view the data as meaningful, useful, and following the research protocols appropriately?

After having considered these general considerations, we now consider three specific data analysis approaches using in interpretive intercultural communication research including grounded theory, constant comparative analysis, and thematic analysis. Other data analytic approaches for data analysis include narrative analysis, conversational analysis, EOC, and interpretive phenomenological analysis. Grounded theory is a continuum of practices that are inductive and iterative aimed at recognizing categories and concepts in texts in order to integrate them to formal theoretical models according to Corbin and Strauss in 2008. They begin with the observations, experiences, and stories, and through a process of coding, analysts identify a theoretical model to fit the data. Another important approach that interpretive scholars use is that of constant comparative analysis (CCA). CCA has often been used as a part of grounded theory, but it is now being used separately to analyze cross-cultural and intercultural communication. CCA is used to balance the etic perspective (participant as outsider) with the emic perspective (participant as insider) to ensure balance between cultural readings and theoretical frameworks. CCA ensures that all data in the relevant set are compared with all other data in the same set to make sure that no data are dismissed on thematic grounds. Further, CCA tries to accommodate the most relevant theories though they may appear disparate. A final prominent approach is thematic analysis. Thematic analysis is a flexible and yet rigorous approach of identifying and analyzing patterns or themes of meaning from data. In 2006 Braun and Clarke identified a six-step process for conducting thematic analysis.

Critical Methods

From the critical perspective, relationships between cultural groups are often characterized by dominance and resistance. Communication between groups is based on certain understanding of culture and ethnicity that is fixed, **reified**, and essentialized and is informed by certain cultural assumptions that tend to be rooted in Euro-American traditions and worldviews. Hermans and Kempen argued in 1998 that dominant approaches to knowledge favor static conceptualizations of culture. It is the creation of these static categories in which the Western understanding of the rest of the world dominates the intercultural relations that results in the reification of culturally homogeneous "ethnic" and racial groups. Consequently, this orientation undermines ways in which the self is understood in different cultures.

Critical and feminist scholars have consistently raised questions about power imbalance between researchers and researched in the field, suggesting that if researchers fail to explore how their personal, professional, and structural positions frame social scientific investigations, researchers may inevitably reproduce dominant gender, race, and class biases. This section illustrates postcolonial ethnography and critical discourse analysis as approaches for intercultural discovery from the critical lens. Additionally, we introduce the role of self-reflexivity and consciousness-raising in the context of methodological concerns from the critical perspective.

Methods

A variety of approaches to critical issues exist such as critical race theory, decolonizing and indigenous methodologies, engaged methodologies, and performative methodologies. In this article, we explore two prominent methods to illustrate some of the key elements to critical approaches given that we cannot cover all of them: postcolonial ethnography and critical discourse analysis.

Postcolonial ethnography seeks to disrupt and restructure established academic practices and modes of knowledge development and dissemination. It attempts to do this by pointing out that gender roles, academic institutions, racial binaries, and other power structures are not apolitical. Postcolonial ethnography seeks to question the reification and valorization of supposed objective, scientific, and disembodied knowledge formations. Instead they seek to find alternate and embodied knowledge forms that accommodate the subjective and the personal.

While postcolonial and third world feminist scholars point to myriad ways in which relations of domination infuse ethnography, they also offer some guidance for negotiating power inherent in the practice of fieldwork. This guidance takes the form of feminist geopolitics, which involves not only questioning hegemonic structures and dominant power structures but also offering alternatives to those structures. Postcolonial scholars argue that the practice of ethnography among marginalized groups is historically tainted by ethnocentric biases in traditional ethnographic practice and research as Collins noted in 1990. Further, as philosopher Sandra Harding emphasized in 1998, ethnocentrism is structured into the institutional and academic practices so as to produce relationships oppressive to indigenous cultures in the so called first world as well as third world countries.

An example of postcolonial inquiry is that of an ethnographic encounter. As a part of this inquiry, the company that the researchers studied, Ddesign, had to develop prototypical home water purification filters. The site of their study was various villages in India where they were supposed to study the feasibility of home water purifiers among the economically deprived households of the villages. The researchers later were told that when Ddesign first started their study, they had notions of privations in the lives of the householders. During their study, they found that the reality was quite different from their preconceptions. They realized that the definitions of privations that the company personnel had were not applicable to the people or to their living conditions. In fact, the researchers were told by the company personnel that the villagers had a very different worldview from that of the personnel. Thus, the researchers and the company personnel realized that one group's notions of well-being and happiness were not necessarily applicable to another group no matter how universal those notions might be.

A second approach is critical discourse analysis (CDA). The creative combining of different approaches of lived experience, texts or discourses, and the social and political structures of power has resulted in popularity of cultural studies as a critical site for different modes of enquiry. According to Fairclough in 1995, "many analysts are becoming increasingly hesitant in their use of basic theoretical concepts such as power, ideology, class, and even truth/ **falsity.**" In recent social scientific research, there has been a turn toward language or, more specifically, toward discourse. According to the feminist critical scholar Michelle M. Lazar in 2005, discourse is a "site of struggle, where forces of social (re)production and contestation are played out." Critical discourse analysis is known for its overtly political stance and deals with all forms of social inequality and injustice. It includes the study of processes premised on the acts and discursive interactions of individuals and groups on which both the local and international contexts bring to bear their limits in the production of legislation, news making, and other such products of discursive interactions as van Dijk noted in 2008.

An example of critical discourse analysis in intercultural communication research is Chen, Simmons, and Kang's study in 2015 of identity construction of college students. The authors contextualize their study in an era of "post-racial" utopia resulting during the Obama administration. They coin the term "Multicultural/multiracial Obama-ism (MMO)" to reflect this era and the prominent frame of colorblindness and multiculturalism prominent in media discourse. They examined 65 student essays about three cultural identities that stood out in a particular context. They analyzed the essays using CDA and found three frames that support this construction of post-racial utopia: **meritocracy**, identity as self-chosen, and equality of opportunity despite privilege. They critique these frames and identify implications for teaching about intercultural communication and identity in the classroom.

Data Analysis and Methodological Concerns

Key methodological issues in the critical approach are the role of reflexivity, consciousness-raising, and limitations/possibilities of the reflective approach. A sociology-of-knowledge approach to critical scholarship reveals the role of reflexivity as a source of insight. Reflexivity means the tendency of critical scholars to reflect upon, examine critically, and explore analytically the nature of the research process. To some extent, this tendency toward reflection is part of a tradition of attention to what Kaplan referred to as "logic-in-use" or the actual occurrences that arise in the inquiry, idealized and unreconstructed. Feminist and critical epistemology carries this tradition of reflection further by using it to gain insight into the assumptions about gender and intercultural relations underlying the conduct of inquiry. This is often accomplished by a thoroughgoing review of the research setting and its participants, including an exploration of the investigator's reactions to doing the research.

One of the ways in which reflexivity is employed involves the concept of consciousness-raising, a process of self-awareness familiar to those involved with the women's movement. Underlying much of the reflexivity found in feminist scholarship is the notion found in the earlier work of scholars such as W. E. B. DuBois and Paulo Freire that consciousness of oppression can lead to a creative insight that is generated by experiencing contradictions. Under ideal circumstances, transformation occurs, during which something hidden is revealed about the formerly taken-for-granted aspects of intercultural relations.

Consciousness-raising is employed in various ways by the critical scholar. The first way is through attention to the consciousness-raising effects of research on the researcher. Consciousness-raising is also involved in discussions of ways in which the research process influences subjects of the inquiry. Some authors view the research act as an explicit attempt to reduce the distance between the researcher and subjects according to Collins in 1990. These approaches have provided critical and feminist researchers with a way to tap collective consciousness as a source of data and have provided participants in the research process with a way to confirm the experiences that have often been denied as real in the past. The applications of critical consciousness-raising and reflexivity can be seen in discourses surrounding terrorism and counterterrorism. This application can be seen in the study by Schmid in 2013 about **radicalization**, deradicalization, and counter-radicalization. Schmid has observed that the usual causes such as poverty, social inequality, oppression, and neglect by the West have not been empirically tested satisfactorily, yet they are believed to be the primary causes of radicalization. The study provides three levels of analysis that can be used to understand how "radicals" are born and how that complex construction can be interrogated: the micro level, dealing with the individual level in terms of identity and self-reflection; the meso level, which deals with the socio-political milieu surrounding the individual; and the macro level, which refers to the larger society and governance that affect the individual. Further, these three levels of analysis can also be used to see how the **continuum** from radical to political undesirable and terrorist can be studied.

Finally, there are limitations and possibilities of reflective practice. Critical researchers use self-reflection about power as a tool to deepen ethnographic analysis and to highlight the dilemmas in fieldwork. The call for reflective practice has also been informed by critiques of postcolonial theorists who argue for self-reflexive understanding of the epistemological investments that shape the politics of method. Cultural studies scholars have also questioned the call to reflective practice, arguing that taken to the extreme, "constant reflexivity" can make "social interaction extremely cumbersome." In contrast, the call to "accountability" is said to offer a more collective approach than the "individual self-assessment of one's perspective" that the term "reflexivity implies." However, from point of ethnographic practice, it is seldom clear to whom one should be "accountable," and therefore the term reflective practice seems to be appropriate.

Reflective practice indicates both individual self-assessment and collective assessment of research strategies. Hurtado emphasized in 1996 that a "reflexive mechanism for understanding how we are all involved in the dirty process of racializing and gendering others, limiting who they are and who they can become" is a necessary strategy to help dismantle domination. Such reflective strategies can help ethnographers bring to the surface "their own privilege and possible bias" as well as "addressing the difference between different constituencies" within the communities they study.

Integrating Social Science, Interpretive, and Critical Research Methods

Each set of methods presented in this chapter has strengths and limitations. They address specific purposes that collectively are all important for the field of intercultural communication. Moreover, integrating the research methods provides richer insights than using any method by itself. However, these integrations still may have limitations in exploring non-Western contexts. Thus, this section explores integrations of the methods and alternative methods for intercultural inquiry.

Integrations of Methods

The integration of research methods involves using different types of methods at different phases according to Cresswell and Plano Clark in 2011. In this manner, the methods are used one after another (or concurrently) depending on the research question associated with the larger research program. Four phasic designs are most prevalent: (a) qualitative/interpretive methods used to create a quantitative (social science measure); (b) qualitative (interpretive and critical) methods used to embellish quantitative findings (Big Quant, Little Qual); (c) quantitative methods used to embellish qualitative findings (Big Qual, Little Quant); and (d) social science, interpretive, critical methods used conjointly. Space limitations prohibit us from providing examples of all of these approaches, so we detail two of them.

Zhang and colleagues provided in 2007 an example of how to create a cross-culturally valid measure of a construct. Their purpose was to measure teacher immediacy. Teacher immediacy is the psychology closeness that is communicated from a teacher to a student. There exist different measures of immediacy, but Zhang and Oetzel argued in 2006 that prior Western measures were not applicable in Chinese classrooms (i.e., they did not have conceptual equivalence). To address this issue, they first conducted open-ended interviews with Chinese students to identify themes associated with the meanings of immediacy. This phase of the research involved interpretive research methods as they put primacy on emic meanings. In the second phase, they used the emic meanings to create an operational measure of three dimensions of teacher immediacy (instructional, relational, and personal). This measure was administered to college students, and the data were analyzed with confirmatory factor analysis. The results dimensions were found to be internally consistent and had construct validity as they correlated with existing scales in expected directions. In 2007 Zhang et al. continued the development of the scale by administering the scale to college students in four national cultures: China, Japan, Germany, and the United States. With these data, the authors used confirmatory factor analysis to see if the three-dimensional model of teacher immediacy held up in each culture. They found cross-cultural support for the model and also the construct validity of the scales. Thus, their thorough testing from the interpretive phase to the social scientific phase led to the development of a teacher immediacy scale that has valid dimensions in at least four national cultures.

An example of integrating critical, social scientific, and interpretive methods into the same research program can be seen in the work on whiteness ideology. The project culminated in an edited book that included chapters using the various research methods. Whiteness ideology is the worldview that certain groups have privilege over others. It is labeled whiteness because whites tend to be the privileged groups in most societies. This research group's work primarily focused on ethnic groups in the United States, but some international contexts were examined and other scholars have since examined international contexts as well. One part of the project examined the labels that white people in the United States prefer through a survey. Another part of the project involved two of the team members' integrated interpretive and critical methods to understand how whiteness is used as strategic rhetoric. The volume included other scholars writing from different perspectives as well, and the editors attempted to bring together these various perspectives into a "coherent" picture about whiteness ideology. These scholars asked different questions and used different methods to investigate the same phenomena. Collectively, the research program told a richer and fuller story than any single study could have told. This example illustrates how different research methods can be used concurrently to advance understanding about intercultural phenomena.

Alternative Approaches to Studying Intercultural Communication

Intercultural research using the social scientific, interpretive, and critical methods have offered remarkable insights on a variety of intercultural phenomena. Each of these traditional approaches, however, uses a Euro-Western lens that is predominantly **textocentric**, privileging text, writing, and the lettered word in comparison to oral stories and visuals. We offer here two participatory approaches that, in some sense, hand over the power of the data to the participants. From these approaches, the ontology, epistemology, and axiology of the participants are more important than those of the researchers. Singhal, Harter, Chitnis, and Sharma explained in 2007 that participation-based methodology allows for lateral communication between participants, creates a space for dialogue, focuses on the people's needs, enables collective empowerment, and offers cultural-specific content. In contrast, they note that nonparticipatory methods allow top-down vertical communication, generally focus on individual behavior change, consider the donors' and researchers' goals of greater importance than community needs, and offer cultural-general information. This section discusses three participatory approaches: theater, photography, and community-based participatory research.

Participatory Theater. Based on the dialogic theorizing of Brazilian educator Paulo Freire in 1970 and its application by Augusto Boal in his performative intervention, "Theater of the Oppressed" in 1995, participatory theater can offer researchers an epistemology different from other research methods that rely on data from interviews and focus groups. This approach provides different kinds of data, discursive narratives that can be used to highlight some of the significant generative themes of the research participants.

The Theater of the Oppressed was developed in an effort to transform theater from the "monologue" of traditional performance into a "dialogue" between audience and stage. In 1995 Boal experimented with many kinds of interactive theater. His explorations were based on the assumption that dialogue is the common, healthy dynamic between all humans and when a dialogue becomes a monologue, oppression ensues. Participatory theater is a research tool that produces generative and local knowledge, starting with the use of the body, the container of memory, emotions, and culture. Theater has the ability to provide a useful connection to specific places as well as people. The encounter between the researcher and the researched in the theater space is outside the redundancy of everyday life. As a result, the researcher can see herself and her interactions between and with the researched in a way that is more distant than in everyday life, thus possibly making it easier to become reflexive.

In 1995 Boal developed various forms of theater workshops and performances which aimed to meet the needs of all people for interaction, dialogue, critical thinking, action, and fun. For example, Forum Theater constitutes a series of workshops in which the participants are transformed from a passive audience into the double roles of actors and active audience. They construct dramatic scenes involving conflictual oppressive situations in small groups and show them to the other participants, who intervene by taking the place of the protagonists and suggesting better strategies for achieving their goals. One of the popular research tools used in Forum Theater is role-playing. Role-playing serves as a vehicle for analyzing power, stimulating public debate, and searching for solutions. Participants explore the complexity of the human condition and situate this knowledge in its cultural moment. The aim of the forum is not to find an ideal solution but to invent new ways of confronting problems. A second key tool is discussion. Following each intervention, audience members discuss the solution offered. A skilled facilitator encourages an in-depth discussion with the participants to generate ideas that will help to address issues under investigation.

Participatory Photography. Similarly, Paolo Friere is a pioneer in participatory photography. In 1973, Freire and his team asked people living in a slum in Lima, Peru, to visualize "exploitation" by taking photographs. One child took a photograph of a nail on a wall. While the photograph did not resonate with adults, many of the children strongly supported it. When asked to explain, it was learned that many of the boys in the neighborhood were shoeshine boys in the city. Since the shoeshine box was heavy and they could not carry it to the city, they rented a nail on the wall in one of the city shops. These shop owners charged the boys more than half of each day's earnings as rent. The children expressed that the photo of the nail was the strongest symbol of exploitation. Friere and his team then used this photo to generate a discussion about exploitation and how the community members wished to address it.

Participatory photography, otherwise known as "photo voice" or "shooting back," gives power to the participants, through photographs, to shape their own stories (Wang, 1999). Participatory photography has been used in a variety of contexts (slums, hospitals, schools, villages, etc.) and in different parts of the world. For example, Briski and Kauffman (2004), in their Oscar-winning film, *Born into Brothels: Calcutta's Red Light Kids*, taught the children of commercial sex workers how to take photographs. These children, then, took photos to depict their harsh reality. These powerful images became the foundation of this moving film. Another example is the work of Loignon et al. in 2014 in Canada about the relation between impoverishment and lack of access to primary health care. The researchers recruited four family medicine residents and two medical supervisors to pursue their study. There were eight participants who came from economically underprivileged backgrounds trained in photographic techniques and photo voice philosophy. The researchers were able to realize the importance of primary health care professionals developing greater interpersonal and social acuity. They also realized that their patients were co-participants in the processes of diagnosis, prognosis, and medication. Finally, the researchers were also able to realize that they would be able to develop a greater competency by actually investing a part of their training time in the socioeconomic milieu of the patients they are to serve.

The implications of using participatory photography are significant. This method works best when the participants are given general directions and allowed to play with ideas. It is important for the participants to share their visual stories with the researchers. It is, however, critical for fellow participants in a community to share their stories with each other. The challenge of using photography is that it is, by nature, an intrusive process. With terminology like "aim," "shoot," and "capture," there can be a colonizing mentality in photography. It is particularly important that the participants be sensitive and reflective about how they take photographs of people and objects. While this may be difficult to accomplish across cultures, it is important to seek the permission of the participants before taking their photographs.

Community-Based Participatory Research. Community-based participatory research (CBPR) is a collaborative process where researchers and community members work together at all stages of the research process to address issues that are of importance to the community. Rather than a top-down approach to health and social issues, CBPR focuses on a collaborative and bottom-up approach to identifying and defining problems and developing and implementing solutions (i.e., research "with" rather than "for" or "on"). CPBR is a preferred approach for researchers working with indigenous communities, other communities of color, or other communities facing disparities, which experience similar issues of mistrust for past research issues and social/health inequities. CBPR has goals of developing culturally centered research and interventions, building trust and synergy among partners, building the capacity of all members of the research team, changing power relations among communities and outside entities, developing sustainable change, and improving the social and health conditions of the community.

CBPR is not a method, rather a philosophy of research. CBPR projects can include social scientific, interpretive, and critical approaches and often involve mixed methods. The specific methods meet the needs of the community and the research problem being addressed. The methods should follow key principles of CBPR, including: (a) the project fits local/cultural beliefs, norms, and practices; (b) the project emphasizes what is important in the community; (c) the project builds on strengths in the community; (d) the project balances research and social action; and (e) the project disseminates findings to all partners and involves all partners in the dissemination process.

Conclusion

The purpose of this article was to explore multidisciplinary methodological approaches to intercultural communication research. If our worldview shapes our reality, what we study and how we study phenomena is greatly influenced by our cultural frameworks. We described the traditional approaches to studying intercultural communication, namely, social scientific, interpretive, and critical perspectives. We identified the key ontological, epistemological, and axiological assumptions of each of these perspectives, offered an exemplar for each kind of perspective, types of data collected, and the methodological concerns in each framework. We then explained traditional ways to integrate the social scientific, interpretive, and critical perspectives, offered examples, and explicated the strengths of such integrations. We finally offered three alternative methodological approaches (participatory theater, participatory photography, and community-based participatory research) where the participants shape the scope of the study, interpret the meaning of the data, and offer practical implications for the study.

Historiography

The early history of intercultural communication, including some discussion of research methods, has been covered well by Leeds-Hurwitz in 1990 and Moon in 1996. Leeds-Hurwitz reviewed the early foundation of intercultural communication, which can be traced to the work of Edward T. Hall in the Foreign Service Institute in the 1950s and 1960s. The focus in the earlier years was on descriptive linguistic analysis of micro communication practices (e.g., proxemics, kinesics, and verbal practices) of multiple cultures. These early roots of intercultural communication were influenced by anthropological study of culture (i.e., ethnography).

The 1970s saw the development of the field of intercultural communication, with a focus on culture as race, gender, nationality, and socioeconomic status. The research at this time also reflected the social issues of the 1970s. Methods of research were diverse but predominantly included social scientific and interpretive methods.

The late 1970s and the 1980s saw a change where the focus of culture became nationality and a large emphasis was placed on cross-cultural comparisons. There was a pursuit to develop and apply Western theories to non-Western contexts. Methodologically, the 1980s was dominated by social scientific approaches.

The 1990s brought some backlash against social scientific approaches from interpretive scholars. There was also a rise of critical scholarship which critiqued the social scientific research methods. A number of critical approaches were identified and were especially used to develop theoretical approaches for understanding intercultural communications.

The 2000s brought more balance and integration of the research approaches. The *Journal of International and Intercultural Communication* was founded in 2008. The three editors of this journal to date (Tom Nakayama, Shiv Ganesh, and Rona Halualani) issued editorial statements about the scope of the journal respecting and including diverse methodological approaches.

Text B Thinking Dialectically about Culture and Communication

After Judith N. Martin and Thomas K. Nakayama

A survey of contemporary research reveals distinct and competing approaches to the study of culture and communication, including cross-cultural, intercultural, and intracultural communication studies. Culture and communication studies also reflect important meta-theoretical differences in epistemology, ontology, assumptions about human nature, methodology, and research goals as well as differing conceptualizations of culture and communication, and the relationship between culture and communication. In addition, questions about the role of power and research application often lead to value-laden debates about right and wrong ways to conduct research. Whereas these debates signal a maturation of the field, they can be needlessly divisive when scholars use one set of paradigmatic criteria to evaluate research based on different paradigmatic assumptions. The purpose of this essay is to focus attention on the meta-theoretical issues and conceptualizations that **underlie** these various debates and to explore strategies for constructive inter-paradigmatic discussions.

In order to highlight the various meta-theoretical assumptions of culture and communication research, we first identify four research paradigms based on Burrell and Morgan's frame-work in 1988 categorizing sociological research. Although this framework has been borrowed often by communication researchers and provides a useful "map" to differentiate and legitimate theoretical research, a word of caution is in order. As Deetz noted in 1996, Burrell and Morgan's emphasis on the **incompatibility** of these paradigms has resulted in a tendency to reify research approaches and has led to "poorly formed conflicts and discussions." Therefore, we present this framework, not as a specific categorization system, but as a way to focus attention on current issues and to legitimate the various approaches.

Below, we first briefly describe the framework and the resulting four paradigms. For each paradigm, we identify concomitant meta-theoretical assumptions and research goals, describe how research in this paradigm conceptualizes culture and the relationship between culture and

UNIT NINE
Research Methods of Intercultural Communication

communication and then give examples of current research conducted from this paradigm. It is important to note that the research examples given are illustrative and do not necessarily reflect the scope and depth of each area.

▲▶ Four Paradigms

In 1988 Burrell and Morgan proposed two dimensions for differentiating meta-theoretical assumptions of sociological research: **assumptions** about the nature of social science and assumptions about the nature of society. The assumptions about the nature of social science vary along a subjective-objective dimension, and these categories have been abusively described in communication scholarship. As described by Burrell and Morgan, objectivism assumes a separation of subject (researcher) and object (knowledge), a belief in an external world and human behavior that can be known, described, and predicted, and use of research methodology that maintains this subject-object separation. In addition, subjectivist scholarship sees the subject-object relationship not as bifurcated but in productive tension; reality is not external, but internal and "subjective," and human behavior is creative, voluntary, and discoverable by ideographic methods. Gudykunst and Nishida used this subjective-objective distinction to categorize then-current culture and communication research in 1989.

Burrell and Morgan's less discussed dimension in 1988 describes assumptions about the nature of society—in terms of a debate over order and conflict. Research assuming societal order emphasizes stability and regulation, functional coordination and consensus. In contrast, research based on a conflict or "coercion" view of society attempts to "find explanations for radical change, deep-seated structural conflict, modes of domination and structural contradiction."

According to Burrell and Morgan, the intersection of these two dimensions yields for distinctive paradigms (see Figure 9.1). They use the term **paradigm** to mean strongly held worldviews and beliefs that undergird scholarship, using the broadest of the various Kuhnian meanings. They also identify several caveats: These paradigms are contiguous but separate, have some shared characteristics but different underlying assumptions, and are therefore mutually exclusive.

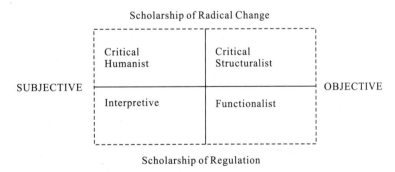

Figure 9.1 Four Paradigms of Culture and Communication Research

It is important to note that research usually adheres more or less to the assumptions of a specific paradigm. For example, as Gudykunst and Nishida pointed out in 1989, probably no contemporary intercultural communication research is strictly functionalist. Rather, it is more useful to think the boundaries among the four paradigms as irregular and slightly permeable, rather than rigid.

Functionalist Paradigm

As discussed by many communication scholars, functionalist research has its philosophical foundations in the work of social theorists such as Auguste Comte, Herbert Spencer, and Emile Durkheim. It assumes that the social world is composed of knowable empirical facts that exist separate from the researcher and reflects the attempt to apply models and methods of the natural sciences to the study of human behavior. Research investigating culture and communication in this tradition become dominant in the 1980s and is identified by various (and related) labels: functionalist, analytic-reductionistic-quantitative, positivist, objective, and traditional.

As noted in Table 9.1, research in this tradition builds on social science research, most notably in psychology and sociology. The ultimate goal is sometimes to describe, but often to predict human behavior. From this perspective, culture is often viewed as a variable, defined a **priori** by group membership many times on a national level, and includes an emphasis on the stable and orderly characteristics of culture. The relationship between culture and communication is frequently conceptualized as causal and deterministic. That is, group membership and the related cultural patterns (e.g., values like individualism—collectivism) can theoretically predict behavior.

Table 9.1 Four Paradigmatic Approaches to the Study of Culture and Communication

Paradigmatic Approaches	Goal of Research	Disciplinary Roots	Culture	Relationship between Culture and Communication
Functional	Predict	Psychology Sociology	A priori group membership	Cansal
Interpretive	Understand	Anthropology Sociolinguistics	Emergent patterns	Reciprocal
Critical Humanist	Locate oppression and strategies for resisting oppression	German critical theory British cultural studies French existentialism	Site of struggle	Contested
Critical Structuralist	Locate and analyze structural oppression	Russian and German Marxism	Societal structures	Contested

Research in this paradigm often focuses on extending interpersonal communication theories to intercultural contexts or discovering theoretically based cross-cultural differences in interpersonal communication, or both. Researchers have also investigated international and cross-national mediated communication and development communication. Most functionalist research is conducted from an "etic" perspective. That is, a theoretical framework is externally imposed by the researcher and research often involves a search for universals.

Probably the best known and most extensively exemplars of functionalist research programs are those conducted by W.B. Gudykunst and colleagues, extending uncertainty reduction theory (recently labeled anxiety-uncertainty management) to intercultural contexts, and communication accommodation theory, a combination of ethnolinguist theory and speech **accommodation** theory. See also extensions of expectancy violation theory and similarity-attraction theory to intercultural contexts.

Another type of functionalist research seeks cross-cultural differences using theoretical constructs like individualism and collectivism as a basis for predicting differences. For example, Stella Ting-Toomey and colleagues have conducted extensive research identifying cultural differences in face management and conflict style. Min-Sun Kim and colleagues have investigated cultural variations in conversational constraints and style.

There are a few research programs like Y.Y. Kim in 1988 and 1995 that do not fit neatly into one category. Although she designates her systems-based theory of cultural adaptation as distinctive from both functionalist and interpretive paradigms, one could argue that this theory is based primarily on functional social psychological research on cultural adaptation, and has generated primarily functionalist research.

Interpretive Paradigm

Culture and communication research in the interpretive paradigm gained prominence in the late 1980s. As noted in Figure 9.2, interpretive (or "subjective") researchers are concerned with understanding the world as it is, and describing the subjective, creative communication of individuals, usually using qualitative research methods. The philosophical foundations of this tradition lie in German Idealism (e.g., Kant) and contemporary phenomenology, hermeneutics, and symbolic interactionism. Interpretivism emphasizes the "knowing mind as an active contributor to the constitution of knowledge." Culture and communication research in this tradition has been described and labeled as interpretive, holistic-contextual-qualitative, humanist, and subjective.

The goal of interpretive research is to understand, rather than predict, human communication behavior. Culture, in the interpretive paradigm, is generally seen as socially constructed and emergent, rather than defined a priori, and it is not limited to nation-state collectives. Similar to functionalist research, interpretivists emphasize the stable, orderly characteristics of culture, reflecting an assumption of the social world as cohesive, ordered, and integrated. Communication is often viewed as patterned codes that serve a communal, unifying function. The relationship between culture and communication is seen as more reciprocal than causal, where culture may influence communication but is also constructed and enacted through communication. Research is often conducted from an "emic" or insider perspective, where the framework and interpretations emerge from the cultural community. The interdisciplinary foundations of this research are found in anthropology and sociolinguistics.

The sociolinguistics theory of Dell Hymes in 1972 has been particularly influential on the strongest exemplar of interpretive research—ethnography of communication studies conducted by Gerry Philipsen and colleagues. They study cultural communication(vs. *intercultural* or *cross-*

cultural communication). That is, their goal is generally to describe communication patterns within one speech community, such as Philipsen's classic study of communication in "Teamsterville" and Donal Carbaugh's numerous studies of U.S. (primarily European American) communication patterns, from "talk show communication" to more general studies.

However, some interpretive scholars are interested in intercultural communication, cross-cultural comparisons, or both. For example, Braithwaite's meta-analysis in 1990 of the role of silence in many cultural groups, Fitch's cross-cultural comparisons in 1994 of directives, and Katriel's studies in 1986 of Israeli and Arab patterns of speaking, M.J. Collier's work on communication competence, as well as Barnlund and colleagues' descriptive studies of contrasts between Japanese and European American communication in 1975 and 1996.

It should be pointed out that some interpretive research programs reflect functionalist elements. One could argue that Collier's work in 1991 and 1996, Hecht and colleagues' research on ethnicity and identity in 1992 and 1993, and Barnlund's research in 1989 on Japanese American contrasts have produced emic, insider descriptions, but also seem to imply behavior as deterministic, sometimes linked a priori to cultural group membership. In addition, some of their studies do explicitly predict behavior, conducted from a functionalist position, but the frameworks and hypotheses are based on previous, emic research findings. Other examples of interpretive theories are coordinated management of meaning, rhetorical studies, and descriptions of African American communication.

Recent culture and communication research reflects a renewed interest in research issues not usually addresses by functionalist or interpretive research. These concerns of context, power, relevance, and the destabilizing aspects of culture have led to research based on the remaining two paradigms. First, there seems to be a growing recognition of the importance of understanding contexts of intercultural interaction. Although functionalist researchers sometimes incorporate context as a variable, and interpretive researchers address "micro" contexts, there has been little attention paid to larger, macro contexts: the historical, social, and political contexts in which intercultural encounters take place.

Secondly, there is an increasing emphasis on the role of power in intercultural communication interaction and research, reflecting current debates among many communication scholars. In functionalist research, power is sometimes incorporated as a variable and is alluded to in some interpretive research, e.g., Orbe's research in 1994 and 1998 on African American male communication as "muted groups communication," and notions of third-culture building. The recognition of the role of power is **commensurate** with a notion of destabilizing and conflictual characteristics of culture. Culture is seen not as stable and orderly, but as a site of struggle for various meanings by competing groups.

Scholars have also pointed out the possible consequences of power differentials between researchers and researched: How researchers' position and privilege constrain their interpretations of research finding. And how voices of research participants (many times less privileged) are often not heard in the studies about them.

Third, there is a recognition that intercultural communication research should be more relevant to everyday lives, that theorizing and research should be firmly based in experience, and in turn, should not only be relevant to, but should facilitate, the success of everyday intercultural encounters. These issues have led to a growing body of research based on Burrell and Morgan's remaining two paradigms in 1988, radical humanist and radical structuralist, both of which stress the importance of change and conflict in society. This research reflects the increasing influence of European critical theory, e.g., Bourdieu in 1991, Derrida in 1976, Foucault in 1980, Habermas in 1970 and 1981, and British cultural studies. These "critical" scholars have influenced communication scholarship, primarily in media studies and organizational communication, but critical ideas have been less integrated into mainstream intercultural communication scholarship. So these two paradigms are less clearly defined. The research goal of both paradigms is to understand the role of power and contextual constraints on communication in order ultimately to achieve a more equitable society. Research in both paradigms emphasize the conflictual and unstable aspects of culture and society.

Critical Humanist Paradigm

As noted in Table 9.1, critical humanist research has much in common with the interpretive viewpoint, as both assume that reality is socially constructed and emphasize the voluntaristic characteristic of human behavior. However, critical humanist researchers conceive this voluntarism and human consciousness as dominated by ideological superstructures and material conditions that drive a wedge between them and a more liberated consciousness. Within this paradigm, the point of academic research into cultural differences is based upon a belief in the possibility of changing uneven, differential ways of constructing and understanding other cultures. Culture, then, is not just a variable, not benignly socially constructed, but a site of struggle where various communication meanings are contested.

Founded largely upon the work by Althusser in 1971, Gramsci in 1971 and 1978, and the Frankfurt school, critical humanist scholars attempt to work toward articulating ways in which humans can transcend and reconfigure the larger social frameworks that construct cultural identities in intercultural settings. From this paradigmatic perspective, there is a rapidly developing body of literature investigating communication issues in the construction of cultural identity. Unlike interpretive identity research, critical research assumes no "real" identity, but only the ways that individuals negotiate relations with the larger discursive frameworks. An example of this research is Nakayama's description in 1997 of the competing and contradictory discourses that construct identity of Japanese Americans.

This scholarship often draws directly from cultural studies scholars like Stuart Hall in 1985, who tells us that he is sometimes called "Black," "colored," "West Indian," "immigrant," or "Negro" in differing international contexts. There is no "real" Stuart Hall in these various ways of speaking to him, but only the ways that others place and construct who he is. His identity and his being are never to be conflated.

Other examples of research in this paradigm are critical rhetorical studies, e.g., Nakayama and Krizek's study in 1995 of the rhetoric of Whiteness, and Morris's account in 1997 of being caught between two contradictory and competing discourses (Native American and White). Finally, there is also a growing body of popular culture studies that explore how media and other messages are presented and interpreted (and resisted) in often conflicting ways. See, for example, Flores's analyses in 1994 of Chicano/a images as represented by the media or Peck's analysis in 1994 of various discourses represented in discussions of race relations on *Oprah Winfrey*. Additionally, very recent postcolonial approaches to culture and communication represent a critical humanist perspective. It should be noted that studies in this tradition have focused primarily on cultural meanings in textual or media messages, rather than on face-to-face intercultural interactions.

Critical Structuralist

Critical structuralist research also advocates change—but from an objectivist and more deterministic standpoint as Burrell and Morgan stated in 1998:

> Whereas the radical humanists forge their perspective by focusing upon "consciousness" as the basis for a radical critique of society, the radical structuralists concentrate upon structural relationships within a realist social world.

Largely based upon the structuralist emphasis of Western Marxists like Gramsci in 1971 and 1978, Lukács in 1971, and Volosinov in 1973, this approach emphasizes the significance of the structures and material conditions that guide and constrain the possibilities of cultural contact, intercultural communication, and cultural exchange. Within this paradigm, the possibilities for changing intercultural relations rest largely upon the structural relations imposed by the dominant structure. As noted in Table 9.1, culture is conceptualized as societal structures. So, for example, interactions between privileged foreign students and U.S. American students cannot be seen as random, but rather are a reflection of structural (cultural) systems of privilege and economic power. These larger structural constraints are often overlooked in more traditional intercultural communication research. When power and structural variables are incorporated into functionalist research (e.g., communication accommodation theory, diffusion of innovation), they are conceptualized as somewhat static, and the goal is not to change the structures that reproduce the power relations.

The focus, like that of critical humanism, is usually on popular culture texts rather than interpersonal interactions. For this reason, this scholarship has traditionally been defined as mass communication and not intercultural communication per se. These scholars largely examine economic aspects of industries that produce cultural products (e.g., advertising, media) and how some industries are able to dominate the cultural sphere with their products. An example is Frederic's study in 1986 on the political and **ideological** justifications leading to the establishment and maintenance of *Radio Marti*, the U.S. radio presence in Cuba. Another example is Nakayama and Vachon's study in 1991 of the British film industry between the World War Ⅰ and the World War Ⅱ. They compare the quality of films produced in Britain and in the United States during this time. Based on a paradigmatic assumption that economic structures constrain the kinds of texts (e.g., films) that are possible, they argue that British films were inferior during this time, due to explicit economic strategies (e.g., Lend-Lease Act) to undermine the British film industry.

We should note that postmodern approaches to communication studies may represent the future of culture and communication research, but at this point, it is too early to articulate the relationship between the framework outlined here and a postmodern position.

▸ Beyond the Paradigms

Understanding these four paradigmatic perspectives allows us to locate the source of many scholarly debates, helps to legitimize and also identify strengths and limitations of contemporary approaches, and presents the possibility of **interparadigmatic** dialogue and collaboration. The source of debates can be clearly seen in the dramatic differences among these four perspectives (see Figure 9.2). How can identifying or acknowledging the existence of these traditions lead to more productive research? There are probably a variety of responses or directions one may advocate with respect to interparadigmatic research. We have identified four positions that we think can challenge our way of thinking about culture and communication research: liberal pluralism, interparadigmatic borrowing, multiparadigmatic collaboration, and a dialectic perspective.

Liberal **pluralism** is probably the most common and the easiest, a live-and-let-live response. This position acknowledges the values of each paradigmatic perspective, that each contributes in some unique way to our understanding of culture and communication. One could point out that research in the functionalist paradigm has provided us with some useful snapshot images of cultural variations in communication behavior, that interpretive research has provides many insights into communication rules of various speech communities and contexts. However, one would also have to acknowledge that because cultures are largely seen as static and cultural behavior as **benign** in those two paradigms, the structural dynamics that support any culture are often overlooked. Critical researchers fill this gap by focusing on important structural and contextual dynamics, but provide less insight on intercultural communication on an interpersonal level.

Although the value of each paradigmatic tradition is acknowledged in this position, there is little attempt to connect the ideas from one paradigm to another, or to explore how ideas from one paradigm may enrich the understanding of research from other paradigms. This is **analogous** to African Americans and Whites acknowledging and respecting both Kwanzaa and Christmas traditions, but never actually talking to each other about the cultural significance of these holidays.

There is a strong belief underlying this position that the best kind of research is firmly grounded in solid paradigmatic foundations. As many have noted, paradigmatic beliefs are strong and deeply felt, a sort of faith about the way that world is and should be, and it takes extensive study and experience to become proficient in research in one paradigm.

A second position is that of interparadigmatic borrowing. This position is also strongly committed to paradigmatic research, but recognizes potential complementary contributions from other paradigms. Researchers taking this position listen carefully to what others say, read research from other paradigms and integrate some concerns or issues into their own research. This is seen in currently functionalist and interpretive research that has been influenced by critical thinking, for example, Katriel's essay in 1995 on the importance of integrating understanding of macro-contexts (historical, economic, political) in cultural communication studies, or Collier's recent essay incorporating notions of history and power differentials in ongoing studies of interethnic relationships and cultural identity. This borrowing is analogous to a traveler abroad learning new cultural ways (e.g., learning new expressions) that they incorporate into their lives back home. However, the researcher, while borrowing, is still fundamentally committed to research within a particular paradigm.

A third position is multiparadigmatic collaboration. This approach is not to be undertaken lightly. It is based on the assumption that any one research paradigm is limiting, that all researchers are limited by their own experience and worldview, and the different approaches each have something to contribute. Unlike the other positions, it does not privilege any one paradigm and attempts to make explicit the contributions of each in researching the same general research question. Though this sounds good, it is fraught with pitfalls. Deetz warned in 1996 against **"Teflon-coated** multiperspectivalism" that leads to shallow readings. Others have warned against unproductive synthetic (integrative) and additive (pluralistic, supplementary) approaches.

Although it would be nice to move across paradigms with ease, most researchers are not "multilingual." However, one could argue that culture and communication scholars are particularly well positioned for interparadigmatic dialogue and multiparadigmatic collaboration; that they, of all researchers, should have the conceptual agility to think beyond traditional paradigmatic (cultural) boundaries. In a way this approach reminds us of our interdisciplinary foundations, when anthropologists like Edward. T. Hall used linguistics frameworks to analyze non-verbal interaction—a daring and innovative move.

Because it is unlikely that any one researcher can negotiate various paradigms simultaneously and conduct multiperspectival research, one strategy is collaborative research in multicultural terms. An example of this is a current investigation of Whiteness where scholars from different research traditions (a critical position, an ethnographic perspective, and a social scientific tradition) and representing ethnic and gender diversity are investigating one general research question, "What does being White mean communicatively in the United States today?"

In this collaborative project we are conducting a series of studies using multiple questions, methods, and perspectives, but, more importantly, different paradigmatic assumptions. However, each study meets the paradigmatic criteria for one research orientation, representing what Deetz described as an ideal research program—where complementary relations among research orientations are identified, different questions at different moments are posed, but at each moment answering to specific criteria of an orientation. This multiparadigmatic orientation permits a kind of rotation among incompatible orientations and has led to new insights about the meaning of Whiteness in the U.S. today.

A fourth position is a **dialectic** perspective. Like multiparadigmatic research, this position moves beyond paradigmatic thinking, but is even more challenging in that it seeks to find a way to live with the inherent contradictions and seemingly mutual exclusivity of these various approaches. That is, a dialectic approach to accepted that human nature is probably both creative and deterministic; that research goals can be to predict, describe, and change; that the relationship between culture and communication is, most likely, both reciprocal and contested.

Specifically, is there a way to address the contextual and power concerns of the critical humanists-structuralists in everyday interpersonal interactions between people from different cultural backgrounds? We propose a dialectic approach that moves us beyond paradigmatic constraints and permits more dynamic thinking about intercultural interaction and research.

Toward a Dialectical Perspective

The notion of dialect is hardly new. Used thousands of years ago by the ancient Greeks and others, its more recent emphases continue to stress the relational, **processual**, and contradictory nature of knowledge production such as Bakhtin in 1981, Baxter in 1990, and Cornforth in 1968. Aristotle's famous dictum that "rhetoric is the counterpart of dialectic" emphasizes the significant relationship between modes of expression and modes of knowledge. Dialectic offers intercultural communication researchers a way to think about different ways of knowing in a more comprehensive manner, while retaining the significance of considering how we express this knowledge.

Thus, a dialectical approach to culture and communication offers us the possibility of engaging multiple, but distinct, research paradigms. It offers us the possibility to see the world in multiple ways and to become better prepared to engage in intercultural interaction. This means, of course, that we cannot become **enmeshed** into any paradigm, to do so flies in the face of dialectic thinking.

We are not advocating any single form of dialectic. The adversarial model utilized in forensic rhetoric may be appropriate in some instances, whereas a more inward, therapeutic model discussed by psychoanalysts may be needed in other situations. Different dialectical forms lead to differing kinds of knowledge. No single dialectical form can satisfy epistemological needs within the complexity of multiple cultures. To reach for a singular dialectical form runs counter to the very notion of dialectical "because dialectical thinking depends so closely on the habitual everyday mode of thought which it is called on to transcend, it can take a number of different and apparently contradictory forms."

Yet, a dialectical approach offers us the possibility of "knowing" about intercultural interaction as a dynamic and changing process. We can begin to see epistemological concerns as an open-ended process, as a process that resists fixed, discrete bits of knowledge that encompasses the dynamic nature of cultural processes. We draw from the work of critical theorists who initially envisioned their theory as a "theory of contemporary socio-historical reality in which itself was constantly developing and changing." For critical theorists, as well as ourselves, there are many social realities that coexist among the many cultures of the world. Thus, "dialectics for critical theory describe how phenomena are constituted and the interconnections between different phenomena and spheres of social reality."

A dialectical perspective also emphasizes the relational, rather than individual aspects and persons. In intercultural communication research, the dialectical perspective emphasizes the relationship between aspects of intercultural communication, and the importance of viewing these holistically and not in isolation. In intercultural communication practice, the dialectical perspective stresses the importance of relationship. This means that one becomes fully human only in relation to another person and that there is something unique in a relationship that goes beyond the sum of two individuals. This notion is expressed by Yoshikawa in 1987 as the "dynamic in-betweenness" of a relationship—what exists beyond the two persons. Research on the notion of third-culture building is one attempt to develop a relational dialectic approach to intercultural interactions.

Finally, the most challenging aspect of the dialectical perspective is that it requires holding two contradictory ideals simultaneously, contrary to most formal education in the United States. Most of our assumptions about learning and knowledge assume dichotomy and mutual **exclusivity**. Dichotomies (e.g., good-evil, subjective-objective) form the core of our philosophical, scientific, and religious traditions.

In contrast, a dialectical perspective recognizes a need to transcend these dichotomies. This notion, well known in Eastern countries as based on the logic of "soku," ("not-one, not-two"), emphasizes that the world is neither monistic nor dualistic. Rather, it recognizes and accepts as ordinary, the interdependent and complementary aspects of the seeming opposites. In the following sections, we apply the dialectical perspective to intercultural communication theory and research.

A Dialectical Approach to Studying Intercultural Interaction

Interpersonal communication scholars have applied a dialectical approach to relational research and identified basic contradictions or dialectics in relational development (autonomy—connection, novelty—predictability, openness—closedness). Although we do not advocate a simple extension of this interpersonal communication research program, we have identified six similar dialectics that seem to operate interdependently in intercultural interactions: cultural—individual, personal/social—contextual, differences—similarities, static—dynamic, present—future/history—past, and privilege—disadvantage dialectics. These dialectics are neither exhaustive nor mutually exclusive but represent an ongoing exploration of new ways to think about face-to-face intercultural interaction and research.

Cultural—Individual Dialectic. Scholars and practitioners alike recognize that intercultural communication is both cultural and individual. In any interaction, there are some aspects of communication that are individual and idiosyncratic (e.g., unique non-verbal expressions or language use) as well as aspects that are shared by others in the same cultural groups (e.g., family, gender, ethnicity, etc.). Functionalist research has focused on communication patterns that are shared by particular groups (gender, ethnicity, etc.) and has identified differences between these group patterns. In contrast, critical communication scholars have resisted connecting group membership with any one individual's particular behavior, which leads to essentializing.

A dialectical perspective reminds us that people are both group members and individuals and intercultural interaction is characterized by both. Research could investigate how these two contradictory characteristics work in intercultural interactions. For example, how do people experience the tension between wanting to be seen and treated as individuals, and at the same time have their group identities recognized and affirmed? This tension is often at the heart of the affirmative action debate in the United States—a need to recognize cultural membership and at the same time be treated as an individual and not put in boxes.

Personal/social—Contextual Dialectic. A dialectical perspective emphasizes the relationship between personal and contextual communication. There are some aspects of communication that remain relatively constant over many contexts. There are also aspects that are contextual. That is, people communicate in particular ways in particular contexts (e.g., professors and students in classrooms), and messages are interpreted in particular ways. Outside the classroom (e.g., at football games or at faculty meetings), professors and students may communicate differently, expressing different aspects of themselves. Intercultural encounters are characterized by both personal and contextual communication. Researchers could investigate how these contradictory characteristics operate in intercultural interactions.

Differences—Similarities Dialectic. A dialectic approach recognizes the importance of similarities and differences in understanding intercultural communication. The field was founded on the assumption that there are real, important differences that exist between various cultural groups, and functionalist research has established a long tradition of identifying these differences. However, in real life there are a great many similarities in human experience and ways of communicating. Cultural communication researchers in the interpretive tradition have emphasized these similar patterns in specific cultural communities. Critical researchers have emphasized that there may be differences, but these differences are often not benign, but are political and have implications for power relations.

There has been a tendency to overemphasize group differences in traditional intercultural communication research—in a way that sets up false dichotomies and rigid expectations. However, a dialectical perspective reminds us that difference and similarity can coexist in intercultural communication interactions. For example, Israelis and Palestinians share a love for their Holy City, Jerusalem. This similarity may be overweighed by the historical differences in meanings of Jerusalem so that the differences work in opposition. Research could examine how differences and similarities work in cooperation or in opposition in intercultural interaction.

For example, how do individuals experience the tension of multiple differences and similarities in their everyday intercultural interactions (class, race, gender, attitudes, beliefs)? Are these aspects or topics that tend to emphasize one or the other? How do individuals deal with this tension? What role does context play in managing this tension?

Static—Dynamic Dialectic. The static-dynamic dialectic highlights the ever-changing nature of culture and cultural practices, but also underscores our tendency to think about these things as constant. Traditional intercultural research in the functionalist tradition and some interpretive research have emphasized the stability of cultural patterns, for example, values, that remain relatively consistent over periods of time. Some interpretive research examines varying practices that reflect this value over time. In contrast, critical researchers have emphasized the instability and fleetingness of cultural meanings, for example, Cornyetz's study in 1994 of the appropriation of hip-hop in Japan.

So thinking about culture and cultural practices as both static and dynamic helps us navigate through a diverse world and develop new ways of understanding intercultural encounters.

Research could investigate how these contradictory forces work in intercultural interactions. How do individuals work with the static and dynamic aspects of intercultural interactions? How is the tension of this **dynamism** experienced and expressed in intercultural relationships?

Present—Future/History—Past Dialectic. A dialectic in intercultural communication exists between the history—past and the present—future. Much of the functionalist and interpretive scholarship investigating culture and communication has ignored historical forces. Other scholars added history as a variable in understanding contemporary intercultural interaction, for example, Stephan and Stephan's prior intergroup interaction variable that influences degree of intergroup anxiety. In contrast, critical scholars stress the importance of including history in current analyses of cultural meanings.

A dialectical perspective suggests that we need to balance both an understanding of the past and the present. Also the past is always seen through the lens of the present. For example, Oliver Stone's film, *Nixon*, was criticized because of the interpretation Stone made of (now) historical events and persons. As Stone pointed out, we are always telling our versions of history.

Collier's investigations in 1998 of alliance in ethnic relationships reveal the tensions of the present and past in ethnic relationships. This and other research reveal the importance of balancing an understanding the history, for example, of slavery and the African diaspora, the colonization of indigenous peoples, the internment of Japanese Americans, relationships between Mexico and the U.S., as well as maintaining a focus on the present interethnic relationships in the United States. How do individuals experience this tension? How do they balance the two in everyday interaction? Many influential factors precede and succeed any intercultural interaction that gives meaning to that interaction.

Privilege—Disadvantage Dialectic. As individuals, we carry and communicate various types of privilege and disadvantage, the final dialectic. The traditional intercultural communication research mostly ignores issues of privilege and disadvantage, although these issues are central in critical scholarship. Privilege and disadvantage may be in the form of political, social position, or status. For example, if members of wealthy nations travel to less wealthy countries, the intercultural interactions between these two groups will certainly be influenced by their differential in economic power. Hierarchies and power **differentials** are not always clear. Individuals may be simultaneous privileged and disadvantaged, or privileged in some contexts, and disadvantaged in others. Research could investigate how the intersections of privilege and disadvantage work in intercultural encounters. Women of color may be simultaneously advantaged (education, economic class) and disadvantaged (gender, race), for example. How are these various contradictory privileges and disadvantages felt, expressed, and managed in intercultural interactions? How do context and topic play into the dialectic? Many times, it may not be clear who or how one is privileged or disadvantaged. It may be unstable, fleeting, may depend on the topic, or the context.

Dialectical Intersections

So how do these different dialectics work in everyday interaction? These dialectics are not discrete, but always operate in relation to each other (see Figure 9.2). We can illustrate these intersections with an example of a relationship between a foreign student from a wealthy family and a U.S. American professor. Using this example, we can see how contradictories in several dialectics can occur in interpersonal intercultural interaction. In relation to the personal/social-contextual dialectic, both the student and professor are simultaneously privileged and disadvantaged depending on the context. In talking about class material, for example, the professor is more privileged than the student, but in talking about vacations and travel, the wealthy student may be more privileged.

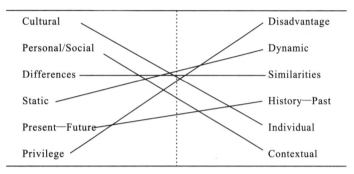

Figure 9.2   Intersections of Six Dialectics of Intercultural Interaction

To focus on another set of dialects, if the topic of international trade barriers comes up, the student may be seen as a cultural representative than an individual and, in this conversation, cultural differences or similarities may be emphasized. When the topic shifts, these relational dialectics also shift—within the same relationship.

These important dialectical relational shifts have not been studied in previous research, and this is what makes the dialectical perspective different from the other three positions identified earlier (liberal pluralism, interparadigmatic borrowing, and multiparadigmatic research). That is, this approach makes explicit the dialectical tension between what previous research topics have been studied (cultural differences, assumed static nature of culture, etc.) and what should be studied (how cultures change, how they are similar, importance of history). The dialectical perspective, then, represents a major epistemological move in our understanding of culture and communication.

▶ Conclusion

In this brief essay we have tried to challenge culture and communication scholars to consider ways that their production of knowledge is related to the epistemological advances made by those in other paradigms. Whereas there cannot be any easy fit among these paradigmatic differences, it is important that we not only recognize these differences, but also seek ways that these epistemological differences can be productive rather than **debilitating**. Information over-load can be **daunting**, but our dialectical perspective offers intercultural scholars, as well as students and practitioners, a way to grapple with the many different kinds of knowledge we have about cultures and interactions.

In his own thinking about dialectical criticism, Fredric Jameson observed in 1971 that there is a breathlessness about this shift from the normal object-oriented activity of the mind to such dialectical self-consciousness—something of the sickening shudder we feel in an elevator's fall or in the sudden dig up in an airliner.

This sudden fall in the ways we think about intercultural communication means letting go of the more rigid kinds of knowledge that we have about others and entering into more uncertain ways of knowing about others.

Applications

1. A Hands-on Approach towards the Application of Research Methods in Academic Paper Writing

Tian, D. X. (2018). A hands-on approach towards the application of research methods in academic paper writing. *Journalism and Mass Communication*, 8(4), 196–214.

Abstract: Based on an extensive summary of existing literature together with a random sampling of 70 graduate theses at the author's university and 30 papers submitted to journals, which the author was entrusted to review, the present paper has addressed the novice researchers' common concern of research method application by defining and categorizing research methods and the related terms, combing and discussing the techniques for qualitative, quantitative, and mixed research methods in accordance with different research questions, and finally illustrating and explaining our viewpoints with real-life samples and comments.

Keywords: graduate theses; hands-on approach; application of research methods; academic paper writing; concern of novice researchers

2. Relational Challenges in an Intercultural Volunteer Program in Jordan: Views from Chinese Participants

Tian, Z. H., & McConachy, T. (2021). Relational challenges in an intercultural volunteer program in Jordan: Views from Chinese participants. *Journal of Intercultural Communication Research*, 50(6), 588–609.

Abstract: Research on international volunteer programs has paid little attention to participants' own situated understandings of intercultural communication experiences in a short-term international volunteer context. The paper reports on a qualitative investigation into the experiences of Chinese participants in a short-term international volunteering program in an elementary school in Jordan which involved co-teaching the English language with partners from the U.S. It focuses on how participants interpreted the challenges of managing communication and building rapport with the children and their volunteer partners, with particular attention to the attribution of difficulties to perceived cultural differences. Findings show that participants struggled to interpret the significance of behavior outside their usual cultural frames of reference and that frequent reliance on dichotomous framings of cultural difference created barriers to rapport.

Keywords: volunteer; Jordan; teaching; intercultural; relational

3. Traditional Chinese Medicine Works: A Politicized Scientific Debate in the COVID-19 Pandemic

Peng, A. Y. Z., & Chen, S. H. (2021) Traditional Chinese medicine works: A politicized scientific debate in the COVID-19 pandemic. *Asian Journal of Communication*, 31(5), 421–435.

Abstract: The COVID-19 pandemic provoked public attention to medical treatments across the world. In China, a debate on the efficacy of traditional Chinese medicine (TCM) took place amid the government's active promotion of it for COVID-19 patients. Rather than addressing such a debate from the perspective of medical science or health communication, this paper explores how TCM was politicized on Chinese social media. The research is based on a case study, collecting data from the most popular Chinese community question-answering (CQA) site——Zhihu. By triangulating content analysis (CA) and thematic analysis (TA), we reveal how nationalist sentiments and dissenting opinions are expressed through approval or criticism of TCM among the Zhihu community. The research findings uncover the political momentum behind the debate by shedding light on how Zhihu users engage with public affairs through medical commentaries. This paper thus contributes to understanding the politicized discourse of TCM in China in the wake of the global pandemic.

Keywords: Covid-19; medical commentary; pandemic; traditional Chinese medicine; Zhihu

Interactive Activities

1. Individually, please finish reading Text A, Text B, and the application abstracts and work out the meanings of the terms in bold type by consulting the dictionary whenever necessary.

2. In pairs, please summarize the content in 2 to 3 sentences of each sub-heading in the unit outlines of Text A and Text B based on your reading and understanding of the texts.

The second paragraph of Text A begins with "Our worldview not only shapes what we see as an interesting problem to study but also the methodology we use to study the problem." What is your worldview or academic paradigm, and what methodology are you going to adopt in your future academic or scientific research projects?

3. In groups, share your gains, comments and suggestions regarding the three application abstracts. Based on your interests, locate and finish reading the full-length papers of your interested abstracts.

4. Q&A: Questions are encouraged about any uncertain or confused part or parts in the unit and seek answers either from other fellow students or the instructor.

5. Complete the Personal Report of Time Orientation, an instrument designed to assess your monochromic and/or polychromic time orientation. Take a few moments and complete the self-assessment for Unit 9.

6. Please locate the full-length papers of the three abstracts and examine **the research design**

of each paper. There are several key terms in research design. Research methodology is the philosophical framework within which the research is conducted or the foundation upon which the research is based. Research approaches are plans and the procedures for research from broad assumptions to detailed methods of data collection, analysis, and interpretation, which can be deductive and inductive. Research methods are the various procedures, schemes, and algorithms in research. Research techniques refer to the behaviors and instruments used to perform research operations such as making observations, recording data, techniques of processing data and the like. In terms of research methods, quantitative and qualitative methods generate different types of data. Quantitative data is expressed as numbers such as units, prices, proportions, rates of change and ratios while qualitative data is expressed as words like statements, paragraphs, stories, case studies and quotations. Quantitative and qualitative methods can be combined in many ways to build on the strengths of both, and minimize their relative weaknesses. Therefore, there is a growing consensus that both are important. This has led to an increased interest in evaluations with mixed methods. Below are the various features and functions of both qualitative and quantitative research methods.

Method	Data	Typical methods of data collection	Analysis	Sampling	Indicators
Quantitative	Numbers	Predefined options and closed questions in surveys, direct measurement, digital data collection	Statistical data methods (averages, correlations, regression analysis)	Large, random samples	Specific, measurable, numeric indicators
Qualitative	Words	Open-ended questions in surveys and interviews, focus group discussions, observation, case studies	Summarisation, reduction and scoring; in-depth analysis of individual cases	Purposive (deliberate) sampling of most interesting cases	Broadly defined qualitative indicators or questions

Method	Milestones and targets	Baselines	Control or comparison groups	Typical monitoring questions	Data storage and processing
Quantitative	Easy to define and to communicate	Numeric collection and presentation of data	Often used in experimental or quasi-experimental methods	How much? How many? How often?	Data stored as numbers; large amount of automatic processing
Qualitative	Hard to define and communicate	Narrative collection and presentation of data	Rarely used in qualitative inquiry	How or why did something happen? For whom?	Data stored as words or as attached reports; less automatic processing

UNIT TEN

New Media and Intercultural Communication

Readings

Text A The Impact of New Media on Intercultural Communication in Global Context

After Guo-Ming Chen

Introduction

The history of human communication began with the oral or spoken tradition. Through the course of history, the **dissemination** of messages progressed from simply the oral tradition, to script, print, wired electronics, wireless electronics and finally digital communication. The greatest change in message dissemination in recent history occurred with the introduction of computers and the Internet in the early 1990s. Since then, this drastic change of communication medium has significantly affected humans' perception of the media, the usage of time and space, and the reachability and control of the media.

In the present age of digital communication, time has been compressed by reducing the distance between different points in space, and the sense of space has led people to feel that local, national, and global space becomes **obsolete**. In addition, the reachability of digital media can now extend to all people, instead of a limited audience. This is significant because without the confinement of time and space, the control of message production and dissemination is no longer a privilege possessed only by church, state, and government, but instead, equally shared by all individuals.

All these innovations in digital media, or so-called new media, have changed and continue to change the way we think, act, and live. For example, digitalization, as a **hybridization** of print and electronic media in a binary code, converts analog to digital that requires a completely different mode of production and distribution.

As Chen indicated in 2007, the impact of digital or new media on human society is demonstrated in the aspects of cognition, social effect, and a new form of aesthetics. Cognitively, new media demands a non-linear nature and the creation of expectations for content, which directly influences the way people use media. Socially, the most manifested impact of new media is the effect of demassification, which denotes that the traditional design for a large, homogeneous audience is disappearing and being replaced by a specific and individual appeal, allowing the audience to access and create the message they wish to produce. Visually, new media brings forth a new digital aesthetic view, which refers to, for example, "interactivity, manipulation, the **pre-purposing** and repurposing of content across media, deliberate creation of virtual experience, and sampling as a means of generating new content," as Chen noted in 2007.

New media is also the main force accelerating the trend of globalization in human society. The globalization trend has led to the **transformation** of almost all aspects of human society. For instance, socially and culturally, globalization has changed the perception of what a community is, redefined the meaning of cultural identity and civic society, and demanded a new way of intercultural interaction. Economically, global competition has enormously intensified. In order to succeed in global business, a company is required to not only understand the local markets in order to meet their global clients' needs, but they must also seek out open markets globally, and foster effective management in global business transactions. In sum, due to the thrust of new media, the global trend creates new social networks and activities, redefines political, cultural, economic, geographical and other boundaries of human society, expands and stretches social relations, intensifies and accelerates social exchanges, and involves both the micro-structures of personhood and macro-structures of community.

From the scholarly perspective, unfortunately, traditional studies seldom connected well or integrated the two concepts of "media" and "globalization." Three established academic fields on the study of the concepts include communication studies, media and cultural studies, and globalization studies. Communication studies began after the World War II and become an academic field during the 1950s in the United States. Beginning with early studies focusing on international communication and speech communication and continuing on to recently developed intercultural communication, communication studies as an academic field tends to ignore the relationship between people and media, or how people use media in different cultural contexts, and how that closely relates to the globalization of human society.

The field of media and cultural studies emerged in the 1970s in Britain on the basis of resisting the dominance of communication studies in the United States, which was more oriented towards the empirical or discovery paradigm. Yet, most British media studies focus on the role media institutions play in the process of globalization. Many scholars in this area tend to take globalization for granted, by not making an effort to theorize the concept. As for cultural studies, originated from the Frankfurt School in Germany, the field suffers from the lack of concern about the impact media has on people. The problems that exist in media studies and cultural studies are like those that appear between the studies of international communication and intercultural communication. As Servaes pointed out in 2008, cultural studies in Europe and in the United States mainly pays attention to cultural issues instead of media issues.

The study of globalization began in the early 1990s, a time when the trend of globalization significantly increased its impact on human society in terms of scope and scale. Nevertheless, although scholars from different disciplines are involved in the study of globalization, and most agreed that without media and communication globalization will not emerge as such a great impetus of the transformation of human society, the role of media and communication in the theorization of the concept of globalization remains vague and less specified. Surprisingly, according to Rantanen in 2006, the contribution of scholars from the field of media and communication to globalization theories is far less than scholars from other disciplines such as

UNIT TEN
New Media and Intercultural Communication

anthropology and sociology.

The separation problem of communication studies, cultural/media studies, and globalization studies in scholarly research has been gradually **alleviated** in recent years, but more studies in this direction are still needed. It is then the purpose of this paper to integrate these concepts through the examination of the relationship between new media and intercultural communication. In order to explore how new media influences the process of intercultural communication, the discussion in this paper contains two parts. In the first part, I explicate the nature of new media and its interdependent relationship with globalization. In the second part, I explain the impact of new media on intercultural communication from different perspectives.

▶ New Media and Globalization

As mentioned above, the rapid development of new media has been the main force accelerating the trend of globalization in human society during the last few decades. With its distinctive and unique nature, new media has brought human interaction and society to a highly interconnected and complex level. Through this convergence the mutual enhancement of new media and globalization has led to the transformation of almost all the aspects of human society. New media being considered "new" is not only because of its successful integration in the form of the traditional interpersonal and mass media, but also because of its new functions that enable individuals to equally control messages in interpersonal media, which allows them to control messages in mass media. New media functionally allows people to interact with multiple persons simultaneously with the ability to individualize messages in the process of interaction.

New media enjoys five distinctive characteristics: digitality, **convergency**, interactivity, **hypertextuality**, and virtuality. First, digitalization is the most prominent feature of new media. New media or digital media dematerializes media text by converting data from analog into digital form, which allows all kind of mathematical operations. New media also makes it possible for a large amount of information to be retrieved, manipulated, and stored in a very limited space.

Second, new media converges the forms and functions of information, media, electronic communication, and electronic computing. The convergence power of new media can be easily demonstrated by the emergence of the Internet in terms of its powerful function embedded in computer information technologies and broadband communication networks. This also leads to the industry convergence displayed by the constant merger of big media companies and the product and service convergence evidenced by the successful connection and combination of media's material, product, and service in the media industry.

Third, the interactive function of new media, i.e., between users and the system regarding the use of information resources, provides users a great freedom in producing and reproducing the content and form of the information during the interaction. In addition, the interactivity of new media makes the interaction among different networks and the **retrieving** of information through different operational systems, both available and convenient. The freedom in controlling the information **endows** new media a great power in the process of human communication.

Fourth, the **hypertextuality** of new media brings forth a global network center in which information can freely move around and spontaneously interconnect. This global network phenomenon has begun to rebuild a new life experience for human beings, which in turn will lead the transformation of economic activities, cultural patterns, interactional styles, and other aspects of human society.

Finally, the cyberspace formed by new media allows people to generate virtual experience and reality. The invisible cyberspace not only induces a gap between reality and virtuality, but also effectuates the free alternation of one's gender, personality, appearance, and occupation. The formation of virtual community that crosses all the boundaries of human society definitely will challenge the way we perceive reality and have traditionally defined identity.

With these distinct features new media pushes the trend of globalization to its highest level in human history. As defined by Steger in 2009, globalization "refers to the expansion and **intensification** of social relations and consciousness across world-time and world-space." In other words, globalization is "a social process in which the constraints of geography on social and cultural arrangements recede and people become increasingly aware that they are receding." It involves the expansion, stretching, intensification, and acceleration of social activities in both objective/material and subjective/human consciousness levels, or different levels of human society, including the entire world, a specific nation, a specific industry or organization, and an individual.

The powerful impact of globalization, enhanced by the advent of new media, is revealed in its dynamic, pervasive, interconnected, hybridized, and individually powerful **attributes**. First, globalization is a dialectically dynamic process, which is caused by the pushing and pulling between the two forces of cultural identity and cultural diversity, or between localization and universalization. Second, globalization is universally pervasive. It moves like air penetrating into every aspect of human society and influences the way we live, think, and behave. Third, globalization is holistically interconnected. It builds a huge matrix in which all components are interconnected with networks. Fourth, globalization represents a culturally hybridized state, which allows cultural transmission via new media to take place at a very rapid rate by **permeating** and dissolving human boundaries. Finally, globalization increases individual power in the new media society, which pluralizes the world by recognizing the ability and importance of individual components.

Together, the dialectically dynamic, universally pervasive, holistically interconnected, culturally hybridized, and individually powerful characteristics of globalization enhanced and deepened by the stimulus and push of the emergence of new media has led to revolutionary changes in people's thinking and behaviors, redefined the sense of community, and restructured human society.

The impact of the integration of new media and globalization can be summarized into five precise effects, namely, a shrinking world, the compression of time and space, close interaction in different aspects of society, global connectivity, and **accelerated** local/global competition/cooperation according to Chen and Starosta in 2000. In other words, boundaries of human societies in terms of space, time, scope, structure, geography, function, profession, value, and beliefs are swiftly changing and transforming into a new pattern of similarities and interconnectedness.

UNIT TEN
New Media and Intercultural Communication

Nevertheless, although the interdependent relationship of new media and globalization is evident, the specific connection between the five distinctive characteristics of new media (i.e., digitality, convergency, interactivity, hypertextuality, and virtuality), and the five manifest features of globalization (i.e., dialectically dynamic, universally **pervasive**, holistically interconnected, culturally hybridized, and individually powerful), remain a valuable research topic for scholars to further pursue. This paper only focuses on the discussion of the relationship between new media and intercultural communication.

The next section first describe the impact of new media on human communication, especially from the intercultural communication perspective, and discusses the present research on the impact of new media on intercultural communication.

▸ The Impact of New Media on Intercultural Communication

With its distinctive features new media has brought human society to a highly interconnected and complex level, but at the same time, it challenges the very existence of human communication in the traditional sense. New media not only influences the form and content of information/messages, but it also affects how people understand each other in the process of human communication, especially for those from different cultural or ethnic groups.

Intrinsically, the new culture hatched from new media creates a continuity gap between traditions and innovations within a culture. Before the emergence of new media, according to Bagdasaryan in 2011, traditions and innovations in human society co-existed in a dynamically **synchronized** way, but the speed and impact of the new media resulted in the inability of traditional values to keep pace with the new cultural values produced by new media. This cultural gap has caused difficulty in understanding or communication between generations and among people in the same culture.

New media also extrinsically breeds communication gaps between different cultural and ethnic groups. The fragmented nature of new media has switched traditional cultural grammar, cultural themes, or cultural maps to a new pattern, resulting in the loss of traditional cultural logic. The rearrangement or restructuring of cultural patterns, or worldview, demands that members of a culture **realign** their communication behaviors within their own community, and to learn a new way of interaction with people from differing cultures. New media fosters a new culture in human society, in which the degree of ambiguity and uncertainty has been **reshuffled** and has reached its highest point, especially in the process of intercultural communication. How to readjust to this new situation and smoothly achieve the goal of mutual understanding for people from different cultural groups in this chaotic stage of cultural change becomes a great challenge for the practical need of interaction in daily life and research in the scholarly community. It is under this circumstance that we see more and more scholars are becoming involved in the investigation of the relationship between new media and intercultural communication.

After examining the extant literature, we found that emerging topical areas in this line of research mainly include three categories: (a) the impact of national/ethnic culture on the development of new media, (b) the impact of new media on cultural/social identity, and (c) the impact of new media (especially social media) on different aspects of intercultural interaction (e.g., intercultural relationship, intercultural dialogue, and intercultural conflict).

▶ National/Ethnic Culture and New Media

As Weick pointed out in 1983, in the international electronic exchange culture plays a significant role in affecting the process and outcome of the interaction. In other words, culture as a communication context may dictate the use of media. Chen found in 2000 that three cultural factors, namely thinking patterns, expression styles, and cultural context, are the three prominent cultural factors that influence how people behave in electronic media, and the three factors are the manifestation of cultural values. Based on the distinction of low-context culture and high-context culture categorized by Hall in 1976, Chung and Chen proposed in 2007 possible communication differences for members in the two groups in the process of electronic interaction (see Table 11.1):

Table 11.1 Differences between Low-Context and High-Context Cultures in E-Communication

Differences	LCC	HCC
Meaning display	explicit	implicit
Value orientation	individual	group
Personal relationship	transitory	permanent
Action base	procedure	personal
Logic	linear	spiral
Message learning time	short	long
Verbal interaction	direct	indirect
Non-verbal style	individualistic	contextual
Idea presentation	logic	reelings
Message style	detailed	simple
Credibility source	authority	communication source

It is assumed that cultural values will influence the social networking process in new media. Hall's low-context and high-context cultures in 1976 and Hofstede's individualism and collectivism dimensions of cultural values in 2001 are two of the most common models used in the study of the relationship between culture and media. For example, Kim, Sohn, and Choi found in 2010 that cultural value **orientations** affect a user's attitude when using new media. Their study demonstrates that although the motives for using social media are similar for students, those in high-context, collectivistic cultures, such as Korean college students, show more emphasis on attaining social support from existing social relationships, while those in low-context, individualistic cultures, such as American college students, tend to show more interest in seeking entertainment rather than social relationships. Moreover, Rosen, Stefanone, and Lackaff as well found in 2010 that, compared to high-context, collectivistic cultures in the process of new media interaction, people in low-context, individualistic cultures tend to emphasize individual achievements and self-promotion to extend their social relations network, though the orientation may trade privacy in the network.

▶ New Media and Cultural Identity

The convergence of new media and globalization brings about at least six new experiences for human beings, including new textual experiences, new ways of representing the world, new relationships between users and new media technologies, new conceptions of the biological body's relationship to technological media, and new patterns of organization and production. These experiences will inevitably challenge the traditional formation and definition of social or cultural identity. In other words, the use of new media is shaking the root of cultural identity by weakening or strengthening the intensity of the relationship between people and community. The time and space compression caused by the convergence of new media and globalization creates a universal cyberspace in which new cultural identity is emerging in different virtual communities.

The new cultural identity formed by new media may not change the traditional meaning of cultural identity as a unique product through interaction in a specific group context, which gives members a sense of belongings to the group, but it will directly challenge the traditional attributes of cultural identity, namely, temporality, **territoriality**, constrastivity, interactivity, and multiplicity. More specifically, cultural identity fostered by new media is no longer a product of historical development (i.e., temporality) confined in an avowal process of people in a geographical place (i.e., territoriality). It may still be a distinct collective consciousness based on the members' sense-making process (i.e., contrastivity). The virtual community is characterized by a higher degree of heterogeneity and a lower level of interconnection according to van Dijk in 1998. In addition, social interaction (i.e., interactivity) as the foundation of developing cultural identity remains unchanged in the age of new media, but the nature of interpersonal and group relationships via social interaction in the virtual community is unlike those constructed from traditional face-to-face interaction. Finally, it is still unknown if the new cultural identity formed by new media will continue to be a multi-faceted concept or practice (i.e., multiplicity), which can contrast with the six facets of traditional cultural identity indicated by Belay in 1996, including sociological identities, occupational identities, **geobasic** identities, national identities, co-cultural identities, and ethnic identities.

In sum, new media continues to establish different kinds of new communities without the limit of time and space, which makes cultural identity more dynamic, fluid, and relativized, and imposes austere challenges to the autonomy and stability of cultural identity. The impact of new media on cultural identity has become one of the issues intercultural communication scholars are most concerned about.

▶ New Media and Intercultural Interaction

The impact of new media on different aspects of intercultural interaction is apparent and has attracted more and more studies from intercultural communication scholars. This part discusses the influence of new media on three common aspects of intercultural interaction in the global context: intercultural relationship, intercultural adaptation, and intercultural conflict.

Intercultural Relationships

New media, especially social media such as Facebook, blogs, MySpace, YouTube, Twitter, and the iPhone, have enabled people from every corner of the world to represent themselves in a particular way and stay connected in cyberspace. It is obvious that the flexibility of information presented and shared in the new media will directly affect, either positively or negatively, the development of intercultural relationships in the virtual community through the creation of a network of personal connection.

Moreover, Elola and Oskoz found in 2009 that in foreign language and study abroad contexts, the use of blogging not only showed a positive effect on the development of intercultural relationships, but also increased the degree of participants' intercultural communication competence. In addition to intercultural relationships on a personal level, social media also helps to establish international business relationships. Nevertheless, new media may also produce a negative impact on intercultural communication. For example, Qian and Scott found in 2007 that revealing too much personal information in blogs, especially negative information about one's friends, employer, and others, tends to jeopardize or cause problems in establishing constructive human relationships intraculturally and interculturally.

Finally, McEwan and Sobre-Denton argued in 2011 that computer-mediated communication can promote and develop virtual **cosmopolitanism** and virtual third cultures. The authors indicated that through the construction of third culture space, a new, hybrid culture is created, in which interactants from differing cultures are able to gather cultural and social information, build online communities, and form intercultural relationships.

Intercultural Adaptation

Because new media enables individuals across the globe to exchange messages for the purpose of understanding people from different cultures, it has become popular for sojourners or immigrants to use new media to communicate with their friends, classmates, and relatives or family members in both their native and host country in their learning process or daily life study. The longer immigrants reside in the host country, the more they communicate with the host nationals via new media, but the frequency of surfing their original country's websites is decreasing. W. Chen also found that the use of new media shows a significant impact on the process of immigrants' intercultural adaptation. In other words, the social interaction conducted through new media by immigrants proves to be a critical element that can determine whether they can successfully adjust to the host country.

In addition, Sawyer and Chen investigated in 2011 how international students use social media and how it affects their intercultural adaptation. The authors found that social media provides an environment for international students to connect with people in both their home and host countries, which in turn helps them strengthen personal relationships and fosters a sense of belonging to the host culture. The use of new media obviously helps international students cope with cultural barriers in the process of intercultural adaptation. The study also found that, due to the influence of culture shock, **sojourners** tend to rely more on social media in the initial stage of arriving in the host country, to keep connected with those people they know in their home country in order to gain a sense of comfort in the new environment. As time moves on, the use of social media was switched to interacting with the host nationals to help them better integrate into the new culture.

Furthermore, Croucher attempted to propose in 2011 a theoretical model through the integration of **cultivation** theory and ethnic group vitality to illustrate the relationship between social networking and cultural adaptation. Croucher successfully generated two propositions: (a) "During cultural adaptation, the use of social networking sites affects immigrants' interaction with the dominant culture," and (b) "during cultural adaptation, the use of social networking sites will affect immigrants' in-group communication." According to the author, the **propositions** provide great potential for future research to investigate the impact of social media on the process of immigrants' adaptation in the host culture, which may include:

Frequency of interaction with dominant culture, their use of dominant and ethnic media, perception of the dominant culture, familiarity with dominant language or cultural norms, identification with dominant or ethnic culture, involvement in the dominant political system, and motivation to acculturate.

Intercultural Conflict

New media provides people and governments with a powerful tool to construct their own image, to define and redefine the meanings of messages, to set the media agenda, or to frame the news or messages. However, cultural dissimilarities result in different ways in media representation on the individual or governmental level. Because the underlying order, perspectives and practical limitations of the media in any society are based on their cultural value orientations, the different forms of media representation tend to reflect the asymmetry of intercultural communication and inevitably lead to the problem of intercultural confrontation or conflict in interpersonal, group, and national levels.

Conclusion

This paper examines the relationship between new media and intercultural communication in the global context. It is argued that new media not only provides a space in which people of different cultures can freely express their opinions and establish relationships, but may also challenge the existence of human communication in **intracultural** and intercultural contexts because of its specific characteristics that are significantly dissimilar to traditional media. With its focus on intercultural interaction, this paper explicates the impact of cultural values on new media, the impact of new media on cultural identity, and the impact of new media on three aspects of intercultural interaction, namely, intercultural relationships, intercultural dialogue, and intercultural conflict. Two implications can be made based on the delineation of this paper.

First, this paper only deals with the directional influence of cultural values on new media, new media on cultural identity, and new media on intercultural interaction. It is plausible that the relationship of new media and other variables discussed in this paper can be mutual. In other words, for future research scholars can examine, for example, the possible impact of new media on the formation of new cultural values, the transformation of or rendering obsolete old cultural values, and the impact of cultural identity on the use of new media. Moreover, in addition to the three categories examined in this paper, the scope of the relationship between new media and intercultural communication can be expanded to other themes, such as the investigation of co-cultural variations in the use of new media to communication within and across cultures, the impact of new media on intercultural dialogue, and the potential use of new media to resolve intercultural conflicts.

Second and finally, because the impact of new media on human society is still in its initial stages, the possible effect of new media on human communication mentioned in the first part of this paper remains dynamic and still lacks systematic studies from scholars. Hence, the impact of new media on intercultural communication discussed in this paper is largely confined to the old model of media functions. How to unlock this limitation and shift from the context of traditional media to new media remains a great challenge for scholars to observe in this line of research. In other words, future research needs to observe and study the question, "Is intercultural communication possible?" raised by Shan in 2010, under the context of new media in global society.

Text B   New Media and Intercultural Communication

After Robert Shuter

Introduction

New media or information communication technologies (ICTs) are **omnipresent** in the 21st century and include the internet, computer-mediated communication (CMC), social network sites (SNSs), mobile phones, Skype, text messaging, online games (MMOGs), virtual worlds, and blogs. With the advent of these new communication technologies, virtual, video, and mobile contact between cultures has increased exponentially, especially between individuals and groups. Face-to-face communication is no longer the predominant mode of intercultural contact. With the assistance of ICTs, individuals and groups can communicate instantly across geo-political boundaries, space, and time. This communications revolution has significant effects and implications for the theory and praxis of intercultural communication.

Intercultural new media studies (INMS) is designed to examine how ICTs affect intercultural communication. INMS examines new digital theories of intercultural contact as well as refining twentieth-century intercultural communication theories, exploring their relevance in a digital world. Composed of two research areas, intercultural new media studies focuses specifically on (a) new media and intercultural communication theory and (b) culture and the social uses of new media. The first area **probes** how ICTs impact theories of communication between people who do not share the same cultural backgrounds which have been traditionally defined as national culture (country) and co-culture (i.e. ethnicity/race). More contemporary definitions of culture and cultural backgrounds include hybridized cultures developed transnationally across geopolitical boundaries due to migration, diaspora, and time/space **reconfigurations** in a digital age. The second area of INMS investigates the relationship between culture and new media: How does culture impact the social uses of new media within and across societies, and in what ways do new media affect culture?

New media and intercultural communication theory raises significant questions about the relevance of theories of intercultural communication that were primarily developed in the 20th century and based on a face-to-face paradigm. For example, these ICC theories include, but are not limited to, acculturation/adaptation, third culture, intercultural dialogue, intercultural competence, cultural identity, stereotyping, high-context/low-context communication, intercultural conflict, intercultural contact, M-time/P-time, ethnocentrism, racism, culture shock, and intercultural relationship development. Consider the impact of new media on cultural identity theory.

According to social identity theory, cultural identity is founded on membership in social groups and is co-created and negotiated as well as impacted by communication and internal and external forces. This conception of cultural identity is founded on twentieth century assumptions about the self in that it's fixed in time and space, based on group contacts rooted in a face-to-face paradigm, and can vary depending on its' salience in a social context. In a new media era of perpetual contact that encourages people to live in virtual spaces with many others, this perspective may not be adequate for explaining the development and maintenance of cultural identity in the twenty first century. In fact, with the advent of the internet, individuals can join virtual cultures, which are technological entities not grounded in time and space. These virtual cultures are referred to as pseudo-communities since they are not bound by time or space and do not rely on face-to-face communication. These virtual cultures have been known to alter pre-existing cultural identities that were usually co-created, negotiated, and developed in concert with social identity theory.

When virtual communities are composed of members with similar backgrounds who may or may not know one another, it's been found that they can preserve pre-existing cultural identities. For instance, research studies have found that cultural members living in foreign settings successfully utilize new media to connect worldwide with other people from their culture, reinforcing their identities and even their religions. Moreover, organic, face-to-face communities in diaspora also seem to successfully utilize social media like Facebook and other new media to reinforce their cultural identities.

Interestingly, research suggests that in virtual communities consisting of American ethnic and racial groups, individuals reinforce their cultural identities in elaborate ways. For example, it's been found that African Americans, Latinos, Native Americans and Vietnamese craft Facebook profiles that deliberately and indiscreetly present their cultural identities. It appears from this research that cultural minorities in the U.S. can be empowered by utilizing social networking sites for ethno-racial identity presentations.

On balance, it appears from the research that cultural identities in virtual communities are not necessarily co-created or negotiated as they generally are in organic communities. Frequently considered pseudo communities, virtual communities are often anonymous and disconnected from time and space, which renders their climates unfavorable for co-creation and negotiation. It's not clear from the research how cultural identities are constructed in virtual communities.

Moreover, preserving cultural identity may be governed by different dynamics in virtual than organic communities. For example, it appears from research that in cyberspace marginalized and minority groups may be able to assert and reinforce their cultural identities in unique and powerful ways that may not be as readily available to them in face-to-face encounters. Given the limited research on identity preservation in cyberspace, it's unclear how this is accomplished and whether/how the dynamics of identity preservation in virtual communities differ from organic communities.

▶ Acculturation, Intercultural Competence, and New Media

There is plentiful research on the processes inherent in adapting to new cultures generally referred to as acculturation. These studies have largely concentrated on how personality, face-to-face communication with in-groups and out-groups, and mass media influence acculturation. This research suggests, on balance, that increased positive communication with the host culture, including consuming its mass media, coupled with moderate and even declining interaction with in-groups, can enhance acculturation. While there is limited research on acculturation and new media, investigations in this area suggest that ICTs may play a positive role in adjusting to new cultures.

Most of the online acculturation studies focus on students living internationally for educational purposes. This body of research suggests that students' successful adjustment to a culture is significantly improved when they receive support on-line from in-groups. Staying connected via the internet with friends, family and even strangers from their home culture can improve students' emotional adjustment to a new society. Interestingly, it's been found that the longer students remain in the host culture, the less likely they are to access home country websites and, instead, reach out on-line to members of the host culture.

Social networking sites like Facebook also appear to enhance acculturation as long as international students and immigrants communicate with members of their home culture and the host culture. Students who use a combination of SNSs and on-line communication to interact with family members and friends tend to have less acculturative stress and adjust more successfully. However, it has been found that SNSs can be an obstacle to acculturation when immigrants rely on them to communicate predominantly with ethnic in-group members. This finding is also consistent with acculturation research conducted on face-to-face interaction; that is, acculturation is enhanced when individuals communicate consistently with members of the host culture.

Interestingly, acculturation is not only affected by face-to-face interaction, mass media exposure, and online support networks, but it's also influenced by the individual's level of intercultural competence. Often defined as awareness of and openness to new cultures, intercultural competence also includes the abilities and skills necessary to navigate a new society. According to past research, competence is fueled by many factors including social communication, pre-departure preparation, and exposure to salient mass media. However, it's clear from the literature that on-line interaction can nurture competence and improve acculturation. For example, on-line contact between second language learners and native speakers not only assists with language acquisition but it also tends to improve cultural awareness and communication skills like asking probing questions, which is a component of intercultural competence. Participation in virtual games like Second Life and World of War Craft has also been linked in a few studies to increased intercultural competence. This is because the players experiment with the skills necessary to adjust to the gaming culture which may improve their competence skills in face-to-face intercultural encounters. However, the impact of virtual intercultural competence on real world interaction has not been established.

It appears that on-line communication and SNSs tend to play a positive role in acculturation and intercultural competence. An invalidating factor, especially for acculturation, seems to be the amount of time individuals engage in on-line in-group communication, with sustained and extensive on-line contact becoming an obstacle to acculturation. While participation in virtual games may have some impacts on the enhancement of intercultural competence, the research is too scanty to establish a connection. Finally, the literature on ICTs and acculturationneed to be carefully considered when revisiting acculturation theories based on a face-to-face paradigm.

▶ Intercultural Dialogue, Third Culture and New Media

The literatures on intercultural dialogue and third culture are abundant with almost of it derived from research on face-to-face communication. Intercultural dialogue entails deep understanding of another person while third culture requires co-joining of their separate cultures, resulting in a more inclusive third space called third culture. To achieve intercultural dialogue and third culture, the literature suggests that communicators must have an open, empathetic, and accepting relationship—characteristics difficult to achieve in face-to-face encounters and even more challenging in virtual communities.

Intercultural dialogue in virtual encounters may be challenged by the anonymous, transitory and sometimes impersonal nature of this type of interaction. This suggests that intercultural dialogue may not be possible in virtual spaces if face-to-face relational requirements are necessary to achieve dialogue. Interestingly, research suggests that intercultural collaboration is quite possible in virtual communities such as collaborative authoring in Wikipedia. Studies on international tele-collaboration among students, which includes blogs, podcasts, Skype and other Web 2.0 tools, indicate that use of multiple new media platforms can create conditions that may lead to intercultural dialogue. In short, virtual collaboration may be a **precursor**, even gateway, to intercultural dialogue.

McEwan and Sobre-Denton suggested in 2011 that it may be possible to achieve the third culture in virtual communities. They argue that **anonymity** and maintaining social distance—characteristics inimical to the third culture in FtF communities—may help achieve the third culture in virtual encounters because they reduce face threats due to social errors and encourage intercultural risk taking. In addition, ICTs provide easy access to culturally diverse others because it's not necessary to leave one's domicile to make contact.

Research suggests that intercultural dialogue and third culture may be possible to achieve in virtual communities but the requirements for attaining both may be different than what was originally proposed in FtF intercultural theories. Not only may anonymity and social distance increase the prospect of achieving virtual dialogue/the third culture but so may the use of multiple new media tools. This suggests that FtF ICC theories of intercultural dialogue and the third culture may need to be **augmented** to be applicable to virtual encounters.

▶ Cultural Stereotyping and New Media

ICC theories of modifying cultural group stereotypes are long standing and emerge predominantly from 20th century research on face-to-face interaction. One of the major theories of altering existing stereotypes is called the contact hypothesis which was developed by Gordon Allport in 1954. It's based on the assumption that under the right conditions intergroup contact can change negative group stereotypes and create positive attitude change. Much research has been conducted on the contact hypothesis since its inception, confirming the original assumptions. These assumptions include the following: for intergroup contact to work (a) group members need to be of equal social status (i.e. social class similarity), (b) possess common goals (i.e. successfully complete a task, (c) be willing to cooperate with one another to complete a task, and (d) engage in personal rather than casual contact over time. Do the major assumptions of the contact hypothesis apply to virtual communities?

Research suggests that digital contact between cultural groups can reduce stereotypes and improve group attitudes. Email has been used successfully to reduce stereotypes between university students from different cultures. For example, Iranian and Canadian students, who were paired as email buddies for multiple weeks and encouraged to exchange pictures and personal information, became more informed about the one another's cultures, changed their negative group stereotypes, and improved their group attitudes. These positive changes were especially prominent when email buddies communicated frequently with one another and shared more personal information. In another study, when Chinese and Japanese university students were paired as email buddies for language learning, certain stereotypes tended to be reduced more than others. Cultural stereotypes based on hearsay and the opinions of fellow learners were more apt to change. In contrast, stereotypes that originated from teachers and native speakers of their languages were more resistant to change.

This research indicates that major elements of the contact **hypothesis** may apply to online encounters. Participants of similar age and status (e.g. university students) who have common goals (e.g. language learning) and cooperate on common tasks are inclined to alter their negative stereotypes. Interestingly, even though email is not considered an effective medium for exchanging personal information with others, students restricted to email are still able to communicate significant information and, hence, alter negative stereotypes. This finding suggests that email may be a more robust platform for communicating personal information in intercultural encounters than researchers have assumed in the past.

Face-to-face interaction is generally considered the most effective medium for communicating personal information to others followed by speaking on the phone. Text based media like email and text messaging are considered less satisfactory to communicate personal data to others. Perhaps email may be more effective in intercultural communication because it removes verbal and non-verbal social cues and, hence, reduces social threat due to fear of making interpersonal errors. Text based communication also allows communicators the time to formulate their ideas before replying to others, which is especially important when people are not interacting in their native languages.

New media are expanding and even challenging basic theories of intercultural communication based on the research reviewed here. It's important that theories of intercultural communication developed in the 20th century are revisited in light of the proliferation of ICTs in the 21st century. Casting a critical eye on 20th century ICC theories should result in more salient theories for a technological age. To ensure the vitality of the ICC discipline, it's vital to review ICC theories through the lens of new media.

Culture and the Social Uses of New Media

Another major dimension of new media and intercultural communication is the many ways culture affects the social uses of ICTs, and how ICTs affect culture. Culture and new media are inseparable; they influence one other in terms of when, where, how, and around whom communicators actually use ICTs. For example, Shuter and Chattopadhyay found in 2010 that communicators from India and the U.S. have quite different rules for text messaging which the authors call **textiquettes.** They found that American men and women tend to send and receive text messages just about anywhere including public spaces like street corners, movie theaters and even classrooms. In contrast, Indian males and females prefer to text message at home among family members and only occasionally in public settings. Interestingly, Indian females are less willing than Indian men, American men, and American women to text message around others; in fact, they prefer to text message when they're alone or with a close friend. The authors suggest that Indian women text message differently than the others because traditional Indian culture does not allow women to communicate in the same ways as men, which also affects when, where, how and around whom they text message.

Culture also affects how mobile phones and laptops are used at work and school. In research conducted in Denmark and the United States, it was found that Danes tend to use their mobile phones around their bosses significantly more than do Americans, who try to avoid utilizing their phones near superiors at work. Studies on ICT use in university classrooms found that American students use their mobile phones in class much more than Danes and prefer that their instructors determine class policies for ICTs. In contrast, Danish university students would rather not have rules regulating use of ICTs in class and are significantly less supportive than Americans of instructors determining classroom digital policies. Differences in American and Danish ICT use at work and school appear to emerge from variations in cultural values, which are defined as preferred behavioral outcomes of a society, according to Shuter and Chattopadhyay in 2014.

Decades of research on intercultural communication have demonstrated that cultural values affect communicators' face-to-face interaction with others. Cultural values like individualism and collectivism, for example, have been linked to differences in interpersonal behavior of Asians and North Americans, according to Geert Hofstede in 1980, a major researcher on cultural values. Given extensive past research that cultural values are foundational to communicative behavior, it's not surprising that they also affect how communicators in different cultures utilize ICTs.

In the case of Danes and Americans, they differ in how they view authority. Danes possess a more equalitarian authority value than Americans who tend to be significantly more hierarchical. This difference in authority values is best **exemplified** by Triandis and Gelfand in 1998 who classified Americans as vertical individualists because they emphasize gaining status through competition. In contrast, Danes are considered horizontal individualists since they avoid status and emphasize equality, conforming and not sticking out. These authority values are reflected in American preference for instructors to develop class policies to manage laptops and Smartphones, and Danish desire not to have these class policies. It is also evident in American reluctance and Danish willingness to use their mobile phones at work in front of their bosses.

The connection between cultural values and the social uses of new media is called a socio-cultural theory of new media. It argues that cultural values affect various aspects of ICT use including when, where, how and among whom they are utilized. This theory draws from extensive research on cultural values and human behavior and applies this research to how communicators use new media platforms such as mobile phones, laptops, blogs, and multiplayer online games.

The socio-cultural theory of new media also argues that ICTs can challenge and even alter a society's cultural values. For example, Shuter found in 2010 that text messaging in India challenges traditional Indian gender values about the roles of men and women. For example, Indian women who text in public tend to receive negative treatment from Indian men who are strangers. Typically, Indian men make harsh comments to Indian women who text in public; sometimes, these comments are accompanied by unwanted touching and grabbing. In India this type of behavior is called eve teasing and refers to men who treat women disrespectfully in public settings like street corners, public transport, and even schools. Since mobile phones empower people to communicate with anyone at any time, women who text message are eve teased in India because Indian men perceive texting as a threat to traditional female gender role.

Future studies on culture and new media should focus on developing intercultural theories on the social uses of new media. In contrast, the current trend is to examine ICT behavior through the prism of new media theories that are supposed to apply to all cultures such as media richness theory. This theory, for example, argues that all new media platforms, regardless of culture, have inherent limitations as to the amount and type of information they can effectively handle, which is called "richness." Text messaging, according to this theory, is suited for short, impersonal messages while phone calls are preferred for longer more personal information. Although this seems reasonable, richness theory may not apply to many cultures and settings. East Asians, especially Chinese and Japanese, prefer phone calls when communicating short impersonal messages to their bosses because text messaging is generally viewed as an impolite way to communicate with authority figures. Current theories of new media are no substitute for formulating and refining culture-based theories that attempt to explain socio-cultural influences on the social uses of new media.

Applications

1. Intercultural New Media Studies: The Next Frontier in Intercultural Communication

Shutter, R. (2012). Intercultural new media studies: The next frontier in intercultural communication. *Journal of Intercultural Communication Research*, 41(3), 219 – 237.

Abstract: New media are transforming communication across cultures. Despite this revolution in cross cultural contact, researchers in communication and the social sciences have largely ignored the impact of new media on intercultural communication. This groundbreaking article defines the parameters of a new field of inquiry called Intercultural New Media Studies (INMS) which explores the intersection between new media and intercultural communication. Composed of two research areas: (a) new media and intercultural communication theory and (b) culture and new media, INMS investigates new digital theories of intercultural contact as well as refines and expands 20th century intercultural communication theories, exploring their salience in a digital world. Intercultural new media studies promise to increase our understanding of intercultural communication in a new media age and is the next frontier in intercultural communication.

Keywords: intercultural new media studies; frontier; intercultural communication; parameter; new digital stories

2. New Media and Political Communication in Asia: A Critical Assessment of Research on Media and Politics, 1988 – 2008

Lo, V. H., & Wei, R. (2010). New media and political communication in Asia: A critical assessment of research on media and politics, 1988 – 2008, *Asian Journal of Communication*, 20(2), 264 – 275.

Abstract: This study focuses on reviewing research on the interplay between new media and political communication in Asian societies. To assess the state of the discipline of political communication and how the research advances knowledge of the role and impact of media in politics, this study content-analyzed articles concerning media use in political arenas in Asian societies that were published in 10 leading communication journals between 1988 and 2008. Results reveal that the social science paradigm was the leading paradigm of inquiry, accounting for the majority of research in these journals. The analysis also indicates that most articles were theory-driven and survey was the most frequently used method. American or U.S.-based authors dominated new media and political communication research in Asia. Implications of these trends are discussed with the goal to shed some light on new directions for future research.

Keywords: new media; political communication; Asian communication research; research paradigm; new directions

3. Online Media and Intercultural Communication

Vujović, M., & Obradović, N. (2017). Online media and intercultural communication. *Philosophy, Sociology, Psychology and History*, 16(1), 51–61.

Abstract. The emergence of the Internet has led to tectonic changes in all aspects of human life, and certainly the most important ones occurred in communication and information. The term "Global Village", which was first used by Marshall McLuhan in his "Report on the project of understanding new media" in 1960, seems to be more current today than ever. The emergence of online media, social networks and many other applications has enabled people to connect and communicate no matter where they are on the planet. However, despite all the positive effects that communication networks have brought with them, there are many negative aspects of intercultural communication that have been retained to the same or even greater extent, creating the so-called "noise" or disruption of communication. One of the best examples of this is the comments in the online media. This is an essential segment of online journalism, and it proved to be a fruitful intercultural communication channel, which is why this paper will put special emphasis on the readers' comments.

Keywords: online media; intercultural communication; comments; information; readers' comments

Interactive Activities

1. Individually, please finish reading Text A, Text B, and the application abstracts and work out the meanings of the terms in bold type by consulting the dictionary whenever necessary.

2. In pairs, please summarize the content in 2 to 3 sentences of each sub-heading in the unit outlines of Text A and Text B based on your reading and understanding of the texts.

3. In groups, share your gains, comments and suggestions regarding the three application abstracts. Based on your interests, locate and finish reading the full-length papers of your interested abstracts.

4. Q&A: Questions are encouraged about any uncertain or confused part or parts in the unit and seek answers either from other fellow students or the instructor.

In today's digitalized information age, main stream media have been getting increasingly merged with social media. What suggestions do you intend to make to facilitate the mergence of the two so as to integrate the strengths of both?

5. Complete the Personal Report of the Dimensions of Privacy Questionnaire, an instrument designed to measure the types of privacy preferred by individuals. Take a few moments and complete the self-assessment for Unit 11.

6. Please find a qualitative research paper and a quantitative research paper concerning the

relationships between new media and intercultural communication. Then, pay close attention to the wording and functions of the **research questions** (RQ) and **hypotheses** in the two research papers. Research questions are relevant to normative or census type research (e.g., How many of them are there? Is there a relationship between them?). They are most often used in qualitative inquiry though their use in quantitative inquiry is becoming more prominent. A hypothesis is defined as a guess or a hunch or an assumption. In other words, a hypothesis is a conjectural statement of the relation between two or more variables. Just as conclusions must be grounded in the data, hypotheses must be grounded in the theoretical framework. A research question poses a relationship between two or more variables but phrases the relationship as a question while a hypothesis represents a declarative statement of the relations between two or more variables. Both the research question and hypothesis either support or refuse an existing theory but the main difference between the two is that a research question is formulated in the form of a question whereas a hypothesis is an assumed solution to a problem in the form of a statement. Another main difference between the two is that a research question is a form of the researcher wondering about the workings of the world while a hypothesis is an educated guess on the outcome of the study.

UNIT ELEVEN

Intercultural Relationships and Conflicts

Readings

Text A Culture, Communication, and Conflict

After Judith N. Martin and Thomas K. Nakayama

▶ Introduction

The need to understand intercultural conflict seems more important now than ever. One thing we can be sure of is that conflict is inevitable. Conflicts are happening all around the world, as they always have, and at many different levels: interpersonal, social, national, and international. In this text, we use our **tripartite** framework (social science, interpretive, and critical) to examine and understand intercultural conflict. The social science approach focuses on how cultural differences cause conflict and influence the management of the conflict, primarily on the interpersonal level. The other two approaches—interpretive and critical—focus more on intergroup relationships and on cultural, historical, and structural elements as the primary sources of conflict. These three approaches emphasize different aspects of the individual-contextual dialectic and the need to view conflict on all three levels: the interpersonal, societal, and international. We first define what we mean by conflict and intercultural conflict and then describe each of the three approaches. We conclude the chapter with practical suggestions for understanding and improving our intercultural conflict skills.

▶ Characteristics of Intercultural Conflict

Conflict is usually defined as involving a perceived or real **incompatibility** of goals, values, expectations, processes, or outcomes between two or more **interdependent** individuals or groups. The complexity of intercultural conflict can be seen in the current debate, discussed in previous chapters.

There is no reason to seek a single source for conflict. By taking a dialectical approach to thinking about conflict, you can see how various forces—economic, social, political, religious—may all play different roles at different times. Yet, when confronted with such conflicts, how should society respond? How should you respond? What are the characteristics of **intercultural conflict**? How does intercultural conflict differ from other kinds of conflict? One unique characteristic is that intercultural conflicts tend to be more ambiguous than intracultural conflict. Other characteristics involve language issues and contradictory conflict styles.

Ambiguity

While some conflicts are seen unambiguously as conflicts by parties involved (e.g., Israelis and Palestinians), this and many other conflicts are seen in very different ways by the individuals and groups involved. For example, when 49 people were murdered in an Orlando, Florida nightclub in June 2016, there were varying views of the causes and proposed solutions. Some saw it as a hate crime—caused by the gunman's anti-gay prejudice. Some saw it as a clash of cultures and religions, United States (Christianity) and Islam, and refused to acknowledge the anti-gay element. Others saw it as an attack on freedom of all individuals. Still others saw it primarily as the actions of a deranged individual with a history of mental illness and unresolved anger issues. The proposed solutions to the conflict—more gun control **legislation** or more protection/rights for gay Americans—depended on one's view of the cause as Healey stated in 2016.

In some interpersonal contexts, individuals may not even agree there is a conflict. A student, Tabbetha, reported an ongoing conflict at work with one of her co-workers, an older gentleman, in the customer service department. She thinks the co-worker doesn't like her very much and they frequently disagree about how to handle certain customer complaints. Part of the problem is that she doesn't really get what is going on between them—she's not sure if it's her age, her gender, or if he's having a bad time in his personal life, and so she is not sure how to handle the situation.

Language

Issues surrounding language may be important to intercultural conflict. One student, Stephanie, described a situation that occurred when she was studying in Spain. She went to an indoor swimming pool with her host family sisters. Being from Arizona, she was unaccustomed to swimming in such cold water, so she went outside to sunbathe. Her "sisters" asked her why she didn't swim with them. Stephanie explains:

> At that point I realized they thought I should really be with them.... I didn't know how to express myself well enough to explain to them.... I tried, but I don't think it worked very well. So I just apologized.... I did basically ignore the conflict. I would have dealt with it, but I felt I did not have the language skills to explain myself effectively, so I did not even try.... That is why I had such a problem, because I could not even express what I would have liked to.

When individuals don't know the language well, it is very difficult to handle conflict effectively. At the same time, silence is not always a bad thing. Sometimes it provides a **"cooling off"** period, allowing things to settle down. Depending on the cultural context, silence can be very appropriate.

Contradictory Conflict Styles

Intercultural conflict also may be characterized by a combination of orientations to conflict and conflict management styles. In 1999 Communication scholar Sheryl Lindsley interviewed managers in maquiladoras—sorting or assembly plants along the Mexican-U.S. border—and found many examples of conflict. For example, Mexican managers thought that U.S. managers were often rude and impolite in their dealings with each other and the workers. The biggest difference between U.S. Americans and Mexicans was in the way that U.S. Americans expressed disagreement at management meetings. One Mexican manager explained:

> When we are in a meeting together, the U.S. American will tell another manager, "I don't like what you did."... Mexicans interpret this as a personal insult. They have a difficult time understanding that U.S. Americans can insult each other in this way and then go off and play golf together.... Mexicans would be polite, perhaps tell the person in private, or make a suggestion, rather than confronting.

As Lindsley points out, the conflict between the Mexican and U.S. American managers in their business meetings needs to be understood as a dialectical and "layered" process in which individual, dyadic, societal, and historical forces are recognized.

▶ The Social Science Approach to Conflict

Perhaps if everyone agreed on the best way to view conflict, there would be less of it. But the reality is that different orientations to conflict may result in more conflict. In this section, which takes a social science approach, we identify cultural influences in approaches to conflict, different types of conflict, and different strategies and tactics for responding to conflict.

A key question is: Is open conflict good or bad? That is, should conflict be welcomed because it provides opportunities to strengthen relationships? Or should it be avoided because it can only lead to problems for relationships and groups? Other questions are: What is the best way to handle conflict when it arises? Should individuals talk about it directly, deal with it indirectly, or avoid it? Should emotions be part of the conflict resolution? Are expressions of emotions viewed as showing commitment to resolving the conflict at hand? Or is it better to be restrained and solve problems by rational logic rather than emotional expressiveness? Also consider the following questions: How do we learn how to deal with conflict? Who teaches us how to solve conflicts when they arise? How we answer all of these questions depends in large part on our cultural background and the way we were raised.

Cultural Values and Conflict

One general way to understand cultural variations in intercultural conflict resolution is to look at how cultural values influence conflict management. Face negotiation theory links cultural values to facework and conflict styles. **Facework** refers to specific communication strategies we use to "save" our own or another person's face and is a universal concept; how we "do" facework varies from culture to culture and influences conflict styles. Communication scholar Ting-Toomey and her colleagues have conducted a number of studies showing that people from individualistic societies tend to be more concerned with saving their own face than another person's, so they tend to use more direct conflict management styles according to Ting-Toomey and Oetzel in 2002.

In contrast, people from collectivistic societies tend to be more concerned with preserving group harmony and with saving the other person's face (and dignity) during conflict. They may use a less direct conversational style; protecting the other person's face and making him or her look good is considered a skillful facework style. These face concerns lead them to use a more

accommodating conflict style. However, some evidence indicates that not all collectivistic societies prefer indirect ways of dealing with conflict. How someone chooses to deal with conflict in any situation depends on the type of conflict and the relationship she or he has with the other person. For example, Kaori, a Japanese student, recounted a conflict she had with her U.S. American friend, Mara, when the two were working together on a sorority project. Mara seemed to take a very competitive, individualistic approach to the project, saying things like, "I did this on the project," or referring to it as "my project." Kaori became increasingly irritated and less motivated to work on the project. She finally said to Mara, "Is this your project or our project?" Mara seemed surprised, tried to defend herself, and eventually apologized; the two women then continued to work on the project and put the conflict behind them. This example is supported by a study that showed that while Japanese young people said they would avoid conflict with strangers or acquaintances, like Kaori, they were more willing to deal openly with conflict and work through conflicts with ingroup members like close friends.

Family Influences

Most people deal with conflict in the way they learned while growing up—their default style. A primary influence is our family background; some families prefer a particular conflict style, and children come to accept this style as normal. For example, the family may have settled conflict in a direct, engaging manner, with the person having the strongest argument (or the biggest muscle) getting his or her way, and preserving his or her own self-esteem, rather than helping the other person "save face." Or, we may prefer to sacrifice our own self-esteem in order to preserve the relationship.

Sometimes, people try very hard to reject the conflict styles they saw their parents using. For example, suppose that Maria's parents avoided open conflict and never discussed what was bothering them. Their children learned to avoid conflict and become very uncomfortable when people around them use a more expressive style of conflict management. Maria has vowed she will never deal with conflict that way with her own children and has tried very hard to use other ways of dealing with conflicts when they do arise in her family. It is important to realize that people deal with conflict in a variety of ways and may not have the same reasons for choosing a certain style.

Family conflict can also arise from generational differences in immigrant families that reflect intercultural differences. In Western Europe, Muslim immigrant girls are sometimes punished by their families for being too Western. Other immigrant families may have conflicts over arranged marriages, dating, and other cultural expectations that may highlight differences between the country of origin and the new homeland.

Intercultural Conflict Styles

Given cultural background and values as well as family influences, how do people specifically respond to conflict situations? In 2005 Conflict expert Mitchell Hammer has systematically investigated this topic and proposes a four-style framework, based on two primary dimensions (direct/indirect and emotional expressiveness/restraint). Let's see how this works.

Direct and Indirect Conflict Approaches. This **direct/indirect approach** to conflict is similar to the direct/indirect language dimension we discussed earlier. There it was applied specifically to language use, whereas here it represents a broader conflict resolution approach. Some cultural groups think that conflict is fundamentally a good thing; these groups feel that it is best to approach conflict very directly, because working through conflicts constructively results in stronger, healthier, and more satisfying relationships. Similarly, groups that work through conflict can gain new information about members or about other groups, defuse more serious conflict, and increase group cohesiveness.

People who take this approach concentrate on using very precise language. While they may not always feel comfortable with face-to-face conflict, they think that it's important to "say what's on your mind" in a conflict situation. The goal in this approach is to articulate the issues carefully and select the "best" solution based on an agreed-upon set of criteria. However, many cultural groups view conflict as ultimately destructive for relationships and do not think that a direct approach to conflict resolution is useful. For example, many Asian cultures, reflecting the influence of Confucianism and Taoism, and some religious groups in the United States see conflict as disturbing the peace. For instance, most Amish think of conflict not as an opportunity for personal growth, but as a threat to interpersonal and community harmony. When conflict does arise, the strong spiritual value of **pacifism** dictates a nonresistant response—often avoidance or dealing with conflict very indirectly.

Also, these groups think that when members disagree they should adhere to the consensus of the group rather than engage in conflict. In fact, members who threaten group harmony may be sanctioned. One writer gives an example of a man from the Maori culture in New Zealand who was swearing and using inappropriate language in a public meeting:

> A woman went up to him, laying her hand on his arm and speaking softly. He shook her off and continued. The crowd now moved back from him as far as possible, and as if by general agreement, the listeners dropped their gaze to their toes until all he could see was the tops of their heads. The speaker slowed, faltered, was reduced to silence, and then sat down.

These people tend to approach conflict rather indirectly. They concentrate on the meaning that is "outside" the verbal message and tend to be very careful to protect the "face" of the person with whom they disagree. They may emphasize vagueness and ambiguity in language and often rely on third parties to help resolve disagreements. The goal in this approach is to make sure that the relationship stays intact during the disagreement. For example, they may emphasize the past history of the disputants and try to build a deeper relationship that involves increased obligation toward each other.

Emotional Expressiveness/Restraint Approaches. A second broad approach to conflict management concerns the role of emotion in conflict. People who value intense and overt displays of emotions during discussion of disagreement rely on the **emotionally expressive approach.** They think it is better to show emotion during disagreement than to hide or suppress feelings; that is, they show emotion through expressive non-verbal behavior and vocalization. They also think that this outward display of emotions means that one really cares and is committed to resolving the conflict. In fact, one's credibility is based on the ability to be expressive.

In addition, people who believe in the **restraint approach** think that disagreements are best discussed in an emotionally calm manner. For these people, it's important to control and internalize one's feelings during conflict and to avoid non-verbal emotion. They are uncomfortable with emotional expression and think that such expressions may hurt others. People who use this approach think that relationships are made stronger by keeping one's emotions in check and protecting the "face" or honor of the other person. Credibility is demonstrated by maintaining tight control over one's emotions.

These two approaches to conflict resolution reflect different underlying cultural values involving identity and preserving self-esteem and "face." In the more individualistic approach that sees conflict as good, the concern is with individuals preserving their own dignity. The more communal approach espoused by both Amish and Asian cultures and by many other collectivist groups is more concerned with maintaining harmony in interpersonal relations and preserving the dignity of others. For example, in classic Chinese thought, social harmony is the goal of human society at all levels—individual, family, village, and nation.

It is possible to combine these approaches and come up with four different conflict resolution styles that seem to be connected to various cultural groups: the discussion style, the engagement style, the accommodating style, and the dynamic style.

The **discussion style** combines the direct and emotionally restrained approaches and emphasizes a verbally direct approach for dealing with disagreements—to "say what you mean and mean what you say." People who use this style are comfortable expressing disagreements directly but prefer to be emotionally restrained. This style is often identified as the predominant style preferred by many white Americans, as well as by Europeans, Australians, and New Zealanders

The **engagement style** emphasizes a verbally direct and confrontational approach to dealing with conflict. This style views intense verbal and non-verbal expression of emotion as demonstrating sincerity and willingness to engage intensely to resolve conflict. It has been linked to some African Americans and southern Europeans (France, Greece, Italy, Spain), as well as to some people from Russia and the Middle East (Israel). This approach is captured in the Russian proverb, "After a storm, fair weather; after sorrow, joy."

The **accommodating style** emphasizes an indirect approach for dealing with conflict and a more emotionally restrained manner. People who use this style may be ambiguous and indirect in expressing their views, thinking that this is a way to ensure that the conflict "doesn't get out of control." This style is often preferred by American Indians, Latin Americans (Mexicans, Costa Ricans), and Asians. This style may best be expressed by the Swahili proverb, "Silence produces peace, and peace produces safety," or by the Chinese proverb, "The first to raise their voice loses the argument." In this style, silence and avoidance may be used to manage conflict. For example, the Amish would prefer to lose face or money rather than escalate a conflict, and Amish children are instructed to turn the other cheek in any conflict situation, even if it means getting beat up by the neighborhood bully.

Individuals from these groups also use **intermediaries**—friends or colleagues who act on their behalf in dealing with conflict. For example, an African American student at a U.S. university was offended by one of his classmates who disphayed contempt of the black people. The African

American student went to the international student advisor and asked him to talk to his classmate about the contempt. People who think that interpersonal conflict provides opportunities to strengthen relationships also use **mediation**, but mainly in formal settings (lawyers, real estate agents, therapists), which we will discuss later in the unit. It is often difficult for people who are taught to use the discussion or engaging style to see the value in the accommodating style or in nonviolent approaches. They see indirectness and avoidance as a sign of weakness. However, millions of people view conflict as primarily "dysfunctional, interpersonally embarrassing, distressing and as a forum for potential humiliation and loss of face." With this view of conflict, it makes much more sense to avoid direct confrontation and work toward saving face for the other person.

The **dynamic style** is an indirect style of communicating along with a more emotionally intense expressiveness. People who use this style may use strong language, stories, metaphors, and third-party intermediaries. They are comfortable with more emotionally confrontational talk and view credibility of the other person grounded in their degree of emotional expressiveness. This style may be preferred by Arabs in the Middle East.

Cautions about Stereotyping. As with any generalization, however, it must be remembered that all conflict resolution styles can be found in any one cultural group, and while cultural groups tend to prefer one style over another, we must be careful not to stereotype. Also, these cultural differences may depend on a number of factors, including (a) whether regions have been historically homogeneous and isolated from other cultures, (b) the influence of **colonization**, and (c) the immigration history of different cultural groups. For example, there is much more African influence in the Caribbean (compared to Central and Latin America), resulting in a more direct and emotionally expressive approach (engagement style) than in Mexico—where people maintain a more indirect and emotionally restrained approach (accommodation style). And there is great variety within the cultures on the African continent, accounting for tremendous variation in conflict resolution styles.

It is also important to recognize that people deal with conflict in a variety of ways for a variety of reasons. Conflict specialists William Wilmot and Joyce Hocker warned in 2010 that we should not think of preferred styles as static and set in stone. Rather, they suggest that purely individual styles really do not exist because we are each influenced by others in interaction. Therefore, our conflict management styles are not static across settings and relationships. For example, people may use a discussion style at work and accommodating style at home, or they may use an accommodating style at work and an engagement style at home. And they may use different styles with different partners. For instance, with co-workers, individuals may tend to collaborate and work through conflict issues in a more direct way; with the boss, they may tend to employ more accommodating strategies. In addition, our styles often change over the course of a conflict and over the life span. For example, individuals who tend to avoid and accommodate may learn the benefits of engaging and working through conflicts.

Gender, Ethnicity, and Conflict Styles

Our gender and ethnicity may influence how we handle conflict. Some research shows that men and women do tend to behave in stereotypical ways in some contexts: Men using a more engagement conflict style, whereas women use a more accommodating style. This may reflect the fact that in many cultures, women are socialized to focus on relationships and to be more accommodating and indirect in their interaction, while men are socialized to be more competitive. However, it may be that these gender behaviors are context-specific. Some research shows that the pattern may be reversed in heterosexual, romantic relationships—women tend to engage in more negative (competitive) conflict strategies, and men tend to avoid conflict with their romantic partners.

Ethnicity may also influence conflict style. At least one study showed that Asian and Latino Americans tended to use accommodating and third-party conflict styles more than African Americans and that Asian Americans also tended to use more accommodating conflict tactics than European Americans according to Ting-Toomey et al. in 2000.

The relationship among ethnicity, gender, and conflict management is even more complex. In their study of African American and European American women's views on workplace conflict, communication scholars Lynn Turner and Robert Shuter found in 2004 that African American women viewed workplace conflict more negatively, more passively, and with less optimism about a positive resolution than European American women.

It is important to remember that, whereas ethnicity and gender may be related to ways of dealing with conflict, it is inappropriate (and inaccurate) to assume that any one person will behave in a particular way because of his or her ethnicity or gender.

▶ Interactive and Critical Approaches to Social Conflict

Both the interpretive and critical approaches tend to emphasize the social, cultural, and historical aspects of conflict. In these perspectives, conflict is far more complex than the ways that interpersonal conflict is enacted. It is deeply rooted in cultural differences in these contexts. Further, a dialectical perspective requires a more complex consideration of types and contexts of conflict. Social conflict arises from unequal or unjust social relationships. Consider, for example, the recent uprisings of immigrant youths in Europe. In 2005, 2007, and again in 2012, rioting of young people erupted in Paris, cars were torched, and buildings burned. In the summer of 2011 and again in 2016, young people in London, England rioted with widespread looting and destruction to property. How do we understand this conflict? A social science approach may view the conflicts as stemming from cultural differences (generational, ethnic, racial, religious), and these differences certainly play a role.

For example, some experts say it's just hooliganism pure and simple: young undisciplined looters lashing out against society. And some point out the religious element, describing the conflict as rooted in Islamic discontent with the West, particularly in France, because many of the rioters come from Islamic backgrounds. And in both France and England, many of the **rioters** were ethnic and racial minorities. However, the interpretive and critical perspectives suggest that we look beyond cultural differences to economic, political, and historical contexts and underscore the point that disputes are often more complicated than they first appear. We can invoke the various dialectics to illuminate the complexity of this conflict.

UNIT ELEVEN
Intercultural Relationships and Conflicts

The rioting in both England and France started with those economically marginalized in society (i.e., the common denominator in both countries); the perpetrators come from poor neighborhoods. Sociologist Nora Fellag suggested in 2014 that the riots, more than anything, revealed "the ongoing isolation and alienation of minorities who continue to be excluded from the resources that necessarily lead to greater equality and integration into larger society [...], clustered in the suburbs of big cities with poor housing, limited job opportunities and underfunded, over-crowded and academically inferior schools, remain largely marginalized and have great difficulty achieving upward mobility."

In addition to economic marginalization, many ethnic and racial minorities feel excluded from French and English society. Unlike the United States and Canada, where there is an expression (not always realized) that anyone can become American or Canadian, immigrants in France, particularly of African heritage, can never really become French; they remain forever on the societal periphery.

Fellag argued in 2014 that the problem lies in the French constructing the North Africans always with a religious "Muslim" label, "the tendency of policy-makers and citizens to rhetorically and systematically categorize French Magrehibis [citizens from North Africa] as 'Muslims'—a title not without real consequences... Paradoxically, 'native' Algerians of Jewish backgrounds were granted full French citizenship upon Algerian independence, but not those of Islamic origin." While immigrants in the United States have generally more easily assimilated into the larger U.S. society, tensions between communities of color and police and anti-immigrant attitudes, particularly directed at Muslims, have led some to question our ability to realize a peaceful multicultural society.

For these reasons, the rioting points to deep social and cultural conflict. In England and France, officials had warned of tensions in many neighborhoods; as long as these cultural groups remain **marginalized**, alienated, and largely unemployed. These cultural conflicts are likely to continue. Some believe this kind of violence is one of the few ways that society can be **provoked** into interrogating social inequities and begin the long process of changing any society. There are no easy solutions to these conflicts. In England and France, there have been some attempts to change the economic and cultural conditions underlying the social conflict, including renovating neglected neighborhoods and trying to connect with local Muslim leaders. U.S. Federal Bureau of Investigation (FBI) agents are also engaging with community and religious leaders (imams) in U.S. Muslim neighborhoods like Dearborn, Michigan—to decrease chances of disaffected youth from becoming radicalized and to send messages of acceptance and inclusion. However, there are other forces at work. After several terrorist attacks in 2015, the French government extended emergency powers, outlawed any public demonstrations, made more than a thousand raids, detained many people, and are even surveilling many Muslims who are not terrorists. Likewise, some in the United States are calling for restricting the civil liberties of U.S. Muslims. The point here is that there is no reason to seek a single source for conflict. In a sense, then, the economic contexts, the cultural identities and belongingness, and the political and religious contexts all work together to shape these conflicts. By taking a dialectical approach to thinking about these riots, you can see how these various forces—economic, social, political, religious—may all play different roles simultaneously.

Social Movements

Some conflict may be motivated by a desire to bring about social change. In **social movements**, individuals work together to bring about social change. They often use confrontation as a strategy to highlight the injustices of the present system. So, for example, when African American students in Greensboro, North Carolina, sat down at white-only lunch counters in the 1960s, they were pointing out the injustices of segregation. Although the students were nonviolent, their actions drew a violent reaction that, for many people, legitimized the claims of injustice. The women's suffrage movement of the early 20th century is another example of a social movement, a mass effort to win women the right to vote in the United States. Many similar contemporary social movements give meaning to conflicts. These include movements against racism, sexism, and homophobia and movements in support of animal rights, the environment, free speech, and civil rights.

College campuses are likely locations for much activism, and a 2016 survey of college students found that 8.5% of all students (and 16% of black students) said there was a "very good chance" they would participate in a protest while in college. These numbers were the highest ever recorded since the survey began in 1967 and the report goes on to say that in more than 50 schools, "student protesters made demands to right what they see as historic wrongs—demands for greater faculty diversity, new courses, public apologies, administrators' **oustings**." The tactics included hunger strikes, **boycotts**, walkouts, marches, occupying administrative offices, as well as social media strategies. Much of the protests focused on racist incidents including fraternity parties where members are invited to dress up and "go back to da hood," offensive statues (and building names) on campus honoring 19th century white supremacists and pro-slavery graduates/benefactors.

Many interpersonal conflicts arise and must be understood against the backdrop of large-scale social movements designed to change contemporary society. For example, Jacqueline, from Singapore, is annoyed by U.S. Americans who comment on how well she speaks English because English is her first language even though she is ethnically Chinese. She used to say nothing in response; now sometimes she retorts, "So is yours," reflecting her struggle against the stereotype that Asians cannot speak English. In this context, the social movement against racism gives meaning to the conflict that arises for Jacqueline.

There is, of course, no comprehensive list of existing social movements. They arise and dissipate, depending on the opposition they provoke, the attention they attract, and the strategies they use. As part of social change, social movements need confrontation to highlight the perceived injustice. Confrontation, then, can be seen as an opportunity for social change. In arguing for a change, Dr. Martin Luther King, Jr. emphasized in 1984 the importance of nonviolent confrontation:

> Nonviolent resistance is not a method for cowards; it does resist.... (It) does not seek to defeat or humiliate the opponent, but to win his friendship and understanding. The nonviolent resister must often express his protest through noncooperation or boycotts, but

he realizes that these are not ends themselves; they are merely means to awaken a sense of moral shame in the opponent.

Although nonviolence is not the only form of confrontation employed by social movements, its use has a long history—from Mahatma Gandhi's struggle for India's independence from Britain, to the civil rights struggle in the United States, including Black Lives Matter, to the struggle against apartheid in South Africa. In each case, images of violent responses to nonviolent protesters tended to legitimize the social movements and delegitimize the existing social system. For example, in the resistance to **apartheid** in South Africa, when the government reacted with brutal force to strikes and boycotts, this led to condemnation and economic punishment by the international community. "Nonviolent power did not by itself bring down the curtain on white rule, but it discredited the regime's authority." More recently, some images of police in military gear confronting peaceful protestors in Ferguson, Missouri and Baton Rouge, reacting against police killings of black men, were also powerful.

Historical and Political Contexts

Most of us recall the childhood saying "Sticks and stones may break my bones, but words will never hurt me." In fact, we know that derogatory words can be a powerful source of conflict. The force that many derogatory words carry comes from their historical usage and the history of oppression to which they refer. As we noted earlier, much of our identity comes from history. It is only through understanding the past that we can understand what it means to be members of particular cultural groups. For example, understanding the history of Ireland helps give meaning to Irish American identity.

In Kyrgyzstan, a nation in Central Asia, conflicts between the Uzbeks and the Kyrgyz (two different ethnic groups) broke out in 2010. These ethnic conflicts took place in Osh, which is a part of the fertile Fergana Valley, near the Uzbekistan border. Ethnic clashes are not new to this area, but "the clashes are the worst ethnic violence to hit southern Kyrgyzstan since 1990, when several hundred people were killed. Kyrgyzstan was then part of the Soviet Union, which sent in troops to quell the unrest."

The historical context is an important part of understanding this conflict. The Fergana Valley is inhabited primarily by Uzbeks, Krygyz, and Tajiks. This fertile valley has been culturally diverse for thousands of years and has seen the influx of peoples from Europe and Asia. More recently, under the Soviet Union, the valley was divided by the establishment of three Soviet Socialist Republics: Uzbekistan, Tajikistan, and Krygyzstan, whose borders split the valley but did not follow along the lines where the ethnic groups lived. Once the Soviet Union collapsed, and the republics became independent, the ethnic composition of these new nations became more significant. Because of this history, "the valley remains an ethnic patchwork, and minority enclaves, like that of the Uzbeks in Osh, have been scenes for violence."

So the violence that broke out between the two ethnic groups in 2010 was embedded in a long history of tensions between these ethnic groups—tensions that go back hundreds of years, but which have been exacerbated by creating national borders and independent nations that put various ethnic groups together in imbalanced ways. The thousands of refugees and the many people who died in the conflict create a new history that will be difficult to easily overcome in the future. Indeed, some observers believe that there is an even larger political context that prevents a more responsible government from arising in Kyrgyzstan: "outside powers..., who covet the region's extensive natural resources of natural gas and hydro power, and the United States, with its base in Kyrgyzstan, show little interest in fostering more responsible rule."

These dynamics are at work all around the world. Historical **antagonisms** become part of cultural identities and practices that place people in positions of conflict. Whether in the Middle East, Northern Ireland, Rwanda, Uganda, Nigeria, Sri Lanka, East Timor, Kosovo, or Chechnya, these historical antagonisms lead to various forms of conflict.

When people witness conflict, they often assume that it is caused by personal issues between individuals. By reducing conflict to the level of interpersonal interaction, we lose sight of the larger social and political forces that contextualize these conflicts. People are in conflict for reasons that extend far beyond personal communication styles.

Managing Intercultural Conflict

Given all the variations in how people deal with conflict, and the historical, political elements of intercultural conflict, what are the strategies for effective conflict management/resolution? While there are no easy answers, this section provides some useful strategies for both individuals and groups. We first provide some strategies for dealing with interpersonal conflict and also outline characteristics of productive and destructive approaches to conflicts for both individuals and groups. In the final part of the unit, we describe additional strategies for dealing with difficult conflicts: Mediation and Peacebuilding.

Dealing with Interpersonal Conflict

In searching for effective strategies for dealing with interpersonal conflict, we can apply the principles of dialectics; sometimes, we may need to step back and show self-restraint. Occasionally, though, it may be more appropriate to assert ourselves and not be afraid of strong emotion. Here, we offer seven suggestions for dealing with interpersonal conflict:

(a) Stay centered and do not polarize.

(b) Maintain contact.

(c) Recognize the existence of different styles.

(d) Identify your preferred style.

(e) Be creative and expand your style repertoire.

(f) Recognize the importance of conflict context.

(g) Be willing to forgive.

Let's look at these guidelines in more detail.

Stay Centered and Do Not Polarize. It's important to move beyond traditional stereotypes and either-or thinking. Try not to view other's motives as simple and **antagonistic** and your own as complex and reasonable. Try to be open to a third alternative perspective that might bring you to a mutually acceptable solution.

The parties involved must practice self-restraint. It's okay to get angry, but it's important to move past the anger and to refrain from acting out feelings. For example, Jenni and her co-worker both practiced self-restraint and stayed centered in a recent disagreement about religion. Jenni explains:

> My friend is a devout Catholic, and I am a devout Mormon. She asked me about where we get some of our doctrine and how it relates to the Bible. We never really solved our differences, but compromised and "agreed to disagree." This was necessary to keep our friendship and respect as co-workers. I felt bad that she couldn't see the points I was coming from. I do think it turned out for the best, though, because we don't feel tension around each other.

Maintain Contact. This does not mean that the parties have to stay in the conflict situation—sometimes it's necessary to step away for a while. However, the parties should not cut off the relationship. Rather, they should attempt a dialogue rather than isolate themselves from each other or engage in fighting. Dialogue differs from conversation in that it assumes the transformative power of speaking and being understood; it involves listening and speaking, not to persuade, but to clarify—even to clarify and truly understand an opposing viewpoint. Quality dialogue is attentive, careful, and full of feeling.

Dialogue is possible only between two persons or two groups whose power relationship is more or less in balance. Dialogue offers an important opportunity to come to a richer understanding of intercultural conflicts and experiences. Our student Cameron experienced an intercultural conflict in an accounting class in which his maintaining contact paid off. He was placed in a group with three Japanese students who were all friends. He recalls:

> Right from the beginning things were quite awkward; their mathematics abilities far exceeded mine. After only two days, they had met twice without me and completed part of the assignment. I had been left out of the decision-making process.

Rather than avoiding the problem, however, he decided to invite them all over to his house to talk about the project. Everyone was able to loosen up and discuss what had gone wrong, and the conflict was handled productively: "Although I was unhappy with the way things went during the earlier parts of the project, the end result was three new acquaintances and an A in accounting."

Recognize the Existence of Different Styles. Conflict is often exacerbated because of the unwillingness of partners to recognize management style differences. The heart of the question is how to reconcile these different styles, particularly when dealing with difficult issues like interracial relations, gay and lesbian rights, abortion rights, and so on. One approach is to "maintain civility," stressing that when **contentious** issues arise, it's most productive to be polite, respectful, and maybe even avoid direct confrontation. As we've discussed earlier, this approach would be very accepted among many cultural groups. However, some Western scholars contend that this emphasis on civility actually constructs barriers to productive understanding and reinforces the very inequality and injustice it portends to address. Mayo says that civility works precisely because it maintains the distance it initially appears to bridge—and is not the way people build close relations. For example, if gay and lesbian students or other minority students complain about homophobia on campus, they may be seen being "uncivil"—making an issue of something that, in polite society, ought to be ignored. Mayo and others advocate a more direct, expressive style—suggesting that we should not be afraid of "incivility" and anger, rather it is in moments of listening to and giving space to angry voices that conflicts can be resolved and hurt feelings soothed.

An example that illustrates these different styles occurred during a Diversity, Racism, and Community meeting in Compton, Los Angeles. There were many diverse community groups in attendance and the atmosphere was tense, when a middle age white man spoke confidently and gently about all the experience he had with multicultural groups and how he did not like anger. A young black man said he thought the white man didn't know what he was talking about. The white man ignored him and finally the black man stood up and spoke vehemently about his experiences of discrimination in the local community and his disappointments at not being listened to. The white man turned his body away, repeatedly saying he was open to anyone but refusing to talk to an "angry" person.

The multiracial facilitating team pointed out the contrasting assumptions underlying the behavior of the two men: different conflict styles and perceptions. The white man thinking that one needs to be calm to debate, the black man perceiving the white's man style (civility and calmness) as communicating a hidden message: don't upset me about issues that aren't mine. The engaging style demonstrated by the black man was that one can be emotional and rational in dealing with conflict, and, in fact, one should be emotional about topics one really cares about.

This particular combination of differing but complementary styles often results in damaged relationships and frozen agendas—the rational/avoiding-emotional/ confronting "dance." Other combinations may be problematic but less overtly damaging. For example, two people with assertive emotional styles may understand each other and know how to work through the conflict. Likewise, things can work if both people avoid open conflict, particularly in long-term committed relationships. Jointly avoiding conflict does not necessarily mean that it goes away, but it may give people time to think about how to deal with the conflict and talk about it.

Identify Your Preferred Style. Although people may change their way of dealing with conflict based on the situation and the type of conflict, most tend to use the same style in most situations. For example, Tom and Judith both prefer an avoiding style. If we are pushed into conflict or feel strongly that we need to resolve a particular issue, we can speak up for ourselves or for others. However, we both prefer more indirect means of dealing with current and potential conflicts. We often choose to work things out on a more personal, indirect level.

It is also important to recognize which conflict styles "push your conflict button." Some styles are more or less compatible; it's important to know which styles are congruent with your own. If you prefer a more confronting style and you have a disagreement with someone like Tom or Judith, it may drive you crazy.

Be Creative and Expand Your Style Repertoire. If a particular way of dealing with conflict is not working, be willing to try a different style. Of course, this is easier said than done. As conflict specialists William Wilmot and Joyce Hocker explained in 2010, people often seem to get "frozen" into a conflict style. For example, some people consistently deny any problems in a relationship, whereas others consistently **escalate** small conflicts into large ones.

There are many reasons for getting stuck in a conflict management style, according to

Wilmot and Hocker. The style may have developed during a time when the person felt good about himself or herself—when the particular conflict management style worked well. Consider, for example, there is a high school athlete who develops an aggressive style on and off the playing field, a style that people seem to respect. A limited repertoire may be related to gender differences. Some women get stuck in an avoiding style, whereas some men get stuck in a confronting style. A limited repertoire also may come from cultural background—a culture that encourages confronting conflict or a culture (like Judith's and Tom's) that rewards avoiding conflict. A combination of these reasons is the likely cause of getting stuck in the use of one conflict management style. For example, even though Tom and Judith prefer an avoiding style, we have occasionally found it effective to be more assertive and direct in intercultural conflicts in which the dominant communication style was more confrontational.

In most aspects of intercultural communication, adaptability and flexibility serve us well—and conflict communication is no exception. This means that there is no so-called objective way to deal with conflict. Many times, as in other aspects of relationships, it's best simply to listen and not say anything. One strategy that mediators use is to allow one person to talk for an extended time while the other person listens.

Recognize the Importance of Conflict Context. As noted earlier in this unit, it is important to understand the larger social, economic, political, and historical contexts that give meaning to many types of conflict. Conflict arises for many reasons, and it is misleading to think that all conflict can be understood within the interpersonal context alone. For example, when one student, George, went home for a family reunion, everyone seemed to be talking about their romantic relationships, spouses, children, and so on. When George, who is gay, talked about his own partner, George's uncle asked why gay people had to flaunt their lifestyle. George reacted angrily. The conflict was not simply between George and his uncle; it rests in the social context that accepts straight people talking frequently and openly about their relationships but that does not validate the same discussion of romantic relationships from gay people. The same talk is interpreted differently because of the social context.

People often act in ways that cause conflict. However, it is important to let the context explain the behavior as much as possible. Otherwise, the behavior may not make sense. Once you understand the contexts that frame the conflict, whether cultural, social, historical, or political, you will be in a better position to understand and conceive of the possibilities for resolution. For example, Savina, who is white, was shopping with her friend Lashieki. The employee at the cash register referred to someone as "that black girl," and Lashieki, who is African American, demanded, "Why did they have to refer to her as that black girl?" Lashieki's response can only be understood by knowing something about the context of majority-minority relations in the United States. That is, whites are rarely referred to by color, whereas people of color are often defined solely on the basis of race.

Be Willing to Forgive. A final suggestion for facilitating conflict is to consider forgiveness. This means letting go of—not forgetting—feelings of revenge. Teaching forgiveness between estranged individuals is as old as recorded history; it is present in every culture and is part of the human condition. In fact, recent research suggests that both revenge and forgiveness are instinctual and universal among humans and both have developed as adaptive mechanisms in human evolution.

At the same time, forgiveness is also a basic human instinct that has also served humans well. And it is not always bad to retaliate when someone has done us a great wrong... but not helpful to hold a grudge forever. At a very fundamental level, forgiveness ensures that we get along with both family and close friends and helps establish and maintain cooperative relationships with nonrelatives, and, overall, forgiveness is the best strategy for human beings in the long term—it can deliver freedom from fear and freedom to resume normal, peaceful relations. In fact, it is in our self-interest to forgive. Psychologists point out that blaming others and feeling resentment lead to a victim mentality and may actually lead to stress, burnout, and physical problems. Forgiveness, on the other hand, can lead to improved physical health.

As cooperation on a group level evolve, revenge and forgiveness are not on opposite sides, they are on the same team. You can't be easy-going all the time, you can't be vengeful and spiteful all of the time.... "In social **dilemmas** that pit the short-term gains of selfishness against the long-term gains of cooperation, evolution favors the organism that can be vengeful when necessary, that can forgive when necessary, and that has the wisdom to know the difference."

There are several models of forgiveness—most include an acknowledgement of feelings of hurt and anger and a need for healing. Communication scholars Vince Waldron and Doug Kelley proposed in 2008 a dialectical approach to forgiveness, particularly applicable because forgiveness is a complex process, often with many contradictions. They identify four dialectical tensions: remembering versus forgetting (it may be good to forget the transgression while, at the same time in some relationships, it may be productive to remember so as not to get involved in repeat of conflict); heart versus mind (tension between strong emotional response to conflict and sometimes needing to engage a more intellectual, cognitive approach to forgiveness); trust versus risk (forgiveness is sometimes a process of rebuilding trust and reducing future relational risk; and mercy versus justice (perhaps the most fundamental dialectic; trying to let go of hostile feelings, extending mercy to the transgressor and, at the same time, a letting go of a desire for revenge and **retribution**).

In a dialectical forgiveness **loop**, forgiveness is seen as socially constructed and based in communication. If someone is in a stressed relationship, he or she can create actions and behaviors that make forgiveness seem real, balancing these dialectical tensions; then he or she can communicate this to the other person, enabling the relationship to move forward. It is easier to forgive when one can see the offender as someone who is careworthy, valuable and safe and when the vengeful impulse has been satisfied to some degree, perhaps knowing that an offender has been punished. So an important part of apologizing and asking for forgiveness may be making **compensation**, ensuring some measure of restorative justice.

The importance of compensation in preventing violent revenge and encouraging forgiveness can't be overstated. Cross-cultural studies of pre-modern cultures found that many had developed compensation strategies and forgiveness rituals for quelling revenge, which often included accepting "blood money" as an alternative to killing a murderer or one of his or her relatives, as well as compensations and gift exchanges. Restorative justice conferences as part of the forgiveness process can play an important role in the criminal justice system. They are extremely effective at reducing the desire for revenge and fostering forgiveness and "give people the chance to process the traumatic experience and talk to their offenders in a safe nonthreatening way." "The **restorative** justice movement is another great example of an institution that brings out people's best selves in the aftermath of conflict and violence... It works because it enables people to use their evolved moral intuitions to address the pain of crime in the mega-societies in which most of us live..."

Civil wars that end in forgiveness and reconciliation have four processes: redefine affected people's identities, implement countless small actions, process of public "truth," justice short of revenge (legal consequences, amnesty, reparations). An example of forgiveness on a national level involves the National Sorry Day and the Journey of Healing, which serve to acknowledge and apologize for the wretched treatment of Aboriginals by non-Aboriginal Australians. Another example is the Truth and **Reconciliation** Commission in South Africa, formed to investigate and facilitate the healing of racial wounds as a result of apartheid. The committee hears stories of the atrocities that were committed, but the ultimate goal is forgiveness, not revenge. So how do we escape the historical, political, and social forces that entrap us in conflict and work toward a more peaceful society and world? Earlier in the unit, we outlined some strategies for dealing with interpersonal conflict. Let's now turn our attention to several other responses to conflict situations.

Mediation

Sometimes two individuals or groups cannot work through conflict on their own. They may request an intermediary, or one may be assigned to intervene. In some societies, these third parties may be rather informal. In Western societies, though, they tend to be built into the legal and judicial system. For example, lawyers or counselors may act as mediators to settle community or family disputes.

Contemporary Western mediation models often ignore cultural variations in conflict processes. Fortunately, more scholars and mediators are looking at other cultural models that may work better in intercultural conflicts. Augsburger suggested in 1992 that the culturally sensitive mediator engages in conflict transformation (not conflict resolution or conflict management). The conflict transformer assists disputants to think in new ways about the conflict—for example, to transform attitudes by redirecting negative perceptions. This requires a commitment by both parties to treat each other with goodwill and mutual respect. Of course, this is often much easier said than done. Behavior can be transformed by limiting all action to collaborative behavior; this can break the negative cycle but requires a commitment to seek a **non-coercive** process of negotiation even when there has been intense provocation. For example, in the recent Northern Ireland agreement, mediation resulted in commitment by most people to change the vision of Northern Ireland, in spite of horrendous provocation on the part of some extremists.

Traditional societies often use mediation models based on non-direct means. The models vary but share many characteristics. Although North American mediation tends to be more formal and structured, involving direct confrontation and communication, most traditional cultural models are more communally based, with involvement by trusted leaders. Indirect communication is preferred in order to permit individuals to save face. In addition, the process is more dynamic, directed toward resolving tension in the community—the responsibility of the disputants to their larger community is central.

Augsburger provides the example of mediation in the Gitksan Nation, in northwest British Columbia, where mediation of disputes begins with placement of the problem "in the middle of the table." Everyone involved—including those in authority and the witnesses—must make suggestions in a peaceful manner until they come to a decision all can live with. Even conflicts ending in murder are resolved in this consensus-oriented fashion. For instance, "land would be transferred as compensation to help deal with the pain of the loss. The murderer might be required to give up his or her name and go nameless for a period to show respect for the life taken." Eventually, however, the land or anything else that was given up would be returned, "when the pain has passed and time has taken care of the grief." Augsburger points out that this traditional communal approach to mediation is based on collectivistic beliefs that make individualistic solutions to conflicts unacceptable.

Contemporary mediators have learned some lessons from the traditional non-Western models, and mediation is used increasingly in the United States and other countries to resolve conflicts. Mediation is advantageous because it relies on the disputing parties' active involvement in and commitment to the resolution. Also, it represents the work of all involved, so it's likely to be more creative and **integrative**. Finally, mediation is often cheaper than adversarial legal resolution.

Peacebuilding

Some of the conflicts described in this unit involve longstanding and violent intergroup conflicts that have lasted for decades, often between ethnic or religious groups within the same geographic area (e.g., Palestinians and Israelis, Sunni and Shia Muslims in Iraq and other countries, Hindus and Muslims in India, Serbs and Croats in former Yugoslavia, Greeks and Turks in Cyprus). These conflicts, where neighbors or sometimes members of the same family are on different sides of the conflict, are particularly horrific and have devastating psychological effects—often enduring for generations.

Experts stress that these types of longstanding "intractable" conflicts require special communication processes and a reframing of the problem and the enemy. For example, communication scholar Don Ellis suggested in 2015 that, in "fierce **entanglements**" the other side should not be considered as an enemy that needs to be destroyed, but as an adversary that needs to be engaged. In addition, both sides need to reframe the problems such that solutions require interdependence and engagement in "reasonable and skilled disagreement." Thus, communication is essential and needs to take place at all levels, from informal intercultural community dialogue groups to high-level government negotiation and diplomacy.

After years of working with these types of conflicts, communication scholar Benjamin Broome has developed a particularly effective approach for improving these difficult situations—

facilitated intergroup dialogue. As we described earlier, dialogue differs from conversation, in that it focuses on the *power* of speaking and being understood; it involves listening and speaking, not to persuade, but to clarify—with a goal of truly understanding an opposing viewpoint.

Intergroup dialogue is one of several strategies of **peacebuilding,** (working toward equilibrium and stability in a society so that new disputes do not escalate into violence and war). The idea behind the facilitated intergroup dialogue, and peacebuilding, is that government leaders alone cannot negotiate a true peace in these types of conflict. Rather, the general population and civic leaders must also be involved. Dr. Broome has conducted countless dialogue workshops and programs in the United States and all over the world—particularly on the small island of Cyprus where Cypriot Turks and Greeks have been in (often violent) conflict for years.

The facilitated intergroup dialogue process usually begins with bringing together members from the two sides—persons, often community leaders, who are interested in working toward peace. Sometimes presentations are made by each party describing their view of the conflict. Then a three-phase systematic dialogue, an exchange of ideas and perceptions, is conducted— facilitated by an impartial third party expert, like Ben Broome. The first step involves analyzing the current situation that affects peacebuilding efforts, the second is building a collective vision for the future, and finally developing a specific action plan to achieve peaceful collaboration. Each phase is carefully facilitated with the goal that each side really listens to and tries to understand the opposing side's views. As you can image achieving a vision and plan that everyone agrees to in situations where both sides feel tremendously hurt and victimized by the other is not easy!

In spite of these challenges, Broome and others who use this peacebuilding approach have seen success in reducing intergroup conflict and note that it's very important for facilitators to acknowledge the power relations and relative privilege or lack thereof of each group and also the role of strong emotion in conflict situations.

Text B Understanding Intercultural Conflict Competence: Multiple Theoretical Insights

After Stella Ting-Toomey

Introduction

Intercultural conflict frustrations often arise because of our lack of necessary and sufficient knowledge to deal with culture-based conflict communication issues competently. Our cultural ignorance or ineptness oftentimes clutters our ability to communicate appropriately, effectively, and adaptively across cultural lines. As the global economy becomes an everyday reality in most societies, individuals will inevitably encounter people who are culturally different in diverse workplaces and relationship-building situations. Learning to manage such differences mindfully, especially in intercultural conflicts, can bring about multiple perspectives and expanded visions in the conflict encountering process.

This text is developed in six sections. The first section provides an overview of the contents of the different sections. The second section summarizes three theoretical approaches that hold potential promises to explaining and organizing the complex layers of intercultural conflict issues. The three conceptual approaches which are reviewed are: social ecological theory, integrated threat theory, and face negotiation theory. The third section discusses critical issues related to the criteria and components of intercultural conflict competence. The fourth section addresses the critical role of mindfulness and offers a set of reflective questions in prompting a mindful transformation process in shifting our **ingrained**, culture-based conflict assumptions to alternatives insights and viewpoints. The fifth section recommends some specific identity threat management and facework management strategies in promoting intercultural conflict competence. The sixth section proffers directions for future theorizing and researching on the motif of intercultural conflict competence.

Intercultural conflict is defined in this chapter as the perceived or actual incompatibility of cultural values, situational norms, goals, face orientations, scarce resources, styles/processes, and/or outcomes in a face-to-face (or mediated) context. Both the appropriateness and effectiveness features, together with the interaction adaptability feature, are part of the intercultural conflict competence criteria. If inappropriate or ineffective conflict behaviors continue, the miscommunication can very easily spiral into a complex, **polarized** intercultural conflict situation.

More specifically, intercultural conflict competence refers to the mindful management of emotional frustrations and conflict interaction struggles due primarily to cultural or ethnic group membership differences. The larger the cultural distance, the more likely the escalatory conflict spirals will spin into **entangled**, chaotic mode of biased attributions and defensive emotional reactions. The outcome goal of competent conflict practice is to transform ingrained culture-based conflict knowledge, habits, and skills from an ethnocentric viewpoint to an ethno-relative perspective. Culture, from this backdrop context, is defined as a learned system of traditions, symbolic patterns, and accumulative meanings that fosters a particular sense of shared identity-hood, community-hood, and interaction rituals among the aggregate of its group members. Both cultural and individual conditioning factors in conjunction with multilayered situational factors shape intercultural conflict competence antecedent factors, process, and outcome.

▶ Two Intercultural Conflict-Related Theories

After half of a decade of researching and theorizing about intercultural conflict, many scholars have developed well-designed and well-tested theories to explain intergroup attitudes and general communication and particular conflict styles across cultures, as Gudykunst noted in 2005. For the purpose of this particular chapter and because of space limitations, I have selected three theories that hold theoretical and research promises in explaining intercultural conflict and intercultural conflict competence for the next generation.

The four criteria for my selection of particular theories include: (a) the theory has strong explanatory or framing potentials in deepening our understanding of a complex, intercultural conflict case on multiple levels of analysis; (b) the theory covers some intriguing angle on intercultural/intergroup conflict encounter and can be connected in a meaningful direction with the intercultural conflict competence theme; (c) the theory has been systematically researched in a variety of cross-cultural or intercultural-intergroup conflict settings and displayed a reasonable sense of cross-cultural validity; (d) the theory has heuristic function for bridging intercultural conflict theorizing process with conflict competence practice issues. I have selected the following three theories for a synoptic review and discussion in this section: social ecological theory, integrated threat theory, and conflict face-negotiation theory.

The Social Ecological Theory

Intercultural conflict is a multilevel and multi-contextual phenomenon. While past intercultural studies tend to use either a macro-level lens or a micro-level view to analyze intercultural conflict, the social ecological perspective pays particular attention to multiple levels of analysis of a complex intercultural conflict case. A multilevel, contextual perspective in analyzing an intercultural conflict case provides the opportunity to understand (and possibly challenge) what are the deeply-held assumptions of a particular cultural conflict worldview or practice. A multilevel theorizing process may illustrate that a particular intercultural conflict case contains both consistencies and inconsistencies at multiple levels of analysis. Additionally, a multilevel perspective helps to illustrate the multitude of factors that shape cultural worldview level, institutional-level, immediate community level, and individual-level concerning conflict decoding process within and across distinct levels.

More specifically, in utilizing a social ecological multilevel theoretical framework, there are four levels of research analytical units: macro-level analysis, exo-level analysis, meso-level analysis, and micro-level analysis. In 1979 Brofenbenner viewed these four social ecological contexts as nested Russian dolls with reciprocal causal effects influencing each sphere. The macro-level analysis refers to the larger sociocultural contexts, histories, worldviews, beliefs, values, and ideologies that shape the individual outlooks and the various embedded systems under this broad umbrella. The term exo-level (external environment emphasis) analysis refers to the larger, formal institutions (e.g., government agency system, courtroom system, health care system, or school system) which hold power resources and established personnel to enforce or modify policies, standards, and existing procedures. These exo-contexts often have filtered (as versus direct) influence on the individual conflict behaviors and reactions. On the other hand, the meso-level analysis refers to the broad-based non-immediate units (e.g., media influence) to the immediate units' influence such as local church group, extended family unit, workplace setting, third-party witnesses that have a direct impact on the individual's conflict attitudes and behaviors and the recurring conflict interactions. Finally, the micro-level analysis refers to both intrapersonal-level (i.e., personal and social identity-based issues, attributions, and conflict emotions) and interpersonal-level features (e.g., the ongoing team conflicts, or the actual discourse and non-verbal face-to-face conflict encounters) plus the actual settings in which the individuals live out their daily lives. It also emphasizes the importance of how individuals act as active agents to construct meanings and interpretations of a given conflict communication event. In addition to the macro-system, exo-system, meso-system, and micro-system of analysis, Brofenbenner also later added a fifth context, the chronosystem-level of analysis. This level refers to the evolution phases, transitions, patterns, and consequences of developmental conflict changes over time.

The social ecological framework is an interdisciplinary approach that gained momentum in the mid 1960s and early 1970s to better address the influences of cultural and social contexts on human behavior and development. In recent years, in family communication, Ihinger-Tallman and Cooney used the social ecological framework in 2005 to discuss the family system both as an institution and as a small group and to describe how the study of family should be understood within the nested historical, social class, and racial contexts. In the health care communication setting, for example, violent behaviors within intimate partner relationships in Native American communities were analyzed via macro, meso, and micro connective factors.

Core Principles and Analytical Concepts. On a broad level, Stokols explained in 1996 that the social ecological perspective consists of five core principles. First, communication outcomes are influenced by the cumulative effects of multiple physical, cultural, social, and temporal factors. Second, communication outcomes are also affected by individual attributes and specific situations. Third, social ecology incorporates concepts from systems theory, such as interdependence and homeostasis, to further understand the relationship between individuals and their broader contexts. Fourth, social ecology recognizes not only the interconnections among multiple settings, but also the interdependence of conditions within particular settings. Fifth, the social ecological perspective is interdisciplinary, involves multilevel domain analysis, and incorporates diverse methodologies. The key analytical concepts under the social ecological perspective are parallels and discontinuities, and cross-level effects.

Parallels and Discontinuities. In examining the **reciprocal** causation between the individual and the environment (e.g., intergroup conflict in a community setting), two specific types of relationships between and among levels of analysis can be probed: (a) parallels and discontinuities, and (b) cross-level effects. On the parallels and discontinuities relationship type, parallel models (also known as isomorphic models) posit that the relationship between and among variables (e.g., concepts such as apology and forgiveness) at one level (e.g., interpersonal reaction level) will be the same or similar at another level (e.g., the larger institutional/governmental reaction level) in terms of magnitude and direction. In contrast, when different types of relationships or reactions are found among concepts at different (or in opposite direction) levels, these are described as discontinuities.

Cross-Level Effects. On the "cross-level" relationship type, studying intercultural conflict at any single level underestimates the fact that individuals, organizations, communities, and cultures are interconnected. Multilevel theorizing is influenced by the principles of interdependence and hierarchy from general systems theory. General systems theory emphasizes that different analytical levels are nested structures organized hierarchically. Given this assumption, three types of cross-level effects should be considered: (a) top-down effects, (b) bottom-up effects, and (c) interactive effects.

"Top-down effects" refer to how the larger cultural/institutional forces shape the intercultural conflict stance or practice—from the macro-level, the exo-level, the meso-level, to the micro-level. From this top-down effect viewpoint, individual conflict ideologies and practices are shaped by the various layered structures in which people are nested hierarchically (e.g., does the larger cultural worldview or institutional level emphasize the communication phenomenon of apology or forgiveness and does the effect spill downward to the lower levels?). Bottom-up effects focus on how lower levels (e.g., individuals and interpersonal relationships) affect higher levels (e.g., workplace/media, institutional policies, and then cultural change). These types of effects are not as prevalent in the literature as are top-down, but they are no less important. Interactive effects involve simultaneous and mutual effects at more than one level. In some cases, the effects of one level (e.g., culture) moderate the outcomes at another level (e.g., family policies). Top-down or bottom-up effects differ from interactive effects in that the former assumes some sort of cumulative effect passing down (or up) from one level to the next in a systematic fashion, and that interactive effects assume simultaneous process impacts at multiple contextual levels.

In any intercultural conflict situations, group membership identity threats and communicative face threats can occur at multiple levels of conflict struggles.

The Integrated Threat Theory

Throughout the years, Stephan and Gudykunst have collaborated closely together and influenced each others' ideas in their respective development of the integrated threat theory and the anxiety/uncertainty management theory. Integrated threat theory fuses various affective theories in the social identity and intergroup prejudice literature and emphasizes one key causal factor on prejudice and intergroup conflict—namely, feelings of fear or threat. Feelings of fear or identity threat prompt intergroup animosities and conflicts. Feelings of fear or threat are closely aligned with Gudykunst's notions in 2005 on anxiety management issues and ineffective communication concepts.

The integrated threat theory can serve as a combined macro-level and ex-level conflict theory that explains intergroup or intercultural antagonism. Macro-level and exo-level theory factors refer to the "big picture" historical, socioeconomic, and institutional factors that frame intergroup relations in a society. According to the integrated threat theory, four antecedent conditions prime the various perceived threat types. Four antecedent conditions are prior conflict history, ignorance or knowledge gap, contact, and status. According to Stephan in 1999, intergroup conflict history is "the single most important seedbed of prejudice." More important, past intergroup conflict history serves as a backdrop to current intergroup contact relations. The more damaging and protracted the past conflict, the more perceived threats and prejudiced attitudes exist in the intergroup relations.

Second, intergroup knowledge gap or ignorance of the out-group refers to the fact that when intergroup members know very little of each other or think they know too much (i.e., based on their over-generalized, stereotypic lens), they are likely to perceive the other group as threatening in the context of intergroup hostility situation. One of the important knowledge gaps under this antecedent condition is the language fluency gap and, in particular, the socio-pragmatic language usage knowledge gap in context. By socio-pragmatic language knowledge gap, the concept refers to the importance of fusing language fluency (e.g., conveying respect versus disrespect linguistic codes in an appropriate tone of voice), situational knowledge fluency (e.g., when and to whom and in what situational context and with what timing the disrespect or identity threat codes should be directed or restrained), and cultural fluency (e.g., a deep mastery of cultural dimensions such as individualism-collectivism values, or small-large power distance values) in communicating with the unfamiliar others during the antagonistic conflict situation. By not having the socio-pragmatic fluency of appropriate and effective discourse usage in a polarized conflict context, even minor intergroup irritations can escalate into major conflict misunderstandings and explosions.

Third, the type (positive vs. negative) and frequency of intergroup contact also shape feelings of security or insecurity, familiarity or unfamiliarity, and trust or mistrust between members of different identity groups. The more positive and personalized the contact, the more likely members of both groups can see the "human face" beyond the broad-based identity group categories. The more negative and surface level the contact, the greater the perceived negative stereotypes and prejudice justifications. Fourth, societal/group membership power status refers to both institutional power dominance/resistance issues and individual power perception issues. On the institutional power level, dominant group members in a society can be perceived as controlling the key political, economic, and media functioning of a society. On the individual power level, it can refer to how high-status group members view low-status group members in a society or in a particular institutional setting (and, vice versa). Oftentimes, "high-status" or dominant group members may want to reinforce their own power positions and not want to give up their power resources. They might also worry about hostility or competition from the "low-status" (i.e., in the packing order of the societal or institutional power scheme) minority group members in snatching away their precious resources in the community.

Minority group members might, indeed, resent the power resources or positions amassed by the dominant group members. They might already experience the historical legacy of inequality, injustice, prejudice, and unfair treatment weighted on them. Thus, for some minority group members, they are often emotionally frustrated because of the uneven playing field. The wider the cultural relation schism and the wider the perceived power schism, the more anxiety or fear is being generated in the escalatory conflict cycles. These antecedent conditions can either escalate or de-escalate the perceived threat level in intergroup conflict.

Identity Threat Types. The four basic identity threat types that lead to escalatory prejudice and conflict cycles are intergroup anxiety, negative or rigid stereotypes, tangible/realistic threats, and perceived value/symbolic threats. The theory also emphasizes subjectively perceived threats posed by the other "enemy" group. The first type of threat, intergroup anxiety/anticipated consequences, often arises in unfamiliar intergroup encounter processes. In intergroup encounters, people can be especially anxious about anticipated negative consequences such as negative psychological consequences (e.g., confusion, frustration, feeling incompetent), negative behavioral consequences (e.g., being exploited, harmed), and negative evaluations by out-group members (e.g., rejection or being identified with marginalized out-group members). Individuals have anticipated intergroup anxiety because they are concerned about potential face threats or their identities being stigmatized, embarrassed, rejected, or even excluded in intergroup contact situations. Emotional fear or anxiety is usually heightened and intensified when there exist intergroup historical **grievances**, low or little prior intergroup contact, or contact that is consistently antagonistic or reinforcing existing negative stereotypes.

The second type of threats, rigid stereotypes or negative stereotypes, poses as threats to the in-group (especially the dominant in-group) because in-group members typically learn negative images and traits of out-groups through the mass media and secondhand sources. These negative images can generate negative self-fulfilling prophecies and expectations and thus arouse negative intergroup encountering processes and outcomes. Rigid positive stereotypes can also be considered as a potential intergroup threat because of the fear that this particular group is taking over the educational system, the technological field, or the medical health care profession. Overly positive and negative stereotypes can activate both dominant-minority and minority-minority intergroup conflicts in a multicultural society. This rigid or inflexible stereotypic mentality leads to a third type of identity threat.

The third type of threats, tangible/realistic threats, refers to perceived content threats from the out-groups such as the battle for territory, wealth, scarce resources, and natural resources and also the perceived threats and competitions of economics, housing, education placements, and/or political clouts. The fourth type of threats, perceived values/symbolic threats, is founded in cultural/ethnic membership differences in morals, beliefs, values, norms, standards, and attitudes. These are threats to the "standard way of living" and the "standard way of behaving" of the dominant in-group. Out-groups who hold worldviews and values that are different from the in-group threaten the core value systems of the in-group, which may then lead to **fossilify** in-group ethnocentrism and out-group avoidance or rejection. Values or symbolic threats can be experienced by minorities, disadvantaged groups, and subordinate groups, as well as by majority groups. Research studies testing the four threat types demonstrated that three (i.e., intergroup anxiety, tangible threats, and values/symbolic threats) of the four threat types consistently predicted prejudice and attitudinal animosity from mainstream, dominant group (e.g., European Americans) toward minority groups (e.g., African American, Asian American, and Mexican American groups) and also immigrant groups (e.g., Cuban American immigrants) in a multicultural society.

In sum, intergroup anxiety and fear can color our biased expectations and intensify our perceived identity threat levels in dealing with culturally dissimilar strangers or what we consider as our "enemies." On the macro-level of analysis, if the backdrop of the intergroup relations evokes continuous, **acrimonious** hostilities, it is difficult for identity group members to come together with a clean slate. With historically tainted glasses and competition for scarce resources, members from dominant and minority groups might view each other with certain mistrust, suspicions, disrespect, and face annihilation outlook (e.g., vicious verbal attacks and name-calling cycles).

▶ Intercultural Conflict Competence: Critical Issues

Drawing from Spitzberg and Cupach's original conceptualization of interpersonal communication competence and also research in the broader intercultural communication competence domain,

Wiseman conceptualized in 2003 general intercultural communication competence as involving the "knowledge, motivation, and skills to interact effectively and appropriately with members of different cultures." Deardorff in interviewing 23 scholars and trainers in the intercultural communication field, identified in 2006 the most preferred definition of intercultural competence as "the ability to communicate effectively and appropriately in intercultural situations based on one's intercultural knowledge, skills and attitudes."

Canary and Lakey argued in 2006 for the importance of the twin criteria of "appropriateness" and "effectiveness" in assessing conflict competence. They comment that communication can be judged as competent "only within the context of a relationship or situation because the context determines the standards of appropriateness that must be met" and that "communication can be appropriate without being effective and effective without being appropriate." Thus, conflict facework competence can best be understood as a contextual package that includes the development of a deep knowledge structure of the cultural-framed social setting, the key conflict parties' socio-cultural and personal identities, conflict speech event, and the activation of culturally appropriate and effective facework negotiation skills in respect to all the situational and multi-layered features.

Conflict Competence Criteria

The criteria of perceived interactional appropriateness, effectiveness, and adaptability can serve as the evaluative yardsticks of whether an intercultural communicator has been perceived as behaving competently or incompetently in a conflict situation. Appropriateness refers to the degree to which the exchanged behaviors are regarded as proper and match the expectations generated by the insiders of the culture. To behave appropriately in any given cultural situation, competent communicators need to have the relevant value knowledge patterns of the larger culture that frame the particular conflict situation. They also need to apply the specific situational knowledge schema of what constitutes proper or improper, and respectful or disrespectful communication patterns that promote optimal constructive outcome. Thus, the criterion of "appropriateness" is conceptualized as a culture-sensitive application process in which individuals have mastered the deep knowledge structures and the situated language codes of the culture-based values and behaviors.

The criterion of effectiveness refers to the degree to which communicators achieve mutually shared meaning and integrative goal-related outcomes through skillful interactional strategies in the various intercultural negotiation phases. To be perceived as effective intercultural communicators, individuals need to have a wide range of verbal and non-verbal repertoires to make mindful choices and cultivate creative options. Interactional effectiveness has been achieved when multiple meanings are attended to with accuracy and in an unbiased manner, and mutually desired interaction goals have been conjointly worked out in a strategic and inclusive manner.

More important, appropriateness and effectiveness criteria are positively interdependent. When one manages a problematic situation appropriately, the "good faith" proper and respectful behaviors can induce interaction effectiveness. Likewise, when one promotes integrative-inclined mutual-goal outcome, the integrative posture can maximize the perceived effectiveness criterion and further induce cooperative interaction responses from the other cultural party.

In addition, Ting-Toomey argued in 2005 that the criterion of perceived communication adaptability should be included as a third yardstick in assessing intercultural conflict competence. To behave both appropriately and effectively in managing a diverse range of intercultural conflict situations, one needs to be mentally and behaviorally flexible and adaptive. Communication adaptability refers to our ability to change our interaction behaviors and goals to meet the specific needs of the situation. It implies cognitive, affective, and behavioral flexibility in dealing with the intercultural conflict situation. It signals our attunement of the other conflict party's perspectives, interests, goals, and conflict communication approach, plus our willingness to modify our own behaviors and goals to adapt to the emergent conflict situation. Communication adaptability connotes dynamic code-switching ability in an intercultural conflict interaction scene. Dynamic cross-cultural code switching refers to the intentional learning and moving between culturally ingrained systems of behavior.

Conflict Competence Components

Individuals from contrasting cultural communities often bring with them different value patterns, verbal and non-verbal habits, and conflict interaction scripts that influence the punctuation points of competent versus incompetent conflict behaviors. Sharpening the knowledge, mindfulness, and conflict communication skills of the intercultural negotiators can enhance their pragmatic competencies. According to the conflict face-negotiation theory, culture-sensitive knowledge, mindfulness, and constructive communication skills constitute the key features of the intercultural conflict competence components.

Of all the components, knowledge is recognized as the most important component that underscores the other components of competence. With "culture-sensitive knowledge," communicators can learn to uncover the implicit "ethnocentric lenses" they use to evaluate the "bizarre" behaviors in an intercultural conflict scene. With culturally-grounded knowledge, individuals can develop an accurate culture-sensitive perspective and learn to reframe their interpretation of a conflict situation from the other's cultural frame of reference.

Mindfulness, from the IC conflict competence component framework, means the willingness to attend to one's internal cultural and personal communication assumptions, cognitions, and emotions and, at the same time, becoming exquisitely attuned to the other's communication assumptions, cognitions, and emotions. Mindful fluency requires us to tune into our own cultural and personal habitual assumptions in scanning a problematic interaction scene. It also refers to the willingness to learn from the unfamiliar other. To be mindful of intercultural differences, individuals have to learn to see the unfamiliar behavior from multiple cultural angles. The discussion of the particular characteristics of mindfulness and mindful transformation process will be presented in the next section.

Constructive communication skills refer to our operational abilities to manage a conflict situation appropriately and effectively via skillful language, verbal, and non-verbal behaviors. Many communication skills are useful in enhancing intercultural mediation competencies. Of the many possible operational competence skills, for example, skills such as deep listening, mindful reframing, de-centering, face-sensitive respectful dialogue skills, and collaborative conflict negotiation skills are competent communication practices. In hooking the knowledge component with the conflict skills' component, the theme of mindfulness plays a critical role in moving an intercultural conflict negotiator to enhance ethno-relative consciousness.

The Role of Mindfulness in Developing Conflict Competence

Mindfulness: Eastern and Western Orientations

According to Langer's concepts of mindfulness in 1989 and 1997, mindfulness can include the following characteristics: (a) learning to see behavior or information presented in the conflict situation as novel or fresh, (b) learning to view a conflict situation from several **vantage** points or perspectives, (c) learning to attend to the conflict context and the person in whom we are perceiving the behavior, and (d) learning to create new categories through which conflict behavior may be understood. Applying this Western mindfulness orientation to intercultural conflict, the perspective suggests a readiness to shift one's frame of reference from an ethnocentric lens to an ethno-relative lens, and the possibility to understand a conflict episode from the other person's cultural frame of reference.

On the other side of the spectrum, mindfulness, from an Eastern Buddhist orientation, means empting our mindset and learning to listen deeply without **preconceived** notions, judgments, and assumptions. Through an Eastern philosophical lens, mindfulness means learning to observe an unfolding conflict episode with one-pointed wakefulness and watchfulness. It means being fully present—attending fully to our own arising emotions and the cultural disputants' conflict assumptions, worldviews, positions, interests, and arising emotions. It also means listening deeply with all our senses open and all our perceptual filters unclogged.

Mindful Transformation Questions

We can also use some critical reflective questions to guide our conflict transformative "U" learning process. For example, if a disputant in an intercultural mediation session was constantly using silence or indirect response to every question a mediator asked during the conflict storytelling phase, the mindful transformative questions that the mediator can process within herself or himself are:

First, what are my cultural and personal assessments about the use of silence in this particular mediation scene (a content reflection question)? Second, why do I form such assessments and what are the sources of my assessments (a process critical reflection question)? Third, what are the underlying assumptions or values that drive my evaluative assessments (a premise-value question)? Fourth, how do I know that they are relevant or valid in this conflict context (a premise-self-challenge question)? Fifth, what reasons might I have for maintaining or changing my underlying conflict premises (an identity transformation question)? Sixth, how should I shift my cultural or personal premises into the direction that promotes deeper intercultural understanding (a mindset transformation question)? Seventh, how should I flex adaptively on both verbal and non-verbal conflict style levels in order to display facework sensitive behaviors and to facilitate a productive common-interest outcome (a behavioral transformation question)? The first three questions are based on Fisher-Yoshida's work in 2005 concerning the importance of engaging in deeper double-loop thinking in analyzing the role of self-in-conflict context. The last four questions are an extension of Ting-Toomey's mindful identity transformation work in 2005.

We engage in an ethnocentric viewpoint when we view our own cultural way of communicating as the most proper way of communicating, and we view the unfamiliar conflict communication practices of other cultural groups as improper and incorrect. Ethnorelativism, on the other hand, means the capacity to view conflict communication behaviors from the other person's cultural premise and understand why people behave the way they behave from their cultural value orientations' perspective (Bennett & Bennett, 2004). These seven questions can also be applied to our own intentional **transformational** process in dealing with diverse individuals in the intercultural mediation session.

Recommendations for Competent Conflict Practice

Managing Identity Threats

The focal ideas on intergroup conflict competence focus on the reduction of emotional or identity threat and promoting accurate knowledge between the two polarized identity groups. Stephan recommended in 2003 some possible remedies to lighten the perceived emotional anxiety and intergroup threat loads: (a) gaining accurate knowledge of major cultural value difference dimensions to enhance mutual understanding and decrease ignorance, (b) promoting information about overriding human values (such as family security, respect, and compassion) common to all cultures in order to decrease prejudice about outgroup members, (c) pursuing accurate data concerning the exaggerated nature of people's beliefs concerning the scarcity of resources in a conflict situation, (d) creating or developing superordinate identities so that both cultural groups can realize the connected humanistic souls that exist between them; and (e) reminding people of the multiple social categories or overlapping circles to which they belong.

Additionally, setting up opportunities for two or more identity groups to engage in cooperative learning techniques (e.g., team-building activities and working on positive interdependent tasks) would help both groups to see the "human face" beyond the broad based stereotypic group membership labels. Cooperative learning techniques include face-to-face active communication engagements between dominant group and minority groups in solving an interdependent problem and that the outcome holds positive reward incentive. More importantly, both groups should be able to experience some concrete interdependent contributions to the problem-solving task. Cooperative learning techniques also have built-in semi-structured time to promote friendships and a mutual personalized sharing process. Thus, the contact condition should allow individuals to get to know each other on a personalized, culture-sensitive sharing level as versus superficial, stereotypic level. Lastly, the intergroup contact process should be strongly supported by key authority figures or change agents in the organization or the community and, hopefully, with adequate resource funding. In these cooperative settings, the positive goal interdependence between cultural/ethnic groups has been identified as the key causal factor in accomplishing positive interpersonal relationship and achievement outcome.

Managing Facework Vulnerability

According to Assumption 7 of the conflict face-negotiation theory, intercultural facework competence refers to the optimal integration of knowledge, mindfulness, and communication skills in managing vulnerable identity-based interaction scenes appropriately, effectively, and adaptively. Intercultural mediation competence can also borrow from the twin standards of communication appropriateness and effectiveness. An intercultural mediator has acted appropriately when both cultural disputants view that the mediator has communicated skillfully and displayed adaptive facilitation styles so that both disputants feel included in the mediation session. Concurrently, the mediator also has moved the conflict parties forward productively or effectively and helped them to reach a do-able, mutual-interest outcome.

To behave appropriately in a mediation session, competent mediators need to internalize the relevant value knowledge patterns and the in situ operational language patterns of the larger cultures and the ethnic heritages of both conflict parties. They also need to apply culture-sensitive situational norms in understanding the holistic conflict story. To be perceived as effective mediators, the intercultural mediators need to have linguistic, verbal, and non-verbal elastic skills to confront, to conjure, and to know when to "manage" the mediation process and when to "let go" of the mediation process and let the disputants take over the process.

More important, appropriateness and effectiveness criteria reciprocally influence one another. When the mediator uses a culture-sensitive approach to mediate the mediation session, the "good faith" respectful behaviors can induce cooperative and effective outcome. Likewise, when the mediator skillfully moves the disputants from one stage of the mediation process to another stage, her or his effective facilitation skills can elicit respect from both the disputants toward each other and toward the mediator herself or himself. For example, in mediating conflicts with Asian cultural members, mediators may want to heed the following guidelines: (a) Asian disputants may emphasize a strong benevolent conflict approach in entering a mediation session; (b) they may expect that the mediator is there to serve as a benevolent, authoritative figure and who is there to give them the solution to a conflict problem; (c) Asian disputants are oftentimes face-sensitive in disclosing private information—they may not feel comfortable engaging in direct conflict storytelling and self-disclosure unless some emotional ties or trust have been established; (d) they may not see the distinction between substantive conflict issue and relational conflict issue—they may tend to see both data sets as an integrative whole; (e) they may not feel comfortable with the free-wheeling brainstorming techniques in the problem-solving phase especially under time pressure; and (f) they may need to claim "face victory" in front of their own ingroups.

On the other hand, competent intercultural mediators must also learn to validate the face claims or social self-images of the Western disputants via the following strategies: (a) Culturally astute mediators need to spend more time in the 'introduction' mediation stage to educate the both the Asian and Western disputants about the importance of displaying cultural sensitivity to all conflict parties in the mediation session; (b) they may want to address the possibility that individuals in the room may have different culture-based and personal-based conflict style approaches and preferences; (c) They may also want to emphasize that indeed their mediator role is neutral, impartial, and objective so that they can match the expectancies and concerns of disputants who subscribe to a strong "impartial" conflict approach; (d) they need to develop full mindfulness in serving as well-balanced traffic conductors in balancing the talk times between the Western individualists and the reticent Asian collectivists; (e) they may want to educate the Western disputants about the difference between low-context and high-context communication tendencies according to Hall in 1983—with the Asian disputants' communication tendencies in "contexting" their conflict story before getting to the core substantive conflict issues; and (f) they may also need to role-model adaptive communication styles so that both the Asian and Western disputants can observe first-hand how to engage in appropriate and effective culture-sensitive dialogue. Finally, mediators may want to team up with other intercultural experts and conduct co-mediation sessions when there are strong linguistic and deep-rooted cultural animosities exist between the polarized cultural group factions.

Conclusion

This text advocates the importance of understanding the multiple layers of intercultural conflict—from a macro identity threat perspective to the micro-level of how individuals manage facework violations issues across languages and cultures. It also emphasizes the importance of understanding socio-pragmatic discourse usage in promoting skillful intercultural conflict management. Both international insider and outsider research collaboration efforts are urgently needed to understand the rich **fabric** of the different designs and the golden threads that constitute the complex intercultural conflict competence system. From the narrative approach to the functional-quantitative approach, more theoretical efforts from both indigenous and cross-cultural comparative perspectives are needed for us to truly hear the multiplicity of voices, stories, and melodies of the storytellers from diverse situational conflict contexts, and from a diverse range of gendered, social class, and racial/ethnic global communities.

Applications

1. Bridging the Divide: Cross-Cultural Mediation
Mahan, N. L., & Mahuna, M. J. (2017). Bridging the divide: Cross-cultural mediation. *International Research and Review*, 7(1), 11-22.
Abstract: The article strives to contribute to the growing field of conflict resolution by analyzing contrasting cross-cultural perceptions through insights from multiple areas to resolve

intercultural conflicts and disputes. Western-centric mediation techniques are dissected in **juxtaposition** to indigenous methodologies in degrees of (a) substantiality and its prominence in indigenous communities; (b) connectivity in the ability for these methodologies to resonate within other cultures; and (c) determinism through application to aid in the manifestation of possible resolutions. By analyzing various global indigenous systems, we argue individualistic and collectivist mediation techniques often lack synergy between peoples in cross-cultural conflicts, which can lead to miscommunication. In this paper, we present the Cross-Cultural Mediation Model and methodology for managing conflict that incorporates a wide variety of mediation techniques found throughout the world at every level of society.

Keywords: culture; cross-cultural; mediation; collectivism; individualism; conflict resolution

2. Management of Intercultural Conflict: A Preliminary Study of Chinese Managers and Western Subordinates

Chen, L., & Cheung, C. F. K. (2008). Management of intercultural conflict: A preliminary study of Chinese managers and western subordinates. *Intercultural Communication Studies*, XVII(4), 17-35.

Abstract: This paper reports a study of intercultural conflicts between Chinese managers and Western subordinates. Through field observation and in-depth interviews, it is found that Chinese managers tended to switch conflict strategies while Western subordinates kept theirs rather consistently even though they were at a lower organizational status. Chinese managers reported "power" as the biggest influencing factor in determining intercultural conflict management strategy, whereas Western subordinates claimed "face" to be the most important factor. Some previously reported cultural patterns were confirmed in intercultural superior-subordinate conflicts, whereas a degree of adaptability was also evident in the context.

Keywords: intercultural conflict; Chinese managers; Western subordinates; conflict strategies; influencing factors

3. Managing Cross-Culture Conflicts: A Close Look at the Implication of Direct versus Indirect Confrontation

Brett, J., Behfar, K., & Sanchez-Burks, J. (2014). Managing cross-culture conflicts: A close look at the implication of direct versus indirect confrontation. In N. Ashkanasy & K. Jehn (Eds.), *Handbook of Conflict Management Research*, 136-154. London, United Kingdom: Edward Edgar.

Abstract: This study discusses the meaning, cultural significance, and consequences in terms of resolution of conflict and preservation of face, and reputation of direct versus indirect confrontation of conflict. The analysis of the study shows that scholars should not oversimplify the deep distinctions between direct versus indirect confrontation in terms of the motives underlying the use of direct versus indirect approaches, or in the forms of non-verbal behavior, in verbal behavior, and third-party intervention that are characteristic of each. Furthermore, the study suggests that labeling an approach as "indirect" is somewhat of a Western bias because only those primed to take a direct approach view it as indirect; those who are primed to notice indirect communication find very clear messages in all forms of indirect confrontation. Different preferences for acknowledging, expressing, and engaging in conflict do not mean that real confrontation is not happening.

Keywords: resolution; conflict; direct vs. indirect confrontation; distinction; messages

UNIT ELEVEN
Intercultural Relationships and Conflicts

Interactive Activities

1. Individually, please finish reading Text A, Text B, and the application abstracts and work out the meanings of the terms in bold type by consulting the dictionary whenever necessary.

2. In pairs, please summarize the content in 2 to 3 sentences of each sub-heading in the unit outlines of Text A and Text B based on your reading and understanding of the texts.

3. In groups, share your gains, comments and suggestions regarding the three application abstracts. Based on your interests, locate and finish reading the full-length papers of your interested abstracts.

4. Q&A: Questions are encouraged about any uncertain or confused part or parts in the unit and seek answers either from other fellow students or the instructor.

5. Complete the Personal Report of the Self-Face, Other-Face, and Mutual-Face Concerns, an instrument designed to measure the degree of your concern with the three different faces. Take a few moments and complete the self-assessment for Unit 11.

6. Please refer back to Text A, Text B and one of the full-length papers of the three abstracts and examine the **rationale** in relation to the **significance**, and **purpose** of the texts. The rationale of a study or research is the justification of that study. It clarifies the reason or need for conducting the study based on what is missing or the gaps in the existing literature. Besides indicating how the specific project fits within the developing body of knowledge, it also explains which specific groups of people can benefit from the research. When describing the rationale, researchers should examine what impact the study might have not just on the academic or scientific community but also on the general public and additionally on how it will impact lives or the environment. The difference between rationale and significance is that rationale asks the question: Based on what is already known and published in the literature of your subject, does your planned experimental approach have a logical reasoning? On the other hand, significance asks the question: If your experimental approach goes well and yields quality results, how will the results contribute to what is already known (academic significance) and/or application in reality? The difference between rationale and purpose of a study is that rationale involves stating the reasons for which one is undertaking a study or asking a specific question of what the study is all about whereas the purpose of a study provides readers with what they can expect to know or come away with after reading the study. In simple terms, rationale is an explanation for an action whereas purpose is the objective or what you want to achieve from doing your study or research.

UNIT TWELVE

Acculturation, Culture Shock, and Intercultural Communication Competence

Readings

Text A Acculturation, Culture Shock, and Intercultural Communication Competence

After James William Neuliep

▲ Acculturation

Acculturation is the term used to describe what happens when people from one culture enter a different culture. Many years ago, acculturation was defined by Robert Redfield, Ralph Linton, and Melville Herskovits as "those phenomena which result when groups of individuals having different cultures come into continuous first-hand contact with subsequent changes in the original culture pattern of either or both groups." John Berry, well known for his work on acculturation, argues that in practice, when two different cultural groups engage in continuous contact, one of the two groups will induce more change than the other. For example, when immigrants enter the United States, they are probably going to experience more change than the people already living here. Berry also distinguishes between acculturation at the group level and at the individual level. He contends that the distinction is important because not all members of the group experience the same levels of acculturation.

According to Berry, in pluralistic, diverse societies such as the United States, three factors bring cultural groups together: mobility, voluntariness, and **permanence**. For example, regarding mobility, some groups experience acculturation because they have moved into a new culture—as is the case for immigrants and refugees such as the Hmong people of Laos, who came to the United States. Other groups experience acculturation because they have had a new culture thrust on them, as is the case for indigenous peoples such as Native Americans/American Indians. Some groups enter acculturation voluntarily, such as Mexican immigrants to the United States, whereas others experience acculturation involuntarily, as did African slaves brought to the United States. Finally, some groups will experience a relatively permanent acculturation change, as Black Americans and Mexican Americans have, whereas others face only temporary acculturation, as do exchange students studying abroad or expatriates in temporary job transfers. Berry maintains that despite the sometimes dramatic differences in circumstances of acculturating groups, the overall acculturation process is universal across groups.

Acculturative Stress

Most people experience a degree of stress and strain when they enter a culture different from their own. Acculturation is often marked by physical and psychological changes that occur as a result of the adaptation required to function in a new and different cultural context. People adapting to new cultures face changes in their diet, climate, housing, communication, role prescriptions, and media consumption, as well as in myriad rules, norms, and values of a new and (relatively) dissimilar culture. Moreover, such persons are isolated from familiar social networks and may experience problems with language, unemployment, and discrimination. The stress associated with such changes, known as acculturative stress, is marked by a reduction in one's physical and mental health.

Many immigrant groups in the United States experience acculturative stress. A rather substantial body of research has documented the effects of acculturative stress on America's largest microcultural group, Hispanics/Latinos. Alexis Miranda and Kenneth Matheny point out that among Hispanics/Latinos, acculturative stress is related to decreased **self-efficacy** expectations, decreased career aspirations, depression, and suicidal ideation (especially in Hispanic/Latino adolescents). In their work with Hispanics/Latinos, Julie and David Smart have observed that acculturative stress is associated with fatalistic thinking. They argue that acculturative stress has a lifelong effect on Hispanics/Latinos' psychological well-being, decision-making abilities, occupational effectiveness, and physical health. They contend that for Hispanic/Latino immigrants, the most significant aspect of acculturative stress is the loss of social support from the family. They maintain that this loss is particularly intense for Hispanics/Latinos because of their collectivistic orientation. In fact, Hispanic/Latino women may be more likely than men to suffer from acculturative stress because their roles are clearly prescribed in their native culture. In the United States—an individualistic, equality-based society—women's roles are more open and unspecified. Joseph Hovey, in his work, found that family **dysfunction**, separation from family, negative expectations for the future, and low income levels were significantly related to higher levels of acculturative stress.

In an interesting line of research, Emeka Nwadiora and Harriette McAdoo investigated acculturative stress among Amerasian refugees in the United States. Amerasians are individuals born of U.S. servicemen and Vietnamese or Cambodian women during the Vietnam War. Because of their mixed racial background, these children were considered half-breeds and social outcasts in their homeland. In 1987, Congress passed the Amerasian Homecoming Act, permitting all Amerasians and their immediate families (including wives, half-siblings, and mothers) to immigrate to the United States. Nwadiora and McAdoo report that Amerasians have faced pervasive prejudice in the United States, often by Asians, Europeans, and especially Black Americans. In their research, they found that the Amerasians experienced acculturative stress in the areas of spoken English, employment, and limited formal education. They also report that gender and race had no significant impact on acculturative stress.

Berry also argues that the degree of acculturative stress experienced by people adapting to new cultures varies according to the similarities and dissimilarities between the host culture and the immigrants' native culture. To the extent that the cultures are more similar than different, less stress is experienced. Individual personal traits also play a role in the manifestation of acculturative stress. Berry notes that such characteristics as one's degree of previous exposure to the new culture; one's level of education; one's sex, age, language, race, and income; and one's psychological and spiritual strength all affect acculturative stress. A well-educated woman from the United States may experience more acculturative stress than a well-educated man from the United States when entering a culture that does not recognize sexual equality (either socially or legally).

A Model of Acculturation

Acculturation is not unilateral; it is an interactive process between a culture and groups of people. When individuals or groups of individuals enter a new culture, they are often changed by the culture, but they also impact the culture in return. For example, although Mexican immigrants face challenges imposed on them by the dominant culture, their presence has changed the United States' cultural milieu, especially in places such as Texas and California. Young Kim's model of cultural adaptation takes into account both individual and cultural factors that affect acculturation. Kim argues that acculturation is not a linear, one-way process; rather, an interaction occurs between the stranger and the host culture. Kim argues that the role of communication, the role of the host environment, and the role of predisposition best explain the acculturation process (see Figure 12.1)

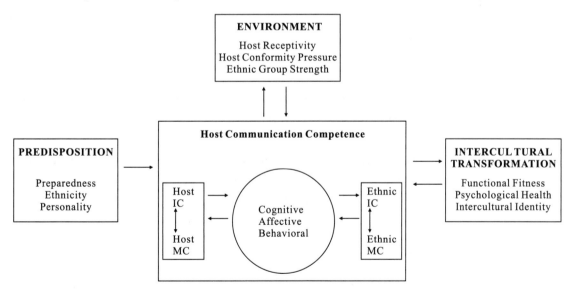

Figure 12.1 Kim's Model of Cross-Cultural Adaptation

At the core of the model is host communication competence. This includes how much the individual knows about the host culture (i.e., cognitive)—for example, the degree to which the newcomer understands the host language's rules and norms, knows effective and understands appropriate conflict resolution strategies. The affective component refers to how motivated the individual is to initiate and develop host culture relationships (i.e., approach avoidance tendencies). The behavioral component refers to the actual interaction between the newcomer and host persons. Participating in relationships, engaging in conflict resolution, and exposing oneself to the mass communication of the host culture can enhance and facilitate the acculturation process. Kim also argues that while in the host culture, adaptation is facilitated by maintaining interpersonal and mass communication (i.e., Host IC and Host MC) with the host culture but also maintaining interpersonal and mass communication (i.e., Ethnic IC and Ethnic MC) with one's native culture.

Predisposition factors also affect acculturation. Kim argues that newcomers enter into their new culture with varying degrees of readiness or preparedness. How much people know about their new culture, their ability to speak the language, the probability of employment, and their understanding of the cultural institutions will have a dramatic effect on their acculturation process. Newcomers' ethnicity will also play a role in the pace of their acculturation. Kim uses the term ethnicity to refer to the inherited characteristics that newcomers have as members of distinct ethnic groups. Such characteristics include race and language. For example, because of their ethnicity, Japanese may have a more difficult time acculturating to the United States than would a person from Great Britain. Finally, Kim argues that certain personality characteristics affect the individual's acculturation process. Age, for example, has been shown to affect acculturation. Generally, young persons adapt more quickly to new and different modes of behavior than do older persons, who may be set in their ways. Karmela Liebkind found that among Vietnamese refugees in Finland, younger generations maintained much more positive attitudes about acculturation than did older generations. Liebkind explains that the Finnish values and practices of gender equality and egalitarian parent/child relationships contrasted sharply with Southeast Asian values of hierarchical familial relationships and filial piety. In the traditional Southeast Asian family, children are taught to be loyal. They are obligated to show respect and obedience to their parents. Wives are expected to rear the children and serve their husbands. Not having been completely enculturated into Vietnamese society, the younger generations of the refugee Vietnamese families found it much easier than did their parents to acculturate into Finnish society.

Kim argues that the environment plays a key role in the acculturation process. The degree to which the host culture is receptive to strangers is important. Certain factions in the United States, for example, believe the country should close its borders to immigrants. Given the tensions in the Middle East, U.S. citizens sometimes face hostilities when they enter certain countries. Host conformity pressure is another factor. The extent to which natives within the host culture exert pressure on newcomers to conform to their culture's values, beliefs, and practices can facilitate or alienate the newcomers. In the United States, for example, people expect that newcomers will speak English. In fact, some members of the U.S. Congress have introduced legislation that would make English the official language of the United States. Ethnic-group strength refers to the amount of influence the newcomer's group wields in the host culture. Clearly, some ethnic groups are more powerful than others politically, economically, and socially. Because of their numbers, Black Americans and Hispanics/Latinos have become powerful ethnic groups in the United States. Kim notes that as ethnic-group strength increases, members of the ethnic group may encourage newcomers to maintain their native ethnic heritage and pressure them not to conform to the host culture. Hence, newcomers may feel pressure from the host culture to adapt, while simultaneously facing pressure from their native ethnic group to preserve their ethnic heritage.

Finally, to the extent that the adaptation process is successful, the individual develops a functional fitness; that is, they are able to accomplish goals that perhaps prior to leaving they were not. The individual develops a kind of psychological health—a sense of accomplishment and confidence in having adapted to different surroundings. Finally, many returning expatriates take on a kind of intercultural identity in that their character and personality have grown and matured.

Modes of Acculturation

For acculturation to occur, there must be contact between the members of the host culture and the newcomers. Berry argues that such contact needs to be continuous and direct. He maintains that short-term accidental contact does not generally lead to much acculturation. Moreover, the purpose of contact between the two groups is an important consideration. Berry points out that acculturation effects may vary according to whether the purpose of contact is colonization, enslavement, trade, military control, evangelization, or education. The length of contact is also a factor, as are the social or political policies of the mainstream culture as they relate to the immigrant group (i.e., political representation, citizenship criteria, language requirements, employment opportunities, and so forth).

Berry points out that an individual's level of acculturation depends in part on two independent processes: the degree to which the person approaches or avoids interaction with the host culture (i.e., out-group contact and relations) and the degree to which the individual maintains or relinquishes his or her native culture's attributes (i.e., in-group identity and maintenance). On the basis of these two factors, Berry has identified four modes of acculturation: (a) assimilation, (b) integration, (c) separation, and (d) marginalization (see Figure 12.2).

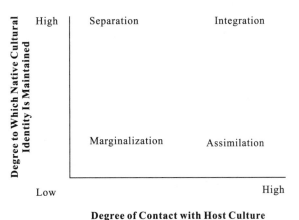

Figure 12.2 Modes of Acculturation

To the extent that the individual desires contact with the host culture (and its various microcultures) while not necessarily maintaining an identity with his or her native culture,

assimilation occurs. According to Hardin Coleman, the individual loses his or her original cultural identity as he or she acquires a new identity in the host culture. During assimilation, the individual takes on the behaviors and language habits, as well as practices the basic rules and norms of the host culture. There is an ongoing effort to approach the dominant culture while discontinuing the values, beliefs, and behaviors associated with the native culture. Coleman argues that the defining property of the assimilation mode is that the individual endeavors to acquire the values and beliefs of a single cultural group, with the ultimate goal of becoming indistinguishable from other members of the host culture. The individual will seek interaction with members of the host culture and build social networks with them.

On the other hand, some people desire a high level of interaction with the host culture while maintaining identity with their native culture. This kind of acculturation is called integration. In this mode, the individual develops a kind of bicultural orientation that successfully blends and synthesizes cultural dimensions from both groups while maintaining an identity in each group. Coleman maintains that people practicing this mode of acculturation take part in activities that allow individuals from different groups to interact without the obstacle of social hierarchies. **Presumably**, integration is associated with less acculturative stress and conflict. To be sure, an individual's successful integration of cultural skills and norms does not mean that the person relinquishes his or her native cultural identity. In fact, Coleman contends that the development of the bicultural identity is what leads to a successful life in a bicultural context. In other models of acculturation, this mode is called pluralism or multiculturalism. This mode of acculturation guides many of the social and legislative efforts in the United States' educational and affirmative action statutes.

When individuals prefer low levels of interaction with the host culture and associated microcultural groups while desiring a close connection with, and reaffirmation of, their native culture, the mode of acculturation is called separation. Here, the individual resists acculturation with the dominant culture and chooses not to identify with the host cultural group. At the same time, the person retains his or her native cultural identity. Coleman argues that people choosing separation may harbor animosity toward the host culture as a result of social or historical factors. Such persons generally focus on the perceived incompatibility between their native culture and the host culture. Although the values and beliefs of the host culture are **eschewed**, the individual may take on selected behaviors of the host culture for purely functional reasons (e.g., to get a job). Coleman suggests that separated persons communicate almost exclusively with their own group while actively avoiding participation in situations with members of the host culture. Some Black Americans and Native Americans/American Indians, for example, prefer not to identify with the dominant White culture because of past racism and the country's history of slavery. In some models, the separation mode is labeled segregation.

The fourth type of acculturation is marginalization. Marginalization occurs when the individual chooses not to identify with his or her native culture or with the host culture. In many instances, **marginalized** people give up their native culture only to find that they are not accepted by the host culture, to which they would choose to acculturate if given the opportunity. These persons experience **alienation** from both cultures. Often, they feel a sense of abandonment.

Dysfunctional behaviors (e.g., alcoholism or drug abuse) are often seen in marginalized people. Black Americans, Asian Americans, and Hispanic/Latino Americans often feel marginalized in U.S. culture. Acculturative stress is often found among marginalized groups.

Another possible acculturation mode, articulated by Richard Mendoza, is cultural **transmutation.** In this mode, the individual chooses to identify with a third cultural group (microculture) that materializes out of the native and host cultural groups. For example, a youth may choose to join a gang or some other kind of microcultural outlet. Although similar to separation, cultural transmutation is different in that a new cultural identity is created. In other models of acculturation, this is called fusion. Gay and lesbian groups are a good example of the cultural transmutation mode of acculturation. In this mode, individuals have left their native heterosexual groups and immigrated into homosexual contexts. Religious groups are another example of acculturative transmutation. Many religious communities merge the values, beliefs, and behaviors of diverse religions into a new religion.

Acculturation in the United States

The two largest ethnic populations in the United States are Hispanics/Latinos and Black Americans. In 2015, about 13% of the population in the United States were Black Americans and just over 17% were of Hispanic/Latino origin. For these groups, acculturation refers to the degree to which they participate in the cultural traditions, values, beliefs, and norms of the dominant White society; remain immersed in their own unique cultural customs and conventions; or participate in both. As Hope Landrine and Elizabeth Klonoff comment, some microcultural groups remain highly traditional, whereas others are highly acculturated. Highly traditional Hispanics/Latinos and Black Americans differ significantly from White people in a variety of values and behaviors, whereas highly acculturated Hispanics/Latinos and Black Americans do not.

Social scientists are beginning to understand that the degree of acculturation for microcultural groups within the United States is associated with a variety of social and medical problems, such as alcoholism, cigarette smoking, drug abuse, and HIV/AIDS related knowledge, attitudes, and behaviors. According to Landrine and Klonoff, many studies have found that levels of acculturation among Black Americans play a significant role in their behavior and are more influential than education and income combined. For example, they point to studies that have found that low levels of acculturation among Black Americans are significantly related to type of coping strategy used to handle stress, social support, depression, suicidal ideation, cigarette smoking, food-related attitudes and eating disorders, knowledge of AIDS transmission, and performance on neuropsychological tests. They also note that Black Americans tend to score significantly lower than White people on two subtests of an IQ test called the Wechsler Adult Intelligent Scale-Revised (WAIS-R) and on subtests of a neuropsychological battery, but that racial differences disappear when acculturation was taken into account. In other words, as Black Americans become more acculturated, they score equal to white people on these scales.

Moreover, microcultural group acculturation is tied to methods of conflict resolution (e.g., belligerent behaviors), willingness to use counseling, career development and work habits, and educational achievement (i.e., increased absences, lower grades). The more marginalized or segregated the group, the more likely its members are to experience physical and mental health problems and the less likely they are to seek out appropriate avenues to handle them. Landrine and Klonoff maintain that ethnic differences observed in the United States might be better understood as degrees of acculturation. According to Landrine and Klonoff, understanding a microcultural group's level of acculturation has the potential to diminish racist beliefs about ethnic differences and to increase our knowledge of such differences as a symptom or exhibition of culture.

In an effort to better understand maladaptive attitudes and behaviors among the various microcultural groups in the United States, researchers have devoted considerable attention to assessing levels of acculturation. The Acculturation Rating Scale for Mexican Americans (ARSMA) was first published in 1980. The scale was recently revised and is used to assess Mexican American acculturation according to Berry's four modes of acculturation—namely, integration, assimilation, separation, and marginalization. It is designed to be completed by persons of Mexican or Hispanic/Latino origin. As with other microcultural groups, some Black Americans are more acculturated than others. Landrine and Klonoff have also developed an instrument called the Beliefs and Attitudes Scale that is designed to measure levels of Black American acculturation. They argue that within the microcultural context, acculturation refers to the degree to which microcultural groups (e.g., Black Americans, Asian Americans, Native Americans/American Indians) participate in the traditional values, beliefs, and practices of the dominant White culture, remain **immersed** in their own cultural traditions, or blend the two traditions. Black Americans who complete the instrument are asked to indicate their preference of their religious beliefs and practices, their experience with traditional Black American foods and games, any relevant childhood experiences, superstitions, interracial attitudes, and cultural mistrust of the White majority, their experiences with "falling out," their adherence to Black American family values, and their family practices. This scale is designed for Black Americans in the United States and is not applicable to other microcultural groups.

The two scales discussed here are valid indices of acculturation for Hispanics/Latinos and Black Americans and indicate that cultural diversity can be measured reliably. Such measurements give us a better understanding of an individual's perceptual context. The more we know about a person's individual level of acculturation, the better able we are to provide culturally competent services to him or her.

▶ Culture Shock

When people move to a new culture, they take with them the values, beliefs, customs, and behaviors of their old culture. Often, depending on the degree of similarity between the old and the new culture, the values, beliefs, customs, and behaviors of the native culture clash with those of the new culture. This can result in disorientation, misunderstandings, conflict, stress, and anxiety. Researchers call this phenomenon culture shock. Michael Winkelman defines culture shock as a multifaceted experience that results from the numerous stressors that occur when coming into contact with a different culture. Anyone can experience culture shock, although some are more prone to it than others. Winkelman maintains that culture shock can occur with immigrant groups—such as foreign students and refugees, international business exchanges, Peace Corps volunteers, and social workers entering new communities during crises—as well as with members of microcultural groups within their own culture and society. Expatriate professors teaching abroad often describe their experiences using the term education shock.

Anthropologist Kalervo Oberg was the first to apply the term culture shock to the effects associated with the tension and anxiety of entering into a new culture, combined with the sensations of loss, confusion, and powerlessness resulting from the forfeiture of cultural norms and social rituals. Likewise, Winkelman points out that culture shock stems from the challenges associated with new cultural surroundings in addition to the loss of a familiar cultural environment. Culture shock appears to be a psychological and social process that progresses in stages, usually lasting as long as a year. Most models of culture shock include four stages. The first model of culture shock, developed by Oberg nearly 50 years ago, incorporates a medical metaphor and terminology—beginning with the incubation stage, followed by crisis, leading to recovery, and finishing with full recovery. William Smalley's model begins with a fascination stage and then moves through hostility, adjustment, and biculturalism. Alan Richardson's four-stage model includes elation, depression, recovery, and acculturation. Daniel Kealey's model incorporates exploration, frustration, coping, and adjustment phases (see Table 12.1).

Table 12.1 Table of Culture Shock Models

Oberg(1954)	Smalley(1963)	Richardson(1974)	Kealey(1978)
1. Incubation	1. Fascination	1. Elation	1. Exploration
2. Crisis	2. Hostility	2. Derpression	2. Frustration
3. Recovery	3. Adjustment	3. Recovery	3. Coping
4. Full recovery	4. Biculturalism	4. Acculturation	4. Adjustment

Most models of culture shock describe the process **curvilinearly**, or by what Sverre Lysgaard called the "U-curve hypothesis." Elaborating on the U curve, Professor Kim Zapf asserts that culture shock begins with feelings of optimism and even elation that eventually give way to frustration, tension, and anxiety as individuals are unable to interact effectively with their new environment. As they develop strategies for resolving conflict, people begin to restore their confidence and eventually recover and reach some level of acculturation.

The initial stage of culture shock, usually called something like the tourist stage or honeymoon stage, is characterized by intense excitement and euphoria associated with being somewhere different and unusual (see Figure 12.3). Winkelman asserts that this stage is typical of that experienced by people who enter other cultures temporarily during honeymoons, vacations, or brief business trips. The stresses associated with cultural differences are tolerated and may even seem fun and humorous. During the tourist phase, the newcomers' primary interactions with their new cultural environment are through major cultural institutions, such as museums, hotels, western restaurants, and so forth. This phase may last weeks or months but is temporary. In some instances, the tourist phase may be very short, as when newcomers are confronted with drastic changes in climate or hostile political environments. Eventually, the fun and excitement associated with the tourist phase give way to frustration and real stress, or active culture shock. Failure events once considered minor and funny are now perceived as stressful. Winkelman maintains that culture shock is partially based on the simultaneous effects of cognitive overload and behavioral inadequacy that are rooted in the psychological and physical stresses associated with confronting a new environment. The new environment requires a great deal of conscious energy that was not required in the old environment, which leads to cognitive overload and fatigue. People also experience role shock in that the behaviors associated with their role in their native culture may be dramatically different from the behaviors for that same role in the new culture. Finally, people may experience personal shock in the form of a loss of intimacy with interpersonal partners. In describing the second phase of culture shock, Winkelman notes:

Things start to go wrong, minor issues become major problems, and cultural differences become irritating. Excessive preoccupation with cleanliness of food, drinking water, bedding, and surroundings begins. One experiences increasing disappointments, frustrations, impatience, and tension. Life does not make sense and one may feel helpless, confused, disliked by others, or treated like a child.

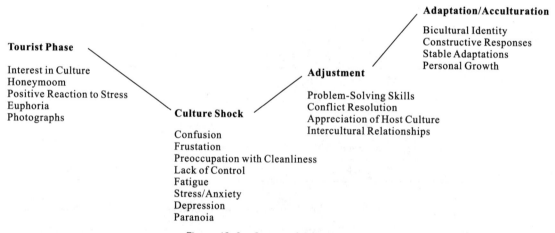

Figure 12.3 Stages of Culture Shock

Stephen Rhinesmith notes that during the culture shock phase, people feel helpless, isolated, and depressed. Paranoia—in which newcomers are convinced that their troubles are deliberate attempts by the natives to disrupt their lives—is also a typical response to culture shock. In this phase, people may develop irrational fears of being cheated, robbed, or even **assaulted**. The degree to which one experiences culture shock varies from person to person. Walt Lonner has identified six factors that affect the nature of culture shock experienced: (a) control factors, (b) interpersonal factors, (c) organismic/biological factors, (d) intrapersonal factors, (e) spatial/temporal factors, and (f) geopolitical factors. Arza Churchman and Michal Mitrani have added three additional factors: (a) the degree of similarity between one's native and new culture, including the physical environment; (b) the degree and quality of information about the new environment; and (c) the host culture's attitude and policies toward immigrants (see Figure 12.4).

UNIT TWELVE
Acculturation, Culture Shock, and Intercultural Communication Competence

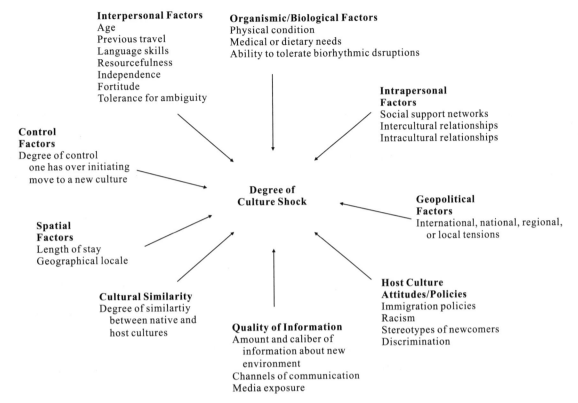

Figure 12.4 Factors That Affect Culture Shock

Some people never recuperate from the crisis stage of culture shock and return home or isolate themselves from the host culture by restricting their interaction with it, such as by fostering only intracultural relationships (e.g., in a military base or university setting). When the lines of communication with the host culture are severed, there is little hope of acculturation or recovery from the crisis stage. The third phase of culture shock is typically called the adjustment phase, or reorientation phase. Here, people eventually realize that the problems associated with the host culture are due not to deliberate actions by the natives but, rather, to a real difference in values, beliefs, and behaviors. At this stage, people actively seek out effective problem-solving and conflict-resolution strategies. They begin to develop a positive attitude about solving their problems. As Winkelman notes, the host culture begins to make sense, and pessimistic reactions and responses to it are lessened as people recognize that their problems are due largely to their inability to understand, accept, and adapt. Typically, the adjustment phase is gradual and slow, and often people relapse into mini-crisis stages. The final stage of culture shock is labeled the adaptation or acculturation stage. At this point, individuals actively engage the culture with their new problem-solving and conflict-resolution tools, and they experience some degree of success.

Kim argues that to the extent that people acculturate to their new culture, they experience cultural transformation. They possess a degree of functional fitness in which the external demands of the host culture are met with appropriate and consistent internal responses. Moreover, they develop a level of competency in communicating with the natives. As a result of their successes, people also acquire psychological health, take on an intercultural identity, and foster a sense of integration with their host environment.

W-Curve Models of Reentry Culture Shock

As mentioned earlier in the unit, most models of culture shock contain four phases in the U-curve tradition. But many people who have lived outside their native culture argue that they experience a kind of reentry shock when they return home. Adrian Furnham and Stephen Bochner's "W-curve" model of culture shock contains two U-curves—the initial culture shock experienced when the traveler enters a new culture and a reentry shock U-curve (see Figure 12.5).

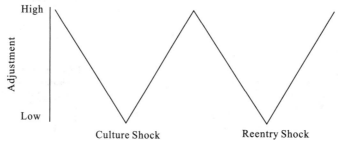

Figure 12.5　W-Curve Model of Reentry Culture Shock

In other words, when people return home after an extended stay in a foreign culture, they experience another round of culture shock, this time in their native culture. Furnham and Bochner note that students returning from study abroad often report a reentry shock phenomenon. Some students fear that they will be treated differently by their "stay-at-home" peers, friends, and parents when they return. In addition, because they have successfully acculturated themselves to a foreign culture, they essentially have to **reacculturate** to their native culture. Students frequently report that the nature of long-term international travel transforms them. When they return home, they are different; they have taken on new perspectives and are able to see the world through different lens. Students lament that communicating to their friends and families about their experiences abroad is often difficult.

Strategies for Managing Culture Shock

If you are traveling to a new culture for the first time, you will likely experience some kind of culture shock. The level of intensity will vary. In addition, the duration of your culture shock will depend on your ability to manage it. Probably the best piece of commonsense advice is to do your homework and be prepared. Successful management of culture shock depends on an awareness of its symptoms and the degree of its severity. Winkelman maintains that sometimes people falsely attribute their problems to sources other than culture shock. He argues that people have a tendency to deny that they are experiencing it. His advice is that one should accept the fact that virtually all atypical problems that occur during acculturation are caused or exacerbated by culture shock. Zapf has developed a questionnaire called the Culture Shock Profile to assess the intensity of culture shock an individual is experiencing. Please keep in mind that everyone experiences some degree of culture shock when entering a new culture for some length of time. Zapf recommends that the Culture Shock Profile be taken several times during the first year of one's move—specifically, after the first month, sometime during the fourth or fifth month, and then after a year. If managed appropriately, most culture shock is significantly reduced after a year.

Indicators of Success in the Intercultural Context

Considering the warning signs previously indicated, there are also keys to success in overcoming acculturative stress and culture shock. Karen van der Zee and her colleague Jan Pieter van Oudenhoven have written extensively about the factors that contribute to an individual's ability to cope with acculturative stress and culture shock. Through their years of study, van der Zee and Oudenhoven have identified five personality dimensions directly linked to success in long-term intercultural encounters. They argue that these five dimensions increase an individual's professional performance, personal adjustment, and social integration during acculturation across a variety of settings, including employee effectiveness on the job, successful immigration, relational satisfaction among **expatriates** and their families, and the academic performance of students studying abroad. These five dimensions are cultural empathy, open-mindedness, social initiative, emotional stability, and flexibility.

As we learned earlier, experiencing pure **empathy** toward another is impossible, but here cultural empathy refers to an individual's sincere attempt to identify with, understand, and sympathize with the feelings, thoughts, and behaviors of the individuals from the new culture with whom he or she is living and interacting. Van der Zee and Oudenhoven point to research indicating that cultural empathy is positively associated with psychological adjustment in a new culture. Open-mindedness refers to the individual's motivation and ability to delay or defer judgment when confronted with the different behaviors or values of a new culture. When confronted with cultural differences, often our initial response is to reject them. Like cultural empathy, open-mindedness is associated with psychological adjustment and also satisfaction with life in the new culture. Social initiative refers to the individual's tendency to approach social situations.

Recall from the beginning of this book that intercultural communication is **replete** with uncertainty, and uncertainty is associated with anxiety, which often leads to avoidance. Individuals who are willing to approach communicative situations tend to integrate better into their host culture than do those who avoid such situations. While maintaining relationships with family and friends from home is absolutely fine, establishing relationships with members of your host culture is one of the best ways to ensure a successful intercultural experience. Emotional stability refers to the individual's ability to remain composed when faced with novel and stressful conditions. To be sure, you will confront many situations that appear unusual and even strange. Your ability to remain calm and poised will serve you well. Finally, flexibility refers to your ability to transition from or replace those thoughts, feelings, and behaviors that have become almost second nature to you in favor of new strategies to deal with everyday situations. Van der Zee and Oudenhoven assert that rather than fearing new and unknown situations, individuals should try to seek them out and view them as a challenge rather than a threat.

Intercultural Communication Competence

One of the fundamental goals of this book is to help you become a competent intercultural communicator. Intercultural communication competence is defined as the degree to which you effectively adapt your verbal and non-verbal messages to the appropriate cultural context. When you communicate with someone from a different culture, to be interculturally competent you will have to adjust and modify the kinds of verbal and non-verbal messages you send. This process requires that you have some knowledge about the person with whom you are communicating, that you are motivated to communicate with him or her, and that you have the appropriate verbal and non-verbal skills to encode and decode messages.

Interculturally competent people successfully and effectively adapt their verbal and non-verbal messages to the appropriate cultural context. For the most part, competence is perceived in an individual rather than inherently possessed. In other words, an individual may appear competent to one person but not to another. Moreover, intercultural competence varies from situation to situation. That is, a particular American may be quite competent while interacting with Chinese people and relatively incompetent when interacting with Germans. Verbal and non-verbal appropriateness and effectiveness are two important qualities of intercultural competence. According to Brian Spitzberg, appropriate behaviors conform to the rules, norms, and expectancies of the cultural context.

For example, when greeting a Japanese person in Japan, one is expected to bow. The rules associated with bowing are determined by one's status (e.g., age, sex, occupation, education). The person of lower status bows lower and longer than the person with higher status and typically does not make direct eye contact. Effective behaviors are those that successfully perform and accomplish the rules and norms. For example, to the extent you are able to bow correctly, your behavior will be perceived as effective and competent. As we have seen throughout this book, the appropriateness and effectiveness of verbal and non-verbal messages vary considerably across cultures. Behaviors considered appropriate in one culture may not be wholly appropriate in another culture.

A Model of Intercultural Competence

Spitzberg and his colleague Bill Cupach argue that there are three necessary and interdependent **ingredients** of communication competence: (a) knowledge, (b) motivation, and (c) behavior. The model of intercultural competence presented in this text includes these three dimensions along with a fourth component, situational features. In this model, intercultural competence is the potential outcome of four interdependent components of the intercultural communication encounter. Each component influences and is influenced by the other three.

The Knowledge Component. The knowledge component of intercultural competence consists of how much one knows about the culture of the person with whom one is interacting. To the extent that people have knowledge about other cultures, they are more likely to be perceived as competent (although there is no guarantee!). Consider your own general cultural awareness.

UNIT TWELVE
Acculturation, Culture Shock, and Intercultural Communication Competence

To be perceived as culturally knowledgeable, minimally, one should have some comprehension of the other person's dominant cultural values and beliefs. In addition, one should know whether the other person is from an individualistic or collectivistic, high-context or low-context, large or small power distance, and high or low uncertainty avoidance culture. In the model of intercultural competence, verbal and non-verbal scripts are also a part of the knowledge component. Communication theorist Charles Berger argues that verbal and non-verbal scripts (or plans) guide communication action. Scripts are like blueprints for communication that provide people with expectations about future communicative encounters with others. Berger and Jerry Jordan have argued that knowledgeable communicators develop and maintain a repertoire of scripts that enable them to comprehend and predict their actions and the actions of others. They have demonstrated that people store scripts in long-term memory. According to Berger and Jordan, when anticipating interaction with others, communicators establish goals. They search their long-term memory for instances when they have tried to accomplish similar goals and then access a script or plan that was successful in achieving those goals in the past. The frequency and similarity with which a particular script has been used facilitates access to it. In never-before-encountered situations, people may possess vicariously based scripts. Perhaps one has witnessed a similar event by watching a film or reading a comparable account. The more plans one has, the better equipped one is to enact them.

Cognitive simplicity and rigidity refers to the degree to which individuals process information about persons from different cultures in a simplistic and rigid manner. Kim includes this dimension in her model of intercultural conflict. According to Kim, people with simplistic and rigid cognitive systems tend to engage in gross stereotyping. Moreover, such individuals may have narrowly defined and inflexible categories. Narrow categorizers tend to make more negative and more confident judgments about other people, particularly those from other cultures. Such persons probably think dogmatically (i.e., are narrow-minded). Metaphorically, a person with a simple and rigid cognitive system sees the world with blinders on, like a racehorse. Obviously, the competent communicator would possess an open and flexible cognitive system. The person with a simple and rigid system would not be perceived as competent.

As discussed before, ethnocentrism is the extent to which one perceives one's own group as the center of everything and judges other groups with reference to it. **Ethnocentrics** tend to create and reinforce negative attitudes and behaviors toward outgroups. Judgments about in-groups and out-groups almost always are biased in favor of the in-group at the expense of the out-group. Furthermore, ethnocentric groups see themselves as righteous and exceptional and view their own standards as universal and moral. Outgroups are seen as immoral, subordinate, and impotent. Ethnocentrism is clearly an obstacle to intercultural communication competence. The ethnocentric person most likely possesses narrow categories and a simple and rigid cognitive system. In his research, Rich Wiseman found that ethnocentrism was the strongest predictor of general cultural understanding. That is, higher levels of ethnocentrism were associated with less general cultural understanding. Higher levels of ethnocentrism were also related to less positive regard for other cultures.

The Affective Component. The affective component of intercultural communication is the degree to which one approaches or avoids intercultural communication—that is, one's level of motivation to interact with others from different cultures. A central feature here is intercultural communication apprehension (ICA). ICA is defined by Jim Neuliep and James McCroskey as the fear or anxiety associated with either real or anticipated interaction with persons from different cultures.

Persons high in ICA tend to avoid interacting with others from different cultures. As mentioned in unit 1, because they are seen as strangers, people from different cultures may seem unusual and novel. This difference can create tension and anxiety, which, in turn, can lead to avoidance. In addition, some people may be positively predisposed to initiate intercultural interactions even when they are completely free to choose whether or not to communicate. This predisposition, labeled by Jeffrey Kassing, is called intercultural willingness to communicate. You can assess your individual level of intercultural willingness to communicate by completing the Intercultural Willingness to Communicate Scale.

Kim has argued that one's ability to cope with stress also affects one's approach-avoidance tendencies. Because of the potentially inordinate uncertainty of intercultural communication, anxiety levels may be high as well, leading to increased stress. Some people handle stress well, whereas others do not. William Gudykunst and Kim maintain that to be an effective intercultural communicator, one needs to tolerate ambiguity to a certain degree. The more one is able to manage stress and endure **ambivalence**, the more likely one is to initiate intercultural communication and to be an effective and competent intercultural communicator. The knowledge component and the affective component of intercultural competence are interdependent in that the more knowledge one has, the more likely one is to approach situations involving intercultural communication. The increase in knowledge generally leads to an increase in motivation. Likewise, the more motivation one has, the more likely one is to pursue interaction with people from different cultures, thereby learning more about them and their culture and increasing one's knowledge.

The Psychomotor Component. The psychomotor component of intercultural communication is the actual enactment of the knowledge and affective components. The elements of the psychomotor component are (a) verbal and non-verbal performance and (b) role enactment. Verbal performance is how people use language. A person may know a great deal about the language of the host culture but not be able to engage in a conversation.

Many foreign exchange students in the United States come here not to learn more about English but to practice using it in actual conversations. A U.S. student who recently returned from a year's stay in Japan reported that she had been paid handsomely for hourly conversations with Japanese. People would come to her apartment and pay her simply to converse in English about trivial subjects for 60 minutes. These Japanese had all the knowledge they needed about English but wanted to sharpen their performance skills. Knowing and being able to use a second language certainly increases one's perceived competence when interacting interculturally. Language scripts and plans that reduce uncertainty are of particular importance. The psychomotor function is where one puts the scripts and plans into action. If one does not speak the language of the host culture, then at the very least, one should know some of the basic

UNIT TWELVE
Acculturation, Culture Shock, and Intercultural Communication Competence

greetings, requests, and routines used frequently in that language.

Non-verbal performance is also an important part of the psychomotor component. Here, the individual needs to pay close attention to the **nuances** of the kinesic, paralinguistic, haptic, olfactic, and proxemic codes of the other culture. As with verbal knowledge and performance, one may have knowledge of a particular culture's non-verbal mannerisms but may not be able to execute them. Hence, before traveling to a foreign country, it might be wise to polish and refine your repertoire of non-verbal skills. For example, before traveling to Japan, you might practice bowing with family members or friends. Keep in mind also that how you smell will affect how others perceive you. Many cultures feel that U.S. citizens smell antiseptic because of our frequent use of soaps, perfumes, and so forth. As mentioned earlier, we have a tendency to mask the natural odor of the human body, and this custom seems strange to many other cultures.

Role **enactment** refers to how well one executes the appropriate verbal and non-verbal messages according to one's relative position and role in the host culture. The behaviors that professors in the United States enact in the classroom may be misinterpreted or seen as improper in classrooms in other cultures. Managers must be particularly careful about the types of strategies they employ across cultures. Men and women should know how their sex roles vary across cultures. U.S. women returning from abroad frequently comment on how badly they were treated. The freedoms U.S. women have gained are not shared by women across the globe. A female student who recently returned from a semester of study in southern Italy recounted her experience:

> I couldn't believe how the men acted toward me and my friends. When we would walk through town, they would whistle and hiss at us. Everyone told us that this was how they treated women and to just get used to it.

As we have seen throughout this text, the verbal and non-verbal behaviors expected for certain sex and occupation roles vary considerably across cultures. In particular, understanding these two role positions is key to becoming interculturally competent.

Situational Features

The fourth component of intercultural competence is the actual situation in which intercultural communication occurs. Remember that a person may be perceived as competent in one situation and not in another. Perceived competence varies with the situation. Some of the situational features that may affect competence include, but are not limited to, the environmental context, previous contact, status **diferential**, and third-party interventions. Recall from the above the influence of the environment on communication. Some situations may have higher information loads than others, which may affect your motivation and ability to enact appropriate verbal and non-verbal behaviors. Highly loaded situations may increase anxiety and reduce your motivation to approach another. In addition, you should have some knowledge of the host culture's perception of time and space. If you are lucky enough to be invited into someone's home, keep in mind that the use of space in homes varies dramatically across cultures. In some of her work, Kim discusses the importance of previous contact and status differences.

Because of the dynamic nature of competence, any previous contact you may have had with a person from another culture may enhance your perception of competence. Competence and trust take time to establish and build, and your competence will grow as you interact more with the people of your host culture. Conversations with persons from other cultures provide a particularly rich source of data for you. The more contact you can have with these people, the more likely you will be to learn about them (knowledge) and feel comfortable (affective) interacting with them, thus enabling you to master your verbal and non-verbal skills (**psychomotor**).

Although you may have sufficient knowledge about another culture and be motivated to interact, status differences may require you to take on multiple modes of behavior. Certain verbal and non-verbal strategies may be more or less appropriate, depending on whether you are interacting with someone of lower, equal, or higher status. In the United States, we have a tendency to minimize status differences. In other cultures, one's status determines the order of speakers and the types of codes to use in a given situation. Because your status may be high in one situation and low in another, you should be mindful of how the communication will vary accordingly.

The addition of a third party may noticeably change the dynamics of the situation and, hence, your competence. All of a sudden, your status may go up or down, as might the status of the person with whom you are interacting. The gender of the third party may also alter the situational features. Topics that were appropriate just a moment ago may now be unfit for discussion. The competent communicator keeps a sharp eye on the changing characteristics of the situation and adapts his or her verbal and non-verbal communication accordingly. The model of intercultural competence provided in Figure 12.6 depicts the knowledge, affective, **psychomotor**, and situational features as interdependent. This means that as one component changes, the others are affected as well. Generally, as knowledge increases, one's motivation to approach

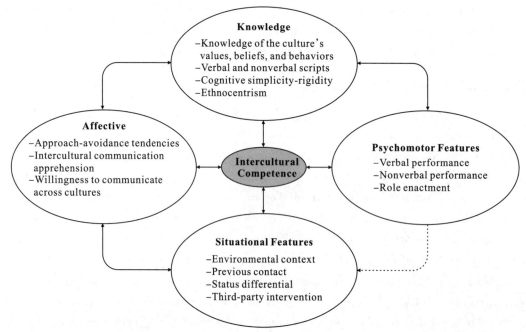

Figure 12.6 Model of Intercultural Competence

increases. As motivation increases, one is more likely to engage in behaviors. If the behaviors are successful, one learns more about intercultural communication, which serves to further increase motivation. And the cycle continues.

▶ Summary

Leaving your native culture for a new one can be one of the most rewarding, yet challenging experiences of a lifetime. Upon relocating to a new culture, everyone goes through a process of acculturation—that is, a process of cultural change that results from ongoing contact between two or more culturally different groups. For some, this process can be particularly difficult, whereas for others, it is relatively easy. Acculturation is in large part a function of how much interaction one chooses to have with members of the new culture and how much of the old culture one desires to maintain. Virtually everyone experiences some degree of culture shock when entering a new culture for an extended period of time. Culture shock results in feelings of disorientation, misunderstandings, conflict, stress, and anxiety. Often, a traveler experiences the same feelings upon returning home. In addition to discussing its causes and symptoms, this unit has offered several strategies for assessing and managing culture shock. Although culture shock sounds awful, understanding its causes, symptoms, and effects is the first step in alleviating the severity you might experience. Generally speaking, most students who travel abroad experience only minor levels of culture shock.

Finally, one of the foremost goals of this book is to help you become a competent intercultural communicator. As defined in this unit, intercultural communication competence is the degree to which you effectively adapt your verbal and non-verbal messages to the appropriate cultural context. This unit has presented a model of intercultural competence that includes knowledge, affective, psychomotor, and situational components. To be a competent intercultural communicator, you must have some knowledge about the person with whom you are communicating, you need to be motivated to communicate with people who are different from you, and you need to engage in appropriate and effective verbal and non-verbal skills to encode and decode messages. You also need to be sensitive to the situational features that influence the verbal and non-verbal messages you send. It is hoped that you, after having read this text, are more knowledgeable about culture, are more motivated to enter into new cultures and establish relationships with persons from different cultures, and have gained some communication skills. Although challenging, intercultural communication is one of the most rewarding life experiences you will ever encounter.

Text B Understanding and Assessing Intercultural Competence: A Summary of Theory, Research, and Practice

After Castle Sinicrope, John Norris and Yukiko Watanabe

Introduction

In its broadest sense, intercultural competence can be defined following Fantini's definition in 2006 as "a complex of abilities needed to perform effectively and appropriately when interacting with others who are linguistically and culturally different from oneself." Throughout the literature, researchers and **theoreticians** use a range of more or less related terms to discuss and describe intercultural competence, including intercultural communicative competence (ICC), transcultural communication, cross-cultural adaptation, and intercultural sensitivity, among others. What all of these terms attempt to account for is the ability to step beyond one's own culture and function with other individuals from linguistically and culturally diverse backgrounds. College foreign language and study abroad programs play a unique role in offering students the opportunity to develop their intercultural competencies. The acquisition of such competencies may be important not only for individual enrichment and communicative proficiency but also for providing future educators, professionals, and leaders with the capabilities necessary for promoting successful collaboration across cultures.

In this report we summarize theory and research on intercultural competence, paying particular attention to existing approaches and tools for its assessment. We also review examples of the assessment of intercultural competence in the specific contexts of general education and college foreign language and study abroad programs (Deleted for the lack of space here; please read the original report if you really need it.) It is our hope that these resources will provide a useful basis to foreign language (and other) educators as they seek to understand and improve the intercultural competencies of their students.

▲ Theoretical Frameworks for Intercultural Competence

Background

Historically, a major focus on intercultural competence emerged out of research into the experiences of westerners working abroad in the 1950s, 1960s, and early 1970s. This early research was typically motivated by perceived cross-cultural communication problems that **hampered** collaboration between individuals from different backgrounds. In the late 1970s and 1980s, the contexts for intercultural competence research expanded to include study abroad, international business, cross-cultural training, expatriates living overseas, and immigrant acculturation. During these formative years, research on intercultural competence utilized assessments of individuals' attitudes, personalities, values, and motives, usually through short self-reports, surveys, or open-ended interviews. The purpose and focus of ICC assessment using

UNIT TWELVE
Acculturation, Culture Shock, and Intercultural Communication Competence

these tools centered around four main goals: "(a) to explain overseas failure, (b) to predict overseas success, (c) to develop personnel selection strategies, and (d) to design, implement and test sojourner training and preparation methodologies" according to Ruben in 1989.

Today, intercultural competence research spans a wide **spectrum**, from international schools to medical training, from short study abroad programs to permanent residency in foreign cultures. The purposes of research also range widely, from the selection of appropriate participants for sending abroad to cross-cultural mediation to the determination of learning outcomes associated with a variety of educational experiences. As the focus and purpose of intercultural competence research has expanded, approaches to its description and assessment have evolved as well, from short attitude and personality surveys to more complex behavioral self-assessments, performance assessments, **portfolio** assessments, and others. At the same time, nearly twenty years after Ruben declared in 1989 the "need for conceptual clarity," a multiplicity of frameworks and approaches to defining and assessing intercultural competence persists today. Thus, although the broad range of theories and models provides language educators with a variety of approaches to understanding and investigating intercultural competence, it also **complexifies** the task of communicating about related ideas in a systematic and consistently interpretable way.

By way of example, Table 12.2 presents 19 terms that have been utilized as alternatives for discussing intercultural competence. Though often used interchangeably with the most frequent labels of intercultural competence, intercultural communicative competence, intercultural sensitivity, and cross-cultural adaptation, each alternative also implies additional nuances that are often only implicitly addressed in research.

Table 12.2 Alternative Terms for Intercultural Communicative Competence

transcultural communication	international communication	ethnorelativity
cross-cultural communication	intercultural interaction	biculturalism
cross-cultural awareness	intercultural sensitivity	multiculturalisn
global competitive intelligence	intercultural cooperation	pluralingualism
global competence	cultural sensitivity	effective inter-group communication
cross-cultural adaptation	cultural competence	
international competence	communicative competence	

Hammer, Bennet, and Wiseman attempted to overcome some of the murkiness of ICC definitions in 2003 by drawing a major distinction between intercultural sensitivity and intercultural competence. From their perspective, intercultural sensitivity is "the ability to **discriminate** and experience relevant cultural differences" whereas intercultural competence is "the ability to think and act in interculturally appropriate ways." Their distinction between knowing and doing in interculturally competent ways offers a fitting prelude to the themes that have emerged from most contemporary work on ICC. In the following sections, we introduce four major frameworks for conceptualizing intercultural competence. Additional theoretical frameworks for intercultural competence are described briefly as well, but the main focus in this report is on those approaches that have served as bases for assessments developed to gauge intercultural competence. Following the overview of theoretical frameworks, we then turn to their operationalization in research and assessment in Section 3.

Ruben's Behavioral Approach to Intercultural Communicative Competence

One of the earliest comprehensive frameworks was Ruben's behavioral approach to the **conceptualization** and measurement of intercultural communicative competence. In contrast to the personality and attitudinal foci of previous approaches, Ruben advocated a behavioral approach to linking the gap between knowing and doing, that is, between what individuals know to be interculturally competent and what those individuals actually do in intercultural situations. It is not uncommon for an individual to be exceptionally well-versed on the theories of cross-cultural effectiveness, possess the best of motives, and be sincerely concerned about enacting his role accordingly, yet be unable to demonstrate those understandings in his own behavior.

For these reasons, Ruben argued in 1976 that to understand and assess individuals' behaviors, it would be necessary to employ "measures of competency that reflect an individual's ability to display concepts in his behavior rather than intentions, understandings, knowledge, attitudes, or desires" (p. 337). Ruben theorized that observing individuals in situations similar to those for which they are being trained or selected would provide information for predicting their performances in similar future situations.

Based on findings in the literature and his own work, Ruben identified in 1976 seven dimensions of intercultural competence:

(a) Display of respect describes an individual's ability to "express respect and positive regard" for other individuals.

(b) Interaction posturer efers to an individual's ability to "respond to others in a descriptive, non-evaluative, and nonjudgmental way."

(c) Orientation to knowledge describes an individual's ability to "recognize the extent to which knowledge is individual in nature." In other words, orientation to knowledge describes an individual's ability to recognize and acknowledge that people explain the world around them in different ways with differing views of what is "right" and "true."

(d) Empathy is an individual's ability to "put [himself] in another's shoes."

(e) Self-oriented role behavior expresses an individual's ability to "be flexible and to function in [initiating and harmonizing] roles." In this context, initiating refers to requesting information and clarification and evaluating ideas for problem solving. Harmonizing, on the other hand, refers to regulating the group status quo through mediation.

(f) Interaction management is an individual's ability to take turns in discussion and initiate and terminate interaction based on a reasonably accurate assessment of the needs and desires of others.

(g) Lastly, tolerance for ambiguity describes an individual's ability to "react to new and ambiguous situations with little visible discomfort."

For assessment purposes, Ruben operationalized the seven dimensions with observational procedures and rating scales. These were subsequently employed and further developed by additional researchers. Ruben's call for a behavioral model and the assessment of behavioral outcomes, that is, describing an individual's competence based on observed actions, can also be regarded as a precursor to performance assessments of ICC. In sum, from Ruben's perspective in 1976, ICC consists of the "ability to function in a manner that is perceived to be relatively consistent with the needs, capacities, goals, and expectations of the individuals in one's environment while satisfying one's own needs, capacities, goals, and expectations," an ability that is best assessed by observing an individual's actions rather than reading an individual's self-reports.

European Multidimensional Models of Intercultural Competence: Byram and Risager

Based on their experiences in the European context, Byram and Risager have also theorized multidimensional models of intercultural competence in 1997 and 2007 respectively. In *Teaching and Assessing Intercultural Communicative Competence*, Byram proposed in 1997 a five-factor model of intercultural competence comprising the following:

(a) The *attitude* factor refers to the ability to relativize one's self and value others, and includes "curiosity and openness, readiness to suspend disbelief about other cultures and belief about one's own."

(b) *Knowledge* of one's self and others means knowledge of the rules for individual and social interaction and consists of knowing social groups and their practices, both in one's one culture and in the other culture.

(c) The first skill set, the *skills of interpreting and relating*, describes an individual's ability to interpret, explain, and relate events and documents from another culture to one's own culture.

(d) The second skill set, the *skills of discovery and interaction*, allows the individual to acquire "new knowledge of culture and cultural practices," including the ability to use existing knowledge, attitudes, and skills in cross-cultural interactions.

(e) The last factor, *critical cultural awareness*, describes the ability to use perspectives, practices, and products in one's own culture and in other cultures to make evaluations.

Byram further clarified that the interaction factor (skills of discovery and interacting) includes a range of communication forms, including verbal and non-verbal modes and the development of linguistic, sociolinguistic, and discourse competencies.

Building on Byram's theoretical foundation, Risager proposed in 2007 an expanded conceptualization of intercultural competence. She argued that a model for intercultural competence must include the broad resources an individual possesses as well as the narrow competences that can be assessed. Risager claimed her model to be broader in scope; however, it is noteworthy that the 10 elements she outlined are largely manifested in linguistic developments and proficiencies:

(a) Linguistic (**languastructural**) competence

(b) Languacultural competences and resources: semantics and pragmatics

(c) Languacultural competences and resources: poetics

(d) Languacultural competences and resources: linguistic identity

(e) Translation and interpretation

(f) Interpreting texts (discourses)

(g) Use of ethnographic methods

(h) Transnational cooperation

(i) Knowledge of language as critical language awareness, also as a world citizen

(j) Knowledge of culture and society and critical cultural awareness, also as a world citizen

Extending ideas from these foundations, Byram and other European researchers have collaborated to combine existing theories of intercultural competence as the basis for developing their own assessment tool. Named INCA (intercultural competence assessment), the research project has adopted a multidimensional framework. Their overall model consists of two sets of dimensions, one for the assessor and one for the examinee, with three skill levels for each dimension: basic, intermediate, and full. From the assessor's point of view, intercultural competence consists of 6 different dimensions, as defined by the INCA assessor's manual:

(a) Tolerance for ambiguity is the ability to accept lack of clarity and ambiguity and to be able to deal with it constructively.

(b) Behavioural flexibility is the ability to adapt one's own behavior to different requirements and situations.

(c) Communicative awareness is the ability [...] to establish relationships between linguistic expressions and cultural contents, to identify, and consciously work with, various communicative conventions of foreign partners, and to modify correspondingly one's own linguistics forms of expression.

(d) Knowledge discovery is the ability to acquire new knowledge of a culture and cultural practices and the ability to act using that knowledge, those attitudes and those skills under the constraints of real-time communication and interaction.

(e) Respect for otherness is the readiness to suspend disbelief about other cultures and belief about one's own.

(f) Empathy is the ability to intuitively understand what other people think and how they feel in concrete situations.

From the examinee's point of view, intercultural competence consists of three dimensions, in a simplified version of the assessor's model:

(a) Openness is the ability to be open to the other and to situations in which something is done differently (respect for others + tolerance of ambiguity).

(b) Knowledge is the characteristic of not only want[ing] to know the 'hard facts' about a situation or about a certain culture, but also [...] want[ing] to know something about the feelings of the other person (knowledge discovery + empathy).

(c) Adaptability describes the ability to adapt [one's] behavior and [one's] style of communication (behavioral flexibility + communicative awareness).

Given the assessment orientation of this ICC framework, the different dimensions have not only been explained theoretically, as above, but have also been given concrete descriptions for each skill level. For example, Table 12.3 provides descriptions for each level of the first dimension, tolerance for ambiguity.

Table 12.3 Skill Levels for Tolerance for Ambiguity Dimension

Basic	Intermediate	Full
Deals with ambiguity on a one-off basis, responding to items as they arise. May be overwhelmed by ambiguous situations which imply high involvement.	Has begun to acquire a repertoire of approaches to cope with ambiguities in low-involvement situations. Begins to accept ambiguity as a challenge.	Is constantly aware of the possibility of ambiguity. When it occurs, he/she tolerates and manages it.

Beyond the INCA project, the multidimensional approach and the dimensions Risager and Byram ascribe to intercultural competence can be seen in both commercial assessment tools (Cross-Cultural Adaptability Index) and non-commercial assessment practices. Key to these European-oriented frameworks, and distinct from Ruben's early work, is the emphasis on acquisition of proficiency in the host culture—moving well beyond the ability to interact respectfully, non-judgmentally, and effectively with the host culture.

Bennett's Developmental Model of Intercultural Sensitivity (DMIS)

In the North American context, a different model of intercultural competence has been widely discussed, researched, and explored in recent years: Bennett's Developmental Model of Intercultural Sensitivity (DMIS). On the basis of research in the 1970s and 1980s, Bennett developed a dynamic model to explain how individuals respond to cultural differences and how their responses evolve over time.

The Developmental Model of Intercultural Sensitivity (DMIS) consists of six stages grouped into three **ethnocentric** stages [the individual's culture is the central worldview, (a) to (c)] and three ethnorelative stages [the individual's culture is one of many equally valid worldviews, (d) to (f)], as follows:

(a) In the first ethnocentric stage, **denial**. The individual denies the difference or existence of other cultures by erecting psychological or physical barriers in the forms of isolation and separation from other cultures.

(b) In the second ethnocentric stage, defense, the individual reacts against the threat of other cultures by denigrating the other cultures (negative stereotyping) and promoting the superiority of one's own culture. In some cases, the individual undergoes a reversal phase, during which the worldview shifts from one's own culture to the other culture, and the own culture is subject to **disparagement.**

(c) Finally, in the third ethnocentric stage, **minimization**, the individual acknowledges cultural differences on the surface but considers all cultures as fundamentally similar.

(d) During the acceptance phase, the individual accepts and respects cultural differences with regard to behavior and values.

(e) In the second ethno-relative stage, adaptation, the individual develops the ability to shift his frame of reference to other culturally diverse worldviews through empathy and pluralism.

(f) In the last stage, integration, the individual expands and incorporates other worldviews into his own worldview.

Together, these six stages comprise a continuum from least culturally competent to most culturally competent, and they illustrate a dynamic way of modeling the development of intercultural competence.

In the past ten years, Bennett's Developmental Model of Intercultural Sensitivity has served as the basis for several assessment tools addressing intercultural sensitivity and cross-cultural competence, both commercially available and locally developed. Although Bennett does not explicitly describe the role of communication in the development of intercultural sensitivity, he references communication as a developmental strategy, particularly in the ethnorelative stages:

> Participants moving out of acceptance are eager to apply their knowledge of cultural differences to actual face-to-face communication. Thus, now is the time to provide opportunities for interaction. These activities might include dyads with other-culture partners, facilitated multicultural group discussions, or outside assignments involving interviewing of people from other cultures ... Communication practice could refer to homestays or developing friendships in the other culture.

A Culture-Generic Approach to Intercultural Competence

The most recent developments in intercultural competence theory have emerged in the research of Arasaratnam and Doerfel (2005). In their work, Arasaratnam and Doerfel call for a new, culture-wide model of intercultural communication competence. Previous models, they argue, have often been subjective and limited by the cultures of the individuals involved in their conceptualization and assessment. Instead of imposing factors and dimensions in a top-down fashion, Arasaratnam and Doerfel have adopted a bottom-up approach, in which themes and dimensions come to light in interviews. To identify these themes, they conducted a semantic network analysis of interview transcripts with 37 interculturally competent participants. Participants were affiliated with a large university and included U.S. students ($N=12$) and international students from 14 different countries ($N=25$). U.S. students were selected based on their involvement in international student organizations, study abroad programs, and international friendship/host programs. During the interview, participants responded to the following prompts:

Q1: How would you define intercultural communication?

Q2: Can you identify some qualities or aspects of people who are competent in intercultural communication?

Q3: Can you identify some specific individuals whom you think are particularly competent in intercultural communication and say why you perceive them as such?

Q4: What are aspects of good communication in your culture/opinion?

Q5: What are aspects of bad communication in your culture/opinion?

Semantic analyses of participants' answers revealed four to five dominant clusters of words for each question. For example, definitions of intercultural communication (Q1) included: (a) able, cross, language, talking, verbal, cultural, and religious; (b) backgrounds, countries, across, message, ideas, understand, and coming; (c) beliefs, group, information, exchange, individuals, communicating, outside, and town; and (d) communicate, cultures, different, people, ethnic, two, differences, and trying. Based on semantic analyses for all five questions, Arasaratnam and Doerfel identified 10 unique dimensions of intercultural communicative competence: heterogeneity, transmission, other-centered, observant, motivation, sensitivity, respect, relational, investment, and appropriateness. Although this approach has not led to the development of widely practiced assessment methods, it promises a culture-generic, bottom-up approach to eliciting definitions and dimensions of intercultural competence that may be used in future assessment tools.

Other Theoretical Approaches to Intercultural Competence

In addition to the theoretical approaches described above, at least three other models have been conceptualized and investigated: anxiety/uncertainty management by Gudykunst in 1993, 1998; an integrative system's theory by Kim in 1993; and identity negotiation by Ting-Toomey in 1993.

In anxiety/uncertainty management (AUM), Gudykunst argued in 1993 and 1998 that individuals experience both anxiety and uncertainty when interacting with foreign cultures. In order to adapt, individuals must develop the ability to manage their anxiety through mindfulness. For Gudykunst, mindfulness includes identifying and focusing on the sources of anxiety, which may include concept of self, reaction to host culture, situations, and connections with the host culture. In Kim's integrative model in 1993, cross-cultural adaptation is seen as an interactive and integrative process, in which the individual is dynamic, "never a finished product but, instead...in the business of growing and maturing." Her model comprises six different dimensions including communication competence, social communication, environment, predisposition, and intercultural transformation. Individuals who experience cross-cultural adaptation undergo phases of acculturation (acquiring elements of the host culture) and **deculturation** (unlearning elements of the old culture) in a cyclic pattern of stress-adaptation. Lastly, Ting-Toomey's negotiation model in 1993 includes three components that contribute to adaptation when individuals are faced with foreign or unfamiliar settings: cognitive, affective, and behavioral factors. These components "contribute to effective identity negotiation and outcome attainment processes," and enable individuals to interact with strangers. Although these models for intercultural competence have been theorized, none (to our knowledge) has led to the development of assessments for estimating levels or degrees of intercultural competence. Nevertheless, they do offer further insights into the factors that may be related to learners' development of ICC.

In sum, the difficult-to-pin-point nature of intercultural competence has led to a range of definitions, theories, and models that have served as the basis for different approaches to its assessment. Some models stress the communicative nature of intercultural competence, while others emphasize an individual's adaptation and development when confronted with a new culture, and still others focus on empathic and tolerant reactions to other cultures. Ultimately, these models seek to explain the types of skills and abilities individuals need to function in culturally diverse settings and the processes they undergo in developing the needed skills and abilities for being interculturally competent. How such skills and abilities might best be observed and understood is the focus of the next section.

Assessing Intercultural Competence

In recent years, intercultural competence and intercultural sensitivity research has flourished in a variety of contexts: doctors in sensitivity training programs, expatriates living abroad, students in international schools, and students in study abroad programs. This section summarizes major assessment approaches that have been utilized in the study of intercultural competence.

Studies Using Indirect Assessment Tools for Intercultural Competence

Before 1996, a handful of researchers developed their own scales for survey research, such as the Behavioral Assessment Scale for Intercultural Competence (BASIC) and the Intercultural Sensitivity Inventory (ISCI). The ISCI utilized responses on a self-report instrument to assess individuals' abilities to interact and modify their behavior in cross-cultural situations. By contrast, the BASIC instrument was used by observers to assess individuals' cross-cultural communication competence based on their actions. More recently, two commercial procedures/scales have dominated the research landscape: the Intercultural Development Inventory (IDI) and the Cross-Cultural Cultural Adaptability Inventory (CCAI). However, recent years have also seen the sustained use of non-commercial and locally developed assessment practices including the Intercultural Sensitivity Index (ISI) and the Assessment of Intercultural Competence (AIC). Furthermore, innovative researchers sometimes have developed their own assessment scales in combination with commercially available scales or as replacements for commercial assessment tools like the IDI and the CCAI. In the following sections we review these various instruments and procedures in turn, providing example items, scales, and procedural notes.

Behavioral Assessment Scale for Intercultural Competence. The Behavioral Assessment Scale for Intercultural Competence (BASIC) was developed from Ruben's pioneering work in behavioral approaches to ICC. In Ruben (1976), observers used 4-point and 5-point Likert scales to assess individuals on each of the seven dimensions: display of respect, interaction posture, orientation to knowledge, empathy, self-oriented role behavior, interaction management, and tolerance for ambiguity. Table 12.4 shows an early version of the scale used for assessing the "interaction posture" dimension.

Table 12.4 Example Item from **Precursor** to BASIC: Interactive Posture

Instructions: Responses to another person or persons in an interpersonal or group situation range from *descriptive*, *nonevaluating* to *highly judgmental*. Indicate on a 1 to 4 continuum which interaction pattern was most characteristic during the observation.

An early factor-analytic study of the scales revealed three clusters, described by Ruben as three types of participants: Types Ⅰ, Ⅱ, and Ⅲ. Type I participants showed high tolerance for ambiguity, high interaction management, and high respect plus base personal knowledge, and Ruben called these participants competent cross-cultural communicators. Type Ⅱ participants, with some respect, some tolerance for ambiguity, and some degree of empathy plus low self-oriented role behavior and low interaction management, were described as a mixed behavioral

UNIT TWELVE
Acculturation, Culture Shock, and Intercultural Communication Competence

group with potential for successful cross-cultural communication. Type Ⅲ individuals, with high self-oriented role behavior plus low orientation to knowledge, low interaction management, low group maintenance, low empathy, low tolerance for ambiguity, and low interaction posture, were described as individuals who might face difficulties when attempting to communicate cross-culturally.

The detailed description of the table is as follows.

Highly Evaluative. The individual appears to respond to others' verbal and non-verbal contributions in a highly judgmental and evaluative manner. He or she appears to measure the contributions of others in terms of a highly structured, predetermined framework of thoughts, beliefs, attitudes, and values. Reponses therefore communicate clearly whether the individual believes others to be "right" or "wrong." Reactions are made in declarative, often dogmatic fashion and will closely follow the comments of others, indicating little or no effort to digest what has been said before judging it.

Evaluative. The individual responds to others verbally and non-verbally in an evaluative and judgmental manner and measures the responses and comments of others in terms of a predetermined framework of thoughts, beliefs, attitudes, and values. The framework is not totally rigid but does provide a clear basis for determining whether others' contributions are "right" or "wrong." Reactions to others tend to follow fairly closely on the heels of termination of discussion by other interactants, but there is some break, indicating a minimal attempt to digest and consider others' ideas before responding positively or negatively.

Evaluative-Descriptive. The individual appears to measure the responses of others in terms of a framework based partly on information, thoughts, attitudes, and feelings gathered from the particular interaction and the individuals involved. He or she offers evaluative responses, but they appear to be less than rigidly held and subject to negotiations and modification. The time lapse between others' comments and the individual's response suggests an effort to digest and consider input before reacting either positively or negatively.

Descriptive. The individual responds to others in a manner that draws out information, thoughts, and feelings and provides evaluative responses, but only after gathering sufficient input so that the evaluative framework fits the individual(s) with whom he or she is interacting. He or she asks questions, restates others' ideas, and appears to gather information prior to responding evaluatively.

Subsequently, Ruben and Kealey expanded in 1979 the behavioral model to nine dimensions by dividing *self-oriented role behavior* into three distinct dimensions: *task-related roles*, *relational roles*, and *individualistic roles*. They then analyzed assessments of pre-deployment and one-year post-deployment individuals and their spouses moving and living abroad. Results revealed that three dimensions were the best predictors of how participants reacted to immersion in a new culture, also known as *culture shock*: orientation to knowledge, relational role orientation, and empathy. Ruben and Kealey also found that two dimensions, display of respect and interaction management, predicted how participants adjusted to their surrounding culture.

Finally, two other dimensions, moderate task-related and low individualistic role behavior, also correlated with the individuals' abilities to function effectively in the host culture. Building on Ruben and Kealey's work, Koester and Olebe adopted and further developed the nine BASIC scales in 1988, adding an overall score based on the nine individual scales. In their 1988 study, Koester and Olebe focused on rephrasing the scales for untrained raters by reducing sentence length and nominal forms, eliminating redundancies, avoiding technical language, and clarifying main ideas. Table 12.5 shows an example of BASIC scales.

Table 12.5 Revised BASIC Example: Interaction Posture

4. *Descriptive*. My roommate responds to others in a manner that draws out information, thoughts, and feelings. *She or he provides evaluative response, but only after gathering enough information to provide a response that is appropriate* to the individuals involved. She or he asks questions, restates others' ideas, and appears to gather information before answering evaluatively.

Koester and Olebe found in 1988 that untrained observers (university students living in dorms) were able to use the rephrased scales to evaluate their roommates. They reported correlations between a global measure of intercultural communication effectiveness (not described in their study) and each individual BASIC scale as ranging from $r=.10$ (individualistic roles) to $r=.51$ (empathy). When the individualistic role scales were excluded, the correlation between the overall BASIC score and communication effectiveness was $r=.62$. Koester and Olebe interpreted this correlation as support for the claim that BASIC provides a good measure of intercultural communication competence. Unfortunately, they did not provide the prompt or tool that elicited the communication effectiveness score or explain how the overall BASIC score was computed. Despite limitations, the study showed that untrained peers can use the BASIC scales to provide a picture of an individual's intercultural communicative effectiveness based on their familiarity with the individual's behavior.

Intercultural Sensitivity Inventory. The Intercultural Sensitivity Inventory (ICSI) was developed to measure an individual's ability to modify behavior in culturally appropriate ways when moving between different cultures. In particular, the inventory was used in comparing behavior in an individualistic culture (United States) versus a collectivistic culture (Japan). The self-report instrument comprised 46 questions on a 7-point Likert scale with the following descriptors: 1=very strongly agree, 2=strongly agree, 3=agree, 4=not decided, 5=disagree, 6=strongly disagree, and 7=very strongly disagree. The instrument was divided into two parts. In the first part, participants were asked to respond to the same 16 questions while imagining living and working in (a) the United States and (b) Japan. In the second part, participants responded to 14 generic items on flexibility and open-mindedness. Table 12.6 shows several sample items from the ICSI. A business orientation in Bhawuk and Brislin's research is clear from these items, the majority of which deal with interactions in the work-place.

In their study in 1992, Bhawuk and Brislin administered the survey to two groups of participants, MBA students and graduate students living in international dormitories. To examine the potential effects of social desirability—a phenomenon in which respondents perform on the basis of what they believe is socially acceptable rather than as an accurate depiction of their behaviors—Bhawuk and Brislin also administered the Marlow-Crowne Social Desirability scale.

Correlations between the Marlowe-Crowne scale and the total ICSI scale were relatively low ($r=.35$ for MBA students and $.37$ for graduate students), suggesting that participants were not overly affected by social desirability when answering items. Overall results from the study showed that participants with three or more years of cross-cultural experience exhibited a greater degree of intercultural sensitivity. No difference, however, was shown between the MBA students and the graduate students living in international dormitories.

Table 12.6 Sample Item from Intercultural Sensitivity Inventory (ICSI)

Individualism and Collectivism Ties	
For items 1-16, imagine living and working in the United States. Go over the items again (calling them 17-32) while imagining that you are living and working in Japan.	
Item	Statement
1	When I disagree with a group, I would allow a conflict in the group to remain, rather than change my own stance on important issues.
3	I prefer to be direct and forthright when dealing with people.
5	I am very modest when talking about my own accomplishments.
7	If I want my subordinate to perform a task, I tell the person that my superiors want me to get that task done.
13	It is important to develop a network of people in my community who can help me out when I have tasks to accomplish.
16	If I want a person to perform a certain task I try to show how the task will benefit others in the person's group.
Flexibility and Open-mindedness Items	
Item	Statement
33	When I am living abroad, I assess situations as quickly as I do when I am living in my own country.
36	I do not like to receive unannounced visitors at my home.
38	We all have a right to hold different beliefs about God and religion.
44	I would not allow my subordinate to promote his nephew if there is someone marginally better than him. The person who is better must be promoted at all costs.
46	While living abroad, I spend most of my personal time with people from my own country.

Based on their findings, Bhawuk and Brislin concluded that individualism and collectivism (i.e., the main components of the ICSI) can be used to estimate intercultural sensitivity. Furthermore, their work suggested that individuals may require three or more years of cross-cultural experience to attain a level of cross-cultural competence that is desirable for international business operations. The role of language competence and developmental aspects of intercultural competence over time were not considered in the Intercultural Sensitivity Inventory.

The Intercultural Development Inventory. The Intercultural Development Inventory (IDI) is based on Bennett's Developmental Model of Intercultural Sensitivity (DMIS) and has been used to assess the intercultural competence of high school students at international schools, university students abroad, and physician trainees. Studies by the developers have also examined the scales in detail. The IDI is a 50-item self-assessment with five-point Likert scales using the following descriptors: 1=disagree, 2=disagree somewhat more than agree, 3=disagree some and agree some, 4=agree somewhat more than disagree, and 5=agree. Table 12.7 shows sample IDI self-assessment items.

Table 12.7 Sample Items from Intercultural Development Inventory

	Developmental Stage	Sample Item
1	Denial	Society would be better off if culturally different groups kept to themselves.
2	Defense	People from other cultures are not as open-minded as people from my own culture.
3	Minimization	People are the same despite outward differences in appearance.
4	Acceptance	It is appropriate that people from other cultures do not necessarily have the same values and goals as people from my culture.
5	Adaptation	When I come in contact with people from a different culture, I find I change my behavior to adapt to theirs.
6	Integration	*no example provided*

In-depth evaluations of the Intercultural Development Inventory (IDI) and studies using the instrument have lent support to the validity and usefulness of the IDI for estimating changes in intercultural competence. Results from Straffon's (2003) one-time administration of the IDI revealed that 97% of high school students attending one international school were categorized in the acceptance and adaptation stages of the DMIS, the fourth and fifth stages respectively. His findings also indicated that the level of intercultural sensitivity, as measured by the IDI, was positively correlated with the time students had attended the international school. However, note that correlations were low for section and overall scores on the IDI (ranging from $r=.12$ to $r=.19$), suggesting only a marginal relationship with time at the school.

The Cross-Cultural Adaptability Inventory. The Cross-Cultural Adaptability Inventory (CCAI) has also been used to assess study abroad experience and sensitivity training for medical students, as well as the effects of experiential training on cross-cultural adaptability. The CCAI scales were developed by Kelley and Meyers in the early 1990's. Although they have published several manuals, only limited information on the underlying theory or development of the model is accessible.

As described in Williams, the Cross-Cultural Adaptability Inventory (CCAI) is a "training instrument designed to provide information to an individual about his or her potential for cross-cultural effectiveness". The CCAI consists of four dimensions that measure an individual's ability to adapt to different cultures: (a) emotional resilience, (b) flexibility and openness, (c) perceptual acuity, and (d) personal autonomy.

  (a) The emotional resistance dimension reflects an individual's ability to cope with stress and ambiguity and recover from mistakes and unexpected turns of events with a positive attitude and resourcefulness.
  (b) The second dimension, flexibility and openness, assesses an individual's openness to

UNIT TWELVE
Acculturation, Culture Shock, and Intercultural Communication Competence

others and flexibility with regard to new and unfamiliar situations.

(c) **Perceptual acuity**, the third dimension, assesses both behavior and perception with emphasis on the individual's ability to interpret communication cues (verbal and nonverbal) cross-culturally.

(d) The final dimension, personal autonomy, measures both the individual's sense of identity and his ability to respect differing cultural values.

Overall cross-cultural adaptability is calculated by summing responses to the four dimensions, as measured with a 50-item survey of items using six-point Likert scale self-ratings with the following anchors: 1=DNT (definitely not true), 2=NT (not true), 3=TNT (tends to be not true), 4=TT (tends to be true), 5=T (true), DT (definitely true). Examples to illustrate the four dimensions can be seen in Table 12.8.

Table 12.8 Sample Items from Cross-Cultural Adaptability Inventory (CCAI)

Dimension	Items(k)	Sample Item
Emotional resilience	18	When I am working with people of a different background, it is important for me to receive their approval.
Flexibility and openness	17	If I had to adapt to a slower pace of life, I would become impatient.
Perceptual acuity	10	I pay attention to how people's cultural differences affect their perception of me.
Personal autonomy	7	I feel free to maintain my personal values, even among those who do not share them

Mixed results have emerged from studies that used the Cross-Cultural Adaptability Inventory (CCAI) to measure change in individuals' intercultural competence. In their research on the impact of study abroad, Kitsantas and Meyers found in 2001 statistically significant differences between study abroad and non-study abroad groups for all four dimensions and total score. Prior to the study abroad program, minimal differences were shown between the experimental group (study abroad) and the control group (non-study abroad). Similarly, Goldstein and Smith found in 1999 differences between control and experimental groups along all four dimensions; however, they followed a post-test only design and, therefore, their results may or may not have been attributable to the hands-on, cross-cultural experiences.

The Intercultural Sensitivity Index (ISI). Based on Bennett's theoretical framework of the Development Model of Intercultural Sensitivity (DMIS) and multidimensional models of intercultural competence in 1993, Olson and Kroeger developed in 2001 their own instrument for measuring global intercultural competency, the Intercultural Sensitivity Index (ISI). The instrument's items represent not only the six stages of the DMIS (denial, defense, minimization, acceptance, adaptation, and integration) but also three dimensions of global competency (substantive knowledge, perceptual understanding, and intercultural communication). Sample items for both theoretical orientations follow in Table 12.9 and Table 12.10. The total number of items and the number of items for each dimension were not reported. Each question is answered on a five-point scale (note that the scale-point descriptors were not provided in the study).

Table 12.9 Sample Items for Bennett's Developmental Model of Intercultural Competence

	Stage	Sample Item
1	Denial	I feel most comfortable living and working in a community where people look and act like me.
2	Defense	I believe that aid to developing countries should be targeted to those efforts that help these countries evolve toward the types of social, economic, and political systems that exist in the United States.
3	Minimization	I understand that difference exist [*sic*] but believe that we should focus on similarities. We are all human.
4	Acceptance	I believe that verbal and non-verbal behavior vary across cultures and that all forms of such behavior are worthy of respect.
5	Adaptation	I have two or more cultural frames of reference, and I feel positive about cultural differences.
6	Integration	I am able to analyze and evaluate situations from one or more chosen cultural perspectives.

Table 12.10 Sample Items for Global Competency

Dimension	Sample Item
Substantive knowledge	I think that the choices one makes at home have relevance for other countries and vice versa.
	I am linguistically and cultural competent in at least one language and culture other than my own.
Perceptual understanding	I appreciate how people from other cultures are different from me.
	I question my own prejudices as well as national and cultural stereotypes.
Intercultural competence	I incorporate the attractive aspects of other cultures into my way of doings things.
	I have the ability to deal flexibly with and adjust to new people, places, and situations.

Olson and Kroeger piloted their survey with faculty members of the New Jersey City University and found that 69% self-rated at 4 or 5 on the scale for stage 4, acceptance. Next highest, 44% self-rated at 4 or 5 on the scale for stage 5, adaptation, while 17% self-rated at 4 or 5 on the scale for stage six, integration. None of the respondents rated themselves high on the scale for stages 1 or 2, denial and defense respectively, and only 10% rated themselves highly on stage 3, minimization. Olson and Kroeger provided two explanations for these results. First, the faculty at New Jersey City University live in a diverse and metropolitan area. Second, only 10% of 500 faculty members responded to the survey. Olson and Kroeger argued that individuals in stages of denial and defense might be less likely to complete and return such a survey, thereby depressing the numbers for the lower end of the scale.

Only one other study, Williams (2005), was identified that employed the ISI, which was used in combination with CCAI to assess and compare the intercultural communication skills of students before and after study abroad programs. Williams found that students who studied abroad averaged an 11.28 increase on the ISI (out of a potential 192 points). Despite these positive findings, Williams concluded that the results should be interpreted cautiously given the self-study format, the small sample size, the broad scope of study abroad programs, and the moderate reliability of the ISI ($r=.56$ on the pretest; $r=.67$ on the posttest). For future research, she suggested longitudinal studies with improved assessment instruments.

The Assessment of Intercultural Competence (AIC). In another approach, the Assessment of Intercultural Competence (AIC) was also developed in-house for specific purposes. The Federation of the Experiment in International Living (FEIL) developed the scale as a first step in a larger project of exploring and assessing the intercultural competence outcomes of its programs. As the basis for its research, the FEIL researchers proposed the definition of intercultural competence as "a complex of abilities needed to perform effectively and appropriately when interacting with others who are linguistically and culturally different from one's self," as Fantini noted in 2006. Within this definition, Fantini specified different components: characteristics of intercultural competence, domains of intercultural competence (relationships, communication, and collaboration), dimensions of intercultural competence (knowledge, attitude, skills, and awareness), language proficiency, and developmental level.

In initial research on this recent assessment, two-way procedures (self and other-reported) and hour-long interviews were employed. In total, the self-assessment instrument consisted of seven sections and 211 items. Participants for the research were British and Swiss individuals in FEIL volunteer projects in Ecuador, including both alumni, current volunteers, and project mentors. Topics ranged from personal characteristics to intercultural abilities, as shown in Table 12.11 below. Questions on a 0–5 point scale had descriptors ranging from 0=none/not at all to 5=extremely high/well.

Fantini presented findings from the self-assessment instrument, the AIC, and interview data from participants. He interpreted results to provide evidence for overall improvement in intercultural competence. To support the validity of these findings, he reported reliability estimates of 0.70 and greater and factor loadings of 0.60 and greater for each item on each of the four dimensions of intercultural competence: knowledge, attitude, skills, and awareness. Using the alumni interview data, he completed fine-grained analyses to address assertions underlying the intercultural competence model in the AIC, such as: ICC is a complex of abilities, learning the host language affects ICC development, and all parties in intercultural contact are affected to some degree and in various ways. Evidence in the interview data offered support for most of the assertions that were researched. Future development plans for the AIC include revising the instrument and expanding its use to other cross-cultural contexts.

Overview of Indirect Assessment Tools for Intercultural Competence. Table 12.12 summarizes major indirect assessment tools that have been developed for estimating intercultural competence. Existing tools consist mostly of self-reports, in the form of surveys, with a focus on multiple dimensions that comprise the overall construct of ICC. One exception to this generalization is the other-assessment tool, BASIC, which includes assessment by others using pre-specified guidelines and scales. Another exception to this generalization is the IDI, which measures an individual's development along a continuum of ICC rather than dimensions of an overall ICC construct.

Table 12.11　Sample Items from Assessment of Intercultural Competence (AIC)

No.	Section	Items(N)	Sample Items ask respondents to...
1	About the respondent	37	*provide name, nationality, gender, education level, past intercultural relationships, etc.*
2	Personal characteristics	28	*rate themselves as they perceive themselves in their own cultures and as they believe their hosts perceived them in the other culture (0-5)* **example characteristics:** 1. intolerant 2. flexible 3. patient 4. lacks sense of humor 5. tolerates differences
3	Motivation and options	18	*rate level of interest and characterize motivation towards host culture (0-5)* **example levels of interest:** 1. Before arriving 2. Mid-way through the experience **example motivations** 1. Sometimes wanted to return home 2. Desired to adjust as best as you could
4	Language proficiency	15	*describe proficiency at beginning and end of stay (yes or no)* **example proficiency items:** 1. no ability at all 2. able to satisfy immediate needs with memorized phrases
5	Communication styles	47	*compare their responses to situations in their own and in the host culture* **example situation:** When disagreeing in my/the host culture, I prefer 1. to be told directly and openly about the problem no matter the consequences. 2. not to speak openly so as to not offend anyone. 3. not sure.
6	Intercultural areas	12	*rate their situations (0-5)* **example situation:** I was able to communicate in Spanish with 1. my host family. 2. my host colleagues. 3. other host natives.
7	Intercuhulal abililies	54	*rate intercultural abilities at the beginning and the end of the program for knowledge, attitudes, skills, and awareness (0-5)* **example of knowledge ability:** I could contrast important aspects of the host language culture with my own. **example of attitude ability:** I demonstrated willingness to interact with host culture members. **example of skills ability:** I adjusted my behavior, dress, etc., as appropriate, to avoid offending my hosts. **example of awareness ability:** I realized the importance of my, negative reactions.

Table 12.12 Indirect Assessment Tools for Intercultural Competence

Assessment Tool	Format	Constructs
Behavioral Assessment Scale for Intercultural Competence (BASIC) Ruben, 1976; Ruben & Kealey, 1979; Koester & Olebe, 1988	7 – 9 questions 4 – point and 5 – point scales	display of respect interaction posture orientation to knowledge empathy self-oriented role behavior interaction management tolerance for ambiguity
Intercultural Sensitivity Inventory (ICSI) Bhawuk & Brislin, 1992	46 questions 7 – point scale	individualism ties collectivism ties flexibility open-mindedness
Intercultural Development Inventory (IDI) Hammer & Bennett, 1993	50 questions 7 – point scale	denial defense minimization acceptance adaptation integration
Cross-Cultural Adaptabilily Inventory (CCAI) Kelley & Meyers, 1995	50 questions 6 – point scale	emotional resistance flexibility and openness perceptual acuity personal autonomy
Global Competency and Intercultural Sensitivity Index (ISI) Olson & Kroeger, 2001; Williams, 2005	30 questions 5 – point scale	denial defense minimization acceptance adaptation integration substantive knowledge perceptual understanding intercultural competence
Assessment of Intercultural Competence (AIC) Fantini, 2006	multiple survey components	knowledge attitude skills awareness

Concerns with Self-Assessment Instruments. Some researchers have voiced concerns over the potential short-comings of the self-report formats that characterize most of the indirect assessment instruments. Findings in Altshuler et al. revealed in 2003 a "discrepancy between participants' self-perception of their intercultural awareness and sensitivity and their actual abilities." To control for the likely influence of social desirability, Hammer et al. in 2003 and

Bhawuk and Brislin in 1992 administered the Marlowe-Crown scale. Correlations between Marlowe-Crown's social desirability scale and responses on the IDI and ICSI did not reveal any substantial relationships between assessment responses and social desirability. Despite such findings, researchers continue to doubt the ability of individuals to provide accurate self-assessments.

According to Arasaratnam and Doerfel in 2005, the issue with self-assessment may not be that individuals choose to respond inaccurately, but that they may not be able to respond accurately: "a major short-coming in studies in the past is that often participants who have little experience in intercultural situations are asked for self-reports of behavioral choices in hypothetical intercultural situations." Although this factor may not apply in post-study abroad or post-training assessments, it could affect the pre-study abroad and pre-training results that are used as a baseline to determine individual gains in intercultural competence. Despite potential theoretical and methodological drawbacks, self-report surveys remain the most widely practiced form of indirect assessment, owing to the availability of ready-made instruments and the speed and ease of data collection and analysis.

Direct Assessments of Intercultural Competence. Direct and combined assessment designs are not as common as indirect assessments of intercultural competence, which may be due largely to the time-consuming nature of collecting and analyzing direct assessment data. Nevertheless, these approaches potentially offer more complete assessments of intercultural competence because they can provide more detailed, nuanced, and individualized accounts while avoiding many of the issues inherent in indirect or self-report assessment approaches discussed above.

Direct Assessment Tools. Direct approaches to assessing ICC include performance assessment, portfolio assessment, and interviews. Common to these is the elicitation of an individual's ability to display intercultural competence in his or her behavior, whether in real-time situations (performance assessment), in reflections and collections of work (portfolio assessment), or in one-on-one conversations with interlocutors (interviews).

Proponents of direct assessment suggest including performance assessment because it reveals an individual's ability to use any acquired intercultural competence in real-time situations. For example, to assess the skills of discovery and interaction, Byram and Morgan utilized an interview with a native speaker on a personal topic in 1997. Before the interview, interviewees prepared for a discussion on the topic of regional identity. During the interview, they were asked to explain how their feeling of social identity was related to their place of origin. After the interview, they were encouraged to reflect on the content and form of their discussion, which could also include self-assessing their skills via analysis of audio-recordings of the task.

Ruben advocated in 1976 performance assessments in which individuals are observed in situations that are similar to what they will face in the future. If these situations are not naturally occurring, they can be created "using a simulation, game, or structured experience." However, Ruben did not provide a suggested list of potential simulations, games, or structured experiences. In his study, nineteen participants were observed during a seven-day intercultural adaptation training program, which was aimed at preparing the participants for upcoming cross-cultural assignments. Staff members completed the BASIC scales using their observations of

UNIT TWELVE
Acculturation, Culture Shock, and Intercultural Communication Competence

participant behavior during formal and informal parts of the program, including training sessions, coffee breaks, cocktail hours, and meals. Based on the description of the study, it is unclear whether participants were aware that their intercultural competence performance was being evaluated.

Others have emphasized the potential of portfolio assessment for gauging intercultural competence. Jacobson et al. argued in 1999 that learning is not always quantifiable and may be represented best by self-selected work. In their study, the process of developing a portfolio encouraged students to reflect on their evolving intercultural competencies, thereby increasing the potential for learning and growth. The final product was assumed to represent the students' intercultural competence level at the end of the research period. To guide the portfolio process, participants in Jacobson et al. received the following directions in 1999.

Learning to communicate in a new culture is like learning a new type of art. Words alone cannot really show what you have learned, and there is no simple way to take a test or give yourself a grade that will show what you have learned. Instead, think of good examples from your experiences in this country that show what you have learned about communicating in the culture here.

Although portfolio entries for some students were encouraging, in that they showed how students developed and grappled with their understanding of and ability to adapt to cultural phenomena (e.g., small talk and the meaning of time and punctuality in the United States), Jacobson et al. noted two limitations: (a) selective representation of students' intercultural ability, as the students themselves chose examples that represented them in particular ways; and (b) confusion over the concept of a portfolio, because some students did not follow the directions for the portfolio assignment. Many students focused their portfolios on broad cultural differences between their home countries and the United States instead of focusing on more narrow issues of intercultural communication. Despite these drawbacks, Jacobson et al. concluded that portfolios can provide a useful alternative means for assessing intercultural competence.

In 1997 Byram also advocated portfolio assessments for estimating the dimensions of attitude, skills of interaction/discovery and relating/interpreting, and critical awareness. However, Byram did not provide concrete ideas or examples of portfolio assessment designs. Similarly, Pruegger and Rogers suggested in 1994 the use of content analysis of personal documents. In this approach, three-page follow-up papers were analyzed for positive change, mixed change, no change, and no comment after cross-cultural training.

Finally, interviews may also function as a form of direct assessment, both as a means for eliciting authentic performances, or as a supplement that adds rich layers to the preliminary results of indirect assessments. During in-depth interviews, Fantini used the following questions to elicit data on the nature and development of intercultural competence in 2006.

Q1: What abilities do you think are important toward intercultural success?
Q2: To what extent did you develop these abilities? Why or why not?
Q3: Was learning of the host language important to your success? Why or why not?
Q4: What impact did this intercultural service experience have on your life?
Q5: How and to what extent have you utilized any of these abilities in your own life and

work?

Q6: Any additional comments?

Similarly, Straffon utilized in 2003 the following questions and responses as a basis for comparison to indirect assessment results in his analysis:

Q1: What do you think is more important to pay attention to, cultural differences or cultural similarities?

Q2: When you encounter a cultural difference, what is your first reaction?

Q3: What does the word culture mean to you?

▲ Conclusion

In sum, it is apparent that notions of intercultural communication and associated competences are of increasing importance, not only as outcomes of foreign language and study abroad programs, but also as fundamental targets of adult and higher education. Faculty, programs, institutions, and society at large are coming to value the capacity of individuals to think and act beyond their particular cultural circumstances. Assessment should play a key role in helping educators to understand and improve students' ICC capacities, providing an empirical basis for tracking development, motivating learning, examining outcomes, and indicating areas for instructional improvement. However, it is also apparent that there is large variability in the available practices that have been recommended and implemented for assessing ICC, and these assessment forms depend considerably on the particular models of ICC adopted. While commercial and non-commercial assessments are readily available, they clearly differ (sometimes dramatically) in terms of what gets assessed and what interpretations may be made on their basis; accordingly, their use in any given program will also have **differential** impact on the teaching and learning that occurs. For any individual foreign language program, then, a key first step in deciding on how best to assess ICC will be to determine: (a) the specific purposes or uses to which the assessment will be put; and (b) the particular local conceptualization of ICC that characterizes what is to be learned and/or how learners are intended to change. With these foundational decisions achieved, FL programs and faculty will be in a much better position to select among the array of possibilities reviewed in this report, seeking a fitting alignment between assessment method, the particular version of ICC learning in question, and the ways in which assessment can be put to use in making sure that ICC leaning really happens.

Applications

1. Relationships of the Dimensions of Intercultural Communication Competence

Chen, G. M. (1989). Relationships of the dimensions of intercultural communication competence. *Communication Quarterly*, 37(2), 118 – 133.

Abstract: This study has been designed to investigate the relationships between the dimensions and components of intercultural communication competence. In this study, 149 international students and 129 American people have been used as respondents. Significant relationships have been predicted. Results from correlation and canonical analyses have shown that the two hypotheses were supported. Limitations and directions for future research were also discussed.

Keywords: intercultural communication competence; personal attributes; communication skills; psychological adaptation; cultural awareness

2. Intercultural Communication Competence and Acculturation among International Students in Central China

Ngwira, F. F., Mapoma, W. T. H., Hong, J., Sariyo, S., Kondowe, W. (2015). Intercultural communication competence and acculturation among international students in central China. *Intercultural Communication Studies*, XXIV(2), 61 – 83.

Abstract: Each year, increasing numbers of international students enroll in Chinese universities, yet no literature is available on their intercultural communication competences (ICC) and acculturation status. The study aimed at investigating these two key concepts at Central China Normal University. Two dimensions of intercultural communication competence (affect and behavior) and two dimensions of acculturation (attitude towards maintenance of one's culture and attitude towards contact with other cultures) were employed to measure and analyze the two research constructs. A representative sample of 302 international students shows that Asian international students are less motivated to adapt than other students from other continents. In addition, time and education level do not seem to be sufficient factors in facilitating adaptation. Furthermore, the most preferred acculturation strategy is found to be integration. Finally, attitude towards contact positively correlates with affect and behavior. However, there is no relationship between attitude towards cultural maintenance and the two dimensions of ICC. These findings suggest that a better understanding of intercultural communication competence and acculturation, as well as of factors that help facilitate adjustment to the new culture, are essential in assisting Chinese universities to come up with effective programs that enhance contact between cultures.

Keywords: Intercultural communication competence; acculturation; demographic factors; cultural diversity; international students

3. Intercultural Communicative Competence (ICC) Revisited

Orsini-Jones, M., & Lee, F. (2018). Intercultural communicative competence (ICC) revisited. In M. Orsini-Jones & F. Lee (Eds.), *Intercultural Communicative Competence for Global Citizenship*, 7 – 23. London, United Kingdom: Macmillan.

Abstract: This chapter documents the evolution of the concepts of communicative competence (CC) and intercultural communicative competence (ICC) and discusses how the advent of the World Wide Web and the widespread use of computer mediated communication (CMC) are affecting the re-conceptualization of ICC. It highlights the importance of integrating tele-collaboration into the HE curriculum for the purpose of developing a global citizenship competence for the digital age in higher education (HE). The concept and features of ICC for global citizenship are explored.

Keywords: communicative competence; intercultural communication competence; computer mediated communication; cyber-pragmatics; global citizenship

Interactive Activities

1. Individually, please finish reading Text A, Text B, and the application abstracts and work out the meanings of the terms in bold type by consulting the dictionary whenever necessary.

2. In pairs, please summarize the content in 2 to 3 sentences of each sub-heading in the unit outlines of Text A and Text B based on your reading and understanding of the texts.

3. In groups, share your gains, comments and suggestions regarding the three application abstracts. Based on your interests, locate and finish reading the full-length papers of your interested abstracts.

4. Q&A: Questions are encouraged about any uncertain or confused part or parts in the unit and seek answers either from other fellow students or the instructor.

Whatever you major is and whatever jobs you may take in your future, you are sure to encounter opportunities to interact with people from other cultural backgrounds. What is your understanding of a competent intercultural communicator and how do you plan to continue improving your intercultural communication competence?

5. Complete the Personal Reports of The Intercultural Communication Competence Scale, an instrument designed to describe how you think, feel, and behave when interacting with people from different cultural backgrounds. Take a few moments and complete the self-assessment for Unit 12.

6. To check your understanding of the readings in this book and to demonstrate your achievements in this course, research papers are probably assigned during the semester. To facilitate your paper writing, please save and refer to the following paper outline:

Paper Outline

Title

1. Introduction:
    1.1 Attention-getter
    1.2 Mini-literature review and gap identification
    1.3 Clear idea(s) about the topic with a preview of the main points
    1.4 Rationale, underlying reasons, or intentions for the research

2. Literature Review
   2.1 Literature review (Chronological; topical; or the order of climax)
   2.2 Gap (necessity for further study; "However, ...")
   2.3 Research questions or hypotheses (based on 1.3 and the literature review)
3. Theoretical Framework(s)
   3.1 Introduction to the theory
   3.2 Existing applications (or occasions)
   3.3 Fitness for application in the present study
4. Research Methods
   4.1 Methods to collect data (secondary: facts, examples, cases, or study results or other scholars; primary: survey, interview, experiments)
   4.2 Methods to analyze data (close reading; discourse analysis; comparison and contrast, ...; SPSS, Chi-square, t-test, regression ...)
   4.3 Reasons for choosing the selected data the using the methods for analysis
5. Findings and Discussion
   5.1 Research findings in accordance with the research questions and/or hypotheses
   5.2 Analysis and interpretations of the findings based on the theoretical framework (How helpful is the theoretical framework, how have the findings enriched the theoretical framework, or is there anything beyond the scope of the theoretical framework?)
6. Conclusion
   6.1 Brief summary of the research findings (The purposes of the study were to find ... The findings are threefold ...)
   6.2 Implications (theoretically; practically)
   6.3 Limitations and suggestions for future research
7. Works Cited/References

Glossary of Intercultural Communication Studies

A

Acculturation Difficulty   A problem stemming from an inability to appropriately adapt to a different culture or environment. The problem is not based on any coexisting mental disorder.

Achieved Status   Social status and prestige of an individual acquired as a result of individual accomplishments (cf. ascribed status).

Adaptation   Adaptation is a process of reconciliation and of coming to terms with a changed socio-cultural environment by making *adjustments* in one's cultural identity. It is also a stage of intercultural sensitivity, which may allow the person to function in a bicultural capacity. In this stage, a person is able to take the perspective of another culture and operate successfully within that culture. The person should know enough about his or her own culture and a second culture to allow a mental shift into the value scheme of the other culture, and an evaluation of behavior based on its norms, rather than the norms of the individual's culture of origin. This is referred to as *cognitive adaptation*. The more advanced form of adaptation is *behavioral adaptation*, in which the person can produce behaviors appropriate to the norms of the second culture. Adaptation may also refer to patterns of behavior which enable a culture to cope with its surroundings.

Adaptation Level   Individual standards of comparison for evaluating properties of physical and social environment such as crowding and noise.

Advocacy View   Advocacy view of applied anthropology is the belief that as anthropologists have acquired expertise on human problems and social change, and because they study, understand, and respect cultural values, they should be responsible for making policies affecting people.

Affirmative Action   Affirmative action refers to positive steps taken to increase the representation of minorities (racial, ethnic minorities and women in general) in areas of employment, education, and business from which they have been historically excluded.

Age Discrimination   Age discrimination is discrimination against a person or group on the basis of age. Age discrimination usually comes in one of two forms: discrimination against youth, and discrimination against the elderly.

Age Set   Group uniting all men or women born during a certain historical time span.

Aggregate   Any collection of individuals who do not interact with one another.

Alternative Medicine   Any form of medicine or healthcare practices which are not within the jurisdiction of the official health care delivery system nor legally sanctioned.

Ambient Environment   Changeable aspects of an individual's immediate surroundings, e. g. , light, sounds, air quality, humidity, temperature etc.

Ambient Stressors Factors in the environment that contributes to the experience of stress.

Anchor A reference point for making judgments. In social judgment theory, anchor is the point corresponding to the center of the latitude of acceptance.

Animism The belief that souls inhabit all or most objects. Animism attributes personalized souls to animals, vegetables, and minerals in a manner that the material object is also governed by the qualities which compose its particular soul. Animistic religions generally do not accept a sharp distinction between spirit and matter.

Anthropology The study of the human species and its immediate ancestors. Anthropology is the comparative study of past and contemporary cultures, focusing on the ways of life, and customs of all peoples of the world. Main sub-disciplines are physical anthropology, archaeology, linguistic anthropology, ethnology (which is also called social or cultural anthropology) and theoretical anthropology, and applied anthropology.

Apartheid A system of racial segregation used in South Africa from 1948 to the early 1990s. Though first used in 1917 by Jan Smuts, the future Prime Minister of South Africa, apartheid was simply an extension of the segregationist policies of previous white governments in South Africa. The term originates in Afrikaans or Dutch, where it means *separateness*. Races, classified by law into White, Black, Indian, and Colored groups, were separated, each with their own homelands and institutions. This prevented non-white people from having a vote or influence on the governance. Education, medical care and other public services available to non-white people were vastly inferior and non-whites were not allowed to run businesses or professional practices in those areas designated as *White South Africa*.

Arbitration Third-party assistance to two or more groups for reaching an agreement, where the third party or arbitrary has the power to force everyone to accept a particular solution. ?

Arranged Marriage Any marriage in which the selection of a spouse is outside the control of the bride and groom. Usually parents or their representatives select brides or grooms by trying to match compatibility rather than relying on romantic attraction.

Ascribed Status Ascribed status refers to a position in society which is the result of a fixed characteristic given at birth, such as gender or social class.

Assimilation A process of consistent integration whereby members of an ethno-cultural group, typically immigrants, or other minority groups, are "*absorbed*" into an established larger community. If a child assimilates into a new culture, he/she gives up his/her cultural values and beliefs and adopts the new cultural values in their place. Originates from a Piagetian (Swiss Developmental Psychologist JEAN PIAGET, 1896 – 1980) term describing a person's ability to comprehend and integrate new experiences.

Assimilation Effects Shifts in judgments towards an anchor point in social judgment theory.

Attachment Theory A theory of the formation and characterization of relationships based on the progress and outcome of an individual's experiences as an infant in relation to the primary caregiver.

Attitude Evaluation of people, objects, or issues about which an individual has some knowledge.

Availability Heuristic The tendency to be biased by events readily accessible in our memory.

B

Belief System   The way in which a culture collectively constructs a model or framework for how it thinks about something. A religion is a particular kind of belief system. Other examples of general forms of belief systems are ideologies, paradigms and world-views also known by the German word *Weltanschauung*. In addition to governing almost all aspects of human activity, belief systems have a significant impact on what a culture deems worthy of passing down to following generations as its cultural heritage. This also influences how cultures view the cultural heritage of other cultures. Many people today recognize that there is no one corrects belief system or way of thinking. This is known as relativism or conceptual relativism. This contrasts with objectivism and essentialism, both of which posit a reality that is independent of the way in which people conceptualize. A plurality of belief systems is a hallmark of *postmodernism*.

Biculturalism   The simultaneous identification with two cultures when an individual feels equally at home in both cultures and feels emotional attachment with both cultures. The term started appearing in the 1950s.

Bi-ethnic   Of two ethnic groups; belonging or relating to two different ethnic groups. Usually, used in reference to a person. For example: if a person's father is French and mother English, she is bi-ethnic though not biracial. See also *biracial*.

Bilingual Education   Teaching a second language by relying heavily on the native language of the speaker. The background theory claims that a strong sense of one's one culture and language is necessary to acquire another language and culture.

Bilateral Kinship Calculation   A system in which kinship ties are calculated equally through both sexes: mother and father, sister and brother, daughter and son, and so on.

Biological Determinists   Those who argue that human behavior and social organization are biologically determined and not learnt.

Biracial   Of two races. Usually, used to refer to people whose parents come from two different races, e. g., father is Chinese and mother English.

Bottom-up Development   Economic and social changes brought about by activities of individuals and social groups in society rather than by the state and its agents.

Bride Price   The payment made by a man to the family from whom he takes a daughter in marriage.

C

Complementary Medicine   Traditional or alternative health beliefs or practices which are brought into a healing practice to enhance the dominant healthcare modality.

Corporate Culture   The fundamental philosophy of an organization is determined by its corporate culture. The behavior and actions of individuals within a corporation illustrate the existing culture of that organization.

Capital   Wealth or resources invested in business, with the intent of producing a profit for the owner of the capital.

Capitalist World Economy   The single world system, committed to production for sale, with the object of maximizing profits rather than supplying domestic needs. The term was launched by the

US historical social scientist, Immanuel Wallenstein.

Capitalism Economic or socio-economic system in which production and distribution are designed to accumulate capital and create profit. A characteristic feature of the system is the separation of those who own the means of production and those who work for them. *The Communist Manifesto* by Karl Marx and Friedrich Engels first used the term Kapitalist in 1848. The first use of the word capitalism is by novelist William Thackeray in 1854.

Caste System Hereditary system of stratification. Hierarchical social status is ascribed at birth and often dictated by religion or other social norms. Today, it is most commonly associated with the Indian caste system and the *Varna* in Hinduism.

Charlie Non-derogatory slang term used by American troops during the Vietnam War as a shorthand term for Vietnamese guerrillas. Shortened from *"Victor Charlie"*, the phonetic alphabet for Viet Cong, or VC. It was also a mildly derogatory term used by African Americans, in the 1960s and 1970s, for a white person (from James Baldwin's novel, *Blues for Mr. Charlie*).

Chiefdom Kin-based form of sociopolitical organization between the tribe and the state. It comes with differential access to resources and a permanent political structure. The relations among villages as well as among individuals are unequal, with smaller villages under the authority of leaders in larger villages; it has a two-level settlement hierarchy.

Clan Form of unilateral descent group based on stipulated descent. A clan is a group of people united by kinship and descent, which is defined by perceived descent from a common ancestor. As kinship based bonds can be merely symbolical in nature some clans share a *"stipulated"* common ancestor.

Clash of Civilizations A hotly debated theory publicized by Samuel P. Huntington with his book *The Clash of Civilizations and the Remaking of World Order*. He argues that the world has cultural fault lines similar to the physical ones that cause earthquakes and that people's cultural/religious identity will be the primary agent of conflict in the post-Cold War world.

Collateral Household A type of expanded family household including siblings and their spouses and children.

Collectivism Individualism/collectivism is one of the Hofstede dimensions in intercultural communication studies. Collectivism pertains to societies in which people from birth onwards are integrated into strong, cohesive in-groups, which throughout people's lifetime continue to protect them in exchange for unquestioning loyalty. (Hofstede, G., 1991).

Colonialism The political, social, economic, and cultural domination of a territory and its people by a foreign power for an extended time.

Communism A political theory of Karl Marx and Friedrich Engels. Communism is characterized by the common ownership of the means of production contra private ownership in capitalism. The Soviet Union was the first communist state and lasted from 1917 to 1991.

Complex Societies Complex societies are usually nation states; large and populous, with social stratification and centralized forms of governments.

Consanguineal Kin A blood relative. An individual related by common descent from the same individual. In most societies of the world, kinship can be traced both by common descent and through marriage, although a distinction is usually made between the two categories. The degree of consanguinity between any two people can be calculated as the percentage of genes they share through common descent.

Contact Zone　The space in which transculturation takes place—where two different cultures meet and inform each other, often in highly asymmetrical ways.

Core Values　Basic, or central values that integrate a culture and help distinguish it from others.

Cosmology　Ideas and beliefs about the universe as an ordered system, its origin and the place of humans in the universe through which, people in that culture understand the makeup and the workings of all things.

Counterculture　A sociological term used to describe a cultural or social group whose values and norms are at odds with those of the social mainstream. The term became popular during the youth rebellion and unrest in the USA and Western Europe in the 1960s as a reaction against the conservative social norms of the 1950s. The Russian term *Counterculture* has a different meaning and is used to define a cultural movement that promotes acting outside the usual conventions of

Cross Cousins　Children of a brother and a sister.

Cross Cultural　Interaction between individuals from different cultures. The term cross-cultural is generally used to describe comparative studies of cultures. Inter cultural is also used for the same meaning.

Cross-Cultural Awareness　Cross-cultural awareness develops from cross-cultural knowledge as the learner understands and appreciates the deeper functioning of a culture. This may also be followed by changes in the learner's own behavior and attitudes and a greater flexibility and openness becomes visible.

Cross-Cultural Communication　Cross-cultural communication (also referred to as *Intercultural Communication*) is a field of study that looks at how people from differing cultural backgrounds try to communicate. As a science, Cross-cultural communication tries to bring together such seemingly unrelated disciplines as communication, information theory, learning theories and cultural anthropology. The aim is to produce increased understanding and some guidelines, which would help people from different cultures to better, communicate with each other.

Cross-Cultural Communication Skills　Cross-cultural communication skills refers to the ability to recognize cultural differences and similarities when dealing with someone from another culture and also the ability to recognize features of own behavior, which are affected by culture.

Cross-Cultural Competence　The final stage of cross-cultural learning and signals the individual's ability to work effectively across cultures. Cross cultural competency necessitates more than knowledge,

Cross-Cultural Knowledge　Cross-cultural knowledge refers to a surface level familiarization with cultural characteristics, values, beliefs and behaviors. It is vital to basic cross-cultural understanding and without it cross-cultural competence cannot develop.

Cross-Cultural Sensitivity　Cross-cultural sensitivity refers to an individual's ability to read into situations, contexts and behaviors that are culturally rooted and consequently the individual is able to react to them suitably. A suitable response necessitates that the individual no longer carries his/her own culturally predetermined interpretations of the situation or behavior (i. e.

good/bad, right/wrong).

Cultural Alienation　The process of devaluing or abandoning one's own culture or cultural background in favor of another.

Cultural Anthropology　The study of contemporary and recent historical cultures among humans all over the world. The focus is on social organization, culture change, economic and political systems and religion. Cultural anthropologists argue that culture is *human nature*, and that all people have a capacity to classify experiences, encode classifications symbolically and teach such abstractions to others. They believe that humans acquire culture through learning and people living in different places or different circumstances may develop different cultures because it is through culture that people can adapt to their environment in non-genetic ways. Cultural anthropology is also referred to as social or socio-cultural anthropology. Key theorists: Franz Boas, Emile Durkheim, Clifford Geertz, Marvin Harris, Claude Levi-Strauss, Karl Marx.

Cultural Boundaries　Cultural boundaries can be defined as those invisible lines, which divide territories, cultures, traditions, practices, and worldviews. Typically, they are not aligned with the physical boundaries of political entities such as nation states.

Cultural Components　Attributes that vary from culture to culture, including religion, language, architecture, cuisine, technology, music, dance, sports, medicine, dress, gender roles, laws, education, government, agriculture, economy, grooming, values, work ethic, etiquette, courtship, recreation, and gestures.

Culturally Competent Healthcare　Healthcare practice which recognizes the importance of cultural beliefs and practices in restoration and maintenance of health, and thus adapts, modifies and reorients perceptions and practices within a bio-medical setting in response to the cultural background of the patient.

Cultural Competency　The ability to respond respectfully and effectively to people of all cultures, classes, ethnic background and religions in a manner that recognizes and values cultural differences and similarities.

Cultural Construct　The idea that the characteristics people attribute to social categories such as gender, illness, death, status of women, and status of men is culturally defined.

Cultural Convergence　An idea that increased communication among the peoples of the world via the Internet will lead to the differences among national cultures becoming smaller over time, eventually resulting in the formation of a single global culture. One outcome of this process is that unique national identities will disappear, replaced by a single transnational identity. Henry Jenkins, a professor at the Massachusetts Institute of Technology, USA coined the term in 1998.

Cultural Cringe　Cultural cringe refers to an internalized inferiority complex of an entire culture. This leads people of that culture to dismiss their own culture as inferior to the cultures of other countries. In 1950 the Melbourne critic A. A. Philips coined the term Cultural cringe to show how Australians widely assumed that anything produced by local artists, dramatists, actors, musicians and writers was inferior to the works of the British and European counterparts. The term cultural cringe is very close to cultural alienation or the process of devaluing or abandoning one's own culture or cultural background in favor of another.

Cultural Determinists　Cultural determinists are those who relate behavior and social organization to cultural or environmental factors. The focus is on variation rather than on universals and stresses learning and the role of culture in human adaptation.

Cultural Diffusion The spreading of a cultural trait (e. g. , material object, idea, or behavior pattern) from one society to another.

Cultural Dissonance Elements of discord or lack of agreement within a culture.

Cultural Diversity Differences in race, ethnicity, language, nationality or religion. Cultural diversity refers to the variety or multiformity of human social structures, belief systems, and strategies for adapting to situations in different parts of the world.

Cultural Evolution Theories that have developed since the mid-19th century, which attempt to explain processes and patterns of cultural change. Often such theories have presented such change as progress, from earlier forms (*primitive*, *less developed*, *less advanced* etc.) to later forms (*more developed*, *more advanced*). These schemes usually have reflected the ethnocentrism of the theorists, as they frequently put their own societies at the pinnacle of progress.

Cultural Identity Cultural identity is the identity of a group or culture, or of an individual as her/his belonging to a group or culture affects her/his view of her/him. People who feel they belong to the same culture share a common set of norms.

Cultural Imperialism Cultural imperialism is the rapid spread or advance of one culture at the expense of others, or its imposition on other cultures, which it modifies, replaces, or destroys—usually due to economic or political reasons.

Cultural Landscape The natural landscape as modified by human activities and bearing the imprint of a culture group or society including buildings, shrines, signage, sports and recreational facilities, economic and agricultural structures, transportation systems, etc.

Cultural Materialism Cultural materialism is a theoretical approach in Cultural Anthropology that explores and examines culture as a reflection or product of material conditions in a society. Cultural materialism is a variation on basic materialist approaches to understanding culture. The Anthropologist Marvin Harris is a famous representative.

Cultural Norms Cultural norms are behavior patterns that are typical of specific groups, which have distinct identities, based on culture, language, ethnicity or race separating them from other groups. Such behaviors are learned early in life from parents, teachers, peers and other human interaction. Norms are the unwritten rules that govern individual behavior. Norms assume importance especially when broken or when an individual finds him/herself in a foreign environment dealing with an unfamiliar culture where the norms are different.

Cultural Relativism The position that the values, beliefs and customs of cultures differ and deserve recognition and acceptance. This principle was established by the German anthropologist Franz Boas (1858 – 1942) in the first few decades of the 20th century. Cultural relativism as a movement was in part a response to Western ethnocentrism. Between World War I and World War II, Cultural relativism was the central tool for American anthropologists in their refusal of Western claims to universality.

Cultural Resource Management (CRM) Cultural resource management is the branch of applied archaeology which aims to preserve archeological sites threatened by prospective dams, highways, and other projects.

Cultural Rights Cultural rights is the idea that certain rights are vested not in individuals but in larger identifiable groups, such as religious and ethnic minorities and indigenous societies. Cultural rights include a group's ability to preserve its culture, to raise its children in the ways of its ancestors, to continue practicing its language, and not to be deprived of its economic base by the nation-state or large political entity in which it is located.

Cultural Safety Cultural safety refers to an environment that is safe for all people. An environment where there's no denial of or challenge to their identity or to who they are. It is a space that embraces the differences between people and allows for a shared experience of respect, acknowledgement, and understanding.

Cultural Sensitivity Cultural sensitivity is a necessary component of cultural competence, meaning that we make an effort to be aware of the potential and actual cultural factors that affect our interactions with others.

Cultural Traits Distinguishing features of a culture such as language, dress, religion, values, and an emphasis on family; these traits are shared throughout that culture.

Cultural Universality General cultural traits and features found in all societies of the world. Some examples are organization of family life; roles of males, females, children and elders; division of labor; religious beliefs and practices; birth and death rituals; stories of creation and myths for explaining the unknown; *rights* and *wrongs* of behavior etc.

Cultural Universalism Cultural universalism is the assertion that there exist values, which transcend cultural and national differences. Universalism claims that more primitive cultures will eventually evolve to have the same system of law and rights as Western cultures. Cultural relativists on the other hand hold an opposite viewpoint, that a traditional culture is unchangeable. In universalism, an individual is a social unit, possessing inalienable rights, and driven by the pursuit of self-interest. In the cultural relativist model, a community is the basic social unit where concepts such as individualism, freedom of choice, and equality are absent.

Cultural Values The individual's desirable or preferred way of acting or knowing something that is sustained over time and that governs actions

Culture The shared values, norms, traditions, customs, arts, history, folklore and institutions of a group of people. "Integrated pattern of human knowledge, belief, and behavior that is both a result of an integral to the human capacity for learning and transmitting knowledge to succeeding generations." The etymological root of the word is from the Latin "colere" which means to cultivate, from which is derived "cultus", that which is cultivated or fashioned. In comparison of words such as kultur and zivilisation in German, culture and civilization in English, and culture and civilization in French the concepts reveal very different perspectives. The meaning of these concepts is however, converging across languages as a result of international contacts, cultural exchanges and other information processes.

Culture Shock A state of distress and tension with possible physical symptoms after a person relocates to an unfamiliar cultural environment. This term was used by social scientists in the 1950s to describe, the difficulties of a person moving from the country to a big city but now the meaning has changed to mean relocating to a different culture or country. One of the first recorded uses of the term was in 1954 by the anthropologist Dr. Kalervo Oberg who was born to Finnish parents in British Columbia, Canada. While giving a talk to the Women's Club of Rio de Janeiro, August 3, 1954, he identified four stages of culture shock—the honeymoon of being a newcomer and guest, the hostility and aggressiveness of coming to grips with different way of life, working through feelings of superiority and gaining ability to operate in the culture by learning the language and finally acceptance of another way of living and worldview.

D

Daughter Languages　Daughter languages are languages developing out of the same parent language; for example, French and Spanish are daughter languages of Latin or Bengali and Hindi are daughter languages of Sanskrit.

Debriefing　Open discussion at the end of a study or experiment when the researcher reveals the complete procedure and background to the subject and explains the reasons for any possible deceptions that may have taken place and were necessary for the success.

Demarginalization　The process which facilitates a marginal or stigmatized space becoming normalized so that its population is incorporated into the mainstream.

Descent Group　Descent group is a permanent social unit whose members claim common ancestry. Usually this is fundamental to tribal society.

Differential Access　Differential access refers to unequal access to resources, which is the basic attribute of different social structures from chiefdoms and states.

Diffuse　Diffuse/specific is one of the value dimensions proposed by Trompenaars & Hampden-Turner. It shows *how far we choose to get involved*. In a very diffuse culture, a large part of the life is regarded as *private*, where other persons without explicit consent have no access.

Diffusion　Diffusion is the borrowing of cultural traits between societies, either directly or through intermediaries.

Dimensions of Diversity　Dimensions of diversity in humans includes, but is not limited to: culture, gender, age, ethnicity, nationality, geography, lifestyle, education, income, health, physical appearance, pigmentation, language, personality, beliefs, faith, dreams, interests, aspirations, skills, professions, perceptions, and experiences.

Diversity　The concept of diversity means understanding that each individual is unique, and recognizing individual differences along the dimensions of race, ethnicity, gender, sexual orientation, socio-economic status, age, physical abilities, religious beliefs, political beliefs, or other ideologies. Primary dimensions are those that cannot be changed e.g., age, ethnicity, gender, physical abilities/qualities, race and sexual orientation. Secondary dimensions of diversity are those that can be changed, e.g., educational background, geographic location, income, marital status, parental status, religious beliefs, and work role/experiences. Diversity or diversity management includes, therefore, knowing how to relate to those qualities and conditions that are different from our own and outside the groups to which we belong.

Diversity Initiative　Sets of policy, definitions, action-plans and steps to map out, support and protect diversity in different dimensions such as age, gender ethnicity etc. in any organization, society or area.

Dominant Culture There is usually one dominant culture in each area that forms the basis for defining that culture. This is determined by power and control in cultural institutions (church, government, education, mass media, monetary systems, and economics). Often, those in the dominant culture do not see the privilege that accrues to them by being dominant "norm" and do not identify themselves as being the dominant culture. Rather, they believe that their cultural norm.

Dowry A marital exchange in which the wife's family provides substantial gifts of money, goods or property to the husband's family. The opposite direction, property given to the bride by the groom, is called dower.

E

Egalitarianism Affirming, promoting, or characterized by belief in equal political, economic, social, and civil rights for all people. One of the seven fundamental value dimensions of Shalom Schwartz measuring how other people are recognized as moral equals.

Embeddedness One of the seven fundamental value dimensions of Shalom Schwartz describing people as part of a collective.

Enculturation Enculturation is the process whereby an established culture teaches an individual its accepted norms and values, by establishing a context of boundaries and correctness that dictates what is and is not permissible within that society's framework. Enculturation is learned through communication by way of speech, words, action and gestures. The six components of culture learnt are: technological, economic, political, interactive, and ideological and worldview. It is also called socialization (Conrad Phillip Kottack, *Cultural Anthropology*).

Endogamy Endogamy is the practice of marrying within one's own social group. Cultures that practice endogamy require marriage between specified social groups, classes, or ethnicities. Strictly endogamous communities like the Jews, the Parsees of India and the Yazidi of Iraq claim that endogamy helps minorities to survive over a long time in societies with other practices and beliefs. The opposite practice is exogamy.

Equity, Increased A reduction in absolute poverty and a fairer or more even distribution of wealth in a particular society or nation state.

Ethnic Competence The capacity to function effectively in more than one culture, requiring the ability to appreciate and understand features of other ethnic groups and further to interact with people of ethnic groups other than one's own.

Ethnic Group Group characterized by cultural similarities (shared among members of that group) and differences (between that group and others). Members of an ethnic group share beliefs, values, habits, customs, norms, a common language, religion, history, geography, kinship, and/or race.

Ethnicity Belonging to a common group with shared heritage, often linked by race, nationality and language.

Ethnocentrism Belief in the superiority of one's own ethnic group. Seeing the world through the lenses of one's own people or culture so that own culture always looks best and becomes the pattern everyone else should fit into.

Ethnography A research methodology associated with anthropology and sociology that systematically tries to describe the culture of a group of people by trying to understand the natives'/insiders' view of their own world (an emic view of the world).

Ethnology Cross-cultural comparison or the comparative study of ethnographic data, of society and of culture

Ethnomusicology The comparative study of the music's of different places of the world and of music as a central aspect of culture and society.

Ethnosemantics The study of meaning attached to specific terms used by members of a group. Ethnosemantics concentrates on the meaning of categories of reality and folk taxonomies to the people who use them.

Exogamy The custom of marrying outside a specific group to which one belongs. Some experts hold that the custom of exogamy originated from a scarcity of women, which forced men to seek wives from other groups, e.g., marriage by capture. Another viewpoint ascribes the origin of exogamy to totemism, and claim that a religious respect for the blood of a totemic clan, led to exogamy. The opposite of exogamy is *endogamy*.

Expatriate Someone who has left his or her home country to live and work in another country. When we go to another country to live, we become expatriates or expats for short.

Extended Family The relatives of an individual, both by blood and by marriage, other than its immediate family, such as aunts, uncles, grandparents and cousins, who live in close proximity and often under one roof. Extended families are very common in collectivistic cultures. This is the opposite of the nuclear family.

Family of Orientation Nuclear family in which one is born and grows up.

Family of Procreation Nuclear family established when one marries and has children.

Feminity Masculinity/feminity is one of the Hofstede dimensions. Hofstede defines this dimension as follows: "femininity pertains to societies in which social agenda roles overlap (i.e., men and women are supposed be modest, tender, and concerned with the quality of life)".

Feudalism Hierarchical social and political system common in Europe during the medieval period. The majority of the population was engaged in subsistence agriculture while simultaneously having an obligation to fulfill certain duties for the landholder. At the same time the landholder owed various obligations called fealty to his overlord.

First Nation The indigenous population of Canada, excepting the Inuit or Métis people. The term came into common usage in the 1980s to refer mostly to Canada's aboriginal people, most of who live around Ontario and British Columbia.

G

Gender Discrimination Gender discrimination is any action that allows or denies opportunities, privileges or rewards to a person on the basis of their gender alone.

Glass Ceiling The term glass ceiling describes the process by which women are barred from promotion by means of an invisible barrier. In the United States, the Glass Ceiling Commission has stated that women represent 1.1 percent of inside directors (those drawn from top management of the company) on the boards of Fortune 500 companies.

Gender Roles The tasks and activities that a culture assigns to each sex.

Gender Stereotypes Gender stereotypes are oversimplified but strongly held ideas about the characteristics, roles and behavior models of males and females.

Gender Stratification Unequal distribution of rewards (socially valued resources, power, prestige, and personal freedom) between men and women, depending on their different positions in a social hierarchy.

Generalized Reciprocity The principle that characterizes exchanges between closely related individuals. As social distance increases, reciprocity becomes balanced and finally negative.

Genetic Marker A known DNA sequence of the human DNA. Genetic markers can be used to study the relationship between an inherited disease and its likely genetic cause.

Genitor Biological father of a child.

Global Culture One world culture. The earth's inhabitants will lose their individual cultural diversity and one culture will remain for all the people.

Globalization A disputed term relating to transformation in the relationship between space, economy and society. The International Monetary Fund defines globalization as "the growing economic interdependence of countries worldwide through increasing volume and variety of cross-border transactions in goods and services, free international capital flows, and more rapid and widespread diffusion of technology." Meanwhile, The International Forum on Globalization defines it as "the present worldwide drive toward a globalized economic system dominated by supranational corporate trade and banking institutions that are not accountable to democratic processes or national governments."

H

Helping Behavior Prosocial behavior that benefits others more than the person. Different from prosocial cooperation, in which mutual benefit is gained.

Hierarchy One of the seven fundamental value dimensions of Shalom Schwartz measuring the unequal distribution of power in a culture.

High Context and Low Context Cultures According to Hall (1981), all communication (verbal as well as nonverbal) is contextually bound. What we do or do not pay attention to is largely dictated by cultural contexting. In low-context cultures, the majority of the information is explicitly communicated in the verbal message. In high-context cultures the information is embedded in the context. High-context and low-context cultures also differ in their definition of social and power hierarchies, relationships, work ethics, business practices, time management. Low-context cultures tend to emphasize the individual while high-context cultures places more importance on the collective.

Historical Linguistics Also called diachronic linguistics, Historical Linguistics is the study of how and why languages change.

Holistic Emphasizing the importance of the whole and the interdependence of its parts. Interested in the whole of the human condition: past, present, and future; biology, society, language, and culture.

Holocultural Analysis A paradigm of research for testing hypotheses "by means of correlations found in a worldwide, comparative study whose units of study are entire societies or cultures, and whose sampling universe is either all known cultures or all known primitive tribes".

Human Rights　　Human rights refers to the basic rights and freedoms to which all humans irrespective of countries, cultures, politics, languages, skin color and religions are entitled. Examples of human rights are the right to life and liberty, freedom of expression, and equality before the law, the right to participate in culture, the right to work, the right to hold religious beliefs without persecution, and to not be enslaved, or imprisoned without charge and the right to education.

Hybridity　　Refers to groups as a mixture of local and non-local influences; their character and cultural attributes is a product of contact with the world beyond a local place. The term originates from agriculture and has for a long time been strongly related to pejorative concepts of racism and racial purity from western colonial history.

Hyperdescent　　The practice of determining the lineage of a child of mixed race ancestry by assigning the child the race of his more socially dominant parent (opposite of Hypodescent).

Hypodescent　　A social rule that automatically places the children of a union or mating between members of different socioeconomic groups in the less-privileged group. In its most extreme form in the United States, hypodescent came to be known as the "one drop rule", meaning that if a person had one drop of black blood, he was considered black. The opposite of hypodescent is hyperdescent.

I

Imaginary Geographies　　The ideas and representations that divide the world into spaces and areas with specific meanings and associations. These can exist on different scales e.g. the imaginaries that divide the world into a developed core and less developed peripheries or the imagined divide between the deprived inner city and the affluent suburbs (Sibley).

Imperialism　　A policy of extending the rule of a nation or empire over foreign nations or of taking and holding foreign colonies by forceful conquest.

Independent Invention　　Appearance of the same cultural trait or pattern in separate cultures as a result of comparable needs and circumstances.

Indigenized　　Adapted or modified to fit the local culture.

Indigenous Peoples　　Those peoples native to a particular territory that was later colonized, particularly by Europeans. Other terms for indigenous peoples include aborigines, native peoples, first peoples, Fourth World, first nations and autochthonous (this last term having a derivation from Greek, meaning *sprung from the earth*). The UN Permanent Forum on Indigenous Issues estimates range from 300 million to 350 million as of the start of the 21st century or just fewer than 6 percent of the total world population. This includes at least 5000 distinct peoples in over 72 countries.

Individualism　　Individualism/collectivism is one of the Hofstede dimensions in intercultural communication studies. He defines this dimension as: "individualism pertains to societies in which the ties between individuals are loose; everyone is expected to look after himself or herself and his or her immediate family".

International Culture　Cultural traditions that extend beyond the boundaries of nation states.
Integration　The bringing of people of different racial or ethnic groups into unrestricted and equal association, as in society or an organization; desegregation. An individual integrates when s/he becomes a part of the existing society.
Interpretive Approach in Cultural Anthropology　Regards culture as texts, to be read and translated for their thick meaning. Clifford Geertz is an example of those who represents this approach.

J

Jati　A local subcastes in Hindu India.
Joint Family Household　A complex family unit formed through polygyny or polyandry or through the decision of married siblings to live together with or without their parents.
Jook Sing　A Chinese term used to refer to American Born Chinese of either U.S. or Canadian birth. Meaning hollow bamboo in Cantonese, it suggests that the target of the remark may be Chinese on the outside, but lacks the cultural beliefs and values that would make them truly Chinese.

K

Kinesics　The study of non-linguistic bodily movements, such as gestures, stances and facial expressions as a systematic mode of communication.
Kinship Calculation　The system by which people in a particular society reckon kin relationships.

L

Language　The primary means of communication for humans. It may be spoken or written and features productivity and displacement and is culturally transmitted.
Levirate　Custom by which a widow marries the brother of her deceased husband.
Life Expectancy　The length of time that a person can, on the average, expect to live.
Life History　Life History provides a personal cultural portrait of existence or change in a culture.
Liminality　The critically important marginal or in-between phase of a rite of passage.
Lineage　Unilineal descent group based on demonstrated descent.
Lineal Relative　Any of ego's or principal subject's ancestors or descendants (e.g., parents, grandparents, children, grandchildren) on the direct line of descent that leads to and from ego.
Linguistic Anthropology　The descriptive, comparative, and historical study of language and of linguistic similarities and differences in time, space, and society.

M

Magic　Use of supernatural techniques to accomplish specific aims. Common in many societies. Example: Folk magic, Witchcraft or Voodoo.
Mana　Sacred impersonal force in Melanesian and Polynesian religions.
Masculinity　One of the Hofstede dimensions. Hofstede defines this dimension as follows: "masculinity pertains to societies in which social roles are clearly distinct (i.e., men are supposed to be assertive, tough and focused on material success whereas women are supposed to be more

modest, tender and concerned with the quality of life)".
Mater   Socially recognized mother of a child.
Matriarchy   A society ruled by women. There is consensus among modern anthropologists and sociologists that a strictly matriarchal society never existed, but there are examples of matrifocal societies. There exist many matriarchal animal societies including bees, elephants, and killer whales. The word matriarchy is coined as the opposite of Patriarchy.
Matrifocal   Mother-centered society. It often refers to a household with no resident husband-father.
Matrilineage   Line of descent as traced through women on the maternal side of a family. In some cultures, membership of a specific group is inherited matrilineally. For example, one is a Jew if one's mother (rather than one's father) is a Jew. The Nairs of Kerala, India are also matrilineal.
Matrilocality   Customary residence with the wife's relatives after marriage, so that children grow up in their mother's community. The Nair community in Kerala in South India and the Mosuo of Yunnan and Sichuan in southwestern China are contemporary examples.
Meritocracy   A system of government based on rule by ability or merit rather than by wealth, race or other determinants of social position. Nowadays this term refers to openly competitive societies like the USA where large inequalities of income and wealth accrued by merit rather than birth is accepted. In contrast egalitarian societies like the Scandinavian countries aim to reduce such disparities of wealth.
Mestizo   A term used to refer to people of partly Native American descent from Spanish.
Minority Group   A group that occupies a subordinate position in a society. Minorities may be separated by physical or cultural traits disapproved of by the dominant group and as a result often experience discrimination. Minorities may not always be defined along social, ethnic, religious or sexual lines but could be broad based, e. g., non-citizens or foreigners.
Monoethnic   Belonging to the same ethnic group.
Monotheism   Worship of an eternal, omniscient, omnipotent, and omnipresent supreme being. Judaism and Islam are examples.
Morphology   The study of form. It is used in linguistics (the study of morphemes and word construction).
Monochronic   E. T. Hall introduced the concept of Polychronic/Monochronic cultures. According to him, in monochronic cultures, people try to sequence actions on the *one thing at a time* principle. Interpersonal relations are subordinate to time schedules and deadlines.
Mulato   A term used for people of partly African descent. Originates from Spanish.
Multiculturalism   A belief or policy that endorses the principle of cultural diversity of different cultural and ethnic groups so that they retain distinctive cultural identities. The United States is understood as *a mosaic* of various and diverse cultures, as opposed to the single monolithic culture that results from the *melting pot* or assimilation model. Pluralism tends to focus on differences within the whole, while multiculturalism emphasizes the individual groups that make up the whole. The term multiculturalism is also used to refer to strategies and measures intended to promote diversity. According to Wikipedia, the word was first used in 1957 to describe Switzerland, but came into common currency in Canada in the late 1960s.

Multiracial The terms multiracial and mixed-race describe people whose parents are not the same race. Multiracial is more commonly used to describe a society or group of people from more than one racial or ethnic group. Mulato (for people of partly African descent) and mestizo (people of partly Native American descent) in Spanish and métis in Canadian French (for people of mixed white and original inhabitants of Canada descent) are also used in English.

Myth Story told in one's culture to explain things like the creation of the world, and the behavior of its inhabitants.

N

Nation Earlier a synonym for ethnic group, designating a single culture sharing a language, religion, history, territory, ancestry, and kinship. Now usually a synonym for state or nation-state.

National Culture Cultural experiences, beliefs, learned behavior patterns, and values shared by citizens of the same nation.

Nationalities Ethnic groups that have, once had, or wish to have or regain, autonomous political status (their own country).

Nation-State A symbolic system of institutions claiming sovereignty over a bounded territory. The Oxford English Dictionary defines *nation-state*: a sovereign state of which most of the citizens or subjects are united also by factors which define a nation, such as language or common descent. Japan and Iceland could be two examples of near ideal nation-states.

Négritude Black association and identity. It is an idea developed by dark-skinned intellectuals in Francophone (French-speaking) West Africa and the Caribbean. ?

Neolocality Postmarital residence pattern in which a couple establishes a new place of residence rather than living with or near either set of parents.

Nuclear Family A household consisting of two heterosexual parents and their children as distinct from the extended family. Nuclear families are typical in societies where people must be relatively mobile e. g. , hunter-gatherers and industrial societies.

O

One-World Culture A belief that the future will bring development of a single homogeneous world culture through advances and links created by modern communication, transportation and trade.

Open Class System Stratification system that facilitates social mobility, with individual achievement and personal merit determining social rank.

Overinnovation Characteristic of projects that require major changes in the daily lives of the natives in the target community, especially ones that interfere with customary subsistence pursuits.

P

Paradigm The set of fundamental assumptions that influence how people think and how they perceive the world.

Paradigmatic View　An approach to science, developed by Thomas Kuhn, which holds that science develops from a set of assumptions (paradigm) and that revolutionary science ends with the acceptance of a new paradigm which ushers in a period of normal science.

Parallel Cousins　Children of two brothers or two sisters.

Particularity　Distinctive or unique culture trait, pattern, or integration.

Participant Observation　Technique for cross-cultural adjustment. This entails keeping a detailed record of your observations, interactions and interviews while living in a culture that is not your own. Participant observation is also a fundamental method of research used in cultural anthropology. A researcher lives within a given culture for an extended period of time, to take part in its daily life in all its richness and diversity. The anthropologist in this approach tries to experience a culture from within, as a person native to that culture is presumed to.

Participative Competence　The ability to interact on equal terms in multicultural environments so that knowledge is shared and the learning experience is professionally enhancing for all involved. Even when using a second language, people with high participative competence are able to contribute equitably to the common task under discussion and can also share knowledge, communicate experience, and stimulate group learning to benefit all parties.

Particularism　One of the value dimensions as proposed by Trompenaars & Hampden-Turner. It reflects the preference for rules over relationships (or vice versa). Particularist societies tend to be more flexible with rules, and acknowledge the unique circumstances around a particular rule.

Pater　Socially recognized father of a child though not necessarily the genitor or biological father.

Patriarchy　Political system ruled by men in which women have inferior social and political status, including basic human rights.

Patrilineage　Line of descent as traced through men on the paternal side of a family each of whom is related to the common ancestor through males. Synonym is agnation and opposite is matrilineage.

Patrilocality　Customary residence with the husband's relatives after marriage, so that children grow up in their father's community.

Peers Pressure　The influences that people of the same rank, age or group have on each other. Under peer pressure a group norm of attitudes and/or behaviors may override individual moral inhibitions, sexual personal habits or individual attitudes or behavioral patterns.

Periphery　The weakest structural position in the world system.

Personal Space　Humans desire to have a pocket of space around them and into which they tend to resent others intruding. Personal space is highly variable. Those who live in a densely populated environment tend to have smaller personal space requirements. Thus a resident of a city in India or China may have a smaller personal space than someone who lives in Northern Lapland. See also *Proxemics*.

Phonetics　The study of speech sounds in general; what people actually say in various languages.

Phylogenetic Tree　A graphic representation of evolutionary relationships among animal species.

Plural Society　A society that combines ethnic contrasts and economic interdependence of the ethnic groups.

Polyandry　A variety of plural marriage in which a woman has more than one husband.

Polytheism　Belief in several deities who control aspects of nature. The ancient Greeks believed that their gods were independent deities who weren't aspects of a great deity.

Polychronic　The concept of polychronic/monochronic cultures was introduced by E. T. Hall. He suggested that in Polychronic cultures, multiple tasks are handled at the same time, and time is subordinate to interpersonal relations.

Postcolonial　Refers to interactions between European nations and the societies they colonized (mainly after 1800). "Postcolonial" may be used to signify a position against imperialism and Eurocentrism.

Postmodern　Describes the blurring and breakdown of established canons (rules, standards), categories, distinctions, and boundaries.

Postmodernity　Postmodernity refers to the condition of a world in flux, with people on the move, in which established groups, boundaries, identities, contrasts, and standards are breaking down.

Post-Partum Sex Taboo　The prohibition of a woman from having sexual intercourse for a specified period of time following the birth of a child.

Power Distance　One of the Hofstede dimensions of national cultures. "The extent to which the less powerful members of institutions and organizations within a country expect and accept that power is distributed unequally".

Power Geometry　The notion of power geometry is a product of globalization and refers to the ways that different groups of individuals interact at different scales, linking local development to national, international, and global processes.

Prejudice　Over-generalized, oversimplified or exaggerated beliefs associated with a category or group of people. These beliefs are not easily changed, even in the fact of contrary evidence.

Progeny Price　A gift from the husband and his kin to the wife and her kin before, at, or after marriage. It legitimizes children born to the woman as members of the husband's descent group.

Protoculture　The simplest or beginning aspects of culture as seen in some nonhuman primates.

Proto-language　A language ancestral to several daughter languages. Example: Latin or Sanskrit.

Proxemics　The study of human perception and use of space. Proxemics tries to identify the distance and the way the space around persons are organized. In some cultures, people are comfortable with being very close, or even touching each other as a normal sign of friendship. In other cultures, touching and sitting/standing very close can cause considerable discomfort.

Purdah　The Muslim or Hindu practice of keeping women hidden from men outside their own family; or, a curtain, veil, or the like used for such a purpose.

Q

Qualitative Research　Qualitative research involves the gathering of data through methods that involve observing forms of behavior e. g. , conversations, non-verbal communication, rituals, displays of emotion, which cannot easily be expressed in terms of quantities or numbers.

Quantitative Research　Quantitative research is the systematic scientific investigation of quantitative or measurable properties and phenomena and interrelationships. Quantitative research aims to develop and employ hypotheses, theories and models, which can be verified scientifically.

Questionnaire　Survey research technique in which the researcher supplies written questions to the subject, who gives written answers to the questions asked.

R

Racism　Theories, attitudes and practices that display dislike or antagonism towards people seen as belonging to particular ethnic groups. Social or political significance is attached to culturally constructed ideas of difference.

Ranked Society　A society in which there is an unequal division of status and power between its members, where such divisions are based primarily on such factors as family and inherited social position. This is in contrast with egalitarian society, which aims to minimize such unequal divisions.

Reciprocity　One of the three principles of exchange. It governs exchange between social equals and is a major exchange mode in band and tribal societies. Since virtually all humans live in some kind of society and have at least a few possessions, reciprocity is common to every culture. Reciprocity is the basis of most non-market economies.

Relativism　A willingness to consider other persons' or groups' theories and values as equally reasonable as one's own.

Rites of Passage　Culturally defined activities (rituals) that mark a person's transition from one stage of life to another. These aim to help participants move into new social roles, positions or statuses. Puberty, wedding, childbirth are examples.

Ritual　Behavior that is formal, stylized, repetitive, and stereotyped. A ritual is performed earnestly as a social act. Rituals are held at set times and places and have liturgical orders.

S

Sample　A smaller study group chosen to represent a larger population.

Sapir　Sapir-Whorf hypothesis (SWH) (also known as the linguistic relativity hypothesis) is a theory that different languages produce different ways of thinking. It postulates a systematic relationship between the grammatical categories of the language a person speaks and how that person both understands the world and behaves in it.

Scapegoating　The directing of hostility towards less powerful groups when the actual source of frustration or anger cannot be attacked or is unavailable.

Schema　An organized pattern of knowledge, acquired from past experience, humans use to interpret current experience.

Script　A conceptual representation of a stereotyped sequence of events.

Self-Awareness　A psychological state in which individuals focus their attention on and evaluate different aspects of their self-concepts. These can vary from physical experiences to differences between Ideal self and Real self.

Self-Categorization　The process of an individual spontaneously including herself or himself as a member of a group.

Self-Schema　Cognitive generalizations about own self. These guide and organize the processing of self-related information.

Semantic differential technique   A method of measuring attitude in which test subjects rate a concept on a series of bipolar scales of adjectives.

Sexism   Discrimination or prejudice against some people because of their gender.

Simulation   A research method that tries to imitate crucial aspects some real-world situation in order to understand the underlying mechanism of that situation.

Slavery   The most extreme, coercive, abusive, and inhumane form of legalized inequality where people are treated as things or someone's property.

Social Distance   The degree of physical, social or psychological closeness or intimacy to members of a group like ethnic, racial or religious groups.

Social Exclusion   The various ways in which people are excluded from the accepted norms within a society. Exclusion can be economic, social, religious or political.

Social Inhibition   Social inhibition happens when the presence of other people causes a decline in a person's performance. Also called Social Impairment.

Social Judgment Theory   A theory of attitude change which emphasizes the individual's perception and judgment of a persuasive communication. Central concepts in this theory are anchors, assimilation and contrast effects, and latitudes of acceptance, rejection and non-commitment.

Social Learning Theory   A theory that proposes that social behavior develops as a result of observing others and of being reinforced for certain behaviors.

Social Support   Help and resourced provided by others for coping.

Socialization   A process of behaviors accepted by society.

Sociofugal Space   Settings created to discourage conversation among people by making eye contact difficult. E. g. , side by side seating in waiting rooms.

Sociolinguistics   The study of relationships between social and linguistic variation or the study of language (performance) in its social context.

Sociopetal Space   Setting that encourage interpersonal interaction through increased eye contact. E. g. , cafés, cocktail lounges.

Stereotypes   Stereotypes (or *characterizations*) are generalizations or assumptions that people make about the characteristics of all members of a group, based on an inaccurate image about what people in that group are like. For example, Americans are generally friendly, generous, and tolerant, but also arrogant, impatient, and domineering. Asians are humble, shrewd and alert, but reserved. Stereotyping is common and causes most of the problems in cross-cultural conflicts.

Stigma   A term describing the condition of possessing an identity which has been branded "spoiled" or discredited identity by others. Examples of negative social stigmas are physical or mental handicaps and disorders, as well as homosexuality or affiliation with a specific nationality, religion or ethnicity.

Stratification   Characteristic of a system with socioeconomic strata, sharp social divisions based on unequal access to wealth and power.

Stratified Society   A society where there is an unequal division of material wealth between its members.

Strength   Power, status or resources associated with a social influence agent in social impact theory.

Stress An imbalance between environmental demands and an organism's response capabilities. Also the human body's response to excessive change.

Structuralism There has been a number of forms of structuralism in the history of anthropology.

Structural-functionalism Structural-functionalism approaches the basic structures of a given society as serving key functions in meeting basic human needs. Another form of structuralism, developed by Claude Levi-Strauss, argues that social/cultural structures are actually rooted in the fundamental structure of the human brain, which generates basic building-blocks of social/cultural systems. In this approach, culture is studied for its deeper meaning to be discovered in the careful structural analysis of meaning in myth and ritual.

Sub-Culture A part or subdivision of a dominant culture or an enclave within it with a distinct integrated network of behavior, beliefs and attitudes. The subculture may be distinctive because of the race, ethnicity, social class, gender or age of its members.

Symbolic Racism A blend of negative affect and traditional moral values embodied in e. g., the Protestant ethic; underlying attitudes that support racist positions.

Syncretism Blending traits from two different cultures to form a new trait. Also called *fusion*. This occurs when a subordinate group molds elements of a dominant culture to fit its own traditions.

Syntax The arrangement and order of words in phrases and sentences.

T

Taboo A strong social prohibition with grave consequences about certain areas of human activity or social custom. The term originally came from the Tongan language. The first recorded usage in English was by Captain James Cook in 1777. Some examples of taboo are dietary restrictions such as halal or kosher, restrictions on sexual activities such as incest, bestiality or animal-human sex, necrophilia or sex with the dead etc.

Third World A term used to describe those regions of the world in which levels of development, applying such measures as GDP, are significantly below those of the economically more advanced regions. The term is increasingly seen as an inadequate description of the prevailing world situation since it fails to describe a significant amount of internal differentiation and development.

Traditional Medicine Medicine and healthcare practices which originated in a particular culture, and have been practiced by an ethnic or cultural group centuries in the country of origin or of emigration.

Trait Trait describes regularities in behavior, especially with reference to an individual's personality.

Transculturation A term coined by Fernando Ortiz in the 1940s to describe the phenomenon of merging and converging of different cultures. It argues that the natural tendency of people is to resolve conflicts over time, rather than aggravating them. Global communication and transportation technology nowadays replaces the ancient tendency of cultures drifting or remaining apart by bringing cultures more into interaction. The term Ethnoconvergence is sometimes used in cases where transculturation affects ethnic issues.

Tribe A type of social formation usually considered to arise from the development of agriculture. Tribes tend to have a higher population density than bands and are also characterized by common descent or ancestry.

U

Uncertainty Avoidance One of the Hofstede dimensions, which he defines as "the extent to which the members of a culture feel threatened by uncertain or unknown situations".

Uncertainty of Approval Measures how much any member of a group is concerned about getting acceptance from other group members.

Under-Differentiation In developmental anthropology, it refers to planning fallacy of viewing less-developed countries as an undifferentiated group. Ignoring cultural diversity and adopting a uniform approach (often ethnocentric) for very different types of project beneficiaries. In Linguistics it is the representation of two or more phonemes, syllables, or morphemes with a single symbol.

Unilineal Descent Matrilineal or patrilineal descent.

Unilineal Descent Group A kin group in which membership is inherited only through either the paternal or the maternal line.

Universal Something that exists in every culture.

Universalism One of the Trompenaars & Hampden-Turner (1997) dimensions describing the preference for rules over relationships (or vice versa). In a Universalist culture, a rule cannot be broken and is a hard fact, no matter what the relationship with the person is. People in universalistic cultures share the belief that general rules, codes, values and standards take precedence over particular needs and claims of friends and relations.

V

Validity The extent to which a measure represents accurately what it is supposed to represent.

Variables Attributes (e.g., sex, age, height, weight) that differ from one person or case to the next.

Vertical Mobility Upward or downward change in a person's social status.

Visual Dominance Behavior The tendency of high-status positions to look more fixedly at lower-status people when speaking than when listening.

Vividness The intensity or emotional interest of a stimulus.

W

Wealth All a person's material assets, including income, land, and other types of property. It is the basis of economic and often social status.

Westernization The acculturative influence of Western expansion on native cultures.

Worldview The English translation of the German word Weltanschaung. Also called World View.

X

Xenophile A person attracted to everything that is foreign, especially to foreign peoples, manners, or cultures.

Xenophile The belief that people and things from other countries must be superior.

Xenophobe A person who is fearful or contemptuous of anything foreign, especially of strangers or foreign peoples or cultures.

Xenophobia The belief that people and things from other countries are dangerous and always have ulterior motives. Xenophobia is an irrational fear or hatred of anything foreign or unfamiliar.

Y

Yang Yin and yang are two opposing and complementing aspects of phenomena in Chinese philosophy. Yang qualities are hot, fire, restless, hard, dry, excitement, rapidity, and correspond to the day.

Yin Yin and yang are two opposing and complementing aspects of phenomena in Chinese philosophy. Yin qualities are characterized as soft, substantial, water, cold, conserving, tranquil, gentle, and corresponds to the night.